MARKETING
from scratch

DAVID STRUTTON

KENNETH THOMPSON

UNIVERSITY OF NORTH TEXAS

THE PRINCIPLES *You* REALLY NEED TO KNOW

Kendall Hunt
publishing company

Kendall Hunt
publishing company

www.kendallhunt.com
Send all inquiries to:
4050 Westmark Drive
Dubuque, IA 52004-1840

 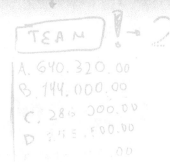 

DEDICATION

For my father, Jack Strutton, who taught me everything needed to write this book, at times even using words.
—David Strutton

For Patricia. Without her understanding and support this book could not have been completed.
—Kenneth Thompson

Contents

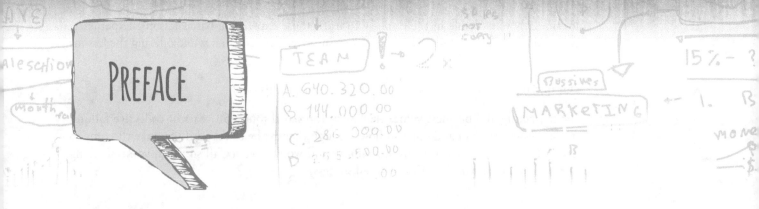

PREFACE

→ Why Care about Marketing—and This Book?

The first rule of story-telling is "make me care." Makes us think that the first rule of writing a book is that the tome should be worth caring about. This book is worth caring about because it solves a problem that many of you don't even know you have. The problem is this: Most people know less about marketing than they think. Yet most people need to know more about marketing than they assume. And in this particular situation your "need-to-know" has nothing to do with whether you succeed in a course that does not intrinsically interest all of you.

The fact is, you engage perpetually in marketing. Regardless of what you do or eventually do for a living or with your life, you are a marketer. So what, you may think. Actually, the fact that you are a marketer is a big deal. Your ability or lack of ability to market yourself and your ideas well will change the arc of your professional and personal life for better or worse.

Everybody, everywhere is selling something—his or her ideas, self, or values. And everybody, everywhere, is buying or has already bought something. Do you want more power, influence, and success; all the result of your own ethically and socially responsible behaviors, of course? More friends, status, material goods, experiences and, yes, more money? Would you like to make better decisions? You each surely want all these things. Consequently, you need to learn how to do marketing better. You need to fully learn *Marketing—from Scratch*. Imagine how much could be lost if you don't.

You're also a marketer because you engage constantly in *exchanges*. The opportunity and need to create, sustain or strengthen *exchange relationships* is not important just to you. Exchange is similarly important to marketers; in many ways the creation and cultivation of exchange relationships is the overarching purpose of every marketing activity. Exchange is the core marketing concept; exchange is what every firm continuously strives to develop, sustain or strengthen. If you already understand how to manage exchange relationships successfully, congratulations. Life has likely rewarded you accordingly. But if you admit there's room for improvement in how you create, manage and strengthen the key relationships in your life then marketing—and *Marketing from Scratch*, designed from birth to split the difference between Old School Principles and Digital Age Applications—was made for you.

Marketing from Scratch is largely based on the experiences of two authors who collectively have created, taught, and executed marketing principles *for more than 50 years*. Scary *italicized* phrase this, but true. Human beings, including all marketing students, are unique amongst all creatures residing on earth in their ability to learn from others' experiences. The experiences of others can so often prove quite the gift. But only if the receiver is open and subsequently pays attention to the present. Unfortunately, human beings, including many university students, are similarly remarkable in their ability to learn those experience-based lessons. Experience, as is well known, is a tough teacher. You see, she gives the tests first while offering the lessons only later.

Our initial piece of advice: Don't ignore the lessons in this book.

The marketing and business values that we've learned through 50 years of collective failures and successes weave in and out and flow through the text below. And if you take the time to learn what we have learned from our failures you won't have to fail so much yourself, along what we all hope is your path to eventual success.

Chapter 1
You Need This Stuff: Core Concepts and Principles

Marketing success comes easier for people or firms who consistently demonstrate three abilities. First, marketing success follows from the ability to "stand-out" rather than "fit-in." Standing out in a positive, appealing, or determinant way, of course. Marketers of all types have realized how the importance of standing-out for some time. Experts, for example, recently discovered that during the 1920s New York City builders routinely added four to six more floors than originally planned per skyscraper project just to stand out favorably from other buildings already around them in the skyline. The price differentials that tenants subsequently paid to work or live in the tallest building in the district attests to the success of their scheme to "stand-out."

The second prerequisite to marketing success derives from the ability to make "old-things-seem-new" or "new-things-known." When hugely exciting stories are repeatedly told, they grow less and less exciting, which is a major reason why formerly passionate couples often stop having sex with the passage of time. Yet this woe need not arise if those couples read this book, which specializes in making-old-things-appear-new, again. (We exaggerate, a bit, to make a point.) Then there is the stone-cold fact that nothing new in this world—no idea, person, product or place—has ever been accepted, purchased, or used without customers first being aware of the new or old thing.

The third sure-fire precursor to marketing success originates from the ability to develop and deliver new things. Yet simply introducing new stuff is never enough. The new idea, product, person, service, experience, or place also must be genuinely useful to, or perceived as such, by customers. Not that many years back one knew he or she needed to text, constantly. Now, students risk expulsion from important lectures because their desire to receive and send texts—still a relatively new product—has grown into an irresistible need.

The catch, of course, and yes, there usually is a catch, is that none of these abilities come easily to marketers. But mastering the ideas and principles and examples introduced throughout this book can take you or your Firm a long way down the path to success.

These three factors are each critical to marketing success because all human brains are wired to operate at one and only one of three levels at any given point in time. The three levels are: I will, I won't, or I want. While each level is relevant, (marketers do care about our "wills" and "won'ts"), human wants are surely most important to marketers.

Wants are critically important to us humans, too, because, as an ever-popular book[1] suggests, four things in this world are never satisfied. First, there is the leech. Leeches will continue sucking blood from animal hosts until they pop. They always want more; they are never satisfied. Second, there is the empty grave. The graveyard always cries out for more. Death is utterly democratic, exactly one out of one people on earth today will participate in the process.

Third, fire. The bigger a fire gets, the more it wants to consume, and fire will never quit until fuel or oxygen is exhausted. Fourth, the empty womb (and we did not mean to write "room").

However, the book of Proverbs was not really discussing insects, dirt, or fire, as you surely know. The book was actually referencing us humans. We humans represent a fifth entity in this world that is never satisfied.

Fact: Most humans, no matter how much they have, want more. Our intrinsic selves are genetically programed to want. Personalize the sentence that you just read. What is happiness to you? One answer, taken from the famous television show *Madmen*, is that happiness "is a moment in time before we want something else to create more happiness." Can you relate? For most of us, happiness is more about anticipation of a moment than it is about the reality of the moment. In some ways most of us, at least some of the times, are big empty holes waiting and indeed yearning to be filled up. Marketers are quite aware of this fact, and frequently leverage their awareness in ways that benefit them and, at least occasionally, harm us as consumers.

By the way, as an aside, happiness is supposedly most likely to present in the lives of those who have something to do, something to look forward to, and someone to love. However, since that line of reasoning is only loosely related to this book, consider that a freebie.

In addition, most humans, too often, want the wrong things. More sugar, salt or fat, anyone? Often the easiest path to marketing success is to provide people what they **want**, even if what they want is not good for them, rather than what they actually **need**. This topic is addressed again in succeeding chapters.

Madonna, the 1980s' "Beyoncé/Taylor Swift/Lady Gaga" and one-time "Like a Virgin" performer who morphed into a "Material Girl" was right when she sang: "We're all living in a material world." Fortunately or unfortunately, marketers are there to help us stuff our closets with things we often do not need and frequently cannot afford.

These circumstances, along with the fact that humans are always unsatisfied, merge to create a world in which successful marketing ought to prove comparatively easy: Identify what people want that they do not currently have and then give it to them. Unfortunately, life, business, or marketing is rarely that simple. If were they, this book could end now.

→ Another Path Toward Certain Marketing Success

iPods allow users to carry a huge selection of hand-picked tunes around with them as they travel wherever, whenever. There was a time not so long ago when this specific problem-solving capability was unique. Prior to the introduction of MP3 technology, the world's consumers had no idea they needed to carry thousands of songs on a 24/7/365 basis on their person. At the time of introduction, the world's music lovers were already listening to their favorite music and were satisfied with the media that delivered their favorite music to them. Yet once this new solution was widely available, demonstrably easy to use, and priced at levels customers felt were appropriate, many people quickly had a "problem." Apple had created a solution for a problem that the general marketplace did not even realize existed. That is, Apple had followed a proven path to certain marketing success; i.e., create a solution and then "sell the problem." The outcome, of course, has been very good for customers, Apple, and Apple's shareholders.

More controversially, consider this data taken from a study reported at an American Psychological Association (APA) conference in 2010: 24% of college students sampled in a survey reported taking psychiatric medication in 2009, compared with 11% of college students in 1998.[2] Over an 11-year-period, did US college students become twice as likely to suffer psychiatric problems? Or, is it possible that the major US drug marketers—often called Big Pharma—became extremely proficient at making (and marketing) new antidepressant medications that purportedly provided pharmaceutical solutions to depression-related problems during the years 1998–2009? Is it possible, perhaps likely, that once a supposed pharmaceutical solution to a psychiatric problem existed, more and more psychiatric problems were somehow diagnosed or otherwise suspected to exist? Might Big Pharma and legions of physicians have teamed up to promote the need; that is, diagnose more problems among younger patients? Whenever more drugs are purchased, each party clearly wins so readers should draw their own conclusions. Still, the questions merit consideration insofar as they reinforce how successful marketers can become when they create a solution and then market a problem that the solution can solve.

Now, if the APA is accurate, about 24%+ of students reading this book are taking psychiatric medications, and it is not in our interests to upset anyone. Many psychiatric problems are real indeed. Instead, we seek to motivate everyone to think, and understand that at times:

> *Marketers can develop and promote solutions to problems that did not previously exist in the mind of the market (until the product/solution was available), and in the process create perceptions that a problem exists.*

A fourth way to ensure marketing success is to create a solution and then convince a targeted market segment that it has the problem that can be solved by the new solution. A delicate and sophisticated process, to be sure, but one that many marketers have pulled off over the years. Just ask Starbucks, Facebook, YouTube, Netflix, or Instagram.

Marketing is an extraordinarily powerful and important business function and activity. Marketing can facilitate good (ethical and socially responsible) outcomes. Marketing can generate outcomes that are difficult to defend (too much obesity, acceptance of unethical ideas, or excessive greed). We learn more about the whys and hows of the good and bad in chapters that follow.

→ A Market Full of Paradox

A paradox exists whenever two competing and often contradictory ideas, assertions or positions hold equal claim to the truth. Here is one paradox: most, indeed nearly all, Americans have less than they want. Yet nearly all Americans have more than they need. Indeed, even poor people in the US often seem to have cigarettes, smart phones, and flat screen televisions.

Many US consumers (and from this point forward unless otherwise indicated we assume consumers are Americans) live on a "hedonic treadmill" (hedonic means pleasure-seeking), where people are temporarily satisfied with whatever new thing they wanted and received but then quickly find themselves lustfully lunging forward to wanting something else that is new. Next thing you know you have 39 pairs of shoes or nine guns and still want more. These conditions are good for marketers, making for a genuinely target rich environment. They may or may not prove bad for the psyches and souls of consumers, yet beyond question, these human tendencies are seen as good rather than bad for the US economy. The more customers buy, or conversely, the more marketers sell, the better the economy does.

→ Holes, Problems, and Solutions: Each Begets Success

You should realize by now that marketing success, at corporate or personal levels, is also based on a marketer's ability to develop and deliver solutions to customers' problems. Whichever Firm (hereafter, "Firm" refers to all manner of Marketing Organizations) or person delivers the best solution ("best" as defined and perceived in the mind of the customer) is the Firm or person that will close the sale and create or strengthen customer relationships.

Which is why the answer to the question "What exactly is a customer buying when she visits Home Depot and purchases a quarter-inch drill bit?" is highly informative. The right answer, perhaps surprisingly, is she is purchasing a one-quarter inch hole. (She is not buying a brand or a purposed piece of steel.) Why does she *need* to purchase a one-quarter inch hole? The answer is simple: she has a problem for which the solution is a quarter-inch hole. The most successful marketers are those who realize they must continuously perform as want and need satisfiers, or alternatively, as problem-solvers. We repeat, marketers, the successful ones at least, view themselves a want and need satisfiers, or as problem solvers.

All marketing organizations understand this simple criterion for success. Take the Marine Corps in its recruiting practices; Sprouts, in its ability to market healthier food options at even healthier prices; Gillette, a 124-year-old Firm that has succeeded on a grand scale by charging much higher prices than competitors generally have charged during each of those 13 plus decades; Las Vegas, as a flat place in a far-from-anywhere often burning-hot desert that successfully sucks away billions of hard-earned consumers' dollars annually; the Republican or Democratic political parties, in their ability to successfully convince large chunks of their targeted market segments on the idea that this immigration, unemployment, or terrorism problem can actually be solved if you vote for the right candidate.

We challenge you, right now, to name an organization that does not engage in marketing. Better still, name a successful organization that has flourished for a while whose success is not grounded in large part in effective marketing. If you really try to do this, you will quickly learn such organizations are fewer than you likely suspect.

→ Marketing Principles/Fundamentals and Laws

This book does not distinguish principles from fundamentals. Principles or fundamentals both tell us what works. Using either name, you always must master principles or fundamentals before you can achieve excellence because without said mastery, you are unlikely to achieve excellence. This would prove a voluntary misfortune: First, because the fundamentals and principles to achieve excellence are present in this book and second, because excellence is a prerequisite to marketing success.

Please note: the marketing world is an extraordinarily competitive arena. It's not quite "kill or be killed," but it's close enough in many markets or geographic areas to not quibble about the difference. The world has shrunk (think technology), customers have gotten smarter (think technology) and customers have many more choices available than was true only a few years ago (think globalization).

Laws, by contrast, tell us what we can and cannot—or should or should not—do. Laws keep us in bounds. Laws operate in a fashion similar to how bowling alleys use child bumpers to keep kids' balls from the gutter. Laws also permit people to discriminate more easily between right and wrong decisions; and choose right more readily than wrong.

Nine Marketing Laws, each geared toward facilitating marketing success, follow. Most originate from the work of Al Reis and Jack Trout.[3]

- *Law 1: Leadership.* This law suggests Firms, or more correctly their products and brands, must be "first to market" for them to secure a good chance of remaining "first in the mind" of the market. (More about that, later.) Charles Lindbergh, for example, was the first person to fly an airplane nonstop across the Atlantic Ocean. He traveled from Garden City, New York to Paris, France, in 1927. Even today most undergraduates, a market segment not known for its historical acumen, know the name Lindbergh. Why? Because he was first. The second person to fly solo across the Atlantic was Bert Hinkle. How well known is Mr. Hinkle today?
Crickets.
Which brings us to …

- *Law 2: Category.* This law suggests that if your Firm cannot be "first to market" (and as a practical matter, how many Firms or brands or products can be first?), then they should establish a category in which they or their product or brand can be first. Amelia Earhart remains well known, even today, for two reasons. Each reason is relevant. Ms. Earhart was the first woman to fly an airplane across the Atlantic. She was, in brief, the "first in her category"—in this case, her gender— to accomplish this feat. The second reason Ms. Earhart remains relevant is that she was first in her category to be lost at sea while flying across the world. Similar to Malaysian Airlines Flight 370, she vanished without a trace in 1937. However, being first in a category is not enough to ensure lasting success. Say hello to Janet Guthrie, the first woman to compete in the Indianapolis 500.
Who?
Which brings us to …

- *Law 3: The Mind.* If a Firm cannot be first to market, or cannot establish a category in which to be first, it still might become "first in the mind" (of the market). This is synonymous with having "top of the mind" awareness. Here, we should consider Danica Patrick. Despite having never come close to winning a race during her four plus years of competing as a NASCAR driver, she would still be the first person—actually, the first human brand—to come to mind for most Americans who know about but are not fans of NASCAR and its products or values. This is because, as will you discover later, perceptions truly matter …

This discussion of the mind and the importance of brands or products earning a top-of-mind position in the mind of the market is so crucial we will leave our list for a moment. Please consider viewing the mind, particularly your mind, as an organ that somehow contains millions of ladders. Each ladder is comprised of numerous rungs. Simple question: Would you, as a marketer, want your brand to occupy a bottom or near-bottom rung in the mind of the market, or would you want your brand to occupy a top, or near-top, rung? The answer, of course, is obvious. Otherwise, when a problem arises for which your particular brand/product is one of many possible solutions your brand/product will not even have a place in the evoked set—also often called the consideration set—of consumers.

This is important. If a brand of beer (e.g., Samuel Adams) does not occupy one of the top three rungs on the beer ladder that resides inside the average beer drinker's mind, there is little to no chance that the Sam Adams brand will be chosen when a beer drinker encounters a problem s/he believes is best solved by beer. The event just described, by the way, is known as "top-of-the-mind" awareness.

Consumers, like you, are hurried, harried people. They live fast lives during fast times. We usually do have or typically will not allocate the time to sit around deliberating in a highly engaged or thoughtful manner which among the possibly dozens of market solutions will best resolve our problem. Instead, we will usually briefly consider the one, two, or possibly three brand alternatives that might solve our problem for which a nice cold beer is the best solution. (Beer, if you think about it, solves many problems for many consumers. Refreshment for the thirsty, confidence for the insecure, a buzz for the bored, a comfort for the lonely, and temporary clarity for the uncertain.) Those two or three options (products or brands) that consumers consider constitute their evoked—or consideration—set of brand solutions.

Which is exactly why the Coors, Budweiser, or Miller brands continue to advertise long after most of the world is aware of their existence and understands their purported differences. Coors, Budweiser, and Miller understand they must remain "top-of-mind" amongst potential and actual American beer drinkers. They likewise understand they must do what is possible and reasonable to keep the Samuel Adams brand out of their current customers' minds.

- *Law 4: Perceptions.* This law suggests to us that marketing is a war, battle, or competition (listed tougher to gentler) that is waged and won or lost in the minds of customers in the marketplace. This mind-space battle is waged—and subsequently won or lost—based on customers' perceptions. Shakespeare wrote "There is nothing either good or bad, but thinking makes it so." This is why one spouse in a family earning $300,000+ annually could conclude, perceptually, that a Mercedes is obviously the only right and proper vehicle, while the other spouse is every bit as happy or satisfied with an ancient, beat-up, but reliable Hyundai. Neither spouse is right; neither spouse is wrong. Each spouse simply differs in his or her perceptions. Moreover, those perceptual differences can make all the difference for the past, present, or future success or failure of a brand. Fortunately, marketers can and do, and in pursuit of their own best interests should, shape perceptions.

Human beings perceive (look at and attempt to make sense of) the world in an active, ongoing, never-ending process. During that process, "meaning-creation" or "sense-making" takes place. In due course, the perceptions that arise influence and actively bias our decisions. This always happens, albeit usually without our being consciously aware of the process. Perceptions, and the marketer's ability to create and manage them, really matter. Consider, for example, that about 80% of what we see exists behind (rather than before) our eyes as we make sense of what we have seen or experienced. To illustrate what we mean, please note that fairness has little to do with absolute equality. Fairness is about your specific perception of equality. Your perception of what is fair likely differs from the person beside you. Not in "differs-worse" nor in "differs-better"; just differs. One other thing to learn about perceptions: At critical points, we all make choices based on our perceptions of which alternatives provide the most value to us and best supports our self-interests. The criteria on which most of our discretionary choices are based usually come down to these two factors.

Can marketers shape your perceptions? Of course. Do they? Again, yes. Do they shape them for better or worse, in ways that help or hurt us? You already surely know the answer.

- *Law 5: Focus.* Before we discuss focus, please note our first four laws lay out like dominos insofar as if a Firm is unable to achieve leadership advantage, it still might achieve category leadership. But, if category advantage proves unattainable, it might earn mind-based, or what we later described as positioning, advantages, where success is ultimately determined by winning a victory in a battle of perceptions. Focus as a Law, by contrast, is something that all Firms can aspire to and achieve, but only when those Firms are highly creative. The Law of Focus is also the Law of Ownership, as in "owning something." Owning *what where*? The "what" is a word; the "where" is in the mind.

To illustrate this point, consider that Starbucks currently owns "coffee" in the United States. UPS once owned "brown," which was nice. UPS, however, now also owns "logistics," which is a more desirable word to own. Kleenex owns a product category called facial tissues, similar to how Band-Aid owns, particularly in the minds of children, a category otherwise known as adhesive strips. Yet when you cry, you rarely ask for a facial tissue. It is usually a Kleenex, please. When children bang-up their knees, few have ever screamed "Mama get me an adhesive strip!" Kids go right to the brand (Band-Aid) that owns the word.

Google owns "search." Facebook currently owns "social networking." Twitter, we suppose, owns "Tweets." FedEx stills owns "overnight," which is great for them and great for you if your problem involves how best to ship packages overnight. Owning something in a market's mind is important. Says Sara Blakely, owner and founder of Spanx: "I keep saying this to the team: We've got to own something. If we own butts, and then branch out from there, that's O.K. You don't want to limit yourself to butts in the customer's mind, but you don't want to become everything to all people too quickly."[4] (A brand that owns butts; the mind boggles.)

- *Law 6: Attributes and the Law of the Opposite.* One sure thing about attributes: every product has them. This is important because attributes deliver benefits and value and without perceived or actual benefits or value there can be no product. Value, in turn, contributes to the problem-solving capacity of any product. Consider, for example, a brand of toothpaste. Brand A might feature and emphasize in its marketing communication i.e., its promotions a cavity-fighting attribute. Yet according to the Law of the Opposite, a creative marketing competitor could emphasize an opposing attribute, say, whiter teeth, to distinguish or differentiate its brand B from the original brand A. Moreover, toothpaste brand C or brand D could differentiate their toothpastes' distinguishing values by emphasizing other attributes, such as fresher breath, enhanced kiss-ability, its war on gingivitis, or elimination of plaque. This list of opposing but equally appealing attributes, at least equally appealing to different customer groups or segments could go on.
  Then there is ….

- *Law 7: Concentration.* In football, the low man wins. Despite possibly being physically smaller, slower, or weaker, the low man can still prevail in football because he is able to concentrate his strengths against his opponent's comparative weaknesses. He has gained, and exploited, leverage. Similar conditions can prevail in the midst of marketing competitions between Firms. The smaller, under-resourced Firm can defeat larger, better-resourced Firms through judicious leveraging, if it targets its relative strengths at its competitors' relative weaknesses. Were this not true, the young Microsoft may have never prevailed against IBM; the young Google may have never prevailed against Yahoo; or the young Nike may have never prevailed against Converse. Yet these now iconic brands obviously did win. Each Firm won because it leveraged its ability to create appealing customer value faster, better, and less expensively than did larger, better-known and better-financed competitors. Young Microsoft, Google, and Nike also conquered their competitors because they attacked IBM, Yahoo, or Converse, exactly the way that Facebook vanquished Myspace.

The last two Laws do not necessarily follow directly from the preceding seven Laws. Yet each remains important in its own right.

- *Law 8: Candor.* In business, marketing, branding, and product development, as well as promotion or even the supply chain, things will go wrong. Sometimes the fault is yours; sometimes other factors are responsible, although error-prone Firms should rarely point the finger at anything other than themselves. The law of candor suggests that when bad stuff happens, individuals or Firms should react by taking responsibility when they are to blame. Individuals or Firms should act like full-grown, mature, responsible adults.

Tiger Woods failed to act responsibility as his sexual indulgences incrementally, but persistently, came to light. Instead, Tiger delayed, denied, deflected, obfuscated, and lied. By contrast, David Letterman did take ownership and full responsibility. He discussed his serial sexual dalliances on his show the day when the scandal broke. (Note: each man once was and remains a human brand, which is why each incident is introduced.) The brand image that had been carefully crafted by Tiger Woods and his marketing team has never fully recovered. The brand image of David Lettermen was barely and only temporarily dinged.

What the National Football League will do, and how the various incidents of spousal (Ray Rice), child (Adrian Peterson) and player-on-player abuse (i.e. abusing their own and opponents' brains; i.e., Junior Seau) will play out remains to be seen. The League appears to be taking full responsibility as a mature and responsible marketer, as it should. However, it remains hard to tell and difficult to predict what the future portends, a circumstance that logically brings us to our final law.

- *Law 9: Unpredictability.* Yogi Berra was a baseball old-timer famous for uttering mala-propisms (i.e., statements that seemingly did not make any sense until they made perfect sense. For example, when discussing left field, or the sun field at Yankee Stadium, Yogi said "It gets late early out there." When discussing a popular restaurant: "Nobody eats there anymore because it is too busy.") Serendipitously summing up the Law of Unpredictability, Yogi once said, "Making predictions is really difficult, especially when they are about the future."[5] Making predictions about your competitors, customers, or the environment really is difficult. Even if one Firm stole a competitor's business plan the task would prove daunting because plans never work out as predicted, either. But Firms should still try to predict, through marketing research and other information-gathering tools that are available to marketers. A little knowledge about the future is better than no information at all.

→ What Is Marketing?

Most people would respond to this question by saying marketing entails "selling," "advertising" or both, and not much else. In reality, however, marketing is far more than just selling or advertising. In fact, advertising and selling are merely part of a larger "promotional mix" and the promotional mix includes a variety of other tools such as sales promotion, publicity, and public relations. The promotion mix, in turn, is only one of four components of the overall "marketing mix" (Exhibit 1.1). The marketing mix, which is often called the "Four P's of Marketing includes:

- Product: conceptualizing, planning, and designing the products or services that will be sold
- Price: setting and managing the prices of products or services to deliver value to customers
- Promotion: developing the integrated communications program required to communicate the product or service to intended customers
- Place (Distribution): disseminating products or services through appropriate "channels of distribution" to make them available to customers.

Marketing features an array of disparate activities. These brief descriptions, in fact, merely scratch the surface.

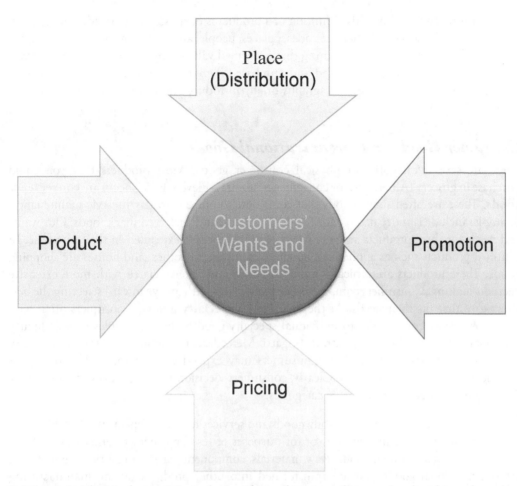

Exhibit 1.1 *The Marketing Mix is the specific combination of inter-related and interdependent marketing activities employed by organizations to meet objectives.*

→ Marketing: A Process of Managing the Marketing Mix

The definition of marketing provided below emphasizes that marketing is a process. The act of marketing involves a series of activities performed by businesses to create value and generate exchanges that deliver one or more types of utility to buyers. The marketing activities that create these exchanges and deliver utilities are known collectively as the marketing mix. The marketing mix is equivalent to a set of tools. Marketers employ these tools to create, satisfy, and manage demand for their goods and services within targeted markets. Targeted markets are better described as target segments. A good chunk of the book discusses these marketing mix tools, in order that readers might better understand how to use them. Notably, when Firms change one element of their marketing mix, they create an entirely new marketing mix.

What is a "Product"?

Although we address the role of **product** as a marketing mix component later, we should provide early insight here regarding how this book uses the term. For our purposes, a product is any "bundle of attributes that is capable of satisfying customer wants and needs." All products possess a set of characteristics or attributes that can satisfy a specific configuration of customer wants and needs. This definition of a product is purposely very broad. Products can be other than physical goods. Services, ideas, places, people, and even "causes" are marketed as products. Products encompass anything that is deemed valuable by actual or potential buyers (i.e., prospects) that can be marketed and purchased (i.e., sold and bought) in a buyer-seller exchange process. The next few paragraphs briefly introduce you to the diversity of the term "product."

Consumer Goods and Organizational Goods

There are several categories of physical consumer goods. Most products that you could purchase in grocery (Albertsons) or convenience stores (7-Eleven, E-Z Check) are **convenience goods**. These are often staple goods that contribute to our day-to-day lifestyle maintenance. Examples include laundry detergents, breakfast cereals, and packaged snack foods. Our wants and needs for these products are very basic and little effort is expended in their purchase. In contrast, products such as appliances, notebook computers, clothes, and houses are shopping goods. These products are typically more expensive and are associated with more extensive decision-making. Consumers compare brands and prices with an eye toward selecting the best alternative that fits their needs. At the extreme are **specialty goods**. Consumers often have strong preferences or loyalties to individual specialty good brands. Examples include luxury automobiles (e.g. BMW, Audi, Ferrari, Bugatti, Mercedes, etc.), designer clothes and jewelry (e.g. Armani, Rolex, and Cartier). Consumers may expend considerable effort to acquire specific brands of specialty goods. Clearly, consumers' decision-making processes will be very different for products in these three categories.

Businesses and other organizations buy goods and services for use in operating their Firms, in producing other goods and services, or for purposes of reselling them to other buyers. Such products are organizational goods. Raw materials, component parts, and fabricating materials are organizational goods that are transformed into other products during manufacturing processes. Installations (capital equipment) and accessory equipment are products responsible for this manufacturing transformation. Some accessory equipment and operating supplies are employed both in the production of other products and to facilitate day-to-day operations.

Products purchased by organizational buyers, whether the buyer is a local farmer, small businessperson, or executive in a major corporation, are purchased much differently than consumer goods. Organizational buyers generally exercise greater care in the decision process because of the higher costs and risks associated with organizational products. Mistakes in buying can cost millions of dollars and potentially bankrupt a company.

Services, People, Ideas, Places, and Causes All Are Products

Products can be typical household services such as Orkin for pest control services, Roto-Rooter for drain cleaning, Jiffy Lube for oil changes, LA Fitness in health clubs. Business organizations, of course, also purchase services. Many of the same services available to consumers are also applicable to organizations. Pest control, heating and cooling, plumbing, and laundry services are examples. Other specialized services are geared strictly to organizations. For example, consider the professional consulting and research services provided by the Boston Consulting Group, McKinsey, Accenture, and Booz Allen Hamilton. These Firms specialize in conducting marketing and other forms of research for their clients, as well as offering expert advice and solutions covering a wide range of business problems. Examples of additional professional services offered to organizations include engineering, banking, accounting, investment, logistics, and human resources.

Products can be places. Travel agencies market places. They are in business to sell travel packages to business and consumer markets that make it easy, enjoyable, and affordable to visit the places people want to go. In fact, many attractive destination resort cities, states, and countries have established government and/or private organizations to encourage tourism. These organizations work in conjunction with travel agencies to provide consumers with attractive travel and vacation packages.

Products can be people and ideas. At your last job interview, you were both the product and the marketer! You were marketing yourself to your prospective employer, trying to convince the recruiter that you were the ideal candidate to satisfy the Firm's needs! In return for your valuable services, you anticipated that they would offer an attractive salary and benefit package, as well as provide you with substantial career opportunities. Politicians market themselves and their ideas. The Internet has opened a major new communications medium that politicians can use to obtain continuous exposure with various "publics." President Obama's election team was adept at using the Internet to reach large numbers of young voters who were very receptive to his message of "hope and change." No political candidate can hope to run a successful campaign today without a strong Internet presence with heavy reliance on social media. Finally, products can be "causes." Tune in to television at any time of the day. You will encounter commercials that advocate social causes and/or solicit donations for charitable organizations.

→ Marketing: Defined

So what is marketing? Various similar definitions exist. Three useful ways of defining and describing marketing follow. Note their similarities, not their differences.

> *Marketing is the performance of business activities that direct the flow of goods and services from producers to consumers.*

This definition is useful. However, it is too limiting. Marketing is more encompassing than this.

> *Marketing is a business function and a collection of processes designed to create, communicate, and deliver value to customers and to manage customer relationships in ways that benefit the Firm and its various stakeholders.*

This definition is more useful; it is certainly more complicated and inclusive.

We encourage you to concentrate on the third and simpler definition that follows. Please note the bold words. Each is a key concept in marketing. Understanding what each word means here provides a useful initial foundation that should enhance your future understanding, and prospects for success, as you progress through this book and course.

> *Marketing is a social and managerial process through which individuals and groups obtain what they need or want by creating and exchanging value with others.*

The word "social" implies that marketing is an activity that involves people, both individually and collectively, and that the marketing activity itself entails human interaction. The word "managerial" implies marketing, as an activity and business function, requires strategies and tactics, the development and execution of goals and objectives and metrics, and the allocation and utilization of resources. Typically, in this book, resources consist of the 3-T's: Time (of a Firm's employees, primarily), Talent (again, primarily, of a Firm's employees), and Treasure (a Firm's financial resources). Note that any organization's resources are necessarily limited and finite. Even marketing organizations as large as the US Federal Government have limited resources, as evidenced by the nearly $17 billion deficit it is trying to manage as of this writing.

The word "process" implies that marketing activities are ongoing, essentially never-ending, in nature. This notion fits in logically with marketing principles such as "sell customers once and service them [well] forever," "creating and sustaining loyal customer exchange relationships," or "continuous improvement and/or perpetual innovation." Innovation, not coincidentally, is another key marketing idea, and a concept explored in subsequent chapters. For now, however, we can view an innovation simply as something that is new *and* useful.

The word "individual" implies that marketing exists to satisfy the wants and needs, and in the process solves the problems, of individual consumers. We are all consumers. To the extent that you have ever purchased or acquired any product; used or consumed any product; or finally, rid yourself or disposed of any product, you are a consumer. When marketers target consumers, they are engaged in Business-to-Consumer or B2C marketing.

The word "groups" implies that marketing also exists to satisfy the wants and needs, and solve the problems, of customer groups. These groups of customers usually are other organizations that are somehow engaged in marketing. Note that every organization markets and, therefore, is a marketing organization. Churches, schools, governmental agencies, corporations, community clubs, and so-forth are marketing organizations. When marketers target groups, they are typically involved in Business-to-Business or B2B marketing.

Marketers exist to satisfy customers' "needs." In many ways the word needs is interchangeable with the word "problems"—and the marketer's ability to solve customer's problems. But for now, let us stick with needs. Needs, for our purpose, can be defined simply as "states (or conditions) of felt deprivation." You understand how it feels to be deprived of something, right? For example, water, sleep, food, sex, love, a sense of belonging (fitting in), a sense you are safe and so forth are all common needs. Marketers do not have to create needs. Nor, fundamentally, can marketers create needs. Each need mentioned above would exist even if no marketing existed anywhere in the world.

Marketers similarly exist to satisfy customers' **wants**. Our human wants are essentially endless, as discussed above. Marketers certainly can and do create new wants for us on a routine basis. No one wanted a smart phone until the device existed on planet Earth. Arguably, no one actually needs a smart phone. It just feels like you do because wants, over time, can transmogrify into needs. Wants are "the shape (or form) that needs take as the need is influenced by individual personalities and the environment."

Is marketing part of the environment in which customers are influenced and make decisions? Certainly, and thus we see how marketing both creates and shapes needs over time. Culture is also part of the environment, and contributes to the fact that if the same customer demographic, say, 18–22 year old males are raised in different cultures, for instance, the United States as opposed to the Southeast Pacific island nation of Bali, they will want different foods when they experience the hunger need. The American, when hungry, is likely to want pizza or a burger, fries and Coke. Whereas the Bali is likely to want pork, beans, and mango juice. Same need; radically different wants.

While they differ, wants and needs still relate to one another. A want exists as a specific satisfier of a given need based on customers' experiences, resources, motives, cultural background, and personality. One way to illustrate the distinction between wants and needs: "I need food. But I want a steak."

The word creating means to create something. What you may not know or understand right now is that the marketer's job, as executed through various means and methods and in various contexts, is to create and capture value. The primary tools that marketers use to create and capture value are the product, promotion, the price, and something called the supply chain—the Marketing Mix. (More about each of these marketing mix elements later.) The primary means used by marketers to create and capture value is exchange, a critical concept already introduced in the foreword.

The word **exchange** is defined simply, but critically, as "a get and give." What is typically "gotten" in an exchange? A product and its accompanying values. What is typically "given up" in an exchange? Usually, money, but other forms of value might be substituted. Regardless, in exchange, some sort of value always must be received by each party in exchange for the provision of some other sort of value. Quid pro quo. Value for value, always.

Finally, then, **value**. Value may be best and most simply defined as the ratio between the benefits that a customer gets and the costs that a customer incurs in order to obtain those benefits. Value, then, should be defined from the perspective of customers. Another way of describing value is as follows: Products deliver benefits, benefits provide solutions, and solutions have value because they solve customers' problems, or satisfy their wants or needs.

Consider this: Air conditioners have no value, not even in Texas in August. However, cool air, the benefit/solution generated by air conditioners, has value. Alternatively, lawn fertilizer has no value, not even to customers who care passionately about yards. Green grass, the benefit—or the solution to the problem of having a brown lawn—delivers value.

Marketing Never Occurs in a Vacuum

Marketing occurs inside Firms, between Firms, and inside something called supply chains. Marketing occurs anytime and anywhere buyers are engaging or considering engaging in exchange relationships. Marketing occurs inside churches, synagogues, or temples; marketing even happens inside classrooms; that is, when you actually learn something valuable there. For the most part, however, marketing occurs inside markets. Defined simply, a market is the entire set of actual or potential customers for any product.

Defined more technically, a market is a group of people or organizations that:

- Possess wants and needs (or problems) that must be satisfied (or solved).
- Possess sufficient financial resources (i.e., money) to exchange in return for products that can satisfy those wants and needs, or solve those problems.
- Are willing to engage in exchange for purposes of acquiring the products and value that will satisfy their wants and needs, (or solve their problems).

Marketing cannot and will not occur unless **markets** exist for the products or services being marketed or sold. Markets are individuals or organizations that need and want the goods/services offered by marketing organizations. **Consumer markets** consist of individuals who buy goods and services for their own use. In **organizational markets** businesses purchase products that are required for engaging in business operations or for resale to others. A business user may buy a computer system to automate its inventory management, buy equipment to support its manufacturing processes, or buy supplies (office, janitorial, etc.) used to support daily operations. Producers buy parts and materials that will be combined during the manufacturing process in order to make other products. Their intention, in turn, is to sell those products directly to consumers or to other businesses. Wholesalers and retailers are part of the organizational market when they buy finished goods that they resell to the next level of the distribution channel.

Governmental agencies acquire goods and services for use in operating their organizations. The US Federal Government is the world's largest customer for goods and services. Specifically, the Department of Defense (DoD) spends billions of dollars to purchase equipment and services for our national defense. The projected 2015 budget for the DoD exceeded $631 billion.[6]

Non-profit organizations are markets for a wide variety of goods and services needed to staff, manage, and operate their organizations. Finally, various "publics" are markets. A good example is the voting public, a market targeted by politicians wishing to exchange their ideas for votes. Another example is the local community in which a business operates. Businesses often treat citizens of these communities as "customers" to whom they direct advertising messages that are geared to creating good will and enhancing corporate image. For example, subsequent to the oil spill in the Gulf of Mexico, BP has directed a range of promotions to different publics (including local communities) to sway public opinion about its operations and to enhance its corporate image. Many Firms treat employees and other internal and external stakeholders as "markets," toward whom they direct many forms of communications and "services."

The Importance of Managing Customers' Expectations

As noted, marketing products provides solutions. These solutions offer benefits. Benefits deliver value. From there, the value delivered can exceed customer expectations, correspond exactly to what customers expect, or fall short of customers' expectations. Knowing this, savvy marketers likewise understand that they should manage expectations in ways that profit their customers as well as themselves. These marketers understand a concept known as "under-promising and over-delivering" (value).

Avomaster, for example, is a Keller, TX based Firm that develops and markets avocado-based dishes. Walmart purchases a chicken-avocado meal from Avomaster, a meal that purportedly contains 6.75 ounces of chicken. Avomaster, however, is actually misrepresenting reality; it is under-promising and over-delivering because the Firm actually delivers 7.25 ounces of chicken. Without knowing why, Avomaster's customers experience more satisfaction than they expected. This extra dollop of satisfaction redounds to their benefit and to the benefit of the Firm itself. That little extra bite of chicken, in fact, may actually delight customers. Astute businesspeople likewise routinely over-promise and under-deliver in terms of promised project completion. At times, when they promise a Friday—yet deliver a Thursday—delivery, businesspeople can come across as heroes because they have exceeded their customer's expectations.

⟶ The Marketing Concept

Marketing thought and practice has evolved dramatically since the Industrial Revolution (pre-twentieth century.) This evolutionary process culminated in one of the most important concepts in modern marketing thought—the **Marketing Concept**.

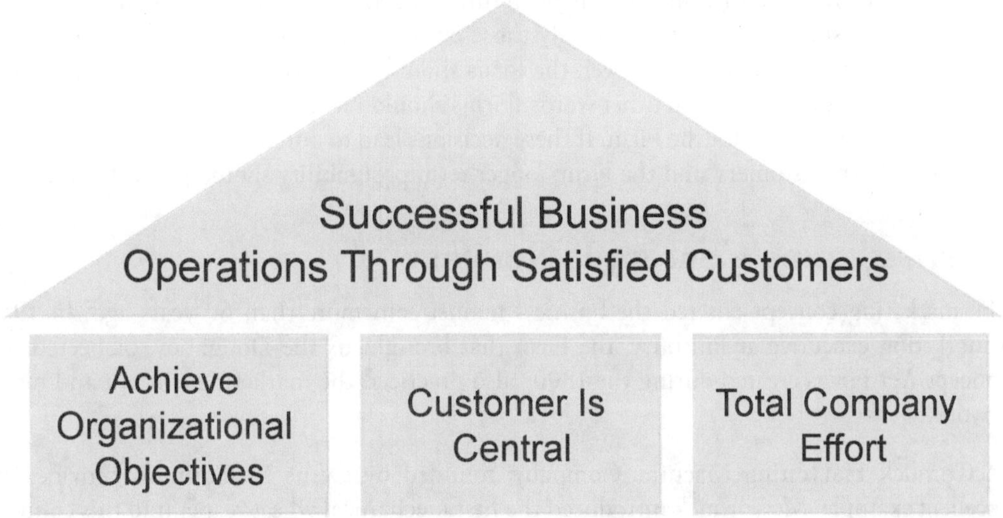

Exhibit 1.2 *Elements of the Marketing Concept, a business philosophy that focuses the Firm's efforts on satisfying customers' want and needs.*

The Marketing Concept Is a Business Philosophy

The marketing concept is a business philosophy that places an emphasis on the customer—and the identification and satisfaction of the customers wants, needs and problems—as the focal point of all business operations. This orientation has three fundamental premises (Exhibit 1.2): Firms must be customer-oriented, a total company effort is required, and the effort must be profitable.

Firms Must Be Customer-Oriented

First, and foremost, the marketing concept dictates that Firms must be **customer-orientated** in conducting all of their operations. The customer must be the focal point of everything the Firm does. Firms must remember that they are in business to identify and satisfy customer needs. Firms should strive first to determine what the market wants and needs, and then tailor their marketing mix offerings such that they satisfy those customer wants and needs.

A Total Coordinated Company Effort Is Required

For the philosophy to work, everyone in the Firm should believe in and practice the marketing concept. All business functions (not just marketing functions) must be coordinated and focused on the central goal of achieving customer satisfaction. Put another way, application of the Marketing Concept should entail an integrated company-wide effort and this starts with top management. If senior leadership does not believe in the Marketing Concept, it will not happen. Many Firms say they believe in the Marketing Concept, however, often they are just paying lip service to it. They may believe in it, but practice another business philosophy. Hypocrisy abounds. A hypocrite, after all, is the kind of fellow who would complain there is too much violence and sex on the shows he DVRed.

The Firm Must Be Profitable

Firms must remain profitable as they strive to satisfy their customers' wants and needs. More generally, the Firm's coordinated and customer-centric marketing efforts must help it achieve key organizational objectives. These objectives typically encompass profitability objectives such as stock prices, return on investment, return on sales, and market capitalization. This suggests Firms should select or target only those customer groups for which it possesses the resources to serve effectively. Moreover, the focus should be on long-term profitability rather than short-term profitability. In other words, Firms should recognize that some decisions may result in short-term loses for the Firm. If these decisions lead to outcomes that support the best interests of both customers' and the Firm, longer-term profitability should generally follow.

The Marketing Concept Is Not New

The marketing concept entered the business mainstream more than 60 years ago. In 1951 a marketing executive at Pillsbury, the Firm that brought us the Doughboy, pioneered the concept. Yet Firms created during the 1800s also practiced the marketing concept and made it work.

McCormick Harvesting Machine Company, founded by Cyrus McCormick, provides an excellent example. McCormick introduced the first mechanical wheat reaper into this country just prior to the Civil War (Exhibit 1.3). His reaper is now viewed as one of the most important inventions of the 19th century, and is credited with helping the North win the Civil War. McCormick believed in the marketing concept, although he never called it that. McCormick understood that successful commercialization of the reaper would require more than just making a great product. He realized an entire marketing program was required to demonstrate the value of his reaper and make it a practical reality. McCormick developed compelling sales demonstrations to overcome initial sales resistance. He implemented installment payment plans, post-sale product service, standardized parts, off-season servicing, and full product warranties. In fact, McCormick issued one of the first product recalls, was among the first to use full-color ads, and employed a comprehensive set of brochures to promote his products.

Exhibit 1.3 *Cyrus McCormick's wheat reaper at a presentation in Virginia, middle 19th century.*

→ A Historical Take on Marketing Practice

The Marketing Concept is hardly the only philosophy that has guided modern businesspeople. It is but one point in the ongoing evolution of business and marketing thought, an outgrowth of earlier business philosophies, many of which have been lost to history.

Overview of Alternative Business Philosophies

Exhibit 1.4 summarizes the major business philosophies and orders them on an evolutionary time-line. The time-line begins, roughly, just prior to 1900. It extends through today. The production orientation (production concept) is the oldest business philosophy. This philosophy eventually evolved into the selling orientation (concept). The selling concept dominated the 1930s. The marketing concept, in turn, evolved from the selling concept during the early 1950s. The societal marketing concept and relationship marketing are the latest stages in marketing thought.

The Production Orientation

The production orientation's basic premise was that companies producing quality products at affordable prices should succeed. Such products, supposedly, would "sell themselves." (The good ole days; this rarely happens today.) The production orientation philosophy suggests Firms should minimize production and distribution costs, and maintain acceptable levels of quality. As costs decreased, Firms enjoyed the opportunity—not always exercised—to charge lower prices.

Henry Ford's famous Model T automobile illustrates the heyday of the production orientation (Exhibit 1.5). Henry Ford founded his namesake Ford Motor Company in Dearborn, Michigan, and invented the modern production line. By developing efficient assembly lines,

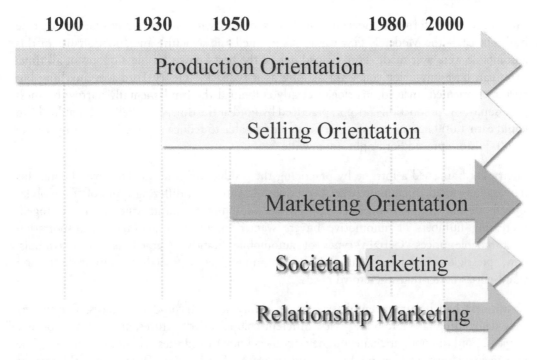

Exhibit 1.4 *The Evolution of the Marketing Concept.*

Exhibit 1.5 *The Classic Ford Model T.*

Ford lowered the Model T's production costs from an original $800 to just under $300. The consequences were huge. Suddenly, affordable automobile-driven transportation was available to average American consumers.

The not-so-secret formula underpinning Ford's success with the assembly line was that he built one car—the Model T. Few variations on the basic structure and functionality of this automobile were ever made. Ford coined one of the best-known business quotes of all time: "You can have any color you want as long as it is black." Henry Ford was anything but customer-oriented. Instead, his slogan clearly embodied the fundamentally narrow business philosophy, the production concept, practiced by Ford at the time. Ford believed that his Firm could earn 1,000 new customers every time he was able to reduce production costs by a mere $1.00. History proved Ford right, for a while.

Henry Ford amassed a fortune by practicing the production concept. However, he and his namesake ignored changing market conditions. As more and differing types of automobiles spread throughout US markets, consumers' automotive wants and needs changed. Increasing numbers of automotive buyers wanted more than just basic transportation at affordable prices. Certain types of automobile brands emerged as status symbols; new, prestigious products that satisfied consumers' egos, social-communications, and stand-out-as-better-than-the-crowd needs.

Consumers had begun to emphasize image utility in their product choices. Consumers were demanding far more body styles, different colors, added features, and a variety of new services. Ford did not anticipate and never fully acknowledged these changing demands. The management team at General Motors did, however. By the end of the 1920s, the upstart General Motors' sales dramatically raced ahead of Ford. They remain there to this day.

The Model T exemplifies a situation where the production concept worked, for a while. The production concept worked and still might, when products are in the early stages of their life cycles. This was surely the case with automobiles at the dawn of the 20th century. Under these circumstances, consumers' wants and needs with respect to the new product remain basic. Consumers were mainly interested in affordable transportation during the heyday of the Model T; a car designed and built to satisfy only the most basic or fundamental transportation needs. When cars were still in their infancy, Firms could succeed by producing limited ranges of product options, maximizing production and distribution efficiencies and, of course, lowering costs. Lower costs generally lead to lower prices, or at least give Firms the option of pricing lower and still earning acceptable profit margins.

Eventually, however, if new product categories succeed, the markets created by their successes always mature. (Stories, once told, cannot help but grow old.) Those once new markets fragment as new customers segments seeking new, exciting, and obviously different types of values emerge. Customers, in brief, begin to want more than just the basic product. Firms that fail to track changing wants and needs, and continue to execute based on now far-less-relevant business models—outdated marketing philosophies—face rocky roads going forward.

The Selling Orientation Takes Over

The production orientation dominated business thought and practice until the early 1930s. Drastic changes in supply and demand relationships arose during this time because of the Great Depression. The supply of goods suddenly exceeded the demand for goods. Consumers stopped buying things simply because they were available. The US economy struck near rock bottom as unemployment reached nearly 30% of the population. Firms faced no choice but to evolve. One consequence of this evolution was that a new philosophy of conducting business emerged: the selling concept.

Products, even good ones, rarely sell themselves. Customers must be convinced to buy; this was the message preached by the selling concept. Firms sought to maximize their sales revenues by aggressively promoting their products in order to stimulate demand. "Hard sell" became the norm rather than exception. An assumption that people would not buy products unless encouraged prevailed. The intensity and sophistication of marketing promotional and communication efforts ramped up materially. Firms pumped huge resources into advertising, hired larger sales forces, and trained them to push products relentlessly. Sounds like a bad time to be a customer, and it probably was.

The Marketing Orientation Emerges

The selling orientation predominated in the US until the early 1950s. At that point, customers essentially rebelled, rejecting the notion that businesses should force products on them. This was the dawn of the post-World War II era. America stood astride the world as its sole undefeated superpower. Consumers' discretionary incomes had risen. Products had become more sophisticated. The business environment was now far more complex and competitive. Consumers turned toward businesses that were more responsive to their wants and needs, and in a land of plenty (of seemingly equally good product choices), they rejected those Firms that were not.

The marketing concept, as we know it today, slowly but persistently emerged as the dominant business philosophy. General Electric was among the first Firms to endorse the "marketing concept" and use it as a guiding business principle. CEO John McKitterick announced: GE's business philosophy was driven by the goal of satisfying customers' identified needs, rather than bending the customers' will to fit the needs of the company.[7]

The marketing concept begins with the Firm "thinking about" customers and their wants, needs and problems. The philosophy's core premise is that Firms first must identify exactly the exact sorts of marketing values that customers want and need. Then, and only then, should Firms develop and deliver these now-obviously desirable "solutions" to willing and perhaps even anxious customers. The ability of Firms to achieve these two related outcomes generally depends on the proficiency with which they conduct thorough marketing research that yields actionable insights. Effective marketing programs rarely emerge unless marketers thoroughly understand the marketplace. Effective marketing programs are marketing mixes that are capable of creating and delivering differentiating customer value.

The Societal Marketing Concept

A new school of philosophical marketing thought emerged during the early 1980s. Its prevailing wisdom was that the marketing concept was dated. Academics and practitioners believed the marketing concept no longer adequately accounted for dramatic social and cultural changes that were emerging. The marketing concept had become old; it needed a makeover as a newer, sexier, more relevant and consequently more useful version of its old self. The **societal marketing concept** rose from this concern.

The societal marketing concept extends the marketing concept by challenging organizations to conduct marketing operations more (socially) responsibly. The societal marketing concept, at its core, asks Firms to consider the ethical and societal consequences of their actions as they identify and satisfy customer needs.

The driving emphasis for the societal marketing concept remains constant: profitably satisfy customer wants and needs. Never forget that Firms exist to satisfy customers and earn returns for their investors; no or low profitably is never an option. However, adherent Firms strategies shifted slightly as they began market based on the new philosophy. Firms became more concerned with the long-term interests of society as they developed and managed marketing mixes. Firms closely examined each marketing mix element to determine whether what is happening there sustained or perhaps elevated the long-term societal welfare. Achieve this end, experts argued, and Firms' reputation and branding power would each improve. Then Firms could earn even higher profits.

In response, some Firms refrained from marketing certain products. Others dramatically changed how they promoted certain products. Society logically continues to question the marketing of tobacco products and alcoholic beverages. Tobacco marketers one day may have to remove traditional cigarettes from the US market. Is it mere coincidence that the industry has recently and successfully introduced e-cigarettes? Doubtful. As hugely successful marketers, even if they enjoy the advantage of marketing an addictive product (nicotine), the tobacco industry understands the value of making old-things-seem-new (tobacco as nicotine delivery vehicle), new-things-known (e-cigarettes), and standing-apart by offering something that new and healthier. (As if.)

Then there is the modern marketing of alcohol, a product that kills more people and wreaks more lives and families than cigarettes do, year after year. Because the world grew less ignorant of this, marketers now routinely deliver advertisements promoting the idea that targeted customer groups should consume beer more responsibly. Messages like "don't drive if you drink," "drink moderately," or "designated driver" have been around so long that those words do not sound strange to most of you. Trust us, at one time they did. Other products were aggressively "de-marketed." More messages are evident in a wide range of media that directly attempt to reduce the consumption of cigarettes, drugs, and alcoholic beverages.

Relationship Marketing

The 1990s heralded the era of **relationship marketing**. Relationship marketing extends the marketing concept and societal marketing philosophies, along with marketing practice itself, to include building:

- Stronger, longer-term, more mutually-beneficial relationships with consumers and
- Stronger, longer-term, more mutually beneficial relationships with business partners.

The idea of building stronger customer relationships is hardly new. Benjamin Franklin's Philadelphia print shops thrived as they were guided by this exact premise from around 1740 to 1776. The same notion also drives the marketing concept. Then again, great value is available to anyone or anything that is capable of making the old appear new, again.

What is unique to relationship marketing is the idea of extending marketing relationships to business partners. The implication is that developing strong relationships with our business partners (suppliers and distributors) will lead to facilitate better supply chain arrangements, higher levels of cooperation, less conflict, and increased efficiency. When this happens, everyone wins, especially ultimate consumers. (Cliché alert: we just referenced "win-win.")

Relationship marketing requires that Firms treat everyone as if they were customers. This customer-like embrace includes partnering Firms or people who supplied the marketer with goods and services, or supply chain intermediaries who acquire goods and services from one another for purposes of reselling them to their own customers. Driven by the goal of building longer-term, mutually beneficial relationships with as many organizations and individuals as possible, Firms developed marketing strategies that purposefully delivered desirable value to partners and customers throughout the entire supply chain. Decisions guided by relationship marketing no longer focus intently on optimizing one Firm's power and position at the expense of other Firms or customers' power or position. Instead, marketing decision-makers seek to optimize efficiency throughout the entire supply chain in ways that benefit and confer new value to all supply chain partners.

→ How and Why Marketing Works (So Well)

Much of what marketing Firms do is done to identify and characterize (i.e., profiling) potential market segments. Once those potential market segments are classified and prioritized, the next marketing task to influence those segments to engage in exchange relationships. Customers will usually choose the outcome that they perceive will deliver them the most value. Their perceived receipt of value incentivizes or motivates customers to make choices that marketers would prefer them to make. The final task of marketers, then, is convince those segments that their Firm can deliver those exact values. Firms achieve this persuasion by skillfully managing their marketing mixes.

Marketing Firms succeed by creating valued exchanges between themselves and the market segments they target and serve. Marketing Firms presumably offer the sorts of goods and services that deliver the sorts of values that markets perceive are desirable. In return for their opportunity to acquire these values, markets must give back something of value to the marketer, generally in the form of money (e.g. dollars). Both ends receive value resulting in the exchange process. Marketers make money and markets receive goods, services, or ideas that satisfy the wants and needs of customers who comprise those markets (Exhibit 1.6).

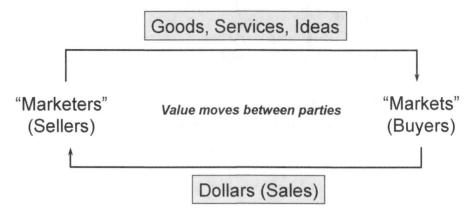

Exhibit 1.6 *Marketing Involves Exchange.*

Goods, services, and money flow between marketers and the markets they target. So too does information. This information actually knits together buyer and seller relationships, and the Business-to-Business (B2B) relationships that emerge between Firms in the form of supply chains. Marketers communicate with markets via a wide range of promotional media informing them of the product's availability and its benefits. Marketers also employ promotional messages to build images for their brands, in other words, develop personalities or positions for brands in consumers' minds.

Markets similarly communicate with marketers. By speaking with their feet, they tell marketers whether they did a good or bad job. Of course, the level of sales generated for a product is a major means by which markets communicate how well marketers have performed. Greater sales tend to suggest that the marketer is on track; low or declining sales suggests there might be a potential problem.

The market also communicates with the marketer via complaint behaviors. Unhappy or dissatisfied customers issue complaints toward sellers in various ways. An increasingly important avenue for filing complaints is via the Internet. A growing number of consumers communicate their concerns to marketers via e-mail or dedicated customer service web pages set up by Firms. Social media, such as Facebook, Twitter, You Tube, and Instagram are major venues for communicating likes and dislikes voiced by consumers. One of the more interesting uses of the Internet for voicing complaints consists of web pages built by dissatisfied customers. Customers that are having a hard time getting their complaints appropriately reconciled by marketers are using web pages as a way of broadcasting their dissatisfaction with the offending company.

Valuable Exchanges Create Utility for Customers

Utility is another important term to insert into your marketing vocabulary. Utility is the want-satisfying, need-satisfying, or problem-solving ability of a product or service. Marketing is responsible for creating and communicating most of a product's inherent utility. Marketing programs that succeed in creating satisfying exchanges with customers provide these customers with utility in the process. For our purposes, five distinct types of utility exist (Exhibit 1.7).

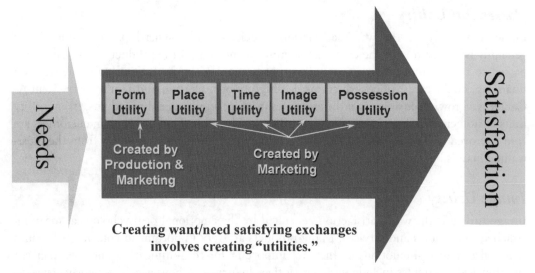

Creating want/need satisfying exchanges involves creating "utilities."

Exhibit 1.7 *Exchange, Utility, and Satisfaction.*

Form Utility

Form utility is the want-satisfaction generated by the physical characteristics of the product. The better the job the product does in delivering on the customer's needs and wants, the greater the product's form utility. For example, consider a car. A car's physical characteristics deliver form utility. The primary need served or satisfied by cars is transportation. Cars give customers the ability to move efficiently from point A to point B. When a particular car brand does a better job of satisfying the transportation need, that brand delivers higher amounts of perceived form utility. Form utility is derived primarily from the production function. However, marketing does provide input by using research to identify the benefits and physical attributes desired by customers.

Place Utility

Place utility is the want satisfaction associated with making the product available where customers exactly want to buy and to acquire it. Customers interested in obtaining place utility are often interested in convenience. They typically do not want to go out of their way to obtain products and services. These consumers are often willing of pay more for products and services in return for this convenience. Examples of marketing organizations and activities catering to place utility are convenience stores, in-home delivery, and in-home shopping (such as shopping via the television, telephone shopping, or shopping via the Internet). Indeed being able to place orders and accept delivery for products in one's home has to be the ultimate place utility!

Time Utility

Time utility relates closely to place utility. They go hand in hand. Time utility is the satisfaction gained from having the product available when you want to buy it. Time utility encompasses the desire for immediate gratification. Just as with place utility, customers are often willing to pay more in order to quickly obtain products and services. Examples of marketing activities that accommodate the desire for time utility are fast checkout lanes in grocery stores, drive-through windows at fast-food restaurants, ATMs, next day or one-hour turn around by cleaners, vending machines, and, of course, the convenient shopping available at local 7-Eleven's and neighborhood grocery stores.

Possession Utility

Possession utility is the want satisfaction associated with ownership. Possession utility generally is achieved with the customer acquires ownership of the product i.e., when title is passed to the customer. Marketers generate possession utility by facilitating ownership via financing, credit cards, price reductions, leasing options, renting, and rent-to-own. Rent-A-Center is a growing business that differentiates itself by providing enhanced possession utility to its customers with its rent-to-own plan called its Flex Plan. Under this plan, customers are "pre-approved to buy new and "like-new" pre-rented home furnishings today from the most-wanted brands."[8]

Image Utility

Image utility is the want satisfaction generated by the emotional or psychological meaning attached to products and services. Many products are very important to consumers because they reflect personal emotions or they are important for communicating one's self-concept (Exhibit 1.8). Examples include designer clothes, luxury cars, houses, and expensive jewelry. Consumers are willing to pay quite a bit more than the product probably is worth in exchange for its image utility.

Besides You, Who Does Marketing?

Businesses Are Marketers

Marketing organizations are Firms that sell goods and services to ultimate consumers. Walmart and Target stores sell products to consumers who use them in their daily lives.

Another category of Firms market to other businesses. These Firms engage in "business-to-business (B2B or B-to-B) marketing." Such "businesses" sell goods and services to other "business" customers that employ these goods and services in their day-to-day operations.

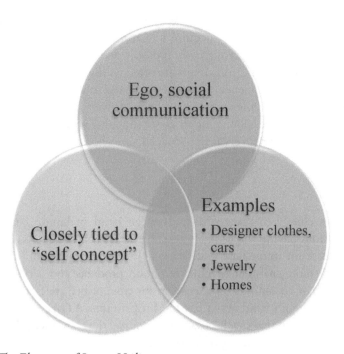

Exhibit 1.8 *The Elements of Image Utility.*

These customers are "business users." There are, for example, hundreds of businesses that supply General Motors (GM) as an organizational buyer (business user) with the equipment, parts, materials, supplies, and services that GM uses in its daily operations.

Some businesses buy products from their suppliers and simply resell them, unchanged, to other businesses. These business marketers are "re-sellers." Fleming Foods, for example, is a wholesaler of grocery products. Fleming Foods buys food and other grocery and related products from its suppliers and then resells these products to its retail store customers.

Non-Business Organizations Are Marketers

This book primarily focuses on marketing as a process conducted by business organizations. The actual act of marketing, however, is much broader than that. For starters, most people reading this are also marketers insofar as most readers would enjoy having more influence and power. Right? The most basic ways to acquire or execute more influence and power in your lives are present within most of the principles that drive this book. Learn them, and benefit accordingly.

Yet myriad other types of organizations engage in marketing. One category is the nonprofit organization. Charitable organizations, churches, some hospitals, some museums, and foundations are nonprofits. The American Red Cross exists to provide disaster relief in communities or regions stricken by natural and manmade disasters. The Red Cross relies on donations and government subsidies to provide these services. Big Brothers and Big Sisters (BBBS) is another charitable organization established to help disadvantaged children growing up in single parent households. BBBS' ability to aid these children depends entirely on contributions from businesses and private individuals.

Nonprofit organizations typically provide products, services, or ideas to their respective customers and publics. Some products and services may have prices attached to them; the values provided by nonprofits are not necessarily free. However making a profit is not an objective. The focus is on generating revenue to cover operating costs. Moreover, nonprofit organizations may engage in extensive promotional activities such as advertising on television, radio, as well as various printed and social media. The point here is that these non-business organizations engage in the same marketing activities as do traditional profit-oriented business Firms!

Government Agencies Are Marketers

Federal, state, and local government agencies also "market." Too much, in the opinions of many. Governmental agencies provide goods, services, and ideas to a wide range of "customers," including the general voting public. An excellent example is the Department of Defense. The Army, Navy, Marines, and Air Force each advertise in a variety of traditional and social media in an attempt to recruit new soldiers, sailors, marines, and airmen. The fundamental product or service offered is a career in the military. For example, consider the typical Marines Corp advertisement. An attractive life style is promoted that is supposed to appeal directly to potential recruits' self-concept. Military advertisements often stress self-concept and other emotional content. Indeed, the slogans employed by different armed services clearly emphasize emotional needs such as feelings of accomplishment and fulfillment ("Be all you can be."—Army; "Aim high."—Air Force), life experiences ("It's not just a job, it's an adventure."—Navy), pride ("The few, the proud."—Marines). However, the military also sells other products such as educational programs that allow individuals to learn useful trades that may be useful in the civilian community.

Individuals Are Marketers

Ordinary people are also marketers. For example, politicians are notorious for marketing themselves and their ideas. TV commercials promoting the images and ideas of specific politicians are commonplace. Most of these assume a comparative approach in which candidates compared themselves directly against their competition, usually while also tearing down the quality of that competition.

Consider the home page of the White House (www.whitehouse.gov). The site provides information about the White House, its history, visitation hours, and a range of interesting trivia and anecdotes. However, it also is a venue for "marketing" existing, pending, and proposed programs and legislation. Try searching other politicians' web pages. It should be apparent that these people are marketing themselves and their ideas, as well as providing information as a public service.

Finally, consider yourself as a marketer. You market yourself on many occasions and in many ways. During job interviews, you should market yourself by demonstrating to prospective employers the range of values that you can offer. The objective is to market the match between your skills and the needs of the company you are targeting as your future employer. You may market yourself via social media, such as Facebook or LinkedIn or your personal charm, wit or intellect.

→ You Should Learn

What are the most important things to learn in this class and from this book? (Hint: each is so important that you will not be tested on many of these things.)

1. The marketing concept applies to almost everything in life.
2. Communication skills such listening, writing, and speaking (and listening) really matter in marketing and business.
3. Marketing or interpersonal impressions really matter. In particular, first impressions are important because you never get a second chance to make a good first impression.
4. Almost everything you do has marketing implications.
5. "Everyone" never represents an acceptable marketing segment or target market.
6. Knowledge is the fundamental source of competitive advantage.
7. Change is inevitable, and will not arrive in a straight line.
   a. Change will be directly or indirectly resisted by someone; usually, by many.
   b. Change does not always represent progress, but change is always necessary for progress to occur.
   c. If you are really smart, you will always stay ahead of change and then, in effect lead the change.
8. All successful companies have one thing in common: they are customer-focused and heavily committed to marketing. These Firms make promises. More importantly, these Firms keep all promises they make.
9. Nothing happens in business until someone sells something.
10. The Firm or person who, throughout their lives, delivers the most value, wins almost every time.
11. Marketing is a part of all our lives, for better and for worse.

Endnotes

1   The Bible, Proverbs 30.

2   "College Students Exhibiting More Severe Mental Illness, Study Finds," *American Psychological Association*., August 12, 2010, http://www.apa.org/news/press/releases/2010/08/students-mental-illness.aspx, Accessed June 12, 2015.

3   Jack Trout and Al Reis, *Positioning: The Battle for Your Mind* (New York, NY: McGraw-Hill, 1981).

4   Alexandra Jacobs, "Sooth Moves: How Sara Blakely Rehabilitated the Girdle." *The New Yorker*, March 28, 2011, http://www.newyorker.com/magazine/2011/03/28/smooth-moves, accessed June 12, 2015.

5   Retrieved from: http://www.brainyquote.com/quotes/authors/y/yogi_berra.html

6   National Defense Budget Estimates for FY 2015. Office of the Under Secretary of Defense (Comptroller), April 2014. Retrieved from: http://comptroller.defense.gov/Portals/45/ Documents/defbudget/fy2015/FY15_Green_Book.pdf

7   Joseph P. Guiltinan and Gordon W. Paul, *Marketing Management. 5th Ed.* (New York: McGraw-Hill, Inc., 1994), 5-6.

8   Retrieved from: http://www6.rentacenter.com/how-rac-works/how-rent-a-center-works?

Chapter 2

Marketing Strategies: A Philosophical and Historical View

The word "strategy" is derived from the ancient Greek stratēgós, meaning "military commander," a description that remains appropriate today. Indeed, successful marketing strategies typically share much in common with successful military campaigns. Strategy entails the art and the act of creating power. Effective strategies allow planning units (a marketing Firm, a person, team, politician, nation, or armed service) to secure more value from a competitive situation than the original balance of power between the competing units suggested was possible. In strategic marketing contexts, this power and value would usually arrive in the form of competitive advantages. When strategies prove genuinely effective, the competitive advantages may prove sustainable.

Emu and kangaroos are both native to Australia. The emu is a large flightless bird; imagine a less attractive ostrich with a larger tail. The kangaroo, more famously, is a large marsupial characterized by powerful oversized hind legs and a pouch for its young. The latter animal is generally deemed cute and lovable, the former not so much. Yet each animal is prominently featured on Australia's Code of Arms. The reason why is important, relevant to this discussion, and driven by the one trait that these seemingly unrelated animals share: neither creature can take a step backward. Each animal is all-straight-ahead, all-the-time, just like the worldview, beliefs, and values that pervade throughout their native land. Australia remains resolute in its commitment to growth, improvement, and progress; the nation is utterly committed to moving forward. Hence, the nation's symbolic homage to two animals that can move only forward makes perfect sense.

Strategies should outline where the marketing Firm is going, how it will get there, and what will be accomplished after arrival. Strategies are all about growth, about moving forward, about laying-out a roadmap that permits planning entities to achieve reach their goals.

→ The Two Levels of Business Strategy

Business strategies can be classified, developed, and executed at two discrete levels. Strategic planning, at its core, forces development of an overall corporate or organizational strategy. The general strategic intention of these top-level, overarching (think umbrella-like) organizational-wide plans is to:

- Meet and beat competitive threats, and
- Ensure the long-term survival and eventual growth of the Firm.

Growth is critical to any Firm. To illustrate, consider the shark. What happens to sharks when they stop moving forward continuously? They drown because they can no longer breathe. Firms should think and act like sharks as they develop and execute their strategies. There is an ongoing need to move forward continuously.

At the second functional or **strategic marketing planning** level, tactical decisions are made about:

- Which products to produce or update (change in some manner), and
- How to promote, price, and distribute these products effectively.

In other words, tactical or tactical decisions about how best to manage the marketing mix are made. When Firms decide which products to produce, they are required to make other planning decisions. Specifically, Firms must simultaneously determine the:

- Market (i.e., target segments) they will enter and in which they will compete.
- Types of customer wants, needs, and ultimately problems they will satisfy or solve.
- Competitors against which they will compete.

Worth noting, when Firms decide which market segments they will target and serve, those Firms are also deciding who their competitors will be. The importance of these five decisions to any Firm's prospects for success would prove difficult to overstate.

A brief discussion about what constitutes a "product" appears also appears appropriate at this time. A product can be defined as anything developed or delivered by a Firm that a) potentially offers value to some customer or customer group and b) can be offered to those customers as part of an exchange relationship. Products could include tangible products, intangible services, an idea, person, or place or, as noted, anything else that might offer value to anyone. This point is important to understand. An expansive, but absolutely appropriate, view of what constitutes a product is in place throughout the following chapters.

→ Ten Universal Strategic Laws

Strategic planning processes require that senior leadership carefully examine and analyze where their Firms have been (the past), where their Firms are now in terms of their current Strengths and Weaknesses (the Present), and where their Firms logically should go given the Opportunities and Threats that they soon may face (Future). A famous Irish Proverb summarizes the capabilities and mindsets that strategic leaders hopefully possess or can cultivate as they execute strategic planning processes: "May you have the Foresight to know where you are going, the Hindsight to know where you have been, and Insight to know when you have gone too far."

In other words, the ability to move quickly combined with the wisdom to move fast with patience; leadership qualities that are not inherently contradictory. Seven strategic laws follow. Each is designed to promote one or more additional strategic leadership qualities inside leaders as they attempt to develop strategic marketing plans.

- *Strategic Law 1: Remain Grounded in Logic.* Strategists, operating in any decision-making setting, should always pursue logical marketing solutions. In its heyday (i.e., prior to its 2005–2011 era of overexpansion), Starbucks preferred to locate new stores near dry cleaners or movie rental stores. This plan for expansion was logical. After all, each neighboring retailing venue requires two visits, drop-offs and pick-ups. Starbucks eventually overextended, of course, by arguably placing too many competing stores too close to each other. Part of strategic planning success is based on knowing when to stop, to declare victory, not for purposes of going home but with the strategic intention of introducing some other product that offers alternative value to new or existing market segments.

- *Strategic Law 2: Always Account for Technology.* Movie rental stores, ironically, generally no longer exist. Technologically-driven innovations obsoleted the industry's business model, and the industry's marketing leaders responded too slowly to save themselves. Technology always has its say as well as, seemingly, its way. It creates new business opportunities at approximately the same rate it closes the door on dated business models. The role and impact of technology should be given special attention considered as strategies are developed. As this is written, technology remains the incredibly fertile mother of myriad changes, opportunities and threats, and growing/shrinking strengths/ weaknesses for myriad Firms. Technology, like emus, kangaroos, and sharks, is always moving forward.

- *Strategic Law 3: Accept but Accommodate Certain Uncontrollable(s).* Strategists, again logically, should never spend an excessive amount of time trying to change things they cannot control. Time, of course, is a finite resource, not to be wasted. Strategists instead should allocate more time to thinking and doing something about factors they can control. Marketers, for example, cannot control the pre-existing beliefs and attitudes of customers. Nor can marketers typically change those beliefs and attitudes. But marketing strategists still must account and make accommodations for such uncontrollable factors. This is one reason why planning for the management of target marketing efforts and the development of marketing mixes that deliver differing customer values is so crucial to successful marketing planning.

- *Strategic Law 4: Gold Rules.* When developing strategies plans, marketers should usually dance close to revenue and/or cost lines. Goals and tasks should prioritize goals and tasks based on their anticipated contributions to revenue (growth), costs (savings), and, ultimately, profits (enjoy them). Assuming they remain socially responsible (Chapter 4), marketing strategies should, with apologies to *Jerry McGuire*, "show [them] the money!"

- *Strategic Law 5: Manage Two Types of Risk.* Strategists must evaluate the potential risks and returns associated with all planning options. When planning, marketers should consider two types of risk. The first: "sinking the boat." The second: "missing the boat." "Sinking the boat" entails the risk of ruining a Firm by making a bad strategic bet. "Missing the boat" entails the risk of permitting a great strategic opportunity to cruise by because strategists missed, ignored, or were unwilling to shoulder the risk necessary to pursue it.

Historically, Firms appear more prone to "missing the boat." Many Firms have proven almost instinctively predisposed toward cutting marketing expenditures when problems or their possibility appear on the horizon. Cutting marketing expenditures in this manner is usually a bad idea. Ask Chrysler, long one of the Big-3 domestic (i.e., US based) automakers. Chrysler cut back dramatically on marketing expenditures (i.e., investments in new product development, promotions, brand management or training) at various points during the 1970s and then again during the 1990s. Since then, domestically, the Firm has remained seemingly chained into a weak third place among US auto marketers. Or ask Post cereals, one of the Big-3 domestic cereal makers along with Kellogg's and General Mills. Post cut marketing spending to the bone during the 1930s. At the time Post was the leading cereal marketer in the United States. But the Firm quickly collapsed to a third-place market share position and remains there to this day.

When they engage in strategy decision-making, marketers should also consider the Waterline Principle, which was authored by Bill Gore. Gore suggests that marketing strategists should imagine they are on a ship in the middle of the ocean. Marketing planners should further visualize that if any decision they make goes bad it will blow a hole in their ship. Now, if marketers blow a hole above the waterline (where the ship will not take on water and possibly sink), the hole can be patched, planners and their Firm can learn from the experience, and sail on in the knowledge that neither will repeat the mistake again. But if marketers blow a hole below the waterline, a deluge of water will rush in, pulling the boat toward the ocean floor. If the hole is big enough, the ship will sink fast. There is no chance to learn from your mistake. The strategic marketing planning lesson: As marketing planners make decisions, it is more than acceptable to make big bets. Generally speaking, this is how people and Firms get ahead and ultimately win big. But people or Firms should avoid making bets that would blow holes beneath their ships waterline if the decision goes wrong. Our recommendation, marketing planners should be carefully-aggressive, if that is not too much an oxymoron.

Two additional thoughts appear relevant. First, unless they consciously commit to the learning task, no guarantee exists that humans will learn from their mistakes. We humans are unique amongst the world's animals in our ability to learn from the mistakes of others and perhaps even more exceptional is our ability to ignore the lessons.

Second, none of these recommendations are offered as absolutes. Consider this: another axiomatic, and obviously historically grounded truth, is that if you or your Firm does not embrace the possibility of great failure you and it are far less likely to ever experience great success. Still, strategic planners should only take big risks when prospects of pain and gain— the ratio between likely gain and likely pain—are favorable enough to compel them to comfortably do so. Speaking of risk, we come to our next strategic guidelines.

- *Strategic Law 6: Distinguish between Uncertainty and Risk.* Why would intelligent strategic thinkers at powerful Firms damage their interests through such voluntary actions? The answer may relate to the distinction between risk and uncertainty. Risk describes a situation where planners have a sense of the range and likelihood of possible outcomes. Uncertainty describes a situation where not only it is unclear what might happen, it is also unclear how likely all the various outcomes are. Strategic marketers must distinguish uncertainty from risk. Only then can the types of risks that market- ers must manage be more fully revealed. The management of uncertainty is always part of strategy development and execution. But that management process will unfold more efficiently once the various sources and types of uncertainties are identified.

We won't go so far as to write: no guts, no glory. No, doing that would prove too cliché. But we would invite all future strategic planners reading this text to consider this cliché: Often, in business or in life, the great risk is not taking any.

- *Strategic Law 7: Accept that Some Problems Are Wicked.* Sometimes, marketers have no choice but to develop strategies aimed at resolving truly wicked strategic problems that are confronting the Firm. Wicked strategic problems include challenges so persistent, pervasive, or slippery that strategies often deem them insoluble. Examples of wicked strategic problems include:

  1. Balancing long-term goals with short-term demands (pressures). Business professors preach about how important it is to manage for the long run. But businesspeople, especially marketers, live in a what-have-you-done-for-me-lately world. And in a country where a $17,000,000,000 (that is, 17 billion) federal deficit exists as a sure

indicator that government is living for today absent much concern for future generations, who are we can criticize businesspeople who are more concerned about the short term?

2. Balancing the pursuit of profits with the desire to be socially responsible. Few people wake up wanting to ruin the environment for future generations. Yet strategic decisions designed to help one's great-grandchildren might take food from one's children's mouths. See, it is not just the government that appears overly concerned about the short run, the here-and-now.

3. Finding completely unclaimed new market space. The type of space, or gap, in the market where customers' problems are not being resolved and where your Firm and its products could be first-to-market or first-in-a-category.

4. Determining how best to multiply success and creativity by leveraging diversity of opinion and expertise through cross-functional collaboration; that is, getting marketers, engineers, accountants, new product developers and designers to all play well with one another inside the same organization. As we will learn in future chapters, the best ideas usually result when good ideas from diverse areas of thinking (say, accounting and marketing) come together and generate new ideas.

5. Protecting profit margins and sustaining market shares within increasingly commoditized business sectors. As products (from steel to pork bellies to smart phones) slide toward commodity states, achieving differentiation becomes more difficult. Thoughtful and creative marketing strategists should realize how diligently and purposefully they should work to avoid having the products they market turn into commodities or products that prove difficult to differentiate.

6. Or, simply, balancing the need for higher manufacturing quality with the desire for lower production costs.

- *Strategic Law 8. Often No One Best Solution Exists.* When attempting to strategically solve truly wicked problems, the solutions eventually agreed upon are rarely completely right or completely wrong. Instead, solutions will more likely prove merely better or worse. Perfectly strategic solutions will almost never be found for truly wicked problems. Engineering- or accounting-type minds are welcome to apply for and would likely excel in their execution of strategic level marketing decision-making roles. But the sort of person who assumes one-best-answer exists for every vexing marketing problem will likely be frustrated in the role because this is simply not true for those charged with successfully marketing products to human beings who not only are prone to making irrational buying decisions, but are prone to making purchasing decisions in predictably irrational ways, as economist Dan Ariel would say.

Planners would likewise benefit from remembering and acting in accord with the following words: "Contentious strategic problems are best solved not by imposing a single point of view at the expense of all others, but by striving for a higher order solution that integrates the diverse perspectives of all relevant constituencies." This perspective is attributed to Mary Parker Follett, circa 1857, who served as intellectual mentor to the famous strategy Professor Peter Drucker.

- *Strategic Law 9: Watch Those Assumptions.* During planning processes, strategists must remain vigilant about their assumptions. In business or in life, often it is not what we don't know that hurts us. It is instead that which we assumed we knew for certain. Watch those assumptions when developing or executing strategies.

- *Strategic Law 10: Relationships are Huge.* One assumption should always prevail; relationships are important. Creating and sustaining exchange relationships are always absolute keys to marketing success. Everything that Firms or individuals might do strategically in order to achieve or sustain marketing success relates directly or indirectly to relationships and exchange. Customers never owe anything to Firms. Instead, Firms always owe strategic commitments to create and deliver something of value to customer that they perceive is worth paying for; that's exchange, the basis for any marketer-customer relationship.

→ Business Strategy: What History Teaches Us

Each of the following quotes relates directly or indirectly to business and marketing strategy. The value of each quote follows from what it indicates, intimates, or implies about the value, necessity, or importance of strategy.

- "Failing to plan is like planning to fail."—UCLA basketball coach John Wooden.

John Wooden's statement implies that if you want to ensure the failure of your Firm or yourself, don't plan. A hugely successful basketball coach, Wooden cared so much about getting the details right that he even taught his players the best way to put on their socks. He also taught his players to "move quickly, with patience." This counsel surely should apply to marketers, too, whenever they detect an opportunity or threat through SWOT analyses. (More about SWOT analyses follow in Chapter 3.)

- "Plans are nothing, but planning is everything."—General and US President Dwight D. Eisenhower.

General Eisenhower's statement implies that plans rarely, if ever, work out the way they are supposed to on paper. Put another way, as another well-known military quote reveals, "No plan survives the first smoke of battle." Or as former World Champion heavyweight fighter Mike Tyson put it: "Everybody's got a plan until he gets punched in the nose." All three quotes are both relevant and true because circumstances change, mistakes are made, and enemies (or in this context, competitors) fail to respond as anticipated.

But none of this undermines the value and importance of planning. The planning act itself forces consideration of alternative contingencies to pursue, if things don't work as planned. The true value of planning is not that anticipated results somehow arrive seamlessly. This would only occasionally be true. Instead planning is valuable because engaging in the act of planning itself generates knowledge and insights about the marketplace, competitors and customers. And these insights, regardless of what happens to the plan, can contribute mightily to any Firm's ultimate success. Knowledge, you see, is often the ultimate asset, weapon, and source of advantage in contemporary marketing contexts.

- "A good plan, violently executed today, is better than a perfect plan next week"—General George Patton.

What General Patton was suggesting, well before the aphorism morphed into business cliché, is that strategists and their Firms should "never let the (pursuit of the) perfect be the enemy of the good." Patton's comment implies that Firms must be opportunistic when opportunities arise. Firms should strike fast and hard against their competitors as soon as they are able rather than waiting for the perfect time. When a threat arises, take whatever remedial or evasive actions appear appropriate. But do so now, rather than waiting too long.

Patton's take on strategy flips conventional planning wisdom on its ear. Prevailing thinking about strategy and plans, as presented in most texts, is that Firms should set big goals (sometimes called BHAGs—Big Hairy Audacious Goals) and then do whatever is necessary to achieve them. In fact, this approach is similar to many recommendations that follow below in this chapter.

But there are alternative ways to think about strategy. Instead of setting goals first, Firms may consider scanning their environment continuously (more about this in Chapter 3, too). The purpose of this scanning is to identify opportunities promising large payoffs at low costs. Only then should Firms establish their goals.

French Emperor Napoleon Bonaparte did exactly this during the first half of his brilliant military rise. Civil rights icon Dr. Martin Luther King followed this alternative strategic approach when he opportunistically exploited an unplanned bus boycott in Montgomery, Al, during 1954–1955. Rosa Park's refusal to sit at the back of the bus triggered a spontaneous city-wide boycott of buses among African-Americans. As noted, this boycott was not part of any plan. But when opportunity arose, unexpectedly and surreptitiously, the then still young national civil rights movement quickly exploited it. Changing goals rapidly, Dr. King quickly positioned himself as the face of non-violent civil rights brand and elevated awareness of such inequalities throughout the nation. His new plan culminated with the history-changing Civil Rights Act of 1964.

Non-violent protest was the **core competency** that drove the ultimate success of Dr. King's movement. This concept was borrowed from Mahatma Gandhi's leadership of non-violent protests that liberated India from its British oppressor in 1947. Moreover, non-violent protest works only when protesting against a rational and reasonably moral opponent or oppressor. Non-violent protests against North Korea, today, or Nazi Germany or Soviet Russia in the past, would have inevitably lead to disaster. The strategic takeaway: Plans inevitably must align with the spirit of their times and character of their environment or be doomed to failure. Marketing strategies should continuously strive to develop the right plan for the right context.

Technology is deeply embedded in the "spirit of our times," our *zeitgeist*. And technology, of course, changes everything. Should a professor ask, "In what ways has technology changed business?" you should reply, respectfully, a better question would be "In what ways has technology not changed business?" Technology is the ultimate one-way street. Technology influences how Firms communicate with Firms, how Firms communicate with customers, and how customers communicate with Firms.

Technology is the primary reason why in the future (say, one minute from now) the big (Firms) will not automatically eat the little (Firms). Instead, the fast will eat the slow. The act of planning helps Firms move faster.

What about you? What's your plan to improve your tempo?

- "When absolute superiority is not attainable produce a relative one at the decisive point by making skillful use of the resources you have."—General Carl von Clausewitz.

In this single quote General von Clausewitz, a renowned Prussian military strategist, provided three key points of counsel to any organization engaged in planning. First, Firms should attack competitors at their weakest points. The act of planning, as well as analysis, will often prove necessary to identify those weak points.

Next, Firms should concentrate on doing what they do best. That is, Firms should consciously cultivate a distinctive core competency (i.e., non-violence protest, as exploited to their advantage by the civil rights movement). And then, Firms should exploit these differences in ways that permit them to deliver differentiating value in the marketplace.

The various branches of the US Armed Forces understand this principle and leverage it to their advantage. Open water is a forbidding barrier to the US Army, while on the ground, it is Army-Strong. Fortunately, when the challenge is water the Navy is available. The Navy's core strength is water every bit to the extent that the Army's core strength is ground. Of course, the Marine Corps can deliver hell to waterborne and landlocked enemies alike.

Firms should focus on their strengths. Standing down from our warlike footing, consider In-N-Out Burger, a hugely successful provider of marketing value. In-N-Out believes so much in value of focus that apart from drinks it only features three menu items: burgers, fries, and milkshakes.

Focus matters greatly. When Starbucks lost its mojo a few years back (not just because the Firm almost certainly over expanded), it was because they had also lost their focus on coffee. The plan of selling CDs and/or sandwiches whose smell distracted from the coffee aroma were not cutting it. Starbucks has since regained its focus on the coffee mojo.

Finally, the counsel of von Clausewitz speaks to the fact that strategists should institute measures to carefully steward always limited resources or what has already been labeled the "3 T's:" time, talent, and treasure. Consider the allocation of time, for example, in the context of planning. The results are in. Studies show one of one people on earth dies. Time is irreplaceable. And even were it not, humans only receive 168 hours per week. There is never enough time to waste it. As noted, what is your plan? The question matters, as denoted in the next quote:

- "If you don't know where you are going, any road will get you there."— Anonymous.

Firms should view strategies as maps to desirable destinations. But first, a Firm must identify intentional destinations. This is where missions, and goals and objectives, come into play, along with metrics—or measurements—that permit planners to measure progress in route to those desirable destinations.

Measurements are an underappreciated aspect of strategy. But the omission of metrics from any strategy would be an unforced error, insofar as people or firms generally perform to their metrics. Measuring performance improves performance. But measuring is not enough. A value must also be assigned by the firm on the performance being measured. The question of whether the return (i.e., the value) the Firm is receiving in exchange for its strategic investment of time, personnel, or money in pursuit of a particular strategy goal or priority must be answered. If the answer is positive (customer service improved), plans should be in place to reward the responsible parties. If the answer is negative (customer service failed to improve), plans should take responsible parties to task.

- "The man who chases two rabbit's catches neither."— Chinese Proverb.

The value, power, and virtue of simplicity in strategic settings would prove difficult to overstate. Firms should focus ruthlessly on performing the one, two, or possibly three things that they must do well in order to succeed. Beyond that, they usually should outsource the performance of other functions to other Firms. This is what Apple does. Apple, at its core, only executes three key functions. But it performs those functions (i.e., idea creation, design, and branding) exquisitely well. Apple has consciously simplified its business model and relentlessly applied it to as many opportunities as possible.

- "Chance favors the prepared mind."— Louis Pasteur.
- "Dig wells before you are thirsty."— Chinese Proverb.
- "Luck is where opportunity and preparation meet."— Roman philosopher Seneca.

These quotes speak directly to a singular value that inevitably contributes to strategic success. The value, of course, is preparation. Planning not only requires preparation, it also creates preparation. Pasteur's statement suggests that Firms should get ready, in order to be ready when opportunities or threats arise. Then, as the Chinese Proverb infers, Firms won't delay initiating necessary action and lose the moment.

The famous swimmer Michael Phelps is 6'4" tall, weighed 186 pounds (when competing), has hands/feet as long as flippers, short legs and a long torso. Like most world-class swimmers, he is built like a fish. Olympic caliber swimmers never emerge unless they have already won the aquatic genetic lottery. But Phelps also trained diligently since age 8. To date he has won 19 gold medals, far and away the most in history. Was he lucky, good, or prepared?

- "We don't have a strategy, yet."— President Barrack Obama.

The President, speaking in 2014, was referring to the terrorist organization known as ISIS. He spoke truthfully about the fact that the United States had not determined how to address the ISIS problem. The voting marketplace generally reacted negatively toward this "no-strategy-here" admission. The brand image of the Democrat Party (i.e., a strategic marketing planning entity, as well as a brand and product!), as a whole, clearly suffered as a consequence. Republicans (the Democrat's primary marketing competitor) made unprecedented gains in House of Representatives, Senate, and Gubernatorial elections during the 2014 election cycle. The implication: Firms of all sizes, scales, and scopes should have a plan. And even when you don't have a plan, don't make public pronouncements about the fact.

- "If you don't have (or cannot create) a competitive advantage, don't compete."— Jack Welch, former CEO of General Electric (GE).

GE has been a marketing powerhouse marketer for decades. The Firm successfully marketed everything from light bulbs to locomotive engines to the brainy parts of nuclear weaponry. But GE experienced a serious sales decline during the 1980s prompting Welch to address the executives who were managing G.E.'s myriad **Strategic Business Units (SBUs)**. (A SBU is the smallest unit inside any Firm for which independent strategic planning can be done. An SBU could be an entire Firm, a division inside a Firm, or a product category family within the Firm) Welch said, "You need to become more creative in your development and delivery of differentiating value to customers and earn a competitive advantage"—or else. Creativity is but one key to product differentiation, but hugely important one. And individuals can become more creative through planning. More about this key topic follows in later chapters.

Virtually any product, no matter how similar it is to competitive offerings, can be differentiated when marketers are sufficiently creative. Take salt, for example. Salt is the most plentiful mineral on earth. Salt is salt; no differences separate one from another grain. But don't tell that to Morton Salt, who successfully differentiated its brand more than 100 years ago. Morton did this through the creative use of a blue cylinder-like container, a little girl, a yellow rain slicker, and the immortal positioning words: "When it rains it pours." Since that time Morton's has owned the table salt market. And all the while Morton's brand of salt, which is fact is no different from any other brand of salt, has commanded a materially higher price than competitor brands.

→ Why Strategy Is Useful

The act of developing a business or marketing strategy is inevitably useful. This is because the effort:

- Encourages systematic and forward-looking thinking within a Firm.
- Forces planners to create, clarify, and prioritize goals and objectives.
- Leads to more efficient coordination of efforts within a Firm.

- Leads to more efficient allocation of resources inside Firms.
  - Resources: Any physical, organizational, human, temporal (time) or financial asset that enables the Firm to generate and execute strategies that improve its efficiency and effectiveness in the marketplace.
  - Resources = time, talent, treasures (again, the "3-T's").
- Provides clear performance metrics for Firms.
  - In turn, the presence of these metrics facilitates managerial control and establishing accountability; that is, who is responsible for what?
- Helps Firms identify, understand, and respond more quickly to environmental changes and suddenly or gradually emergent opportunities and threats.
- Forces more careful consideration of the entire environment in which a Firm operates, as well as deliberation about customers and competitors who also exist as key dimensions of any Firm's environment.
- Increases the likelihood that the Firm is working-on-the-right-things and doing-those-right-things-right.
- Uncovers new ideas and areas for growth and improvement.
- Provides a safe harbor in which decision-makers can engage in possibility-thinking; i.e., considering and evaluating heretofore outside-the-box approaches.

Relevant Thoughts on Goals and Goal-Setting

The notion that Firms should be managed based on objectives or goals has been broadly accepted since at least 1954. At that time Peter Drucker suggested leaders establish the Firm's overall goals, and then, in discussion with each worker, establish and agree upon a subset of goals or objectives that align what those workers were supposed to do with the Firm's overall goals. These goals, according to Professor Drucker, should be SMART: Specific (precision and clarity matters greatly), Measurable (because what gets measured is what gets done), Actionable (steps can be identified to achieve the objectives), Realistic (the goals may stretch the Firm's collective abilities and resources, but are still reasonably attainable), and Time-sensitive (a time-line for completion of the objectives is always present).

Some critics, eventually including Drucker himself, have since suggested this approach is overly bureaucratic. Others suggest that when Firms focus only on outcome goals (for example, increasing year over year revenues by 20%) their ideal goals still remain uncertain. At times it thus may be preferable to establish indirect goals, and work forward in terms of planning once those indirect goals are achieved. A Firm, for example, may decide first to collect specific data. Then, after analyzing that data, decision makers have more exacting insights available about the nature and scope of what their goals ideally should be.

Beyond question, however, having well-defined objectives in place improves employee performance. Employees guided by clear and simple goals, on average, perform markedly better than employees whose only guidance was, say, "do your best." Clear and simple goals permit individuals, work teams, and Firms to focus better on more important tasks; to evaluate their performance against established benchmarks; to determine whether to maintain or change the current course of planned action; and to experience satisfaction and enhanced motivation when goals are reached and rewards are distributed.

The absence of clear, simple, and SMART goals is likely to trigger undesirable side effects. For starters, employees are more likely to neglect important issues and tasks. They are also more amendable to unethical or risky behaviors and more likely to experience less motivation as they operate in work environments burdened by uncertainty and dispute over which paths are best pursued. To improve performance, goals should be set more frequently and be more transparent to the rest of the Firm. Given today's technological tools, crowdsourcing might be employed to secure greater assurance that the goals are neither too difficult nor too easy to achieve. Innovative marketing managers might consider separating goal setting from performance reviews that influence raises and bonuses. This action alone would give employees at least implicit permission to truly challenge themselves and consequently sometimes fail. Google, for example, expects its goals to be met only 60–70% of the time.

Relevant Thoughts on Decision Making Itself

Here, near the end of this opening conversation about strategy, we should acknowledge that strategic success always boils down to the ability to make good decisions. Roughly speaking, there are only four steps in any decision.

First, strategists must perceive (make-sense of) the relevant situation. If the situation is relevant it will offer either opportunity of a threat.

Second, strategists should think up and prioritize all possible courses of action in response to the opportunity or threat that is embedded in the decision.

Third, strategists should calculate which action is in the best interests of the Firm.

Fourth, and finally, strategists should decide which action to pursue.

Experts have long assumed that step three is most important. This assumption is based on the premise that most strategists engage in rational economic-like calculations and attempt to maximize their own self-interests. But more recently, events increasingly suggest that the first step, the perceptual or sense-making step is most important. At first blush, it appears that perceiving a situation correctly should prove rather easy. Just look around and see what is happening. But the activity that appears most simple is probably actually the most complex; this is because most of the action occurs below the level of our conscious awareness. Making sense of the world is an active, perpetually ongoing process of "meaning-creation" that shapes, influences, and actively biases the other three steps of this comparatively simple decision-making chain. In the end, then, strategists need to become aware of their own biases.

→ Accounting for Porter's "Five Strategic Forces"

A leading strategic thinker, Michael Porter, notes that every Firm is subject to five forces and should consider each as it develops strategies. The five forces are: the competitors or rivals that the Firm currently faces, the threat of new competitors, the threat of substitutes for the Firm's current products, the bargaining power of suppliers (suppliers exist as part of any Firm's supply chain, a topic discussed later in detail), and the bargaining power of customers.

Within that environment, every Firm must choose a strategy. Insofar as every successful Firm possesses and is able to exploit some element of uniqueness, the overarching goal of that Firm's strategy is to find or develop that uniqueness and then capitalize on it. Only three ways exist for Firms to achieve that measure of uniqueness or what educated marketers commonly think of as differentiation. Firms can achieve uniqueness by:

- Earning low cost advantage in the minds of the segments they target,
- Differentiating greater customer intimacy within the segments they target, or
- Dominating a niche or market segment by establishing technological advantage.

More discussion about these three paths to differentiation and positioning success will follow in subsequent chapters. But for now, it is enough for readers to understand that trying to do some of each usually prevents a Firm from fully realizing the benefits of any of these strategies. As a result, the strategizing Firm usually loses sales and/or brand equity and/or pricing power and/or market share. Focus, as always, remains critical to Firms or people as either is developing and executing strategies.

CHAPTER 2A APPENDIX

→ Lessons from Extreme Strategic Marketing Rivalries

Marketing strategies are often comparable to the strategies that warring parties create in as they prepare for battle—a point emphasized during the chapter you just completed. One sentiment prevails across all strategic military contexts: when possible, never fight a "fair fight." Harsh, but absolutely true. Why would anyone ever plan to fight—to compete against—an enemy or competitor who enjoys a good chance of destroying you? Thus marketing and military strategies alike realize they should carefully choose their enemies (competitors). The choices strategists make may permit or prevent their future success, and survival.

The various US Armed Services (i.e., the Army, Navy, Marine Corp and Air Force) have always strenuously sought to avoid a fair fight, one waged between equally well-equipped, prepared, or motivated opponents. Better to crush than be crushed by your enemies and possibly rebuild or coop them later. One way for Firms to ensure that they never have to fight a "fair fight," as they prepare to wage marketing competitions, is to out-strategize their competitors: to use resources more effectively; to move faster to acquire the best terrain first (notably, those positions often exists inside the minds of targeted customer groups); to outflank or outthink (which generally comes down to out-creating) one's opponents. So if Firms are able to muster and exploit their power through their strategic marketing plans in ways that provide them with unfair advantages against their competitors, we say, all the better. That is, as long as the Firm consciously elects to fight in an ethical and socially responsible manner.

Most wise marketers understand this military/marketing strategic intersection and act accordingly. But sometimes even the best marketers have taken the warlike hostility a bit too far. Certain of these extreme strategic marketing rivalries are discussed below.

Sometimes the competing Firms failed to play fair but still performed ethically. At other times the competitors were well-matched and competed fairly and ethically with one another. Unsurprisingly, at times the strategic marketing competitions described below reflect no-holds-barred marketing competitions where each opponent was utterly committed to winning, no matter what the costs. And frequently, as demonstrated below, those costs were extremely high.

But at this point, who are we to judge? Because each set of business rivalries is instructive. Each delivers unique strategic lessons. Moral posturing and the provision of opinions about what is right or wrong on various topics, as authors tend to do, is well and good. But when moral posturing is replaced by an honest (reliable, valid, unbiased) reporting of what has historically transpired, the results often yield useful insights. Moral posturing, one could argue, represents the way authors would like the world to work; whereas the type of historical summary of several fierce strategic marketing strategies demonstrates how the marketing world actually does work. Besides, we save our moral and ethical posturing for Chapter 5.

Playing Strategic Hard Ball

The distinguished grey-haired gentleman genius credited with bringing electric light to the world, Thomas Edison, once wantonly and publically murdered an innocent elephant, Topsy. He did so on one fine day in January 1903. In public. In front of thousands. The killing was performed strategically as a part of a corporate promotion.

The ten-foot-tall Topsy was executed to illustrate the dangers of his primary competitor's brand of electricity current. In the original AC/DC showdown, Edison and his Firm, Edison General Electric and his rival, Nicola Tesla and his firm, Westinghouse, launched a strategic marketing throw-down that lasted for decades. But this event was not the culmination but simply one episode in an ongoing brutal marketing war involving these two rivals. Not satisfied with killing Topsy, Edison then turned his DC current's attention toward the execution of a criminal, in an effort to demonstrate the superiority of his brand in the first electric chair. The execution required eight minutes, two attempts and was broadly criticized. George Westinghouse, the founder of Tesla's Firm, said (paraphrasing) "they should have an ax instead" [to execute the man].

Edison, the mentor, felt he had been scored by Tesla protégé. Tesla, the protégé, felt he had been cheated out of money and recognition that he rightfully earned while working for Edison, and history suggests he was right. Tesla's AC electric current ultimately won the marketing battle; Edison won the war. His Edison General Electric eventually morphed into the GE that is so well known and powerful, today. Long after Tesla and Edison had died, the feud carried on until the 1980s, when GE choose the right CEO, Jack Welch, and Westinghouse choose poorly, and soon was no more.

Phil Knight, founder, owner and acknowledged marketing maestro of Nike, was slowly but steadily losing a marketing war with, as well as marketing share to, Reebok during 1984. Then, betting on the future, he signed a hoops player who had left college one year early to join the National Basketball Association (the NBA). The player's name was Michael Jordan. The competitive advantage accruing from Mr. Jordan's personal brand's strategic affiliation with the Nike brand continues to change marketing history to this day.

From the start Mr. Jordan, rightfully reputed to be the most fiercely competitive player in NBA history as well as, at one time, the most powerful personal brand in the world, apparently knew how to strategically manage his image from the jump. When asked, during the signing event, whether he preferred Coke or Pepsi, Michael (as a 22 year old) instantly opined: [Why choose?] … "they both taste great." At early age Mr. Jordan understood there is never a reason to alienate a potential sponsor, or for that matter, customer. This strategic savvy has characterized Michael ever since. Jordan has repeatedly been asked to endorse particular Democrat political candidates. He always steadfastly refused, retorting simply: "Republicans buy shoes, too."

Great strategic marketing conflicts make for interesting story, which is fun. But great marketing rivalries have also changed the world.

Surely, most students would shudder at the thought of facing life without smartphones or the Internet. But that likely would be your life now if the little-engine-that-could, MCI, had not challenged the enormous ATT and its monopoly power in 1974.

By the last two years of his life Steve Jobs was working with Bill Gates on several new products. During the preceding 30-something years, however, Jobs and Gates had competed fiercely with one another in a titanic strategic-struggle over whose vision of the computing world would prevail. Their rivalry, too, changed the act of your life as a consumer, businessperson, and one who communicates with other "friends"—however and whatever that term has evolved to mean today in a Facebook world.

Finally, air travel, particularly its international variety, painful as it has become, would be much worse still had European-based Airbus and US based-Boeing not gone at each other with hammers and tongs for decades. At least their products, passenger airplanes themselves, have improved as a result of their rivalry.

Game Changer

Competition, at any level, forces all Firms to elevate their strategic game. Even the losers, for whom failure usually is not fatal but rather an opportunity to learn, usually benefit from business marketing competitions. Moreover, competition surely helps consumers and other Firms because of the wonderful customer solutions that unrelenting strategic competitions can stimulate. Competitors—or rivals and thus rivalries—are, after all, one of Porter's "Five Strategic Forces" as referenced originally in Chapter 2.

Yet competitive pairs sometimes engage so intensively with one another that they become blinded by their intense strategic focus on each other. As a consequence they may unconsciously co-create planning contexts where each misses out on various other should-have-been-obvious marketing opportunities. Consider, for example, Coca-Cola, Inc. and PepsiCo, Inc., each unquestionably ensconced amongst the most strategic and successful marketers in American history. The two giants have competed head-to-head for their share of customer hearts, mouths, and wallets since the 1890s. To suggest that neither Firm likes the other is an understatement. A circumstance which, against all odds, may explain why neither Firm markets the best-selling energy drink in both the United States and throughout the world. That prize goes to the Salzburg, Austria-based Red Bull.

This same sort of myopic focus likely also explains why another pair of powerful Firms strategically focused nearly exclusively on each other for decades. That is, they maintained this myopic focus until the 2000s arrived. Then, seemingly out of the blue, General Motors and Ford Motor Company finally realized Toyota and other Japanese brands such as Nissan and Honda had not just incrementally stolen their former US market share. The Japanese Goliaths had also taken the majority of their profits. How? The former underdogs had methodically developed and executed strategic marketing plans that enabled them to develop marketing mixes that consistently delivered higher quality vehicles at lower prices to the US market. Lower prices and higher quality is a differentiating value likely to appeal to myriad market segments. Patriotic obligations are one reason for Americans to buy domestically-produced vehicles. Clearly superior financially-driven values apparently are an altogether and far more persuasive reason to buy foreign.

To this day, the two domestic automakers continue to hate— and likely focus too exclusively— on each other. Ford Marketing Chief, Jim Farley, recently said: "I hate them [GM] and what they stand for." Around the same time, former GM Chairman Dan Akerson suggested "holy water" be sprinkled on the ailing but still iconic Ford Lincoln brand, closing by saying: [For Lincoln] "It's over." The Lincoln brand has not left the market, yet, but you get the point.

Perhaps Ford and GM executives should refocus their rivalry imposed hate, and their strategic efforts not just on fighting each other fairly, but also encountering the Japanese, Korean and

European competitors whose strategy continue to produce more winning—or should we write, differentiating—value.

Strategic Takeaway

Marketing is a highly competitive game. Marketing is also a strategic competition. The game of marketing likewise rewards patience, balance, and an outward-looking, scanner-like, perspective. Finally, marketing, the game, punishes unwarranted hatred.

Marketing strategy is a game that ostensibly is played by competing firms. But not really; in fact, not at all. Firms never compete with other Firms. Instead teams of human beings who lead and represent each Firm compete with other teams of human beings doing the same things for their Firms. Thus the human element, and humanity's concomitant emotions, play an important role in the development and execution of successful strategic marketing plans.

There are seven human emotions: love, happiness, fear, anger, sadness, desire, and hatred. Worth noting, four of these emotions are definitively negative, while the sixth, desire, is often cast as such. Malice is every bit as much a part of human nature as is kindness. But my hating you or your Firm is analogous to me drinking poison and hoping you and your Firm die. Takeaway One: respect, don't hate your competitors.

On the flip side, sometimes what you hate is what makes you great. So, Takeaway Two: if hate you must (after all, haters gonna hate, right?) then choose who or what you hate carefully. Witness, for instance, the arc-of-history-altering technologies and products fomented by the great Steve Jobs-Bill Gates strategic rivalry. So choose carefully what you hate because you are likely to become it yourself. Gates and Jobs choose their archenemies well.

Which brings us toward consideration of the strategic value that can accrue to those strategic planners who exercise patience and achieve balance as they develop and execute the plans that prove necessary to meet and beat their competitors.

Takeaway Three: moderation, balance, in almost all things is a good thing. Successful strategic planners generally think as people of action but act like a people of thought. Successful strategic planners, whether they realize it or not, overcome the Focusing Illusion, meaning they understand, overtly or not, that few things in business—no competitor, customer, or problem—are as important or as bad as you think they are while you are thinking about them. In other words, when it comes to planning successfully, strategists rarely suffer from potentially damaging delusions or obsessions about their primary rivals.

CHAPTER 3
DEVELOPING AND EXECUTING STRATEGIC MARKETING PLANS

The strategic marketing planning process, on its surface, appears simple. The marketing planning process features the following steps:

- Analyzing marketing opportunities: What and where are the best opportunities? From the start of this process Firms should realize that no Firm or product can be all things to all people. No product has ever been made or marketed that everyone wants or needs *and* can also afford. (There are many people who would want a Ferrari, but can all of these people afford a Ferrari?) Consequently, marketers must target carefully.

- Selecting target markets (or selecting market segments): This step entails identifying the customer segment(s) that the Firm is best equipped to target and pursue; these customer groups, effectively, represent the best marketing opportunities. The ability to identify the unmet needs, unrecognized wants, and/or unsolved problems of the customer segments that have been targeted should drive any planning efforts that are developed at this point.

- Developing and eventually executing the marketing effort: This step entails deciding how best to manage the Firm's marketing mix in order to create and deliver the most appealing sorts of value to target markets.

Firms generally seek to satisfy the needs of multiple target markets. **Target markets** are the groups or market segments of customers that the Firm is best prepared to pursue because of differentiating value that it is able to deliver. These segments are generally homogenous in nature. Their homogeneity means that the segments typically share certain characteristics such as the same age, ethnicity, attitudes, zip codes, etc. And the fact that the segments are homogeneous means they are more likely to respond in a similar fashion (either positive or negative) to the differentiating value that Firms are able create through their marketing mixes. Value, in turn, is defined as the hopefully positive difference between what a customer gains (a "get") from owning/using a product and what it costs the customer (a "give") to acquire the product. Please note, value is tied to exchange; here, the exchange relationship between customers and marketers. Exchange, also involves two parties who elect to engage "in a get and a give."

Its billion plus users engage continuously in an exchange relationship with Facebook. Facebook gets all your personal information (which Facebook uses for other marketing purposes), postings of all your pictures, tags for all your friends, and so, forever. In return, Facebook optimizes your social life. And that is pretty much that.

The marketing mix, as previously discussed and shown again in Exhibit 3.1, is also called the "4P's." The first P is the product. Products deliver value, satisfy customer needs, and/ or solve their problems. The order in which the next three P's—promotion, place (also called distribution) and price—are considered does not matter. What matters instead is that strategies are developed that permit the Promotion and Place elements to be managed in ways that create value for both customers and the Firm or, in the case of Price, captures value from customers for the Firm. Notably, when marketing managers change any one of the 4P's they create an entirely new marketing mix; one that delivers a new and unique sort of value to targeted market segments.

When a Firm is marketing services (as opposed to tangible products) the marketing mix is often treated as if it featured three additional "Ps." The three new Ps are: the *People* (who perform or provide the service), the *Physical environment* (in which the service is delivered) and *Process* (or the process through which the service is developed and delivered). There are various reasons why services are often marketed differently from products, and these reasons will be discussed in latter chapters.

Marketing mixes should be managed as tools through which Firms establish distinctive positions for their products (brands). Market positions are complicated to explain, but genuinely important to understand. In marketing a position can alternatively be described as:

- An image or mental representation that customers develop about the characteristics associated with the product (because, after all, positions are developed in the collective mind of the targeted market).
- The collective perception of targeted market segments about the product's ability to satisfy their needs.
- The manner in which the product measures up against, or is perceived as more or less desirable than competing products available in the market.

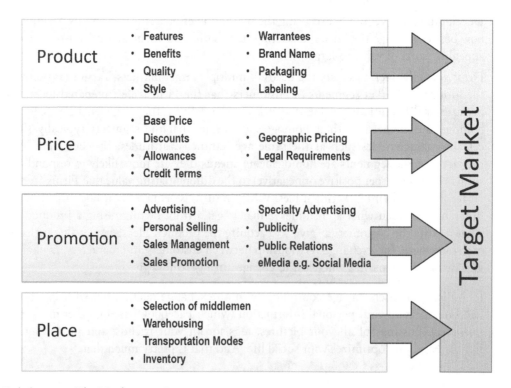

Exhibit 3.1 *The Marketing Mix.*

In some ways the primary purpose of any marketing strategy is to create a unique and uniquely desirable position for the Firm's products. Notably, when Firms create desirable positions for their products they have also effectively differentiated those same products.

→ So What's a Marketing Strategy?

A **target market**, a sought-after and desirable market position, and the marketing mix used to reach this target market with differentiating value are collectively referred to as a marketing strategy. As noted, Firms usually target more than one market segment. This implies, in turn, that multiple marketing strategies are frequently developed and subsequently executed by a single Firm. The Firm's marketing objectives, its marketing strategies, and its associated implementation and control activities are referred to as the Firm's marketing program.

The need to design and implement the best possible marketing program is the most important task facing any Firm. And we do mean ALL Firms. Absent sound marketing objectives, strategies, and supporting implementation and control (metrics) programs, Firms will inevitably fail in the market place. We encourage students to take a moment and attempt to identify a successful Firm that has sustained its success without also having successful marketing programs in place. Trust us, you will not be able to identify many, if any, Firms.

The marketing manager's job is to develop and execute this marketing strategies and programs. Marketing management entails the process of developing, implementing, and controlling marketing programs. Marketing managers must identify attractive target markets to serve and guide the Firm as it develops and implements marketing mix activities that will convert targeted market segments into profitable customer groups.

→ The Strategic Marketing Planning Process

Marketing managers engage in a sequence of activities that is called the strategic marketing planning process. Exhibit 3.2 summarizes the steps in this process.

Identify and Select Market Opportunities

The first and probably most critical step in the process is to identify possible market opportunities for the Firm. A potential market opportunity exists anywhere there is an unfilled need or unsolved problem in the marketplace that the Firm believe it can profitably satisfy or solve. As students move forward through this book they would benefit from thinking about needs-as-problems or problems-as-needs. Unsolved problems or unsatisfied needs each exist as potential market opportunities to any marketer who is able to address them successfully. When a Firm conducts a **Market Opportunity Analysis (MOA)** it is attempting to identify a customer group that possesses a specific need (problem) that can be satisfied by offering these customers a particular marketing mix. The MOA activity itself is subsumed under the more general **SWOT** analyses (Strengths, Weakness, Opportunities, and Threats) activity.

SWOT Analysis

The execution of strategic planning processes involves a SWOT analysis. Decision-makers (i.e., the strategic planners) should evaluate the Strengths and Weaknesses that exist within their Firm during SWOT analyses. Planners should subsequently develop and execute strategies that permit them to exploit their Firm's strengths. Weaknesses, on the other hand, impose constraints on what planners can do as they develop and execute marketing strategies.

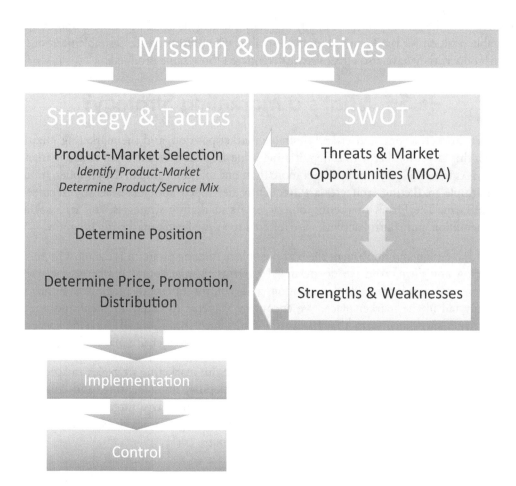

Exhibit 3.2 *The Strategic Marketing Planning Process.*

During SWOT analyses, decision-makers also evaluate the Opportunities and Threats that exist outside the Firm. These opportunities and threats would exist even if the Firm did not exist. Opportunities or threats emerge as a consequence of the presence of uncontrollable environmental trends that are moving in favor of or against the best interests of a Firm. Gasoline prices at the pump rise or fall based on the whims of the market. General Motors, as large and powerful as it is, is unable to control the rise and fall of gas prices. Yet falling gas prices exist as an opportunity for the Strategic Business Unit at GM that is responsible for making and marketing trucks and other sports utility vehicles at the Firm. Just as the same falling gas prices represent a threat to GM's hybrid car divisions. GM's planners must account for the likelihood that retail gasoline prices will rise or fall as they engage in strategic marketing planning, because their estimates of this particular threat or opportunity should impact what sorts and how many vehicles they produce, and how they promote and price each of them. (Note, reference was just made to three of the 4 P's.)

MOA exists as part of the "opportunities" aspect of SWOT analyses. For Remington Arms, a manufacturer that produces guns and ammunition, the threat of gun control legislation is taken seriously and factors heavily into its planning processes. Curiously, the threat of gun control actually increased short-run sales for Remington. But if highly restrictive gun control legislation to ever pass, the longer-term marketing prospects for Remington would be substantively impacted, as would its strategic planning processes. Still, for Firms such as Remington, a crisis is a terrible thing to waste. For genuinely strategic marketers, so are opportunities, threats, and problems, even those that appear uncontrollable.

SWOT analyses focus on analyzing the current state of the Firm's marketing efforts along with current and future environmental trends that pose threats as well as present opportunities to any Firm. Mindful of this, the SWOT should be conducted as a series of separate, but related, analyses. Specifically, the SWOT should consist of industry and competitor analyses, environmental analyses, market and customer analyses, current marketing programs analyses, demand analyses, and critical resources analyses. The meaning and implications associated with each are discussed below.

Industry and Competitor Analysis

SWOT analyses would normally begin with a thorough examination of the principal industry within which the Firm operates. This analysis includes how Firms in the relevant industry compete with one another and how those Firms "compete" with Firms in closely allied industries. This analysis, along with the environmental analysis, should identify the major threats and opportunities faced by the Firm. The primary purpose is to investigate:[1]

- The nature and intensity of competitive interaction in the industry, including trends related to numbers of competitors.
- The existence of powerful suppliers that may make pricing and price-related demands that adversely affect industry margins.
- The existence of entry or exit barriers that tend to prevent competitors from easily entering or leaving the industry.
- The existence of substitute products that may directly or indirectly compete with the products current produced by Firms in the industry.
- The fundamental channel structures and supply chain and logistics processes that prevail within the industry and, culminating in
- The nature of industry cost structures that determine which value-added stages within their supply chains represent the greatest costs to Firms.

Another purpose of this industry and competitor analysis investigation is to identify the **Key Success Factors (KSFs)** that prevail within the relevant industry. KSFs are characteristics (essential skills or assets) that appear most likely to prove critical as prerequisites for success within market sectors in which the Firm is competing. Firms that possess or able to acquire these KSFs will enjoy a distinct competitive advantage.[2]

Competitor analyses focus on defining the major competitors in the industry. Competitors should be investigated for purposes of identifying who they are, their modes of operation, and their relative strengths and weaknesses. The resulting insights may determine much of the Firm's subsequent marketing strategy. Classifying the potential threats posed by specific competitors entails examining all facets of their marketing programs. Strategic Firms should identify competitors' target markets, market positions, and marketing mixes. Valuable information about competitors can be gathered through various readily-available sources of information. Such sources might include but are certainly not limited to popular press articles, advertisements, stock reports, or conversations with customers, suppliers or Firms that partner with the competitor.

The ability to identify and evaluate the marketing strategies of key competitors probably offers the quickest means through which Firms can gain actionable insights about the market and about what is required to successfully satisfy customers in that market. By examining how competitors operate a Firm can:

- Identify how the market is currently segmented by examining differences in customer groups served by different competitors.

- Identify the basic wants, needs, and problems that specific market segments are experiencing, and gain insight into how effectively those wants, needs, and problems are currently being addressed by key competitors.

- Identify customer groups whose needs and problems are underserved or not satisfied at all.

- Identify competitors' market positions and the differentiating marketing mix and value factors that contribute most to their positions. The planning Firms can then determine how best to position its products in ways that "differentiate" them in a "determinant" fashion from competitors. More about the important meaning and implications of the word determinant to follow in latter chapters.

- Assess the likely effectiveness of different pricing, promotion, product/service and distribution strategies by examining how effectively similar strategies have worked for competitors.

- Identify which elements of the Firm's current marketing mix should be changed to satisfy current customers more effectively.

Environmental Analysis

A thorough analysis of the Firm's external environment will identify changes and trends on the horizon that may generate additional opportunities and threats. The external environment is comprised of various dimensions, including the economic, social, natural, and political-legal environments. The early identification of threats better prepares the Firm to minimize or eliminate their negative impact on the Firm. Indeed, these threats can sometimes be converted into market opportunities. The marketing environment subject is addressed in greater detail in the following chapter.

Current Market and Customer Analysis

The purpose of market and customer analyses is to determine how current and prospective target markets for existing or proposed products are structured, and how best to characterize (profile) customers in those markets. Managers begin by examining existing target markets to determine how well current customers are being served. The Firm's current markets and its positioning strategies are examined in order to identify shortfalls and areas for improvement. The purpose of this analysis is to: (1) determine the extent to which ongoing opportunity exists in markets that are currently served by the Firm and (2) explore new markets to ascertain their potential opportunity for the Firm. Key issues that should be explored during market and customer analyses include:

- Customer wants and needs with respect to existing products or services, or products and services that could be developed by the Firm, in current and new markets.

- The characteristics (i.e., features, attributes, and benefits) of the product or service that customers view as most important inside current and new markets.

- The existence of possible market segments in current or new markets.

- Characteristics (demographics, attitudes, lifestyles, wants, needs and problems) of buyers in different market segments in current and new markets.

- The reasons why customers buy the basic product and why they may buy one brand rather than another.

Current Marketing Programs Analyses

Here, detailed analyses of the Firm's current marketing programs are undertaken. First, the Firm's current marketing mix should be carefully examined. The purpose of this examination is to identify what the Firm is doing right (e.g., keep-on-keeping-on, perhaps even with the allocation of additional resources) or wrong (e.g., areas for upgrades and improvements).

Ultimately, recommendations must be made regarding how any problems identified during this analytical stage can be corrected. Information for these analyses is obtained from discussion with key personnel inside the Firm, its financial records, journal and magazine articles, advertisements, and other public documents. This step usually takes the most time to execute.

Demand Analysis

The purpose of the demand analysis is to forecast potential demand for the Firm's existing and potential products in existing and prospective target markets. As a result, managers ultimately are faced with the always-challenging task of forecasting industry sales, company sales, and sales for specific products or services. Challenging indeed, because as pointed out in the last chapter, Yogi Berra once said, making predictions is difficult, especially when they are about the future. That is supposed to be funny, and it is, but you should also get the point.

The basic questions that must be answered at this stage are:

- Market and/or market segment size in terms of unit and dollar sales in current and new markets.
- Potential market share for the Firm's products in current and new markets.
- Anticipated actual sales in specific target markets.

Various tools are available to enhance the effectiveness of this forecasting process. These tools range from simple qualitative "seat of the pants" estimates to very sophisticated statistical techniques. The forecasting task generally proves easiest for products that the Firm is currently selling to well-established markets. Unless major changes are afoot for one or more elements of the marketing mix or major changes in important environmental variables that may threaten or enhance anticipated affect sales are uncovered, forecasts can be executed through time-series extrapolations from products' sales during previous periods.

By contrast, the task of forecasting sales for new products is fraught with far more uncertainty. Indeed, sales forecasts for newly-developed and launched products often amounts to guesswork. In such cases, one can sometimes back into reasonable forecasts by determining the minimum level of sales needed in order to achieve a specific return on investment or to cover fixed operating costs. Armed with knowledge of past sales data for the entire industry as well as select competitors, the strategist may be able to subjectively, yet with a sufficient degree of accuracy, estimate the likelihood that this minimum level of sales can be achieved.

Critical Resources Analyses

The SWOT analysis should end with an audit of the Firm's critical resources. An analysis of how well the Firm currently is utilizing its resources to serve current markets, as well as the Firm's capacity to exploit new market or environmental opportunities, is conducted. Key resources examined would include available capital or access to capital, technical and managerial expertise, plant and equipment, and the adequacy of the Firm's organizational structure for serving each potential market. In one or another form, each resource type can be summarized in the always limited Time, Talent, and Treasure within any operational Firm.

Careful attention should paid to identifying strengths and weaknesses possessed by the Firm relative to its ability to serve current and future markets, particularly in comparison to competitors' capabilities to deliver the same services to the same markets. Specific attention should also be allocated toward identifying potential sources of differential competitive advantage or assets or skills possessed by Firms that give them distinct, enduring advantages over competitors. As such, these advantages often emerge from KSFs. Assets might include virtually any resource possessed by a Firm that elevates it to a position of relative strength in comparison to competitors. Examples include:

- Strong brand name identification, brand equity, and the associated pricing power that generally follows these initial two assets.
- Differential access to capital, human resources, raw materials, or distribution channels.
- Patents or other forms of legal protection for critical technologies.
- Cost advantages stemming from scale economies or experience curve effects.

The sort of skills that can function as sources of differential competitive advantage can include anything the Firm "does exceptionally well, such as manufacturing or promotion, which has strategic importance to that business."[3]

Market Opportunity Analysis

Market opportunity analysis (also known as **MOA**) entails the systematic search for and analysis of opportunities.[4] The critical limiting factor in this quest is profitability. Any potentially targeted market presents a prospective opportunity to any Firm only to the extent that the Firm can successful pursue the opportunity at a profit to the Firm. (Those readers who are highly engaged may note the implicit reference here to the marketing concept, wherein Firms are highly focused in their efforts to satisfy wants, needs, and problems of customers, but only under those conditions where those wants, needs, and problems can be satisfied through ways that prove profitable to the Firm.)

However, the focus must be on long-term profitability. Entrepreneurs, for example, should seek opportunities that enhance the long-term viability of the Firm, rather than opportunities that merely provide short-term boosts to their bottom line. While appealing because it promises quick solutions to the Firm's financial problems, this type of opportunity would only rarely represent the best long-term strategic alternative.

Identifying market opportunities requires an organized scanning, or assessment, of the relevant marketing environment. One purpose of this analysis is to identify customer groups (segments) whose needs, for some reason, have not yet been met. Such opportunities for growth can be straightforward, such as continuing to market the same products to current target segments already served by the Firm, but marketing those products more effectively by changing some aspect of the marketing mix in ways the deliver new and appealing value to current customers. Indeed, current target markets are generally the first place that Firms should examine when seeking new opportunity. These so-called market penetration opportunities entail the least risk.

At the growth spectrum's other end, Firms may decide that their best opportunities lie in developing entirely new products for new markets, customer segments that differ substantially from those the planning Firm is already experienced at serving. These latter opportunities are referred to as market diversification opportunities. Naturally, these are much riskier for the Firm to pursue.[5]

The Importance of Mission and Goals

The range of market opportunities examined by any Firm should be constrained by its mission. A Firm's **mission** specifically designates and directs the sort of opportunities the

Firm should or should not pursuit. The **mission statement** guides the Firm toward opportunities that are consistent with what it currently pursues or could pursue in the future.

Good mission statements tend to have the following elements in common. They:

- Focus on satisfying customers' needs.
- Indicate a distinctive competency "owned" by the Firm.
- Are neither overly broad nor too narrow.
- Are realistic, specific, suitable for the environment in which the Firm operates, and motivating.

A mission statement should define in the fewest possible words any Firm's reason for existence. The mission should embody the philosophies, ambitions, and mores (these designate acceptable or unacceptable behaviors) for the Firm. Any Firm that operates without a mission runs the risk of wandering through the world without an ability to verify whether it is on its intended best course. This is because the Firm's strategic goals, by definition, must be compatible with its mission. Goals should be established in ways that permit the Firm to take advantage of its strengths and overcome its weaknesses. **Goals** ensure that the Firm does what is necessary and appropriate to secure the resources and establish the means (approaches) and methods necessary to measure progress toward achieving its mission. The Firm's goals provide useful metrics and benchmarks against which to measure progress or the failure to move forward successfully. Goals should feature a time line, a will-be-completed by specific date metric.

Focus on Satisfying Customer Needs

Most Firms traditionally defined their missions in product or technological terms.[6] A Firm, for example, may state its mission as "we manufacture high quality mechanical pens and pencils" (product definition) or "we are a Firm that is committed to remaining at the forefront of semiconductor technology" (technological definition). Firms that define their missions in this manner have been accused of engaging in **marketing myopia** (short-sightedness and/or tunnel-vision), in that this type of mission statement may excessively restrict the range of market opportunities that they can examine. In turn, this myopic view may cause them to ignore highly profitable opportunities.

Theodore Levitt suggested Firms should define their missions from a market perspective. The mission should focus on satisfying customers' wants and needs, rather than on building products. Levitt cites the railroad and movie industries as classic examples of Firms that "missed-many-boats" (see Chapter 2) by defining their missions too narrowly based on a product perspective. The strength of railroads, traditionally defining their mission as building and running railroads, was greatly diminished by the advent of the internal combustion engine and the new modes of transportation that this technology spawned. Remember, technological advances of any significant magnitude almost always represent threats to some industries and opportunities to others. The railroad industry would have been better served by defining its mission from a transportation (market needs) perspective.

Similarly, the movie industry traditionally defined its mission as making movies. If the industry stated its mission as developing entertainment content,[7] it would not have fallen so far behind in the race to develop and distribute Internet-mediated entertainment and informational content.

Examples of Firms that have redefined their missions by changing from a "product" or "technology" focus to a market focus include:

- Xerox Corporation, which redefined its mission from producing copy machines to a "supplier of automated office systems."[8]
- Bally Manufacturing, which changed its mission from being a "manufacturer of video games" to "leisure and entertainment."[9]

Build on Distinctive Competencies

A good mission statement should not only build upon but also leverage and exploit the Firm's **distinctive competencies**. In other words, the mission statement should highlight and be grounded in things that the Firm does exceptionally well, particularly in comparison to its closest competitors. Good mission statements should direct the Firm into new market areas where it has a particular expertise or possesses particular resources that provide it with a competitive advantage.

Not Too Broad or Too Narrow

Narrow definitions, like many product-based missions, are overly restrictive. By focusing the Firm on building and selling specific products, opportunities for substitute products that meet the same market needs may be overlooked. By contrast, mission statements that are too broad may lead or push Firms into uncharted waters far removed from their areas of distinctive competency. Kotler provides an excellent example, one involving a producer of lead pencils: If the Firm envisioned itself as a marketer of writing devices, "it might expand to the production of pens and other small writing instruments." Yet if the same Firm views its mission as one where its charge was to market writing equipment, it might elect to produce "typewriters and other equipment that facilitate writing." The broadest concept of its business is that it is a communications company, and this would be stretching things too far for a lead-pencil manufacturer."[10]

The following mission statements are appropriately grounded in the core competencies of their respective Firms. Their missions also emphasize customers' needs and are neither overly broad nor narrow. The following mission statements exemplify the essence of excellence:

- Ritz Carlton: "to create a memorable experience (for our guests)."
- FedEx: "to create a satisfied customer at the end of each transaction."
- Southwest Airlines: "to become the world's most loved, most flown, most profitable airline while connecting people with what is important in their lives through friendly, reliable and low-cost air travel."
- Facebook: "to give people the power to share … and make the world more open and connected."
- Krispy Kreme: "to touch and enhance lives through Kristy Kreme."
- Komatzu (a Japanese manufacturer of heavy construction equipment): "to surround Caterpillar." (the Peoria, IL, manufacturer of heavy construction equipment). The inspiring and highly-focused mission statement, launched decades ago, motivated Komatzu to place dealerships in close proximity to Caterpillar dealerships over the entire globe. In the process, due to Komatzu pricing advantage and quality equivalence, the marketing strategies that followed for the Japanese marketer almost put the American icon out of business. The only thing that saved Caterpillar from bankruptcy, and just barely, was the power of its brand and huge concessions agreed to by its unionized workforce.

Other Strategic Models Guiding Opportunity Identification

The Firm's mission statement delimits while concurrently focuses the search for new opportunities. However, several additional strategic models exist that also provide first-rate guidance in the search for opportunities. The most widely used models are Ansoff's **Product-Market Expansion Grid**[11] and the Boston Consulting Group's **Growth-Share Matrix**[12].

The Product-Market Expansion Grid

Most opportunities for market growth (remember the shark, the emu, and the kangaroo) will fall into one of four categories defined by the Market-Product Expansion Grid. Illustrated in Exhibit 3.3, the four categories of opportunity defined by the Product-Market Expansion Grid are determined by two criteria. The first is a "market" dimension (think horizontal or vertical axis) based whether or not the market is currently being served by or is new to the Firm. The second is a "product" dimension or axis. This dimension is similarly interpreted. Are we intending to market products that we currently sell, or are we going to market a product that is new to the Firm? Based on these two dimensions, the four types of market opportunities are referred to as market penetration, market development, product development, and diversification.

Market Penetration Opportunities

Market penetration is a strategy whereby the Firm continues to sell its existing products to its existing customers. Marketers attempt to sell more of the same product to the same market. That is why the strategy is called market penetration. It is an attempt to penetrate a market in greater depth; an attempt to gain market share, generally at the expense of competitors.

A range of marketing mix tactics can be employed to do this. Price can be lowered to stimulate added demand. Coupons, rebates, and buy-one-get-one-free (BOGO) offers, are all commonly-employed promotional and pricing tactics. Advertising new uses for products can be very effective at stimulating added consumption. Consider a past ad for Morton Salt in which the salt is formed in the shape of a fish with the caption: "Eats Fish Odors." With this ad Morton is implying that salt can be used for more than just cooking or seasoning. The ad shows consumers how the product helps in neutralizing nasty odors. Morton clearly is attempting to sell more product (salt) to the same market!

A classic example of the same tactic is illustrated by Arm and Hammer's baking soda. Baking soda has a wide range of common household applications for odor removal including refrigerators, kitchen sinks, carpeting, and kitty litter boxes. And, this is just the tip of

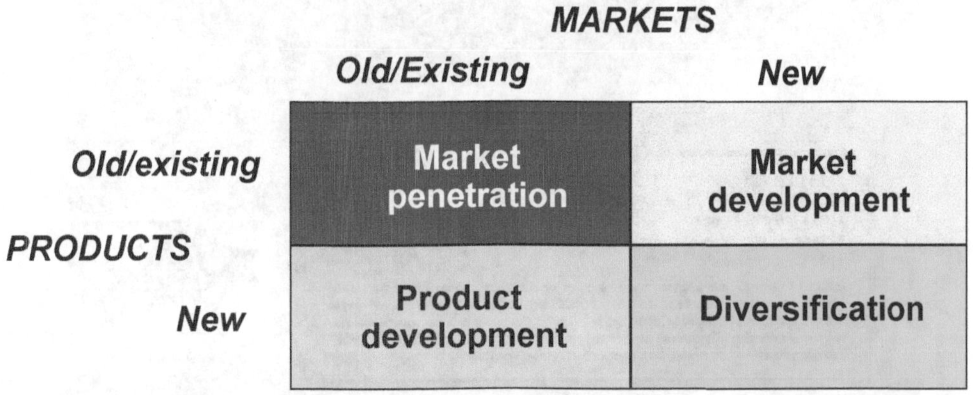

	MARKETS	
	Old/Existing	**New**
Old/existing	Market penetration	Market development
PRODUCTS		
New	Product development	Diversification

Exhibit 3.3 *Ansoff's Product-Market Expansion Grid.*

the iceberg. Arm & Hammer has extensively promoted baking soda's use for a myriad of household and personal care applications including as an underarm deodorant, toothpaste, laundry detergent additive, etc.

The ad in Exhibit 3.4 for Cool Whip Lite offers a recipe for how this product can be used in a multi-layered cake. This is a common approach for stimulating additional sales of food products to the same customer base. Another classic example of this strategy is illustrated with Kellogg's Rice Krispies Treats. The recipe proved so popular that consumers now can buy Rice Krispies Treats as a separate, dedicated product. Such recipes that suggest new uses for products resulting in increased consumption.

Market Development Opportunities

A **market development** opportunity is a search for new markets for a Firm's existing products. The most logical and common application of market development is illustrated with geographic expansion; looking for new geographic areas in which to sell the Firm's existing products. For example, in 2014 Merck's Consumer Health Division expanded its Bion 3 brand into Brazil. Its strong sales and leadership position in other key markets, including Chile, Belgium, and France provides Merck with a foundation to leverage its products into a number of key emerging markets.[13]

Courtesy Kraft Foods

Exhibit 3.4 *Cool Whip Lite: New Ways to Use Cool Whip.*

Market development can be pursued in other ways. Firms can seek new market segments to serve with current products. Post Cereal pursued what it deemed a market development opportunity when it targeted adult markets concerned with cancer prevention with its Bran Flakes brand. Bran and other high fiber foods apparently reduce the odds of developing colon cancer. Post and other producers of high fiber foods took advantage of this debate to create a market development opportunity.

Johnson & Johnson's Baby Shampoo was traditionally promoted as the ideal option for washing a baby's hair. The shampoo was promoted as a gentle, mild formula that would not burn the child's eyes. Attracted to the same benefits, mothers began using it themselves, prompting Johnson and Johnson to actively market to this new market segment.

Gerber's Singles was a failed attempt to market baby food to geriatric adults. The product was nothing more than the Firm's existing line of baby food repackaged for the geriatric market. Gerber's decision to target the elderly market was based on the observation that the elderly are sometimes characterized by chewing and digestive problems that are similar to those that babies experience. Unfortunately, the elderly market was not receptive to the idea of eating baby food. The product was abandoned after a short period of time.

Product Development Opportunities

A **product development** opportunity entails developing entirely new products, or at least modifying and upgrading existing products, that deliver new and useful value that increases the desirability of the products within market segments that the Firm already targets and serves. This strategy often involves making minor changes to existing products and marketing them as new. This approach, called line extensions[14], is frequently the easiest and least risky approach to new product development. Pine-Sol's introduction of alternative scented versions of its classic cleanser illustrates these points.

The product development strategy is commonly employed by Firms that make and market consumer package goods. Procter & Gamble, for example, sells a number of different lines of consumer goods, generally with multiple brands represented in each line. P&G's line of laundry detergents contains a number of entries, each bearing a different brand name. These **flanker brands**[15] are chemically similar and only minor differences exist between them. Most importantly, many are marketed to the same customer segments. Clearly this is a product development strategy that has been very successful!

Diversification Opportunities

Diversification opportunities are those in which a new product is targeted to a new market. Diversification opportunities imply a departure from the typical products and markets targeted in the past. As a result, this strategy is the most risky growth alternative.

Diversification opportunities often assume the form of brand extensions. Here, Firms attempt to employ and leverage the value (e.g., name recognition, brand loyalty, brand equity) of their family brand to launch new products in product categories that are also new to the Firm. For example, Turtle Wax, known mainly for its automotive polishes attempted to penetrate a new consumer market with a shoe polish bearing the Turtle Wax brand. Turtle Wax used its existing brand name to help it launch shoe polish, leveraging off the image of its existing products to induce trial and speed adoption of the new product (Exhibit 3.5).

Courtesy Turtle Wax, Inc.

Exhibit 3.5 *Turtle Wax Shoe Polish.*

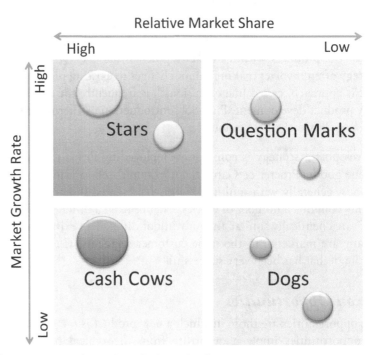

Exhibit 3.6 *Boston Consulting Group's Growth-Share Matrix.*

BCG Growth-Share Matrix

The Boston Consulting Group's growth-share matrix (Exhibit 3.6) is one of several business portfolio models. Originally developed by the BCG for application to Firms' strategic business units (SBUs), the matrix can also be applied to groups of products and brands in the Firm's portfolio.

We assume for this discussion that the unit of analysis is a given Firm's products or brands. The matrix is based on two key strategic dimensions: ***Relative market share*** and ***market growth rate***. Relative market share is the Firm's proportion of the sales for specific products/

brands sold by a Firm relative to total sales for the industry. Think of relative market share as an indicator of the strength of the Firm's product offering compared to the largest competitor in that market. Market growth rate is the annual growth rate of the market in which the product/brand competes. It is a measure of the relative attractiveness of that market. The matrix is comprised of four quadrants:

- *Stars* are those products/brands which possess high market share and compete in a market that is growing at an above average rate. The Firm in question has two products that qualify as stars, where the sizes of the circles represent the relative proportion of the Firm's annual sales generated by each product. Stars require continued investment to nurture their growth. Eventually, if stars continue to perform well, they will evolve into cash cows.

- *Cash Cows* are products that possess high market share but exist in lower growth markets. Generally, such markets are more mature than markets in which stars compete. However, the continued viability of these markets and the substantial market share possessed by cash cows mean that these products/brands will generate substantial resources for the Firm that can be reinvested into other products, such as up and coming stars. Our hypothetical Firm has one cash cow that accounts for a high proportion of its sales. Excess resources generated by this product will be reinvested into other products in the matrix.

- *Question Marks* are those products that exist in attractive markets, but possess limited market share. There is, therefore, some doubt as to the product's longer-term viability. The question is whether the question mark should continue to be nurtured with resources in hopes that it will become a star. Our Firm has two products in this quadrant. These products will require continued careful planning and monitoring to improve their performance. Firms possessing substantial resources are wise to maintain a number of products in this quadrant as not all are likely to survive. Those that do not perform well are likely to move into the last quadrant of the matrix—dogs.

- *Dogs* exist in low growth markets and possess relatively little market share. These products are clearly the poorer performers in the Firm's portfolio. Normally, dogs are doomed to be phased out and the resources previously dedicated to them will be transferred to other products in either the star or question mark quadrants.

→ Product-Market Identification & Selection

Searching for market opportunities generally entails identifying relevant **market segments** within broader **product-markets**. Product-markets are essentially defined in the same manner that markets were defined as in the last chapter. We prefer the term product-market because, in reality, markets only exist for specific products.[16] It makes little sense to speak of a market without also identifying the specific product under consideration for the market.

Broader product-markets tend to be larger and more heterogeneous in nature, meaning that they typically consist of large numbers of consumers or buying Firms who possess diverse wants, needs, or problems with respect to the specific products and services under consideration. Associated with these differing wants, needs, and problems are diverse combinations of consumer characteristics, such as differing demographic profiles, beliefs and attitudes, lifestyle preferences, and media preferences. The strategic takeaway: there is no way that any single Firm could ever hope to target the entire product-market with a single product and its concomitant marketing mix, including its promotion, its pricing, and its distribution.

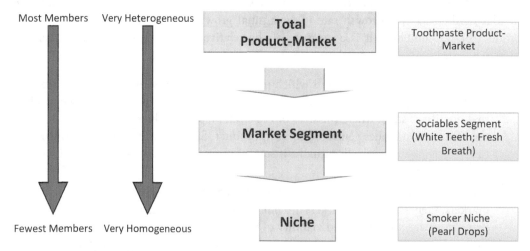

Exhibit 3.7 *Relationship Between Product-Markets and Market Segments.*

Identifying Market Segments

Due to the inherent diversity that is present within these broader aggregate product-markets, marketers typically face situations where the product-market must be divided. That is, segmented into more homogeneous submarkets called market segments. A market segment is a smaller group (subset or submarket) of consumers or organizations drawn from a larger market. Within a market segment consumers (or organizations) tend to have similar wants, needs, and purchasing-related characteristics. As noted, their similarities, the traits and characteristics these potential groups of customers share in common, makes them more likely to respond in the same fashion to any Firm's marketing mix-driven values.

Market segmentation, then, is viewed as the process of subdividing these larger, diverse markets into smaller more homogenous submarkets or market segments. In fact, levels of market segments can exist. Each level becomes increasingly more homogeneous or more similar with respect to numbers of consumers and their consumption-related traits and other characteristics.

The smallest operational market segment at the end of this chain is the niche. The potential customers that are classified as part of a niche are highly similar to one another in their respective consumption-related characteristics. The relationship between product-markets and market segments is illustrated in Exhibit 3.7.

An example taken from a classic study of the toothpaste market illustrates these relationships. The overall product-market for toothpaste is very diverse. Consumers possess a diversity of wants/needs for toothpaste products. Similarly, these consumers are highly diverse in their demographic and consumption-related characteristics. It is one or more of these market segments that Firms eventually select as market targets or target markets.

Analyzing Market Opportunities

Once a market opportunity has been identified, its potential is assessed by systematically addressing two basic questions:

1. Does the opportunity offer profit potential for the Firm?
2. Does the Firm possess the resources to take advantage of the opportunity?

Answering the first question requires due diligence on the part of the marketing manager. As a minimum, the answer requires a thorough understanding of the following issues:

- The customer's needs and buying behavior for this type of product or service.
- Likely demand for the product or service to be offered.
- Probable costs for producing and marketing the product or service to the targeted customer group.
- How the Firm's product or service compares with competing products or services.

The market opportunity analysis typically yields multiple possible markets or market segments that hold the promise of profit potential. However, these market opportunities will not and should not be viewed as equally attractive by marketing managers within the Firm. Nor will the Firm possess the resources to take advantage of them all. Opportunities must be ranked in terms of their "fit" with the Firm's mission, goals and objectives, resources and capabilities, as well as their profit potential.

Firms often have additional objectives that serve as screening criteria for market opportunities. For example, two opportunities may appear to offer equally attractive profit potential. Moreover, the Firm may enjoy the financial and managerial resources to successfully pursue each opportunity. But one opportunity may be incompatible with the Firm's goal, as underscored in its mission, of providing only environmentally safe products to customers. In this case, the Firm's environmental goals act as an additional screening criterion for culling out opportunities. These sorts of "qualitative" criteria have become increasingly important to decision makers as they evaluate major strategic decisions. Given growing societal concerns about consumer value and safety, concerns over the environment and quality of life, and prospective customers' understandably renewed skepticism about major institutions, Firms can no longer focus exclusively on bottom line results. Stated differently, if Firms elect to focus solely on bottom line results at the expense of other non-financial considerations, their profits will almost inevitably suffer, particularly over the longer run.

Planning the Product and Service Mix

The existence of a market opportunity presupposes that the Firm has envisioned a specific product and/or service that can satisfy the needs and/or solve the problems exhibited by the market in question. Developing the best product/service combination to serve the target market is probably the most critical component of the marketing mix. Firms must develop a quality product/service that is capable of generating customer need/want satisfaction in a manner that distinguishes the product/service from competing offers. This means finding some characteristic, or set of characteristics, that provide the product/service with superior quality and/or performance vis-à-vis competitors.

Products and services exist on a continuum. Most tangible products possess a substantial service component. For example, consumer durables, (e.g., cars, dishwashers, microwave ovens, etc.) are primarily viewed as products, but feature substantial service dimensions such as warrantees, service contracts, delivery, credit terms, etc. Similarly, most services also offer a tangible product component. For example, pest control services primarily market the labor and expertise required to get rid of customers' bug problems. But, in the process, they employ very tangible products such as the chemical pesticides, traps, etc. to control these bugs. What should be understood here is that product design means that marketing managers must focus on the "total product." And the total product often includes the tangible physical dimensions of the product as well as its more intangible service-related aspects.

Table 3.1 • *The Scope of the Product Management Decision*

Product Item	Description
Benefits	The benefits the product provides to customers that fulfill their needs and expectations
Attributes	The specific attributes or characteristics the product must possess to provide customers with the desired benefits
Branding	Family brand vs. individual brand Specific brand name to use Brand mark or logo
Legal Protection	Trade marking Copyrights Licenses
Packaging	Desired functions of the package Package design and costs Package labeling Legal obligations with labels Package disposition and recycling
Quality Level	Desired level of quality the product should possess
Product Safety	Design and build in safety features Test to ensure safe to use.
Warranties and Guarantees	Warrantee coverage for the life of the product
Life Cycle Management	How the product should be managed over its life cycle in terms of features, services, quality levels, branding, pricing, etc

Major questions that must be addressed when determining the product/service to provide range from identifying basic features to include in the product to considerations involved with establishing the product's brand name and its packaging. Table 3.1 summarizes many of the deciding making areas that must be addressed. Not all of the considerations listed in Table 3.1 necessarily are required for every marketing program. But of course, additional items may exist that are not featured in the table that marketing managers still may believe are pertinent to their specific marketing context. These and additional decision-making areas are addressed in greater detail later in the book.

Identifying the Desired Market (Product) Position

A key to success in today's extremely competitive markets is the ability to **position** products and services in prospect customers' minds such that those products are perceived by customers as being distinct from and better than competing products and services. Very simply, a product's position is its image. It is the mental picture customers form about the Firm's product in terms of its characteristics or features, the benefits it delivers, and what it offers relative to competing substitutes.

Firms should spend considerable amounts of energy deciding on the correct position their brands should occupy in consumers' minds. Firms generate positioning or image statements that are intended to guide strategy development by communicating to customers and company employees how the Firm wants its products to be perceived in the collective mind of the market. Some Firms consider positioning critical enough to suggest their targeted position in their mission statement. Brinker International, the parent Firm of Chili's Bar and Grill and Maggianos, Little Italy restaurants, in its 2011 Annual Report emphasizes that it is in the business of "serving the world a great taste of life through the power of welcome."* The Firm subsequently underscores that "Our great team members are the biggest differentiator from our competitors"…."It is our team members at all levels within the organization who create memorable experiences for our guests, day-in and day-out"….Chili's mission "begins and ends with the smart and talented people at Brinker. They are the ones who drive operational excellence, culinary innovation, value for our guests and, ultimately, positive growth for our company."[17] In the end, we see that growth thing again.

→ Developing Pricing, Promotional, and Distribution Programs

In addition to the product/service's fundamental ability to satisfy customer needs, how the product is priced, distributed, and promoted contribute dramatically to the likely success of the product. All elements of the marketing mix must work together logically to achieve the product's desired market position and the Firm's marketing objectives. Each marketing mix factor, say, price (which can be higher or lower relative to competitors), must be consistent with what is happening with each of the others, say, product (and its level of quality, or distribution, and the quality or appeal of the stores used to retail the product) in order to generate a synergistic effect that sets apart effective marketing strategies from less effective alternatives.

Pricing Element of the Marketing Mix

The scope of the pricing decision is summarized in Table 3.2. Pricing decisions fundamentally revolve around setting the list or base price for the product/service. Determining this price is a complex process. Multiple factors and considerations are evaluated. These should include, at a minimum, the Firm's pricing objectives, customers' perceptions of value, competitors' prices, and the costs of production and marketing. The marketing manager must project the likely demand and profitability associated with alternative pricing levels. Finally, thought must be given to the prospect of using a wide array of discount and allowance schedules; the use of any pricing promotions, such as coupons and rebates; how shipping and handling should be charged and how it will affect the final price for the product; and any legal constraints that may affect pricing activities. Pricing is the marketing mix element that most likely to be managed badly.

Table 3.2 • *The Scope of the Pricing Decision*

PRICING ELEMENT	DESCRIPTION
Pricing Objectives and Strategies	Pricing objectives reflect the Firm's overall marketing objectives and guide the pricing decision. Strategies include the pricing mechanisms by which these objectives will be achieved.
Customer Demand and Perceptions of Value	Decision makers must estimate the likely demand at prices under consideration. Demand estimates combined with cost projections allow the Firm to predict profitability.
Method by Which Price Will Be Set	Techniques used to actually set base price fall into three categories: cost-based, demand-based, competition-based. Firms generally employ considerations from all three areas.
Competitors' Pricing and Possible Reactions to Prices	All aspects of pricing are affected by how competitors set their prices and how they may react to prices set by the Firm.
Discount and Allowance Schedules including: Quantity Discounts Trade Discounts Cash Discounts and Credit Terms Promotion allowances	Numerous discounts and allowances exist that Firms may offer at different levels of the distribution channel. These generally are deductions from list price and affect profitability.
Laws Affecting Pricing	Legal restraints govern many aspects of pricing, ranging from price fixing to the use of loss leaders and other promotions.
Geographic Pricing	Base price often must be adjusted to allow for shipping and handling costs that vary by geographic area.
Price Promotions	A wide number of promotional incentives amount to price reductions including coupons, rebates, and cents-off offers.
Product Line Pricing	The pricing of one product in the seller's line affects how price must be set for other products in the line.

Promotion Element of the Marketing Mix

The major promotion decisions facing marketing managers are essentially communications decisions. Promotion essentially entails communicating to customers about the product and its merits. The major promotion tools available to marketing managers, referred to as the **promotion mix**, include advertising, personal selling, sales promotion, and public relations. Decisions must be made with respect to how each of these communication tools should be employed. Table 3.3 summarizes the major promotion decision areas faced by marketing managers for each element of the promotion mix.

Advertising is often conflated with promotion, as if advertising was all there is to promotion. In reality, advertising is merely one component of the overall promotion function. More specifically, advertising is the dissemination of information through non-personal paid media, such as radio, TV, newspapers, magazines, outdoor billboards, etc. Advertising decision areas essentially revolve around the steps involved with creating an advertising campaign. An

Table 3.3 • *The Scope of the Promotion Decision*

PROMOTION ELEMENT	DESCRIPTION

Promotion Objectives
Specific promotion objectives are set that identify what we want promotion to accomplish for us.
Objectives determine what promotional elements will be employed
	Sales Promotion
	• Determining sales promotion objectives
	• Selecting the types of sales promotion activities to use:
	  • P-O-P devices
	  • Samples
	  • Specialty advertising
	  • Premiums and trading stamps
	  • Coupons
	  • Trade shows and exhibits
	• Evaluating the effectiveness of sales promotions

Advertising considerations • Identifying the target audience • Defining advertising objectives • Selecting the advertising platform or theme • Selecting the advertising budget • Developing a media plan • Creating the advertising message including copy and artwork • Executing the advertising program • Measuring advertising effectiveness • Define advertising objectives	**Public Relations and Publicity** • Establish public relations and publicity objectives. • Select messages and vehicles • Assess the effectiveness of public relations and publicity efforts
Personal selling considerations • Determining the number and types of sales people required. • Establishing sales force objectives • Recruiting sales personnel • Training sales personnel • Compensating sales personnel • Motivating sales personnel • Identifying and managing sales territories • Controlling and evaluating sales force efforts	

advertising campaign is the collection of specific ads and media used to reach specific target audiences. The advertising decisions that must be addressed during the marketing planning process range from determining the role that advertising should play in the total promotion mix and the appropriate advertising objectives, to deciding on specific advertising themes, copy, media scheduling, and associated budgets.

Advertising is a non-personal, one-way form of communication. Personal selling is just the opposite. Personal selling, unsurprisingly, is quite personal. This promotional mix element is designed to inform or remind customers about the product and its merits and then to persuade them to buy. In terms of resource allocation, personal selling generally receives the lion's share of the promotion budget, particularly for the sales of industrial goods and services, making the selling function one of the more important elements of many Firms' promotion mixes. Today's salespeople are often viewed as highly rewarded consultants who help their clients solve their business problems. In this vein, today's salespeople do not sell products. They sell solutions to problems. Accordingly, a major objective of today's personal selling efforts is to build long-term relationships with customers; to build a high level of trust in the sales person and his or her ability to work for the customer as well as his or her own Firm. Only by focusing on developing this kind of rapport can the Firm build the image and credibility that leads to repeat sales and continued viability in the market place. Personal selling decision areas range from deciding on the type of sales force desired to considerations on how to monitor and control the personal selling effort.

Sales promotions consist of special types of promotion tools that are intended to encourage sales of a product or service. They tend to be short-term in use and supplement advertising and personal selling efforts through the targeted provision of incentives to customers and prospective customers. Sales promotions can be targeted to consumers or middlemen (i.e., corporate members of Firm's supply chains). Examples of sales promotions aimed at consumers are coupons, games, contests, specialty advertising, point-of-purchase displays, and free samples. Trade promotions include promotion allowances, free goods, push money (also called "spiffs"), trade shows, conventions, and cooperative advertising.

Most Firms use sales promotions to support advertising and personal selling efforts. In recent years, the monies that Firms spend on sales promotions has exceeded their expenditures on advertising. In 1987, sales promotion expenditures surpassed the $100 billion mark, accounting for over 64% of the average promotion budget.[18] As indicated in Table 3.3, marketing managers must make decisions in several areas concerning sales promotions. The beginning point is to identify the specific objectives sales promotions are expected to accomplish. Management then can select the specific sales promotion tools to use as well as decide how to implement and monitor the effectiveness of the total sales promotion effort.

Public relations and **publicity** are closely interrelated. Publicity is typically subsumed under the Firm's public relations efforts. Public relations efforts require deliberate planning efforts on the part of Firms to obtain goodwill and/or promote a positive image for the Firm and its products with various publics. Another purpose of public relationships is to strengthen or sustain the Firm's or brand's relationships with those publics during times in which the image of the Firm or its brand is threatened. Think brand names such British Petroleum, Lance Armstrong, Tiger Woods, Bill Cosby, or the National Football League with its 2014 domestic abuse and head injury problems, and you understand how to the need to achieve such outcomes is likely to arise. "Publics" of primary concern include entities such as customers, stockholders, employees, unions, environmental groups, the media, governmental agencies, and members of the local community.

By contrast, publicity is often unplanned and can be negative as well as positive. Publicity generally is in the form of news stories in mass media (TV, radio, newspapers, etc.) or promotional "plugs" provided by someone during an interview or speech aired in the mass media.[19] As with sales promotions, public relations and publicity are employed to support the larger advertising and personal selling efforts in the Firm. In fact, public relations efforts can be more cost-effective than advertising.

Marketing decision makers should determine the role that public relations and publicity will play in the promotion process. Specific objectives are established to identify exactly what public relations or publicity promotions would be expected to accomplish in a given context. The appropriate public relations tools then are selected to attain these objectives. The major public relations tools available to marketing planners include news releases, speeches, sponsored special events, written materials including annual reports, brochures, and newsletters, audio-visual materials such as films as well as public service activities.

Distribution Element of the Marketing Mix

Table 3.4 summarizes many of the distribution or supply chain issues with which marketing managers must grapple on an ongoing basis. A **distribution channel** is the set of organizations responsible for moving the product and its ownership from one end of the channel (producers) to the other end (consumers). As implied, the traditional term "distribution channel" has largely given way to the contemporary term "supply chain."

Decisions must occur in several major areas, including setting distribution objectives, determining the range of distribution functions that must be performed, deciding on the basic form of the supply chains—distribution channel(s)—to be used to reach the target market, and how the goods should be physically distributed to customers. In the process of making these decisions, myriad federal, state, and local laws exist that must be factored into any decisions that are made. These traditional laws must be considered because they set restrictions on and generally govern the relationships in which channel, or supply chain, members typically engage. The legal penalties for violating these laws can prove harsh.

→ Implementing and Controlling Marketing Programs

The implementation of strategic marketing programs requires close coordination between all areas of the Firm. All departments must be charged with the responsibility of making the Firm's marketing program work; notably, this is entirely consistent with the principles of the marketing concept. Implementation involves the day-to-day "grunt" work that makes effective marketing happen in the Firm. Effective implementation is critical for an effective marketing effort; however, it is difficult to achieve. Often it proves easier to devise effective marketing programs than it is to actually bring these programs to fruitful life.[20] Effective implementation depends on possessing the correct organizational structure and having an effective management control system.

The success of most Firms' marketing implementation processes depends in large part on ensuring that those manning key positions are charged with the correct specific responsibilities. Different organizational structures are available for implementing marketing processes within Firms. Regardless of their specific forms or the products they market, Firms should generally:

- Encourage specialization to foster greater efficiency.
- Establish formal lines of authority and communications channels between people and departments.
- Simplify and avoid the "over-formalization" of marketing process. Too much formalization would tend to impede effective communications, timely decision-making, and quick responses/reactions as pressing problems inevitably arise.

Table 3.4 • *The Scope of the Distribution Decision*

Channel Item	Description
Channel Objectives	Channel objectives are the goals that planners have for their distribution system. Objectives are set for such things as intensity of distribution coverage, customer service levels, total costs of distribution, and relationships between channel members. Channel objectives will determine, in part, the types of functions that channel members must perform.
Channel Functions	What channel distribution related functions must be performed? The specific functions that must be accomplished to ensure that product or service is appropriately available to customers will guide the channel structure and channel member selection decisions.

Channel Structure
• Types channels to employ
  • Single channels
  • Dual or multiple channels
• Selection of specific middlemen
  • Wholesalers
  • Agents
  • Retailers
	Channel structure decisions relate to identifying the specific channel or channels that will be used to move products and services to customer groups. A channel is the simply the group of organizations that assist the flow of goods from producers to consumers. For most applications the channel is nothing more than the set of companies (producers, wholesalers, agents, and retailers) that work together to place products in the hands of consumers.

Legal Restrictions and Considerations	There are numerous federal and state laws that affect distribution activities. Major areas of laws consist of those that regulate horizontal price fixing, vertical price fixing, exclusive dealing, exclusive territories, and tying contracts. Planners must understand and allow for the major laws relevant to their industries.
Supplier Evaluation and Selection	A Firm's suppliers often are an integral part of the channel of distribution. This is particularly true for retailers and wholesalers who buy products for resale. Planners must evaluate suppliers with respect to key criteria that reflect or predict their likely performance in the channel.
Physical Distribution • Warehouse numbers and types • Inventory quantities & locations • Transportation mode • Order Processing • Protective Packaging • Materials Handling	Physical distribution includes all activities for the physical movement of goods through the channel of distribution. The various activities that must be planned relate primarily to the transportation, storage, and handling of goods. The Firm's primary distribution goal should be to mold a physical distribution system that delivers the desired level of customer service at the lowest possible total cost to the Firm.

Effectively responsive management control systems designed to monitor day-to-day marketing activities can identify potential problems before they truly break-bad. These managerial control systems should generally feature the following elements:

- A budgeting system that provides the necessary financing, information, and measurement systems capable of delivering timely and accurate data that proves useful in decision-making and identifying potential problem areas.
- Reward systems that appropriately reward personnel for making correct decisions.[21]

The Marketing Plan

The content of the marketing plan should parallel the steps in the strategic marketing process. The marketing plan, in essence, exists as a blueprint and/or roadmap for the process. The marketing plan functions as a mechanism through which marketing managers formally outline how the strategic marketing process should unfold within the Firm. There is no universally agreed upon format for marketing plans. We prefer the format outlined in Table 3.5. This approach is as good as any and better than most.

The Executive Summary

The plan begins with an executive summary. The executive summary provides a concise overview of the plan. While it is presented first, the executive summary is always written last. This section is typically one or two pages in length and should exist as a stand-alone document. Just as its name implies, executive-level decision makers should be able to glean the major strategic and financial implications of the plan from this section.

SWOT Analysis

A brief discussion of the SWOT should follow. This discussion should highlight the processes that were used. The sources of information used in developing the SWOT insights. Most details from the SWOT will be relegated to an appendix to the plan.

Summary of Market Opportunities and Threats

The culmination of the SWOT is a thorough understanding of the opportunities and threats faced by the Firm. The details are specifically summarized in this section. Later sections of the plan will identify strategic options available to the Firm for exploiting its major opportunities and reducing or eliminating major threats.

→ Marketing Program Focusing-Objectives

This section outlines the major marketing objectives that will guide the formation of a strategic focus and subsequent action programs. These "focusing-objectives" are established for the marketing program, considered as a whole, and are generally expressed in terms of what the marketing program should accomplish. As a result, focusing-objectives tend to be broad, often reflecting the basic purpose for which the marketing plan is written. Focusing-objectives for marketing plans would commonly reflect the following outcomes:

- Introducing new products in specific target markets.
- Stimulating sales growth for products whose sales have reached a plateau.
- Establishing new businesses serving specific markets.
- Implementing new promotional programs to increase sales in existing target markets.

Table 3.5 • *Overview of the Contents of a Marketing Plan*

SECTIONS IN THE PLAN	DESCRIPTION
Contents	Table of contents for the plan.
Executive Summary	Concise overview of the plan.
SWOT • Industry and Competitor Analysis • Environmental Analysis • Marketing Programs Analysis • Market and Customer Analysis • Demand Analysis • Critical Resources Analysis	A description of past, present, and future conditions in each area as they impact the profitability of the marketing effort. The analysis in these areas taken together comprises the Market Opportunity Analysis.
Summary of Market Opportunities and Threats	Based on the situation analysis. Summarizes the major market opportunities presented to the Firm. Also summarized are the major threats to the Firm that may require a change in marketing strategy.
Marketing Objectives	Identification of the goals the Firms wishes to achieve by serving the selected market(s). Includes financial and non-financial.
Marketing Strategic Focus	A concise description of the strategic focus the Firm intends to employ to achieve its marketing objectives.
Target Market(s) and Market Position	Identification of the customer groups the Firm intends to serve. Identification of the desired image for the Firm and its products relative to competitors.
Marketing Action Programs • Product/Service Plan • Promotion Plan • Pricing Plan • Distribution Plan	A detailed presentation of the specific objectives, strategies, and tactical activities in each area of the marketing mix required to implement the overall marketing strategy.
Budget and Financial Analysis	Detailed breakdown of the costs associated with each action program and additional financial analysis such as break-even analysis, cash flow statements, incremental analysis, cannibalization analysis, etc.
Monitoring and Control Program • Monitoring procedures • Information sources • Contingency plans	Detailed description of the methods and sources of information that will be used to monitor progress on the plan and allow for corrective action in the event of problems.
Appendices	Supporting materials as required.

As an example, consider the first objective: introducing a new product into a specific market. Once the actual objective was written into a marketing plan it would be more precise; it would also provide additional information that clarifies, in a quantifiable manner, what this objective entails. The objective may read:

> *Launch our new brand of mouthwash targeted to our existing customer base. Within six months of the launch achieve break-even with an estimated overall 3% market share. Within the first year of launch, achieve a 10% ROS with an estimated 5% market share.*

This example highlights some important points about focusing-objectives. Focusing-objectives are usually expressed in terms of desired levels of sales, market share, return on investment (ROI), and other profitability measures. Focusing-objectives should also satisfy the general criteria used for all business objectives; they should be measurable, attainable, and timely. In other words, focusing-objectives should be expressed in quantitative terms. Planners should feel confident that the objective(s) can be achieved within a specific time-frame.

Focusing-objectives are generally couched in terms of anticipated market share, sales volume, and profitability levels. But Firms are increasingly emphasizing societal welfare priorities in their focusing-objectives, particularly with respect to their commitments to environmental protection and consumer safety.

Objectives that are linked with specific elements of the marketing mix are usually avoided at this stage. Objectives in these latter areas tend to be dependent on the more general objectives set at this stage. Eventually, specific supporting objectives will be identified in each area of the marketing mix.

Marketing Strategic Focus

A pyramid of objectives and strategies should be established that begins with the Firm's overall corporate focusing-objectives and strategies and then filters down to those set for the marketing programs and individual elements of the marketing mix (specific marketing actions). The marketing strategic focus provides a general overview of how the Firm's focusing marketing objective(s) will be achieved. The broad strategies identified at this time become the basis for constructing specific marketing action programs.

The marketing strategic focus is derived from, and should be consistent with, focusing-objectives and strategies identified for the organization as a whole. This is particularly crucial in multi-product Firms that may have multiple Strategic Business Units (SBUs). In turn, the marketing strategic focus will determine specific strategies and actions for elements of the marketing mix—product, price, promotion, and distribution.

As a minimum, the marketing strategic focus should identify target markets that will be served, the market positions that will be sought, and generally describe how these markets will be served and the desired positions achieved. The choice of target markets and desired market (product) positions are important enough to place in their own section of the marketing plan where they will be given a detailed discussion, as shown below.

Target Market(s) and Desired Market Position(s)

The next two sections of the plan outline the Firm's specific marketing strategies. A marketing strategy consists of the a) target market the Firm elects to serve, b) combined with the market position sought in these market segments and c) the marketing mix that will be used to create the desired position. The primary emphasis in this section is to:

- Specifically identify the Firm's target market(s).
- Identify and justify the desired market position in each target market.

The justification for the desired market position amounts to an explanation of why the stated position is desired. This explanation first should identify the specific image desired for the product or service in terms of how it will deliver desired benefits. This explanation should likewise explain how this specific market position will effectively differentiate the product or service from currently existing competitors.

Marketing Action Programs

This section features action programs, also known as tactical actions, for each element of the marketing mix. The action programs make-up the bulk of the marketing plan. Each action program identifies the primary objectives, specific strategies that will be pursued, and the detailed activities or actions that will be performed, when they will be accomplished, who will accomplish them, and how much performance will cost. At a minimum, there will be an action program for each major element of the marketing mix. In reality, multiple action programs will be developed for each mix element.

The costs associated with each action program comprise the majority of the budget cited in later sections of the plan. The action program section is the longest and most detailed section of the marketing plan, particularly if the plan is to be used to guide operations rather than provide an overview of an intended marketing program for another plan, such as a business plan targeted to investors.

→ Marketing Program Budget and Supporting Financial Analyses

Good marketing programs cost money. The marketing program must feature a detailed breakdown of how much each action program will cost to implement. The marketing program budget functions as a major control that ensures the marketing program is progressing as desired.

Supporting financial analyses also are presented in this section. Break-even analyses, cash flow analyses, pro-forma income statements, balance sheets, and cannibalization analyses are normally included in marketing plans. Generally, the results of the specific analysis are examined, along with their implications. However, details are relegated to an appendix. For example, the budget section may contain reference to a pro forma income statement, citing appropriate numbers from the spreadsheet, but the actual spreadsheet is contained in an appendix.

Monitoring and Control Program

The action programs previously discussed outline how things will be done. The monitoring and control programs are employed to ensure that right action programs are properly implemented and indeed are appropriate given the Firm's objectives. This section specifies the kinds of information that should be collected, who should collect the information, and how that information should be used to ensure that things are going well.

The control process requires that results somehow be compared with a standard or baseline. The plan's action programs provide a large share of the baseline against which actual performance is compared. Each action program has an associated set of objectives and an implementation time line. By comparing actual results against this time line, progress can be tracked and decisions can be made should changes be required in either how the plan is implemented or in the plan itself.

Remember that the marketing plan is a dynamic tool. Changes can still be made to the plan, even after Firms are well into the implementation stage. Circumstances and unanticipated events that require adjustments to the plan are inevitable. Remember, as noted previously: Making predictions is difficult, particularly when they are about the future. One can never anticipate everything.

The budget is a major control mechanism. By having a carefully developed budget, a standard is established against which the results of our actions can be compared as the plan is actually executed. If actions exceed budgeted amounts, corrective action may have to be taken to bring costs into line. Alternatively, the budget may have to be re-examined to make it more realistic.

Other control tools include:

- The sales forecast made as a part of the demand analysis.
- Comparison of actual market share to market shares anticipated based on industry and sales forecasts.
- Comparison of cost-to-sales ratios actually obtained with those anticipated based on sales forecasts and budgeted costs.
- Various customer and dealer attitude surveys. Conducting these surveys involves simple marketing research and should be specifically planned for as part of the monitoring and control process.

Endnotes

[1] This discussion is adapted from David A. Aaker, *Strategic Marketing Management* (New York: John Wiley & Sons, x1991), 26.

[2] Ibid. 27.

[3] David A. Aaker, *Developing Business Strategies, 2nd Ed.* (New York: John Wiley & Sons, 1988), 5. Aaker refers to sources of differential advantage as "sources of competitive advantage" or SCAs.

[4] The term market opportunity analysis or MOA has been adopted from—Robert B. Woodruff, "A Systematic Approach to Market Opportunity Analyses," *Business Horizons* (August 1976): 55–65.

[5] Market penetration and diversification are two areas of opportunity explored by Ansoff in the Product-Market Expansion Grid. See H. Igor Ansoff, "Strategies for Diversification," *Harvard Business Review* (September–October 1957): 113–124.

[6] Philip Kotler and Gary Armstrong, *Principles of Marketing, Fourth Edition* (Englewood Cliffs, NJ: Prentice Hall, 1989), 29.

[7] Theodore Levitt, "Marketing Myopia," *Harvard Business Review* (July-August, 1960): 45–56.

[8] Derek F. Abell, *Defining the Business: The Starting Point of Strategic Planning* (Englewood Cliffs, NJ: Prentice Hall, 1980), 4–6.

[9] Kathleen Deveny, "Bally Is On a Winning Streak," *Business Week* (December 2, 1985): 30–31.

[10] Philip Kotler, *Marketing Management, 5th Ed.,* (Englewood Cliffs, NJ: Prentice-Hall, Inc. (1991), 47–48.

11 H. Igor Ansoff, "Strategies for Diversification," *Harvard Business Review* (September–October 1957): 113–124.

12 Bruce D. Henderson and Alan J. Zakon, "Corporate Growth Strategy: How to Develop and Implement It," in *Handbook of Business Problem Solving*, ed. Kenneth J. Alpert (New York: McGraw-Hill, 1980), 1-3–1-19.

13 "Product Innovations and Geographical Expansion Drive Sustained Merck Consumer Health Business Growth," *Business Wire* (September 29, 2014). http://www.businesswire.com/news/home/20140929005060/en/Product-Innovations-Geographical-Expansion-Drive-Sustained-Merck#.VG0DCdZDymE.

14 Line extensions are new products introduced into the same product line using the Firm's family brand.

15 Flanker brands are new products in a Firm's existing product line that have been given unique brand names rather than the family brand.

16 David W. Cravens, Gerald E. Hills, and Robert W. Woodruff, *Marketing Management* (Homewood, IL: Irwin, 1987), 102.

17 Retrieved from: http://www.brinker.com/company/Brinker2011/annualreport2011.pdf

18 Len Strawzewski, "Promotion 'Carnival' Gets Serious," *Advertising Age* (April 27, 1988): S1–2.

19 William J. Stanton and Charles Futrell, *Fundamentals of Marketing* (New York: McGraw-Hill, 1987), 482.

20 Philip Kotler and Gary Armstrong, *Principles of Marketing, 5th Ed.* (Englewood Cliffs, NJ: Prentice Hall, 1991), 545.

21 David A. Aaker, *Strategic Marketing Management, 2nd Ed.* (New York: John Wiley & Sons, 1988), 315–320.

THE MARKETING ENVIRONMENT

CHAPTER 4

One author recently spent 70 minutes driving alongside a magnificent fiord called Lake Wikatipu. The fiord began at the foot of New Zealand's Mt. Cook, flowed some 50 miles as it wound through precipitous mountains, and emptied into the South Tasman Sea. On average the fiord is two miles wide and more than 1,000 feet deep. Lake Wikatipu was formed— carved, actually—as a consequence of the retreat of Ice Age glaciers some 14,000 years ago. Mt. Cook remains capped by one of the world's largest glaciers. Heard of America's Great Lakes, right? All five bodies of water are huge. Each is also glacially-constructed. Glaciers impose consequences on their surroundings. They shape and reshape environments.

But glaciers also experience the consequences of change in their surrounding environments. Glaciers directly "suffer" problems (they shrink, as many currently are) or "reap" benefits (when they expand) as their adjacent environments transform e.g., when the weather warms/ cools or there is more or less precipitation. At net, glaciers change their environment at the same time they are impacted by changes in their surrounding environment.

Exactly the same description applies to marketers. Marketing behaviors, strategically driven or not, generate marketing consequences that impact the larger environment. Changes in marketers' environments generate consequences that impact their success or failure, and ought to influence the strategies that marketers create and the decisions they make. Four takeaways:

- The relationship between a glacier and its environment is highly comparable to the relationship that exists between by any marketing Firm and its environment.
- Marketers and Firms are impacted by their environments.
- Their environments are affected by the decisions that marketers make and the behaviors (usually customer consumption behaviors) that those decisions inspire.
- Because decisions always generate behaviors which produce consequences, choose wisely!

Thus perpetual environmental scanning, especially regarding changes in environments, should be conducted with due diligence before and during the times when marketing strategies are developed, and during the times in which those plans are executed.

→ The Past Is Never Past

Many of you are "preparing for jobs that do not exist where you will use technologies that have not yet been invented."[1] It is thus crucial for you to look around in order that you might understand the purpose of the past. This is because the practically functional insights that you, or for that matter, your Firm develop about the past and present will increase the likelihood that you or your Firm, will succeed in what promises to prove a continuously disruptive and consequently unsettling future.

But the future will not prove nearly as unsettling for those people or Firms who have adequately prepared for its arrival. You can never predict your Future. But you can create far better or worse futures for yourself (your Firm) dependent on the decisions you make right now.

Understanding the past to discover the future? Absolutely, the past is usually the best guide to what is likely to happen to you (your Firm) in the future. Chinese philosopher Confucius said: "Study the past if you would define the future."[2] Confucius was certainly correct, in part because US writer William Faulkner pronounced: "The past is not dead. In fact, it is not even past."[3]

Understanding the past is valuable because the resulting insights point out places, we call them **opportunities**, where you or your Firm should go. But it not is a GPS device that tells you how to get there and corrects you when you are wrong. An understanding of the past likewise points out places that you or your Firm should seek to avoid. We call these places **threats**.

As British historian Edward Gibbon wrote, "Still, history (the past) is the best guide to what will likely occur in the future."[4] As for us, we more simply encourage you to make personal or marketing decisions *now* as if you are looking back from the future upon the consequences that emanated from yesterday's, from your *past*, decisions.

Consider one simple illustration you all understand: good or bad decisions you make about what to eat *now* will result in a healthier or unhealthier you in the *future*. There is no question but that this is true. We acknowledge, however, that our suggesting one should look toward *future* health consequences when making *present* day dietary decisions and one actually electing to do it are two different things. For all our sakes, we hope all of us choose well.

→ A Good Choice; One Good Decision

One important choice all marketers should make is to pay meticulous attention to what is going on around their Firms in the moment. Attend to the present, for as British author George Orwell presciently wrote in the book *1984*, "He who controls the present controls the past, and he who controls the past controls the future."[5] We write, again more simply, take advantage of the informational and strategic gift that is the present by observing and living more fully in it. The present unquestionably represents a gift waiting to be opened for anyone reading this now. Why else would the exact moment you are reading this be called the "present?"

To provide your Firm the gift of the present, make the conscious decision now to power down and live more beyond those little screens that dominate too much of too many people's time. Yes, there certainly is good to be found in those machines, but generally not enough to justify all the time dedicated to them. Decide, for example, to walk, talk, and look around through metaphorical windows that reveal things happening around you or your Firm in the actual world rather than looking down continuously toward little devices residing near your lap. Face it, your own lap is usually just not that interesting or useful. But, looking incessantly down there has made Millennials spiritually, emotionally, and intellectually weaker than preceding generations, according to scientists who have studied the matter.[6]

People never can exactly predict the futures in which their firms will be marketing and whether they will fail or succeed. This is true even though this predictive ability is exactly what one should strive for when studying the environment and the reason why the Marketing Environment is studied in the first place. But, as noted, most Firms can create futures more to their liking, and live in them. That is, they can achieve these desirable futures if they properly assess, analyze, aggregate, and act upon information they purposely gather about their Firm's past and present circumstances. But to achieve these desirable outcomes people first must strategically establish their Firm's goals. Goals mark out where we want our Firms to be and what we want them to become. Then go for it. A successful marketing life, just like any successful life, truly is a "being" (managing the present) and a "becoming" (managing toward the future).

→ Managing on the Horizon

Marketers, to be as successful as possible, should live their professional lives on the horizon. Horizons provide vantage points from which people can look back (or around) to see what has happened and what worked well or failed miserably. From the same vantage points, people can also look forward to determine what their Firm has the capacity to make happen next.

Are you gathering a sense of the extent to which people, Firms, or even nations who do not plan well for their futures tend to not do well when they arrive at those futures? Hopefully, your understanding is growing. Nothing will age faster than your future, if you have not prepared for it. Because this is true, you must keep scanning forward from your vantage point on the horizon—visualizing what your future could and should be.

We call this visualizing activity **environmental scanning**. More about the subject follows.

Did You Know?

- The average American woman is 5'5" tall and weighs 163 pounds.
- The average American female model is 5'11" and weighs 117 pounds.
- Most fashion models are thinner than 98% of American women.
- On any given day, almost one-half of American women are dieting.
- Four of five American women report they are dissatisfied with their appearance.
- Meanwhile, most marketers of female apparel design their clothes as if they will be worn exclusively by models, with their abnormal dimensions, rather than by typical female consumers possessing normal dimensions.[7]

Why should marketers care about such fashion and sizing matters? Apparel marketers and all relevant fashion constituencies (designers, the media, the press, entertainment, and the arts) should care about the fact that such a high percentage of American women are not having their apparel-related wants and needs satisfied, or problems solved, by most contemporary marketers of women's apparel. Those marketers are missing out on a lot of green.

More to the point in this context, most apparel marketers who target women are currently missing out on a tremendous environment opportunity. Or are the environment conditions described above, which relate to customers or potential customers, more an environmental threat for apparel marketers?

What about American Men...and Fashion?

Because readers may be speculating (as we believe you should), we will tell you: the average American male weighs 192 pounds. At that poundage, he is, on average, at least slightly overweight. But he also is far less concerned about his weight and, for that matter, clothing than the average American female consumer. Are these two facts threats or opportunities for marketers?

Before answering, ask yourself whether female or male apparel fashions are driven more by social, cultural, or entertainment trends? We assume you know the answer. Ask, as well, in which gender-based demographic segment (male versus female) do styles and fads come-and-go more quickly. Again, we know you know the answer. Finally, ask: in which demographic segment is clothing, on average, built to be more durable. The answer to this final question, obviously, is male. Because, on average, males want, or at least are satisfied, to wear the same stuff longer.

It pays, literally, when marketers understand the important customer dimensions of their environment, in this case, the customers who constitute their primary target market segments. Moreover, it particularly pays to understand what the unsatisfied wants or needs, or resolved customer problems are within these segments right now, at this exact moment in time, in the present. Those segments, you should understand, are where the best opportunities to engage in successful new product development exist.

By the way, the answer to our initial question about the two facts related to men, their weight and their clothing wants, need, and problems is: These facts, these environmental differences between female and male apparel consumers, represent both opportunity and threat to apparel marketers.

More Environmental Differences—and Their Consequences

American men are not only far less concerned, on average, about their weight or clothing choices. They are also less concerned about working hard enough to successfully get into or out of college than are women. Consequently, American men graduate college at much lower rates than American women, and the gender gap continues to widen.[8] At the same time, an American male is much more likely to serve time in prison than an American female, for what either trend is worth.

These gender-based environmental differences, it turns out, are worth quite a lot. Each still emerging trend or environmental change difference exercises a tremendous impact on the:

- Growth and productivity of the entire US economy;
- Norms, beliefs and behaviors that prevail through US society and culture; and
- Current welfare and future prospects of US children, just for starters, because we could have gone on.

Naturally, these two gender-based environmental trends present any number of environmental opportunities to American marketers who are best able to identify and embrace these trends and subsequently manage their segmentation, targeting, and positioning (or marketing mix) efforts in response to these trends. Or, these trends create environmental threats for American marketers who fail to identify or ignore these trends, or create the wrong strategic responses.

Examining the Consequences

Context is frequently important when making business or marketing decisions, living life, or attempting to describe the myriad consequences that emerge as a result of one straightforward, apparently simple environmental trend: men doing worse in school than women. The trickle-down effect of this trend is, in part, a reduction in the number of marriages between American men and women. And this effect, in turn, may have further trickle-down effects on other aspects of the economy. How is this so? The context is this. Men often marry down in terms of their partners' social standing or economic potential/ current financial worth in exchange for the value associated with the perceived or actual physical attractiveness of their marital partner. Female college graduates rarely marry down to men whose economic prospects are not at par or superior to their own. This tendency also characterizes women who never attend college. They rarely marry down, either.

Safe to say, women are more strategic in their marital consumption choices than are men. With good cause, because it remains true that getting ahead professionally and economically in the contemporary marketplace without college degrees is tough for males and females, but it is tougher still for males because their former muscle-related work, which once paid enough to support a family, generally no longer exists and no longer pays high wages (on average). These blue-collar jobs have been replaced by pink-collar cubical-bound jobs, for which men are often unsuitable. Yes, Bill Gates, Steve Jobs, and Mark Zuckerberg did it without a college degree. But each was also a genius and lucky. Each was born at the right time and place in human history, where their specific talent, motives, and the technologies available in their respective presents (meaning time) cohered in ways that rarely happen. Few people have been simultaneously intelligent and fortunately-right-place-right-time (for them and consumers) as this tech trinity.

Therefore, women who graduate from college right now, today, are less likely than they were only recently to get married soon or at all. Consequently, there are currently fewer marriages between American men and women. This first socio-cultural environmental consequence is a whopper in terms of its associated consequences. Its impact of this consequence is analogous to throwing a large rock straight up and having it come straight down deep into a calm lake and watching the water ripple out in increasing circles.

The only sort of human coupling that can develop those new products called children is a heterosexual exchange; a special marketing exchange that, like all exchanges, exists and pivots based on a giving/getting of value (sperm and egg). We assume you knew this. (By stating the obvious at this point we are neither discounting nor ignoring gay or lesbian marriage.)

This natural fact about child manufacturing proves critical in the context of this discussion. Back to traditional marriage: in 2012, for the first time in US history fewer than 50% of Americans older than 21 years were married.[9] Since then, the percentage of heterosexually married couples has further declined. Moreover, the median age (half of marriages above this age, half below) of first marriages has never been higher for brides (26.8 years) or grooms (28.8 years).[10] These environmental trends are also important. Just as behaviors always generate consequences, one consequence always generates additional behaviors and new consequences—the toss-a-big-rock in a still-lake thing, again.

A second socio-cultural and ultimately economic consequence of this marital trend is that more US children than ever before in history are born out of wedlock. Consumers still will have sex, regardless of their marital status. The physiological motives or needs that create the desire for sex, as your examination of Chapter 6's discussion of Maslow's hierarchy of needs will reveal, are relentless. The sex drive is rightfully listed amongst human beings—consumers'—most pressing needs.

Notably, less than 10% of births to college-educated American women are out of wedlock. For mothers without a college degree, the number is greater than 50%.[11] Here, a third socio-cultural consequence, one associated in no small measure with consumers' educational status, is revealed.

Children produced outside of marriage, on average, experience more educational and social problems. They also possess less self-control, again, on average.[12] That lack of self-control, again on average, exacerbates or causes the first two problems. These children consequently are less employable in modern economies as they age into their futures. (Note, we know, as you should understand, that there are many exceptions to each of these correlations.) But a fourth socio-economic consequence arises naturally.

Employers, like consumers, only "buy" people as employees when they believe that the new purchase of an employee, who is truly just a product, will add value to their Firm. Consumers, you will learn, rarely purchase anything unless they perceive the value that they will acquire from using or giving the product exceeds the value of the money that currently resides in their pockets. Decision-makers must give-up value in order to get value. In most situations, most people would never give-up money unless they perceive they are "winning," e.g., they think they are getting more back than they gave up in return for the new product—or employee.

Uneducated or undereducated people bring less value to any employer's table. Uneducated or undereducated people are thus less likely to be hired, or, if hired, more likely to be paid less. This is a marketing thing, you see. It is an exchange of values thing, again. Everyone, certainly you, will make the decisions they perceive will deliver the most value to them, every time.

Other more direct economic consequences that follow from the consequence of fewer Americans getting married as a consequence of fewer men graduating from college are that fewer houses will be sold. On average, again, singletons find it more difficult to afford or get home mortgages. For those still keeping count, this is the fifth economic consequence.

No sense stopping there, however, because as a sixth, seventh, or eighth consequence fewer construction jobs are available, less lumber is harvested and refined, and the need for trucks or trains or barges to transport that wood diminishes, meaning that the entire US economy performs at a lower level than would be the case if more men graduated college and more women got married. Or, we could have reported that fewer washing machines, life insurance policies, expensive items of furniture, luxury vacations or restaurant meals will be sold. All because, on average, singletons are not nearly so powerful an economic engine as is a dual earning or even a single earner married couple.

In retrospect, if any marketer had carefully evaluated the consequences of this beginning environmental trend, these effects would have been as predictable as they were inevitable.

→ Fortunes Rise, Fortunes Fall

This singular environmental trend (men graduating at lower rates) has created wonderful opportunities for certain marketers. McDonald's, whose specialty is selling fast-food-cheap, is doing well. Rent-A-Center (RAC), headquartered in Plano, TX, is also doing extremely well. RAC succeeds on an impressive scale because it provides ready-made solutions to the problems of US consumers who cannot afford to purchase the household goods they want right now. But many of those same US consumers feel they need those things, just the same. As their short-term needs become sufficiently pressing, RAC's customers become more willing to pay whatever higher long-term price is necessary to obtain those items, now, in the short-run.

Cliché alert: human natures are what they are. By this we mean: over time, humans constantly convert simple wants into pressing needs. Many marketers, such as RAC, do a magnificent job of exploiting this human tendency.

Yet the fortunes of other Firms, indeed entire industries, have undoubtedly been damaged by the aforementioned educational and marital trends. The sales of Zales Jewelers, Kay Jewelers (after all, every Kiss begins with "K", a promotional branding and positioning slogan) or even Tiffany Jewelers come to mind. The *getting* (purchasing from a store) and the *giving* (to the female partner) of a diamond ring in a typically highly ritualized exchange process is a direct consequence of most marriage proposals in the United States.

When marriage proposals decline, fewer diamond rings are sold. This is another negative *economic consequence* for marketers. Impending and actual marriages generate profoundly positive financial consequences for Firms who market finer foods, wines, flowers, wedding planning services, accommodations, and transportation services. We again see how one environmental event, multiplied by hundreds of thousands, generates consequences that create wave-like effects through entire economies, cultures, and markets. We should also note the extent to which the entire relational world is nothing more than an intricately networked series of marketing exchanges.

Branding Thoughts

Speaking of Tiffany: has the branding power of any firm ever been so polished for so long (since 1961) by a relative cipher of a movie? (Yes, the movie is *Breakfast at Tiffany's*.) The answer is probably not.

But the real point we hope you learn here follows from the lesson about the sustainable *branding power* that can emerge when the right marketing medium (a movie and a spokesperson, the never-aging iconic ingénue that was Audrey Hepburn) delivers the right message at the right time to the right audience. Even today, more than 50 years later, knowing-men know that when they give a diamond enclosed in a little blue box they are demonstrating a full measure of love and devotion. Or at least Tiffany, through its powerful marketing machine, has so convinced much of the civilized male and female consumer worlds.

Naturally these men are required to pay an extra high price for that "full measure" of their demonstrated love. But they generally do so consciously and willingly, motivated in each case not by the "power of love" but rather by the fact that they and their female recipients were inspired by the power of branding.

Discerning readers might cynically suggest this is because, unlike love, "A Diamond is Forever." But these words do not actually capture Tiffany's branding position. The "Forever" brand imagery has been South Africa-based De Beers Diamonds' positional stake-in-the-ground since 1948. Tiffany, by contrast, has relied on the branding power of its "Little Blue Box" seemingly forever.

→ Managing Environmental Opportunities and Threats

Marketing efforts to identify environmental opportunities should begin with a strategic examination of what might be trending in various relevant dimensions of the Firm's environment. This "looking-around-process" is called **environmental scanning**. Why should Firms engage in environmental scanning? The answer is similar to the response that the 1930s-era bank robber Willie Sutton provided when newspaper reporters asked, post-capture: "Willie, why did you rob all those banks?" Mr. Sutton's answer, logically: "That's where the money is."[13]

The marketing environment is also where the potentially most advantageous opportunities or most damaging threats facing the Firm exist. Firms that detect these environmental opportunities before their competitors do and then exploit them by strategically shifting their segmentation, targeting, and positioning efforts before those competitors can respond should make more money. This is the first reason why firms should engage in environmental scanning.

In the same fashion Firms that are able to detect environmental threats before their competitors, and subsequently are first to react strategically in response to its negative consequences, should be able to negate or avoid the worst of those threats. First-responder Firms will generally lose less money, or perhaps lose nothing at all. Threats that are properly anticipated and appropriately addressed may transform into opportunities in disguise. As the adage suggests, "A crisis is a terrible thing to waste." This is the second reason why firms should engage in strategic planning.

→ Key Marketing Success Factors

A future is rapidly arriving in which bigger Firms will be less likely to destroy or "eat" smaller Firms. That is, unless those smaller Firms want to be eaten, in other words, acquired whole. This is already happening. Just ask Instagram and Whatsapp, each of which was happily gobbled up by Facebook for approximately $1 billion and $19 billion, respectively.

Instead, *faster* firms are much more likely to destroy or devour *slower* competitors in today's world. Physical size provides certain indisputable advantages to those who possess it in American football. (Lest we forgot, the rest of the world calls what we call "soccer" football.) But in American football (and in hand-to-hand combat) smaller men who get lower, arrive faster, and thus secure leverage will prevail against bigger men, most of the time.

Along a similar vein, information that is acquired through environmental scanning should be fed directly into the Firm's marketing information system (MkIS) for use in its ongoing strategic planning processes.[14] The resulting operational and actionable knowledge should allow those Firms to get lower, move faster, gain leverage, and win their marketing competitions.

The ultimate secret formula for achieving sustainable marketing success is much the same as a three-part "secret formula" for achieving sustainable life success:

- First, you or your Firm should accept change as a permanent condition, meaning that change is a constant, like death and taxes.
- Second, accept that you or your Firm should willingly adapt constantly in response to ever changing environmental circumstances.
- Three, understand the degree to which dynamically disruptive environmental conditions facilitate continuously arising opportunities, threats, and problems for you or your Firm to exploit, avoid, or solve.

→ Environmental Opportunities and Threats, Defined

An **environmental opportunity** entails any environmental trend that is moving in ways that support the best interests of a Firm and its current strategy and mission. For example, global fuel prices trending higher represent an opportunity for the hybrid car strategic business unit (SBU) at General Motors.

An **environmental threat**, defined, entails any environmental trend that is moving against the best interests of a Firm and its current strategy and mission. For example, fuel prices that are trending higher represent a threat for the sport utility vehicle SBU at General Motors.

As this simple illustration demonstrates the same environmental trend can be viewed as an opportunity or threat, even within the same Firm. Then again, this is always true. People's point-of-view, even their perceptions of good or bad or right or wrong, usually depends primarily on their "points-of-viewing." Yet there is more to this truth than that. Even the most challenging threat, for example, could be converted into a relative opportunity for Firms if they identify and respond more quickly and effectively to the threat than their competitors.

You probably know the phrase "the cutting-edge," as in, Firms should operate on the cutting-edge in terms of their awareness and understanding of the likely consequences associated with environmental trends (opportunities or threats) that it uncovers through environmental scanning efforts. We largely agree, while differing slightly, with this premise. Our small disagreement arises because Firms who are equivalent to each other in everything else can still create sustainable competitive advantages for themselves by managing the environmental scanning process and operating on the *bleeding*, rather than cutting, edge of environmental changes. *Bleeding-edge environmental* trends are so fresh and new that any "cuts" they elicit are still hemorrhaging.

Firms that practice bleeding-edge environmental scanning may not always be completely right. It is true that when you operate on the bleeding edge, you are likely to bleed occasionally—ouch. But such Firms would always be first-movers in their respective market spaces. And as you already know, genuine advantages generally accrue to those Firms that are first-to-market with anything—an idea, insight, or product—that offers or promises new and useful value.

Own the Trend When It Is Your Friend

Firms should always attempt to own the trend when it is their friend. Levi Straus absolutely understood this rule in 1986, when it strategically introduced its long-since iconic Dockers brand of pants. Levi Straus's senior management, according to lore, had just identified new independent research findings that suggested the productivity of professional workers increased materially when they could dress more casually at work. To this point in time US male professional workers invariably dressed, well, professionally—suits, ties, white shirts. Soon after this study, however, an idea called Casual Fridays was born. Dockers arrived nearly simultaneously, through a planned market entry.[15]

The exactly right product was made available at exactly the right time because Levi Straus had anticipated this environmental trend. In taking ownership of this friendly trend Levi had quickly leveraged its denim expertise, which is really just an expertise in cotton, and developed a true innovation (i.e., it was both new and useful) best described as casual dress pants. Through its Dockers brand, Levi's changed the men's pant market forever by developing an **intersectional product** that truly threaded the needle. Like Goldilocks and The Three Bears, Dockers split the difference between too-casual (blue jeans) and too-dressy (suit pants) and managed to get things "just right." Levi's took ownership of the environmental trend toward more casual professional men's work wear. The trend here, an opportunity, *was their friend*.

While there has been the occasional bump in the road during the intervening 30-something years, the Dockers brand has largely dominated its market. As Levi's should have, because this was a market that Levi Strauss had earlier created, by itself. Despite the sometimes manic efforts of competitors such as Haggar, Liz Claiborne, Polo, Tommy, Perry Ellis, J. Crew, Dickies, or The Gap to catch up, none ever really has. First-to-market, first-in-mind; these old marketing principles are often the best marketing principals. Because, while environments such as culture, society, technology, or the economy change continuously, human nature never really changes.

Environmental anticipation, of the sort that Levi Straus demonstrated, is critical to marketing and business success in general. No person or Firm can wait for an opportunity to become obvious. They should instead go all-in "bleeding-edge", most of the time. In modern marketing it rarely makes sense to simply be, think, or act like everyone else is being, thinking, or acting. Instead, environmentally attuned marketers should be, think, and act different, better and yes, faster than competitors.

Is It Opportunity or Threat?

Firms should ask five questions during the environmental scanning process:

- First, is this environmental trend an opportunity or threat?
- Second, why is this trend an opportunity or threat?
- Third, for whom (which business unit) inside our Firm is this trend an opportunity or threat?
- Fourth, should our Firm respond strategically to this opportunity or threat?
- Finally, how should our Firm respond, if the preceding answer was "yes"?

Consider the five environment trends listed below as we discuss whether these are opportunities or threats, and for whom.

"Kids these days just want to live in their own f---ing little worlds watching Netflix and getting obese"—The Economist, 2014.[16]

This environmental trend, like the others following it, represents both an opportunity and a threat. If your Firm operates in the salty snacks (the kind you can munch while you watch or play at life), smart devices (so these experiences can be shared with others experiencing the same things), online games, or health care industries, we hope you're enjoying these halcyon days. For example, overweight kids are more likely to become heavy adults and heavy adults are more likely to get sick. Consequently, as noted, the future prospects for health care providers appear increasingly bright.

But if your Firm competes in, say, the classic US sports equipment industries, you might be lamenting those days, not so long ago, when far more kids brought gloves and baseballs; basketballs, or basketball shoes for sport not for fashion; footballs, cleats, or mouth guards; or even soccer balls, hockey sticks and skates, tennis racquets, or swimsuits because they wanted to play the game. While neither games nor sports has dried up and blown away, smaller proportions of young American consumers are participating in either. This environmental trend represents a threat to any Firm attempting to market any of these products.

"There has been a huge increase in social pressure to become a good parent"—The Economist, 2014.[17]

With observations such as the one offered just above, this trend, cited in the same magazine is trending heavily. It is a small wonder that anxious parents are now apparently trying so hard to improve their "products." (We joke, we joke; maybe). But in all seriousness, this environmental trend clearly exists as an opportunity for any Firm attempting to market any product that makes baby or junior/missy smarter, healthier, more articulate, more socially adept, more resilient, or better looking. Child psychologists or youth-oriented life coaches, for example, must be dancing in the street. Marketers who own and/or manage the highest-end, more academically oriented day care centers should be similarly delighted.

The only entities threatened by this trend, likely, are those parents themselves, struggling as they are against all odds to create sustainable perfection out of imperfect human clay. Who knows, perhaps marital counselors or adult psychologists are rubbing their hands in anticipating the never-ending task of convincing the parents that "the kids are alright"—with apologies to The Who and Julianne Moore/Ann Benning movie of the same name—even if the parents aren't.

> *Written in 2011, "Total U.S. payrolls today amount to 131 million, a figure that is lower than it was at the beginning of the year 2000, even though our population has grown by near 30 million"*—US News & World Report 2011[18]

The problem, unfortunately, is that the work-force participation and under-employment rates remain so high that they overwhelm and negate any perceived decline in the reported unemployment rate.

The net of this economic trend is that too many Americans have less money to spend and higher doubts about their economic prospects in an uncertain future. Consequently, more US firms have fewer customers poised, willing, and able to purchase from them. This low workforce participation trend represents a threat across essentially the entire spectrum of US for-profit and not-for-profit businesses sectors.

The consequences also flood over to educational and political domains. Older American adults are re-entering or graduating from college in greater numbers and proportions than at any point in American history. This is because these mature consumers were wise and experienced enough to discern the value that the hiring workplace ascribes to higher education.

Or consider, for example, the Republican marketing machine. The Grand Old Party i.e., Republican's traditional brand name, made unprecedented gains in the number of House of Representative seats it holds during the 2012 and 2014 election cycles. Republican marketers now hold more House seats than at any time since the 1920s. The subtle and not-so-subtle consequences of the low-work-force-participation trend created a situation where the brand position of the Democratic marketing party became untenable in the eyes of consumers who decided to vote them out. Yet if the Republican brand does not reverse this environmental trend it faces the same marketing consequences during the 2016 election cycle.

One dirty secret: politicians can do little to change this rate. Lower US workforce participation rates are almost entirely due to the role that technological environmental trends have played in eliminating menial work, muscle work, or work featuring ample redundant motion.

But for retailers such as the The Dollar Store, Dollar General, Everything's a Dollar or even Big Lots, this specific trend has made the past seven or so years "your time." Underemployed, unemployed, or anxious consumers have had their needs well served by these and other retailers. These providers have made it their mission to solve the purchasing problems of poorer U.S. consumers. And, through masterful management of their supply chains, they have consistently achieved their missions.

A major consequence, at least partially due to this environmental trend, is that 27.7% of American consumers are obese. Another 35.3% are overweight but not obese. (Obese implies one's Body Mass Index [BMI] is greater than 30%.). Meanwhile, being overweight is still not viewed as a good thing, although the once new cultural trend is becoming the new normal. At net: 63% of Americans were considered obese or overweight in 2014.[19]

Obesity is the leading cause of disease, illness, and preventable death in the entire world. But what does this mean for marketers? As far as opportunities go, this environmental trend represents an unparalleled opportunity to an entire industry, just as it represents a huge threat to another.

This heavyweight trend implies, more directly, that were a pharmaceutical marketer able to create a diet pill that actually worked sans grave damage to consumers' hearts, bowels, and/or energy levels, the opportunity to reap trillions in profits would prove so delicious that everyone could quit and go home. Most pharmaceutical marketers operate and compete inside the so-called Big Pharma. Globally, Big Pharma consists of 12 firms, including (based on highest to lowest revenue) Johnson & Johnson, Novartis, Roche, Pfizer, Sanofi, GlaxoSmithKline, and Merck.[20]

Any specific marketing solution to the obesity problem, which to some degree clearly has been worsened by marketing practices, is unlikely to arrive soon—if ever. Indeed, while the obesity problem has probably grown about as much as possible the problem does not appear likely to shrink anytime soon. Not in a marketing world where calorie-dense branded foods (Wendy's burgers, Pizza Hut pizza, Frito-Lay potato chips and any brand's French fries, Pepsi soft drinks, Skippy's peanut butter, etc.) are what sell best because they are generally fattier, saltier, and sweeter, all while being lower in cost than healthier dietary alternatives. The fact remains: humans instinctively crave more sugar, higher fat, salt and, naturally, lower prices. This sugary, fatty, salty, lower-priced combination of values makes fast food one of the easiest things in the world to market successfully. Various highly successful national brands—Coca-Cola, McDonalds, Burger King, KFC, Taco Bell, Dominos, etc.—have each already carved out their differentiating positions. Now their seemingly simple task is to retain their marketing positions and loyal customer bases. Yet this endeavor will prove increasingly challenging as various environmental factors such as regulatory/legislative forces, educational initiatives, and public interest group efforts are uniformly trending against them, attempting to undermine their marketing efforts.

Meanwhile, US consumers live in a nation where they enjoy the full sovereign right to eat what they want so long as they are willing to accept the fact of how much they may lose as a consequence of how much they have gained. As noted, the same premise of freedom does not necessarily apply to marketers. Just ask those marketers who sell soda in New York City, where *Big Gulps* are no longer so big at a skinny 16 ounces, maximum.

Be mindful, however, that historically this amount is still a large quantity. The original Coca-Cola came in a 6.5 ounce bottle; the original McDonald's soft drink size was a full 7 ounces. These are not misprints. Each statistic underscores how cultural and societal norms/standards change slowly but inexorably until one day Americans wake up and believe that 64 ounces of sugary soda is actually normal—because it is!

Frogs, it is said, can be placed in an uncovered pot full of lukewarm water (swamp temperature?) and, if the water is heated up slowly enough, they will never jump. As the water begins to boil, they are cooked. Culture, as part of any marketing firm's environment, often changes in much the same manner. It transforms incrementally, essentially imperceptibly but steadily, over longer or shorter periods of time until one day a Firm wakes up, finds it is operating in a different world, and that its "frog" is cooked. That is, unless the Firm has engaged continuously in environmental scanning.

Suffice it to report at this point that the fast food industry and its set of usual governmental/ regulatory suspects are scrambling to devise strategies that will permit them to deliver healthier but still tasty product alternatives to an anxious marketplace.

> *The percentage of Americans who regularly attend a church, mosque, temple, or synagogue is lower than at any point in US history, and trending further down year by year.[21]*

Religion, along with other secular or anthropological disciplines such as psychology, sociology, philosophy or marketing share one thing in common: an abiding awareness of people's unhappiness and dissatisfaction, usually with themselves. But religion is unique among these other institutions of philosophical thought. Religion actually promises a genuine solution to much but not all of our personal unhappiness and dissatisfaction. And the modern American customer environment, if nothing else, is chock-full of unhappy and dissatisfied souls. This trend is also undeniably true and highly relevant to religious marketers who generally teach their customers to stop pursuing every single one of their selfish impulses while exercising more restraint. As Buddha taught: a craving for things outside ourselves creates, as a consequence, an unhappy and ultimately fruitless search for security and more unhappiness and dissatisfaction.

This environmental trend thus represents a huge opportunity for those religious marketers who prove capable of properly packaging, promoting, positioning and subsequently delivering their version of a solution to masses of consumers who are yearning for greater happiness and more sustainable states of satisfaction. That value would prove worth a high price to most consumers. Fortunately for religious marketers, the price of introducing greater religiosity to one's consumer life is generally quite low.

As far as marketing threats, we see few indeed. Except, perhaps, for the occasional golf courses' loss of business (on Sundays, for Christians, the "Sunday people"; Saturday for Jews (the "Saturday people"); or Friday, for Muslims, the "Friday people"). At their cores each of the world's five major religions essentially teach, as one of its key principles, "May you be better people." There is nothing threatening about that at all.

→ Micro- and Macro-Environments

Every Firm faces a series of **microenvironments**, which include:

- An internal environment consisting of all entities (i.e. departments and functions) within the Firm
- Customers and prospective customer relationships
- Relationships with suppliers, other supply chain intermediaries or resellers, which could include retailers
- Relationships with various *publics*, which could include investors (shareholders) or public interest groups, such as the media or regulatory agencies, who may or may not support the general mission and goals of the Firm
- The Firm's competitors

Signs of changes in any of these relationships, as would emerge as a result of environmental scanning, could prove harbingers of delight or trouble. If delight is apparent, Firms should keep doing what is engendering the delight. If trouble appears, Firms should at least consider addressing its underlying causes. Each of these *microenvironments* is addressed in far greater detail in various following chapters. This is why these micro-environmental factors will not be formally discussed in the remainder of this chapter.

Every Firm simultaneously operates in a **macroenvironment**, consisting strictly of environments external to the Firm (Exhibit 4.1). The Firm's macroenvironment consists of cultural trends, which might, for example, include the green movement; demographic trends, which might include the decline in marriage discussed above; economic trends, which could include a currency that is declining or increasing in value; technological trends, which might include almost anything, today; or governmental/regulatory trends, which might be exemplified by increases in capital gains taxes. Collectively, these macroenvironmental trends will almost surely bring opportunities and/or threats to every Firm's doorstep. Each is discussed in greater detail below.

Exhibit 4.1 *Macroenvironments can dramatically affect the Firm's operations.*

→ Key Macro-environments and Trends

Cultural Environment and Trends

New York Times editorialist David Brooks recently wrote: "In some ways, each of us is like every person on earth; in some ways, each of us is like the members of our culture and group; and, in some ways, each of us is unique."[22] Related to Brooks' first phrase, while there may be products (a Rolls Royce, a huge house, or nearly a month playing and learning in New Zealand) that everyone would love to own, consume, or experience, not everyone can afford them. So, the fact that each human being is in some ways like every other person on earth is of little interest to marketers as they engage in segmentation, targeting and positioning efforts.

Related to the editorialist's closing phrase, many Firms presumably would love to serve and satisfy every consumer in the world. But too many unique people exist in the world for any Firm to successfully serve them all. No Firm can customize the value delivered through its marketing mix that many times.

Which leaves us with Brooks' middle phrase: "in some ways each of us is like members of our culture and group." This phrase directly underscores the reason why cultural norms and trends, and particularly the bleeding edges of those trends, are so important to marketers. The fact that people who belong to particular cultures or subcultures are so similar to each other makes cultural and subcultural groups important to marketers.

Culture exists and operates as an emergent market system. A culture emerges whenever a group of people who share one, two, or possibly, three or more characteristics in common establish a pattern of interaction with each other. These people collectively determine those norms, beliefs, or behaviors that are deemed right or wrong; appropriate or inappropriate, within their group or culture. Should you call a woman a "ho", or should you call her "ma'am?" Cultural membership determines the appropriateness of either label. And once a culture exists, it influences how the individuals in it behave. This point likewise underscores why culture and cultural trends are so important to marketers.

Contemporary US consumers' cultural-based consumption appears to operate on almost Pavlovian-like instincts. You should already know about Pavlov and his dogs but, in summary, the Russian Professor Pavlov is the father of classical conditioning, a form of behavioral learning, as in ring-a-bell and make-a-dog-salivate. Which a dog will invariably do once it has been conditioned to do so through the learned association of bell ringing and food, a reward, arriving.

Many US consumers appear almost classically conditioned by cultural surroundings to respond in ways similar to Pavlov's dogs. Just ring a bell, as in announce a sale, and watch the customers flood in, in a culturally-conditioned response. Many US consumers are responding classically to an acquisition and consumption culture that has taught them one of the surest measures of love, happiness, and self-worth are the objects we purchase or give. And we can never have enough goods or services, or give enough to others, to satisfy our intense craving for more, and indeed, satisfy our craving for higher consumption-induced status. In a society in which most of everyone's needs are met, everyone rich and poor must be kept feeling perpetually deprived, and in turn often perpetually bound up in debt, to keep this Pavlovian response going. For better or worse, this is one of the cultural consequences that marketers experience and can exploit, should they decide to do so. For better or worse, this is also a cultural consequence that threatens the financial and emotional well-being of many consumers who are raised and acculturated in the modern American culture.

The practice of marketing is simultaneously shaping and reflecting American culture and society. Similarly, culture and society are simultaneously shaping and reflecting what is happening with marketing. Recall the glacial metaphor that was used to open this chapter because it applies most readily in this context.

Culture is a social force that influences consumers' behaviors and marketers' key success factors in more ways than can be easily imagined. Culture encompasses the set of values, ideas, and attitudes that are acquired and shared by members of groups. Cultures exist and function as lenses—one might imagine really thick eyeglasses—through which cultural groups perceive and make sense of the world. People who hail from different cultures can experience the same event at the same time, but assign widely divergent meanings to what is happening. Those folks from different cultures could likely also broadly accept/brusquely reject what is happening during an event based on their originating cultural affiliation. A "small-town-boy" from Gun City, Texas (a real town) might have an entirely different take on an emergent fashion trend than might a "big-city boy" from Dallas, Texas or Chicago, Illinois.

There is, for example, an American cultural group; just as there are Turkish, Chinese, or British cultural groups. But English, Scottish, Irish, and Welsh subcultures exist within the broader British culture. Or, to extend the point, Australian or New Zealand subcultures similarly exist as comparatively similar subsets within the broad British culture. Christchurch, New Zealand (another real town) is described right now as being more fully English in its customs, values, and beliefs than any city in England.

The United States is certainly no stranger to subcultures. A partial list of ethnic-group based subcultures that abide within the broader American culture would include Hispanic-Americans, African-Americans, and Asian-Americans. The membership of each subculture shares much in common with the broader US culture; these respective subcultural memberships also share much in common with Asian-, Hispanic- or African-Americans. Yet the Asian-American subculture itself is quite diverse in its beliefs, attitudes, and behaviors. Consider that Indians, as South Asians, and Chinese dominated nationalities such as China, Taiwan, South Korea, or Thailand are each tossed together in an extremely broad Asian-American bucket even though American consumers who hail from each of these cultures often think, act, and consume differently from each other.

Regional subcultures also exist inside the United States. There is no doubt but that Californians, on average, differ from New Yorkers who differ from Texans in many of each group's shared values, ideas, and attitudes. Far more trucks and SUVs, for example, are purchased in Texas than California or Ohio, where foreign cars and four-door domestic sedans, respectfully, are likely to be purchased. And, there is likewise no question that the values of Northern and Southern Californian consumer groups tend to differ from each other.

Culture and its Effects on Marketing Practice

Subcultural memberships are critical to marketers as they develop and execute their segmentation and targeting efforts. Subcultures, you should understand, frequently exist as ready-made market segments. Once discrete subcultures are identified, Firms might decide to determine a unique and uniquely desirable marketing mix and then target its unique value to the respective subcultures. Consider, for example, how their subcultural group membership affects the dietary choices of various US groups. Or for that matter, consider how many different ethnic restaurants exist and compete successfully in the broader American culture.

Three Important Cultural Trends

Key US cultural ideas, values, and attitudes are trending in predictable and unpredictable ways. For example, attitudes about the role of men and women in the workplace are actually converging. That is to say, male and female attitudes about men and women in the workplace are becoming more, rather than less, similar. If this trend continues the behavioral purchasing patterns of men and women for many non-gender driven purchases will eventually be quite similar.

During the last 10 years American attitudes toward gay and lesbian marriage have changed with incredible speed. Amongst consumers less than 40 years of age the matter is generally settled. The idea that prevails amongst this age group is akin to the notion of "so what," that gays or lesbians have the same opportunity to be as unhappy as anyone else. Even growing percentages of the older US demographic is warming to the idea that gay/lesbian marriage is acceptable.

Marketers who have publically objected to gay/lesbian unions have increasingly faced various threats from other corporate, public interest, or governmental sources. Of course, the day after Chick-fil-A was "outed" for taking a stand against gay marriage[23], it experienced the largest day of sales in its history. Not all subcultural groups, obviously, have so readily accepted gay and lesbian marriage.[24]

After suffering through two large recessions during the last 14 years, US consumers have become increasingly value-conscious. One strategic implication is that Firms are being forced to step up their game as they devise and execute their positioning and branding strategies. Incrementally determinant (i.e. difference-making) value could assume the form of lower prices, higher quality, faster marketer responsiveness to customer problems, faster delivery, new superior product features, customer rewards and incentives, delivery, and/or better warranties—as they devise and execute their positioning and branding strategies. The form of its arrival does not necessarily matter; what does matter is that this "extra" arrives. More retailers, for example, are actually authorizing employees to grant negotiated discounts to customers who ask for them. Now that you have read this perhaps you will be the one doing the negotiating.

Demographic Environment and Trends

Some experts suggest the Democrat Party is little more than a demographic party comprised of minorities; union, governmental, and educational workers; and gays who have little in common other than their seeking a larger portion of what a bigger or more intrusive government can provide. The Democrat Party is also the majority party for women. No criticisms here; this combination of demographic constituencies has proven sufficient to permit Democrats to win the popular vote in five out of the last six Presidential Elections. There is a strong probability that it will be enough to win the popular vote again in 2016. Why? Because *demographics is destiny*, particularly for the category of marketers called politicians and their handlers, brand managers, communication directors, and spokespeople. All these people, including the politicians, are nothing more and nothing less than marketers.

Demography is a catch-all cultural measurement. The term "demographic" should be viewed as a description and a measurement of some key aspect of a particular population at a given point in time. Demographics, as you might expect typically trend up or down.

Demographics can be viewed as a wide, deep bucket. Demographic trends—what's up, down, or stagnant—function as powerful, shape-shifting forces. These forces should influence the Firm's strategies and certainly will influence the fortunes of entire industries (automotive, health care, fashion, restaurants and hospitality, entertainment and the media, construction, banking and financial, technological, etc.). The demographic bucket, for example, involves improving income levels, generally measured within regional-, cultural-, ethnic-, education-, profession-, or gender-based US consumer segments. The Southern and Southwestern regions of the United States are growing proportionately wealthier at the expense of the Midwestern and Northeastern regions, as the businesses and citizens of these latter two regions migrate south. This trend itself is driven by one controllable environmental trend (taxes are inevitably lower in the south, as is usually true of housing prices) and one uncontrollable trend (the South is warmer).

Our demographic bucket will also contain changes in *age distributions* as they trend throughout a culture and its attendant population. The US population is simultaneously growing younger and older. The U.S. population is growing younger in large part because various rapidly growing immigrant consumer segments are reproducing at increasingly higher rates. Educational programs, as well as certain other youth-centric industries (PlayStation or X-box, Six Flags or Disney World, anyone), are likewise profoundly impacted.

The United States is simultaneously growing older because huge numbers of aging Baby Boomers generally have many productive years yet to live. Baby Boomers consist of post World War II babies born between 1946 and 1964. This most famous demographic cohort continues to inexorably pass through American society like the proverbial swallowed pig passes through the body of a python. Eventually the Baby Boomer cohort will pass from history. But, for now, the generation continues to break existing and establish new cultural norms, more so than any generation before or after its arrival. Although the wealth of the Boomer cohort was dramatically affected by the last recession, it still accounts for about 50% of consumer spending and holds 75% of the nation's financial assets. As the Boomer population continues to age, by the year 2030 18% of the total US population will be over the age of 65 years.[25] The marketing implications associated with an aging Baby Boomer cohort are intensely affecting the healthcare and pharmaceutical sectors, housing markets, the leisure and travel industry, the investment and financial sectors, and various social welfare programs offered by federal and state governments.

Younger aged and smaller cohorts, Gen X and Millennials, are hot on the heels of Boomers. The youngest tracked cohort, Millennials range in age from 18 to 34. Many are just now moving into adulthood. According to a recent Pew research report, Millennials are characterized as relatively detached from organized politics. Nearly 50% declare themselves as Independents, although they tend to vote heavily Democratic and demonstrate strong liberal views on many political and social issues. Less than 30% have any formal religious affiliation. They are extensive users of social media and the Internet in general. Indeed, Pew characterizes this cohort as "digital natives" as they are the first generation that has not had to adapt, post-hoc, to digital innovations. As a result of the economic recession of 2008 and 2009, combined with the effects of globalization, technological changes affecting the workforce, and student loans, this cohort is burdened by debt. It is amazing that this cohort remains optimistic about the future.[26]

In between the Millennials and Boomers is Generation X (Gen X), ranging in age from 35 to 49. According to Pew, this cohort tends to be ignored when reporting on occurrences of demographic, social, and political merit. "They're smack in the middle innings of life, which tend to be short on drama and scant of theme."[27] Although Millennials and Boomers exhibit dramatic differences, Gen X possesses traits of both of its sister cohorts. It is literally "stuck in the middle" in terms of its demographic profile. For example:

- *Ethnic diversity*—61% are white, compared to 57% and 72% for Millennials and Boomers, respectively.

- *Marital Status*—36% get married between ages 18 and 32, compared to 26% and 48% for Millennials and Boomers.

- *Religious affiliation*—21% declare no specific religious affiliation. This compares with 29% for Millennials and 16% for Boomers.

Gen Xers also demonstrate a similar middle ground with respect to their views on political and social issues:

- *Bigger Government*—43% express a preference for bigger government and more services. Boomers show the least preference at 32% with Millennials' preferences for a larger government hitting a whopping 53%.

- *Illegal Immigration*—23% of Gen Xers believe that illegal immigrants should not be allowed to remain in the United States. This compares with 16% for Millennials and 30% for Boomers.

- *Patriotism*—64% of Xers view themselves as very patriotic. Contrast this with 49% for Millennials and 75% for Boomers.[28]

As noted above, changing ethnic distributions resulting from immigration have impacted age distributions in regions of the United States. Changes in the sizes and geographic dispersion of different *ethnic groups* also belong in this demographic bucket. Changes occurring in three ethnic groups are of paramount concern: Hispanic-Americans, Asian-Americans, and African-Americans. More than two in five school age students in Texas currently boast a Hispanic heritage. The percentage is growing rapidly. Nationally, the Hispanic demographic segment, or subculture, surpassed the African-American segment as the second largest minority segment in the United States several years ago. The Hispanic population in the United States is growing about five times faster than non-Hispanic ethnic segments.[29] Much more will be said about significant trends in these three ethnic groups as we explore aspects of consumer behavior in a later chapter.

Educational levels as they rise/fall or remain higher/lower amongst particular ethnic segments or even male-female gender categories (as discussed above), are a powerful demographic force affecting most of the marketing landscape. Changes in educational levels, as characterized by shifts in key demographic metrics, generate a rippling effect of consequences among consumer and business segments, generating opportunities and threats for individual Firms and even entire industries.

Demographic-based segmentation matters greatly, as does demographic-based targeting, positioning, messaging and product-development. The demographics of the segment or segments it is targeting are one thing that every marketing Firm should understand. There are comparatively few "always" or "absolutes" in marketing practice, marketing theory, or this book. But this is one of them.

Women who are college-educated and black annually purchase more books than any other target segment.[30] And no one would know this unless relevant demographic information was compiled on who buys what books and when. One potential marketing lesson for the publishing industry: create and distribute even more books that black women would be prone to like.

Each demographic trend noted above is domestic in its origins and implications. Highly similar trends exist throughout international markets. Major US Firms frequently develop unique customized marketing mixes that are specifically targeted at various foreign markets. For example, if a US car marketer intends to sell its vehicles in Great Britain, Australia, New Zealand or, for that matter, the Bahamas it needs to relocate their steering wheels to the right side. International marketers need to understand these idiosyncratic facts and track relevant demographic trends inside the specific national populations they were targeting.

Economic Environment and Trends

The economic conditions that prevail within a given market, in both present and predicted future forms, should instruct and inform most important marketing decisions Firms make. An economy, similar to a culture, is also an emergent market system. For that matter so is political polarization, rising health care costs, and bad marriages.

Emergent market systems are simultaneously bottom-up and top-down. They should be studied differently, as autonomous, distinct wholes and as nested networks of relationships. Relevant economic factors that Firms might logically track could include rising or (in theory it could happen) falling health care costs. Or, for that matter, rising or falling levels of income, unemployment rates, work force participation, consumer debt, domestic or foreign currencies, home ownership levels, gross domestic products, foreign or domestic debt ratios, foreign or domestic stock markets, and the list could go on.

Why track such trends? Because each factor may well influence the types of products that business or consumer customers are willing or able to buy. Similarly, they may affect the prices consumers are willing or able to pay, the types of stores or online shopping venues consumers are more or less likely to frequent, or the types of marketing communications (messages) that are most effective.

Three distinct types of marketing strategies may prove appropriate when the local, regional, or national economies are doing well, promise to do better soon, or are experiencing clear and present duress: continue to invest in promotion and new product development (NPD), innovative promotions, and environmental scanning.

Continue to Invest in Promotion and NPD

One Firm's economic threat might prove another's economic opportunity. Marketing and business history has shown those Firms that maintain or even increase their marketing expenditures despite the presence or threat of economic distress have gained significant market share versus competitors who cut their promotional and/or new product development expenditures. South Korea-based Hyundai Motors made huge gains in the US marketplace by following such a strategy. Hyundai spent more and developed more new products during the 2008–2011 Great Recession, and gained share from the domestic and Japanese automakers that it has yet to relinquish. Similarly, during the 1929–1939 Great Depression, two leading breakfast cereal marketers kept investing heavily in new product development and promotion. Kellogg's and General Mills surged ahead in market share while the third major cereal producer, Post, failed to follow suite, lagging significantly behind both Kellogg's and General Mills in terms of sales, market share, and profits.[31]

Innovative Promotions

Of course in the case of Hyundai, being first to market with clever *innovative promotions* such as "if you buy a car and then lose your job, we will take it back" (and forgive your loan) didn't hurt, either, during the depths of the more recent Great Recession. General Motors followed suit as fast as it could but ended up looking just like what it was: a second place finisher trying to play catch up and wishing it had initiated this promotional tactic first. Hyundai gathered all accolades and "attaboys". General Motors was accorded a haughty "nice-try, but you're late," by the national press.

Scan That Environment

Identify the economic trend as friend or foe. Then get ahead of it. Finally, stay ahead. Hyundai has excelled at this approach since it was first-to-market with the reassuring and value-adding promise of a 100,000-mile, bumper-to-bumper warranty coverage on every new Hyundai vehicle sold. This strategy proved a marketer's delight. It spoke directly to both the quality of the vehicle being marketed and the customer-oriented qualities of the Firm marketing it.

Technological Environment and Trends

Technology encompasses all the inventions and innovations that emerge from various sources and enter cultures, economies, and markets. Inventions can be defined simply as something that is new. Innovations can be defined with a bit more panache as something that is new and useful—useful particularly in terms of their ability to solve existing or new problems. (Additional discussion about the innovation/invention topic follows in Chapter 11.)

Technological inventions and innovations generally emerge from engineering or applied scientific research. One thing to understand about most contemporary and thus still emergent technological systems is that they have made the world of information far more dominant than it once was. The degree to which new technologies are more or less likely to be adopted and used regularly varies based on such things as gender and age cohort. For example, Millennials, as you already know, have been labeled "digital natives" because they have grown up with technology, rather than being forced to adapt to that technology.

Every successive wave of new technologies threatens and actually often destroys existing products, business models, Firms and at times entire industries. For example, no ice-making industry exists anymore, yet for most of the last century the industry was a dominant player. This so-called "creative destruction" process was first described by Austrian economist Joseph Schumpeter in the 1950s, who also coined the currently fashionable term "entrepreneur" at the same time.[32] Creative destruction unfolds naturally as existing products, services, ideas, or processes are replaced or quickly become outmoded as new, superior technologies are introduced.

New technological environmental trends also often create myriad opportunities for new-to-the-world (today, commonly known as "start-up") Firms to thrive. Those same technological trends also routinely yield opportunities for existing Firms who are able to identify the trend before their competitors and leverage the insight to their advantage. Yet technological changes are extremely difficult to predict. The primary reason is because such environmental changes often emerge from basic scientific advances, which themselves are difficult to chart.

Technology is a one-way street; it is always moving forward. Marketers, to win and at times to merely just survive, must stay as close as possible to the front edge of technology as it inexorably moves forward. Technological trends and events and technological driven innovations (which at times seem to capture most innovations)—all of which may occur outside the Firm or even its industry—still have the potential to impact strategy development and the success or failure of strategies once they have been developed. At the most basic level, technology continuously impacts how Firms connect and communicate with consumers and how consumers connect and communicate with Firms. These technological trends and events may, and indeed often should, stimulate *innovation* inside Firms.

As noted in Chapter 11 the crucially important *innovation* topic is discussed in greater detail. For now, however, it is sufficient to understand that innovations include products, services, or ideas that are both new and useful. For a new product, service, or idea to be described as an innovation, it must be able to deliver new, differentiating value to current or different target markets. Few, if any, Firms can thrive or even survive for long without the successful introduction of innovations.

Let's examine books, an old technology, and e-book readers, a still emergent technology in most environmental contexts and among many demographic segments. Books are, in their own right, an utterly spectacular technology, developed and used to refine and advance thought and knowledge; a technology that actually changed the arc of history and human relationships when Johannes Gutenberg invented the printing press in 1440.

Once the printing press was created it made books, and the information and ideas contained within them, more widely available among common people. (Yes, we know we're discussing books but many scholars agree the printing press is the most impactful new technology of the last 1,000 years.)

The printed book remains an excellent means of channeling information from writer to reader. But the e-book can send information back as well. Isn't that clearly superior?

Still, somehow, the printed book remains a highly competitive technology. It is portable. When you drop a book on the sidewalk it does not break. The book features high-resolution pages. Books never trouble their owners because of a short battery life or the need to plug them in. Plus, in the eyes of many, they look great on the shelf. These are five incontrovertibly and clearly sustainable competitive advantages for the book.

Competing with this simple technology, one that seemingly offers the simplest possible solution for the marketing problem of how to convey information (a tact which, according to Albert Einstein and Occam's Razor, is always a good idea), has proven surprisingly difficult for technology-based firms and e-reading devices that essentially have tried to displace the book.

However, analogies about how technology has caused the relative decline of the music and newspaper industries come up short. The music industry's traditional business model collapsed in part because the bundle of values it was marketing fell apart. Consumers did not want to buy an album holding 12 songs on which they only liked two or three once the technology was available to grab only those two or three songs. Technology also enabled consumer piracy or, less controversially, gave consumers the opportunity to share. An additional benefit to consumers, but what about to the recording industry?

The rapid decline of newspapers and magazines was driven by the decline of initial readership—a decline not paralleled by books—and the subsequent decline in advertising revenues generated by these print media (newspapers or magazines) for Firms that owned them. The retail (cover) price of newspapers and magazines has never covered the costs of acquiring, agglomerating, presenting and printing the news, informational or editorial content, and then delivering a bulky paper product to the point at which an actual buyer-seller exchange occurred. No, all along, it had advertisers paying the bill. But, with the technologically-induced loss of readership, advertisers abandoned these traditional media. But not so the book; the sense of the book as a fundamental, old-school technology-based channel through which culture flows from the past to present and onward into the future, apparently will endure.

Notwithstanding, when it comes to its status as an environmental trend, technology kicks butt and writes names—and is able to remember them forever. In perhaps its most far-reaching environmental consequence, the passage of time and growth of technology has expanded the number of non-zero sum relationships in **Business to Business** (or **B2B**) markets. That is to say, technology has made possible more relationships in which both parties can win, if they cooperate and collaborate, or in which both Firms will lose if they fail to cooperate and collaborate. The technological revolution that continues to engulf us all has placed more and more people and Firms in non-zero sum relationships, at greater and greater distances, often across far-flung ethnic, natural, and religious bounds. If you are struggling to ascertain the implications for you and your Firm's future, you should continue to struggle until you identify the answer. More discussion about this exact issue follows in Chapter 12.

But, for now, remember: a free-market, capitalistic society is an ingenious form of connectedness. The universal goal that prevails inside these markets/societies is to sell more goods, services, and ideas to as many people as possible and consequently reap the rewards associated with the value you provide if your Firm does these things well in an ethical and socially responsible manner. To thrive in higher competitive capitalistic marketplaces, however, businesses and other organizations must constantly seek and acquire competitive advantages. One of the best, yet still one of least predicable, places to find these advantages is on the bleeding-edge of technology. That is, if your Firm can continue to dance along that particular razor's edge.

Finally, in a man-bites-dog version of the glowing news we somehow have come to always expect about technology, we personally believe that in many ways modern technology has proven a big disappointment. Experts on the subject from the 1950s and 1960s thought there would be flying cars by now, or that by now consumers would be enjoying the benefits of devices that both fed and walked our dogs when they had to stay an hour late at work. Instead, the bulk of contemporary innovations are merely enabling us to do something in different ways that we human beings had already mastered thousands of years ago. This something is, yes, talk to one another. Who cares if we now have 12 ways to communicate with each other when neither user says little more than "not much; what about you … did you see my *selfie*?"?

The major marketing and consumer life changing benefits of technological innovation probably arrived between 1870 and 1900. This is the era when electricity, the internal combustion engine, and running water with indoor plumbing came into being. These technological trends led to other innovations such as air-conditioning, hygienic cleanliness, high speed transport, mass communication, home appliances, and cultural changes such as higher female workforce participation and decreasing marital rates that we now take for granted (or are learning about for the first time).

Governmental and Regulatory Environments and Trends

One thing to understand from the start about the environmental role played by the Federal government (hereafter, government) is that it does not produce anything. The government instead only takes, aggregates, and redistributes value that it receives, in the form of taxes, from the productivity of businesses and citizens. This ever-trending issue, not surprisingly, relates to how much taxation is too much taxation. As was true of other environmental trends, this environmental issue sometimes works against and sometimes supports the best interests of Firms.

The "it depends" portion of this proposition depends on who the Firm is and in what industrial or business or educational or organizational sphere a Firm operates. The oil and gas industry and the myriad drilling, refining, and distribution (think Keystone Pipeline) corporate entities that support it has been a special target for governmental sanctions during President Obama's administration. This is true of the entire US coal industry, whose survival prospects have been ravaged by governmental fiat.

Despite these onerous initial descriptions, the government also exits to protect the free and fair interests of various Firms and individuals whose interests genuinely need to be protected. These protections also arise as a consequence of the redistributive process. The government, for example, eliminates or regulates monopolies. Consumers and other corporate competitors rightfully cheer. Price discrimination and collusion are both illegal. The government supports consumerism, a movement that began in the 1960s. Consumerism exists to elevate the influence, rights and power of consumers in relation to the influence, right and power of marketers. The major legislative actions affecting marketing in the United States are summarized in Table 4.1. More will be said about specific legislation affecting marketing and business as appropriate in follow-on chapters.

Table 4.1 • *Major Legislative Actions Affecting US Businesses*

Legislative Action	Description
1890 Sherman Antitrust Act	Prohibits the formation of monopolies and other actions that effectively restrain trade and interfere with competition in markets.
1906 Food and Drug Act	Formed the Federal Drug Administration and gave it the power to regulate the sale of adulterated food products and poisonous patent medicines. Set requirements for accurately labeling such products. Outlawed the sale of products that were unsafe or ineffective.
1914 Clayton Act	Enhanced the Sherman Antitrust Act by setting more stringent prohibitions against price discrimination, exclusive dealing, and the use of tying contracts.
1914 Federal Ttrade Commission Act	Established the Federal Trade Commission which overseas interactions between businesses to ensure fairness. Authorized to issue "cease and desist" orders to curb unfair trade practices related to advertising and pricing.
1936 Robinson-Patman Act	Supplements the Clayton Act and strengthens prohibitions against price discrimination. Allows FTC to restrict the use of certain discounts and allowances unless they are offered on a proportionate basis to buyers.
1938 Wheeler-Lea Act	Empowered the FTC to regulate the advertising of food and drugs. Declared all misleading, unfair, or deceptive practices to be illegal, regardless of injury to competition. Primarily intended to apply to false and misleading advertising.
1946 Lanham Trademark Act	Protects brand names, trademarks, and service marks.
1966 Fair Packaging and Labeling Act	Dictates how consumer product packages are to be labeled with respect to contents and producer.
1972 Consumer Product Safety Act	Established the Consumer Products Safety Commission, which is tasked with setting and enforcing safety standards for consumer products.
1991 Americans With Disabilities Act	Established that it is illegal for organizations to discriminate against anyone with disabilities with respect to public transportation, accommodations, and telecommunications.

The government also elevates the welfare of, and provides a safety net for, consumers needing such values at particular points in time in their lives. This governmental function allows consumers who otherwise would lack the resources to continue to purchase necessary goods and services. This redistributive process, where, for example, taxation on younger workers pay for social security paid out for older, retired workers, generally benefits the entire market economy.

When nations have strong central governments and strong civil societies they can usually develop the ability to address most challenging problems. A general balance or equilibrium between these two forces has traditionally characterized the United States. But if any country becomes deficient along one or both of these dimensions or gets out of balance (particularly in terms of too much or too little government), watch out. The long- and short-term consequences for the overall economy, and thus for marketers, would be severe.

The addition or elimination of legislation that imposes regulatory constraints will inevitably impose major strategic threats or opportunities on Firms. (Note how threats just preceded opportunities for the first time in this discussion. The implication: governmental regulations are more likely to impose threats than opportunities for most Firms.) Regardless, any Firm's broader marketing and business strategies and decisions will likely be directed and influenced by regulatory forces.

Regulation, defined, entails restrictions that governmental entities impose on Firms' marketing or more general business conduct. These regulations exist to protect Firms from each other and consumers from Firms. Most governmental regulations are net-positive in their consequences. Freer and fairer competition between and among Firms is promoted if not assured. Additional, generally safer, choices and more accurate product/marketer information is made available for consumers as they ponder or make purchasing decisions. Governmental prohibition of various compounds from food, cosmetics, or fuel products, for example, has materially affected the marketing and business strategies of McDonalds, Mary Kay, and Exon-Mobil for decades.

Competitive Environment

The importance of out-gunning one's competitors and owning environmental trends to attain competitive advantage underscores the need to fully comprehend the nature of the competitive environment. From a macro-economic perspective, there are four basic forms of competition. You may recall these from your basic economics course.

Forms of Competition

A **monopoly** exists when a single competitor virtually owns the entire market. Due to the lack of competitive pressure from other firms and the power monopoly holders can exert on markets, there is little incentive to control prices or improve product/service quality. Few true monopolies exist today as a result of intense government regulation. John D. Rockefeller's Standard Oil was broken up at the turn of the 20th Century with the advent of the Sherman Anti-trust Act. AT&T operated as a government-sponsored telecommunications monopoly until the industry was deregulated by President Reagan in 1980. The US Postal Service, once the only viable postal and package delivery service in the United States, now faces intense competition from UPS, FedEx, and myriad Internet forms of communication. Monopolies are sometimes justifiable in industries where scale economies lead to substantial cost, and therefore price, reductions for consumers. This has been the argument in the past for justifying monopolies by large producers of oil and gas, steel, and telecommunications. However, as conditions in these industries have evolved, monopolies are no longer justified, caving to government and consumer pressures.

Oligopolies occur in industries where there exist a handful of large competitors, each with substantial market share. Taken together, these large Firms dominate sales and market share for the industry. Depending on the industry, there may also be a pool of smaller competitors each of which holds inconsequential market shares. Due to the limited number of large players, each is painfully aware of the moves made by others. Competitors are carefully monitored and strategies and tactics are purposely adjusted to accommodate their actions. Industries prone to oligopolistic competition are those in which large investments in plant and equipment are keys to survival. Examples include the airline industry (American, Delta, United, Southwest), automotive industry (GM, Ford, Toyota, Chrysler, Honda, Hyundai/Kia, and Nissan hold 86% of the US market), wireless industry (Verizon, AT&T, T-Mobile, and Sprint control 90% of the wireless market)[33]; and computing (Lenovo, HP, Dell, Acer Group, Apple dominate 70% of the world market for personal computers). Smaller competitors survive by focusing on providing unique products / services that meet the needs of select sub-segments in these industries.

Monopolistic competition exists in industries characterized by a large number of competitors all vying with each other for market share. No single competitor dominates. Each attempts to compete by changing its products and services to offer a value bundle that helps differentiate it from competitors' offerings. Branding and positioning are the firm's major tools. Price competition tends to be avoided and Firms strive to create unique positions for their brands in consumers' minds. Many industries producing consumer durable goods (clothing and shoes, for example) and nondurable goods (breakfast cereals, snack foods, toothpaste) are characterized by this form of competitive interaction. In the services industries examples include restaurants, health clubs, and destination resorts.

Perfect competition exists in industries characterized by many small companies each producing and selling essentially the same product or service. True situations of perfect competition rarely exist. Agricultural markets tend to come closest. Agricultural markets are characterized by many small producers of products that amount to commodities for which one source of supply is generally undifferentiated from any other (i.e. the output of one producer is no different than that of any other producer of the same product). Significant differences between products from alternative suppliers normally are negligible. However, even in these markets, individual Firms can differentiate their products via branding and positioning. Purdue, for example, is a producer of poultry products. In the 1980s Purdue successfully differentiated its brand based on color, convincing consumers that yellow-skinned chickens were higher quality. Purdue's promotional program emphasized that each bird was quality checked and tagged with a Purdue sticker attesting to that quality. Quality, Purdue claimed, was a result of how their birds were raised and fed.[34]

The Nature and Intensity of Competitive Interaction

How competitive interactions unfold in industries is serious business. Misjudging the sources and intensity of competitive interactions puts Firms at a distinct disadvantage, potentially leading to their demise. Marketers often and inappropriately believe that the only important source of competition is from other Firm's that produce the same kinds of products i.e. rivalry between alternative brands within the same product category. In reality, the sources of competition extend beyond this boundary. Marketers must recognize these additional sources of competition and grasp the factors that drive competitive interactions within their industries.

In general, the intensity of competition within an industry is a function of five forces: rivalry among existing competitors, threat of competitive entry, threats from substitute products, the relative power of suppliers, and the relative power of buyers (Exhibit 4.2).[35]

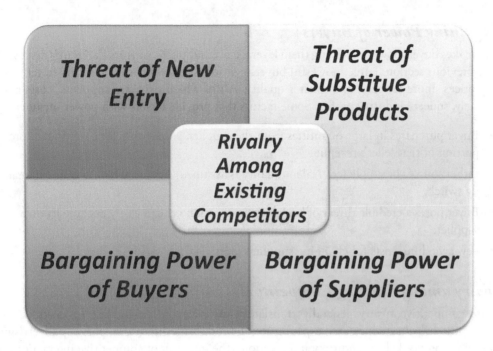

Threat of New Entry	Threat of Substitue Products
Rivalry Among Existing Competitors	
Bargaining Power of Buyers	Bargaining Power of Suppliers

Exhibit 4.2 *Forces That Determine the Intensity of Competitive Interactions Within an Industry.*

Threat of New Entry

The likelihood that new competitors will enter a given industry is a function of the industry's relative appeal in terms of such things as growth potential, profitability, ability to acquire market share; the likelihood of retaliation by existing competitors; and any barriers to entry in place in that industry. Industries with high growth and profit potential will attract new competitors. But, high barriers to entry (e.g. high capital investment requirements, inability to acquire adequate distribution channels, need for scale economies to drive down costs) and the likelihood of retaliation by incumbent Firms tend to discourage entry.

Threat from Substitute Products

A substitute product performs the same or a similar function as an industry's product by a different means. Substitutes are alternative products or services that essentially satisfy the same customer needs or provide the same solutions. Plastics are a substitute for steel and other metals; e-mail can be used instead of fax or express mail. The threat of substitutes, whether they are recognized by Firms or not, place limits on the industry's profit and growth potential for incumbents. Firms astute enough to recognize threats from substitute sources must adjust strategies to position themselves away from these threats. Changes in product performance, quality, and/or changes in marketing programs are essential.

Bargaining Power of Suppliers

Large, powerful suppliers can exert extreme pressure on buyers to capture disproportionate value from the supply chain for themselves. Such suppliers know that their customers have few other options. Some factors that provide suppliers with power include:

- Buyers face very high switching costs should they attempt to change suppliers.
- There are no viable substitute products to which buyers can switch e.g. plastic cannot be substituted for steel.
- The supplier's products are highly differentiated from other sources in terms of quality and/or function.

Bargaining Power of Buyers

What makes buyers powerful, giving them leverage over suppliers, mirrors the factors discussed in the previous section. Large, powerful buyers can force concessions from sellers in terms of lower prices, more services, and greater quality. All of which drive up suppliers' costs and, ultimately, squeeze industry profits. Some factors that provide buyers with power include:

- Buyer purchases in large quantities from the supplier, accounting for a significant proportion of that seller's revenue.
- Other sources of supply (equivalent quality is assumed) exist to which buyers can readily switch.
- Buyer poses a credible threat of backward integration i.e. can easily become its own supplier.
- Few switching costs for changing suppliers exist.

Rivalry among Existing Competitors

Intense competitive rivalry generally translates into lower prices and higher costs. Costs escalate primarily due to increased expenditures in product modifications, plus any advertising and promotion needed to solidify brand position. The intensity of competitive interactions is a function of:

- Stage of the product life cycle. Competitive rivalry increases as products move through the growth stage into maturity and the number of competitors increases. There are strong incentives to "steal" business from one another, meaning that further growth for a single Firm is at the expense of its competitors.
- Firms face high exit barriers, meaning that it is difficult to leave the industry. This situation arises when firms have significant funds tied up in assets that cannot be easily liquidated.

→ The Natural Environment

The earth's resources are bountiful, but not infinite. Many resources are limited, and many cannot be replaced. Eventually, these resources will be consumed. Marketers have to recognize their societal responsibility to help conserve these precious resources. Pollution and raw material shortages pose serious and immediate threats. In some places water and clean air are at a premium. Water, in particular, is critically limited. Not too far in the future, wars may be fought over access to water supplies in third-world countries. Water shortages even affect areas of the United States. Currently, 20% of earth's population lives in places where water is threatened. Estimates are that within 15 years, nearly one third of the world population will face water shortages. Water use has been growing at an accelerated rate in the last century, more than twice the rate of population increase leaving increasing numbers of areas persistently short of water.[36] Wars fought over water don't sound that crazy if you believe this statistic.

At the same time the shortages seen now, and those anticipated in the future, open up tremendous market opportunities for the astute marketing Firms. Resource shortages portend opportunities as well as pose threats. For example, discarded tires accumulating in landfills simultaneously constitute a major environmental threat to the environment and a major opportunity Firms tracking the bleeding edge of environmental change! Companies are fast emerging that have the technology to transform old tires into usable products. Auburndale Recycling Center, Inc. located in Wisconsin, specializes in extracting fuel from old tires. Liberty Tire Recycling Center, Inc. was established as a dedicated scrap tire processing plant for producing high quality alternative fuels. As the largest scrap tire processor in world, Liberty processes over 30% of the nation's discarded tires, turning them into crumb rubber and industrial feedstock for manufacturers, tire derived fuel (TDF) for use in industry, and rubber mulch for landscaping and playground applications.

Similarly, United Electronic Recycling (unitedelectronicrecycling.com) recycles electronic components. Their mission is to recycle all parts of anything electronic that yields zero impact on landfills and the environment. Based in Texas, UER partners with numerous communities and businesses offering a full-service recycling service. A growing business! Stock, anyone?

Concern about the environment has spurred the current "green" (also called **environmental sustainability**) movement and its concomitant marketing opportunities. Examples of products "going green" abound: high efficiency replacement light bulbs, hybrid and electric cars, solar heating systems for homes, crayons made from soy vice paraffin wax (a petroleum product), to name but a few.

Accepting and Exploiting Environmental Change

When examining marketing environments, few things are certain. One near certainty, however, is that few trends evident today will be unfolding exactly the same way next year. In fact, one could safely say change will be the only constant in almost any Firm's relevant marketing environment. People as well as Firms consequently should scan their past and present environments continuously in order to make better predictions about the future.

People, and thus Firms, should also learn that, while change does not always represent progress, change is always necessary for progress to occur. Changes do not always represent threats, either, although humans sometimes appear programmed to receive and respond to change in this manner. We encourage people to embrace changes as natural things, and to subsequently exploit them, particularly those changes emanating from within their relevant micro- and macro-environments. Individuals who manage their Firm's segmentation, targeting, and marketing mix (i.e., positioning) efforts should do so in ways that permit them to take advantage of attractive change-induced opportunities as they arise. Or, to circumvent environmental threats before the Firm is negatively impacted. In either case, the Firm has a higher probability of prevailing in most marketing competitions. This is particularly true when managers engage in the first-mover, inside-out strategic marketing efforts described below.

When engaging in environmental scanning, managers should step outside their Firms and ask:

- What customer wants, needs, and/or problems do we satisfy now?
- What customer wants, needs, and/or problems could we satisfy now? In the future?
- Given our changing environment, what is the gap between those needs we could satisfy in the future and what we do now, and how do we bridge the gap?
- What sustainable competitive advantages do we currently possess?
- Given our changing environment, what sustainable advantages do we need to create?
- Given our changing environment, what old competencies do we need to de-emphasize and what new competencies do we need to create?

This environmental process is akin to "outside-in" thinking, which seems easy and appears to make sense. Yet "outside-in" thinking is clearly difficult to execute because we all live first inside our own minds, and thus "inside-out." But, does difficult mean the same thing as impossible? Naturally, it does not. The sooner one embraces the power and importance of environmental scanning the sooner one can convert from perpetual "inside-out" thinking to the occasional, when necessary, "outside-in" environmental analysis. The information, knowledge, and eventual actionable insights that follow and function as highly valued inputs into the strategic planning process or its execution would surely make the "outside-in" effort worthwhile.

This whole inside-out thinking discussion is more important than many of you likely think. Perhaps you are poised to inherit a great deal of wealth. Maybe you are a great athlete who will play professionally. If neither description applies to you, remember this: Your future wealth is a product of your capacity to think strategically. That means, thinking "inside-out" as well as "outside-in."

Endnotes

1   McLeod, K. F. "Did You Know," accessed May 2015, http://www.huffingtonpost .com/2009/11/22/did-you-know-tracks-progr_n_366803.html.

2   "Study the past if you would define the future" ~Confucius, accessed May 2015, https://jhss10cestoncarino.wordpress.com/2013/02/15/study-the-past-if-you -would-define-the-future-confucius/.

3   Faulkner, W., *Requiem for a Nun* (New York: Random House. 1950)

4   *The "Best of" Edward Gibbon's -Decline and Fall of the Roman Empire*, accessed May 2015, http://www.his.com/~z/gibbon.html.

5   Orwell, G., *Nineteen Eighty-Four* (London: Secker and Warburg,1949)

6   Bauerlein, M., *The Dumbest Generation: How the Digital Age Stupefies Young Americans and Jeopardizes Our Future (Or, Don't Trust Anyone Under 30)* (New York: Tarcher, 2009).

7   Fasanella, K., "Designer Fashions Are Sized Smaller Than Mass Market," accessed May 2015, http://www.vanitysizing.com/archive/designer-fashions-are-sized-smaller -than-mass-market-clothes/.

8   Fisher, A. "Boys vs. Girls: What's Behind the College Grad Gender Gap?" *Fortune* (March 27, 2013), accessed May 2015, http://fortune.com/2013/03/27/boys-vs -girls-whats-behind-the-college-grad-gender-gap/.

9   "Why Marriage Matters-Facts And Figures," accessed May 2015, http://www.foryourmarriage.org/factsfigures/.

10   Ibid

11   Jonathan Vespa, J. M. L., Rose M. Kreider, *America's Families and Living Arrangements: 2012. 2013.* p. 34.

12   Amato, Paul R. "The Impact of Family Formation Change On the Cognitive, Social, and Emotional Well-Being of the Next Generation." *The Future of Children* 15, no. 2 (2005): 75–96.

13   Ralph Keys, *The Quote Verifier* (New York: St. Martin's Griffin, 2007), 143.

14   The marketing information system is discussed in detail in Chapter 6's discussion of marketing information management.

15 "Welcome to the Dockers Khaki Revolution", *Sportswear International*, accessed January 2015, http://www.sportswearnet.com/brandprofile/pages/profiles/dockers/brand.php

16 "Oh! You Pretty Things", *The Economist* (July 12, 2014), accessed January 2015, http://www.economist.com/news/briefing/21606795-todays-young-people-are-held-be-alienated-unhappy-violent-failures-they-are-proving

17 Ibid.

18 Mortimer B. Zuckerman, "Why the Jobs Situation Is Worse Than It Looks", *U.S. News and World Report* (June 20, 2011), accessed January 2015, http://www.usnews.com/opinion/mzuckerman/articles/2011/06/20/why-the-jobs-situation-is-worse-than-it-looks.

19 Justin McCarthy, "In U.S., Adult Obesity Rate Now at 27.7%", *Gallup* (May 22, 2014), accessed January 2015, http://www.gallup.com/poll/170264/adult-obesity-rate.aspx.

20 Eric Palmer, "The Top 10 Pharma Companies by 2013 Revenue", *FiercePharma* (March 4, 2014), accessed January 2015, http://www.fiercepharma.com/special-reports/top-10-pharma-companies-2013-revenue.

21 Kaleem, J. "Americans Exaggerate How Much They Go To Religious Services, According To Study," *Huffington Post* (May 17, 2014), accessed May 2015, http://www.huffingtonpost.com/2014/05/17/religious-attendance-exaggeration-survey_n_5344535.html.

22 David Brooks, "Huntington's Clash Revisited", *The New York Times: The Opinion Pages* (March 3, 2011), accessed January 2015, http://www.nytimes.com/2011/03/04/opinion/04brooks.html? rref=collection%2 Fcolumn%2Fdavid-brooks&_r=0.

23 Hsu, T. "Is Chick-fil-A Anti-Gay Marriage? 'Guilty As Charged,' Leader Says," (July 18, 2012), accessed May 2015, http://articles.latimes.com/2012/jul/18/business/la-fi-mo-chick-fil-a-gay-20120718.

24 Morin, R. "Study: Opposition To Same-Sex Marriage May Be Understated in Public Opinion Polls," *Pew Research Center* (September 30, 2013), accessed May 2015, http://www.pewresearch.org/fact-tank/2013/09/30/opposition-to-same-sex-marriage-may-be-understated-in-public-opinion-polls/.

25 D'Vera Cohn and Paul Taylor, "Baby Boomers Approach 65—Glumly", *Pew Research Center*, accessed January 2015, http://www.pewsocialtrends.org/files/2010/12/Boomer-Summary-Report-FINAL.pdf. See also, Emily Brandon, "10 Things You Didn't Know About Baby Boomers", U.S. News and World Report (January 15, 2009), accessed January 2015, http://money.usnews.com/money/blogs/planning-to-retire/2009/01/15/10-things-you-didnt-know-about-baby-boomers.

26 Pew Research Social and Demographic Trends, *Millennials in Adulthood: Detached from Institutions, Networked with Friends* (March 7, 2014), accessed January 2015, shttp://www.pewsocialtrends.org/2014/03/07/millennials-in-adulthood/.

27 Paul Taylor and George Gao, "Generation X: America's Neglected 'Middle Child'," *Pew Research Center* (June 5, 2014), accessed January 2015, http://www.pewresearch.org/fact-tank/2014/06/05/generation-x-americas-neglected-middle-child/.

28 Ibid.

29 Brown, A. "U.S. Hispanic and Asian Populations Growing, But for Different Reasons," (June 26, 2014), accessed May 2015 http://www.pewresearch.org/fact-tank/2014/06/26/u-s-hispanic-and-asian-populations-growing-but-for-different-reasons/.

30 Callahan, Y. "College-Educated Black Women Are Most Likely To...Read A Book," accessed May 2015, http://www.clutchmagonline.com/2014/01/college-educated-black-women-likely-read-book/.

31 Food & Water Watch, "Grocery Goliaths- How Food Monopolies Impact Consumers,"(December 5, 2013), accessed May 2015, http://documents.foodandwaterwatch.org/doc/grocery_goliaths.pdf.

32 Joseph Schumpeter, *Capitalism, Socialism, and Democracy, 3d ed.* (New York: Harper and Brothers, 1950), 8.

33 Mike Dano, "Grading the Top 10 U.S. Carriers in the First Quarter of 2013," *Fierce Wireless* (May 15, 2013), accessed January 25, 2015, http://www.fiercewireless.com/node/245923/print.

34 *Produce Magazine*, "Perdue's Chickens 'USDA Process Verified': Legit or a Marketing Hoax?" (July 2011), accessed January 2015, http://producemagazine.com/2011/07/perdues-chickens-usda-process-verified-legit-or-a-marketing-hoax/#sthash.S19efZCc.dpuf.

35 Michael Porter, "The Five Competitive Forces That Shape Strategy", *Harvard Business Review* (January 2008), accessed January 2015, https://hbr.org/2008/01/the-five-competitive-forces-that-shape-strategy.

36 United Nations Department of Economic and Social Affairs, "International Decade for Action 'Water For Life' 2005 – 2015," accessed January 2015, http://www.un.org/waterforlifedecade/index.shtml.

Chapter 5

MARKETING ETHICS AND CORPORATE SOCIAL RESPONSIBILITY

Giving customers what they actually want, as opposed to what they should want, has morphed into a source of ethical conflict for many Firms, particularly in the developed world. In fact, various legislative, public policy and consumer protection interest groups remain up in arms about this exact, and apparently logical, marketing strategy. Welcome to the world of present-day marketing, where doing exactly what others want Firms to do can get Firms and their managers called out for purportedly unethical or socially irresponsible corporate practices.

Yet you've already been taught that giving customers what they want, after identifying exactly what those wants entail, is a proven path toward material marketing success. Across the decades the voluminous revenues and profits of McDonald's, Coca-Cola or PepsiCo, or Philip Morris (i.e., the world's largest cigarette marketer) speaks directly to the preceding statement's accuracy. The results are in; they are compelling. Meanwhile, rising rates of obesity, cancer, diabetes, heart disease, environmental pollution, and resource depletion throughout the developed world simultaneously support those who criticize marketers for giving customers exactly what they want rather than what they should want.

Fat carries more than twice as many calories per gram than do carbohydrates or proteins. Even a little fat turns fast-food servings into calorie bombs. But more significantly, from fast-food marketers' perspective, the absence of fat means an absence of "good taste." And without alluring taste there would far fewer fast-food customers.

Sugar, white flour, rice, corn and potatoes—all close friends to fast-food purveyors—are not as calorie-dense as fats. But each quickly enters the bloodstream as glucose, delivering an energy rush (customers like this), followed by an energy crash that leads to a surge in appetite (fast-food marketers like this). Fat, sugar, and problem carbs trigger pleasure and reward meters that exist in human brains because we evolved over tens of thousands of years when starvation was a constant threat. What's a marketer to do? Ignore easy money from willing customers?

So we, as a nation and developed world, have grown increasingly fatter. And with extra fat comes extra heart disease, diabetes and cancers. But is this the fault of marketing firms who, after all, usually simply seeking to satisfy customers and earn fair returns to their investors? Do you see how this corporate social responsibility often is not as clear-cut as causal or uninformed thinkers might assume?

→ Did You Know?

Question 1: Can you think of a good reason why you would choose to piss in a well that you may need to drink from tomorrow?

Probably not. Assuming your answer indeed was "no," please hold this singular thought in your head as you work through this chapter.

Question 2: Can you identify, with certainty, the three factors that will contribute most directly to most readers' future professional success?

Again, your answer is "probably not." No shame in that. Likely, nobody has taught you this success formula, yet. The three factors that contribute most to most people's professional success are:

- The family circumstances into which they were born.
- Their IQ.
- Their self-control.

Question 3: Which of those three factors to future professional success, can you control?

To begin with, no one has ever selected their birth parents. Not going to happen; no control there.

Additionally, experts agree: about 50% of IQ is inherited. The other 50% is environmental; this is the historical nature versus nurture argument. But people cannot control their environment or nurturing while they're growing up, either. Thus your top-end IQ locks-in early in life. Not much opportunity to exercise control present there, either.

Which leaves us, obviously, with one conclusion: the only factor most readers could ever control is their self-control. "Good news," at least. Everything should be able to control their ethical or unethical choices, right?

How can people improve their self-control? Isn't that tendency something you either have or don't have at relatively early in life? In part, this is true. But one path toward improvement entails resisting unethical temptations by consciously avoiding situations that test self-control. People might structure their environments in ways that minimize unethical distractions and immoral temptations.

Consequently it is useful to understand what sorts of situations and environments might challenge your sense of self-control, which is the best we can offer right now for reasons that unfold below. Unfortunately, marketers cannot avoid situations that will best their self-control nor fully structure their environments in ways that eliminate unethical distractions (see Chapter 4. Environmental factors generally exist beyond the influence of marketers.)

Let's pause for a moment in the midst of these opening questions, and insert a statement with which most can agree. Despite all these challenges, we are all basically smart enough to tell the difference between right and wrong, aren't we? The truth is most of us are. There is little doubt about this fact. A condition that leads us to ask:

Question 4: So, why do we have such a hard time choosing or doing right rather than wrong in situations that feature a moral context?

The answer here is simple. Humans struggle mightily when it comes to choosing right, all the time, because we are so bleeping selfish. Or so self-centered, self-absorbed, self-seeking, self-regarding, egoistic, greedy, or just plain "me-first"—insert your own inwardly-focused adjective.

Don't believe us? Take two healthy, happy two-year-olds. Mix in one safe and empty (but closely adult-supervised from a reasonable distance) room. Place the children, seemingly by themselves, into the room. Add one highly desirable toy that only one two-year-old child can play with at a time. How long will it take before a sinner is produced?

Sinners? Thought we were discussing ethics, didn't you? We are actually discussing both. The word "sin" derives from the old Hebrew meaning "to miss the mark." Unethical managers, customers or Firms, as well as sinners, each exist, simply, as "entities" that somehow "missed the mark," by violating standards, norms, rules, customs, mores or guidelines established by a culture (Firms are part of culture), society. or some prescriptive agency (which could include corporate, legislative or religious bodies).

Why are humans so selfish? The answer is revealed through the Latin phrase, incurvitus in se. This theological concept, expounded by Martin Luther during the early 1500s, describes the degree to which human beings are inherently wired to live life "inwardly," focused on serving the self, rather than "outwardly," in service of others. Luther argued humans are selfish because their creator made them that way. Martin Luther was once a Catholic priest. In 1517, he reformed the Catholic Church by founding a Lutheran sect. This "extension" of the original Holy Roman Catholic Church brand subsequently evolved into the various Protestant church brands that exist today.

There are two characteristics associated with human beings that every B2B or B2C marketer should understand. Then, having acquired this discernment, they should leverage the insights in ways that redound to their Firm's advantage—when doing so is ethical. The first characteristic: nearly every person on earth wants to be center of the universe, and indeed often assumes and acts as if s/he is. The second: everybody wants to see the value of each asset they possess go up in value all the time.

Knowledge is power. Knowledge is an operative resource. "Operative" means you can exploit it to your great advantage, once you learn how. Knowledge is an asset whose value grows over time, particularly when people add to it across the years. (Read more books!) Your beauty and strength will fade over time. With this decay, the power that each asset currently brings to you will decline. But the power of your knowledge will not. The power of knowledge expands across the years when people consciously choose to build it.

Knowing what you know now about these all-too-human, nearly universal selfish-motivations, you should also recognize their power. Because, for better or for worse, each motivation— our a) self-centeredness (i.e., almost all humans want all that we can get all the time) and b) desire to have more than the other (i.e., we all want to get more than the other, the neighbor, has)—drives so many consumer (B2B) and business (B2B) decisions. (The pursuit of pleasure or avoidance of pain motivates the majority of our most important decisions.) And wise marketers know how to manipulate each of your motives to their advantage in ways you likely cannot understand right now. (More about motivations follows in Chapter 6.)

We believe, then, that human moral (ethical) decisions or leanings are rarely driven by their morals or even rational thought. Studies of primate behaviors have shown this to be true time and again. We just want more for ourselves, until one day, due to the passage of time and/or accumulation of experience, we may learn that sometimes, enough actually is enough.

Meanwhile, speaking again of that uncomfortable subject religion …

Question 5: Did you know that the world's five great religions—Buddhism, Hinduism, Islam, Judaism, and Christianity—each speak directly and extensively about ethics? Fact is, each religion's leading historical thinkers and doers have always written and spoken more about the ideal or ethical sort of relationship that humans beings should aspire to create with each other than about humanity's religious connection with the higher power variously known by four of these religions as "God." (Buddhists do not believe in a god.)

The well-known summary of the Jewish Law, the Ten Commandants, speak more about the ideal relationship that faithful Jews should strive to create with each other than about the sort of relationship they should establish and maintain with their God. Six of the Ten Commandants speak to how people should behave toward each other. (Love the neighbor as the self.) Only four laws prescribe the sort of relationship that humans should cultivate with their God.

Question 6: Holy cow! Does of this have anything to do with marketing ethics? Actually, every bit of this has everything to do with marketing ethics and, by extension, corporate social responsibility. Most of what business ethics known to be true about ethical decision-making and social responsibility is rooted in one or more religious philosophy.

Read on and learn how and why.

→ What Is Ethics?

Ethics, as a concept, entails moral principles that govern an individual's or a group's behavior. Ethics, as a concept, provides guidelines that should govern decision-making. Ethics should also provide insights about the sorts of issues that should be evaluated by decision-makers when they seek to identify the rights (moral) or wrongs (immoral) choice. When they are present in our personal lives (and we elect to engage them), ethical standards function as mirrors that reflect our imperfections. Ethical standards also act as curbs against our moral faults. Finally, ethical standards offer snapshots of how a moral life should look.

The preceding descriptions of ethics remains appropriate whether business, marketing, or non-business questions about potentially moral or immoral decisions are being assessed. These descriptions of ethics also remain apt even if and when religious issues, which frequently entail ethical and moral decisions, are deliberated. This fact is not lost among religious thought leaders. Christian thought-leader Paul, for example, wrote in a letter to the church at Philippi: "Let each of you look not just to your own interests, but also to the interests of others" (Philippians 2:4).

The great religious texts routinely prescribe that "better-off" individuals or entities (say, a powerful Firm) should look-out-for rather than take-advantage-of "worse-off" individuals or entities (say, the typical, rather under-informed American consumer). After the harvest, leave something behind in the corners of the field for the "widows and the orphan and the foreigner", as the Jewish Old Testament frequently prescribed. So should marketing Firms; that is, if they seek lasting reputations as ethical corporate players.

The Islamic Koran offers another compelling argument for why humans should made decisions and behave ethically: "He who brings a good deed shall have better than it: but those who bring an evil shall be thrown down on their face in the fire" (Sura XXVIL).

The Book of Matthew, on the other hand, speaks directly to an ongoing need to lean toward truth in life or business: "Simply let your 'yes' be 'yes' and your 'no, no'; anything beyond this comes from the evil one" (Matthew 5:37).

The truth is important. Philosophers from across the ages concluded long ago: the world is too small for anything but truth. This sentiment was expressed hundreds of years before the Internet made possible 24/7/365 free-flowing global banter about lies, supposed lies, or rumors that spread at the "speed of the baud." (A baud is the unit used to measure the speed at which information is sent to or from computer-like technologies.)

Fast or not, former football coach and current television analyst Tony Dungy clearly advocates for truth. Speaking on ESPN about the Tiger Woods branding implosion (you recall the details), Dungy said, "Remember, what is done in the dark usually comes to light." As did former New York Senator Daniel Patrick Moynihan, who famously opined about his unethical critics, "People are entitled to their own opinions, but not their own facts."

Marketers and Firms should live in the light. When Firms act otherwise, their reputations and valuations are badly injured. Just ask British Petroleum about what happened when it failed to quickly or fully accept responsibility the recent US Gulf Coast oil spill.

But truth-telling can prove decidedly challenging. When marketers speak the truth, or their sincere interpretation of the truth (because seemingly there can be multiple versions of truth), they are often second-guessed by somebody. So truth-tellers need to feel comfortable doing what they know is the right thing. The truth usually helps truth-tellers in in the end.

Leave (Some) Value on the Table; Spread the Rest Around

Ethical and religious traditions generally counsel that humans should strive to make the world a better place. Whether the good is provided as a prepayment on heaven or an awareness that you've done what moral humans should do, an ethical benefit is usually associated with spreading value throughout the world. This exact recommendation, not coincidentally, applies to marketers; firms as well as individual marketers also benefit materially when they spread value throughout the world.

We reframe this advice into a single idea: Marketers should leave more value on the table than they take from it. That's it. Do this, and marketers will be ethical and socially responsible corporate citizens.

This simple advice is offered so that readers can avoid the helpless feeling they would experience if we counseled them or their Firms to change the world. The world is too huge. There are too many problems. Where would they start?

People who leave more value behind than they take away are doing more than enough. They have mastered the naturally unethical pull of their innate human selfishness. But at the same time, marketers (lest you do not yet realize it, everyone is a marketer, and "marketing is everything," as Harvard professor Regis McKenna wrote) who do this will enjoy additional value in their life, because they concentrated on generating and providing value to others.

Humans aren't just consumers (takers). We're also creators (makers). The people we call creative, or who self-identify as creative, are individuals who actively change the world around them. But the ability to create is not inherently valuable. People can create things that add value or subtract value from the world. So the ethical responsibility to leave more value on the table may seem especially burdensome for creative people precisely because they are the ones most able to take more from the table in the long run. It doesn't take much brainpower to steal a TV. It requires ample thought to misappropriate millions from people for years without getting caught.

With the power to create comes the responsibility to create the right or ethical stuff. The truth, though, is you will also end up better off when you create more value in the world than you take from it. If you focus on creating value in the world and sharing it with others, you end up being more creative and productive than if you focus your creative energy on extracting value from the world. The days of strip-mining value out of people should end, although we acknowledge that is not about to happen. But that marketing strategy worked better when customers had little knowledge or few options. Today, customers can quickly discover less coercive options, and once they do, they're lost forever.

While they harvest existing fields of value, marketers should also plant value-seeds in new fields. Do this, and marketers can nourish themselves while concurrently nourishing others. When the economic costs of growing ideas, products, and services approaches zero (and technology often permits this), there are opportunities to produce more than any single person or family could ever consume on their own. Learn to fish, and you can eat as long as there are fish. Learn to build and grow value, and you can feast as long as you live.

This is not a suggestion that marketers should give things away for free; that's unsustainable, counter-productive and ignores the marketing concept. Businesspeople should take of their families first before they take care of others; i.e., the essence of traditional capitalism. Instead, this counsel exists as a call to focus your passion and creativity on creating value that you can share with others. New values, once people become of aware of and learn a little about them, are often irresistibly glittering lures.

Try these things. You may discover that brilliant, creative and compassionate people lose more by holding too tightly onto what they have and not exchanging value than by leaving more of what they create and have on the table. Create breathtaking stuff, share it, and then leave some value on the table. This is good to do, good for others, and ultimately good for you. Valuable lessons about how to become and stay more creative arrive in Chapter 11.

An Atheist Addresses the Same Principle

Some readers may be uncomfortable with the religious tenor that this discussion recently took. Find solace, then, in the fact that a prominent atheist, Russian emigrant Ayn Rand, who wrote *Atlas Shrugged*, one of history's most influential books, expressed highly similar views. Rand created the philosophy known as Enlightened Self-Interest, another, related ethical view that, when followed, generally fosters marketing success. The philosophy suggests: People or Firms that consciously act to further the interests of others (i.e., the interests of the group to which they belong or seek to serve) are ultimately serving their own self-interests. Stated a bit differently: One of the best ways to accrue selfish gains is by apparently selflessly serving the interests (or satisfy the wants and needs and/or solving the problems) of others.

In marketing contexts, a decision to act in ways that promote enlightened self-interests is generally desirable and entirely ethical. Enlightened Self-Interests, as an ethical philosophy, is also consistent with another deceptively self-serving ethical marketing principle; that is, "Doing Well by Doing Good," which might best be summarized and described as doing well [for oneself] by doing good [for others].

People or Firms can become more enlightened marketers; marketers more inclined to create good for themselves by doing well for others, by following three easily accessible paths: First, ethical marketers should be extremely customer-focused. This customer-focus might entail organizing the Firm's marketing mix efforts from the customer's point of view. This is also a smart marketing strategy.

Panera Bread apparently buys into these principles. During the bottom of the Great Recession, the restaurant chain adopted a "pay what you can" pricing strategy in its St. Louis area stores. Even folks who had lost their jobs, likely especially people who had lost their jobs, still want to have a meal out. Panera Bread, recognizing this, communicated the fact that customers who could not pay full price (or any money) for a meal should pay what they could (or nothing at all). Panera Bread simultaneously asked customers who could afford to pay a little more to do so. This combined promotional and pricing strategy worked; quite well in fact. Restaurants who offered this deal enjoyed higher traffic, higher revenues and profits, and to this day, years later Panera Bread is still reaping enhanced reputational value and brand equity from its decision to do well by doing good. After all, you just read about it!

Second, ethical firms should be extremely value-marketing focused. People or Firms should invest resources in activities that create additional true value for customers.

The onset of autism among American children, for reasons beyond this discussion's scope, has grown rapidly during recent years. Autistic children display a tendency to act-out vociferously when excited, in ways that might disturb others who did not know the child. This circumstance makes it difficult to take autistic children to the movies, even for films produced for and targeted specifically at their age segment. Recognizing this, 124 AMC Movie theatres created a strategy wherein one screen, showing only child-appropriate movies, was made available for autistic children, their family and friends to view films with each other. Again, by doing "good for others", a Firm "did well for itself". Attendance and profits on a per-screen-basis increased, and AMC similarly secured all manner of favorable publicity for its brand.

Three, ethical firms should be perpetually socially-focused. As they develop and execute marketing strategies, Firms (and their strategists) should always hold customers' wants and long-term needs, society's long-term needs, and the Firm's need to earn profits foremost in their minds. And then set about satisfying those needs.

Many people would prefer to eat healthier while also consuming food that is less harmful, or not at all harmful, to the environment. Fast-food ethicist Steve Ells, founder of Chipotle Restaurants, seeks to destroy fast food as we know it by serving pasture-raised pork burritos and steroid/antibiotic-free chicken tacos. By targeting consumers who seek healthier, environmentally-friendlier food, the chain continues to secure huge customer loyalty, revenues, and profits. Another example of a company doing well for itself by doing good works for targeted customers who appreciate those works. The ethical path, pursued over the long-run, almost always works.

→ What Ethical Issues Typically Arise in Marketing?

Those seeking business and marketing decision-making areas in which ethical dilemmas routinely arise generally find an embarrassment of riches. Situations where the deceptively simple question of, well, what is the "right" (moral) as opposed to what is the "wrong" (immoral) decision to make is often less clear than one might assume. These include the right level of organizational involvement in the community, and with which local or national causes.

How involved should any Firm become in its support of local or national causes? Are Firms obligated to their customers? It's true that consumers never owe anything to Firms. But Firms owe it to consumers to create something that generates value that is worth the price assigned to it. Are Firms obligated to their investors? Of course. To their employees? Beyond question. And isn't it inarguably true that when Firms give to local or national social causes they are taking away resources, generally financial, and in the form of savings or rewards, that otherwise would have gone to customers, investors or employees? Ah, yes, but then what about the value and returns that accrue to Firms and corporate brands who rightfully earn reputations as socially-responsible corporate citizens?

Reputation definitely has a measurable value to marketers. The more trust marketers and/or their Firms and brands earn, the more sales and loyalty will be captured. And, other things equal, the higher the Firm's prices can be raised.

Do you see how, in the midst of situations featuring ethical contact, decisions features large swaths of grey, as opposed to absolute black-and-white? Consequently, ethical Firms should give to other local or national causes to the extent that "the give" does not detract from the value they provide to customers, employees and investors.

Another area where ethical issues are likely to arise involves the degree of honesty, truthfulness and fairness in marketing practice that Firms should pursue. For philosophical reasons described below in greater detail Firms do not always face an absolute moral obligation to tell the truth, the whole truth and nothing but the truth to customers or prospective customers. In fact, the list of such situations is rather lengthy. Believe it or not!

A third issue that has been known to create ethical consternation is the use of animals in product testing. Tests that evaluate the safety of cosmetics and personal care products are still extremely common in the United States in products such as mascara, shampoo, lipstick, cologne, and perfumes. Thousands of mice, guinea pigs, rabbits, and rats die annually as a side effect. This is because pain relief is rarely provided to the animal subjects, who are always killed at the end of each test. How do you feel about that? And truth-be-told, there is rarely a completely right or wrong way to answer that question, a description that applies to many ethical dilemmas that marketing mangers or, here, new product developers routinely confront.

A fourth context in which ethical dilemmas frequently arise is the degree of safety built into product design. The well-known branding phrase "Better Living through Chemistry" was borne from the 1935 advertising slogan, "Better Things for Better Living ... Through Chemistry." DuPont Chemical used the slogan, or positioning statement until 1982. At that time, the "Through Chemistry" portion was abandoned. Since 1999, their positioning statement and advertising hook, or big idea, has been "The miracles of science."

Why the transformation? Most experts would agree it is because chemicals and chemistry, despite their myriad benefits for society, rightfully or wrongly earned a bad reputation across the decades. Sometimes fairly, sometimes not, chemicals became increasingly viewed as unsafe.

Which brings us to the ethical question of "how much testing is necessary is necessary to ensure the safety to chemicals?" Please note, with additional tests, come additional costs, and with additional costs and higher prices fewer truly needy customers are able to reap the "miracles of science." Dow Chemical eventually split the ethical difference by raising or lowering the amount of tests to which its chemicals were subjected. Industrial, or business-to-business (B2B) chemicals are not designed to be ingested or absorbed. Instead they are normally transported, used, and disposed of in more controlled situations. Therefore, while product tests are still conducted, fewer tests are conducted than would be the case for chemicals that are used (consumed) by consumers. Ethically appropriate or inappropriate? The answer is surprisingly difficult to identify.

Other areas where ethical issues arrive within Firms:

- Donations to good causes.
- The extent to which a Firm accepts responsibilities for mishaps, mistakes, or spillages associated with the Firm.
- The marketing of addictive products such as tobacco, sleeping pills (Ambien), high-fat (cheeseburgers) or overly-sweet (doughnuts) or extremely-salty foods (frankly, most processed foods).

But of course, what about tobacco? After all, it is the only legal product that, when used as directed, has conclusively been shown to kill, debilitate, and mutilate (ever experience up close the results of throat, gum or mouth surgery) customers. However, tobacco products are legal in the United States and throughout the world, if not on your campus. But is the marketing of tobacco products such as cigarettes ethical? And where do smokers' and nonsmokers' ethical rights begin and end?

The final set of ethical issues that routinely arise inside Firms includes:

- Involvement in arms trade or the so-called "military industrial complex," a phrase that introduced to the American consciousness by President and General Dwight Eisenhower back in 1960. (Ike was also referenced in Chapter 2.)
- Trading with repressive regimes or regimes that generally act against the best interests of the United States as a whole (and thus are "threats" to the United States as we defined environmental threats in Chapter 4).

The iconic American Firm, General Electric, better known today by its summary brand name GE, has been openly trading with Iran for years. Big deal, so what? The "big deal" is that Iran is likely using GE technology as it develops nuclear weapons. The "so what" is Iran's leaders, though not its people, have uniformly engaged in practices or supported causes that have harmed the welfare of the American population for more than 35 consecutive years. The moral right and moral wrong of GE's targeted segment is not up for us to decide or weigh in upon. But note, beyond question, the interests of GE shareholders, mostly Americans, are in conflict with the interests of the United States population, who are all Americans!

→ Can Students or Managers Learn to Be More Ethical?

One might instinctively assume the answer to this question must be yes. Otherwise, why teach ethics? The answer, however, is likely no. Individuals' personal moral compasses are established well before they move into managerial roles or even before they enter university. The psychologist Lawrence Kohlberg suggests that date arrives sometime between 7 and 10 years of age.

But extreme value is still associated with learning more about the favorable long-term consequences that accrue to Firms or individuals who earn reputations for being ethical, fair and honest. In addition, anyone can learn more about the negative long-term consequences associated with making unethical decisions. The world, after all, is genuinely too small for anything but truth, particularly an Internet-mediated world. Finally, at the least, people can learn more about how to make more ethical choices when facing situations where the line between right or wrong is far from clearly evident; situations which, as has already been demonstrated, arise more frequently that many readers might have originally assumed.

The statement "your reputation precedes you" smacks of cliché. But clichés, like stereotypes, usually have a basis in truth. Students can learn that financial and economic studies conducted across decades consistently demonstrate how those Firms that enjoy reputations as ethical and socially responsible players inevitably boast higher stock valuations … because their reputations precede them. Stock valuations are the purest and least biased assessment about what a Firm—and its reputation and brand—is actually worth in always competitive markets.

Students can likewise learn that they (or their Firms) should never act unethically by taking advantage of any buying Firm or consumer, even when they can. That is, unless they or their Firms plan on never doing business with that customer again. Or fail to eventually realize that ethics is not about being clever in a particular moral crisis but about developing, over time, the sort of character that does not realize it experienced an ethical crisis until the crisis has ended. Or ignore the fact that great oaks emerge from little acorns. The point being, today's small Firms or weak consumers may grow powerful presence over time. At which time the now-strong might prove ready, willing and able to give back the evil they got from you when you were the more powerful partner. You see, we hope, how that exchange-relationship-thing remains in play.

Still, Does Everybody Cheat?

The answer is yes; basically everyone does cheat, at least some of time, subject to the simultaneous presence of two "cheat-inducing" conditions. According to the popular 2005 book *Freakonomics*, the conditions are: a) the stakes (i.e., rewards or incentives) that accrue to the "cheater", if s/he gets away with it, are deemed sufficiently high by the prospective cheater, and b) the "cheater" perceives that the risk of getting caught is sufficiently low.

Once decision-makers, operating in marketing or non-marketing domains, elect to step outside the borders of morality, self-interests apparently often become self-justifications. We rationalize, we self-validate; arguing that everyone does it, this was my fair share anyway, looking out for me and mine. Once our decision-making becomes uncoupled from ethical standards, the pragmatic value that we assign to our "selves" can quickly morph into an unbridled pursue of power. At that point, more is never enough. Support for this premise abounds. For example:

- Entire school districts (look across Texas or Georgia a few years back) were found to have cheated by giving students the answers to federally-imposed "No-Child-Left-Behind" standardized tests. (No answers, well very few, will be given in this class.)
- Time and again people were shown, on hidden video, to take the bagel without throwing a buck into the money container.
- Students, armed with increasingly sophisticated technology, are finding new ways to cheat every year.
- Disneyworld stopped allowing families with disabled members to move to the front of long lines during 2013. Too many families were renting disabled people to join their group.

Are Marketers More Prone than Other Business People to Cheat?

Marketers are quite likely to cheat. They are, after all, only human. But marketing decision makers are no more likely to act unethically, to miss-the-mark, than any other managerial type; say, accounting, financial, or supply chain managers. This is because members of those professional groups are only human, too. They therefore are inherently self-interested, as well.

But marketers and marketing practice are more likely to receive ethical criticism from the customers, the media, or other public interest critics. The reason why relates to the "Iceberg Principle." Readers likely understand that only about 10% of any iceberg is actually visible above the water's surface. What part of the iceberg removes the most attention? The part people can see, of course. While marketing activities constitute far more than 10% of most successful firms (probably more than 50%), marketing practice (products themselves, prices, and promotions [marketing communications], because they are out there for all to see and experience, inevitably receives far more public attention than what goes on behind closed doors or inside most Firms' supply chains.

Readers should recall that the Glacier Principle was introduced in the preceding chapter's discussion of the Marketing Environment. Readers should also understand the difference between the Glacier Principle and the Iceberg Principle.

By the way, far more than just Disneyworld customers have been shown to cheat or to act unethically in the midst of their exchanges with Firms. Because it is during buyer-seller exchanges or during the lead up to or aftermath to those exchanges that everything relevant to marketing happens. The recent Great Recession was created, in part, by unethical mortgage bankers and financial marketers who traded deficient and misrepresented mortgage products to each other. And of course, these artificially low-priced variable mortgages were often marketed to customers who could not afford them over the longer-run when interest rates rose. (Mortgage products are always longer-run in nature.)

But without question customers at the time were also routinely trying to cheat marketers. Home buyers did this by knowingly lying about their incomes or asset base and signing up to low interest-rate mortgage products that customers (and their financial marketer!) knew they could not afford to pay off once higher interest rates kicked in. The whole tawdry affair bespoke not so much about the blind leading the blind (cliché alert) as it did about bunches of marketing liars selling to bunches of buyer liars. Talk about collusion.

One more example follows. No one reading this has ever purchased a clothing item or fashion accoutrement to wear at the big Saturday evening wedding, party or event, and returned the item on Monday. But most people reading this text knows someone who has. Yes, this act is also absolutely unethical because it clearly and unduly injures marketers who can no longer ethically sell the same item at its original price. Or course, marketers could choose to not disclose that the product is used, and the chain of lies and deceit would continue.

→ Where Will Ethical Dilemmas Most Likely Arise?

This is an interesting and important topic. But before addressing it, readers should learn three distinctions between ethical and legal behavior. First, ethical standards provide a higher standard for morality than do legal standards. Second, legal standards, while hugely important, simply reflects society's agreement about what represents a moral or immoral act. Think about that: how easy is it to secure societal agreement about anything? Talk about the law representing the lowest common denominator. Talk about compromises that likely devalue the role of truth. Third, then, people or Firms can engage in decision-making and subsequent activities that exist well within the bounds of the law and yet still engage in unethical decision-making and activities. This final point is the most important distinction.

The marketing areas in which ethical dilemmas, unethical allegations and unethical guilt will most likely arise are: Pricing, specifically, price fixing, price discrimination, price skimming, anticompetitive practices, marketing communications, and poor product quality and safety.

Price Fixing

Price-fixing is illegal and unethical. Price-fixing arises when the owners of say, supposedly competing local gas stations, visit and collude with each other, and jointly agree that fuel prices will be set at given levels. Or, as actually happened on multiple occasions in the past, the leadership of the three largest cereal marketers in the United States get together, probably on a golf course, and created a shared monopoly. And in this shared monopoly the leaders agreed their Firms would compete on based promotions (advertising, coupons), branding (Tony the Tiger versus Captain Crunch), or new product development (healthier, more fiber, whole grain), but not price. The opportunity to not compete on price is a complete win if any Firm that is able to achieve it. Because, then, the revenues (income statement top lines) and profits (income statement bottom lines) of such Firms would each grow sustainably. Simple question: ever wonder why those 12 to 15 ounce boxes of highly processed and widely available grain, laced with inexpensive sugar, cost so much?

Price Discrimination

Price discrimination is legal and illegal. It is ethical and unethical. The two preceding sentences were each consciously written. Price-discrimination is characterized by nuance, and comparatively little black and white clarity. Price-discrimination entails charging different prices (higher or lower) for the same product to different customers or customer groups absent any justification to charge different prices due to higher or lower costs of doing business with the customer. Sounds perfectly illegal and unethical, doesn't it. But what about just past 60-year-olds who pay a lower price when they attend movies? Or the fairer sex, who gain free admission (pay no price) on Ladies Night on the Square? Where is the gender equity? Again, the point at which ethical or even illegal ends and unethical/illegal begins is often blurred.

Price Skimming

Price skimming is typically legal and ethical. The rationale is simple: No consumer is ever required to pay full, or "premium" price when Apple or Gillette introduces their latest iPhone or shaving technology to market. Yet many consumers willingly and happily do, and in the case of Apple products actually stand in line at midnight to do so. Price-skimming is also called skimming-the-cream pricing or, as noted, premium prices. Firms that engage in price-skimming are generally about to do so because they have managed the value generated by the rest of their marketing mix (the Product, the Promotion and the Place [or supply chain]) so well that pricing levels have become a less important consideration in the minds of their targeted market segments. Firms that are able to successful execute premium pricing strategies should be held up for praise, rather than ethical criticism, because they typically have managed their marketing mix so well and/or have developed products for which customers willingly pay more.

Anticompetitive Practices

Anticompetitive practices, specifically, situations where Firms knowingly engage in activities that eliminate or lessen competition. This includes collusion—already referenced in situations where gas station owners or cereal firm executives met to set prices—or situations where one marketing Firm or national industry consciously prices below its costs to injure another Firm or domestic industry and/or eventually eliminate that Firm or industry as a competitor. This unethical and illegal practice is called **dumping**.

The Japanese steel industry, whose efforts were heavily subsidized by the Japanese government, was accused of dumping steel into US markets during the 1970s, 1980s and 1990s. Not coincidentally, steel is a conspicuously difficult product category in which to achieve differentiation. Once differentiation becomes more difficult (i.e., the resulting implication is that the market of customers does not discern the presence of positioning and branding differences between US-produced and Japanese-produced steel), any variations in pricing (i.e., at higher or lower levels) become remarkably important to customers. Hence, the power, say we say, of the "big dump."

Marketing Communications

Specific forms of marketing promotional (communication) strategies, including green-washing, pink-washing, bait and switch, and pyramid (sometimes called multi-level marketing) schemes can be unethical in nature. **Green-washing** arises when marketers promise that their particular product is especially beneficial, or at least not harmful, to the environment. Often, however, those promises are lies or, best case, deliver far less environmental value than marketers promise. With good cause, marketers of air travel, toys, home appliances, automobiles, bottled water, laundry cars and fur have frequently been accused of green washing. And this list could have been greatly extended.

Pink-washing, as an unethical marketing practice, is often closely tied to cause marketing such as the Susan G. Komen Race for the Cure [breast cancer], the ALS Foundation [Lou Gering's disease], or the United Way. Good counsel: These days, "think before you pink." The reason why this advice makes sense is because ample evidence exists that suggests Firms often overpromise and under-deliver when the subject is how much of a percentage of their pink product's selling price actually ends up going to support the cause in question.

This type of promising more than is delivered likely recently arose with respect to the Ice Bucket Challenge and ALS, or the National Football League and the Breast Cancer research. In the past, the high proportion of its contributions that went directly to United Way's senior management's reimbursement gave pause. When this pink-wash came to light, many contributors elected to steer their donations toward other charitable alternatives.

Bait and switch practices are grounded in kernels of truth. But the practice should not be view as ethical. Bait and switch occurs when retailers promote the fact that the hottest new, say, technology product, will be available at their fine store this Saturday only, at an authentically attractive price. The truth is that the product actually is available. The further truth, however, only three of these highly desirable products are actually available at this discounted price. Three customers, for example, may end up happy, while the 333 other people who enter the store after 10:10 AM are not, because they have falsely been baited into the store. But as they enter, and find only disappointment, welcoming marketers might ask: Can I interest you, show you, [switch you to] this other brand? The store wins because you walked into the store, and may up end buying something. But customers lose because they did so under false pretenses.

A **pyramid scheme** is a business model able to lure new participants and their monetary investment into the scheme by promising unsustainable payments or returns in exchange for those participants' commitment to bring other people into the scheme. Pyramid schemes often are not based on the generation of any new value, and that basis alone are unethical. They are also illegal, as numerous marketing players in the most famous recent pyramid scheme engineered by Bernie Madoff can attest to while they live out the rest of their natural lives behind bars.

Metroplex-based Mary Kay, the sixth largest direct-selling Firm in the world, operates successfully and ethically based on a variation of a pyramid scheme called multi-level marketing. Mary Kay distributors (called "beauty consultants") can earn income by marketing directly to women in their social network, but also receive a percentage of sales made by people they recruit into the distribution network. Mary Kay distributors must purchase a $100 starter kit in order to qualify. More recently, however, the jury is out regarding this marketing form's ethicality.

Certain types of advertising practices and content, particularly ads that feature an excessive amount of over-sexualized imagery or innuendo, or advertisements that feature products that broadly viewed as immoral and/or harmful. Specifically, marketing efforts that target children, particularly advertisements and the marketing of certain types of products to children are frequently singled out for ethical criticism.

Children, as is well-known, are not equivalent to little adults. Children are substantially less able than adults to distinguish marketing fiction from fact, hyperbole from reality, or products that are fundamentally bad from products that are fundamentally good for them. Children are notably more easily subject to persuasion and manipulation by marketers when those marketers offer unrealistic depictions of how given toys actually perform. The promotion or placement of unhealthy food products in kid's television programing, programming that itself is little more than 30-minute-advertisements for products, or the promotion or placement of junk foods in schools are frequently, and in our view properly, subjected to criticism from professional and amateur ethicists.

Cutting Corners on Product Quality and Safety

There have rarely been better times or places to purchase or consume products than right now in America. But even highly respected brands such as Toyota, General Motors, and Mattel have recently been put on the carpet because of mishaps and even deaths associated with flaws and shortfalls in their products. Too often, amongst too many well-known brands, decisions made by cost-accountants and attorneys have badly (but correctly) degraded formerly glittering brand's equity. Financial decision-makers, in such cases, generally determine it is less expensive to pay off the occasional $1,000,000 lawsuit initiated by injured customers or dead customers' heirs than it is to spend hundreds of millions re-engineering faulty braking, ignition or airbag systems.

→ Three Perspectives on Marketing Ethics

Decisions, ethical or otherwise, generate behaviors. Behaviors produce consequences. The un/ethical decisions made by marketers generate consequences within three distinct domains: consumers, society and culture, and other businesses. Each is examined below.

As readers work through this content they may note how often ethical criticisms are neither entirely accurate nor inaccurate. This tendency frequently characterizes the relationship between marketing and ethics. Clear-cut, black-and-white marketing decision-making contexts arise less often than readers might causally assume. Is this choice moral or immoral? Sometimes it is hard to tell. Moreover, interminable questions about where one group's or person's rights end and another group's or person's rights begin are likely to arise.

Consumer-Related Ethical Criticisms

- Criticism 1: Consumers are harmed through excessively high prices.

Are they? Only, one would suppose, when consumers are actually required to buy excessively priced products. But no one is forced to purchase a Mercedes car, Fendi bag or Harley motorcycle. Various, far less expensive alternatives are available in each category.

Consumers generally opt for more expensive brands because the marketer has done a great job of convincing them that the higher prices are worth it or because consumers want to elevate themselves above the "masses" who cannot afford the prestigious brand. For categories like bikes or bags, high prices do more than just signal quality and performance. The brand also helps consumers develop and communicate their act or aspirational identities to others. Toting a Fendi bag or driving a Harley bike conveys an enhanced message about the self, particularly when she does both at the same time.

Still, situations will arise in the United States where consumers must pay higher prices because lower-priced alternatives or substitute products are not easily available. Here, though, if the price of milk is higher than market average in a store located in a poor neighborhood, is that due to a) a lack of competition, b) the Firm's knowledge that poor people often don't have transportation or c) because it costs more, say, insurance-wise or theft-wise, to do business in poor neighborhoods? Point in fact, it generally does cost more to do business in poor areas. The grey, rather than black-and-white, again prevails.

- Criticism 2: Marketers Engage In Deceptive Practices.

Do they? Yes, some marketers surely do this. The aforementioned circa 2004–2008 US mortgage industry is an example. Should marketers deceive? The answer is no, not ever. To begin with, if marketers honor the principals of the marketing mix, they would never deceive. Additionally, when marketers build sufficient differentiating value into their products before going to market and then promote and place them effectively, they never have to cheat. Moreover, if marketers understood that "what happens in the dark usually comes to light," they would inexorably move away from scams or frauds, because they would realize they could not get away with either. Finally, as noted, one should never piss in a well that one may want to drink from tomorrow.

Relationships, created based on an honored (fulfilled) promise to deliver truly differentiating value, are critical to sustainable marketing success. If marketers want to do business in the world tomorrow, particularly with the same customers or others who know the victimized customer, they better not deceive today. Bad news, criticism, gossip, and the truth all travel at the speed of the Internet.

- Criticism 3: Marketers engage in high-pressure selling.

Of course some marketers knowingly push people to buy things they don't actually need, or to buy something now rather than later. But consumers have been known to desperately want things they don't need. At times that may be because those consumers are, say, trying to climb a social ladder. Or these false needs may arise because a Firm adroitly managed its marketing mix and created perceptions in the customers' minds that they "cannot live without" this specific, for example, home, car, vodka, or loan. The list of products, of course, could have gone on and on. Marketing is, after all, a battle of perceptions that is waged and won or lost in the middles of consumers.

Moreover, consumers actually enjoy the right to not purchase anything they that do not, "upon further consideration," actually want to buy. Every US state features "Cooling Off" laws. These laws come into play when consumers contract to purchase expensive items such as homes or automobiles, and then change their minds. Consumers who change their minds have between 24 and 48 hours to hand back the keys and return the item, presumably undamaged, to the seller—particularly if buyers believe they were pressured into the purchase. The Federal Trade Commission also permits consumers to cancel the purchase, and return the item, for products priced as low as $25.00. This provides protection against what are called "impulse purchases."

- Criticism 4: Marketing firms market shoddy (low quality) or unsafe (dangerous) products.

Do they? Sure, sometimes this happens; at times knowingly, at times not. Mattel, marketer of Barbie dolls and Hot Wheels cars, unwittingly became entangled in a lead paint scandal (lead paint is especially damaging to young children, and young children do place toys in their mouths) right before Christmas. During 2007 Mattel, a US Firm, contracted with a Firm in China who made 83 different toys for it. But the Chinese Firm outsourced the painting of the toys to a second Chinese Firm (as would be normal and expected, because supply chains permit Firms to focus on their particular specialty and expertise). This second Firm acquired the paint from a third Chinese Firm. It was this Firm that deceptively used lead in its paint, because lead paint costs less.

Mattel, according to respected reports, was innocent of any ethical malfeasance. But Mattel paid a heavy price in terms of reputation, brand equity, and other financial costs due to an unethical decision made four levels upstream in its supply chain (the marketing supply chain and its management will be discussed in great detail in Chapter 12). Eventually, about 9,000,000 toys were recalled. This was an un-merry Christmas for Mattel.

Americans are fortunate to live in an era where high quality is pervasive and generally prevails over "cheap" junk. We live during an era in which Firms that don't sell quality products rarely stick around long. (The world is too small to sell crap for long.) One author lived in south Louisiana for 10 years and never ate at a local restaurant where the food did not taste good, usually very good. Restaurants simply could not survive there for long if their food or service was subpar in quality. Most food consumed in those south Louisiana restaurants trended toward the unhealthy due to their fat and salt content, but that's another story.

But the question arises: What is an unsafe product, anyway? Perhaps cigarettes? Well, they're surely dangerous. They are the only product we know, that when used as directed, often kills those who consume it. But cigarettes are legal if not, in our view, ethical. (Cigarettes are also highly addictive, a condition that makes cigarettes easy to market successfully. Just get the consumer to try them two or three times, especially when the victim is young, impressionable and more easily duped. An unethical marketers' dream, if you will.)

But what about beer, wine, liquors? Medical and public policy experts dispute whether smoking or drinking is more deadly, but the point is clear: either can prove unsafe. Giving people want they actually want may represent a sure path to marketing success but it can subject thoughtful and/or moral people pause over how much is enough. Then there are our favorite *"unsafe"* products: ice cream, hamburgers/pizza, HUGE portion sizes in restaurants. Well, yes but … isn't this what consumers want?

The marketing of unsafe products, as an ethical dilemma, gets very fuzzy very fast. Our advice: moderation in all things, please. Too much pleasure can prove painful and perhaps unethical.

- Criticism 5: Marketers pursue a strategy called "planned obsolescence."

Many Firms do, but those Firms should be commended for their ability to make their own appear outdated, before their competitors do it for them. Gillette, a Firm established in 1890 by a man named King Gillette, has pursued this successful marketing strategy across portions of three centuries. Gillette, which always prices at premium levels, introduces one new generation razor after another, always making key competitors play a catch-up game. Then, when Gillette obsoletes a razor in the United States, it begins marketing the old product in European markets, and eventually to other markets throughout the world. The Gillette Flexball, introduced in 2014, is merely the latest of dozens of innovative products introduced by the firm during the last 13 decades.

Video game marketers, as well as Apple, employ this strategy: iPhone 4, 4S, 5, and 6S and on, on, and on. Should marketers engage in such "planned obsolescence"? We believe the answer is yes. Such Firms are marketing very well because they are able to introduce new products for which people are willing to pay more. Remember, consumers are never forced to buy new versions of existing products as they are introduced to the market. The only reason why most consumers buy new versions of existing products is, in fact, if the new products deliver new and highly appealing value.

Socio-Cultural Related Ethical Criticisms

- Criticism 1: Marketers create false needs and excessive materialism in American society.

Some consumers emotionally live or die based on whether they can acquire the latest hottest product. These individuals are experiencing "false needs." Materialism, on the other hand, is a belief that arises among some people that material things (possessions) are more important than spiritual values.

There is no doubt: our human wants are endless. Many consumers abide, metaphorically, as gaping, longing-for more holes that prove incredibly difficult to fill up. Our souls are made to want. Too often, however, consumers want the wrong things. The ethical question, then, boils down to what consumers choose to desire as they strive to satisfy their emptiness. And, over time, what once were just simply wants can transform into powerful needs. Is any of this the fault or doing of marketers? It is not.

But do marketers knowingly exploit this situation? They certainly do. Can effective marketing activities such as branding, product development, and promotions create false needs? Or, do such activities sometimes simply tap into and grow (into needs) wants that already exist? The answer to each question, unsurprisingly, is yes.

- Criticism 2: Marketers create too much cultural degradation.

Cultural degradation, as it relates to marketing practice, might be summarized as too much promotional and advertising clutter, too many assaults on consumers privacy, and too much sexual content being present in marketing messages or content (television program, music, fashion).

One important issue should be re-addressed, a point that was originally made in Chapter 4. Marketers and their practices are influenced by culture. Culture is influenced by marketing and its practice. What marketers do is generally influenced and viewed as acceptable is often influenced by rapidly evolving standards established by American socio-cultural norms. Sometimes, these socio-cultural norms get ahead of marketers. At other times marketers get ahead of established socio-cultural normative guidelines.

Without question there is too much advertising. This is both problem and challenge for consumers and marketers alike. But today there are also Netflix and DVRs or the opportunity to change the channel. But we enjoy watching football for free on television, don't we? Absent advertising, this would not be the case. We also benefit from having more choices and knowing about more each available choice, when we attempt to determine which pill to take, car to drive, or smart phone to use. These, too, are benefits that would not be possible without advertising.

There indeed are too many assaults on consumer privacy, particularly our personal demographic and lifestyle information. But Facebook's entire business model is based on providing private information about you to advertisers. The vast majority of users understand what Facebook and other social networking sites do with the information they load onto the sites. If those users believed what Facebook does is unethical, Facebook would have to stop the practice. Of course, at that point there no longer be any Facebook, at least not in the form that the Firm's billion-plus users have come to expect.

Consider advertising, television shows, fashions, or music. Beyond question, each is far more sexualized than was the case during prior decades. Here we would argue that marketers are simultaneously driving and following emergent trends in their relevant planning environment. Questions of ethicality are usually not relevant. Consumers, after all, can ignore offensive advertising, switch channels, reject fashions, and listen to other music options.

- Criticism 3: Marketing creates situations in which excessive power ends up in the hands of too few people, Firms, or institutions.

One can argue, with cause, that people or Firms should be rewarded what doing what they do better than others in their market (which is really of marketplace of ideas) or domain. Greater power, and its partner, influence, inevitably arise as part of those "rewards." And almost everyone wants more rather than less power and influence.

Should people who started with nothing (Steve Jobs), who started in the middle (Mark Cuban), or who started from the upper-middle class (Bill Gates and Mark Zuckerberg) be rewarded with prodigious power because they created great new stuff that consumers truly wanted? We believe so. Should other Firms or people or products who earned branding equity and pricing power through their innovativeness and willingness to take risks (that paid off) be similarly rewarded? Assuming each entity was marketed ethically, and no evidence exists to suggest otherwise, then each deserves to takeaway value from what they have earned.

- Criticism 4: Marketers are successfully marketing stuff that harms consumers.

Fact 1: Adjusting for population growth, recent US increases in rates of diabetes, cancer, leukemia, heart disease, and obesity are both astounding and disturbing.

Fact 2: Part of this growth follows from the fact that people currently live longer. (Everyone eventually dies from something.)

Fact 3: People are living longer in part because of breakthrough pharmaceutical products and medical advances that innovative marketers created and introduced to the world.

Fact 4: Marketers have gotten better at understanding consumers and how best to manipulate/persuade them into eating too much of a few products that genuinely degrade the health of those consumers. Seriously, there is more comparatively inexpensive salt, fat and sugar made available for ingestion by American bellies today than the uninformed can easily imagine. Serious question, however:

- By providing these products are marketers acting rationally and ethically by offering and promoting things and outcomes that consumers simply crave based on their natural, instinctive responses?

We believe, perhaps surprisingly, the answer is yes. This book is written in America about America. People in the United States, assuming they have enough money, are free to eat whatever they want. Consumers are sovereign, in charge of their own decisions. Consumers enjoy free-will, which is why questions of ethicality should rarely enter food conversations.

Business/Economic Related Criticisms

On this front, ethical criticisms generally entail arguments that marketing practices harm other Firms and reduce competition.

- Criticism 1: Marketers acquire their competitors.

Sometimes marketers do exactly this. Acquisitions of competitors are often initiated as part of broader strategies aimed at acquiring new products, markets, or professional expertise. And often, the competitors that were acquired are delighted about the arrangement. Just ask the employees of Instagram or WhatsApp. The two Firms were recently acquired by Facebook for $715 million and $21.8 billion (yes, the "B: is correct), respectively.

There is nothing inherently unethical about one Firm acquiring another. Besides, the practice of mergers and acquisitions is carefully regulated by US Federal agencies. Thus, when one large Firm attempted to acquire another large Firm and the new larger Firm that emerges might control too large a market share (and thus pricing power and less motivation to innovate), the government would likely rule the planned acquisition illegal.

- Criticism 2: Marketing Firms grow so powerful or their brands become so well-known that either outcome creates barriers to entry.

Barriers-to-entry is an economics term that reflects what can happen when existing Firms become so large, powerful and/or well known that new competitors' ability to enter the industry or market is impeded. Barriers-to-entry could arise within cell phone, home building, or grocery markets. Again, over time, barriers-to-entry may lead to less innovation and/or higher prices. Barriers-to-entry might arise because one dominant Firm enjoys insurmountable competitive advantages. These advantages could include, but would not be limited to name recognition, branding power, superior technology or superior managerial talent, or sole access to key resources.

Yet few to no barriers-to-entry have ever existed that were not penetrated by competitors who developed superior marketing strategies, built better and new products, used exceptional technology, or demonstrated relentless commitments to innovation or lower costs. This asset combination, when bundled, has routinely allowed new kids on the block to move faster than existing Firms that supposedly enjoyed insurmountable advantages.

Domestic automobile marketers once purportedly enjoyed huge barriers-to-entry. They did, that is, until German and Japanese auto makers slowly and then quickly started nearly burying them. Similar descriptions apply to the domestic textile and steel industries. At one time each stood astride the world like giants. Now their mills are difficult to find in the United States. Each has nearly been put down by faster-moving and more agile Asian competitors.

- Criticism 3: Marketing power creates opportunity to engage in predatory pricing.

Marketing power is actually a synonym for brand equity—a key marketing term to which you have not been fully introduced. The primary value delivered by brand equity to Firms that have earned it is pricing power. Pricing power, finally, implies that the Firm can price above the market average without losing sales or market share.

Pricing power should not be conflated or confused with predatory pricing. When Firms have earned pricing power, consumers are willing to pay a little or a lot extra because they perceive the product delivers a little or lot of extra value. The extra value may be real or primarily image-driven. But the incremental value exists. When consumers (in B2C exchanges) or other Firms (in B2B exchanges) buy anything, they typically will only pay an amount roughly equivalent to what they genuinely believe the product or service is actually worth. Good strategies and effective management of marketing mixes create perceptions of higher value amongst targeted customer segments. Customers thus become willing to pay higher prices. Higher prices are not unethical.

Predatory pricing, by contrast, could arise when two or more Firms collude and agree to not compete on the basis of price. Thereafter their prices often rise to what are deemed predatory levels. As noted the Big 3 Cereal Marketers were indicted multiple times in the past for fixing prices in this manner. Their action was clearly illegal. Thus it was also unethical. Predatory pricing might also arise under conditions of marketing scarcity; that is, there is more demand for than supply of a product. If a Gulf coast hurricane is blowing in toward the Mississippi coast, and Jackson, MS (an inland city), hotel owners triple their prices (because "Coasties" must evacuate), the pricing is considered predatory, illegal and of course, unethical.

→ Balancing Consumer and Marketer Rights

Consumers have rights. So do marketers.

This condition is natural. It should be expected. In fact these rights exist as part of the "get" and "give" exchange process that unifies every buyer and seller.

Consumers' Rights

Consumerism is a consumer protection movement. Its goal is to improve or protect the rights and power of buyers in relation to the rights and power of sellers. The father of modern consumerism is Ralph Nader, who wrote a paradigm-shifting book called *Unsafe at any Speed* in 1965. *Unsafe at any Speed* accused the domestic car industry of resisting the introduction of various safety features, such seatbelts, simply because doing so would have raised prices. Time and again, facts suggest automobile marketers of the time came down on the side of saving money rather than saving lives. This book is often mistakenly identified as the book about the Corvair, a rear-engine car whose design was ahead of its time. But its safety standards were emphatically behind the curve.

Largely as a result of this still emergent movement, buyers now enjoy the rights to:

- Not buy something they don't want to buy.
- Expect the product to be safe (except cigarettes? Alcohol? Etc.).
- Expect the product to perform as claimed.

Marketers' Rights

Given that all exchanges features two players (we call them a buyer and seller), and because exchanges always involve a "get" and a "give," marketers have rights, too. Marketers have the rights to:

- Sell anything (so long as what is being sold does not injure anyone or anything).
- Charge any fair price for the product (so long as there is no discrimination against any group of buyers).
- Promote products and spend any amount they can on promotion, so long as what is said is truly accurate or understood to be so outrageous a claim that no sane person would believe it.
- Use any product message they choose, so long as the product message is not misleading or dishonest.
- Use incentive schemes.

Marketers, as referenced earlier, also have the right as well as the opportunity to "do well for themselves" by "doing good for others." Doing well by doing good could include any Firm:

- Supporting the right causes with its time, talent, and treasure.
- Doing exactly what it says it will do, every time. In other words keeping every promise it makes.
- Being environmentally neutral, in worst case, or environmental beneficial, in ideal case.
- Legitimately following each guideline associated with the marketing concept.

Readers will recall that the marketing concept generally prescribes that satisfaction of customer needs come first (as a driving force for the Firm) while the pursuit of mutual gain between customer and Firm is of paramount consideration.

- Being scrupulously ethical in all activities, marketing or otherwise. The ethical goal of "doing well by doing good" surely makes sense most of the time. However, the constant pursuit of this moral standard alone hardly constitutes a viable strategy. Marketing Firms, thus marketing managers, still should be driven by bottom-line considerations. Or, shall we say, when creating strategies or executing decisions Firms should always dance close to revenue and cost lines.
- Finally, "doing good" as a marketer, could and should also entail:

Honestly and completely informing consumers to the extent that they need to be informed to make a good decision.

- Never engaging in the marketing of ethically questionable products or the use of ethically questionable marketing practices.
- Whenever possible, only marketing products that improve customers' quality of life.
- Never marketing products that directly or indirectly injure welfare or well-being of consumers or other customers.

Are Certain Products Inherently More Ethical than Others?

The answer to this question is an unqualified "yes."

Some Firms enjoy the option of marketing products that deliver immediate or long-term satisfaction to customers who consume them. Those same products may also harm or help consumers over the long-term.

Other Firms enjoy the opportunity to market products that offer immediate or longer-term benefits to customers. The same products may never offer any material satisfaction to customers.

The occasional Firm enjoys the opportunity to do both.

Imagine two dimensions, or axis. One dimension captures a spectrum of satisfaction. The spectrum ranges from the immediate to the longer-term. The other dimension captures a range of benefits, the spectrum ranges from the immediate to the longer-term. Do this, and you have created a two-by-two matrix that features four cells (categories). Virtually all tangible products or intangible services can be classified into one and only one of those cells. Some cells, actually, some products classified in the cells, are more "moral" than others. (See Exhibit 5.1.)

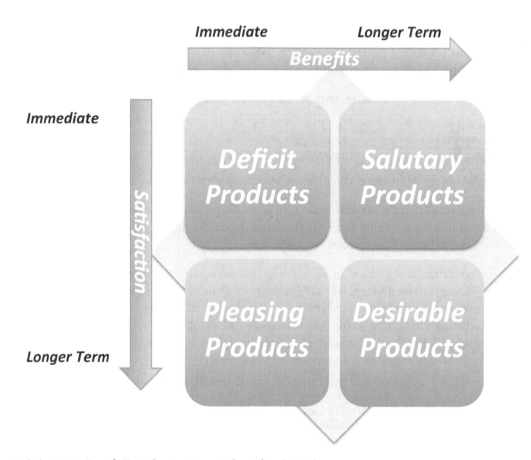

Exhibit 5.1 *Benefit/Satisfaction Matrix for Ethical Products.*

Deficit Products

Deficit products would prove difficult to market because they fail to offer "immediate satisfaction" or "long-term benefit." Diet pills, for example, apparently have never helped dieting consumers lose weight; i.e., they have never delivered the promising long-term benefit. Otherwise, there would surely be a lot fewer overweight people in the United States. Diet pills do, however, materially increase the amount of time users spend in the bathroom. Can you imagine such a morally-challenged product succeeding?

Pleasing Products

Pleasing products, by contrast, deliver immediate satisfaction. Krispy-Kreme or Marlboro Lights come to mine. Both are easily marketed; after they are panaceas to individuals seeking short-term pleasure. And, the "pursuit of pleasure" or the "avoidance of pain" is a prime behavioral motivator for most people. Unfortunately, pleasing products may bring pain over the longer run, which is why the marketing of pleasing products is sometimes deemed less than moral.

Salutary Products

Salutary suggests that at times unpleasant or unwelcome experiences actually generate good (beneficial) longer-term effects. Salutary products are characterized by low immediate appeal (a diminished capacity for delivering short-term satisfaction) and an ability to benefit consumers greatly over the longer-run. For most people exercise programs or broccoli are salutary products. Each ethical product has its niche in the marketplace. But salutary products are generally more difficult to market than pleasing products. Many consumers would rather to live-in-the-moment than plan-for-their-future.

Desirable Products

Desirable products provide immediate-satisfaction and long-run benefits to those who consume them. Classic wool sport jackets (men) or high quality little black dresses (women) are widely viewed as desirable; items that look and feel great as you initially experience them but also provide long-lasting benefits because neither ever goes out of style. This would be a sweet spot for marketers aspiring to do well for themselves by doing well for others (customers). The question is: Can a Firm be creative enough to conceptualize, produce and promote such desirable products?

⟶ How to Become a More Ethical Marketing Manager

In *Improvisation: The Drama of Christian Ethics*, Samuel Ellis suggested "Ethics is not about being clever in a moral crisis but about forming a character that does not realize it has been in a crisis until the 'crisis' is resolved." But it's really not our job to improve your character. Moreover, were this was our job, at this point in your life the task would prove nearly impossible. For better or worse we are rather fully formed beings at this point.

Our job is to teach you, a prospective business leader, how to make more ethical decisions more easily and readily and thus act in more socially responsible fashions more of the time. How valuable is your reputation to you? Does the quality of your reputation influence the type and quality of relationships you are able to develop or sustain? How long did it take for you to develop the reputation you enjoy, assuming you enjoy an admirable reputation? How quickly could your reputation be brought to ruin?

Do you understand that points just made about your reputation apply equally to the reputation of any Firm or brand? That even though the occasional individual or Firm seemingly gets away with shady dealings, over the longer-run, most don't? If your answers are "yes" and "yes," then you surely understand how important ethics and social responsibility is to any Firm or marketing manager.

Four practical approaches exist through which readers can learn how to make more ethical marketing or business decisions more of the time. Each approach is useful. But some are more useful than others.

The Deontological Approach

At its core the apparently daunting word *deontology* means rules. Deontology evaluates the morality of a decision or action based on the decision's or action's adherence to a particular rule. The Hammurabi Code consists of 216 Babylonian (think modern-day Iraq) laws written by the great ruler around 1763 B.C. It is the first known set of deontological do's and don'ts. The Ten Commandments, written around 1100 B.C., are similar to this Code. (Worth noting, Judiasm eventually developed 613 laws, or rules, in an attempt to have a guideline available to discriminate the moral from immoral choice in all possible contexts that feature ethical content.)

Today, marketers, accountants, financial advisors, human resource managers, attorneys, physicians, and for all we know plumbers each have their Codes of Ethics, each designed to address each and every possible ethical dilemma. One problem: Technology, in particular, is creating new opportunities to act unethically faster than professional groups can create and disseminate new rules. Another problem: No one can remember all the rules. Yet another, more pressing shortfall associated with this rule-based approach: In large part due to our intrinsically selfish natures, having these rules simply does not work.

Genuine question, offered for educational rather than shock value: How many Ten Commandments did you break last month? Okay, likely no reader murdered anyone. But did you fail to fully honor your mother or father, covet (experience envy about) something some else had, or bear false witness (lie or misrepresent) about anything or anyone? Don't worry if your answer is more than one. Your authors are right there with you. Having ethical rules in place is a good first step. But rules are rarely enough when the subject is how best to ensure ethical performance for we've already seen how easily rules are broken.

The Utilitarian Approach (Consequentialism)

Most students are familiar with *Star Trek*. And knowing *Star Trek*, you are acquainted with Mr. Spock. Mr. Spock dies during the second *Star Trek* movie, *The Wrath of Kahn* (1982). But more to the point in this context, Spock willingness sacrifices himself in order to save the Starship Enterprise and its crew. Among his dying words: "Remember, the needs of the many outweigh the needs of the few."

Those words capture the essence of utilitarianism as it applies to marketing ethics. Utility is synonym for value. What Mr. Spock was inferring, then, was that the decision that yields the most value for the most people is always the ethical choice, even if some fewer number of people (one, in this scenario) are necessarily hurt.

Whenever marketers make decisions, behaviors result. Those behaviors, in turn, generate consequences. Those consequences may yield good outcomes for some and bad outcomes for others. As long as more people benefit than are harmed, the decision is ethical. While hardly perfect (indeed, Unitarianism is obviously hard on the minority), this approach is typically deemed more useful as a means to identify the moral choice than the deontological alternative. And indeed, in situations where the rule-based method cannot be applied because no rule exists to address the moral contingency in question, utilitarianism is always a viable option.

The Facebook and Your Mother Guideline

This approach is practical and comes highly recommended. Assume that you're in charge, and an ethical quandary arose. You're genuinely struggling to separate the right from wrong choice to make (situations like these do arise in marketing and business). But at the very least you seek to make the least worst unethical decision. The decision you make and the outcomes it yields will be posted tonight on your Facebook page for your Mother, your Facebook "friends," and the rest of your social world to see.

If you're sensing now that you'll be uncomfortable tomorrow when Mom (and the world) sees the report of your decision and its consequences, you're probably too close toward the immoral choice. But if you're comfortable with what she is about to see, you're likely walking as close to ethical as you can given the circumstances in play.

Hamilton and Strutton's Truth-Telling Guideline

The "truth," as we best understand it, and ethical marketing decisions and behavior walk in lockstep as close allies. But marketers always have to be wholly truthful in order to remain ethical. Customers, in either B2C or B2B situations, require accurate information in order to make the best possible decisions for themselves. Said customers do not, however, inevitably need to have all available information in order to make every choice. Brooke Hamilton and David Strutton, writing in the *Journal of Business Ethics*, contend that in marketing contexts, truth-telling amongst marketers means giving customers full and fully accurate disclosure of information to the extent that the information is necessary for the consumer to make a well-informed, well-grounded, and safe decision.

Pharmaceutical marketers face higher truth-telling standards than the marketers of, say, smart-phones, movies, or chewing gum. Because when they consume pharmaceuticals, what customers don't know could kill them, or more likely, make them uncomfortable or sick.

This is exactly why when you encounter a 30-second-long pharmaceutical advertisement on television, you inevitably experience the following sequence. First, 5–6 seconds of imagery and language describes the problem (solved by the drug). Next, another 5–6 seconds of ad content explains how the product solves the problem. Third, 10–12 seconds explained the potential side-effects, which are often nasty. Finally, the problem and the solution are quickly re-encapsulated. More attention is necessarily directed toward explaining what could go wrong than right, because the truth-telling standards are so high. What consumers don't know or understand can hurt them. When selling chewing gum or sneakers, marketers' truth-telling standards are not nearly as high.

All this makes perfect moral and business sense. Marketers, after all, are problem-solvers. But ethical marketers should never make decisions of commission or omission that might transform them into problem-creators.

→ Closing Thought

At the end of this important discussion (because years from now you might not remember the definition of segmentation, but you should remember how to behave more ethically), we leave you with two closing thoughts. The first thought relates to situational ethical values. The second relates to sustainable ethical values.

People guided by situational values generally do whatever situations permit them to get away with, without regard to the wider interests of their Firm or longer-term, usually based on the grounds that for various reasons they care less about the long-run than themselves.

People guided by sustainable values do the opposite; making decisions as if they realize their reputations or their descendants will always exist. They are thus more likely to behave in ways that sustain and lift up their employees, customers or suppliers, the environment, their country and/or future generations they might propagate.

We recommend the latter set of values.

CHAPTER 6
MANAGING MARKETING INFORMATION

This chapter examines marketing information management: the sources and uses of information by marketing managers in their strategic planning efforts as well as in their segmentation, targeting, and positioning efforts. The marketing information that managers acquire and use generally relate to customers, competitors, aspects of the Firm's environment or the marketplace. The key questions answered in this chapter are:

- How do marketing managers obtain key information they need at the right time and in the right form?
- How is this information employed to aid marketing decision-making?

Think back to the model of the strategic marketing process introduced in Chapter 3 (Exhibit 3.2). The successful execution of each step in this strategic and tactical planning process requires access to accurate and timely information. Indeed, quality planning simply cannot occur without such information. SWOT analyses themselves presuppose access to information from within and outside the Firm.

Then, as strategic and tactical plans are launched, information is again required. In fact, accurate, reliable, and timely information may be more critical during the implementation and control of plans. Managers must be able to quickly and correctly assess whether plans are on track, or are going awry. Virtually every decision marketing managers make should be based on the availability of accurate, timely information.

Most large B2C and B2B Firms have mechanisms in place to collect, store, and analyze information. Indeed, these functions are absolutely essential in today's highly competitive global markets. The statement "knowledge is power" is more than mere cliché. Whatever beauty or strength you possess and are able to wield to your advantage in your youth (your 20s and 30s) will fade with time. But the information that you collect now, and over time convert into actionable insights and knowledge, will only grow in power with the passage of time.

A more germane case in point: the 2012 election cycle is considered to be the first Big data-driven presidential campaign. President Obama's marketing team did all the right things right. Prior to the November Election Day a massive database merge was initiated. This meant all critical data were warehoused and made readily available in a single place. The team adopted a "database focus" that broadened their thinking and their approach to the use of metrics. The decision was made early on to measure and track all data that might have any possible relevance to the upcoming campaign and to the likelihood that: a) a given citizen would vote, and b) would vote democrat. A huge treasure trove of data was compiled and mined extensively during the campaign to focus strategy and tactics. Based on data coming into the warehouse on a continual basis, the team ran simulations of the election thousands of times a day. As the campaign progressed and November 6 or election day drew closer, the "dummy election results" were used to refocus and reallocate always finite resources from one state/region where they would have less impact to other states/regions where they would do more good. Just as critical, demographic information was collected and correlated with other voter-based variables that allowed them to more directly target advertising to finely-defined voter segments or "micro-targets."[1]

The successful re-elect President Barrack Obama campaign proved a textbook example of how to segment a voting marketplace, target specific market segments within the broader marketplace, and then position specifically customized values to those segments. More union job promises were offered (positioned) for union workers; promises about more health care for unemployed or underemployed citizens; marital rights for the LGBT community; the prospect of no Keystone Pipeline, for now at least, for environmental activists; immigration promises for various ethnic subcultures, particularly the Hispanic segment; no more or fewer charter schools as a gift for public educators; the list of specially packaged "product values" aimed at identifiable voter; i.e., customer, segments is impressive. The accuracy with which the Obama marketing campaign delivered its messages about these values was likely more impressive still. All this, and indeed the second Obama term in office, was made possible through the re-election campaign's adroit management of market information.

→ Sources of Information for Marketing Decisions

As noted, information is needed for all aspects of marketing decision-making. Next question up: where do Firms obtain the required information? Two major sources of information exist. Some of these sources are internal to the Firm; the others, naturally, are external.

Internal information sources consist of information collected from functional areas (departments) inside the Firm. Internal data sources, for example, include such things as sales data extracted from sales reports, costing data from production and operations, accounting and financial data and projections, customer complaints and inquiries, or even surveys completed by customers who have purchased the Firm's products.

External information sources are usually classified into two basic categories: secondary data and primary data. Secondary data consists of information that has already been collected by someone else, from outside the Firm. Secondary data have (the term "data" is plural) generally been gathered for another purpose, and may only tangentially relate to a research problem faced by the Firm. Secondary data are available from a large number of traditional sources, including libraries. More recently, of course, traditional resources of information have been displaced by Internet and CD-ROM-based information systems.

Primary data are not available in existing (secondary) sources. Primary data consists of new information; such data have not been previously collected by another entity for any other purpose. Instead, primary data are collected through a dedicated study for purposes of addressing a specific research problem or question posed by management. This means marketing research must be conducted to acquire primary data. Three basic research-based techniques are usually employed to collect primary data:

- Survey Research is the most common form of marketing research. Here, a question-naire or measurement instrument is administered to individuals or groups of individuals for purposes of collecting primary information,
- Observational Research entails the direct monitoring of subjects' behaviors through mechanical or human observation. Hidden cameras, Universal Product Code (UPC) scanners, one-way mirrors, and traffic counting devices are commonly employed observation techniques.

- Experimental Research is conducted under controlled laboratory or field conditions. Laboratory experiments are generally used to investigate relationships between important marketing-related constructs. For example, the effects of color on consumers' perceptions of taste or consumer reactions to alternative package designs might be examined. Field experiments often consist of "test markets." Test markets are structured to examine the effects of marketing activities (e.g. changes in one or more elements of the marketing mix) on some outcome variable of interest. Test market investigations usually relate to the introduction and sales of new or existing products.

→ What Is Marketing Research?

Marketing research is a systemic process used to generate reliable and valid information and transform it into a format that marketing decision makers can use. Defined formally, the activity known as marketing research embodies all the tools, techniques, and resources (human talent and expertise, time, money, etc.) that are needed to obtain (collect), interpret (make sense of), and communicate critical information relevant to planning, implementation, and control of all marketing activities within the Firm.

At its core, marketing research is a highly-structured problem-solving process. Marketing research is based on the scientific method. Use of the scientific method requires researchers to first develop and ask carefully defined research questions. These research questions are often called "hypotheses." In the next step researchers collect the exact information in the right form that is required to answer those research questions. This requires reliable and valid measurements. Finally, researchers conduct the right arithmetic, mathematical, or statistical tests that permit the research questions to be answered.

The scientific method ensures that the research is conducted in an objective, unbiased manner. All marketing conclusions or recommendations that are developed through the scientific method are fact-based and empirically-driven. Facts, as the saying goes, are stubborn things; they are supposed to be accurate and free of bias. Empirical means that mathematical and statistical measurements and tests are involved.

→ The Marketing Research Process

The marketing research process consists of five steps, as shown in Exhibit 6.1.

Step 1: Define the Research Problem

The marketing research process begins with the recognition of a marketing-related problem that itself creates the need for a marketing research project. This problem definition is the first, most crucial step in the marketing research process. A problem well-defined, as the saying goes, is a problem half-solved. The converse is also true. If researchers fail to define the research problem accurately, the information they generate through their research efforts has a near zero-chance of actually solving it.

Researchers must distinguish the symptoms of any problem from its causes. This is true for any problem-driven marketing research that is conducted in any domain. Declines in year-over-year sales would usually represent a symptom of a problem, rather than the problem itself, for any Firm. To begin with, causes of this symptom might include a less motivated sales force. Perhaps the sales force is less motivated because the new reward system for salespeople is deficient in some key way, which may be the problem. In addition, the cause of the sales decline symptom may relate to something a competitor did. In this example, assume the competitor

Exhibit 6.1 *The Steps in the Marketing Research Process.*

successfully introduced a new product that negated our Firm's previous advantage in value delivery. That might prove the real problem. Finally, in this example, a new advertising and branding campaign may have simply fizzled. Promotional failures such as these can create year over year sales declines. Perhaps that's actually the real problem.

All of a sudden there are three unique suspects, possible causes, or problems that created the sales decline symptom. The act of distinguishing symptoms from actual problems is surprisingly simple. Just ask why has this symptom occurred? Then, once a probable cause for a symptom (say, in a new example, a distinct decline in traffic on the Firm's website or Facebook page) is identified, ask why did this happen? Then repeat the process of asking why again and again, as many times as is necessary, until the why question can no longer be answered. At that point the Firm has probably identified the real problem. Please note: Firms would generally have to ask "why" two or three times before they have drilled down to and can thus accurately define the real problem.

During Step 1, researchers should also describe and define exactly what they seek to accomplish through this research project. In other words, they should identify their research objectives. Often they are only dimly aware of what the true problem is at this point and cannot, therefore, correctly or fully articulate the project's research objectives. Again, they may be focusing more on symptoms rather than the true underlying problem.

Due to this quandary, correctly identifying the problem may first also require the execution of a thorough situation analysis (Step 2). The collection of additional preliminary data (usually secondary data) may prove necessary in order to define the problem accurately. This is why these two steps of the marketing research process are often executed concurrently. The situation analysis often contributes to changes in the definition of the research problem or the addition or deletion of research objectives.

Step 2: Execute a Situation Analysis

The situation analysis is intended to familiarize researchers with the general problems as well as opportunities that are confronting the Firm. Existing secondary data are collected pertaining to these problems. This information usually relates to one or more aspects associated with a specific environmental dimension (i.e., technology, the marketplace, competitors, new product opportunities) within which the problem emerged.

Situation analyses should begin with a thorough examination of secondary data. The Internet, libraries, government databases, newspaper archives, and other sources can provide a wealth of information. There is usually no reason to move forward with primary data collection (a survey, for example) until after all readily-available secondary sources have been tapped.

Step 3: Design and Conduct the Investigation

This is the most complex step in the research process. This step features four component parts. The Firm that is conducting marketing research must:

- Decide on the type of data needed (primary and/or secondary).
- Determine how the data are to be collected.
- Identify the sample from which data will be obtained (if appropriate).
- Collect the data based on the selected design.

What Type of Data to Use

Secondary Data

In nearly all cases, secondary data should be collected first. In fact, for some studies, the problem may be addressed successfully by using only secondary sources. Secondary data offer definite advantages. First, such data are almost always less expensive to collect than primary data. Moreover, secondary data can be collected quickly and easily. The Internet is a real boon here. During the last 10 to 12 years researchers have used screened devices to access all data sources that once were only available in brick and mortar facilities or printed copy.

Secondary data does present some disadvantages. Remember, secondary data were collected by another entity at an earlier time. And, generally, secondary data were collected with a different purpose in mind. For these reasons secondary data are often outdated, incomplete, or inaccurate. Marketing researchers must ensure that the data do not present these problems before it is used in decision-making. Problems with the quality of secondary data certainly make the data less useful. In extreme situations, secondary data may prove absolutely worthless.

A wide range of secondary data sources is available. An entire course could be dedicated to their examination. As noted, most formerly traditional sources are now available online. You probably are already familiar with many. A few such sources are examined below, focused primarily on the Internet sources summarized in Table 6.1. This discussion begins with sources available from the Federal government.

The Federal government recently rechristened its main Internet portal from "www.firstgov. gov" to "www.usa.gov" (Exhibit 6.2). This site is the main access point to virtually all publically available government websites. The site is searchable using descriptive key words and phrases. Based on search terms entered, the site provides links to the most relevant databases.

Table 6.1 • *Select Sources of Online Secondary Data*

NAME	URL	DESCRIPTION
USA.gov	www.usa.gov	Portal to all publically available government websites, including those maintained by the SEC, Census Bureau, CIA.
Securities and Exchange Commission	www.sec.gov	The SEC provides a wealth of information on its website, which includes access to the EDGAR database of disclosure documents such as 10Ks and other filings.
US Census Bureau	www.census.gov	Site contains a wide range of census data on the US population, businesses, government agencies. Also provides access to key economic indicators. The site is searchable via usa.gov.
Google	www.google.com	Google has a number of popular search engines for general web searches, searches of academic literature (Google Scholar), image searches, and newspaper searches.
Dunn & Bradstreet Business Reports	www.dnb.com	D&B is a premier source of commercial information and prognostication on businesses and business conditions.
Fuld and Company	www.fuld.com	Compendium of competitive intelligence tools and techniques used by companies worldwide. This site is a must for Firm's interested in staying on top of their competitors.
Hoovers Online	www.hoovers.com	Proprietary information on about 18,500 companies and 600 industries. Furnishes access to additional information on nearly 13 million companies from leading providers such as Dun & Bradstreet.
Proquest	www.proquest.com	A multidisciplinary database that searches all ProQuest databases for which a library has a subscription.
Ebsco Host	www.ebscohost.com	EBSCOhost Provides access to various EBSCO databases which can all be searched simultaneously. Available from most university libraries.
Wall Street Journal Online	http://online.wsj.com/home-page	Extensive data on markets, companies, products, environments, trends. A must for all serious business professionals. Subscription required.

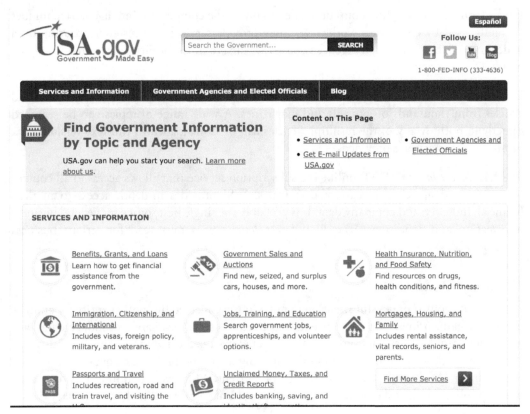

Exhibit 6.2 *Homepage for usa.gov. The primary access point to all Federal government public web sites.*

The Securities and Exchange Commission (www.sec.gov) has an excellent, easily searched website. Probably the most useful component of the SEC site, for our purposes, is the link to the Edgar database. The Edgar database is a repository for most of the financial filings that public companies must submit periodically to the SEC. The SEC site is also searchable via usa.gov.

The US Census Bureau's (www.census.gov) website is loaded with valuable business information. This site provides access to the most current Census of Population, Economic Census of Business, and the Economy, as well as to other census products. Most of the information is free. The site is searchable via usa.gov.

Google's search engines have become a mainstay of business research. Via a number of search engines, Google provides access to many of the same data sources as other, more expensive, electronic sources. In addition to normal web searches, Google offers users the ability to search academic sources (Google Scholar), newspapers (Google News), images, video, and others.

Dun & Bradstreet (D&B) is a premier source of commercial information and projections on businesses and business conditions. Dun & Bradstreet's Business reports (www.dnb.com) are available online. Firms pay a fee to download reports on specific businesses and industries.

Hoover's Online provides proprietary information on over 18,500 companies and 600 industries. It also provides access to select information on 13+ million companies extracted from other providers, such as Dun & Bradstreet. The site provides information download tools that permit users to import data into spreadsheets. Dun & Bradstreet has long been a top-flight source for in-depth analysis of industries, individual Firms, competitors, and customers for decades.

Fuld + Company (www.fuld.com) developed many of the competitive intelligence techniques currently used by companies worldwide. They provide services and resources bearing on a wide range of competitive intelligence issues. This site is a must for Firms interested in staying on top of their competitors.

Proquest and EBSCO Host are portals to a number of databases consisting of abstracts and articles from thousands of journals and magazines. A wide range of topics can be searched directly in both. Many of the resulting articles can be downloaded in full-text version. As a minimum, abstracts are provided.

The *Wall Street Journal* (WSJ) online is a subscription service that allows access to all content in current and up to four years of past issues. WSJ provides in-depth access to market, financial, industry, and company data. It is probably the single best source for general business information and conditions. The *Wall Street Journal* is a must-read for serious business professionals.

Primary Data

Primary data consist of new information not previously collected by another entity for another purpose. Again, primary data are generally collected after all available secondary data have been exhausted. Primary data typically are collected via a dedicated marketing research study that has been developed for purposes of addressing a specific problem or question posed by management. As a result, the data tend to be current. Moreover, assuming the data were properly collected, they should be more focused, accurate, and reliable than secondary data.

Primary data also feature some obvious drawbacks. First, the data are generally much more expensive to acquire. The Firm must either engage a research Firm to collect the data or design and conduct its own data collection study. Most Firms of even middling size do not possess this capability in-house. Second, primary data will require much more time to collect. Most secondary data can be accessed within minutes or hours, given today's electronic sources. By contrast, primary data collection requires formal planning and the subsequent development of a research project; the design and testing of data collection instruments; the allocation of careful attention to ensure that unbiased data are collected from an appropriately selected sample; and meticulous data analysis. These steps are universally time-consuming; sufficiently complicated as to require high levels of specialized professional expertise; and, generally, prove quite expensive.

Determine Data Collection Methods

The next series of steps assumes that any secondary data collected have been gauged insufficient for the task of fully addressing the research question. Consequently, the decision has been made to collect primary data. Three basic techniques are available to collect primary data: observation, survey, and experimentation.

Observational Research

Observational research entails employing trained observers and/or technology to directly observe subject behaviors. Examples of observational research in action include:

- AC Nielsen is a consumer research Firm that specializes in assessing the sizes, characteristics, and viewing habits of TV audiences. Nielsen utilizes observational research for these purposes. Specifically, Nielsen's "people meter" is a digital receiver that attaches to your television. It is equipped with a microprocessor that records who is watching which shows at specific times of day. Technological advances now permit Nielsen to measure audience viewing of online media, such as Netflix and Amazon. com Prime.[2]

- The psycho-galvanometer is essentially a "lie detector." The device monitors subjects' physiological changes. These include changes in heart rate, respiration rate, blood pressure, and galvanic skin response. In consumer research, psycho-galvanometers are used to record consumers' physiological responses when exposed to various marketing stimuli, such as advertisements, new products, and package designs. As such, traditional stimulus-response data are collected through a contemporary device. The assumption is that if and when marketing stimuli arouse (stimulate) consumer emotions, the state of arousal will be recorded on the psycho galvanometer.

- Pupil dilation response (PDR) measurement is similar in function and purpose to the psycho-galvanometer. The PDR measures the amount of pupil dilation that occurs when subjects are exposed to a marketing stimulus (Exhibit 6.3). The underlying premise is that emotional responses triggered as a result of controlled exposure to marketing stimuli (ads, packages, brands, pricing level, new products, spokespeople, etc.) will cause the subject's pupils to dilate. The greater the emotional response, the greater the dilatation.

- The eye movement recorder (EMR), restricted to use in laboratory settings, is a complex and cumbersome piece of equipment that directs a beam of light on the subject's pupil. This light, in turn, is reflected onto anything that is visually scanned by the subject. Eye movement recorders are useful for pretesting different forms of advertising. This technology is especially useful for testing outdoor ads or billboards. This older technology is rapidly being replaced by modern digital projection technologies that introduce more realism into the data collection scenarios. For example,

Eye: © Johanna Goodyear/Shutterstock.com;
Ice cream: © Joao Virissimo/Shutterstock.com

Exhibit 6.3 *The PDR assesses emotional responses to stimuli by measuring corresponding changes to pupil size when exposed to the stimuli.*

Kimberly-Clark has developed a "virtual reality" shopping aisle that mimics exactly what consumers see when shopping in real store environments. The technology allows Kimberley-Clark to quickly and inexpensively test consumers' responses to new products, shelf-space allocation, displays, package designs, price changes, and other product and promotion modifications. Such technologies are proving to be excellent alternatives to traditional test markets.[3]

Additional examples of tools that can be employed for observation research include simple traffic flow counters, in-store video cameras, and mechanical turnstile counters. Internet-based observational techniques include counting visits to websites and tracking click-through rates for online advertisements. Internet cookies are placed on users' computers by advertisers when the advertisers' websites are visited. Cookies record visitors' activities as they connect with given sites. Cookies track pages that are open, time spent on pages, links to other websites, and product purchases made through the site. This technology permits Firms such as Amazon to remember your searches and past purchases in order to offer suggestions for additional products that may interest you. Cookies have been around since 1994. While they're still used extensively, cookies are being supplemented and supplanted by web beacons, flash cookies, history sniffing, and device fingerprinting:[4]

- Web beacons, also referred to as "Web bugs" and "pixels," are small programs embedded in visited web pages. Beacons can track users' activities, including mouse movements and keystroke information, on the infected page. Like cookies, beacons are employed to track movements from page to page on the same or different sites. In the process, user profiles and actionable consumer insights are generated;
- Flash cookies were originally intended to record and save users' flash video playback preferences. More recently, flash cookies are used to surreptitiously re-install regular cookies deleted by users. This type of software effectively evades users' attempts to avoid online tracking;
- History sniffing software records the visited sites identified in the user's browser history. History sniffing code is embedded in ads displayed on web pages users visit. This type of code cannot be deleted by removing cookies;
- Device fingerprinting is the newest and most controversial tracking technology. Every computer, when online, communicates hundreds of details unique to that computer, differentiating it from other computers to which it connects. The unique device information captured includes such things as user preference settings, software configurations, clock settings, screen fonts, etc. Companies use this data to individually identify a computer and then track and profile its users.[5] Scary stuff?

Advantages of observational research

Simple and not-so-simple observation is a marketing research tool that boasts several distinct advantages. First, observation permits recording of what it is that people actually do; marketers are viewing and recording actual behaviors. There is no reliance on what people say they did, or say they will do. People are less likely to "lie" with their behaviors, particularly when they are not aware that they are being observed. Second, observational research often employs mechanical devices to do the observing. This eliminates a great deal of subjectivity from the observation process. The research process permits large amounts of information to be gathered relatively quickly. A good example is the Universal Product Code (UPC) scanner in a grocery store (Exhibit 6.4). As you proceed through the checkout stand, each individual item is scanned for its UPC code (bar code). The scanned information is saved in a database

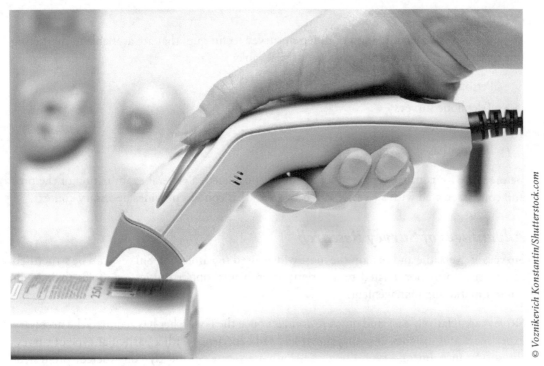

Exhibit 6.4 *The UPC scanner pulls bar code information from packages to track product and brand sales.*

for later analysis. UPC scanners are also employed to collect information about individual consumers' purchasing behaviors. Consumers who participate in consumer-buying panels are given a credit card that contains a personal ID. The ID is keyed to demographic and other information maintained by the marketing research Firm. The information on this card is scanned and recorded along with the UPC data from the products they have purchased. By correlating the UPC product data with the information about the customer that is already on file, marketers learn a great deal about consumer purchase patterns.

Disadvantages of Observational Research

The most serious disadvantage associated with observational research is that, while marketers record what consumers actually did, they generally do not gain insight into why they did it. Understanding why consumers behave the way they do requires an examination of their motives, beliefs, attitudes, and other perceptions. This usually means supplementing observation tools with one or more types of survey-based assessment. With surveys, marketers specifically ask consumers what they think about products and brands. Marketers ask consumers "why they did what they did." Consumers will not always tell the truth (most do, however), but at least they have been asked. A second limitation associated with observational research is some behaviors are not subject to observation. Some consumption behaviors are accomplished in private or in locations where observation techniques cannot be employed. Truly, however, "no one knows what goes on behind closed doors," as Charlie Rich once sang. A third potentially serious drawback centers on the ethics (and legality) involved with using observational techniques. When marketers use devices such as one-way mirrors and hidden cameras to record consumers' behaviors, they run the risk of being charged with unethical or even illegal practices. This is especially true when consumers are not aware they are being observed.

Survey Methods

What follows is an examination of different survey techniques that are available to marketing researchers. Four survey types are generally available:

- Personal (face-to-face) interviews
- Telephone surveys
- Mail surveys
- Internet-based surveys

Before these four survey types are individually considered, a general examination of the pros and cons associated with survey research follows. This content provides necessary context.

Advantages of Survey Research

Surveys are versatile and remain the most widely used research tool. Surveys can be structured to collect information related to a variety of problems, opportunities, or topics that might interest marketing management.

Surveys are relatively easy and quick to conduct once the researcher has acquired the necessary experiences and insights. If management has had experience with a particular type of survey, the survey instrument—typically a questionnaire—can be quickly constructed, pre-tested, and administered, particularly if delivered over the Internet.

Surveys are still the best way to acquire information that yields directly explanatory insight related to the question of why people behave the way they do. Surveys remain the best approach when researchers seek insights about consumers' motives for engaging in certain marketplace behaviors.

Disadvantages of Survey Research

The success of survey research depends heavily upon the primary researcher's skills. A high degree of expertise and experience is required to design and implement a quality survey. Because a typical survey yields large amounts of information, it may be very difficult for managers to pick out the most important information from the mass of data that have been collected and reported.

Surveys are susceptible to sampling error. Generally this is means that the sample is too small or for some other reason is not truly representative of the population from which it is drawn. In either case, the results of the survey generally cannot be generalized back to the population of interest. Essentially, this means that the survey's results are of little value to decision makers.

Improperly developed or administered surveys are subject to systematic errors or biases that arise because something was done incorrectly during the survey process. The wrong questions may have been asked; questions may have been asked in the wrong order; questions may be worded incorrectly. Consequently, consumers who respond to the survey interpret the question as meaning something different than what was intended.

When conducting surveys, interviewers sometimes may say or do something that changes how subjects answer questions. Instead of simply telling the truth, for example, respondents may respond in the way that they believe the marketing researcher wants them to respond. Respondents are trying to be nice, or to please the market researcher, but are actually absolutely confounding the results. Researchers often must disguise their true intentions and should rarely if ever reveal their true feelings about the problem or topic being investigated.

Personal Interviews

Personal interviews are the most flexible survey tools available to researchers. Subjects can be more easily presented with a range of stimuli to which they can be asked to respond. This task is more difficult to accomplish when other survey forms are used. Moreover, researchers can probe subjects further when something interesting, unexpected, or unclear pops up as those subjects respond to the interviewer's questions. The answers provided by subjects are often incomplete. The opportunity to secure additional clarification offers a huge advantage to marketing researchers. Three types of personal interview are examined: focus groups, mall intercepts, and in-depth interviews.

Focus Groups

In a typical focus group, 8 to 12 individuals are recruited and brought into a specially equipped room. The marketing researcher acts as a moderator who "focuses" the group's attention on a specific problem or question. The group session is typically observed through a one-way window and recorded (Exhibit 6.5). Recordings are then content-analyzed on essentially a word-by-word, movement-by-movement (i.e., body language or facial expression) basis. Focus groups yield valuable marketing research insights for various reasons. The most important reason, however, is because 8 to 12 carefully moderated people discussing a problem will generate more and better insights than almost any individual ever would when interviewed in a one-on-one context. Comments made by one person generally stimulate additional thoughts and ideas by others in the group. The major strength of the focus group is the richness of this interaction process. The danger exists, however, that one personality may dominate the entire group. If the moderator permits this to happen, individuals with less assertive personalities may withdraw. As a result, the value of the resulting insights may be degraded.

Courtesy Prairie Research Associates, Inc.

Exhibit 6.5 *Focus group sessions are normally monitored and recorded.*

Focus groups are normally used for exploratory research. The number of individuals in the focus group is generally quite small. This makes it riskier to generalize results from focus group research to larger populations of individuals. Consequently, focus groups are typically used to formulate hypotheses or ideas that are tested in studies that use larger samples of subjects in combination with other survey techniques.

Focus groups are now sometimes conducted online. Online focus groups are less expensive, quicker to execute start to finish, and flexible. Respondents and moderators can log-in and participate from virtually anywhere. Online focus group formats generally entail real-time virtual focus group chat rooms where between six and eight respondents participate simultaneously or asynchronously (i.e., people engaged with the focus questions at different times). Up to 20 respondents can interact on these online bulletin boards over a period of days.

Changes are required when conducting online focus groups. Some simpler, traditional focus group techniques (e.g. sentence completion, memory dumps, brand name recall) can be easily adapted for use in online settings. More complicated focus group activities such as brainstorming, picture sorting, mind-mapping, and controlled sensory tests are limited by the current online technology and require substantial rethinking.[6]

Mall Intercepts

The mall intercept was once a very popular face-to-face survey tool. Many of you have participated in mall intercepts at one time or another. You may recall a person holding a clipboard positioned at a high traffic location in the shopping mall. As you walked by, the researcher may have singled you out from others in the crowd. This is because you appeared to match a "subject profile" used for the specific study at hand. You were then asked a few questions on the spot, or asked to come into the research Firm's office spaces for a more private, and focused interview. Mall intercepts are also employed to recruit subjects for focus group participation. The mall intercept is used to identify candidates and set appointments for the times and locations of the focus groups.

Mall intercepts have become commonplace to the point that many consumers refuse to be interviewed. Consumers actually actively avoid mall locations where the interviewers are stationed. This growing practice calls into question the validity of results emerging from mall intercepts. Because so many people are self-selecting themselves out of the sample, the respondents upon whom the results and conclusions are based may not be representative of the population that was intended for the study.

In-Depth Interviews

In contrast to focus groups in which a number of people are simultaneously interviewed, in-depth interviews are conducted with one person at a time. In-depth interviews can be lengthy. They may require two or more hours to complete. They are surprisingly similar to open-ended, free-ranging conversations.

The purpose of the in-depth interview is to get individuals to reveal as much as possible about how they really feel and to uncover their unconscious thoughts and feelings on the topic of interest. Researchers typically ask probing questions designed to focus the subject's response, which, in turn, often suggests additional questions that can be asked. This cycle is repeated until the researcher is confident that the individual has exhausted his or her thoughts and ideas on the topic.

The total number of people who can be surveyed using in-depth interviews is generally smaller than for focus groups. As was true of focus groups, the insights that are gained through in-depth interviews typically cannot be generalized back to the larger populations from which subjects are sampled. This limitation is the primary reasons why in-depth interviews are normally used during exploratory research.

Mail Surveys

Most readers have participated in mail surveys. When a survey arrives in the mail, if you are interested enough to open the envelope, you may succumb to inertia and actually complete the questionnaire. A self-addressed, stamped envelope is usually included to increase the response-rate for the survey.

The most serious problem associated with mail surveys is their low response rates. Most people view mail surveys as junk mail. When it's obvious a piece of mail is a survey, recipients rarely bother to open the letter. It is immediately tossed. Because of this tendency, various tricks are used to get people to open the mail. Disguising the letter as a check and personally addressing envelopes rather than using mailing labels are just two, among many, techniques used to encourage respondents to at least open the mail.

Of course, getting someone to open the mail is only the first step. Once envelopes are opened, other techniques are used to incentivize respondents to complete the instrument and mail it back. The techniques used to motivate consumers to complete this process include:

- Free gifts included with the letter.
- A promise of a free gift upon completion and return of the survey.
- Phone calls placed ahead of time to respondents informing them of the survey's arrival and requesting that they fill it out and return it.
- A repeat mailing after a period of time if the questionnaire has not been returned by the respondent.
- Making the questionnaire interesting enough so that the individual wants to fill it out and return it.

Response rates may be boosted substantially through use of these techniques. Response rates are often as low as 5 to 10% for initial mail-outs. Judicious use of these techniques can increase response rates into the 20 to 30% range.

The task of finding accurate mailing lists of potential respondents who precisely fit the demographic or psychographic requirements of a study can prove difficult. However, the task has become somewhat easier because of the advent of mailing list brokers. Brokers compile lists from numerous sources and resell them to businesses and marketing research Firms.

Finally, there is a high probability that a significant number of respondents will misinterpret the meaning of the questions contained in the survey. When surveys are used, there is no interviewer present to clarify respondent questions. Consequently, the prospect that respondents will answer the question from a different perspective than was intended is always present. Researchers must be meticulous as they word questions on the mail surveys. Pre-testing the instrument to ensure that each question measures the exact content and only the exact content that it purports to measure is always a good idea.

But the mail survey process is not all-problems-all-the-time. There are distinct advantages associated with the use of mail surveys; otherwise they would not be used. The greatest advantage of mail surveys is probably their relatively low cost. Other than Internet surveys, mail surveys are the least expensive data collection tool available to researchers. Costs are generally limited to the cost of reproducing the questionnaire and conducting the mailing.

Mail surveys also ensure the relative anonymity of respondents. Unless questionnaires have been coded, respondents' names and addresses are not associated with their responses. This anonymity usually increases the truthfulness with which questions are answered. In addition, because an interviewer does not administer the survey, there is no risk of interviewer bias.

Telephone Surveys

Telephone surveys are fast and easy to conduct. Trained interviewers can quickly contact large numbers of people. Speed is enhanced by using computers to dial and/or make initial contact. Once the computer detects an answer to the call, a human interviewer takes over and conducts the interview.

Telephone surveys can be timely. Telephone calls can be made to a sample of potential respondents immediately following some marketing event of interest. Assume, for example, that a Firm tests the recall (i.e., do people exposed to an ad remember it?) of an advertisement that recently aired on a particular television show. To determine whether or not that commercial was seen and what was recalled, the airing could be followed with a series of phone calls to a selected sample of respondents. Telephone surveys are relatively inexpensive. While they cost more than Internet or mailings, they are by less expensive than door-to-door and other types of face-to-face interviews.

There are disadvantages to the use of telephone surveys. Two obvious limitations are their low response rates and the associated declining levels of respondent cooperation. Consumers are fed-up with telemarketing activities in general. As a result, when asked to participate in a phone survey, consumers often refuse to cooperate.

Like face-to-face interviews, telephone surveys are susceptible to the effects of interviewer bias. Interviewer bias arises when interviewers say or do something that changes how respondents answer particular questions. The threat of interviewer bias can be controlled to some degree by good training and supervisory practices. But it can never be completely eliminated. Consumers also are less likely to share confidential, sensitive, personal information over the phone

Finally, and most importantly, the nature of phone service has changed dramatically in the last decade. First, many phone numbers are unlisted, making it nearly impossible to contact all individuals in the sampling frame. Random digit dialing, in which a computer dials phone numbers at random and waits for a response, offers a partial solution to this problem. Second, many consumers have turned to mobile phones as their primary communications medium. Indeed, many homes no longer maintain landline connections.

Internet Surveys

Internet surveys are rapidly replacing mail and telephone surveys. This should not surprise as this approach offers material advantages over each traditional approach while also doing a better job of reaching younger demographics that marketers otherwise find difficult to capture. Online surveys are easy to create and can be administered quickly via email or on the Firm's website. Hundreds, if not thousands, of consumers can be inexpensively reached. Often the only cost is paying someone to develop the survey, post it to the Internet, and compile the results. Each subject's responses are automatically coded and stored, usually in formats that can be analyzed immediately. The three primary online survey applications are Qualtrics (www.qualtrics.com), Survey Monkey (www.surveymonkey.com), and Zoomerang (www.zoomerang.com).

Experiments

Marketing research experiments can be conducted in laboratory or field settings. Field experiments, which marketers more commonly call test markets, are used far more frequently. Marketing researchers can design experiments that permit them to establish "cause and effect" relationships between variables. Typically, researchers manipulate one or more variables. Here, the word "manipulate" means that marketing researchers make systematic changes to these variables. Then researchers can monitor the impact or effects of these manipulations (changes) on other variables. The variables being manipulated are called "independent variables." The variables that are affected or impacted are called "dependent variables."

Laboratory-Based Experiments

The following example illustrates the essence of a laboratory experiment. It is drawn from research that was conducted about subliminal perception. The word "subliminal" means "below the threshold of perception." Subliminal perception means "perception without realization." When consumers perceive at a subliminal level, they are exposed to a stimulus, but are not aware that that they have been exposed. Original theory suggested, however, that the stimulus still has an impact on our mental state and thus possibly on our behavior.

Research on subliminal perception began during the 1950s with James Vicary's classic experiment in a New Jersey movie theater. Moviegoers were repeatedly exposed to subliminal suggestions that were embedded in the film that was shown. The messages "eat popcorn" and "drink coke" were spliced directly into the film. Subjects were exposed once every five seconds to the messages for 1/3,000 of a second each.

Each message occupied only a single frame in the film. But each message was repeated over and over again for the duration of the film. Each message passed so quickly that subjects were not aware they had been exposed. The theoretical assumption, however, was that each consumer would subconsciously become aware of the message. This subconscious awareness, in turn, would trigger a change in subjects' mental states and impact their actual consumption behaviors.

The film was shown to more than 45,000 consumers during a six-week period. Vicary claimed that over the course of the study, sales of Coke rose by 18% and sales for popcorn increased nearly 60%. However, no documentation of the results was provided.[7]

Vicary apparently showed the same film, which featured the same subliminal suggestions, to everyone in the sample. Thus the question, what would have happened to Coke and popcorn sales if no subliminal suggestions were provided, could not be answered. Would sales have been different? No one would ever know because the experiment's design was flawed. There was no "control" group against which his "experimental" group could be compared. The explanatory and predictive ability of the experiment would have improved had a second "control" group of subjects been added. Moreover, if subjects were randomly assigned to each group, a foundation for a more valid experiment would be present.

Here's how this would happen. The experimental group would be exposed to a film containing subliminal messages. The control group would be exposed to the same film absent any subliminal suggestions. The control group film instead would contain blank frames where the subliminal messages should have been located.

Conditions between the experimental and control groups would now be identical, with the obvious exception of the subliminal messages. After the film, subjects in each group could be offered their choice of soft drink. If experimental group subjects choose Coke significantly more often than the control group subjects, an authoritative claim that the subliminal suggestions influenced soft drink consumption behavior could be made.

What results do think such a study would yield? Do you think that subliminal suggestions like this can actually work? Studies similar to the one just described have been conducted with few conclusive results. No evidence currently exists that subliminal suggestions have any impact on consumption behavior.[8]

This is the essence of an experiment. A well-designed experiment gives researchers the ability to control conditions. The only variable that differs is the one whose effect is being tested between the "experimental" and the "control" conditions. In the "experimental" condition, the subliminal message would be included in the film. No subliminal condition would be included in the film in the "control" condition. This presence of the control permits researchers to establish cause and effect relationships between variables in the experiment. Specific cause and effect relationships can be isolated only by ruling out competing causes. Experiments offer the ability to directly observe and measure actual consumption-related behavior.

Experiments have their downsides. Well-designed and executed experiments are time-consuming. They require a great deal of experimenter expertise; consequently, experiments are quite expensive. These drawbacks are particularly true for test market experiments.

Another potential problem arises when laboratory experiments are conducted. Because laboratory experiments conditions are so controlled, they often lack real-world realism. This deficiency makes findings difficult to generalize to other populations, contexts, or times. Realism can be introduced to experiments by taking them into the field. Test market experiments typically have more "external validity." But, at the same time, because they are conducted in the field, it is not always possible to isolate the effects of just the variables we want to investigate. "Competing causes" for the effects that were observed can never be completely ruled out.

Common laboratory-based marketing experiments include:

- Blind taste tests in which, say, different brands of soft drink are compared.
- Package tests in which, say, alternative package designs are compared in terms of their ability to stimulate brand recall.
- Advertising copy tests in which alternative advertising designs, such as billboard designs, are compared for their attention-getting abilities.

Test Markets as Experiments

As noted, because they are conducted in the field, test markets will not provide the degree of control obtained by experiments conducted in a laboratory setting. Consequently, the results of test market experiments must be interpreted cautiously. But test market experiments generally provide greater "external validity" than laboratory experiments. Because test markets are conducted under more realistic market conditions, the results usually can be generalized to other real world settings. A Firm, for example, may conduct test markets in several cities for purposes of projecting expected sales for a newly introduced product. If the test market results are favorable and the test cities are representative of the general target market, the Firm could anticipate similar sales levels throughout the entire market.

There are several types of test markets. They vary in complexity and relative cost. The standard test market is the most expensive. Standard test markets are normally used to forecast sales of new products. A series of test cities are selected that are presumed to be representative of the entire market area to which the product will eventually be commercialized. The product is then introduced into these test cities and marketed just as if the product were being commercialized throughout the entire market. In other words, the product is priced, promoted, and distributed exactly as if it were being fully commercialized.

Let's examine an actual standard test market that was conducted in Colorado and adjacent states during the early 1980s for a new cigarette brand—Eli Cutter. The first ad in the series was ambiguous. It was intended only to grab the readers' attention and tweak their curiosity, containing, as it did, a photo of a scruffy-looking cowboy smoking a cigarette. The headline said "Eli's Coming." At the bottom was the caption "The Man The Legend."

This test market was conducted in multiple cities that were representative of the commercial area in which the new product eventually would be marketed. If the test cities are selected correctly and the test market is conducted properly, the results can be reliably extrapolated (or generalized) to the entire commercial area. Sales results, then, could reasonably be expected to be similar throughout the entire market.

Follow-on advertisements were used to create the Eli Cutter image. These advertisements appeared in multiple media such as newspapers, magazines, and billboards. These follow-on advertisements developed the Eli Cutter story. Each featured the same scruffy cowboy. This tactic provided a constant frame of reference across ads and media. By telling the "Eli Cutter story," these advertisements were developing the brand's position. The advertisements were intended to create an image of Eli Cutter relative to other cigarette brands.

The controlled test market is a scaled-down version of the standard test market. Controlled test market experiments focus on investigating marketing effects that are generated when one or more elements of the marketing mix are strategically changed. Controlled test markets are less expensive and shorter in duration than standard test markets. Controlled test market experiments can be conducted across cities, within individual cities at different locations, or in a single location (e.g. individual retail stores) over a period of time. This latest version is called a "mini-market test."

A classic controlled test market was conducted some years ago to evaluate the effectiveness with which outdoor advertising (billboards) stimulated increased brand awareness. The brand, in this case, was the then current Miss America, Shirley Cothran. The test was conducted for 60 days in 11 market areas on 100 billboards (Exhibit 6.6). The results were startling. Before the study began, only 1.6% of the population knew the actual name of Miss America. By the time it ended, brand, or here name, awareness had increased to over 16%.ix Typical applications of controlled test markets usually involve investigations of the sales effects induced by changes in prices changes, packaging designs, or promotional mix programs.

Mini-market tests are usually conducted inside retail stores in a limited geographic area. Sometimes they are executed within a single retail location. As a result, the mini-market test is much less expensive and less time consuming than larger scale controlled or standard test market experiments. Mini-market tests are usually employed to test the effectiveness of in-store conditions on sales at the retail level. However, marketing research Firms often manipulate the effects of advertising campaigns as they are released through television, radio, print media, or Internet media.

Large marketing research Firms often specialize in the execution of mini-market tests. Such Firms typically arrange for a panel of stores in the relevant market to cooperate in the test. Stores agree to provide specific shelf locations, shelf space, shelf facings, point of purchase displays, and other promotional materials. Stores also agree to raise or lower prices in accord with the research plan. Sales results, which by definition will rise or fall, are usually monitored by scanning UPC codes as consumers complete their transactions.

Then in January 1975, this poster went up and within two months <u>one of every six adults</u> polled knew her name.

Shirley Cothran
Miss America 1975

Exhibit 6.6 *A classic study in brand awareness conducted as a controlled test market in 1975.*

The simulated test market is the quickest and least expensive to execute. (Note the perpetual relationship between research time-spent and research costs-paid.) Simulated test markets are generally accomplished in laboratory rather than field settings. Like controlled test markets, simulated test markets are often used to identify the effects of changes in one or more marketing mix element on sales of existing products. Simulated test markets are also useful when developing estimates of trial and repurchase rates for new products without resorting to the expense of a standard test market.

Subjects for simulated test markets are usually recruited through a process in which they answer various screening questions. When their responses are deemed acceptable, subjects are invited to visit a mock retail store (a laboratory setting). This is where the investigation is conducted. Test subjects are given "cash" and an opportunity to select from among various products arrayed on store shelves. The test, or experimental, product is always one of the product alternatives. Sales for the test product and competing brands are monitored during subjects' visits to the mock retail store. These "mock sales" provide a measure of how effective changes in the marketing program may be for stimulating actual sales.

Identifying the Proper Sampling Procedure

Marketing researchers rarely conduct studies on the entire population of interest.[10] To do so would prove too expensive and time consuming. Instead, researchers do the next best thing. They select a small, but representative, sample from the population of interest. The actual study is then conducted on that sample. Then, based on the results, the sample findings are generalized to the population as a whole. Sample selection is, as you might imagine, a very important decision.

Major Sampling Questions

Three basic questions must be addressed when selecting the sample for any marketing research endeavor:

- Who will be sampled?
- How many people will the sample include?
- How should the sample be selected?

Each question is discussed in detail below.

Who Will Be Sampled

This first question involves identifying the relevant population from which the sample will be selected. The relevant population of interest, also called the sampling frame[11], is a function of the specific research problem under investigation. The research objectives that are selected for and consequently drive the marketing research effort will generally define the scope of the population.

A university, for example, may want to survey the attitudes of individuals who use its automatic course registration system. In this case, the relevant sample frame is existing and potential users of that system. This most likely translates into defining the population as the existing student body at the university. Or consider, for example, a research firm that has been commissioned to investigate how a health club's potential market can be segmented. The relevant population is all existing and potential users of all types of health clubs in that area.

How Many Respondents Should Be in the Sample?

This question addresses the required size of the sample. In reality, samples do not have to be overly large. Smaller, but carefully selected and highly representative samples can certainly provide useful information that is generalizable to the entire population of interest. Various statistical tools exist that tell researchers how large specific samples must be in order for them to provide sufficient levels of statistical confidence that the results truly represent the population. These tools are complicated; so much so that a meaningful discussion of the tools and their statistical properties exist beyond the scope of this book. They are the subject of statistics and other analytical courses.

How Should Samples Be Selected?

The third question addresses how the sample should be selected. The answer is that "it depends" on the purpose of the study. There are two basic types of samples: probability samples and non-probability samples.

Probability Samples.

A probability sample is one in which every member of a population has a known, non-zero probability of being selected. The most common type of probability sample is the simple random sample. When simple random samples are developed, every individual in the population is equally likely to be included in the sample. For example, if there are 1,000 people in a population, each individual has a probability of 1 in 1,000 of being included in the sample.

Probability samples are usually the most desirable from a marketing research perspective. This is because probability samples offer a sound statistical and logical rationale for generalizing findings back to the population from which the sample was drawn. Because each individual included in the sample was selected at random, one can safely assume that the sample is, on average, representative of the population. The sample is representative because every individual in the population had an equally likely chance of being included in the sample.

Stratified random sampling is a form of probability sample in which the population is initially divided into levels. These levels are referred to as strata. A simple random sample is drawn from each stratum. Assume, for example, that a market researcher's goal is to measure income across different occupational categories. Further assume it is important to ensure that every occupational category is represented in the sample. Because some occupational categories may be small in size compared to others, a simple random sample, by sheer chance, might underrepresent or fail to represent some categories. An alternative approach would entail first dividing the population into strata defined by occupational category. Then the marketing researcher could randomly sample from each category (stratum) in proportion to the size of each respective category represented in the defined population.

Cluster (or area) samples are similar to stratified random samples from the standpoint that the population is first divided into groups. However, rather than then randomly sampling within each group, a sample of the groups is selected instead. Then, for those groups selected, marketing researchers either conduct a census on each group or draw a simple random sample from each group. The former technique is sometimes referred to as single-stage cluster sampling. The latter is referred to as multi-stage cluster sampling. A simple example illustrates the single-stage cluster sampling process. Consider a market research project intended to assess consumer reactions to a new brand of mouthwash. The study is conducted in Dallas, Texas. To select the single-stage cluster sample, the city of Dallas is first divided into residential city blocks. Then, a number of city blocks are randomly selected. All consumers in these city blocks are provided with a sample of the new mouthwash on a trial basis. If the researcher sampled a total of 20 city blocks and each city block, on average, had 30 households, the total sample would be 20 x 30, or 600, households. All 600 households will receive the product.

Cluster sampling is often used when it is difficult to identify all individuals in a relevant population. In the mouthwash study example, it was easier to identify city blocks at random on a map of Dallas than it was to identify all individuals that live in the area from phone books or other sources. This specific sampling procedure also tends to be less expensive.

Non-Probability Samples

Non-probability samples are less desirable from a marketing research perspective because there is no statistical basis for predicting the odds with which any given member of a population will be included in the sample. Consequently, researchers cannot count on the sample being representative of any specific population. Thus the results from studies based on such samples cannot be generalized beyond the sample itself. Non-probability samples, therefore, tend to be employed more for less formal exploratory research, rather than applied or primary research. Let's reconsider, for example, our survey of attitudes about the web-based registration system at your university. Rather than selecting a random sample from the entire student body, assume we survey just the students in one section of a basic marketing course. Clearly, these students are not representative of the university's entire student body. Marketing students are predominately business majors at the junior and senior levels and many possessing conservative views. The attitudes of these individuals may be substantially different than those of students at the university as a whole.

This example illustrates one flaw associated with using a convenience sample, which is selected for the "convenience" of the researcher. The decision to employ a convenience sample is often a function of the purpose of the study, the accessibility of individuals in the population, budgets, and time. Convenience samples are often employed for exploratory research in the early stages of more formal projects. Convenience samples are acceptable for this purpose because they will be followed with additional research that employs better sampling methods. When time is short and/or budgets are inadequate to pay for more elaborate sampling methods, the convenience sample may be the only option. Similarly, the population targeted by the study may be too scattered, ill-defined, or otherwise inaccessible. Marketing researchers, at times, may have to use anyone that is available.

Questionnaire Design Considerations

The next step is data collection. The major tasks in the data collection process are designing and administering the data collection instrument. Usually, the instrument is a questionnaire that is either self-administered (a mail or Internet-based survey) or administered by marketing researchers in face-to-face settings. Several critical issues must be considered and addressed while designing the data collection instrument. The more important considerations include:

Construct Validity of Items

Construct validity is the degree to which the variables employed in a study truly measure—or capture—the content that they are intended to measure. For example, questionnaires are generally employed to assess people's beliefs and attitudes about a wide range of topics. A major consideration is whether the questions used accurately reflect these beliefs and attitudes. The wrong wording or inappropriate context for the question may cause it to be interpreted much differently than was intended. If the question is misinterpreted, any information that it produces becomes worthless as a measure of the real construct of interest.

Assume a marketing researcher has the goal of assessing your parents' annual income as part of a survey that examines the factors that influenced your choice of college. However, the researcher administers the questionnaire to you. Remember, the researcher is interested in your parents' actual income as a construct (variable) that may influence your final choice of which college to attend. How likely is it that you can or will accurately assess your parents' annual income in a survey context? The odds are poor. This questionnaire item probably lacks construct validity. This item is unlikely to accurately capture the information actually sought by the researcher.

The wording of questions exercises a dramatic effect on their construct validity. In general, how questions are worded determines the meaning that subjects attach to those questions. Improper wording leads to miscomprehension and can severely bias study results. Individual questions must be examined carefully to ensure that their wording does not mislead, confuse, or overly agitate respondents. Some "do's":

- Wording must be consistent with subjects' level of educational attainment. Never talk over their heads! And remember, the average textbook, including this one, is written at an eighth grade reading comprehension level. Never use a 25 cent word when a 5 cent word would work just as well.
- Wording must reflect cultural, subculture, and ethnic differences.

Format and Scaling of Individual Questions

Survey questions can be asked through a number of different formats. Some formats are more appropriate than others. The appropriateness of any format depends on the type of information sought, the character of the sample used, and the manner in which resulting data will be analyzed. Questions can be divided into two broad types: closed-end and open-end.

Closed-end questions force respondents to select from a pre-determined set of responses. Think of multiple choice questions on an examination. Closed-end questions are easier to code, tabulate, and analyze statistically. As a result, closed-end questions are the questions of choice for most marketing researchers. Numerous formats are available. Those that are used most frequently are shown in Exhibit 6.7.

Open-end questions prompt subjects to respond in their own words. Because these questions allow respondents to voice their own feelings, they produce richer and more revealing responses. But open-ended data are far more difficult to code and analyze. Examples of open-ended questions include word association, sentence completion, story completion, and picture completion exercises. In each example, subjects are given a word, statement, beginning to a story, or a picture and then are asked to add to (write about) what they see. Results then are content analyzed to uncover the underlying motivation or meaning of the responses. Open-ended questions also can be completely open-ended in nature. For example, "How do you feel about how President Obama handled the economy during the first six years of his Presidency?" Or, "What do you think about the fact that Nike has sometimes used suppliers that employ child labor in the production of its shoes?"

Order of Questions, Questionnaire Length, and Instructions

Questionnaires that are too long tend to go unfinished. Subjects get bored or lost in the jumble of questions. Keep questionnaires simple, to the point, and as short as possible. Questions themselves should be sequenced in a manner that walks the subject through a logical progression. Instruments should begin with more general questions. More specific, harder, more personal questions should be placed at or near the end. Instructions that are clearly worded, brief, and that contain examples help subjects move from one section of the questionnaire to the next.

Multiple Choice Scale	Two or more possible choices in which subject selects one or more from list	What is your approximate annual income? [ ] < $10,000 [ ] $10,000 - $20,000 [ ] $20,000 - $40,000 [ ] $40,000 - $60,000 [ ] > $60,000
Rating Scale	Beliefs, attitudes measured as "good" to "bad", "excellent" to "terrible", etc.	My overall impression of this course is: Excellent / Very Good / Good / Fair / Poor □ □ □ □ □
Likert Scale	Beliefs, attitudes measured based extent to which subject agrees or disagrees with items.	My overall impression of this course is EXCELLENT! Strongly Disagree 1 2 3 4 5 Strongly Agree
Semantic Differential Scale	Beliefs, attitudes measured based words that are bi-polar opposites such as "favorable" to "unfavorable."	The way my instructor in this course presented material was _____: Confusing 1 2 3 4 5 Clear

Exhibit 6.7 *Alternative measurement scales typically employed in research questionnaires.*

Bias and Interviewer Cheating

Interviewer cheating and biases are two major potential research problems. Either problem, when present, can destroy the validity of any set of results generated through these primary research techniques. Interviewer cheating is usually a problem with face-to-face surveys, primarily telephone interviews and mall intercepts. For example, consider a scenario where an interviewer conducting a mall intercept has finally succeeded in convincing a mall patron to take the time to participate in a "short survey." Two thirds of the way through the interview the subject gets bored and decides it's time for a skinny latte at Starbucks. The interviewer may simply complete the survey for the respondent. This shortcut has seriously compromised the validity of this consumer's responses and, possibly, the entire study. How do we get around this type of problem? It is not easy. But, close supervision of interviewers and periodic auditing of completed surveys can cut down on the odds that these things will occur.

Several sources of bias are likely to arise in marketing research. Researchers themselves can prove a source of bias, called interviewer bias. Researchers may engage in activities, say things, or provide subtle oral or visual cues that influence how subjects respond to questions. Face-to-face surveys, again, are most susceptible to such biasing effects.

Non-response bias results when a significant portion of the sample does not participate in the study. This normally is most serious with mail and telephone surveys. With mail surveys, of course, many individuals simply trash the questionnaire or, if they open it, they never fill it out or only partially complete it. There is always the chance that people who do not participate, or partially complete surveys questionnaires, differ systematically from those who do fill it out and return it. These differences may substantially bias the results of the study. Similarly, people who refuse to cooperate or are not entirely truthful during depth interviewers or focus groups bias the results of the study. The results are subsequently rendered nearly useless.

Step 4: Data Analysis and Reporting

Data Analysis

After data are collected the next logic step is to make sense out of these data. This is where data analysis begins. The major purposes of data analysis are to:

- Summarize the information that was generated by the study.

With most studies, a large amount of information is produced; too much for marketing researchers to interpret without the use of dedicated statistical techniques. Statistics are the tools that marketing researchers employ to summarize the information contained in large data sets.

- Examine the relationships between variables that were investigated in the study.

The types of statistics employed to summarize data range from simple to complex. Fortunately, most marketing data analysis applications only require the use of simple statistical tools. Descriptive statistics that summarize data central tendency and dispersion, supplemented with the judicious use of simple tables usually suffice. These tables are called cross tabulations or cross tabs and show how one variable relates to another in the study. Cross tabulation is akin to building pivot tables in Microsoft Excel. Indeed, much data analysis required for marketing research can be performed directly in spreadsheet programs such as Excel. Today's spreadsheet software is more powerful than dedicated statistics packages were in the past.

Gender		Crest	Colgate	Total
Men	n	400	833	1,233
	row %	32%	68%	
Women	n	650	372	1,022
	row %	64%	36%	
	Total	1,050	1,205	2,255

Exhibit 6.8 *A simple cross-tabulation showing the hypothetical relationship between brand preference and gender. Can you see the relationship?*

Ages 18 - 30

Gender		Crest	Colgate	Total
Men	n	262	293	555
	row %	47%	53%	
Women	n	243	237	480
	row %	51%	49%	
	Total	505	530	1,035

Ages 30 - 55

Gender		Crest	Colgate	Total
Men	n	262	416	678
	row %	39%	61%	
Women	n	400	142	542
	row %	74%	26%	
	Total	662	558	1,220

Exhibit 6.9 *A slightly more complex cross-tabulation showing the hypothetical relationship between brand preference and gender as moderated by age. How does the relationship between gender and brand preference change when age is considered?*

Exhibit 6.8 contains a simple cross tabulation. The cross-tab depicts the relationship between two variables from a hypothetical study. The variables are gender (male or female) and toothpaste brand preference (Crest vs. Colgate). An examination of the table clearly reveals that Colgate is most preferred by men (68%) and Crest is most preferred by women (64%).

But because different numbers of men and women are in the sample—1,022 women, 1,233 men—the raw numbers may be misleading. Thus it is best to focus on the row percentages. The percentages show the proportion of each gender preferring each brand. When the data are arranged in this format, it is easy to see which brand is preferred by which gender. The simple cross tabulation of the information from the study revealed the relationship quite easily.

Exhibits 6.9 presents a second, slightly more complex, example of how cross tabulations are employed. In this example, a third variable is added to the analysis—age. As a result, the cross tabulation examines the relationship between brand preference and gender. But it also examines how this relationship depends on or changes with subject age. The top part of the table (Exhibit 6.9) examines the relationship between brand preference and gender for people aged 18–30 years. The bottom part of the table looks at the relationship between brand preference and gender for consumers aged greater than 30, but less than 55 years.

For consumers aged 18–30 years it appears that there is really no strong differences in preferences for either brand for men or women. The percentages are close in all cells, probably within the range of statistical sampling error. However, the story is different for those consumers over the age of 30. Distinct differences in preferences again emerge. Men strongly prefer Colgate (80%); women prefer Crest (75%).

The point to learn here is that the addition of a third variable to our analysis (age) clarifies the relationship between brand preference and gender. Apparently, whether men and women prefer one brand over another is highly dependent upon age! Simple cross tabulation of the data was all that was needed to reveal important relationships between the variables.

There are, however, many far more complex statistical tools available for analyzing more complex relationships between multiple variables. These statistical tools are collectively referred to "multivariate techniques" or "multivariate statistics." Multivariate techniques include multiple regression, discriminant analysis, cluster analysis, factor analysis, and multi-dimensional scaling. The specific multivariate techniques employed depend on the nature of the data and the types of relationships between variables that are to be analyzed.

Reporting

Assuming that the results of the data analysis have yielded insight into the research question, these results must be communicated in a coherent manner to the people who will use them. This generally means communicating the information to line managers. Written reports and oral presentations are typically both provided. Care must be taken to ensure that results are communicated clearly and concisely. Too many research reports are filled with jargon and useless details that obscure the more useful information that managers actually need.

Step 5: Follow-Up

The last step in the research process is follow-up. Follow-up is how we determine the study's usefulness to managers. During following up, we determine what was good and bad about the report, and more importantly, how future research can be made more useful to management.

Research: Value versus Cost

A final consideration with respect to conducting marketing research: the value of any information generated by a research project should exceed the costs of obtaining that information for the project to be considered a viable investment. Part of planning a research project involves estimating the cost to conduct the research. Like any other marketing action, research programs must be budgeted. Budgeted costs must be reconciled with the expected value of the information that the project will yield. This may simply be a judgment call: does the value of the information exceed what it will cost to acquire that information? If the answer is "no," the study should be re-evaluated. The marketing research project should be canceled or its anticipated costs reduced.

→ Marketing Information and Decision Support Systems

Marketing research projects presumably generate valuable information that can be used in a timely manner by the Firm and its management. The results of a research project, however, are only one source of information available to Firms. Other sources exist and, along with information provided by research, should be monitored on an ongoing basis. This is the role of the Firm's marketing information system (MkIS).

The MkIS consists of the resources and processes that a Firm uses to:

- Determine the information requirements it needs for decision making.
- Collect that information, and then sort, analyze, and inventory the information.
- Provide the information in timely usable formats to key decision makers.

Frito-Lay, headquartered in Plano Texas, has one of the best Marketing Information Systems in the world. The marketing research component of its overall Management Information System collects and maintains real-time data on its own products and competitors' sales in geographic areas down to the size of the city block. Frito-Lay's system also tracks its purchasing and logistics operations such that it knows in real time the exact locations of all shipments coming into and going out of its warehouses and distribution centers world-wide. Competitor's strategic and tactical behaviors are carefully monitored and tracked as well their relative sales, market shares, shelf-space allocations, share of displays, and actual pricing. The bottom line is that the Frito-Lay MkIS allows it to zero in on any market by product, type of store and geographic location.[12]

The MkIS consists of two major components: (1) the data sources and collection system and (2) the decision support system (Exhibit 6.10).

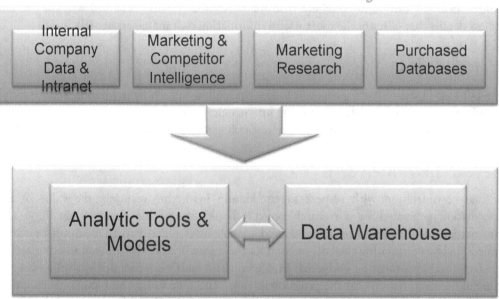

Exhibit 6.10 *The Structure of the Marketing Information System.*

→ Data Sources and Collection System

The data sources available for inclusion in the MkIS include all those internal and external sources examined earlier in the chapter. External sources that are particularly emphasized, as in the Frito-Lay example above, include events unfolding in the Firm's customer, competitor, economic, and legal environments. Trends in these environments are those likely to directly impact the Firm and its viability.

Competitor intelligence is crucial. Many Firms have dedicated personnel and/or departments that track competitors and predict their future actions. Few Firms engage in outright "corporate espionage." (Spying, and software-based surveillance, intelligence-gathering and data-theft) is more a nation thing. China and North Korea do such things frequently, as is surely true of the US government. Hopefully, the domestic government is doing it better.)

But many Firms actively collect information from all available public sources on their competitors' products and operations. Salespeople may be tasked with collecting portions of this information. They operate in the field, are exposed to customers and competitors on a daily basis, and thus should be the first line of information. At Frito-Lay, route salespeople perform this task. Each route salesperson is equipped with a handheld computer employed to take orders, print receipts, and record sales for its products and select information about competitors' products as each retail outlet is visited and stocked.

Firms sometimes hire people to specifically obtain competitor information. In retailing, mystery shoppers are hired to visit the Firm's and competitors' retail operations posing as customers. Or, company personnel may visit competitors' booths at trade shows pumping representatives for information.

The Internet is one of the most important sources of competitor information. The competitor's own website and social media pages (Facebook, Twitter, etc.), consumers' social media postings, news reports, blogs, government data and reports, trade association websites, and industry studies and reports are all available and easily tapped.

→ Decision Support System

The decision support system (DSS) consists of the databases, hardware, software, and procedures that allow managers to tap into data maintained in MkIS databases. A variety of analytic procedures are available in the DSS to allow management (down to the individual manager) to tap into the MkIS and retrieve information organized in the format desired. The information managers extract from the MkIS via the DSS vary from simple financial ratios to complex charts, tables, and reports developed with the use of statistical and modeling software that resides in the DSS.

Some view the MkIS and DSS as separate systems, preferring to view the DSS as the next evolutionary step in IT applications in marketing. If they are viewed differently, the only real difference between them is that the DSS allows individual managers to tap the databases using its powerful analytic procedures tailored to their own individual needs.

The databases housed in the DSS constitute a data warehouse holding information on customers, markets, competitors, the economy, political and legal trends, the environment, and company operations. It contains data from all relevant internal and external environments. Some of the more sophisticated DSS analytics allow managers to data mine the information in this warehouse searching for insights into customer behaviors, market trends, and competitor strategies.

Such data mining processes have yielded significant insight into customer behaviors that have led to major changes in strategic direction for Firms. Harrah's Entertainment has successfully mined its extensive customer data warehouse to aid its development of winning customer incentives. According to Gary Loveman, CEO of Harrah's Entertainment, "We've come out on top in the casino wars by mining our customer data deeply, running marketing experiments, and using the results to develop and implement finely tuned marketing and service-delivery strategies that keep our customers coming back."[13]

Endnotes

[1] Eric Hellweg, "2012: The First Big Data Election," *Harvard Business Review*, (November 13 2012): 1–2, accessed January 15, 2015, https://hbr.org/2012/11/2012-the-first-big-data-electi/.
See also Michael Scherer, "Inside the Secret World of the Data Crunchers Who Helped Obama Win," *Time*, (November 7, 2012), accessed January 15, 2015, http://swampland.time.com/2012/11/07/inside-the-secret-world-of-quants-and-data-crunchers-who-helped-obama-win/.

[2] Keach Hagey and Suzanne Vranica, "Nielsen to Measure Netflix Viewing," *The Wall Street Journal*, (November 18, 2014), accessed January 1, 2015, http://www.wsj.com/articles/nielsen-to-measure-netflix-viewing-1416357093.

[3] Ellen Byron, "A Virtual View of the Store Aisle," *The Wall Street Journal* (October 3, 2007), accessed October 3, 2007, http://online.wsj.com/article/ SB119136645682746972.html. See also Heather Clancy, "Can 3-D Simulation Obsolete the Need for Retail Field Trials?" *Fortune*, (December 19, 2014), accessed January 1, http://fortune.com/2014/12/19/incontext-solutions-3d-simulation/2015.

[4] Laura J. Bowman, "Pulling Back the Curtain: Online Consumer Tracking," I/S: *A Journal of Law and Policy for the Information Society*, 7(3) (2012): 718–48.
Julie Angwin, "The Web's New Gold Mine: Your Secrets," *The Wall Street Journal*, (July 30, 2010), accessed January 8, 2015, http://online.wsj.com/article/ SB10001424052748703940904575395073512989404.html.

[5] Jennifer Valentino-DeVries, "'Evercookies' and 'Fingerprinting': Are Anti-Fraud Tools Good for Ads?", The Wall Street Journal, (Dec. 1, 2010), accessed January 10, 2015, http://blogs.wsj.com/digits/2010/12/01/evercookies-and-fingerprinting-finding-fraudsters-tracking-consumers.

[6] Casey Sweet, "Designing and Conducting Virtual Focus Groups," *Qualitative Market Research: An International Journal*, 4(3) (2001): 130–135.

[7] H. Brean, "What Hidden Sell Is All About," *Life*, (March 31, 1958): 104-114.

[8] For an excellent review of subliminal manipulation see Timothy Moore, "Subliminal Advertising: What You See is What You Get," *Journal of Marketing*, 48 Spring (1982): 38–47.

[9] Robert L. Fitts and Wendell C. Hewitt, "Utilizing the Before and After Control Group Experimental Design to Evaluate an Outdoor Advertising Campaign," *Journal of Advertising*, 6 (1977): 26–28, 39.

[10] If a study is conducted on an entire population, it is referred to as a "census."

11 The sampling frame, technically, is the list of units or elements from which the sample will be drawn. The list can consist of people (the usual case), geographic areas (such as city blocks), companies, or other units. When units for the sampling frame are people, it is equivalent to the "population" as defined in this topic.

12 Alan J. Greco and Jack T. Hogue, "Developing Marketing Decision Support Systems in Consumer Goods Firms," *Journal of Consumer Marketing 7* (1990): 55–64.

13 Gary Loveman, "Diamonds in the Data Mine," *Harvard Business Review*, (May 2003): 1–7.

CHAPTER 6A APPENDIX

→ Moving from Knowledge to Action: A 35,000 Foot View of Marketing Information

The Power of Actionable Knowledge

Knowledge is an operant (i.e. actionable) resource. Knowledge, in fact, may be the most differentiating resource that any modern Firm could ever possess. This is especially true over the long run. Knowledge is the key foundation for achieving sustainable competitive advantage and marketing growth through innovation because innovation is the key to achieving lasting differentiation and marketing power. Should you be surprised then, to read that knowledge is primary source of wealth and power in the modern world, both for Firms and people. Don't believe us? Look around. Do you think that Bill Gates, Warrant Buffet, Mark Zuckerberg, Sheryl Sandberg, Marie Le Pen, Jeff Bezos, Sara Blakely, Barrack Obama, Bill O'Reilly, or the late Steve Jobs got to where they are or were based on good looks or big muscles, alone?

Knowledge is more often caught than taught. Firms and people who seek to become better informed, smarter, more powerful, and ultimately more successful must search for differentiating knowledge in a proactive and strategic fashion. Knowledge, beastly though it is, never walks up to anyone and proudly announced its presence. Knowledge is funny that way: it would rather hide—sometimes in plain sight—than come out into the open where anyone could find it. You must search it out.

The body of knowledge that exists within any particular business domain is a dynamic universe. What should matter most to marketing researchers is not any general body of marketing, consumer, or environmental knowledge, but rather the leading, some say bleeding, edge of knowledge. Marketing researchers must learn how to dance right up to the cutting edge of knowledge. They likewise need to learn how to create the "knowledge-edge" themselves. Making predictions is difficult, especially when they are about the future. But marketing researchers can help create the future by creating the knowledge edge that helps shape the leading edge and the future.

The best marketing researchers likewise know how to create and deliver exactly the knowledge-based insights that marketing planners/managers need. Nothing more, nothing less than what is needed. Truth is, few professionals today have too little information. Too much information is available, literally at their fingertips, to write otherwise. Yet fewer professionals still have all the leading-edge knowledge they need to have in order to succeed at the highest levels.

The best marketing planners/managers, in turn, understand how to leverage this leading-edge knowledge to their Firm's advantage. In a world where information is so readily available, whatever can be done—for either better or for worse—eventually will be done. The only question for any marketing planner/manager is whether the better or worse will be done by or to their Firm.

Marketing is a highly competitive endeavor. Marketing is likewise an activity that rewards patience as well as action. Once they are armed with leading-edge knowledge about customers, competitors, or the relevant environment, marketers should be willing to think like people of action. But their possession and control over leading-edge edge knowledge should also permit them to act like people of thought. This sort of cognitively-balanced managerial practice should permit marketing managers/planners to split the difference between what their Firm ideally could become with what is realistic.

Remember what was written earlier about the nature of strategy. We repeat it here: Good strategy is about getting more out of a situation than the beginning balance of power between competing Firms would suggest is likely or perhaps even possible. The Firm's decision-makers' possession of leading-edge, marketing research-based knowledge will often prove the key ingredient that makes such desirable outcomes a reality.

Propositional and Prescriptive Knowledge

Two types of knowledge are relevant to any Firm. They are, respectively, propositional knowledge and prescriptive knowledge.

Propositional Knowledge

Propositional knowledge is abstract and generalized in nature. The applications of propositional knowledge are broad, as is its value. You never know when a problem in business, in marketing, or for that matter in life, will arise that requires a particular category of propositional knowledge as its solution. A three-part principle is always in play in business, marketing, or life. It is this:

- The more diverse and broader one's base of knowledge becomes, the more interesting and valuable are the connections (intersections) that one can make.
- Those connections or intersections, in turn, are exactly where the most useful solutions to even the most vexing problems will reside. This is always true, by the way, as you learn in Chapter 11.
- All one has to do, metaphorically, is reach in and pick out the best possible solution.

The opportunity to acquire propositional knowledge is another reason for you to travel or read as extensively as possible, as soon as possible. Another reason to acquire such knowledge, of course, is that propositional knowledge contributes to the managers' ability to operate on the leading-knowledge edge as they identify differentiating opportunities for their Firms through marketing research efforts.

Prescriptive Knowledge

Prescriptive knowledge, by contrast, is more narrowly focused. It is often referred to as techniques and know-how. The right techniques and know-how are more than a "nice-to-have" for marketing researchers. The marketing research process and its associated tasks are often extremely complicated and technical in nature. Highly subject-specific bodies of leading-edge knowledge must be understood and enacted by marketing researchers if they are to perform adequately and effectively. We would go so far as to write that having the right prescriptive knowledge (i.e. the proper techniques and know-how) is an absolute "must-have" in any marketing research and marketing planner/manager career.

Propositional and prescriptive knowledge, separately and collectively, are critical to the success of marketing researchers and indeed of all businesspeople. This is because, at their cores, the general practice of business and specific practice of marketing is about making bets on current and future human behaviors—bets on behavioral topics such as which product is most likely to be purchased; which salesperson, as you hire one, is most likely to succeed; or at what price point will the optimal level of customer sales? Marketing researchers, planners, and managers must make informed bets. Bets informed by propositional and prescriptive—and consequently actionable-marketing research based knowledge.

→ Other Ways to Describe Marketing Research

The marketing research process was thoroughly described in Chapter 6. But as the marketing research topic is further examined here, another, higher level perspective is introduced.

Marketing research should be executed as an ongoing process. This process generally involves collecting and analyzing information. The information that is collected and analyzed is usually related to a specific problem or opportunity that is facing the Firm. The marketing research process itself unfolds in two general stages:

- The first stage involves describing/diagnosing the problem or opportunity that is facing the Firm more accurately.
- The second stage involves developing prescriptive inferences regarding how best to strategically address the problem or opportunity through better-informed, more effective management of the Firm's marketing mix.

This two-stage process is similar to what happens when you visit the doctor after a health-related problem has popped-up in your life. Be it a sprained shoulder, runny nose and fever, or colon cancer (the most prevalent cancer, so the example is relevant), physicians usually begin the visit by asking a series of structured questions.

Why all the questions? Essentially, physicians engage in this inquiry to separate symptoms from the true medical problem or problems. Why is this important? Primarily, so that that they diagnose, as quickly as possible, the true source of the problem. Why, again? What's so important about knowing the source—the original cause—of the symptom or problem? Because the fact is that the old saying "a problem well-defined is a problem half-solved" is more than a simple cliché.

Once medical problems and their physical causes are accurately diagnosed, medical practice is probably easier to execute properly than is marketing research practice. The medical solutions for physical problems such as sprained shoulders, runny noses and fevers, or even colon cancer (it's simple: you cut it out, irradiate it, or chemo-therapize it from existence, in some combination) are each already well-known by, they indeed obvious to, experienced physicians.

Not so for the vast array of real or merely perceived emotional, psychological, or physiological problems that customers face or believe they face in their consumer or professional lives. Life is not so simple for marketing researchers and marketing planners whose customer problem-solving tasks, frankly, are far more challenging. That's primarily because human beings operating in either B2B or B2C contexts are often remarkably bad at making important, and less important, decisions. Customers themselves may not even understand the underlying causes of their "problems"; in fact, this is frequently the case. Yet all the while, a primary role of marketing researchers is to determine why customers make the decisions, good or bad, that they make. A true challenge is explaining the what, how, where, when, how many and how often, and of course the why of customer behavior.

Customers, again operating in either B2C or B2B domains, are impressionable, emotional, and irrational—at times, predictably irrational. As if most people did not realize this was true about ourselves, already, think about it. Customers buy things they don't need, often at arbitrary prices that they cannot afford, for silly reasons. Anyone up for jet-boating at $240 for 45 minutes, or at $290 for helicoptering about 8 to 10 minutes in the admittedly beautiful airspace of Queenstown, New Zealand? Apparently, for many, the answer is yes, just because they can. Of course, due to these emotional-driven financial decisions visiting students may be forced to eat too many Kiwi meat pies (not the best food choice, trust us) during much of the rest of their trip.

The decisions that customers make produce behaviors which generate consequences—for better and for worse—every time. Marketing research, for example, has shown that customers linger longer and often spend more when stores play soothing music. Marketing researchers also know that when customers are in a good mood, they are more amenable to persuasion. Would you like a second glass of wine as you experience that high-end vacation home presentation? Marketing researchers likewise understand that customers are often so illogical that they believe price determines the value of something rather than the other way around. Buying and consuming expensive wines just to impress someone else, anyone? Geez—it's just wine! Moreover, the people customers are trying to impress with their expensive tastes and thick wallets may not like them that much, anyway. And marketers know just how likely people are to squander their time, which clearly has its own value, to get something for free. But should people assign a dollar value to their time?

Anyone feeling manipulated about now? If you're not, you're probably not paying enough attention. Read the preceding paragraph again.

Yet their job, the reason they exist, their primary task, the thing that separates great marketing researchers from also-rans is to make sense of these human behaviors and determine why customers or prospective customers make or don't make the sorts of choices that marketing Firms want them to make. Marketing research is an important, serious, and with apologies to Tom Cruise, highly *risky business*. But invariably, with the reality of higher risks comes the prospect of higher returns, as is certainly the case with marketing research activity.

→ Descriptive and Prescriptive Value

Marketing research generates new information or agglomerates existing and sometimes old information. This is important because "information is power."

Realistically, however, information only becomes a source of power or managerial effectiveness after it has been converted into usable or actionable knowledge. Why else would politicians "focus group-test" different ways of presenting issues or staking out various positions before adding or deleting from one or more ideas (which are nothing more or less than new products, as discussed in Chapter 1) to their marketing "stump speeches" or "talking points"? Do you think that the White House marketing communications team (which includes the office's speech-writing team) does this before every speech is delivered?

Politics is marketing; nothing more, nothing less. Politics always has been and always will be marketing. Politics fundamentally involves two activities. The first activity is the artistic development and effective selling of possible versions of the future. The second is the act of developing and marketing those new political products known as people and their ideas as harbingers of these projected futures.

Remember the market-tested political ideas—sloganeering that professional marketers would identify as positioning statements—that drove the 2008 Presidential campaign? The positioning statements "Hope and Change"; "Change You can Believe In"; and the "Fierce Urgency of Now" contributed materially toward the successful introduction and subsequent marketing of a new, essentially unknown, political product to an American voter marketplace. The name of the essentially unknown product: Barrack Obama. As a result a goodly portion of that voting market often became nearly reverential in their regard for this new product. The 2008-era Obama marketing team executed their marketing research efforts and resulting branding, positioning, communication, and promotional messages so well that they gave a significant portion of American voters permission to think more highly of themselves because they thought highly enough of Barrack Obama to vote for those ideas. It's a true win for marketers when they can convince customers to think better of themselves for doing something that marketers want them to do.

Of course by the time the 2012 Presidential re-election campaign rolled around few of those marketing research driven ideas had worked out as promised. So the 2012 marketing research team begin its task early. Over time, as a result of the leading-edge knowledge that was produced, the no longer new political product (President Obama) and his political message were re-positioned, again successfully. The 2012 election proved a true test market for America's voting consumers. For many who were satisfied with emotionally rewarding marketing rhetoric and a promise to get something of value in exchange for giving up nothing of your own because someone else would pay for your value, the choice was clear. And the product that was the President was purchased, again, by a majority of the consumers who decided to vote.

→ The Right Sort of Information Generates Value

Obviously, one can safely conclude that information is important and powerful. Yet despite the widespread recognition of this fact, too many marketers either lack the right sort of information or have too much of the wrong sort of marketing research information to plan and perform at optimal levels of efficiency and effectiveness. Too many marketing planners/managers lack the right sort of information to make the sort of quick and critical decisions that so frequently prove so necessary in today's highly-competitive, ultra-dynamic, increasingly-globalized marketplace.

The right sort of marketing research information must be either descriptive or prescriptive in nature. To generate value and deliver on the promise of increased power, marketing research information must deliver one or the other outcome. This means the marketing information and insights generated by the Firm and its marketing research should describe changing trends (say, customer likes or dislikes, or economic surges or declines) that represent either threats or opportunities to the Firm. Or, the information and knowledge-based insights generated by the Firm should prescribe—dictate or point the way toward—the strategic marketing actions that the Firm should pursue.

Descriptive, also known as diagnostic, information should always come first. Then, and only then, can prescriptive recommendations follow. Just like in the doctor's office, remember? No one can ever know how to resolve a problem or exploit an opportunity until the full dimensions and underlying causes of either are also understood.

Two Equations; Remember Each

The first:

> Better (marketing) information = better (marketing) decisions = better (marketing) performance.

You would agree that this formula might contribute materially to success in your professional life, as well. Right?

The second:

> "Know Yourself (the Firm); Know Your Enemy (the Firm's competitors); and Know Your Terrain" (the markets and environments in which your Firm will engage with competitors), and you should win 100% of your battles."

This counsel was given by the Chinese General Sun Tzu. He wrote these famous words more than 2,000 years ago in *The Art of War*. Sun Tzu's statement, eloquently albeit indirectly, underscores the value of having up-to-date and accurate marketing information. Information about what, you may wonder?

Primarily, information about:

- Competitors, specifically, what are competitors doing, capable of doing, or likely to do with their future marketing strategies. That is, what is likely to happen in terms of competitors' pricing, distribution, promotion and targeting, as well as their new product development, activities?

- Relevant Marketplace and Environmental Trends, specifically, leading-edge knowledge about what is happening in terms of what are, by now, our old friends, marketplace and environmental trends. As you should understand by now, such trends can represent either opportunities or threats. Firms should, as noted, own the trend when it is their friend, and step out of the way when the trend is their enemy or threat.

- Customers, specifically, customers' or prospective customers' likes or dislikes; their demographics; their attitudes, opinions, beliefs, and preferred lifestyle activities (i.e., their psychographics); their preferences, desires, wants, and needs, particularly their unfulfilled desires, unsatisfied wants, or unresolved needs; as well as the motivations that underlie and bolster these traits and tendencies. As discussed in Chapters 7 and 8, this entails marketing research efforts that answer the what, how, how much, when, where and of course all-important why question as it relates to the decision-making and behaviors of B2C consumers and B2B customers.

→ The Value of Knowledge: Revealed Through Statistics

Marketing research efforts are grounded in statistical and probability assessments—efforts to explain what has happened, and why; efforts to predict what is most likely to happen, and why. The fact that statistics and probability assessments are usually in play when marketing research is conducted means that Firms collect information from samples that are supposedly representative of the entire population of interest. This fact was referenced repeatedly in Chapter 6. To collect this information various questions are asked to members of each sample that is investigated. Once the data are collected, various tests are conducted.

Statistical analyses allow often massive amounts to be compressed into a few meaningful numbers. The probability assessments that follow from statistical analyses enable managers to make reasonably accurate decisions in settings that feature imperfect information and substantial uncertainty, in other words, in any marketplace or environment where research is conducted, by measuring the level of uncertainty embedded in a given decision. Consequently, most marketing research-based strategic-marketing-decisions are accurate within a range of around a 5-10% chance of being wrong.

You should also learn the following lesson. Otherwise, you may one day be victimized by not knowing. When working with statistics and computers, researchers too often fall victim to automation and complacency bias. Either bias, when present, can degrade marketing research performance and lead to planning and managerial mistakes.

Automation bias arises when our computers lull us into a false sense of security. Confident that our machines always work flawlessly and are able to handle any problem that pops up, the attention of researchers can drift. They become "complacent." Complacency bias arises when people place too much faith in the accuracy of information provided by computers. They become lazy—or complacent. This complacency- induced trust becomes so strong that we ignore or discount other sources of marketing information or our own judgment that contradicts or invalidates what the machine is reporting.

No matter how technologically adroit marketing researchers are as they develop their prescriptive knowledge they should never discount or overlook the value of a good "walk around" within their markets and with their customers and prospects. Actual reality, rather than computer-generated numbers masquerading as such, is often the best reality-check for marketing researchers.

→ When Should Firms Conduct Marketing Research?

Marketing issues that would normally be addressed through marketing research include, but are not limited to, diagnostic investigations of:

- Brand equity and brand name issues.
- "Cool-hunting" for purposes of making observations and predictions regarding changes in new or existing social or cultural trends.
- Customer satisfaction, in order that Firms might better identify what is working or not working with their products as well as with their competitors' products.
- Concept (idea) testing, as a means to determine whether customers would generally like or be inclined to purchase a new product that the Firm could develop based on the new concept. You haven't learned this yet, but all new products always emerge from a single source, an innovative—that is, a new and useful—idea.
- Price elasticity, or how changes up or down in a product's price affect demand for a given product or product line. More information about price elasticity follows in Chapter 15.
- Test marketing, as noted in Chapter 6, involves small or limited launches of new products or new promotional or branding efforts.
- Positioning research, which entails efforts to ascertain how customers view a Firm's brands and their values relative to competitors' brands and their values.

Sophisticated marketing managers likewise realize they may need to conduct marketing research when their Firm needs to develop operant knowledge and create prescriptive strategic recommendations related to:

- Which market segments exist? (A segmentation and strategic planning research question.)

- Which market segments the Firm should target? (A targeting and strategic planning research question.)

- How the Firm should promote and position its branded products inside these segments? (These are promotional, positional, and strategic planning research questions.)

- Where and how the Firm should acquire or distribute its products? (A place question, inside the context of the marketing mix. More commonly, this is currently known as a "supply chain management" research question.)

- What, if any, new products should be developed in response to competitors' activities, environmental trends, or changing or currently unfulfilled wants and needs of customers? (This a new product development [or "NPD"] research question.)

- What, if any, unsatisfied or less than fully satisfied customer wants exist in the marketplace that the firm is better able than its competitors to solve? (These are targeting, positioning, NPD, and strategic planning-related research questions.)

- What communication channels and what marketing messages should the Firm use to convey key information to its customers and prospects? (This is a promotional research question.)

- At what prices should the Firm's products be offered to the market? (This is a pricing research question.)

- What features and attributes, and thus benefits, of the Firm's existing products need to be changed, added, or deleted, and in what ways? (These are NPD and positioning research questions.)

- Is the Firm satisfying/not satisfying (resolving) any key customer needs? (These are customer relationship management and NPD research questions.)

- Who are the Firm's primary competitors now? Which Firms appear most likely to become the Firm's primary competitors in the future? What are respective strengths and weaknesses of these actual or potential competitor Firms? (These are strategic planning research questions.)

- What features/attributes/benefits associated with our current product line(s) should be changed, added/deleted, emphasized, or de-emphasized in the Firm's NPD and positioning efforts? (These are NPD and positioning research questions.)

- Is the Firm's current branding campaign working, and if not, what should be changed in what ways in increase the likelihood that it works better in the future? (These are brand management and positioning research questions.)

- Is the Firm currently positioning its own brands correctly? What, if anything, about our current positioning strategies should be changed? (This is a positioning question.)

Most marketing managers do not need more information. Most managers simply need better information. They need information that has already been converted into actionable and thus operant knowledge. Yet despite the widespread recognition of this fact, marketing planners/managers often lack either the right sort of information or have too much of the wrong information. In other words, they are missing the sort of leading-edge knowledge that is required for Firms to make the necessarily quick and critical decisions that will facilitate their success. Marketing researchers should take heed of this fact.

→ Knowledge Generated Through Marketing Research Creates ...

The right marketing research-based knowledge creates superior opportunities for Firms to link successfully with customers or prospects through information. Leading-edge marketing research knowledge is generally used to identify and define marketing opportunities. This knowledge is also used to generate, refine, and evaluate marketing activities; particularly segmentation, targeting, and marketing mix management and positioning efforts. Finally, such knowledge should be used to improve marketing as both a business function and ongoing process inside any Firm.

Marketing research specifies the information necessary to resolve customer or Firm problems or exploit any opportunities facing the Firm. Marketing researchers design methods for collecting information. They also implement and manage these collection processes. Finally, marketing researchers summarize and communicate their research findings and implications to Firms for which or within which they work. This is the stage at which marketing researcher also convert raw information into actionable knowledge.

The Firm that possesses superior knowledge and the marketing ability, resources and managerial willingness to act decisively based on that knowledge will generally prevail in the proverbial battle for preferred real estate inside their customers and prospects minds. For as you learned in Chapter 1, the collective mind of the market is exactly where marketing battles unfold. Other things being equal, the Firm that possesses superior knowledge will enjoy the opportunity to develop material sustainable competitive advantage over competitors. Speaking of sustainable competitive advantages (as introduced in Chapters 2 and 3), there are only three ways through which any Firm can achieve them.

→ Sustainable Competitive Advantages

The three ways through which any Firm can create sustainable competitive advantages or enduring points of differentiation in route to more power and greater wealth are through:

- Achieving customer intimacy advantages. The ability of achieving customer intimacy coalesces around the fact that one Firm possesses more actionable leading-edge knowledge about its customers or prospects—their wants, needs, expectations, and problems, in both the present and future—than its competitors possesses about their customers or prospects. When Firms create more intimate relationships with their customers, greater customer loyalty will ensue and the ability to charge higher prices will generally follow. Apple is an example of a Firm that has earned a position of greater customer intimacy in the collective mind of its massive market. Apple loyalists generally assume, rightfully or wrongly, that Apple "gets (understands) them" and their special needs. And the ranks of Apple evangelists are legion.

- Achieving technological advantage. Any Firm that earns technological advantage knows more about what customers want or need in the technological realm. Achieving this advantage requires that the Firm possess the ability (in terms of propositional or prescriptive knowledge) to deliver it. To illustrate, we again go to the well with Apple. Apple has clearly achieved technological advantage in the place that matters the most; i.e., the minds of its customers. The fact that Apple competes at a world-class level in terms of its ability to deliver both greater customer intimacy and greater technological advantage than its competitors is the exact reason why this smallish (merely about 47,000 U.S. employees) company is, at the time of this writing, the most valuable brand in the world.

- Achieving cost-based advantages. To achieve cost-based advantages, Firms must possess knowledge, resource (perhaps patent protected), or supply chain/partnership/economy of scale advantages; each of which is driven, motivated, or strengthened by informational advantages. Again, the key role that leading-edge marketing knowledge plays in developing sustainably winning positions for Firms is self-evident. Notably, Firms that enjoy this status can leverage their cost-based advantages to actually lower their prices to levels their competitors cannot profitably reach. Or, cost-leader Firms can strategically decide to maintain prices at roughly the same levels as competitors while reaping much higher profit margins for themselves. Walmart exemplifies a world-class cost-based leader that opts to pass on its savings to customers in form of lower, albeit not always the lowest, prices across an extremely broad assortment of products. As a consequence, and despite its numerous entrenched enemies, Walmart has also been able to earn tremendous customer intimacy amongst its legions of patrons. Like Apple, Walmart competes at a world-class level on two of three pathways to sustainable competitive advantage and the power and wealth that such differences generate. Similar to Apple, the onetime little Firm from a formerly tiny town in north Arkansas, now stands like a colossus astride the US marketplace.

Chapter 7

Consumer Decision Making and Behavior

You'll likely learn this material more easily if you adopt the mindset that this content relates directly to your life—because it does. Most people pass through their lives unaware that they are surrounded by factors that manipulate and influence their decisions, including the purchasing decisions, they make. But you'll no longer purchase products in a state of relative ignorance after you have studied this chapter. In fact, almost anyone can make better consumption decisions once they understand:

- The forces that influence their choices.
- How much the consumer decisions they make impact their physical, emotional, and economic wellbeing.
- How they frequently use consumer choice to create and express their self-identities.

→ What Is Consumer Behavior?

Consumer behavior refers to the buying behavior of final consumers. Final consumers are individuals who acquire products or services for their personal consumption or for their family's consumption. Consumer behavior (frequently called "CB") also refers to the factors that influence the decisions made by, and the buying behaviors of, final consumers as they acquire, consume (actually use), and dispose of products. Products, you should recall, were previously broadly defined as tangible goods, intangible services, ideas, people, or places, in other words, as anything that is perceived as having value by anyone and that could be used in an exchange.

The consumer behavior topic is hugely important. Year after year more than 70% of the US Gross Domestic Product is generated through the consumption decisions made by domestic consumers. In 2001 President George W. Bush said, in a speech heard by nearly all America because it was delivered right after 9/11, go out and continue to buy stuff.[i] Mr. Bush understood the extent to which American consumers' decisions drove the health of the entire US economy. Thus, his comment was perfectly logical.

Various consumer-related factors influence the CB decisions that consumers make. These factors include, but are not limited to, consumers' demographic, belief and attitude, lifestyle, personality, and family life cycle status characteristics. At a minimum, these factors also would include consumers' wants, needs, and problems, particularly their unsatisfied wants and needs and unresolved problems. Finally, events that exist or are unfolding in consumers' relevant economic, technological, political, social class, cultural or even neighborhood, school, and/or church environments may influence CB decisions.

Take another look at these factors just mentioned and note that marketers generally cannot control them. But marketers should always strive to understand them. In fact, the ability of marketers to successfully identify and develop consumer market opportunities largely pivots based on whether Firms can acquire actionable insights about factors that influence the decision making of the buyers and prospective buyers who comprise the market segments those marketers target and seek to serve.

But there is one major factor that marketers absolutely control: the marketing mix. And the four-pronged element known as the marketing mix surely should influence consumer choice. The marketing mix, you should recall, is a strategic marketing tool used to develop and deliver hopefully differentiating value to targeted consumer segments. These controllable marketing stimuli—the Firm's product, promotion, price, and place—can be strategically managed in ways that shape and influence consumer decision-making. The marketing mix should also be managed such that it favorably impacts consumers' perceptions, beliefs, attitudes about and intentions toward any marketer's products.

Recall, from Chapter 1, that marketing is much more a battle of perceptions than it is a battle between products or brands. Competing marketers fight this perceptual battle and win or lose it inside consumer minds, or more correctly, inside the "collective minds" of consumer segments. Many competitors may be engaged in a specific battle, say, Ford, GM, or Nissan trucks, but the specific product/brand combination that consumers perceive delivers the most value will win this battle.

The world of consumer behavior is that simple, because rational consumers almost always respond to incentives. That is, rational consumers almost always make the choice that they perceive delivers the most value to them. In other words, the choice that best incentivizes them. An incentive is anything that motivates or encourages anybody—in this context, a consumer—to do something. The perception that they will acquire new or extra value from making one product choice as opposed to choosing an alternative product option incentivizes consumers to purchase the blouse, shoes, purse, and/or tattoo that promises more value.

The CB decision-making process sounds simple, we hope, because it is, until it becomes very complicated. This is because, while all humans make rational decisions according to the logical decision-making rules present inside their minds, humans are not all rational in the same way. Presumably, Adolph Hitler perceived the decision to execute six to seven million Jews as completely rational. Yet few others, save his Nazi minions, would agree. The fact not all consumers, each presumably acting rationally in their minds, respond in the same fashion to the same incentives underscores the need for marketers to segment, target, and position their marketing mixes carefully. For this marketing process (as explained in Chapter 9) to effectively work, Firms must understand consumers and the differences that exist between equally rational but divergent consumer segments.

There's more: few consumers are rational all the time. But people always think they are rational in most consumption decisions they make. Trust us, we're not. And beyond that, what one person believes to be a rational choice might be viewed as utterly crazy nuts by others walking beside them. Marketers' sincere efforts to understand what motivates consumers are rarely slam-dunks. One saving grace, however, is that in many ways human beings are actually "predictably irrational," in the words of behavioral economist Dan Ariely.[2] This means, at net, insightful marketers can often predict how specific consumer segments will act irrationally in the same generally anticipated ways at the same time to similar marketing or environmental stimuli. We've curved back toward the axiom that "most people pass through life unaware of the factors that manipulate their decision making."[3]

→ Decisions Made Inside Consumer Minds

Despite these challenges, to no small degree, marketers should study CB in the same fashion and for the same reason that fishermen study fish; that is, to secure useful insights about consumers' behaviors in order to learn how to "catch them" better. Ideally, marketers should also study CB through approaches and for reasons similar to why ichthyologists (fish scientists) study fish; that is, to secure useful insights to understand them (fish or consumers) better so as to serve their needs better; to help them (fisherman or consumers) solve their problems. Successful consumer-marketer = consumer-problem-solver.

When studying consumers, Firms should answer the following questions: *what* consumers buy, *where* consumers buy, *how* and *how much* consumers buy, as well as *when* and *why* consumers buy. Truth-be-told, the first five questions are relatively easily answered in an Internet-mediated and technologically-driven marketplace. Just pay attention, collect relevant data (essentially through point of purchase information), count, and compile.

The sixth question, however, is exceedingly more challenging to answer accurately. This is because the primary reason why consumers do or buy anything is primarily locked away inside the "black boxes"[4] of their minds. These decisions happen inside consumer brains, places that no one can see or easily understand, not even through today's rapidly emerging biometric techniques.

What is known, though, is that consumers always have several choices or options available when making decisions. Decisions routinely made by consumers include:

- Product choices: what or what not to buy. Note: when consumers elect to not purchase anything they have still made a choice.
- Brand choices: again, a "what to buy" choice.
- Dealer/store/website choice: where to buy.
- Purchase timing: when to buy.
- Purchase amount: how much to buy.

Consumers also have to decide whether to:

- Pay attention to or ignore what marketers are saying.
- Like or dislike any product, value, or anything that marketers are saying or offering.
- Evangelize, or spread the good or bad news, to others about their positive or negative experience with products, brands, or stores.

→ A Model of Consumer Buyer Behavior

Exhibit 7.1 models how consumers make decisions. This model organizes the discussion of consumer decision-making and behavior into logical building and learning blocks. Each block and topic header featured in Exhibit 7.1 is discussed below.

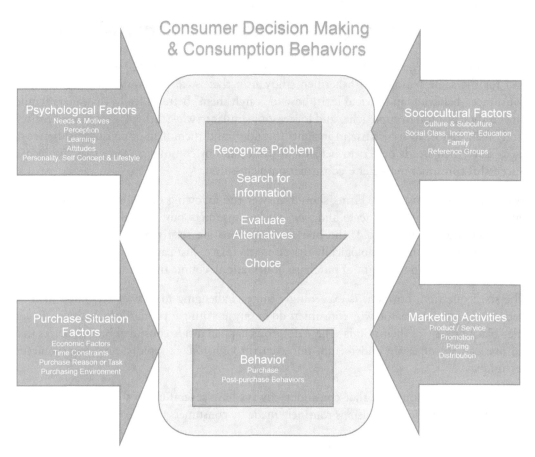

Consumer Decision Making & Consumption Behaviors

Psychological Factors
Needs & Motives
Perception
Learning
Attitudes
Personality, Self Concept & Lifestyle

Sociocultural Factors
Culture & Subculture
Social Class, Income, Education
Family
Reference Groups

Recognize Problem

Search for Information

Evaluate Alternatives

Choice

Purchase Situation Factors
Economic Factors
Time Constraints
Purchase Reason or Task
Purchasing Environment

Marketing Activities
Product / Service
Promotion
Pricing
Distribution

Behavior
Purchase
Post-purchase Behaviors

Exhibit 7.1 *A Model of Consumer Buyer Behavior.*

→ How Consumers Make Decisions

The center block in this consumer decision-making model features the steps in the decision process. Generally, steps in the decision-making process include:

1. *Problem recognition*, or the realization that a purchasing need (problem) exists.

2. *Information search*, or seeking relevant information about products that potentially may satisfy or solve this need (problem).

3. *Alternative evaluation*, or assessing alternative product solutions to determine which one appears most likely to do the best job of satisfying the aroused need (unresolved problem).

4. *Choice*, and subsequent purchase of one or more products based on the prior evaluation process.

5. *Post-purchase processes*, or the cognitive and behavioral responses initiated by consumers as their expectations about the value delivered by the product they selected are exceeded (buyers are delighted), met (buyers are satisfied), or unmet (buyers are disappointed or perhaps apoplectic).

A primary reason why this model is so important is because Firms should be doing different things with their marketing mix as consumers pass through the various stages. During or before Stage 1, for example, marketers should stimulate problem recognition. During or before Stages 2 or 3 marketers should provide information that informs, reminds, or persuades consumers that their product is the "best choice." During or before Stage 5, marketers should take measures as necessary to ensure that consumers expectations are met or exceeded, reinforce to consumers that they have indeed made a "great choice," or make things right if for some reason something went wrong.

The specific steps that consumers follow during the decision-making process may vary depending on the type of product being considered and the purchasing situation faced by consumers. First, the time and effort consumers spend in or allocate toward these five steps also varies for the same reason. BMW may develop and promote its cars so well that a consumer decides right now she has a problem without a Beemer in her garage. While she waits 15 years before she can financially justify acquiring the car, the decision to buy a BMW was made a long time ago. Second, no assumption exists that all consumers pass through all steps. Finally, consumers do not necessarily pass through all steps in the order shown, but the description of the consumer decision making process provided above characterizes how most important consumer decision-making unfold.

The steps presented in Exhibit 7.1 depict an **extensive problem-solving** decision. Consumer decision-making can be arrayed along a continuum. This scale ranges from extensive, more complex decisions, to simpler, more routine, choices (Exhibit 7.2). Extensive CB decisions are complicated, time-consuming, and high-risk. They are "high-involvement" in nature. High-involvement decisions usually feature higher risk, greater costs, and more personal relevance. The issue of personal relevance comes into play because consumers use products to project or advance various dimensions of their self-identity.[5] Automotive, home, major appliance, computer, wedding or prom dress, or expensive jewelry purchases would generally be classified as high-involvement decisions. Yet depending on the purchase occasion, the same product category could be high or low in involvement. Deciding what blouse or shirt to purchase for a special get-away weekend would likely be higher involvement than a blouse or shirt acquired for everyday use.

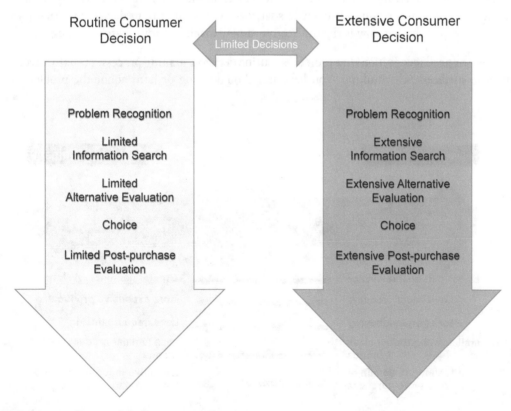

Exhibit 7.2 *Range of Consumer Decisions.*

The decision-making steps involved in lower-involvement, or routine purchases are simplified. Most consumer decisions gravitate toward this end of the continuum. **Routine purchase decisions** would generally include grocery products, gasoline, or Thursday workday underwear. Purchasing, say, a can of green beans or gallon of 2% milk is an inexpensive, low risk, and socially inconspicuous endeavor. No one ever evaluates your worth based on the brand of low-fat milk you might or might not buy. Nor do consumers generally attempt to upgrade how they feel about themselves through the canned vegetables they procure. Similar descriptions would rarely apply to consumption situations where one purchases prom/wedding dresses or special-events clothing; each is too socially conspicuous and potentially risky in nature. The general factors that affect the extent to which decisions are extensive versus routine are summarized in Exhibit 7.3.

The five consumer decision-making stages are each discussed in greater detail below.

Consumer Decision Stage 1: Problem Recognition

The consumer decision-making process begins when people recognize the presence or the existence of a problem. Next thing you know, those consumers potentially need some product to resolve it. When this need is sufficiently strong to prompt consumers to initiate a search for products/brands that can satisfy the need, it transforms into a "motive"; consumers become motivated enough to engage in the CB decision making process. Motives (or drives) are needs that are sufficiently important and pressing to direct individual consumers to seek satisfaction for the need or a solution to the problem that created the motive or drive in the first place.

With extensive decision-making, problem recognition can be instantaneous. Your car breaks down, again, and something needs to be done. Or, problem recognition can grow slowly over time. For example, you may already own a laptop. It works just fine. But, as you encounter friends using newer, faster models or experience advertisements for laptops featuring the latest applications, you may begin to become less satisfied with your current device. Eventually you recognize explicitly that now is the time to buy a new machine. Your search just began.

Problem or need recognition that promotes routine decision-making processes usually involves shallow, surface-level, thinking. You have not thought long or hard about the problem, or

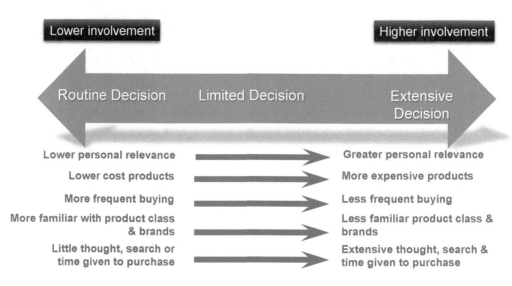

Exhibit 7.3 *Factors Affecting Consumer Decision Complexity and Involvement.*

perhaps not at all until a problem arrives. Problem recognition, in fact, often occurs in retail settings, triggered by a stimulus that you experience. While walking down the breakfast cereal aisle, for example, you notice a display for a new brand of cereal, or a shelf-coupon dispenser offering substantial savings on a preferred brand. Exposure to these marketing stimuli may cause you to recognize that you are nearly out of breakfast cereal and need to restock. No explicit, conscious thought was allocated toward your dwindling cereal supply until you entered the store. (A marketing stimulus is a thing or event, in other words an incentive that prompts specific functional reactions from consumers.)

Problem recognition can be triggered by internal states. Consumers slowly or quickly realize they are hungry, thirsty, cold, or tired. Thus, to solve the emergent problem, they recognize a need exists to eat, drink, get warm, or rest. But what, how or where? These problems must be resolved. Fortunately or unfortunately, marketers distribute and promote, at varying price levels and locations, myriad possible solutions from which consumers can choose.

Consumer needs or problem recognition can be activated through exposure to external stimuli. Consumers may suddenly feel unloved or fear they are missing out (FOMA = Fear of Missing Out) after their "friend" posted about his weekend on Facebook. Or a consumer learns a friend just purchased a new pair of designer jeans. As a result, the consumer decides that it is time to buy a new pair as well. This need was aroused through vicarious experience.

Social media such as Facebook, Twitter, Pinterest, and YouTube may stimulate need arousal based on vicarious experience. The jury is still out on how much influence social media may exert. Based on a survey of 18,000 American consumers, a recent Gallup poll reported that 62% of consumers said Facebook, Twitter, and other social media exercised no influence on their purchasing decisions. Thirty percent said social media had "some influence." Only 5% said social media extensively affected their purchase decisions.[6]

Of course consumers' need recognition can be aroused though exposure to planned marketing activities. These activities could include advertising, promotion, personal selling, direct marketing, or commentary shown on a favorite news program. A consumer experiences a pop-up ad for the iPhone 6+. The promotion extols the phone's improved security and the Apple Pay feature. The consumer was not actually ready to buy a new phone. But her credit card was recently compromised; that's a big problem. So she decided Apple Pay's added security obviously offers a useful solution; that's a big value. Her need recognition was triggered by a marketing stimulus.

Another consumer may be driving down I-35 between Dallas and San Antonio when his car breaks down for the third time this month. The proverbial straw breaks the camel's back; now's the time to trade up to a new used car. In this case, a natural situation event triggered need arousal.

Consumer Decision Stage 2: Information Search

Once aroused, consumers' needs activate information search processes. This stage may or may not occur. But with high-involvement decisions it almost certainly will. When the search does begin, various sources that provide information about available solutions or which solutions are preferable will be accessed. The importance of sources usually varies substantially, depending on individual consumer characteristics or characteristics associated with the problem itself.

The search for alternative solutions typically begins with a memory scan. This is called an internal search. In most purchase situations, consumers possess some prior knowledge about one or more products and/or brands that may meet their needs. This knowledge typically results from prior exposure to advertising and other promotions, past experience with products, and interactions with other consumers who have made similar purchases in the past.

Information received from others, who by definition already exist in the "decider's" social sphere, is typically deemed more trustworthy and credible. This information therefore tends to be more influential. These "others"—who might be friends, family, coworkers, or classmates—usually have no vested interest in the product. Consequently, they have no reason to misrepresent, exaggerate, or lie. Similar descriptions, unfortunately, cannot routinely be applied to marketing-controlled sources.

Low-Involvement Search Processes

Information already stored in memory about viable alternatives may prove sufficient for most low-involvement purchases. Or, external search may be limited to scanning the environment for information that confirms the product's availability and price. An immediate choice can be made. For many low-involvement products, such as paper towels, candy, soft drinks, and other "convenience goods," consumers may skip the information search and alternative evaluation steps, and proceed immediately to actual purchase (choice).

Little prior thought is given to the purchase choice because the risks associated with the product or selecting the wrong alternative are very low. Low-involvement products are relatively less important to consumers. Consequently, consumers willingly accept a range of alternatives, so long as they provide a reasonable level of satisfaction. There is little need to complicate decision-making processes by engaging in additional information search and evaluation. Time, like attention or money, is a scarce resource for almost everyone. Consumers would rarely waste cognitive cash on endless searches for solutions to relatively unimportant problems that are already understood.

This is why marketers of convenience goods should initiate measures to ensure that their brands are among the first to be recalled from memory. Consumers are simply not willing to engage in much information search (internal or external) for low-involvement purchases. Those brands that are recalled first are generally more frequently purchased, underscoring the power of, as well as the need for, promotional strategies designed to create **top-of-mind brand awareness (TOMA)** via repeat advertising across a wide range of media.

This is one reason why Bud, Miller, and Coors continue to advertise so vociferously. These three brands continue to inundate football fans with messages even though each viewer already knows:

- Budweiser is the "King of Beers" (and has Clydesdale horses, too).
- Miller "Tastes Great and Is Less Filling."
- Coors is "Rocky Mountain Brewed," except in Eden, NC (about 1700 miles from the Rockies).

Each beer marketer realizes that its brand must remain "top of the mind" among beer drinking segments if it is to stay tops in market share.

Impulse purchases usually involve low-involvement products. (Consumers make impulse purchases with little to no planning, forethought or, at times, prudence.) This flood of advertising is supported by marketers' liberal use of in-store promotions and displays, coupons, games, contests and other sales promotions, all aimed at increasing consumers' tendencies to purchase impulsively, or encouraging last minute brand-switching. Products purchased under low-involvement conditions are generally distributed through a wide range of distribution outlets. Products must be readily available to reduce the likelihood that consumers will switch to alternative brands.

High-Involvement Search Processes

Internal information search efforts also sometimes prove adequate for higher-involvement consumer decisions. This would most likely occur when consumer are already well informed about the product category. In other words, consumers possess high levels of expertise and confidence about the product and how to use it. Additional external searches would simply waste scarce time.

Brand loyalty reduces the likelihood and degree of external search. This is one reason why brand loyalty is one of the strongest assets any marketer could ever hope to possess. Loyal consumers already demonstrate strong preferences for specific brands. Consequently, they generally believe there is no reason to consider alternatives. Why, then, would loyal consumers pursue additional information?

Exceptions occasionally may arise when expert consumers seek to confirm their expectations. This would be done to minimize any residual perceived risk or anxiety surrounding the purchase. Such consumers implicitly (unknowingly) or explicitly (knowingly) seek to avoid serious post-purchase cognitive dissonance, which is one of marketers' worst enemies, and therefore an outcome Firms seek to avoid.

Consumers, however, do engage in external information searches for most high-involvement purchase decisions. When purposefully gathering information during external search processes, consumers typically rely on printed media (advertising, consumer reports, product brochures, etc.) or personal sources (friends, family, co-workers, classmates). Print media are useful for conveying large amounts of complex information, which is the exact amount and type of information consumers often actively seek when making expensive, risky, or socially conspicuous product decisions. Television and Internet (including social media) advertising generally prove less useful to marketers under these conditions. This is because only limited amounts of information can be communicated through a single advertisement or exposure. More recently, of course, the Internet is becoming increasingly valuable to consumers searching for precisely relevant information associated with extensive, high-involvement decisions.

Non-commercial printed media (e.g. *Consumer Reports*) and personal sources of information (friends, family, co-workers) are particularly important for consumers who lack a high level of expertise with the product category. As noted, such sources are perceived as more credible because they are not trying to "sell." The same cannot be said for commercial advertising. When purchase decisions are perceived as risky, personal sources are generally the most important for assisting novice consumers in their decision-making efforts. Highly risk-averse and/or inexperienced consumers may actually delegate direct decision-making responsibility to a personal source. Teenagers or young people may source one or more of their parents in this fashion when purchasing an automobile. Indeed, they may directly act based on recommendations made by such personal sources.

Certain social or environmental pressures may influence the extent to which consumers search for information. Three are worth noting. First, when consumers are pressured by time to make decisions, they may curtail their information search efforts, even for high-involvement decisions.

Second, physical constraints such as a lack of transportation, limited access to relevant information, or illness may limit consumers' ability to engage in information search. Consumers simply are unable to shop around for information. Given the near universal access to the Internet that prevails today, this limitation is likely less a problem than it once was.

Finally, marketers themselves sometimes try to constrain consumers' search efforts. This would be done for purposes of pressing for quick decision-making (buy-now) based on short-term conditions designed to facilitate purchase of the "coercive" marketer's brand. (Note: coercive marketing tactics may be aggressive but not unethical.)

Such marketing activities reduce the amount of time and effort expended on information search. They might include special limited-time price deals, aggressive personal selling, exceptional warranties, liberal return policies, and point-of-sale devices. These tactics deliver incentives intended to truncate the search process by saying, in effect, "Choose me, now, please." Consumers must weigh the benefits and costs of continuing versus curtailing their search and buying now in order to receive the incentives and values being offered. All part of "free and fair," "get and give," buyer-seller exchange processes.

Consumer Decision Stage 3: Alternative Evaluation

Alternative evaluation and information search essentially occur together; they cannot really be separated into distinct steps. Information about product alternatives is evaluated as it is collected. Consumers instantly evaluate how alternatives measure-up against one another and how the value of each may satisfy their needs.

The evaluation process again is much more extensive for higher risk, complex decisions. Indeed, probably the best way to reduce the level of uncertainty and consequent post-purchase anxiety for the higher involvement purchase is to carefully weigh the alternatives against one another before buying!

When engaged in extensive decision-making, consumers generally employ, even subconsciously, complicated "cognitive decision algebra" to aid the evaluation process. (Cognitive implies mental, intellectual, reasoning-based, thinking sorts of activities are occurring, inside consumers' brains.) Less complex mental processing is employed by consumers when they engage in lower-involvement, routine decisions.

The specific cognitive decision algebra employed by consumers for both extensive and routine decisions has been the subject of much research. This research will continue forever, because it relates to the nearly-impossible-to-answer "Why" question that which was introduced earlier.

Consumer Decision Stage 4: Choice

For extensive problem-solving decision-making, consumers' alternative evaluation processes should culminate with the selection and purchase of one and only one alternative. That is, if consumers choose to purchase something. Remember, when consumers choose nothing at all they have still made a decision. However, any product chosen will always be the one that promises the highest level of expected satisfaction as perceived by the decision maker.

When engaging in lower-involvement, routine decisions, consumers may opt for alternatives that are acceptable, but not necessarily the best choice. Acceptable alternatives may be selected when expenditures of extra time and effort are not, in the decision-maker's perception, worthwhile. Consumers do not always seek to maximize their value by identifying the absolute ideal choice. Buyer-seller exchanges involve tradeoffs.

Brand choices, during routine decision-making conditions, can occur in several ways. Each is consistent with the low-involvement nature of the purchase. Actual brand choice may result from inertia; positive consumer responses to various in-store stimuli; a desire to variety seek; or brand familiarity stemming from exposure to promotional activities, such as advertising.

Inertia, a term that emanates from the physics discipline, infers that an object at rest tends to remain at rest. It is often the easiest response for consumers who have purchased the same brand in the past. Consumer inertia amounts to spurious- or pseudo-brand loyalty in which consumers continue to buy the same brand because that is the brand they always purchase. They perceive that no reason or incentive to switch exists. The product has performed adequately and has not resulted in any dissatisfying experiences.

Consumer inertia, however, is not the same as brand loyalty. Inert consumers will readily switch brands if marketers create or fail to create the right conditions. Out-of-stock scenarios, point-of-sale promotions, alluring coupons, and in-store stimuli can induce brand-switching behavior. This is because little to no emotional commitment to the brand is present; the relationship between consumer and brand is weak.

Variety seeking is the desire to try something new. Consumers can get bored with brands. Many will consciously decide to change brands occasionally. Generally, the decision is made in the store. Upon reaching the breakfast cereal aisle, for example, consumers may decide now's the time to switch from Cheerios to Wheaties. The low risk nature of convenience goods makes this type of decision easy. There is no implication that the consumer was dissatisfied with Cheerios. Indeed, the consumer may switch back to that brand the next time.

Brand familiarity created by repetitive advertising experienced across time may cause consumers to unconsciously pull brands from shelves into their basket. Strong beliefs and attitudes about low-involvement products are not formed prior to purchase and use, if at all. When unfamiliar with a product category, consumers may select brands based on sheer familiarity created by advertising. These outcomes bear witness to the power of repeat advertising for creating top-of-mind brand awareness.

Brand choice implies that purchase of the chosen alternative readily follows. Brand choice and purchase may occur virtually simultaneously for low-involvement products. For grocery products, for example, the chosen item is placed into the shopping cart and paid for in a matter of minutes.

However, for higher-involvement decisions, purchase may not immediately occur. For example, a consumer may have made his decision to buy a specific brand of notebook computer. But he still confronts decisions about financing, the store or site from which to make the purchase, or what options to include (e.g. carrying cases, extra batteries, add-on data drives, etc.) before actually making the purchase. Although tangential to the basic brand decision, they may be equally important. These extra decisions are called instrumental actions.[7]

Purchase also may be delayed, or not happen at all, due to the intervention of **external constraints**.[8] These constraints are typically beyond the control of the consumer and can effectively halt the purchase process, or cause the consumer to revisit earlier stages in the decision making process. For example, the inability to obtain financing for a home or to obtain insurance for a sports car at a reasonable cost may delay or preclude purchase.

Consumer Decision Stage 5: Post-Purchase Behaviors

Consumers proceed into a period of post-purchase evaluation immediately after their actual purchase decision. As they use and experience products consumer evaluation continues. Consumers decide whether they are satisfied. Fundamentally, they are answering yes to one of three questions: Have my expectations been met? (I'm satisfied.) Exceeded? (I'm delighted.) Has the product fallen short of my expectations? (I'm not happy, unsatisfied, and may complain about it.)

Satisfaction increases the likelihood that a repeat purchase will occur. A loyal customer and eventual brand evangelist who spreads the good word about the product may be born. Dissatisfaction decreases the likelihood of either outcome.

In today's intensely competitive environment, Firms are or should be extremely sensitive to customer satisfaction. The relative profitability associated with retaining existing satisfied customers is substantially higher than are profits associated with acquiring new customers. Sell them once, and service them (well) forever, the marketing adage suggests. Studies have documented the negative impacts on the Firm for failing to effectively manage customer dissatisfaction. For every 100 dissatisfied customers, on average only four actively complain to the business. The other 96 simply quit the company. More importantly, each dissatisfied customer will, on average, tell 8 to 10 others about their dissatisfying experiences. This not only translates into lost customers, but makes new customers that much more difficult and expensive to recruit.[9] This is called negative word-of-mouth.

Consumers often experience feelings of doubt or anxiety following purchases; especially those purchases associated with high-risk, high-cost, socially-conspicuous, high-involvement decisions. Was the best choice made? What about the truck, dress, vacation destination, house, job, or boyfriend/girlfriend or wife/husband I did not choose? They all had value, too.

This phenomenon is called post-purchase cognitive dissonance or buyer's remorse. Consumers question whether the best choice was made or even if the purchase should have been made at all. Several factors increase the likelihood that consumers will experience cognitive dissonance after the purchase. As noted, dissonance is more likely to occur when there is substantial risk associated with the purchase. If the product is expensive, tends to strongly reflect social group values, or is functionally complex, perceptions of risk will be higher and post-purchase doubt is more likely to occur. Buyer's remorse is also more likely to exist when the alternatives under consideration were close substitutes for one another and the decision could have gone either way.

Consumers consciously or unconsciously seek to avoid the negative emotional impact of cognitive dissonance. They may avoid information (such as advertisements) about alternatives that were not chosen, or focus only on the negative points in these advertisements. Consumers who decide Dell is for them may avoid or ignore HP advertisements. Or, if exposed to HP advertisements, they may selectively interpret information in ways that magnify the brand's negative characteristics.

Similarly, consumers may reinforce their decisions for the chosen alternative by seeking information about that brand. Knowing this, marketers often develop advertisements directed at recent purchasers to reinforce their choice, thereby helping them reduce the likelihood of post-purchase dissonance. Consumers also may attempt to "sell" the chosen brand to others by building up its good points. Essentially, by convincing others that they (the buyer) made a good decision, they are subconsciously reinforcing the wisdom of the choice in their own mind.[10]

→ Psychological Factors Influence Consumer Decision-Making

The model depicted in Exhibit 7.1 summarized four discrete sets of factors that influence consumer decision-making. Three uncontrollable sets of elements (beyond influence, from the perspective of the Firm) are discussed below. These three factors are psychological, sociocultural, and purchase situation conditions. The fourth, controllable element that also influences consumer decision-making includes marketing activities, or management of marketing mix, which is discussed elsewhere throughout the book

Consumer Needs and Motives

As noted, consumer decision-making processes begin when consumers recognize the existence of a purchasing need or problem. **Needs** are the fundamental forces that cause people to act. Wants result from needs. **Wants** can be viewed as specific satisfiers of the underlying need. For example, you need clothing but want a new pair of 7 For All Mankind jeans.

Wants are learned. Needs are more basic in nature. Aroused needs may cause the consumer to initiate the search for satisfiers of the need. Such aroused needs are called "motives" or "drives"; consumers are motivated or driven to engage in decision-making processes.

Various classification schemes exist that can be used to identify the range of needs and motives that impact human behavior. The most useful and the most widely used scheme is Maslow's Hierarchy of Needs (Exhibit 7.4)[11].

Maslow proposed that people move through a series of motivational states. Consumers themselves begin with the most basic and pressing needs, the ones situated at the bottom of the pyramid. Consumers try to satisfy their most important needs first before moving on to higher-level needs. Basic physical needs comprise the first two levels of the hierarchy. At the bottom are basic physiological needs such as hunger, thirst, and rest. Marketers can target and position food, sports drinks, pharmaceutical products, health care and fitness products to consumers who are experiencing these needs.

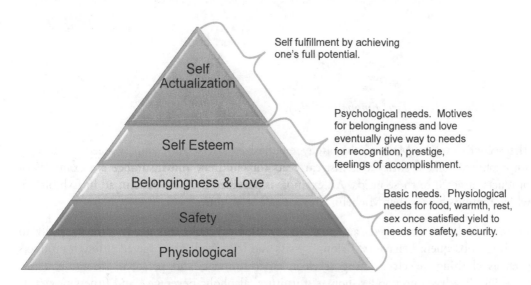

Exhibit 7.4 *Maslow's Hierarchy of Needs has also been called a hierarchy of motives.*

Exhibit 7.5 *Michelin Tires Emphasize Safety.*

The second level in Maslow's hierarchy emphasizes safety and security needs. Safety in automobiles, home security systems, car seats for children, and insurance are examples of products targeted to these needs. An example is provided by the Michelin ad in Exhibit 7.5, which reminds buyers that Michelin tires are safe at all times.

Once these lower level needs are satisfied, unfilled psychological needs arise naturally to motivate subsequent behaviors. Belongingness and love needs are targeted through products such as clothing, jewelry, dating services, entertainment, and personal grooming items. Clothing, jewelry, automobiles, homes, furniture, alcoholic beverages, and fitness programs are examples of products intended to fill needs for self-esteem, prestige, and/or feelings of accomplishment.

At the top of Maslow's hierarchy are needs related to self-actualization. Products directed at satisfying these high-level needs include travel, education, sports, professions, and hobbies. LA Fitness ads that emphasize self-esteem, belongingness, and working together to achieve fitness goals are directed at such higher level needs. The US Army's recruiting advertisements emphasize, "Be all you can be." The University of North Texas' promotes itself as your "Green Light to Greatness."

No assumption or expectation exists that all consumers will be able to satisfy all their needs. There is an assumption that consumers move up and down the pyramid, as some needs are temporarily satisfied and then go wanting. Remember who we are as consumers: rarely-fully-satisfied, yawning-empty-holes, constantly-yearning-to-be-filled-up creatures. This is not exaggeration for effect. This is the truth about us as humans and consumers.

Motivation research investigates consumers' reasons for engaging in consumption-related behaviors and for making the decisions they make. Consumers may or may not be consciously aware of their true consumption-related motives. Increasingly, researchers are determining that, much of the time, consumers are operating in the dark when it comes to their true underlying buying motives. Motivation research presumes that underlying or unconscious motives exist and influence consumer behavior. Motivation research is designed to get at the "hidden" motives; to reveal the inside skinny of the Why question.

The major tools of motivational research are observation, focus groups, and depth interviews. The most useful, but most expensive and time consuming, is direct observation of human behavior. This technique, long used by anthropologists (called ethnographic research) to investigate behavioral patterns driven by cultural differences, can uncover hidden human motives. The tool is equally useful for gaining insights into consumer motivations through direct personal observation or via recorded video. Usually, personal observation is too expensive in terms of cost and time, and few people would be happy having an anthropologist in their household for a month at a time.[12]

Consumer Perception

Perception involves the process by which consumers select, organize and interpret (attempt to make sense of) information. The goal is to create a meaningful, useful picture of what is happening around them. Information is acquired via our five senses. As consumers actively or passively acquire information, they consciously or unconsciously attempt to organize and attach meaning to that information. Our cultural heritage and social class status exercise substantial influence on these sense- or meaning-making activities.

Consumer perceptions are always selective in nature. The alternative is having our heads explode like the Martians did in *Mars Attacks* when they heard Slim Whitman yodel. Humans are exposed daily to too many stimuli to process them all. Consequently, as consumers encounter information, several perceptive filters, or screens, kick in. These filters determine whether that information will be internalized and retained in memory. The vast majority of information to which consumers are exposed is selectively filtered out and discarded. These perceptual filters include:

Selective Exposure
Selective exposure occurs when consumers are exposed to some forms of information but not others. Marketers attempt to overcome selective exposure by ensuring that communications

are placed in media most likely to be viewed by target customers. A common mistake made by many marketers targeting "Millennials" is placing their communications in traditional advertising media, such as TV, when these consumers acquire most information via social media and other Internet sources.[13]

Selective Attention

Selective attention occurs when consumers, once exposed to information, pay attention to only part of that information. Marketers attempt to gain attention by employing entertaining communications in advertising (humor appeals, sex appeals) and by using physical stimuli that tend to stand out (bright colors, sounds, full-page advertisements, etc.).

Selective Interpretation

Selective interpretation occurs when consumers construe information in ways to allow it to fit with existing beliefs and attitudes. Consumers misperceive or misunderstand a large proportion of the information to which they are exposed. An average of 30% of commercial information is misinterpreted by consumers. No communication is immune from such misinterpretation.[14] Marketers strive to ensure that their marketing communications are interpreted as intended. In fact, as discussed further in Chapter 15, communication never actually occurs unless the intended message is understood in the manner the sender intended it to be understood. Advertisements are extensively pretested to ascertain how they will be perceived. The costs of failing to pre-test can be high. A recent Media/Harris Poll suggested more than one third of Americans would not purchase a brand due to exposure to offensive or distasteful advertising.[15]

Selective Retention

Selective retention means that only a portion of the information that makes it through the other perceptual filters is retained in memory. Selective retention is essentially selective memory. How long something is remembered and how much is retained are functions of the importance of the information to the consumer, the extent to which the importance of the information has been reinforced, how often the information has been repeated, and the extent to which imagery has been employed to create the memory.

Consumers tend to retain information longer that is more important to them or that scares them. Fear is a powerful motivator; fear forces us to pay attention. Information that is easily recalled or long-remembered has recently come to be known as "sticky." For marketing communicators, especially advertisers, sticky is usually a good thing. Sticky information often affects our daily existence and is, therefore, regularly accessed in memory. The resulting memory traces tend to be strong and long-lived.[16]

Consumers tend to remember information that is reinforced over time. If information is associated with some type of reward, whether positive or negative in nature, consumers generally remember the information longer. The stronger the reward, the more likely the information will be retained. Assume, for example, you see an advertisement for a pain reliever such as Excedrin Migraine. You buy Excedrin and it effectively relieves severe headaches. A strong reward! You will remember Excedrin Migraine.

Repetition, simply repeating messages, increases the probability that information will be retained. This is why many advertisers repeat advertisements again and again, particularly on television. Television is a low-involvement medium. When consumers watch TV they are generally passive, particularly when commercials arrive. Consumers usually pay little attention to the message, (which is one reason why advertisements are typically jazzed up with sexual imagery, bawdy or evocative humor, and general noise and disconcerting jerkiness.) As a result, with any single airing of a commercial, the consumer is likely to retain very little information. However, over time, as consumers are exposed to repetitions of the advertisement (generally, at least three times), they become more likely to absorb and retain some key pieces of information. Of course, marketers hope consumers retain the brand name and major benefits associated with brand. This type of low-involvement learning, based on repetition, is referred to as iconic rote learning.[17]

The use of imagery in marketing communications promotes greater memory retention. Imagery includes mental representations of actual visual objects and phenomena, as well as sensory representations of words, such as brand names or slogans. Certainly, well-known brand names (such as Coke and Levi) connote well-defined images of what these brands represent, the brands' personalities. Words that connote such images are easier to remember, and memory traces are stickier due to the dual coding of the stimulus.[18]

Consumer Learning

Learning can be viewed as any change in beliefs, attitudes, and behavior resulting from personal experience, mental interpretations, or representations of these experiences, or through observing the experiences of other individuals. Learning is any change in the content or organization of our long-term memory. This means that we learn directly from our experiences and what we think of those experiences. In addition, we learn by observing the behaviors of other people.[19] You learned either when you touched the hot stove or your parents screamed at you to stop.

How consumers learn varies depending on the nature of the learning situation or environment. The distinction between "high involvement learning" and "low involvement learning" situations is particularly important. In high-involvement situations, consumers are motivated to learn. A consumer, for example, may read a magazine or watch a television commercial that describes a product in which they are interested. This high interest level motivates consumers to pay attention and, at times, mentally rehearse the information. The end result is that information will more likely be retained and impact attitudes/potential behaviors.

Low-involvement learning situations, by contrast, exist when consumers demonstrate little motivation to learn information. Low-involvement learning situations arise more frequently than high-involvement learning situations for consumers and students. When people watch television and experience a commercial for a product that they don't care about, they probably won't pay attention. There is little motivation to cognitively elaborate on (actively think about) the information in the ad, let alone retain that information in memory.

Because consumer learning for most products occurs in low-involvement situations, this chapter emphasizes low-involvement learning theories. Two highly respected theories are discussed: classical conditioning and iconic rote learning.

Classical Conditioning

Classical conditioning dates to experiments conducted by Ivan Pavlov in the 1920s.[20] Exhibit 7.6 presents a simple model of how classical conditioning works. Pavlov noted that when his experimental subjects (dogs) were exposed to a natural stimulus (food), which he called the "unconditioned stimulus," a naturally occurring salivation response or "unconditioned response" was elicited. In a series of experiments, Pavlov paired the unconditioned stimulus (food) with a neutral "conditioned stimulus," the sound of a metronome. Each time the dogs were exposed to food, they also heard the metronome (the conditioned stimulus). The pairing

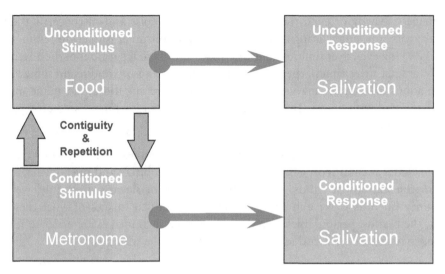

Exhibit 7.6 *The Classical Conditioning Process Employed by Pavlov.*

of the conditioned and the unconditioned stimuli was repeated multiple times. After a series of trials, the dogs eventually learned that the metronome and the food went together; they learned the connection between the two. As a result, when dogs were exposed to the metronome in the absence of food, they still salivated (now referred to as a conditioned response). What was a naturally occurring unconditioned response was now a conditioned response—conditioned to the sound of a metronome.

Associations between conditioned and unconditioned stimuli must be learned. The keys to stimulating this learning are repetition and contiguity. (Contiguity means a paired closeness, or proximate, as in close-to or next-to—Plano is contiguous to Dallas.) The association must be repeated again and again. And, both conditioned and unconditioned stimuli must be presented temporally contiguous to one another; that is, they must be presented at approximately the same point in time.[21]

One of the best examples of classical conditioning at work in advertising is illustrated by the repositioning of Marlboro cigarettes. This is one of the most effective media campaigns in history.[22] Today, the Marlboro brand conveys images of ruggedness, masculinity, and strength. But Marlboro was not always the brand consumers perceive today. When originally introduced, Marlboro was positioned as a woman's cigarette. The brand was promoted and positioned as the "Ivory Tipped Cigarette" that as "Mild as May." The Leo Burnette advertising agency developed a campaign to reposition the Marlboro brand to the male blue-collar market. After experimenting with a number of "macho" images, the agency eventually settled on the American cowboy. Subsequent advertisements effectively linked the Marlboro brand to the cowboy image, despite the fact that across the decades cowboy models kept dying from cancer. (This really happened; look it up.)

The success of the Leo Burnette advertising campaign and the surging sales for the Marlboro brand can be explained from a classical conditioning perspective. The cowboy image was an unconditioned stimulus. Positive consumer feelings evoked by this image were an unconditioned response. The Marlboro brand became the conditioned stimulus that was associated with the cowboy image through repeat advertising with the continual presence of the cowboy in all promotional materials. Because of the effective link created between the cowboy image and Marlboro, the brand itself was able to generate the same positive emotions, or positive affect, originally attributed to the cowboy image alone.

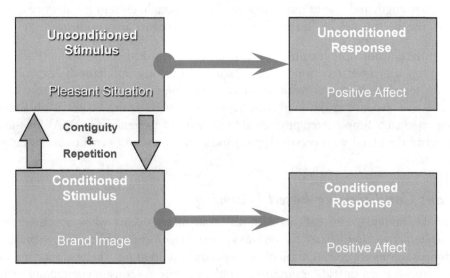

Exhibit 7.7 *The Classical Conditioning Process In a Marketing Context.*

The success of the Marlboro experience can be generalized to how classical conditioning operates in marketing contexts. As illustrated in Exhibit 7.7, given any "pleasant consumption situation," meaning a setting or an event, that is capable of producing positive feelings in consumers, the basis exists for classical conditioning to occur. The pleasant situation is the unconditioned stimulus and its ability to produce positive emotions (i.e. positive affect) is the unconditioned response. If a marketer can succeed in linking its brand's image to the original pleasant situation, the brand may become synonymous in the consumer's mind with the original pleasant situation. As a result, the brand, again by itself, may generate the same positive affective response that was produced by the original happy situation.

A common approach to classical conditioning in advertising is to present a product within the context of an appealing lifestyle setting, as in most perfume and cologne ads. In such ads, the brand is displayed in combination with an alluring lifestyle setting. Such advertisements are selling an image. If the association between the brand and the lifestyle setting is repeatedly demonstrated in other advertisements or promotional media across time, consumers may link the brand with the lifestyle theme. Not only is an attractive image created for the brand, a positive emotional response to the brand also emerges.

Classical conditioning is also illustrated through advertisements that connect brands with sports themes or heroes. Indeed, critics of advertising beer and wine on TV cite the danger of advertisements that continually link drinking with party themes. The fear is that children and young adults are more susceptible to attempts at classical conditioning.

Passive (or Iconic Rote) Learning

Iconic rote learning, also called incidental or passive learning, explains how most consumer learning occurs for low involvement products. Iconic rote learning involves learning the association between two or more concepts in the absence of conditioning.[23] The key element in iconic rote learning is message repetition. Repetition is employed to create a link between a brand name and key benefits delivered by that brand. To illustrate this point, consider the well-known humor appeal for Hefty Zip Bags. The ad depicted a gingerbread character contained in a zip bag being repeatedly dropped and battered, but apparently remaining unharmed. The final comment in the ad was "that's one tough bag!" The "that's one tough bag" theme using the gingerbread character was an effective mechanism for emphasizing the major benefits of the bag: its strength and ease of use. If repeated often enough, even in the absence of focused attention, the message will be "learned" by a large share of the target audience.

On the surface, iconic rote learning appears similar to classical conditioning. Like classical conditioning, it involves repetition. But no stimulus-response mechanism is involved with iconic rote learning. Moreover, with iconic rote learning there is no attempt to stimulate a direct affective response to the marketing stimulus; that is, to the brand. With iconic rote learning, marketers simply attempt to create top of mind awareness (TOMA) for the brand and associate the brand with certain key features, attributes, and benefits that it delivers to consumers.

Operant Conditioning-based Learning

Operant conditioning, also called instrumental learning, occurs when consumers choose between alternative stimuli based on rewards associated with choices they learn to make. These reward mechanisms are crucial to successful operant conditioning. The operant conditioning learning process often unfolds as a result of trial and error. As consumers respond to various marketing stimuli, they learn that different choices are associated with different rewards.

The model of operant conditioning shown in Exhibit 7.8 illustrates its application in a marketing context. The process begins when consumers are exposed to marketing stimuli. Stimuli could include a humorous but informative advertisement, point of purchase (in-store) display announcing drastic short-term price cuts, or a persuasive salesperson. After exposure to the stimulus, a consumer may decide to try or sample the product that has been promoted. Either way, the consumer may have acted impulsively in response to the stimuli. If the consumer liked the product because the experience or its benefits proved gratifying (exceeded expectations), the consumer has received a positive reward. The receipt of this reward reinforces the attractiveness of this specific stimulus-response relationship. The relationship, as perceived,

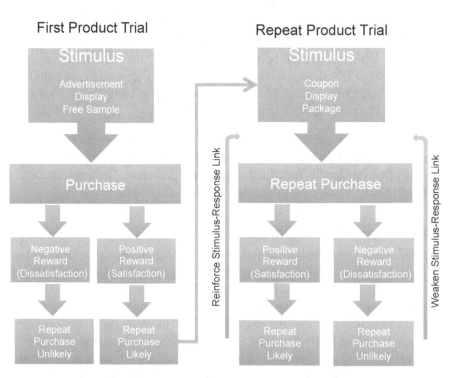

Exhibit 7.8 *Marketers rely on instrumental learning to stimulate trial and repeat purchase behavior.*

is simple: do this one thing, get this other thing. The likelihood that the same consumer response will be repeated during similar shopping occasions naturally increases. Subsequent exposure to additional marketing stimuli may again trigger purchase behavior for the product. If the consumer is again positively rewarded (i.e. the consumer is satisfied with the purchase) an even stronger stimulus-response linkage may emerge, making it increasingly more likely that the consumer will engage in the same purchase behavior in the future.

What if the product experience or its benefits failed to gratify? The consumer would be dissatisfied and repurchase would be unlikely. Negative rewards lessen or extinguish the stimulus-response linkage.

Operant conditioning relies heavily on consumers actually using a product. If not, they cannot experience positive rewards, and learning cannot occur. This is why most marketing promotions are designed to stimulate trial, use, and repeat trial and use of the product. The development of uniformly high-quality new products that deliver unique and useful benefits is also crucial. Otherwise, the learning experiences of consumers will be negative. No learned consumer loyalty or repeat purchases will follow.

Each satisfying experience is assumed to build on previous experiences in operant learning. Thus when learning occurs it becomes increasingly likely that consumers will continue to buy the same brand in the future. This idea is incorporated into an application of operant conditioning known as shaping. The following example illustrates how marketers can shape consumers' behavior. Assume a consumer receives a free sample of a new laundry detergent in the mail. The consumer uses the product and is satisfied. Further assume a coupon worth fifty cents on a second purchase accompanied the free sample. The consumer decides to use the coupon and buys the product a second time. Once more the consumer uses the product and is satisfied. This initial purchase behavior is further reinforced. A third purchase of the brand may be stimulated through an in-store coupon. The consumer may not have planned this latter purchase, but the coupon may generate an impulse buy. Again, the consumer is satisfied with the brand and the stimulus-response behavior is reinforced one more time. The next time the consumer needs laundry detergent he or she may be inclined to pay full price.

Shaping behavior entails walking consumers through a series of steps. These steps begin with a low risk trial of the product. They end with a decision to purchase the product at its full price. Shaping behavior is often used in this manner to reduce the initial risk associated with purchasing new products.

Vicarious Learning

Vicarious learning arises when consumers observe the results of other peoples' decisions/ behaviors/consequences and adjust their consumption behaviors based on the desirable or undesirable outcomes that were observed. Consumers, all of us, continuously see friends using smart phones or wearing designer clothes or jewelry and then evaluate (consciously or sub-consciously) the consequences of our friends' decisions. We decide, again consciously or unconsciously, that we would like to enjoy some of those consequences ourselves or, alternatively, that we would just as soon avoid such consequences.

Such observations and evaluations of others' experiences are an everyday part of lives. This is a normal pattern of behavior that is likely now more prevalent and certainly easier to engage in due to the proliferation of social networking devices such as Facebook and Twitter. And, ready or not, consumers learn more about what products or experiences they would like to have or would seek to avoid as a result of this process.

Most vicarious learning probably occurs in high-involvement situations. However, vicarious learning can also be low-involvement since consumers are constantly exposed to others' behaviors in lower involvement situations. Consumers may pay little or no attention to these behaviors, but the actions can leave memory traces that solidify over time with additional similar observations.[24]

Learning Through Reasoning

Reasoning is the most complex form of learning. Reasoning is the basis by which we gather and evaluate information that is employed in making extended or complex decisions. Reasoning is a high-involvement problem-solving process. Reasoning occurs when new information is collected and is combined with information already in memory for purposes of problem solving. New associations emerge and, in the process, existing concepts are modified or updated or entirely new concepts are created.

Consumer Beliefs and Attitudes

Beliefs and attitudes about products are generated naturally as consumers experience, learn more, and develop insights about those products. Beliefs are descriptive thoughts that consumers have about something; for example, a product, person, idea, place, or an experience. They are less deeply held than attitudes. Beliefs are formed as consumers accumulate knowledge about products' characteristics and their performance. They are generally devoid of emotion (i.e. feelings of good or bad; positive or negative, etc.).

Attitudes, by contrast, capture consumers' relatively enduring, consistent, deeply-held evaluations, feelings, and tendencies held toward a person, idea, place, or an experience. Attitudes are comprised of multiple, bundled, linked, and interconnected beliefs. Thus consumers' beliefs about product characteristics influence their attitudes toward those products. Attitudes, unlike beliefs, capture emotions.[25]

Consumers, for example, may hold beliefs about Harley-Davidson motorcycles related to the brand's country of origin, styling, performance, price, image, reliability, etc. Based on the relative importance of their beliefs on these dimensions, consumers then may form an overall favorable or unfavorable emotional response to the brand. These overall emotional responses are those consumers' attitudes toward the Harley-Davidson brand.

Any marketing effort to create and/or change consumer attitudes will prove challenging. The usual approach is to first attempt to structure or change consumers' beliefs about the product. If successful, a desired attitude may follow. This approach is typically employed when marketers develop new products or reposition existing products in order to enter a new market. Consumers first must be educated on the product's characteristics and benefits before a new attitude can be formed. Beano, for example, was an early entry into the market for products that reduce the gas generated by some food products. The initial communications approach was to identify the benefits of the product i.e. what it would do.

Still, the idea that marketers should routinely attempt to change consumers' attitudes is generally troubling. We cannot in good faith recommend this strategy. Instead, marketers should align the specific product/value that they create, promote, price, and distribute (note a reference to the marketing mix) such that their value propositions align with the preexisting consumer attitudes that dominate within targeted consumer segments. In other words, the

Republican Party should never attempt to position and target even the most appealing pro-life ideas toward target consumer segments whose existing attitudes tilt them leftward toward pro-choice sentiments; i.e., the Democratic Party. Instead, Republican marketers should target consumers in the middle who don't yet possess fully formed attitudes about where a mother's rights end and a child's rights begin.

Consumer Personality

Personality is defined as unique and lasting psychological characteristics that lead consumers to respond in enduring and consistent ways to events and stimuli as each arise in a given consumer's environment. Critical personality traits, at least from the perspective of marketers, include self-confidence, extroversion or introversion, dominance, friendliness or sociability, adaptability, and assertiveness or aggressiveness. The thing about our personalities is that these traits or behaviors generally remain constant across situations. Our personalities reflect who we are. The people who want to answer all the in-class questions asked by the Professor in this course, for example, want to answer all the questions in other courses, too.

Efforts to verify relationships between personality and consumption patterns have yielded mixed results. But the assumption, which remains logical, is that consumers' personality traits impact their preferences for specific products and brands, and affect their decision-making. Consumers often select the products they believe are consistent with or reflective of their personalities.

What is known for certain, however, is that brands have personalities. A brand's personality is its image. Marketers jealously guard their brands' images and attempt to persuade consumers that a desirable "match" exists between their personality and that of the brand. If you're an outlaw, what brand of beer will you drink? If you're male and a lothario (look it up), what clothing brand will you give as a gift to your significant other(s)? Can you keep a secret?

Self-Concept

Personality is related to self-concept. Self-concept is a multi-dimensional construct that captures how consumers feel about and see themselves. Self-concept reflects consumers' personal identity.

The most important dimensions, from the perspective of marketers, are consumers' **ideal-private-self** and **ideal-social-self**. The ideal-private-self encapsulates how consumers would prefer to see themselves. The ideal-social-self captures how consumers would like other to see them. Consumers will change their hair, face, clothing, cars, or even their zip code to move themselves closer to these ideal selves. Many products are characterized by high levels of symbolism that may reflect favorably on consumers' idealized private or social selves. Consumers often buy products in part because the values they deliver reflect or seemingly may further those consumers' ideal private and social selves. You are consuming college and this course because you have an ideal career in mind. You have reasoned, logically we might add, that consuming this education will move you closer to your ideal social and private self.

Marketers strive to establish brand images that align with important dimensions of consumers' ideal self-concepts (Exhibit 7.9). Brand images are designed and communicated to encourage consumers to perceive a match between the brand's image and some dimension of their ideal self-concept. Such matches, in turn, can contribute to the formation of positive attitudes toward

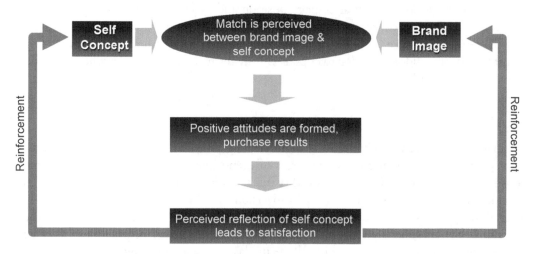

Exhibit 7.9 *Marketers match elements of brand image to consumers' ideal self-concepts to build positive attitudes for brands.*

the brand and, ultimately, a purchase decision. After using the brand, if consumers perceive their self-concept is adequately reflected in the brand, satisfaction may result. Satisfaction, in turn, leads to positive feedback on both brand image and the consumer's self-concept. This feedback is essentially a reinforcing mechanism that solidifies both consumers' perceptions of self, and the fact that their self-concept is reflected in the image portrayed by the brand.

Consumer Lifestyle

Consumer lifestyle entails and captures consumers' patterns of daily living. Lifestyle is measured using three sets of variables. The first category of variables is the activities in which consumers routinely and voluntarily engage during their free time. The second is consumers' interests in things or events happening around them, such as sports, music, fashion, hunting and fishing, books or television, technology and social networking, and so forth. The third is the opinions consumers possess about themselves (including their self-concepts), social or cultural events or trends, political affairs or trends, business, technological and environmental events or trends, and so forth.

Lifestyle, when measured, answers the following question: what do consumers do (activities) and think about (their activities and opinions) in their free time; when they are not working, going to school or taking care of children? Once marketers answer this double-barreled question, they understand more about what products to target or not target toward specific marketing segments (product development and market targeting insights). As importantly, marketers will know what types of communication messages to deliver or not deliver to specifically targeted market segments (positioning and promotional insights). This is why the ability to profile and understand consumer lifestyle segments is so important to marketers.

Lifestyle is a partial extension of self-concept. Many lifestyle-related activities, interests, and opinions result from consumers' desires to achieve their ideal private or social selves. In fact, since lifestyle preferences are measured more easily than self-concept dimensions, lifestyle characteristics are usually employed by marketers to segment and profile consumer segments. Marketing research Firms often specialize in developing lifestyle segments for consumer products. For example, Nielsen's PRIZM service identifies 66 broad lifestyle market segments for product and services based on combinations of consumer demographics (age, income, education, occupation) and lifestyle characteristics. Each resulting segment is fully profiled in terms of product, store, and shopping preferences, as well as media viewing and messaging preferences. Marketers generally refer to these lifestyle activities, interests, and opinions by the acronym AIOs. These measures are collectively referred to as AIO inventories. A single marketing research survey may contain 30–40 AIO measurement items intended to profile consumers' lifestyles.

→ Socio-Cultural Factors Influence Consumer Decision-Making

The wants and needs, decision-making processes, and product preferences of consumers are shaped by trends and events as each unfold in social environments that surround them. These factors include culture and subculture, social class membership, family, and various reference groups. Marketers have little control over these environmental factors. However, they should thoroughly understand their potential and actual effects on consumers' decision-making.

Culture and Subculture

Culture is the broadest factor that influences consumer behavior. Culture is the most basic cause of a person's wants and behaviors. (Not a person's needs, mind you, which remain relatively constant and consistent regardless of cultural circumstance or membership.) Culture is the set or collection of values, beliefs, attitudes, norms, symbols, and customs that consumers share with or learn from other members of their cultural group. Membership in the same culture leads to common behavioral patterns.[26]

Values are the defining ingredients of any culture. A value is an enduring belief that is shared by members of a society that a specific behavior is personally or socially preferred over another. Central cultural values in the United States include strong beliefs in the importance of equality, freedom, the desire for accomplishment, and the pursuit of success. Because they yield common behavioral patterns and are held in common by most members of the society, shared cultural values often become the basis for segmenting markets and structuring marketing strategy. People with similar cultural values often prefer the same kinds of products and may respond similarly to a given marketing strategy.

Culture is important. But the cultural entities that prove most important for marketing managers are the leading edges of trends and movements unfolding inside any culture at a point in time. These trends exist either as opportunities (that marketers should strategically exploit) or threats (that marketers should strategically avoid), particularly when Firms are able to identify the opportunities or threats earlier than their competitors.

Cultural values are enduring, but they certainly evolve over time. Marketers must remain alert for signals of change. The future, as well as the present, generally belongs to Firms that are best prepared react quickly to change. We again see the need that exists for Firms to continuously engage in environmental scanning and strategy planning in response to what they detect.

Cultural shifts can create or destroy market opportunities for new products. For example, existing market opportunities for green products are the result of changing values about humanity's relationship to the environment. Shifting cultural norms about the value and appeal of health/fitness has created lucrative markets for gyms, fitness equipment and attire, nutritional food supplements, and energy drinks. Concurrently, the same cultural shifts threaten to destroy the long-term profitability of the fast food and soft drink industries.

Cultural change can evolve from emerging subcultures. Subcultures are smaller subsets or groups that exist within broader cultures. Members of subcultures may share common value systems based on similar life experiences, ethnicities, religious or political views, or even the teams that they follow (Green Bay Packer cheese-heads, anyone?). Members of subcultures share some values in common with the overall culture. But members also exhibit shared values that are unique to the subculture.

Subcultures often are treated as market segments for products because their memberships share certain values and beliefs in common. And as subcultures grow in size, influence, and power, these shared values can diffuse throughout and affect value systems held by the larger culture as a whole. Myriad subcultures of different sizes exist within the United States. They are often geographically concentrated based on religion or ethnicity. Cajun clusters situated in south Louisiana; high Mormon and Islamic concentrations located in Utah and Michigan, respectively; New Order Amish concentrated in Pennsylvania, Ohio, and Indiana; large Nordic cohorts situated in northern Wisconsin, Minnesota, and Montana; and the huge Hispanic concentration located along the southern border with Mexico exemplify this point.[27]

At times, subcultures can exist inside subcultures. The Hispanic population present in South Florida is primarily Cuban in its ethnic heritage. The much larger Hispanic subcultural cohort that resides in Texas, New Mexico, Arizona, and California is primarily Mexican in ethnicity. The cultural values present within these Hispanic subcultures often diverge as a result. The former segment, for example, votes primarily Republican; the latter segment generally opts for Democrats.

The three most important and rapidly growing subcultural groups in the United States are African Americans, Hispanics, and Asian Americans. The African American population in 2009 comprised 12.3% of the US population. By 2050, this proportion is anticipated to grow to 13%. Several generalizations can be made about African Americans. On average they are younger, less educated, less wealthy, and less likely to be married than the white population. These demographic differences contribute to certain consumption patterns that set apart African Americans from the larger US population; for example, their decision-making as voting consumers.

But African Americans, like Hispanics, are far from homogenous. A Yankelovich study identified 11 distinct market segments within the African American subculture. These segments were created based on differences in income, product and brand preferences, attitudes, and geographic location. The New Middle Class segment comprises 5% of the African American population. This segment generally ranges from 25 to 44 years of age; possesses the highest educational credentials of any segment and, correspondingly, is the wealthiest African American group; lives in suburbs; is technologically-savvy; and enjoys positive attitudes about the future. In terms of their subcultural values, segment membership generally self-identifies as "Black" and believes problems in the Black community are best solved by Blacks.[28]

Hispanic consumers constitute an increasing proportion of the US population. According to the Office of Management and Budget, Hispanic or Latino consumers include any person of Cuban, Mexican, Puerto Rican, South or Central American, or other Spanish culture or origin regardless of race. In 2010, the Hispanic population was about 50.5 million, comprising over 16% of the US population. As the fastest growing ethnic segment in the US, the Hispanic population is expected to grow 167 percent from 2010 to 2050, four times the growth rate of the overall US population.[29]

Hispanic consumers tend to be very family-oriented. When shopping, Hispanics exhibit more brand loyalty than the US population at large. Median household income for Hispanics is higher than that of African American segments. But the segment's income is significantly lower than that of European Americans or Asian Americans. Pointedly, Hispanic median income has grown substantially since 1993 and was the least affected by the economic downturn in 2008.[30] Hispanics exert a rapidly-increasing influence on the US economy. Today's typical Hispanic consumer possesses the ability to move between English and Spanish languages and embraces both cultures.[31]

Asian American consumers constitute the fastest growing consumer segment in the United States, with buying power estimated to reach one trillion dollars by 2017. Asian median household income is the highest of any ethnic group in the United States. The Asian American population is currently about 18.2 million; a 50% increase since 2000. The median household income for Asian Americans is 28% higher than the overall US median. Among Asian Americans, more than 50% of consumers who are older than 25 years of age hold college degrees.

Nielsen reports that 40% of Asian Americans are concentrated in three market areas: Los Angeles, New York City, and San Francisco. Asian Americans are culturally diverse. Note, for example, Chinese and Indian ethnic groups are each considered "Asian." But as a subcultural segment, Asian Americans share certain key values.

Compared to the entire US population, for example, higher proportions of Asian Americans value a successful marriage as among the most important things in life (54% vs. 34%). Asian American children are more likely to be raised in a two-parent married household (80% vs. 63%). These two values function as a two-headed engine that generally drives this American segments' higher levels of prosperity. Children raised in a household where their parents are married perform materially better in school. Correspondingly, more highly educated consumers subsequently perform better professionally and earn higher incomes.

Twenty-eight percent of Asian Americans live in extended family units. These units may include children, parents, grandparents, and other relations. Within the family unit, seniors are highly respected and have considerable input on major family consumption decisions. These consumption decisions include the educational pursuits and targeted professions of their children.[32]

Social Class, Income, and Education

Social classes exist in virtually all societies and are strongly correlated with many consumption patterns and behaviors. The takeaway: consumers from particular social class segments likely respond in similar ways to the same sorts of products, brands, marketing messages, prices, and even retail establishments. (For instance, different social classes are likely to shop at Walmart, Target, Penney's, or at Nordstrom's.) This is because members of specific social classes are more or less likely to "like" the same things. Consumer preferences, and thus their decision-making for certain product categories including clothing, home furnishings, automobiles, resident neighborhoods, leisure activities, or entertainment choices are highly correlated with social class membership.

Social classes are hierarchical rankings that exist in every society in the world. Membership in a particular class is generally a function of income, education, occupation, and accumulated wealth, but would never be determined by any single factor. For example, successful plumbers and general physicians may well make similar incomes. But physicians usually belong to a higher social class due to their profession's prestige and greater educational requirements; unless, perhaps, physicians practice proctology. Then the plumber and physician would at least occasionally address similar issues.

One commonly used classification scheme divides or segments the US population into seven classes:[33]

- *Upper-upper class* consisting of about .3% of the population and characterized by propensity to live in exclusive neighborhoods and buy expensive goods. These people tend to enjoy inherited wealth.
- *Lower-upper class* (1.2%) constitutes the newer social elite by virtue of developing their own wealth. This category includes corporate executives, owners of large businesses, and, to a lesser extent, some professionals.
- *Upper-middle class* with about 12% of the population. Consists of college graduate senior level managers of businesses and professionals.
- *Middle class* comprising 32% of the population. Consists of white- and blue- collar workers earning above average pay. Possesses upper-middle class values and aspirations.
- *Working class* comprising 38% of the population. Features average or below average pay, but live working class lifestyles regardless of income, education, and occupation.
- *Upper-lower class* (9% of the population). Lives just above the poverty level, but not on welfare.
- *Lower-lower class* (7% of the population). On welfare and visibly poverty-stricken and usually out of work, potentially homeless.

Social class status often represents what is known as a positional good in America. For consumers to be or remain on top of the social heap, it is not enough for them to have finer things. Such consumers also must possess things that are finer than anyone else. Someone who buys an expensive watch or automobile to climb the social ladder forces other climbers to buy more to rise up or remain at the same level themselves.

This process, harsh as it may appear, is likely driven by natural factors. Female peacocks get to select male peacocks for the purpose of mating. As you know, male peacocks, not females, boast the extraordinary tails. Which male is she likely to choose? The one with the good-enough tail or, one with a spectacular tail? This whole social striving process is great for marketers, great for the US economy, but is it great for strivers psyches? After all, we are not what we consume … despite what marketers would have us believe.

The Family Unit

The single-most important socio-cultural influence on consumption behavior is the family unit. The family unit itself is the single most important buying center in the entire US economy. A family consists of two or more people related by marriage, blood, or adoption living together in a household. A household, in turn, can hold more than just a family unit. Households can be any size. The unifying characteristic is that one or more people occupy a single dwelling together.

As of 2012, the average number of people per household declined to 2.6 from 3.1 in 1970; 66% of households were single family, down from 81% in 1970; between 1970 and 2012 the number of households consisting of married couples with children dropped from 40% to 20%; during the same period, the number of single person households increased 10 percentage points to 17%.[34] Finally, the same year was the first year in US history where fewer than 50% of adults aged 25 and higher were not married.

Understanding the influence of families and households on consumption is essential. Family directly affects the sale of many products and services that are geared to family use. Many products, such as SUVs, minivans, clothing, furniture, food products, and appliances are clearly targeted to the family unit. Married people buy life insurance together; on average, single people not at all. Married people buy washing machines and dryers together; single people, far less so. Married people with children generally make the consumer choice to invest for their children's education. Single people with children more generally lack sufficient financial resources to make such future-oriented financial decisions.

Aside from such obvious considerations, marketing strategy geared to families and households must also consider how decisions for products and services are made within the family unit. Members of the family unit typically assume different roles with respect to decision-making. These roles include:

- *Influencers:* those having input into the decision in some manner. Children, for example, can dramatically influence decisions for clothing, toys, food products, and travel. Children can initiate the decision, identify the range of alternatives considered, and the final choice.

- *Decision Makers:* the person or persons actually making the decision. Decision-making is often a joint family process. However, individual family members, depending on the product type, can make specific decisions based on their expertise or interests. Males tend to be deciders for automobiles and life insurance. Females are more likely deciders for household items, food, and appliances.

- *Purchasers:* the person or persons who actually buy the product. Purchasers need not be decision makers. For example, the child may have made a decision to purchase a specific video game (with parental permission). His father or her mother may conduct the actual purchase.

- *Users:* the person or persons who use the product. The child will play with the toy purchased by mom. The entire family may use home fitness and entertainment equipment jointly decided on by both parents.

Reference Groups

A reference group is a group of two or more individuals whose beliefs, attitudes, values, norms of behavior, or symbols are used by another person or persons as guides to behavior.[35] Several types of reference groups exist. Those we actually belong to (membership groups) can be primary or secondary. Primary membership groups include family, friends, and colleagues. Associations with members of these groups tend to be strong and interaction is frequent. Members of these groups generally exercise the most influence on others members' value systems and consumer behaviors.

Secondary membership groups include such groups as professional associations, churches, and local organizations. Ties with these group members are weaker and less frequent.

One does not have to be a member of a group for it to exert influence on decision-making and consumer behaviors. Aspirational reference groups, groups whom consumers aspire to be identified or associated with, can impose tremendous effects on consumption behaviors. Product endorsements by celebrity athletes, actors, or musicians can dramatically influence aspirational consumers, who wish to emulate their hero's or role model's choices, to buy endorsed products and brands.

Finally, dissociative reference groups are those which consumers view negatively. Consumers might consciously decide to not buy particular styles or brands of clothing because of the symbolic meanings associated with the stereotypical buyers of these products.

Internet-based reference groups play an increasingly important role in influencing consumption patterns and behaviors. Online social networks consist of groups of people who employ social media to share information, experiences, and opinions.[36] Consumers use these networks to connect with members of existing primary and secondary membership reference groups.

Online social networks are increasingly important for reaching secondary membership groups due to the vast numbers of connections that potentially can be established with other consumers. Major social media used by adult Internet users include Facebook (71%), Twitter (19%), Instagram (17%), Pinterest (21%), and LinkedIn (22%). A recent PEW study reports that 74% of adults use social media. Age seems to be the major factor driving social media use. Eighty-nine percent of adults aged 18–29, 82% aged 30–49, 65% aged 50–64, and 49% aged 65 and over actively engage with social media. Social media engagement across consumers belonging to different income and education segments reveal few differences.[37]

Many marketing organizations have a presence on social media. Marketers' primary objectives are to stimulate interest in their products, drive traffic to their company websites and/or brick-and-mortar (BM) locations, and stimulate electronic word-of-mouth (eWOM) for their products. Traditional word-of-mouth between group members has long been recognized for its contributions to marketing successes. The advent of the Internet and, specifically, social media has radically transformed the influence of WOM processes. eWOM messages can rapidly be replicated, and spread exponentially. Messages originating as one-to-one communiqués can go "viral," reaching millions of consumers within days.

Whether or not messages go viral depends on two communication principles. First, when recipients actively re-send messages to others, they are implicitly endorsing the messages and/or original senders. This, in turn, can translate into a powerful force motivating recommendation and purchase intentions.[38] Second, messages gain credibility as they are passed from one recipient to another. Recipients are likely to pay greater attention to forwarded messages and generally view their content more favorably. Ideally, an information-age electronic alchemy rises, combining the right message with the right medium in ways that inspire truly-viral; that is to say, highly-contagious, effects.[39]

→ Purchase Situations Influence Consumer Decision-Making

The purchasing decision process is subject to several situation-specific factors that can affect the outcome. For example, adverse economic conditions may force consumers to scale down their choice of brands, accept lower-cost brands that are more affordable but not the brands consumers truly desired. This is a "settle-for" choice. Or, consumers may discover they cannot qualify for financing on their new car of choice. Again the consumer is forced to scale down expectations. Rent-A-Center (RAC) recognizes that consumers often face this dilemma when buying furniture. As a result, they provide rent-to-buy options for which customers can more easily qualify.

Time constraints can impact decision outcomes. For example, a consumer may have preferred a leisurely dinner but receives an emergency call from the boss that requires an immediate response. The consumer may settle for take-out and eat on the road.

Other "outside constraints" may terminate or modify consumer decisions. Constraints could include out-of-stock conditions, unanticipated changes in price or financing terms, or the sudden arrival of new information that promotes selection of another alternative.

→ Becoming a Smarter Consumer

As a consumer, you should be aware that:

- Your favorite books, television shows, movies or music rarely provide deep insights into your psychological make-up. But that doesn't mean that marketers don't take advantage of the decisions you make in these arenas. Sometimes, marketers do so for purposes of serving you better, like an ichthyologist. At other times, for purposes of catching you better, like a fisherman who then eats you. This is because these "favorites" point the way toward the market segments in which you most belong. Smart marketers understand that knowing the movies or books you favor reveals insights that can be used to predict your tastes, habits, and ultimately your wants and needs. WATCH OUT: Someone always has you in their targeting sights. Choose your favorites carefully.

- Your anger makes you more optimistic, more prone to taking risks and more likely to buy anything. Don't buy stupidly.

- Your fear makes you more pessimistic and risk-adverse; less likely to buy anything. But modern marketers are awesome in their ability to manipulate your fears in ways that encourage you buy things to elevate your spirits or decrease your sense of danger. Fear the right things.

- Your sadness makes you anxious to buy the wrong stuff; your disgust makes you unlikely to buy anything at all. Avoid each.

- You should limit the number of small or large decisions in your life. A famous study provided unwitting consumers the opportunity to choose one of six jam alternatives or one of 24 jam options demonstrated. More choices are better, right? Wrong. Too many choices negatively impacts the level of satisfaction with the products consumers did choose…when they were able to decide on something. But in most cases too many choices stressed or confused consumers to the point where they chose nothing at all, and walked away frustrated. To become a happier and ultimately more successful consumer, limit your options.

Endnotes

1. Transcript, press conference, New York Times (December 20, 2006), http://www.nytimes.com/2006/12/20/washington/20text-bush.html?pagewanted=all&_r=0.

2. David Ariely, *Predictably Irrational: The Hidden Forces that Shape Our Decisions*, (New York, NY: Harper Collins, 2008), 29.

3. Ibid., 29

4. Historically, the term "black box" is the name used to identify flight recorders that collect data about what happened during fatal passenger plane crashes.

5. For a review of historical thought on involvement see Pirjo Laaksonan, *Consumer Involvement: Concepts and Research* (London: Routledge, 1994).

6. Helen Leggatt, "Does Social Media Influence Purchase Decisions?" *BizReport: Social Marketing*, June 24, 2014, accessed December 15, 2014, http://www.bizreport.com/2014/06/does-social-media-influence-purchase-decisions.html.

[7] Henry Assael, *Consumer Behavior and Marketing Action, 5th Ed.* (Cincinnati: South-Western College Publishing, 1995), 94.

[8] Assael refers to these as "outside constraints." Ibid. 95.

[9] See Valerie Zeithaml, A. Parasuraman, and Leonard Berry, *Delivering Quality Service*, (New York: Free Press, 1990); and I. Singh "Consumer Complaint Intentions and Behavior," *Journal of Marketing* (January 1988): 93–107.

[10] William Cummings and M. Venkatesan, "Cognitive Dissonance and Consumer Behavior: A Review of the Evidence," *Journal of Marketing Research* (August 1976): 303–308.

[11] Abraham H. Maslow, *Motivation and Personality* (New York: Harper and Row, 1970).

[12] Jerry W. Thomas, "Motivational Research," 1998. Retrieved from: http://www.decisionanalyst.com/Downloads /MotivationalResearch.pdf. An excellent review of the basics of ethnographic research is provided by M.D. LeCompte and J. J. Schensul, *Designing and Conducting Ethnographic Research: An Introduction 2nd ed.* (Lanham, MD: Altamira Press, 2010).

[13] Verizon, "Millennials and Entertainment," (March 2014), accessed December 15, 2014, http://www.verizondigitalmedia.com/content/ verizonstudy_digital_millennial.pdf.

[14] J. Jacoby and W.D. Hoyer, "Viewer Miscomprehension of Televised Commercials," *Journal of Marketing* (Fall 1982): 12–31.

[15] MarketingCharts, "Distasteful Ads Hurt Brand Appeal," (Thetford Center, VT: Watershed Publishing, March 26, 2010), accessed December 24, 2014, http://www.marketingcharts.com/traditional/distasteful-ads-hurt-brand-appeal-12414/.

[16] Taken from Del I. Hawkins, Roger J. Best, and Kenneth A. Coney, Consumer *Behavior: Implications for Marketing Strategy, 6th ed.* (Chicago: Richard D. Irwin, 1995), 279.

[17] Iconic rote learning is learning the association between objects in the absence of conditioning. Source: Del I Hawkins and David L. Mothersbaugh, *Consumer Behavior Building Marketing Strategy, 12e.* (New York, NY: McGraw-Hill – Irwin, 2013), 324.

[18] Kim. R. Robertson, "Recall and Recognition Effects on Brand Name Imagery," *Psychology & Marketing*, 4 (1987): 3–15.

[19] Michael. R. Solomon, *Consumer Behavior: Buying, Having, and Being 10th Ed.*, (Upper Saddle River, NJ: Pearson Education, 2013), 83.

[20] Ivan Pavlov, "Conditioned Reflexes," in *An Investigation of the Physiological Activity of the Cerebral Cortex*, ed. G.V. Anrep, (London: Oxford University Press, 1927).

[21] Andrew. A. Mitchell, "Cognitive Processes Initiated by Exposure to Advertising," in *Information Processing Research in Advertising*, ed. Robert Harris (Hillsdale, NJ: Lawrence Erlbaum, 1983), pp.13–42.

[22] Henry Assael, *Consumer Behavior and Marketing Action, 6th Ed.* (Cincinnati: South-Western College Publishing, 1995), 112

23 J. R. Rossiter and A. L. Percy, "Visual Communication in Advertising" in *Information Processing Research in Advertising*, ed. Robert Harris, (Hillsdale, NJ: Lawrence Erlbaum Associates, 1983), 83–126.

Herbert E. Krugman, "The Impact of Television Advertising: Learning Without Involvement," *Public Opinion Quarterly*, 29 (Fall 1965): 349–356.

"Memory Without Recall, Exposure Without Perception," *Journal of Advertising Research*, 1 (September 1982): 80–85.

24 Del I. Hawkins and David L. Mothersbaugh, *Consumer Behavior: Building Marketing Strategy, 12ᵗʰ Ed.* (New York, NY: McGraw-Hill, 2013), 324.

25 Gordon W. Allport, "Attitudes," in *A Handbook of Social Psychology*, ed. C.A. Murchison (Worcester, MA: Clark University Press, 1935), 798–844.

26 Henry Assael, *Consumer Behavior and Marketing Action 2ⁿᵈ ed.* (Boston: Kent Publishing), 285.

27 Joel A. Lieske, "Regional Subcultures of the United States" *Journal of Politics*, 55 (1993): 888–913.

28 Black America Today (Radio One and Yankelovich, 2008). accessed December 15, 2014, http://www.radio-one.com/2008/07/14/largest-national-survey-of-african-americans -provides-surprising-look-at-black-america-today; and, http://www.BlackAmericaStudy .com.

29 Glenn Llopis, "5 Steps to Capturing the Hispanic Market—The Last True Growth Opportunity," *Forbes* (September 3, 2013), accessed 12/20/2014, http://www.forbes. com/sites/ glennllopis/2013/09/03/5-steps-to-capturing-the-hispanic-market-the-last-true -growth-opportunity/.

30 Nick Timiraos, "US Incomes End 6-Year Decline, Just Barely," *Wall Street Journal*, (September 16, 2014), accessed 12/12/2014, http://online.wsj.com/articles/u-s-incomes -edge-higher-as-sluggish-recovery-persists.

31 Glenn Llopis, "5 Steps to Capturing the Hispanic Market."

32 Nielsen Report, "State of the Asian American Consumer," (2012). accessed December 15, 2014, http://www.nielsen.com/content/dam/corporate/us/en/microsites/ publicaffairs/StateoftheAsianAmericanConsumerReport.pdf.

33 Classification scheme adapted from Richard P. Coleman, "Continuing Significance of Social Class to Marketing," *Journal of Consumer Research*, 10(3) (1983): 265–280.

34 J. Vespa, J. Lewis, and R. Kreider, "America's Families and Living Arrangements: 2012," *United States Census Bureau*, accessed December 3, 2014, http://www.census .gov/prod/2013pubs/p20-570.pdf.

35 Definition adopted from Del Hawkins and David Mothersbaugh, *Consumer Behavior: Building Marketing Strategy, 12ᵗʰ ed.*, (New York: McGraw-Hill, 2013), 218.

36 Adopted from Gary Armstrong and Philip Kotler, *Marketing: An Introduction*, 11e. (Upper Saddle River, NJ: Pearson), 132–135.

[37] Social Networking Factsheet, PEW Research Internet & American Life Project (January 2014), accessed December 4, 2014, http://www.pewinternet.org/fact-sheets/social-networking-fact-sheet/.

[38] E. Keller, "Unleashing the Power of Word of Mouth: Creating Brand Advocacy to Drive Growth," *Journal of Advertising Research* 47(4) (2007): 448–452.

[39] D. Strutton, D. Taylor, and K. Thompson, "Investigating Generational Differences in eWOM Behaviors: For Advertising Purposes, Does X=Y?" *International Journal of Advertising* 30(4) (2007): 559–586.

CHAPTER 8

UNDERSTANDING BUSINESS BUYER BEHAVIOR

This chapter focuses on organizational markets and organizational buying behavior. Organizational markets traditionally have been described as **business markets** or **Business-to-Business (or B2B)** markets. Both terms will be employed throughout this book.

The primary distinction between consumer and organizational products derives from the purposes for which goods are purchased (Exhibit 8.1). In other words, the same product can be a consumer or organizational good. Acquire a fluorescent light for personal or household use and it becomes a consumer good. Acquire the same product for use in business operations, for resale to other organizations, or as a part employed in the production or assembly of another product, and the fluorescent light would be designated as an organizational product.

The difference between consumer and organizational *markets* parallels the distinction between consumer and organizational *products*. Consumer markets consist of individuals or groups of individuals who purchase products for personal or household consumption (use). Organizational markets, by contrast, consist of organizations or groups of individuals who

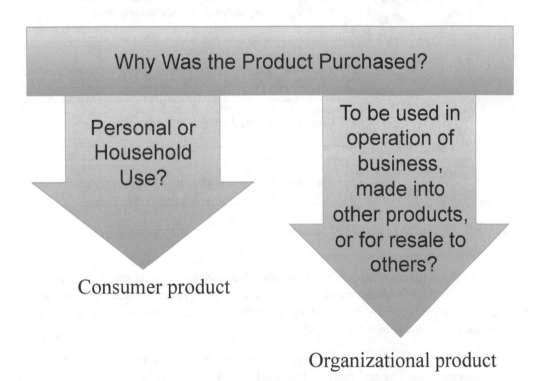

Exhibit 8.1 *Consumer or Organizational Product? Marketers engaged in selling to other organizations are said to be marketing "B2B" i.e. Business to Business.*

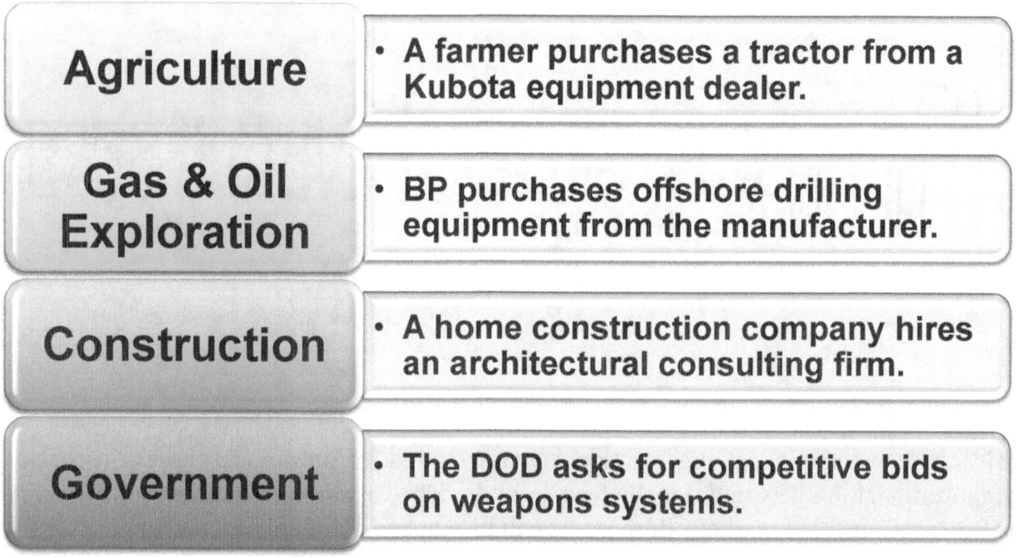

Agriculture · A farmer purchases a tractor from a Kubota equipment dealer.

Gas & Oil Exploration · BP purchases offshore drilling equipment from the manufacturer.

Construction · A home construction company hires an architectural consulting firm.

Government · The DOD asks for competitive bids on weapons systems.

Exhibit 8.2 *Some Examples of Organizational Markets.*

Resellers · Wholesaling Middlemen & Retailers

Manufacturers · Producers of products for resale
· Consumer goods, organizational goods for consumption

Other Producers · Business users producing non-manufactured products.
· Forestry, mining, agriculture, fishing, petroleum.

"Non-Business" · Non-profit organization
· Churches, some hospitals, charities, civic organizations

Government · Federal, state, local government agencies

Services · Services provided to organizations and to consumer users.

Exhibit 8.3 *Types of Organizational Markets.*

purchase products for consumption or use in organizational settings. As noted, B2B products are destined for use in business operations, for resale to other organizations, or for use in the production or assembly of another product or products that flow "downstream" toward end-use customers in the supply chain.

Differences between organizational and consumer markets are illustrated in the examples of organizational products and markets provided in Exhibit 8.2. A farmer who purchases a tractor from a Kubota equipment dealer will use the tractor to produce agricultural products.

In turn, the grain the farmer produces will be sold within local agricultural markets. The farmer's purchase is an **organizational purchase**. The farmer is part of an **organizational market**. When British Petroleum (BP) purchases offshore drilling equipment for oil exploration purposes, BP is part of an organizational market. A home construction Firm that hires a consulting Firm to assist with architectural design has purchased an organizational product. The construction Firm is also part of an organizational market. When the U.S. Department of Defense (DOD) purchases weapons systems it functions in an organizational market and is buying an organizational product.

→ Categories of Organizational Markets

Six categories of organizational markets exist: resellers, manufacturers, other producers, services, non-business, and government markets. Exhibit 8.3 summarizes these types of organizational markets.

The Reseller Market

Resellers are frequently also identified as "middlemen" or intermediaries. Regardless of their label, resellers buy and then resell products downstream toward the next organizational level in distribution channels/supply chains, all in route to ultimate end-consumers. (From this point forward in this Chapter and book the contemporary term **supply chains** is intended whenever the terms **distribution channels** or **marketing channels** are discussed.) Supply chains function as conduits (comprised of linked organizations) through which products are sourced, manufactured or assembled, and finally, transported, inventoried, delivered and ultimately sold to end-use consumers.

During organizational products' passage through supply chains, resellers variously function as agents, negotiators, financiers, wholesalers, warehouses, transportation entities, order processors and, ultimately, as retailers. One or more resellers must perform each of these functions. This is critical. Otherwise, the supply chain would not function efficiently and you would not have coffee, cream and/or sugar, or a cup to mix them in, tomorrow morning.

Resellers normally do not transform products in any way. Usually, products are sold to the next supply chain member without much if any modification. However, resellers certainly add value; which makes sense. Were this not the case there would be no reason for resellers to exist or operate.

Occasionally, resellers bundle products from multiple manufacturers to create value for the next customer in the supply chain. A B2B computer reseller, for example, may bundle computer hardware and software and then offer the total package at a discounted price to its customers. Similarly, resellers may bundle services with products. Best Buy and Office Depot, for example, sell service contracts for most major electronics purchases. This service contract is essentially a warranty that offers additional value beyond the value provided by the product's manufacturer. Best Buy provides its "Geek Squad" service to support sales of its computers and software. Providing such a "value-add" to customers who purchase its services or product bundle differentiates one reseller from competing resellers. The ultimate goal of this marketing strategy, like many others, is to achieve differentiation and competitive advantage.

Resellers also buy products and related services needed to operate their businesses. For example, resellers may purchase janitorial, consulting, or pest control services. They may buy forklift trucks to move products in their warehouses. Resellers may purchase shelves, racks, and other fixtures for displaying merchandise, or a variety of computers, software, and related electronic equipment for recording and monitoring sales. None of these products is re-sold. Each, instead, supports the daily operations of resellers.

The Manufacturer Market

Manufacturers (producers) build products. These products are then sold through supply chains to organizational buyers or ultimate (end-use) consumers. Manufacturers, however, must purchase a wide range of parts, raw materials and, often, services, before they can manufacture anything. Then, to produce new products, these component parts and materials are assembled, combined, and/or processed. Production processes necessarily always encompass numerous value-adding activities.

When purchasing these parts, raw materials or services, manufacturers (who here are buyers) often engage in extensive **value analysis** in conjunction with their suppliers (who here are sellers). Value analysis is executed to reduce or control the costs of component parts and other materials via a careful study of how processes, procedures, and parts might be redesigned and/or standardized across a range of products the manufacturer may produce. Value analysis should lead to improved product quality, which ultimately may differentiate final products that are manufactured and marketed from those of competitors.

Like resellers, manufacturers also purchase goods and services to operate their businesses. Consider, for example, General Motors and Ford. These Firms purchase equipment to be used in their manufacturing processes. Stamping machines, robot welding machines, and inspection stages are among the types of equipment (called **installations**) that are necessary to build automobiles. Like resellers, manufacturers also purchase supporting **accessory equipment** such as computers, desktop printers, and copy machines to support daily operations.

"Other Producers" Market

Other producers, also called **business users**, produce products for consumption. But these products are not manufactured in the usual sense. Other producers typically consist of Firms operating in the mining, construction, agricultural, forestry, and fishing industries. For example, when Exxon-Mobil buys drilling equipment and ships for the exploration, extraction, and shipment of oil it is an "other producer." Farmers, when purchasing equipment or supplies such as seed and fertilizers used in the production of crops for their customers, are business users. Lumber companies, such as Weyerhaeuser, that buy trucks, bulldozers, and other equipment for forest harvesting and milling are engaged in the production of lumber products that will be sold commercially.

The "Non-Business" Market

Non-business or non-profit organizations face many of the same operational problems as traditional for-profit organizations. Organizations in this category include churches, universities, hospitals, charities, and political parties to name but a few. Because these non-business organizations essentially function in the same way as traditional businesses, they face similar purchasing and operating problems. They require similar goods and services for operating their organizations. Moreover, many non-business organizations are becoming increasingly similar to traditional "for-profit" Firms. Indeed, some not-for-profit Firms now designate profitability as a business objective. However, profits aren't distributed to investors or senior management. Instead, profits are retained in the organization to offset future costs and investment.[1]

The Services Market

Service-providers include all Firms that deliver services to supply chain businesses or end-use consumers. Indeed, service-provider Firms out-number manufacturers by a wide margin in the US. Services targeted to other organizations in B2B settings include activities such as consulting, accounting and tax, communications, and transportation/ storage/order processing services. Typical consumer services include pest control, personal care, medical and dental, health clubs, home repair, and maintenance. It is immaterial whether service Firms are selling to other businesses or to ultimate consumers. These Firms are still part of the organizational market because they buy goods and services required to operate their Firms and deliver services to their customers.

The Government Market

The government market consists of government units at federal, state, and local levels. Agencies operating at all levels purchase goods and services used in performing critical government functions. The government market is huge featuring more than 90,000 federal, state, and local units.[2] USA.gov lists 137 independent executive federal agencies with 268 components.[3] Combined federal, state, and local expenditures reached nearly $6.2 trillion in 2013, accounting for nearly 37% of our gross national product.[4]

Government Buying Behavior

The government market features unique buying requirements. Government agencies purchase most of their goods and services via competitive bidding and/or negotiated contracting. Federal, state, and local governments typically engage in a **bid buying** process before making large/important product or service purchasing decisions. The law requires government agencies to seek bids via **requests for proposals** (RFPs). RFPs ask qualified suppliers to submit bids to supply government agencies with needed products and services. The RFP contains all purchasing requirements, specifications, and deadlines that must be satisfied. After they receive bids in response to their RFPs, the law again requires that government agencies only award contracts to bidders who have met specifications and other published requirements at the lowest overall cost.

Unfortunately, this does not always happen. Just ask former New Orleans Mayor Ray Nagin, or three of the last six Governors of Illinois. Each man has or is currently receiving free room-and-board courtesy, again, of the US federal government for his administration's failure to honor this law.

The major source of information on current RFPs for the federal government is the *Commerce Business Daily*. The Federal publication lists business opportunities with the federal government that exceed 25,000 dollars.

Government purchase requests are not always made in the form of RFPs. Requests-for-bids often are directly sent to perspective suppliers based on mailing lists that have been compiled by various agencies. These mailing lists consist of Firms that have contacted governmental buying offices and indicated their desire to be included in future solicitations. Based on these mailing lists, **IFBs** or **Invitations to Bid** are sent directly to interested Firms. IFBs include specifications, instructions for preparation, conditions of purchase, and information concerning delivery and payment schedules for the bid. Contracts again are supposedly awarded to the low-cost bidder whose offer conforms to all requirements on the IFB.

For routine purchases, such as purchases of office supplies and cleaning supplies, lists of approved buyers may exist based on prior RFPs or IFBs. Government agencies may directly purchase from Firms on these lists without soliciting additional bids. However, the size of such "micro-purchases" is generally limited to under $2,500 for the federal government.

Negotiated contracts are used for complex products that must be custom designed for specialized government applications. These products are not typical off-the-shelf products. Instead, these products require extensive research, development, and custom tailoring to satisfy government needs. Defense systems and buildings are common examples. Negotiated contracts are often associated with advanced technologies. Only large, established, and sophisticated suppliers may possess the degree of competence and experience to provide the products and services required. Projects connected with missile systems, military aircraft, capital ships, and other weapons systems illustrate this sort of product. Under unusual circumstances, negotiated contracting may arise for standardized products. Products and services, for example, are often acquired through negotiation particularly when it is impossible to draft adequate specifications or describe the specific product in a standard RFP or IFB.

Government agencies issue a **Request for Quote** (RFQ) to initiate the negotiation process. Responses to RFQs are not offers from sellers. Governmental agencies cannot accept RFQs as bidding contracts. Instead, the government issues them when it does not intend to award a contract immediately but only seeks to obtain price, delivery, or other information for planning purposes. After reviewing responses to RFQs, the contracting officer may negotiate further with Firms that have submitted acceptable proposals.

Sources of Government Buying Information

Finding out how to do business with government agencies is now easier because the key information is available online. For example, the *Commerce Business Daily* is accessible at cbdnet.access.gpo.gov. The US Department of Commerce issues the *Commerce Business Daily* five days a week except on federal holidays. The publication lists proposed government purchases over $25,000 in size, subcontracting leads, contract awards, sales of surplus property, and foreign business opportunities. Most state and local governments have similar publications to the *Commerce Business Daily*.

The *US Government Purchasing and Sales Directory* is a Small Business Administration (SBA) publication. The directory provides a comprehensive guide to all government purchasing and sales activities; lists products and services purchased by the federal government; and identifies the specific agencies involved. Copies of the directory are available through the SBA web site at www.sba.gov.

The Government Solutions Reference Desk (GSRD) is a Website that provides links to other sites, typically government web pages, that provide purchasing information. In fact, the *Commerce Business Daily* and most SBA sites link to the GSRD. The federal government recently contracted for the development of a "one-stop shopping" web site called usa.gov. The Website provides much easier access to information contained in other government web sites.

→ Characteristics of Organizational Markets

Organizational markets differ from consumer markets in several important ways. The following paragraphs examine and explain these differences.

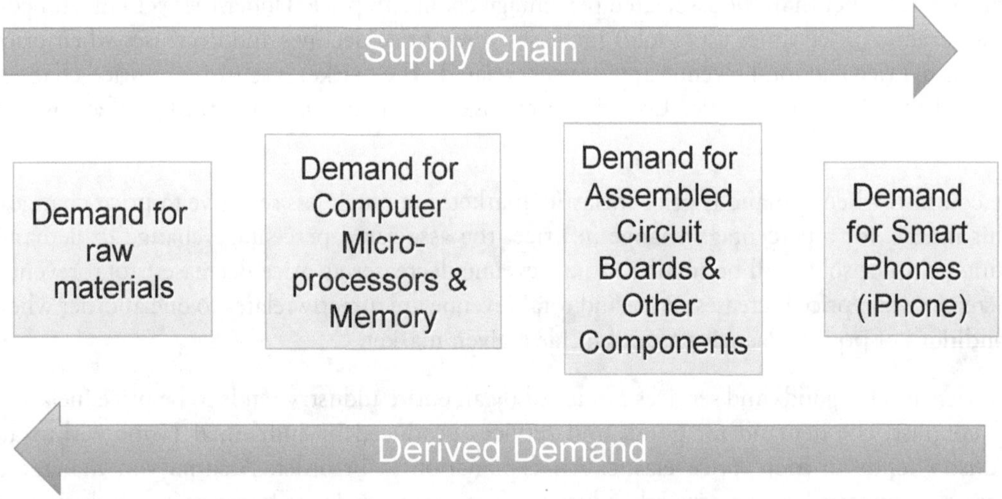

Exhibit 8.4 *Derived demand in the supply chain. The demand for organizational products is ultimately a function of demand for final products sold to consumers.*

Demand Is "Derived"

The demand for goods and services in organizational markets is "derived." Derived demand means that the demand for organizational goods and services is ultimately a function of the demand for consumer goods and services. Exhibit 8.4 illustrates the derived demand concept. Consumer demand for personal computers or smart devices ultimately determines the demand for the parts and materials involved in the manufacture of each product. If consumer sales increase, demand for these products and other in-puts into production processes will increase in lockstep. If consumer demand declines, demand for parts and materials also declines.

Unless demand exists at the consumer level for manufactured goods and services, there will be no demand for these products at the manufacturing and reseller levels inside any supply chain. Manufacturers realize this. Consequently, producers of industrial products that sell primarily to other manufacturers often still advertise directly to ultimate consumers if their product is ultimately destined to become part of a consumer product.

NutraSweet, a product consumers at one time could not buy except as part of another food product, illustrates this point. Monsanto targeted NutraSweet advertising directly at consumers when it first introduced the product in the early 1980s, even though the product was not available in consumer markets. Monsanto understood that if consumers were convinced of NutraSweet's benefits as a substitute for sugar, they would demand NutraSweet in other products. The Firm spent $20+ million on consumer-directed advertising during the first year after NutraSweet's introduction. The investment paid off. By 1990, sales reached $993 million and generated an operating margin of over 20%.[5]

Demand Is Price Inelastic

Organizational demand for goods and services is usually **price inelastic**. Price elasticity of demand captures a market's degree of price sensitivity for specific products. Price elasticity measures how much the demand for a product changes (up or down) as the price for that product increases or decreases. (Chapter 15 also addresses price elasticity.)

When demand is **price elastic**, demand for a product in terms of units sold will shift radically in response to a price change. Specifically, the percentage change in units demanded (sold/

not sold) is higher than the associated percentage change in price. Under these circumstances, total revenue (price times units sold) increases when price declines and decreases when price increases. Price and total revenue are inversely related. The market is sensitive to price-changes when demand is price elastic. Even small changes in price can dramatically affect overall demand.

By contrast, when demand is price inelastic, markets are much less sensitive to price-changes. This means, for a percentage change in price, the associated percentage change in demand (units sold/not sold) will be smaller. Total revenue decreases as price decreases; total revenue increases when price increases. Price and total revenue are directly relates to one another when conditions of price inelasticity prevail inside a given market.

The demand for goods and services produced by an entire industry tends to be price inelastic. By contrast, the demand for goods and services produced by individual Firms within an industry tends to more price elastic. An explanation is in order. Assume you manage a Firm that operates in the apparel industry. Your Firm produces fasteners, a product used to manufacture clothing. Naturally, clothing manufacturers purchase these fasteners from suppliers, and cannot make clothing without them. Clothing producers normally create a wide range of clothing products. Apparel items are sold through traditional wholesalers and retailers to reach ultimate consumers.

Now assume the Firm, and all Firms in your industry, raise fasteners' prices to clothing manufacturers by the same amount. The fastener industry increased its prices, in a uniform fashion, in response to an increase in the commodity price of brass (please note that fasteners are usually akin to zippers). Given these conditions, what will happen to the demand for fasteners in light of this price increase?

As we hope you answered, demand will probably not change much at all. Fasteners are essential to clothing production. No readily available or lower priced alternatives to fasteners exist. Moreover, fasteners account for a relatively small proportion of the total cost of each clothing item produced and ultimately sold to consumers. Even if increases in the price that your and other Firms charge clothing manufacturers is passed on to consumers, any resulting consumer price increases will likely not prove large enough to substantially impact overall consumer demand for apparel. Consumers will continue to buy about the same amount of clothing items as before. As a result, manufacturers of these clothing items will still buy exactly the same number of fasteners that they purchased before. They will pay, willingly or otherwise, the higher price. Because the demand for fasteners is derived, the entire apparel manufacturing industry will still need the same total number of fasteners. That is, unless the price of fasteners rose so high that apparel manufacturers developed a substitute technology.

Individual Firms, however, usually cannot successfully raise prices if the rest of the industry does not follow suit. Raising prices unilaterally would cause apparel manufacturers to shift their purchases to competing fastener manufacturers. Any single Firm that raised price will suffer a decline in sales.

Buy Direct from Producers

Organizational buyers usually prefer to buy directly from manufacturers when possible. This is particularly true for expensive installations and complex items of equipment. Often such products must be custom-designed and require direct support from their producers.

Large retailers and other intermediaries that buy in volume also prefer to buy direct from the manufacturer. By eliminating unnecessary intermediaries in supply chains, substantial savings can occur that may allow the reseller to lower prices to customers and gain a competitive advantage. Walmart, for example, aggressively tries to eliminate intermediaries from its distribution channels by insisting that manufacturers sell products directly to Walmart's corporate buyers. The tremendous buying power of large retailers, such as Walmart, makes it possible for them to insist on such arrangements. These arrangements are one reason why intermediaries sometimes go out of business. (Supply chains sometimes can eliminate intermediaries. But the marketing functions previously performed by the "missing" intermediary still must be executed. Chapter 13 also discusses this issue, but in more detail.)

Close Relationships between Buyers and Sellers

Firms selling to organizational markets normally have much smaller customer bases than do marketers of consumer products. Because of these smaller customer bases, Firms selling products in organizational marketers should be highly attuned to the relationships they develop and seek to cultivate with customers. A Firm's survival may depend on every individual sale. This is particularly true if the seller's customers are large enough to enjoy substantial buying power.

Similarly, organizational buyers usually rely heavily on their suppliers. In many industries, relatively few competent suppliers exist that can provide the goods, services, and expertise needed to support the buying Firm's operations. Organizational buyers consequently expect suppliers to work closely with them in designing products and developing production, distribution, and operational processes and capabilities. Value analysis, as noted earlier, is a major trend that requires this kind of close cooperation.

The need to maintain close working relationships between suppliers and customers has contributed to an ongoing movement toward relationship marketing. Organizational buyers rely on the partnering expertise of industrial sales representatives as they work together to create "best solutions" to the buyers' problems. Sales representatives often function as technical consultants in modern B2B contexts as customers seek total solutions to their purchasing problems.

The close relationships between buyers and sellers in organizational markets often results in reciprocity. Reciprocity, in this context, means that buyers and sellers alternate, or switch, their buyer and seller roles. Practically, this means organizational buyers often select suppliers who also agree to buy from them. The philosophy is "I buy from you if you buy from me." As an example, a furniture manufacturer may choose to buy wood and other materials from a producer who, in turn, agrees to furnish its offices with furniture produced by the manufacturer. Reciprocity agreements are illegal if they overly restrict competition.[6]

Markets Can Be Characterized by SIC and NAIC Codes

Organizational markets are unique in that they can be described by Standard Industrial Classification (SIC) and North American Industrial Classification System (NAICS) codes. The SIC system, being replaced by NAICS, was devised and is maintained by the federal government. The coding scheme classifies every U.S. industry into categories, based on the primary product or service sold. The SIC coding scheme uses only four digits to achieve this. First, all industries are segmented into 10 major divisions using a series of two-digit codes. For example, all Firms related to agriculture, forestry, and fishing receive two-digit SIC codes ranging from 01 to 09. Similarly, all Firms engaged in mining activities receive two-digit codes ranging from 10 to 14. Major divisions then are segmented into more specialized industry categories as the code adds a third and ultimately a fourth digit. The SIC classification is then complete.

The NAICS coding system, by contrast, employs six-digit codes for 20 industry sectors (five product and 15 service sectors). Within these sectors, NAICS categorizes Firms into 1,170 industries compared to 1,004 industries in the 10 sector SIC system. NAICS is quickly replacing SIC, as noted. The remaining discussion thus focuses on NAICS.

How NAICS Works

Where do health clubs fit within this coding system? An online search of NAICS via www.census.gov indicates that health clubs fall under NAICS code 71 for the Arts, Entertainment, and Recreation division (Exhibit 8.5). NAICS 71 is broken down further into several additional categories. One of these, NAICS 713 describes amusement, gambling, and recreational industries. In turn, this specific NAICS holds three categories, 7131, 7132, and 7139. This latter category consists of "other amusement & recreations industries":

- NAICS 71391 describes golf course and country clubs.
- NAICS 71392 contains skiing facilities.
- NAICS 71393 is for marinas, and finally.
- NAICS 71394 describes fitness & recreational sports centers.

How Marketers Use NAICS

NAICS codes can help marketers identify potential organizational customers for their products. The procedure is simple. First, marketers identify the NAICS codes describing existing customers and the NAICS for related industries that may hold potential customers. Once all relevant NAICS codes are identified, the marketer's next step is to use other sources, such as trade directories, to identify the specific names of Firms that possess these NAICS codes. Several directories cross-reference NAICS codes for Firms. These include *Hoovers, Compact Disclosure, The Census of Manufacturers, Dun & Bradstreet's Million Dollar Directory*, and *Industrial Outlooks* (a publication of the Bureau of Industrial Economics).

NAICS codes also aid in segmenting organizational markets. Recall that NAICS codes are used to group together companies that produce the same or similar products. Firms that possess the same NAICS codes logically should face similar production, operating, and,

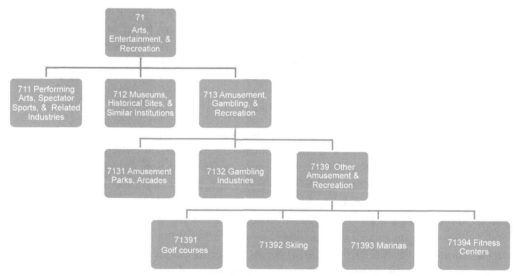

Exhibit 8.5 *NAICS has replaced SICs and the classification scheme for North American Industrial Organizations.*

therefore, purchasing problems. NAICS codes, particularly NAICS at the 5+digit-level, characterize relatively homogeneous groups of Firms. Each NAICS category is equivalent to a market segment.

NAICS is useful for forecasting the demand for products and services. Demand is related to, but different from, the **market potential** for any product. Market potential captures the upper limit of the actual demand for specific goods or services that exists within a particular industry. Market potential estimates the amount of a product that potentially could be sold by all Firms (taken together) in an entire industry if these Firms did everything right and had unlimited budgets. This is clearly a "best case" or ideal scenario.

The estimation process is relatively simple. Assume that a Firm sells industrial equipment to medium and large manufacturers. The Firm seeks to develop new geographic markets. An estimate of market potential for sales of this equipment in these new geographic markets might emerge as follows.

First, the Firm should identify the codes for likely customer industries, as just discussed. Next, the Firm could use secondary sources (as previously described) to identify specific companies with those codes in the targeted geographic areas. These two steps alone would indicate the number of potential customer Firms. The final and critical step is to determine how many pieces of equipment that each customer Firm ideally would need. This step can be achieved through an examination of internal company records. These records should indicate how many pieces of equipment different sizes of existing customer Firms currently use. The size of customer Firms could be measured by counting the number of production workers employed by the Firm, or through other metrics tabulated in the U.S. Census of Manufacturers. For example, the typical customer Firm that purchases this kind of equipment may need three machines per 1,000 workers. The Census of Manufactures summarizes the number of employees for Firms possessing a given NAICS code. A final estimate of market potential can be obtained by multiplying the number of machines needed per 1,000 workers by the number of employees recorded in the Census of Manufactures.

Professional Purchasing

Purchasing personnel in today's organizations are highly trained supply chain management experts. Many purchasing professionals are members of the Institute for Supply Management [ISM]. The ISM offers a dedicated certification program in supply chain management. The Certified Professional in Supply Management (CPSM) program affirms that members possess proficiency in finance, supplier relationship management, and organization global supply chain strategy. This certification program emerged from the older Certified Purchasing Manager's program initiated in 1974, which was the first nationally accepted standard for the purchasing and materials management field.

Systems Buying and Selling

A major trend in organizational buying is the movement towards **system buying**. Here, buyers seek to purchase "total solutions" to their problems. To facilitate this outcome, buyers usually engage (i.e., contract) with a single vendor, as opposed to buying myriad products and services from numerous suppliers. The single vendor earns the purchasing contract and is responsible for sub-contracting to additional suppliers, if required. Initially a government purchasing process, systems buying has filtered down to private enterprise. This new purchasing strategy has imposed tremendous pressure on competing suppliers who must respond with upgraded **system selling** programs that emphasize working closely with buyers to design and deliver "total solutions."

The movement towards systems buying and selling continues to evolve. **Systems contracting** is an outgrowth of systems buying. The systems contracting model applies to marketing suppliers of **Maintenance, Repair, and Operating (MRO)** items. Systems contractors supply entire MRO solutions to buyers. Buyers benefit from systems contracting because it substantially reduces the cost of maintaining the inventory for these items. Over time, the strategy also lessens the time spent on supplier selection decisions. Buyers inevitably also obtain price protection over the term of the contract. This means prices are secure for the duration of the contract; that is, price increases will not occur over a known timeframe, barring cataclysmic or otherwise unforeseen events.

Leasing

Businesses often prefer to lease rather than buy products. Leasing, in the past, was largely restricted to products requiring large financial investments such as heavy construction equipment, large trucks, aircraft, and mainframe computer systems. Leasing arrangements, today, encompass a broader range of products. Leasing offers definite advantages for the lessee (the organizational buyer or customer) and lessor (the organizational seller or marketer):

- Leasing is often less expensive than buying equipment outright. Lease payments may be less than the payment associated with direct purchase of the same item.
- By leasing a product, the lessee can retain investment capital for other applications.
- The performance of leased products are usually guaranteed by repair and maintenance contracts offered by the lessor. This further reduces expenses and cash flow drains.
- Leases agreements typically cover a shorter timeframe than purchases of equivalently products. This provides lessees the opportunity to upgrade technology more frequently and, often, more economically.
- In some cases, distinct tax advantages are associated with leasing. Purchased capital equipment is depreciated over time. In contrast, the amount of lease can be expensed at the lease payment is made; payments are thus treated as an operating expense in their entirety.

From the lessor's perspective, leasing can result in a larger market than if it simply sold products outright. Potential customers who cannot afford to buy products outright often can still afford to lease. Customers, particularly those considering the purchase of large equipment, may be risk averse; i.e., they seek to lower their perceived risk as much as possible. Such customers are, as a result, hesitant to commit to a purchase but may commit to a short-term lease as a means of trying or sampling a product on a limited, lower-risk basis.

→ Organizational Buying Is Often a "Group Process"

The responsibility for making organizational purchases varies across organizations and with type of purchase. Larger organizations generally employ dedicated purchasing managers. They are responsible for managing the acquisition of products and services for the Firm. In fact, larger Firms often employ multiple purchasing managers, referred to as purchasing agents, who specialize in the acquisition of specific product types. Generally, purchasing managers (or agents) are not the only persons involved in making purchasing decisions, multiple people may be involved, either formally or informally. The **buying center** consists of all people involved in the purchase decision process, formally or informally.

→ The Organizational Buying Center

Buying centers usually do not exist as official dedicated buying entities within the Firm. Groups of personnel formally tasked with making specific purchasing decisions are called **buying committees**. Members of such committees may attend meetings, follow specific purchasing protocols, and vote on purchase decisions. The membership of buying committees is normally appointed on an ad hoc basis to evaluate risky, expensive, unique purchases that often are being made for the first time.

Members of the buying center typically perform specific roles related to the purchasing process. Normal purchasing roles include "users," "initiators," "influencers," "gatekeepers," "buyers," and "deciders" (Exhibit 8.6). To be successful, organizational marketers must identify the buying center's members and the specific purchasing-related roles each person performs. Since the buying center is informal, the task can prove difficult. Moreover, one person can perform several critical roles. Similarly, several people may perform the same role in the buying center.

Roles in the Buying Center

Users

Users are people inside the Firm who actually use the product, such as personnel on the production line or in the shipping department. Users can be particularly important sources of information for specifications, alternative products and brands, and how the product can best be used. Users are often responsible for initiating a purchase decision because they have "discovered a better way of doing things."

Initiators

Initiators make specific purchasing requests. Initiators often consist of users, as noted above. Initiators could also include anyone inside the Firm who occupies a position from which to recognize that a problem or need exists.

Role Title	Description of Role
Users	Actually uses the product. May initiate the purchase process. Provides expertise on criteria & alternatives.
Initiators	Request the purchase. May be users. Provides expertise on criteria & alternatives.
Gate-keepers	Power to prevent sellers or information from reaching buying center. Purchasing agents, receptionists, clerks.
Influencers	Supply advice or information for decision. Define specification, evaluate alternatives. Often technicians.
Deciders	Power to make or approve final decision.
Buyers	Formal authority to negotiate contract, arrange terms. Determine specifications, select vendors, negotiate terms.

Exhibit 8.6 *The Roles in the Organizational Buying Center.*

Influencers

Influencers typically are knowledgeable about the product "type" that is under consideration. Such people assist in determining specifications and defining other criteria for use during the purchase decision-making process. Influencers are often supervisory personnel, research and design specialists, or engineers. But, they can also include personnel from finance who control budgets, or others who, because of their position or political power within the Firm, have an important 'say so' about the purchase.

Gatekeepers

Gatekeepers control the flow of information to other members of the buying center, and between the Firm and its vendors. Gatekeepers usually consist of administrative assistants, clerks, and purchasing agents. Identifying gatekeepers in the buying center is important to ensure that key marketing communications reach important players in the buying organization.

Deciders

Deciders make actual decisions about which products to buy. They also decide which vendors to select. Purchasing agents usually make decisions for less expensive, commonly purchased products (i.e. **straight rebuys**). More complex, risky decisions are generally the purview of higher-level managers.

Buyers

Buyers spend more time than anyone with the selling Firm's marketing personnel. They arrange the specific details of the purchase, may negotiate specific terms of the contract, process the paper work, monitor progress on delivery, and engage in any expediting (i.e., speeding things up) that may be required. Usually, someone from the purchasing department performs this function. Again, however, buyers may be upper-level managers for more complex, risky purchase decisions.

Types of Organizational Purchase Decisions

The composition and scope of the buying center varies with the type of buying decision faced by the organization. Complex decisions generally involve more time and effort and have larger buying centers. Simple decisions, on the other hand, may be associated with buying centers that contain only one or two persons.

Exhibit 8.7 offers one way to view the complexity and scope of the buying decision. Three **buy classes** are illustrated: (1) **Straight Rebuys**; (2) **Modified Rebuys**; and, (3) **New Task** purchases. These buy classes are arrayed on a continuum; they are not discreet categories with clear demarcation points between them. However, the types of industrial products highlighted in the Exhibit are representative of each type of purchase decision.

Straight Rebuys

Straight rebuys include simple, recurring purchases of office supplies, parts and materials, and utilities (gas, water, electricity). Firms possess substantial past experience for guiding how decisions should unfold for these products. As a result, few people need to be involved and the scope of the decision remains very limited. Decisions are usually made by purchasing agents. In most cases, no new alternative products or suppliers are evaluated; the purchase order may simply be placed with the vendor that usually supplies these products. This is the most common form of organizational purchase.

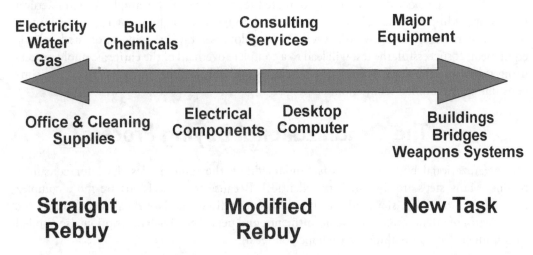

A Continuum

Electricity Water Gas   Bulk Chemicals   Consulting Services   Major Equipment

Office & Cleaning Supplies   Electrical Components   Desktop Computer   Buildings Bridges Weapons Systems

Straight Rebuy   **Modified Rebuy**   **New Task**

Exhibit 8.7 *The "Buy Classes." The size and complexity of the buying center changes with buying situation. There exists a continuum of buying situations ranging between the Straight Rebuy and New Task decisions.*

New Task Purchases

New task decisions for complex, high-risk, first-time purchases of major equipment and production installations occupy the other end of this continuum. Buyers typically have little experience to draw upon for aiding this type of decision. Therefore, substantial information must be gathered and assessed. The range of products and vendors under consideration and the complexity of the evaluation process can be extensive. Because of the nature of the decision, multiple people will be involved and the decision process may require months. Buying centers can consist of 20 or more members for new task purchases.

Modified Rebuys

The modified rebuy is more complex than the straight rebuy, but not to the extreme of the new task. In modified rebuys, limited numbers of alternative products and vendors are considered and a number of people typically will be involved.

The modified rebuy often results from an environmental change that forces a purchase decision. For example, users may identify ways to cut costs, improve quality, or otherwise enhance efficiency. A modified rebuy purchasing process is initiated. "Out suppliers" (i.e., suppliers not currently on the buyer's list of approved vendors) may try to convert straight rebuys into modified rebuys by attempting to demonstrate superiority on critical performance dimensions. The value of knowing who are the users and other initiators in the buying center pays off here for suppliers!

Modified rebuys can evolve from straight rebuys. A modified rebuy may arise because an existing vendor failed to execute a contract or otherwise performed in an unsatisfactory manner. In this situation, blindly placing another order with the same vendor would not serve the Firm's interests. Firms should evaluate alternative providers. The prospect of engaging a new supplier or product is much in play.

Similarly, modified rebuys can emerge from new tasks. The original new task purchase may have been quite complex, requiring substantial time, resources, and personnel to evaluate properly. Subsequent purchases of the same product, however, probably will not require the same commitment. This will be particularly true if the purchase is for a product that will eventually replace older units based on outdated technologies. For example, a manufacturer that is upgrading an assembly line previously dominated by equipment requiring human operators may engage in a new task purchase for a pilot assembly line using automated, robotic equipment. If successful, the test will lead to a complete overhaul of the entire assembly process using the new technology. Subsequent purchases probably will be much less risky and time consuming. A modified rebuy should emerge.

→ The Organizational Buying Process

The organizational buying process is fundamentally the same as described for consumer buying. Many steps are similar, if not identical. Because some decisions are more complex than others, not all decisions will involve all the steps discussed. Nor do all steps require the same degree of attention, resource commitments, and personnel. Each description also applied to consumer decision-making, as we hope you recall.

New task decisions normally involve all seven steps summarized in Exhibit 8.8. For modified rebuys as well as for straight rebuys steps may be abbreviated or skipped entirely. However, one should always recognize that, for every organizational purchase decision, the over-riding objective is to make the decision that is in the best interests of the Firm. As a result, the emphasis when making decisions is on objectivity and maximizing utility. With these caveats in mind, the steps in the organizational buying process are examined.

The Purchasing Problem

Problem or (need) recognition, for example, occurs when users or other initiators suggest costs should be reduced or efficiency improved by investing in new equipment or changing

1 - Recognition of the purchasing problem.
2 - Critical needs & product specifications.
3 - Search for and qualify vendors.
4 - Acquire bids, proposals, solicit presentations.
5 - Analyze proposals, select product & suppliers.
6 - Determine appropriate purchase protocol.
7 - Post-purchase review of products & vendors.

Exhibit 8.8 *Steps in the Organizational Buying Process.*

existing processes. Often, the need to engage in a purchase decision results from a dissatisfying experience with existing products or vendors. Something goes wrong! These "triggers" generally lead to modified rebuys or new task purchase decisions.

In contrast, many purchases result from "automatic" need recognition associated with running low on operating supplies, parts, or materials. Some vendors monitor their customers' inventories and automatically ship additional supplies when inventories reach critical points. Such arrangements are consistent with trends toward systems contracting in which buyers contract with a single vendor to provide all of its maintenance, repair, and operating supply (MRO) requirements. Clearly, this scenario is usually associated with straight rebuy decisions.

Identify Specifications

The second step in the organizational buying process is critical. Organizational buyers must clearly define the specifications and other important selection criteria for both the product and its potential vendors. This process is easy for frequently purchased products. For example, with the straight rebuy for office or janitorial supplies, there is little reason to identify technical specifications. Specifications have already been adequately identified based on past purchase decisions. All that may be required is identification of quantities needed.

In contrast, when engaged in modified rebuy or new task decisions, greater expenditures of time and effort are required to identify solutions needed and establish detailed specifications. Buyers may need to coordinate with engineers and other technicians to identify proper product specifications. **Value analysis** may occur at this stage. An appointed team of technicians may examine high-cost components of products with an eye toward modifying the general design of this product and other products such that they employ common parts. The usual objective of value analysis is to save money. Products and their component parts are critically evaluated with respect to function and design in order to improve quality and, at the same time, lower production and parts/ material costs. Normally, the value analysis team will include purchasing personnel, engineers, and representatives from marketing and finance. Representatives from the seller's organization may also be involved. Their inclusion ensures that suppliers have a better understanding of the buyer's needs and, as a result, are better able to design products that deliver the level of required performance.

Search For and Qualify Vendors

This is a rather simple task for straight rebuy purchase decisions. Vendors are often selected from pre-approved vendor lists, if vendors must be changed. Modified rebuys and new task decisions, however, entail more extensive searches. This is, of course, particularly true for the new task decision. In fact, a major obstacle associated with a new task decision is identifying sources of information about potential suppliers. Sources of relevant supplier data are present in trade directories, can be found by talking to other Firms that may have purchased similar products, or uncovered by conducting Internet searches.

Other potential sources of vendor information include trade advertisements and trade shows. Most industries sponsor trade magazines or journals that are obvious outlets for advertising by companies producing products and services targeted to the industry in question. Similarly, most industries sponsor trade shows that host a variety of potential vendors of products and services to that industry. A typical trade show will have dedicated booth space for a large number of vendors to set up displays for their products.

Marketers of organizational products can do several things to increase their visibility as potential vendors include:

- Getting listed in trade directories that serve the buyer's industry. If directories are available, they are generally maintained by the trade association serving that industry. Again, trade associations are increasingly sponsoring their own Internet web sites, and, therefore can be accessed relatively easily via the Internet. In addition, the *Encyclopedia of Associations*, available in most libraries, will identify many trade associations and other similar organizations.[7]

- Employing aggressive promotion in media targeted to buyers in the industry to ensure their presence is made known. Promotion programs may involve more than just "push" advertising in industry trade magazines. A "pull promotional strategy," where advertising is targeted directly to the product's ultimate users (think NutraSweet), may also prove useful. Push and pull promotional strategies are discussed in greater detail inside Chapters 16 and 17.

- Employing aggressive B2B sales programs that complement push and pull advertising initiatives. Indeed, strong personal selling efforts are probably the most important element of the industrial promotional mix program.

- And, of course, understanding that the best type of promotion is positive word-of-mouth, which is best generated by keeping existing customers satisfied.

Solicit Proposals and/or Bids

The next step is to invite qualified vendors to submit bids and/or proposals. This step is mandatory, particularly for more expensive, high-risk purchases. Major purchasing decisions require detailed written proposals from vendors. Proposals are accompanied by formal sales presentations made by representatives from the marketer's organization. Sales personnel may visit the buyer's organization on one or more occasions prior to scheduling presentations. These visits are used to collect information about the buyer's organization and any specific purchasing needs in order to properly tailor the proposal and the presentation. A well-polished proposal and highly skilled sales presentation team with strong oral communication skills delivering the right message to the right members of the buying center is critical. The skill with which salespeople deliver proposals may prove as important as the content of proposals themselves.

Analyze Proposals, Select Products and Vendors

Organizational buyers are much more likely than are individual consumers to engage in a formal, objective evaluation of alternative products and the suppliers of these products. Because of their technical training and motivation to make the best decision possible for the Firm, organizational buyers will objectively analyze most major proposals. Proposals are compared against one another and against the specifications and other criteria outlined in earlier steps. Because of the complexity of this evaluation process, computer modeling can dramatically reduce the amount of effort involved with the process. A number of computer-assisted decision models and decision-making software are available to the organizational buyer.

Different evaluation (decision) criteria must be in place for products and suppliers. Criteria employed for product evaluation relate to the product's technical specifications, its price, its inherent reliability, durability and other aspects of quality. Other useful evaluation criteria include ease of use, ease of maintenance and repair, and extent to which training may be required to bring employees up to speed on the product. Vendor or supplier-related criteria, in contrast, tend to focus on vendor reputation, purchasing and credit terms, training programs, servicing programs, and general customer relations.

The Purchasing Protocol

Once the choice of products and/or vendors has been made, the buying process turns to consideration of the purchasing protocol or purchasing routine. This step is primarily a "detail-oriented" step in which buying and selling Firms hammer out specifics related to:

- How and when to place the order.
- Generating the appropriate paper work.
- Negotiating details of the contract such as delivery dates and times, credit arrangements, and possible discounts.
- Procedures for tracking, expediting, and inspecting the order once received.

Post Purchase Review

The final, often most important step in the purchase process, is the follow-up review that should occur after the product is in use inside the buying Firm. Buyers generally evaluate the performance of products and vendors, comparing performance against prior expectations. Products/vendors that perform satisfactorily earn repeat business. Organizational marketers that fail to meet specifications and expectations may be eliminated as suppliers and likely will not be considered in later purchase decisions.

Endnotes

[1] Gary M. Grobman. *An Introduction to the Nonprofit Sector 4th Ed.* (Harrisburg, PA: White Hat Communications, 2011)

[2] United States Census Bureau, "2012 Census of Governments: Organization Component Estimates," (Washington, DC: U.S. Census Bureau), assessed November 12, 2014, http://www.census.gov/govs/cog2012.

[3] John M. Kemensky, "Mapping the Contours of the Federal Government," *Administrative and Regulatory Law News* 38 No. 3 (2013): 3–4.

[4] Christopher Chantrill, "U.S Government Spending", (2014), accessed December 6, 2014, http://www.usgovernmentspending.com/total_spending_2013.

[5] "NutraSweet Tries Being More of a Sweetie," *Business Week Archives* (1991), accessed December 6, 2014, http://www.businessweek.com/stories/1991-04-07/nutrasweet-tries -being-more-of-a-sweetie

[6] T. Alejandro, C. Kowalkowski, J. Ritter, R. Marchetti, and P. Prado, "Information Search in Complex Industrial Buying: Empirical Evidence from Brazil," *Industrial Marketing Management* 40 (2011): 17–27.

[7] *Encyclopedia of Associations: National Organizations of the U. S.—An Associations Unlimited Reference Geographic and Executive Indexes*, 50th ed. (Detroit, MI: Cengage Gale, 2011)

CHAPTER 9

SEGMENTATION, TARGET MARKETING, AND POSITIONING

→ Market Segmentation, a Prerequisite to Success

In some ways, everyone reading this book is like everyone else on earth. We're all human beings. Meaning, in brief, we all want to be loved, fed, clothed, safe and for that matter feel "cool." In some ways, everyone reading this book now is similar to fellow members of their core cultural or subcultural group; gender category; social class; professional association; age cohort; and so forth, but substantively different from others not belonging to one or more of those groups. And in some ways everyone reading this book right now is also unique.

The existence and omnipresent nature of these human similarities, differences, and uniquenesses is the primary reason why Firms must "segment" markets well. That is, if those Firms plan to succeed. When engaging in **market segmentation**, Firms deliberately aggregate "similar" consumer or business customers. The act of market segmentation also simultaneously entails a process of deliberate division. Specifically, Firms divide:

- Larger groups of potential customers into smaller groups of actual or potential B2B or B2C customers.

- More heterogeneous groups (hetero means "different") into more homogenous groups (homo means "same") of potential or actual B2C or B2B customers.

- Larger masses of potential or actual customers who are less alike into smaller collections of potential or actual customers who are more alike.

These groups or collections of potential or actual customers are called either **segments** or **market segments**. These homogenous segments are culled from more heterogeneous markets. That the members of these segments are generally similar to one another is important. That the members of market segments generally resemble each another in terms of, say, their beliefs and attitudes; incomes, educational levels or zip codes; or lifestyle preferences is absolutely crucial. This is because the existence of these commonalities implies the membership of these segments will usually:

- Prefer or reject similar products, because the segment membership will be "turned-on" or "turned-off" by the same product features, attributes and benefits.

- Respond more favorably or unfavorably to the same product values and/or promotional messages.

- React in similarly receptive or unreceptive ways to the same pricing strategies.
- Prefer to shop/not shop through the same retailing channels; for example, some segments might prefer traditional brick and mortar stores; others, on-line shopping; others still discount big-box stores, upscale retail stores, etc.

Note that across the preceding four bullet points we purposefully reference the classic marketing mix elements, known as the "4 Ps"—or product, promotion, price, and place.

Almost all Firms should engage in market segmentation. The reason is straightforward. Smart marketing managers and consequently strategically-oriented Firms understand:

- They cannot successfully appeal to all customers or all segments at the same time using the same marketing mix strategies. Too many segment differences, too much human variety, exists out there to think otherwise.
- They should be choosy, "judicious", about the consumers or organizations with whom they seek to develop lasting relationships. Some markets aren't worth the cost to reach. Some customer relationships aren't worth the pain to maintain.
- No such thing as a mass market exists anymore in the U.S.; except perhaps, during four hours on Super Bowl Sundays. But how many Firms can afford more than $6,000,000 to air a 30-second advertising spot? Consequently, Firms must divide and conquer; Firms must pick their spots carefully.

→ Target Marketing, a True Money-Maker

The following adage about fishing should be recalled as Firms develop strategic plans that permit them to market more successfully: Don't just fish where the fish are. Instead, you should fish where the fish are more likely to take your particular bait. Now, let's modify the second statement through the integration of three key marketing terms; the Firm, potentially differentiating values, and the marketing mix, as the only vehicle through which Firms can deliver potentially differentiating value.

Here we go, with the revised saying: Don't just fish where the fish are. Instead, your Firm should fish precisely where the specific types of fish most desired by your Firm live and are more likely to bite on the particular bait—or value—that your Firm offers or one day could offer, if it manages its marketing mix strategically.

This amended adage illustrates how the target marketing and positioning processes ideally could and should work. Assume that your Firm has identified a large number of potentially attractive market segments as a result of its marketing segmentation efforts. In fact, so many segments were identified that it is unreasonable to assume the Firm would have the resources or expertise to successfully satisfy the needs or solve the problems of each segment. Obviously, since the Firm cannot satisfy them all, it must pick and choose its targets. By the way, situations like this are the norm rather than the exception.

You have undoubtedly experienced similar situations. You've likely dined at all-you-can-eat buffets that place more desserts on the bar than you would normally consume in a month. All these sugary, creamy offerings appeared attractive, right? But you held back; you only ate one or, perhaps, two desserts. You strategically targeted your calories. You understood you could not and should not consume everything; you leave some less attractive opportunities on the table.

The act of target marketing unfolds in an analogous fashion. **Target marketing** entails evaluating each of the various segments that the Firm has identified and then deciding, based on these evaluations, which segments to pursue. Or, in marketing-speak, to "target." Target segments with what? Each segment would be targeted with one unique marketing mix. Each marketing mix would be strategically tailored to deliver the exact value or values that the Firm believes customers inside the targeted segment would most likely desire.

Target marketing is where most Firms make or lose a lot of money. Marketers might target only one or two segments that are most likely to respond favorably to the values offered by their existing marketing mix. Alternatively, marketers might target only the one segment that appears most likely to respond favorably to their Firm's revised marketing mix, and the new values this new mix could offer. A Firm might even elect to target multiple market segments it has identified. This targeting option might prove possible depending on the Firm's size, the extensiveness of its product line, and the depth and type of resources the organization has at its command.

Positioning: Why Firms Segment and Target in the First Place

Assume a Firm has decided somewhere between one and five market segments are worth targeting. By the way, most Firms typically target two or three or more customer segments. A given restaurant, for example, might easily target three discrete customer segments:

- The first restaurant customer segment assigns a high value to healthy food choices. Healthy choices are what will attract and satisfy members of this segment. Fortunately, this restaurant can do healthy stuff! Care for a vegetable wrap?

- A second consumer segment exists that assigns greater value to less expensive food choices. The opportunity to eat out while saving money will get these folks into the room. Fortunately, our same restaurant is flexible; please check out its newly-added value menu. Did you hear about the "happy hour" wing deals?

- A third segment of restaurant patrons might value and consequently seek "all-the-taste", "all-the-fun" "all-the-time" with the whole-nine-yards of associated fat, salt, sugar, and alcohol that this menu of food choice options would typically entail. At last, our hypothetical restaurant exclaims—our specialty is making all those delicious bad choices available to our customers! We promise neither broccoli nor asparagus shall ever stalk your table. But would you like extra gravy with your fries and chicken fried steak?

Defining and Developing Positions

Once targeted segments have been selected, the next step is to create a unique and uniquely desirable **market position** in the minds of the prospects or customers who comprise the respective targeted segments. This recommendation is rooted in Chapter 1. Recall, marketing unfolds as a competition or battle that is waged and won or lost in the minds of the market. Well, here we are again. Your Firm should be ready to engage in value-based competition, a battle over whose brand's value is more appealing, and that positioning battle will be fought in the collective mind of the segment or segments the Firm decides to target. But this positioning competition can begin only after the heterogeneous market has been segmented into more homogenous market segments, and one or more of these segments is deemed worth targeting.

A **position** is the mental image that customers or prospective customers develop and hold about specific products, brands and, less frequently, organizations. Marketers develop positions by managing their marketing mixes. Specifically, a marketing mix management approach that determines, develops, and delivers the unique values—or customer solutions—that the Firm:

- Builds into new products or adds to existing products.
- Communicates and emphasizes about its products.
- Integrates into how its products are priced.
- Conveys to targeted customer segments through its supply chains and marketing channels.

Two Perspectives on Positioning

The act of market positioning can be defined from two perspectives. The first perspective is that held by customer segments. The second perspective, naturally, is that held by marketers.

The Customer Perspective

From the customer's perspective, positioning may be described as how customers or potential customers define a product (brand) based on its most important attributes. Alternatively, positioning may be described as the more or less desirable "place" that a product (brand) occupies in consumers' minds as compared to the place or places occupied by competing products (brands). For example, when you encounter the word (brand) "Cadillac" a discrete bundle of perceived attributes undoubtedly comes to your mind. These perceptions may be quite positive in nature, the opposite of positive, or somewhere in-between. At the same time, when you read the words (brands) "Mercedes" or "Jaguar" other bundles of perceptual attributes arise in your mind. Likely, substantially different sets of attributes arose in your mind despite the fact that all three brands designate well-known luxury cars.

Nothing more, nothing less is happening. This is because the Cadillac, Mercedes, and Jaguar brands almost certainly occupy uniquely different places/spaces (positions) in your mind. Cadillac, Mercedes, and Jaguar have successfully or less successfully differentiated their brands in your mind. Remember: successful differentiation generally occurs only after Firms have convinced targeted segments that their brand "is different from" and "better than" competing brands. Hence, our reference to successful or less successful differentiation.

The Marketer Perspective

When evaluated from the perspective of marketers, the act of positioning entails the art of implanting their products' unique benefits and differences; i.e., the brand's differentiating value, in the collective minds of targeted customers. A Firm's marketing efforts always should be executed mindful of the pressing need that exists to develop a unique and uniquely desirable position for its brands in the targeted segment's collective mind. The preceding statement should be viewed as a general marketing principle. Apart from new product development (Chapter 11), every Firm's marketing efforts primarily include segmentation, targeting, and positioning—or marketing mix management—activities.

The Firm's primary positioning goal is to differentiate a brand by building unique bundles of benefits that differentially and favorably appeal to a substantial portion of the prospects or customers who make-up a targeted segment. Think pizza delivery, and *Domino's* wants you to think of its brand first and as the best. Think package delivery, and *UPS* wants you to think of the brown brand, or it is now logistics, first.

These bundles of benefits may be primarily perceptual or absolutely genuine in nature. These benefits should be purposefully designed to specifically satisfy targeted segments' wants or needs, and/or to solve any unresolved problems that prevail within the segment. Ideally, from the marketer's perspective, this set of benefits congeals in ways that make brands appear cooler, more desirable, not just different from but also better than competitive brands and hopefully, in the end, worth acquiring even at substantially higher prices. Apple, Prada, and Tiffany's say hello, and thanks for your loyalty.

Customers Are Doing It for Themselves

Customers will position products in their own minds regardless of whether marketers attempt to do it for them. But obviously, marketers should try to control this process by "doing positioning to customers" before customers "do positioning to them." Most people reading this book are young or youngish. Given this, the Mercedes or Jaguar or likely even BMW or Lexus brands likely occupy more desirable places in your minds than the place that Cadillac occupies. Cadillac is generally positioned in the American market's mind as an older person's ride.

Most of you don't see yourself as old, primarily because you're not, and you don't want to be perceived by others as old. Being perceived by others as "too-old, too-fast" is incompatible with your ideal view of self; your ideal self-concept. Not surprisingly, then, most of you don't aspire to roll in a Cadillac. General Motors has been trying, absent much success, to change Cadillac's positioning status for literally decades. Rather than employing the "Not your father's …" re-positioning statement in its efforts to reinvigorate the Buick brand, GM perhaps should have reserved the phrase for Caddies.

Unique Means Unique, and the Meaning Is Important

There is one other factor to consider now: the meaning of the word: "unique." Unique means the "sole," the "one," or the "one and only." You should understand that something, anything, as in a person, idea, place, product, service, or experience, cannot be somewhat unique, a little unique, or even very unique. Things are either unique, or they are not. Consequently, when positioning within a given target segment, a unique marketing mix, a mix designed to deliver unique benefits, values and solutions in the accurate sense of the word, must be designed for each targeted segment.

You should also remember from Chapters 1 and 3 that when Firms change any part of their marketing mix they create a unique marketing mix.

The Role Played by Marketing Opportunity Analysis

The market opportunity analysis (MOA) concept was introduced in Chapter 3 (Exhibit 3.1). If marketing managers execute the MOA effectively, they are more likely to succeed, as are their Firms. Execute the process poorly, or neglect to execute it at all, and marketing managers may soon be asked to pursue alternative careers. One reason is because marketing managers who fail to execute the MOA effectively are also unlikely to engage in segmentation, targeting, and positioning effectively.

MOAs involve scanning the environment to identify potentially profitable markets that a Firm is currently able to successfully serve. Or one day soon could serve well, if certain strategic changes were enacted within the Firm. The MOA process requires that Firms define and analyze broader product-markets and any submarkets that may exist within this broader market.

As you now know, these submarkets are commonly referred to as **market segments**. Rarely if ever is it possible, or practical, for Firms to target entire markets. Markets, being heterogeneous (dissimilar in nature) are too diverse with respect to customers' wants, needs, and key purchasing-related characteristics. The idea that any Firm could develop a single marketing mix program that would provide the sort of value that would satisfy everyone's needs or solve everyone's problems is laughable. Most of us would likely love to own a Ferrari, for example. But few people can afford one. Consequently, the market, the entire set of potential or actual Ferrari customers, is of little value to the Firm.

Marketers instead generally must identify smaller, more homogeneous (similar), market segments for which they develop specialized values and marketing programs. The market segment or segments Firms decide to pursue are called their target market(s). The act of engaging in market segmentation is entirely consistent with the principles embedded in the marketing mix. Because the process of market segmentation offers managers a precise understanding of the differing customer wants, needs, and problems that dominate within each identified segment, the market segmentation act allows Firms to more precisely allocate their limited resources; namely, their time, talent, and treasures. The more knowledge a Firm possesses about targeted segments, the more likely it is that the Firm can reach the segment with marketing communications (messages) that are meaningful to the people or Firms that comprise the segment. When targeting segments that have been precisely characterized, Firms can custom-tailor products and associated marketing mix programs so as to serve these segments better. Well-informed Firms can develop distinct positions that provide sustainable competitive advantages.

Segmentation in Action

Russell Haley's study of the toothpaste market was first introduced in Chapter 1.[1] Haley characterized the overall toothpaste market as a broad, heterogeneous product-market. There are many different brands of toothpaste available to consumers; toothpastes brands that collectively exist to address a variety of tooth-related needs. And the people who buy toothpaste also possess diverse purchase-related characteristics i.e. they exhibit a range of demographic and psychographic profiles. The bottom line: given the heterogeneous nature of the toothpaste marketplace, no single brand or associated marketing program could possibly serve the entire market effectively. Segmenting this market makes sense.

Market Segments "Levels" Exist

Consider the hypothetical segmentation example highlighted in Exhibit 9.1. This example illustrates the usual situation in defining market segments. It emphasizes that multiple levels of market segments can exist. The process of market segmentation begins by defining the overall **mass market** or **total product-market**, such as the fitness product-market. Such mass markets are generally too diverse to effectively target with a single marketing program. This means that they must be segmented into smaller submarkets.

The Firm's core goal during segmentation is to identify groups of customers within the total product-market that are homogeneous (similar to one another) in terms of their needs; problems, particularly of the unsolved variety; and purchasing-related characteristics. This means subdividing the mass market into a series of market segments. More importantly, this process may require defining multiple levels of market segments going from "macro-segments" to "micro-segments." This later segment is equivalent to our earlier use of the term "niche."

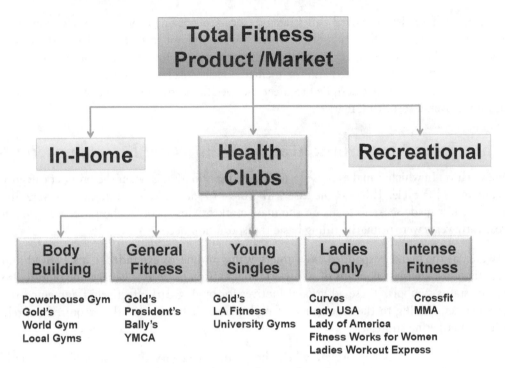

Exhibit 9.1 *Relationship between product-markets and market segments.*

These relationships are evident in Exhibit 9.1. The total fitness product-market is diverse. Many paths to becoming more fit exist, including in-home fitness, recreational fitness, and health clubs. There are more, but we should keep things simple. Each path to fitness can be considered a macro-segment. In turn, each of these segments probably can be further segmented. For example, the segment "gyms" may be segmented further based on the different motives users have for working out in gyms. Each may be considered as micro-segments.

→ Mass Markets, Mass-Marketing, and the Production Concept

At times a Firm may choose not to segment beyond the overall product-market. This might occur, for example, when market segments derived from the mass market are too small to profitably serve, cannot be effectively reached through the promotional communication tools the Firm has available, or are not sufficiently different from one another to justify the creation of dedicated, specialized marketing mix programs to target them. In such cases, Firms may decide to construct a single marketing strategy that targets the entire mass market. Consequently, the Firm opts to target the "average buyer" in the mass market with a single marketing program. This strategy is called a **market-aggregation** or undifferentiated-marketing targeting strategy. In so many words, our Firm has one product, there is one world, and we're going for it.

Mass marketing is rooted in, and complements, the production concept, as defined earlier is this book. The production concept assumes quality products that are priced right will sell themselves. The Firm's major focus becomes one of reducing unit costs while maintaining product quality. Mass production and mass distribution generate scale economies and other production and marketing efficiencies that lead to lower costs and, therefore, potentially lower prices. Henry Ford used this strategy with the Model T. "You can have any color you want as long as it is black." It worked then, but would it work now? Doubtful.

Other Firms have also employed this strategy. Coca-Cola at one time sold only one product in one size in virtually all market areas. There was no attempt to segment the mass market. Coke simply did not have the competition that it faces today. However, the story is now much different. The market has evolved and fragmented. Coca-Cola has a wide range of products in multiple sizes and packages designed to meet the specific needs of multiple market segments within the overall soft drink market.[2]

When Does Mass Marketing and Targeting Make Sense?

One situation in which it makes sense to target the mass market is when the product category is early in its life cycle. This was the case with Ford's Model T. When automobiles were first introduced, it made sense to focus on the mass market. Most people who purchased cars in those early years were primarily filling basic transportation needs.

However, as the market expanded, consumers' wants and needs expanded. Cars evolved into more than just alternative means of transportation, an iron horse as it were; some brands also became status symbols. These additional motives for buying cars effectively fragmented the mass market, leading to the emergence of multiple market segments that required entirely different marketing strategies.

Mass marketing also is appropriate when the product category does not easily lend itself to brand differentiation. For example, most agricultural, lumber, or crude oil products are basically the same regardless of their source. Fresh vegetables, fruits, grains, and milled lumber products are of comparable quality regardless of supplier. More importantly, few differences in consumer needs exist for these products. Similarly, alternate brands of products such as nails, shoe polish, book matches, and table salt are virtually identical commodities in the eyes of most buyers. Consumers view alternative brands as virtually identical. The mass-marketing of these products, which are generically known as commodities, is equally appropriate.

Pros and Cons of Targeting a Mass Market

Certain advantages are associated with targeting a mass market. For starters, treating the overall market as one large market creates a large pool of potential customers. When mass markets are targeted, a large market potential may exist. In turn, this large market potential can yield powerful economies of scale in production, distribution, and promotion that, in turn, can yield cost reductions and lower prices for customers. Few variations on the basic product are manufactured, resulting in longer, more efficient production runs. Warehousing and transportation costs are minimized because systems are geared to distributing a single product. Finally, promotion costs are reduced because only a single, often simple message, needs to be communicated to a single target audience. (The term "economies of scale" is fully defined in Chapter 12.)

Even though the market is treated as a single entity, Firms can still differentiate their brands from those of competitors with some degree of success. This is generally accomplished via promotion as Firms strive to make their brands appear different from and better than competitors' brands. When successful, **product differentiation** can create brand preferences and reduce the degree to which consumers use price as a major criterion for choosing between brands.

Frank Perdue (Perdue Chickens) successfully differentiated his brand of packaged chicken (a supermarket commodity) by focusing on the correlation between skin color (yellow) and freshness in his advertising. Mr. Perdue was famous for appearing as an unsmiling, stern overseer, in his own chicken advertisements. Perdue's ads would always end with the memorable positioning statement: "It takes a tough man to raise a tender chicken." Hey, the positioning statement worked great at the time.

Similarly, Proctor & Gamble's successfully differentiated its Pampers brand disposable diaper (a commodity for many parents) based on its perceived superior absorbency to create one of the world's most valuable brands.[3]

The greatest potential drawback to mass marketing is that customer wants and needs may prove too diverse to employ the "one-size-fits-all" segmentation and targeting strategy. In reality, even most commodity markets can be segmented. For example, gasoline, as a refined crude oil product, is essentially a commodity. But Shell Oil and British Petroleum (BP) have successfully segmented the gasoline market into different grades of fuel (regular, premium) with a variety of additives (ethanol, cleaning agents) that are targeted to different car types as well as different driver types who perceive they have different driving needs. Face it, some people love their cars and thus care for their cars in different ways than others. Hence the presence of fuel gradations and fuel pricing categories, essentially at 20 cent intervals.

The fact remains that firms engaged in mass-marketing are also more susceptible to fierce price competition that undermine all Firms' profit margins. To the extent that customers perceive brands in the product category as essentially equivalent, price probably will drive most customers' purchase decisions. That's generally good for B2B and B2C customers, but generally bad for marketers.

Market Segments within Mass Markets (Macro-segments)

Market segments can be regarded and treated as large identifiable subgroups that are split out from the mass market. Each of these segments is internally more homogeneous than is the mass market. The term homogeneous means that, within each segment, consumers possess similarities in terms of their wants, needs, and purchasing-related characteristics. These purchasing-related characteristics include demographic profiles, personality traits, lifestyle characteristics, social class membership, and a wide range of attitudinal traits.

However, given that similarities do exist within segments, there is still a degree of dissimilarity between consumers within each segment. It is probably better to say that consumers within segments tend to have overlapping (but not identical) wants, needs, and purchasing-related characteristics, Their demographics, personalities, lifestyles, and other traits will be similar, but will not be identical. The marketer's task is to find the key dimensions on which consumers overlap and then create marketing programs that target and appeal to these similarities.

The fitness market introduced earlier in this chapter provides an excellent example of the relationships between mass markets and levels of market segments. The relevant mass-market is the total fitness product-market. Within this market, there are a variety of market segments associated with the different ways that consumers can pursue fitness-related needs. Consumers can stay fit by working out in health clubs, they can work out at home, or they can engage in recreational sports, among others.

Each of these segments is internally more homogeneous with respect to consumer needs and purchase-related characteristics. Health clubs fill a distinct set of fitness needs that attract certain types of customers. The in-home fitness segment fills the needs of a different type of consumer. These customers have needs that overlap with those of people who frequent health clubs, but differences also exist. The latter customers often are more concerned about privacy, cost, and convenience. Consumers in the recreational fitness market are often most interested in the recreational activity itself. Recreational sports, such as tennis, racquetball, baseball, basketball, skiing, etc. fall into this category. Fitness needs may be secondary to the desire to participate in the recreational activity.

Niches (Micro-segments)

Just as macro-segments are derived from larger product-markets, these segments, in turn, can be further segmented. The resulting market segments are called micro-segments or **niches** because each contains consumers that are significantly more similar to one another with respect to customer needs and purchasing-related characteristics than were their parent segments.

Because niches tend to be very narrowly defined, they also tend to be smaller than the market segments from which they were extracted. Moreover, because they tend to be smaller, they also tend to attract less competition. This can prove beneficial. By focusing the Firm's limited marketing resources on satisfying the specific needs of more precisely defined market segments (niches), a differential advantage can be obtained that cannot easily be matched by competitors.

Revisiting our hypothetical fitness product-market example illustrates how the health club macro-segment can be further sub-divided into additional macro- and micro-segments (Exhibit 9.1). A series of additional segments are present within the health club segment. These segments are geared or targeted toward: (1) bodybuilding; (2) general fitness; (3) young singles, (4) ladies only, and (5) intense fitness. The bodybuilding segment provides a good example of a niche. Dedicated bodybuilding clubs exist that amount to "sweat shops" serving the needs of amateur and professional bodybuilders. These clubs focus on traditional free weights with limited machines, support facilities, and services. These clubs operate in marked contrast to clubs such as LA Fitness, Gold's Gym, Bally's, and President's, which cater primarily, though not exclusively, to the general fitness and social needs of young singles. Interestingly, Gold's gym started as a niche operation geared strictly to body builders in Venice Beach, CA. However, when Gold's pursued the franchising route and consequently expanded its operations, the size of its target market expanded in lockstep.

Examples of niche segments are found in many product categories. Bugatti is always a good example. The base price of a 2015 Bugatti is nearly $2,000,000. This company produces a unique, expensive automobile that is targeted to consumers with high discretionary buying power; these consumers comprise a very select market niche.

In financial markets, Green Tree Financial Cooperation specializes in financing the purchase of mobile homes. The Firm effectively developed a marketing program that specifically and successfully targeted this niche (Green Tree was recently acquired by Conseco Financial). Customers in this niche are often lower income buyers with rather unstable job histories. As a result, only a handful of companies are willing to accept the risks associated with financing mobile homes. Because of these inherent risks, Green Tree charges a higher interest rate than people buying regular homes will pay. Green Tree recently has expanded into other high-risk insurance market niches including small aircraft, boats, RVs, motorcycles, pianos and organs, horse trailers, snowmobiles, and four-wheel all-terrain vehicles.

Bases for Segmenting Consumer Markets

The ability to effectively segment larger product-markets into smaller segments requires that Firms find ways to combine consumers into smaller groups based on certain key characteristics that those consumers share in common. As noted, the fact that they share these characteristics implies the members of each segment will generally respond similarly to the marketing mix that the Firm tailors and delivers to that segment. Meanwhile, one segment can easily be distinguished from other segments because these other segments share key characteristics that distinguish them from the first segment.

Before Firms can effectively create market segments they must determine the consumer characteristics or variables that will best "discriminate"—or distinguish or separate—one segment from another. In addition, the variables employed to segment markets also must reflect those characteristics that allow customers in the segments to respond favorably to the marketing mixes tailored to those segments. Generally, this means that the characteristics used to define market segments must somehow be correlated with the different needs and wants of those segments.

Most 65-year-old professional males, for example, could care less about Shayne Oliver's latest fashions. Note that age, gender, occupational status, and educational level (given that most professionals are college graduates) were used to create this segment. Correspondingly, few female (gender), teenage (age), Taylor Swift fans (lifestyle preference) could give a rip about Brooks Brothers' latest line of shirts. So why bother targeting and promoting either fashion to the wrong segment? Not only would the marketing effort be doomed to failure, it would also burn always scarce resources.

The variables that are used to distinguish one segment from another are called **segmentation bases**. Five major segmentation bases are routinely employed to segment consumer markets: geography, demographics, psychographics, and consumer behavior patterns.

Geographic-Based Segmentation

Geographic segmentation entails dividing larger market areas into smaller more precisely delineated areas defined by geographic location. Dividing markets into geographic segments is a convenient surrogate for segmenting based on the benefits sought by consumers or their demographics. Consumers who live in certain geographic locations generally possess similar demographics and needs. Florida has the oldest average population in the United States. Bostonians have, on average, experienced far greater needs to purchase snow shovels than Houstonians. Knowing such obvious geographic shortcuts exist makes it relatively easier to target these geographic locations with discreet and uniquely designed marketing programs.

There are, however, more sophisticated and controversial examples of how marketers exploit consumers' home geographic locations as segmentation bases. RJR Tobacco has divided the Chicago metropolitan market into three segments. The Richmond-based Firm targets three distinct geographic segments with different products and types of promotions because each geographic region is generally home to concentrations of consumers who possess similar demographic characteristics and needs. The North Shore segment, populated by generally better educated, more health conscious consumers receives promotions that feature low-tar brands. The population in the Southeast side of greater Chicago tends to be more conservative. This segment is targeted with ads for Winston. Finally, the predominately African-American Southside of Chicago receives ads placed in black media for the RJR Salem brand, which is high in Menthol.[4]

Geographic segments are established by dividing larger geographic markets using existing political boundaries (voting precincts) or population boundaries (city lines). Segmentation that uses political boundaries essentially creates geographic segments along existing city, county, state, regional, zip code or even country boundaries. Frito-Lay and Coca-Cola employ geographic segmentation when targeting US markets. Both Firms have identified differences in consumer preferences and tastes for their products that are closely associated with regional boundaries. Frito-Lay, by virtue of its extensive MkIS, segments geographic markets down to specific sections of cities in order to respond to changing market and competitive conditions. In cooperation with Texas' anti-litter campaign (Don't Mess With Texas), Coke implemented a dedicated promotional program for Texas emphasizing Texas as a "state of mind" with Coca-Cola Texas—home of the real thing.'[5] Coors beer was marketed for decades only in Colorado and adjoining Rocky Mountain States. Coors, of course, originated in Golden, Co., which you would know if you have ever watched any football game at any point in your life.

Geographic segmentation is evident when local retailers tailor their products and communications to meet the specific cultural, social or even religious idiosyncrasies of local or regional populations. For example, seafood is marketed most heavily in geographic areas where fresh supplies are readily available year round. Kosher foods and brands (e.g., Hebrew National Franks) are more readily available in many northeastern US cities where larger numbers of Jewish consumers live. When you first enter the Walmart in Dearborn, MI, you may be shocked to see barrel-sized containers of fresh dates stationed by the entrance. But you would not be surprised if you already understood that Dearborn is home to more Muslims, percentage-wise (more than 42%), than any other US city. (Assuming, of course, you already also knew fresh dates are highly regarded in the Middle East.)

Climatic differences associated with different geographic areas can drive changes in marketing strategy. For example, SC Johnson employs different formulations of its Raid insect poison for different climatic zones in the United States. This makes sense because the bugs get nastier and more numerous as one travels further south. As a result, different product formulations are required in different climatic regions. Other logical examples of product-markets that are segmented based on climatic differences include markets for sporting goods, heating and cooling equipment, and clothing.

Demographic-Based Segmentation

Demographic segmentation occurs when one or more demographic traits are employed to subdivide a market. Demographic segmentation is widely employed and is probably the most popular form of segmentation for three reasons:

- First, consumers with similar demographic profiles often have similar needs, wants, and product/brand preferences. As noted, preferences for certain foods are highly correlated with one's ethnic or religious ties; think of the importance of kosher foods to Jewish groups. Preferences for music and other forms of entertainment are often similarly related to differences in age, occupation, and educational backgrounds.

- Second, demographic data are easy to obtain. Published demographic information is readily available from a wide range of sources, many of which can now be directly accessed via the Internet. The value of usa.gov is apparent one more time. Recall that usa.gov is the web portal to most publically available information published by the US Government, including data from the Census Bureau.

- Finally, demographic segmentation is commonly employed because it works so well in combination with other segmentation bases. In fact, even when other segmentation bases (such as benefits sought or product consumption rates) are employed, demographics must be used to fully "profile" these segments after they have been created. Many Firms opt to "kill two birds with one stone" and use demographics to simultaneously create and profile market segments.

The typical demographic characteristics used by marketers to create market segments include age, gender, income, race, ethnicity, marital status, family size, and stage of the family life cycle. A few of these are discussed below to illustrate their application.

Segments Based on Age Differences

Marketers create age segments by grouping consumers based on age ranges. For example, American Home Products markets several versions of its Centrum vitamin brand targeted to different age groups. In addition to its adult formula (Centrum Adult), the Firm markets a children's formula (Centrum Kids) and a senior formula (Centrum Silver). The markets for Centrum Adult and Centrum Silver are further segmented by gender. There are different product variants for men and women.

Many companies are retooling their products and marketing activities to fit the needs of the aging Boomer generation. Kimberly-Clark's Depends brand of adult diapers was recently repositioned to reflect attitudinal predispositions in the Boomer generation toward such products. Ads now tout, Depends "Looks and fits like underwear. Protects like nothing else." Kohler, a producer of bathroom-fixtures, adopted rock-climbing terminology to rename its shower "grab bar" as the "Belay" shower handrail, a more acceptable term to Boomers. Across the board, companies are making subtle changes to typefaces (making them larger), modifying store shelves to make products easier to reach, and avoiding some colors on package labels (yellows and blues) that are harder for older eyes to bring into focus.[6]

McDonalds targets children, teens, adults, and seniors through different products and promotional appeals. McDonalds has historically targeted different age groups with diverse types of advertising. Ronald McDonald ads target Happy Meals to children. Most recently, McDonalds has taken steps to better serve the needs of Millennials with McWraps and other higher quality and healthier foods. The jury remains out on whether these healthier options will succeed, but early reports remain far from promising.

Segments Based on Gender Differences

Gender has long been used for segmenting markets for clothing, hair dressing products, cosmetics, and magazines. This seems natural. Men and women have different preferences for such products. Marketers utilize their knowledge of gender differences to tailor different products and promotional programs to each gender category. Procter & Gamble, for example, targets its Secret brand of deodorant specifically to women. Rogaine is targeted mainly to men. However, a Rogaine for Women is also now available. Marlboro and Camel cigarettes are targeted primarily to men. Eve and Virginia Slims are targeted nearly exclusively to women.

Segments Based on Income Differences

Income segmentation will more likely be used for products such as automobiles, boats, clothing, cosmetics, and travel. For the more expensive versions of such products, marketers are primarily interested in targeting higher income consumers due to their greater purchasing power and propensity to be early adopters of new products and technologies. Rolex and Rolls Royce market exclusively to highly affluent consumers. Joy perfume is billed as the "costliest perfume in the world." This Parisian perfume is a classic example of segmenting based on income and positioning using both income and lifestyle. This perfume was historically sold only in upscale department stores, such as Lord & Taylor or Neiman Marcus. Although now sold in many less "upscale" retailing locations, as well as online, Joy still retails at prices in excess of $100 an ounce.

Other retailers purposely target lower income consumer groups. Family Dollar Stores (Exhibit 9.2) is the second largest retailer in the US. Boasting more than 8,100 stores, Family Dollar targets low- and lower-middle income households in urban and rural locations. The Firm's core customer is the female head of household, she is less than 40 years of age, and

Exhibit 9.2 *Family Dollar targets lower income families with affordable products.*

has an annual income less than $40,000. Note that three different demographic bases for segmentation were just referenced. Other Firms that target lower income groups are Walmart, Dollar Tree and, until recently, Korean-based Hyundai.

Segments Based on Family Life Cycle Stage

The stage of the **family life cycle** segmentation approach employs a rich composite of demographic traits to define market segments (Exhibit 9.3). When segmenting based on the family life cycle, Firms specifically recognize that consumers progress through a series of life cycle stages. Traditionally, the life cycle begins with individuals who are young and single. The traditional family cycle ends with consumers who are older and unmarried because their spouse had died. This is the center progression in Exhibit 9.3. Variations on this traditional life cycle exist, reflected in the branches above and below the traditional progression. The consumer membership of each family life cycle stage essentially amounts to a market segment that possesses different wants, needs and problems, and differing product/brand preferences.

Marketers strive to develop products and tailor their marketing programs to address and to serve these differences. A few examples illustrate this point. "Young singles" is an attractive segment for Firms that market sporting goods, sports cars, fashion clothing, entertainment, or recreation. As young singles transition to married life (before they have children), their needs and wants change as they begin building households. Young marrieds place more emphasis on home furnishings and home appliances; durables goods used in a family setting. As children come on the scene, things change even more. Young single parents, in fact, is one of the fastest growing segments reflected in the family life cycle. Given the high divorce rates in the United States and growing propensity to have children outside of marriage, young single parents, often on limited incomes, look for ways to save money. They might generally desire decreased food portions in grocery stores, smaller and more efficient apartments, less expensive but more

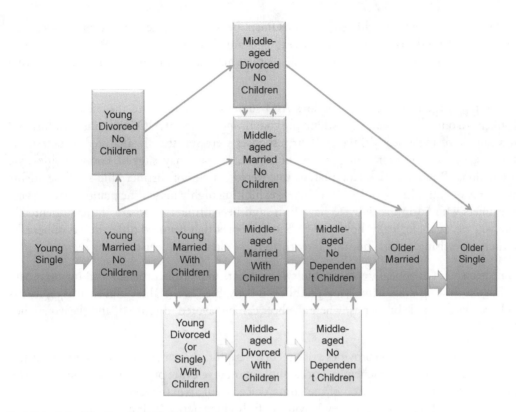

Exhibit 9.3 *The Family Life Cycle.*

convenient childcare, and time-saving appliances. Similarly, seniors are increasingly interested in health care, home security, specialized housing, smaller food portions, and specialized food products.

Psychographic-Based Segmentation

Psychographics, consisting primarily of **lifestyle** and **personality** traits, are frequently used as segmentation bases. Lifestyle segments emphasize differences in how people choose to live their lives, or more specifically, what they choose to do in their free time. Marketers target products or services based on different patterns of lifestyle behaviors. Lifestyle patterns of behaving are uncovered through survey research in which consumers are asked to report their **activities**, **interests**, and **opinions**.

Marketers tease out common patterns in how consumers answer these "AIO" questions. They then classify those people who answered the same questions in a similar fashion into distinct market segments. The underlying rationale for doing so, whose logic is difficult to dispute, is that if consumers:

- Prefer to engage or not engage in the same activities (camping, fishing, nesting at home while binge-viewing DVR-recorded programs, *Breaking Bad*, anyone?)
- Are interested or not interested in the same things (ideas, art, books, sports, music, etc.)
- Hold the mutually compatible or incompatible opinions (about, say, the role that government, guns or God should play in their lives) …

... then the segments to which those consumers belong will generally accept or reject the same sorts of products, promotions, prices, or channels of distribution. We cannot, as you see, divorce ourselves from the integral role that the marketing mix always plays in marketing practice.

For example, the beer industry employs AIO surveys to characterize the life styles of beer drinkers. In one such survey, a questionnaire containing a range of AIO items was administered to a sample of male beer drinkers. Their responses were statistically analyzed to determine the existence of any common patterns of responses that may suggest common life-style orientations. Results of the data analysis uncovered a series of distinct "life-style" segments consisting of "impulsive drinkers," "drinkers exhibiting highly masculine points of view," beer consumers who "drink socially to have fun," and beer drinkers who are "fitness oriented."[7] Can you see, again logically, how specific brands of beer that featured different sets of benefits in their advertising would appeal differently to these alternative beer-drinking segments?

Craft beers tend to appeal to certain lifestyle segments more than others. Drinking craft beer is akin to drinking a fine wine. Most craft beer is consumed in social settings such as taprooms and beer-garden-style breweries, where the beer can be savored, discussed, and the experience shared.[8]

Psychographic information provides a rich set of descriptors that can be used to complement and enrich other segmentation schemes. For example, motorcycles are predominantly purchased by men. However, the male portion of the human race is still an extremely diverse demographic. Motorcycle marketers, think Harley-Davidson, fully characterize their buyers in terms of both demographics and psychographics. The typical Harley-Davidson owner today is not the bad-ass biker type depicted in *The Sons of Anarchy*. Rather, the typical owner conflates the Harley brand with lifestyle expressions of freedom and independence. Harley's dealerships have been completely redesigned to support and bolster this more desirable image, an image that appeals to segments larger and generally more affluent than *Hell's Angels*—although the *Angels* still remain a heck of an audience to marketers of leather and bikes. Harley's now designer stores exude a lifestyle atmosphere. Floor plans are designed to surround visitors with motorcycles. Custom parts, Harley memorabilia, accessories, and clothing lines are prominently displayed. Many stores possess customer lounges complete with Harley videos and games.[9]

Consumer Behavior-Based Segments

Several consumption-related behaviors are routinely employed to segment consumer markets. Product usage rates, product usage occasion, and brand loyalty status come to mind first.

Segments based on product usage rates typically divide consumers of a given product into non-, light-, moderate-, and heavy-users. Snack food or fast-food consumers, for example, are typically segmented in this manner. Marketers often target consumers characterized as heavy users. Why? Because, all else being equal, heavy users (often called the "heavy half") account for the bulk of the sales for a given product. These are often the folks who visit McDonald's frequently, not for the Frappuccino but for Big Mac and Quarter Pounder meals. (Not for nothing is the segment called the "heavy-half.")

The heavy half, however, is often comprised of a relatively small proportion of consumers. The principle involved is called the "80–20" principle. The easiest way to explain the principle in practice is that about 80% of Big Mac sales are accounted for by only 20% of consumers who purchase the product.

Marketers sometimes mistakenly assume the heavy half is the most profitable segment to target. This mistake is called the "majority fallacy"; the false assumption that the heavy half always offers the greatest profit potential. In reality, marketers may be better served by targeting smaller niche opportunities to which they can direct finely tuned marketing programs that provide differential value-based advantages against competitors' related offerings.

When creating market segments based on product usage occasion, the emphasis is on identifying different consumption situations or purchase occasions under which the product is consumed. Different people may purchase and use the same product, let's say wine, for different occasions or in different consumption situations. You may buy wine simply because you and your partner enjoy wine with food, you might buy a different brand of wine because your boss and her spouse are visiting your home for dinner; and, who knows, you might enjoy even a different brand of (more expensive, prestigious) wine because you are celebrating a joyous anniversary or holiday at home with friends. While you might buy the same brand of wine to satisfy the differing expectations that are in play during each occasion, we frankly doubt it.

As a result, opportunities exist for segmenting markets based on such differences in "usage occasions." This is also why airlines, for instance, have segmented their markets into usage occasion segments consisting of people flying for business purposes (business flyers), vacation flyers, and people flying primarily for family reasons. Each segment represents a different usage occasion. Each segment is targeted through different pricing and promotional strategies. Frequent-flyer programs are geared to business travelers to encourage airline loyalty. Super-low fares tied to advanced booking outcomes are used to attract vacation travelers and people flying primarily for family reasons. Cooperative promotional programs with travel agencies, destination resorts, and cruise-lines are commonly employed to provide reduced rates in travel markets.

Markets for more mundane food products can be segmented by usage occasion. For example, orange juice has traditionally been promoted as a breakfast drink. In an attempt to build additional demand for orange juice, the orange grower's trade association promotes the consumption of orange juice at other times of the day. Appropriately, orange juice is positioned as "not just for breakfast anymore."

"Coke in the Morning" is a positioning statement that targets a consumer segment who wants a sugary, carbonated "pick-me-up" rather than coffee when it wakes up. Pepsi experimented with a dedicated product geared to the same usage occasion segment. The product was branded as Pepsi AM during test market. The product was a highly potent version of Pepsi laced with extra caffeine and sugar.[10]

Firms can learn a lot when segmenting consumers by the degree to which they are **brand loyal**. If Firms can determine the characteristics of loyal versus non-loyal customers for their brands and for those of its major competitors, they may be able to find ways to keep their customers loyal and pull non-loyal customers away from competitors. Brand loyalty often is defined based solely on consumers' patterns of repeat purchase behavior. For example, consumers buying the same brand five times in a row have been defined as brand loyal.[11] Brand loyalty has also been defined in terms of the proportion of total purchases within a given product category devoted to the most frequently purchased brand.[12] A problem with such definitions is that repeat purchase patterns may reflect only a spurious loyalty with little attitudinal attachment to the brand. Spuriously loyal consumers can easily be induced to switch to other brands via better prices, coupons, point-of-sale visibility and other incentives.[13]

Brand loyalty has steadily declined amongst American consumers for years. The underlying factors include continuing increases in the number of choices available to consumers; consumers who are much better informed than once was the case about products, thanks to the Internet; and consumers who are increasingly cynical. And the fact that consumers are increasingly cynical is understandable. Why should consumers believe what marketers say in a world where one cannot believe in what politicians, church leaders (here, we reference child sexual abuse scandals), or various celebrity, media, or sports leaders are saying?

Consumer Preference or Predisposition-Based Segments

Markets can be segmented based on differences in the wants, needs, and attitudes of consumers. In our discussion about segmenting the toothpaste market we examined the inherent value in creating **benefit segments**. Firms who target "benefit segments" focus first on identifying and then on satisfying the differing wants and needs that characterize the consumers who constitute each segment. Sometimes, for example, your decision to give another person a watch means that you want him to enjoy the benefit of knowing the time. Other times, you give a person a watch so she can enjoy the benefit of knowing you love her as a friend, lover, or family member. At other times still, you give someone a watch so he benefits from knowing you did not forget the birthday or anniversary. Same watch, conferring different benefits, targeted at diverse consumer segments.

Other consumer predispositions also might lead to meaningful segmentation strategies. Markets can be segmented based on how well-informed or knowledgeable consumers are about a particular product category. Differing promotional mix programs should be used when communicating with consumers who know little to nothing about the product, in contrast to individuals who are already better informed.

Sometimes marketers may seek to distinguish between customers who have experienced specific types of problems with products or brands versus those who have not. Customers who frequently encounter specific types of problems may possess common sets of predictable characteristics. Such conditions would make it not only feasible but also logical to target such segments with different marketing mix solutions.

Segmenting markets based on individuals' media consumption habits seeks to reveal consistent patterns of differences in the types of media preferred (i.e. preferences for specific television shows, radio stations, magazines, newspapers, and online social media). Media consumption patterns, in turn, again may vary across key customer demographic and psychographic traits. This information then can be used to more effectively target advertising and other communications to the customer segments as they are derived.

Bases for Segmenting Organizational Markets

Organizational or business markets can be segmented in the same fashion as consumer markets. Organizations face different marketing challenges depending on geographic locations of their customers. This is particularly true when US Firms compete globally against locally based operations. Firms must modify their products and marketing activities to meet the demands of these localized market areas. For example, Peoria, IL, based Caterpillar Corp. (CAT), the company that makes those huge bulldozers and related equipment, employs a **nested segmentation** scheme that begins with geographic segmentation. Nested segmentation means that a number of segmentation bases are applied hierarchically to more precisely define key market segments. In 2013 approximately 60% of CAT's sales of heavy construction equipment came from international markets. CAT's global markets are divided into North America, Latin America, Asia-Pacific, Canada, and EAME (Europe, Africa, Middle East) classifications. These broader geographic areas are further segmented into smaller geographic locals to identify the best ways to compete in global markets against local and other global competitors such as the Japanese firm Komatzu. However, CAT further segments its geographic markets based on industries served, such as agriculture, construction, forestry, mining, and marine. Different product groups are then targeted to customers in these industries.[14]

The targeted customer organization's fundamental structural characteristics may prove useful for creating market segments. Structural characteristics such as customer industry type (i.e., the industry in which the customer competes), organization size, and the type of technology employed to drive customers' business models can be used to segment organizational markets. Organizations in the same industry, for example, perform similar business functions or services and consequently face the same general production, marketing, personnel, or purchasing problems. As a result, organizations in the same industry often can be treated as a unique market segment. NAICS codes, as you should recall, are employed to categorize business organizations together based on the primary products or services they produce. This is why NAICS codes often are employed to define organizational market segments based on industry type.

Organizations of different sizes typically face different challenges and purchasing problems. This implies, logically, that organizations of the same size can be treated as distinct market segments. The segmenting Firm could measure "size" based on number of employees, sales revenue, number of retail outlets, etc. A customer Firm that employs hundreds of people will require more sophisticated payroll management systems than will Firms that employ, say, 25 individuals.

Potential customer organizations can also be segmented based on their use of different technologies. For example, organizations engaged in computer-aided product design and prototyping are excellent targets for Firms' producing 3D printers for "fast or rapid prototyping." *Stratasys* (stratasys.com) is a leading producer of 3D printers. The Firm targets this still rapidly evolving application and solution to Firms operating in "high tech" aerospace, automotive, defense, medical, architectural, and entertainment industries.

→ Methods for Creating Market Segments

A number of proven techniques and tools exist that can aid marketing managers in identifying market segments. Techniques range between highly complex statistical procedures to simple managerial judgment. A discussion of the available statistical procedures for segmenting markets is beyond the scope of this course. We can, however, examine the simpler judgment-based techniques. One useful and comparatively simple technique is called "hierarchical structures analysis" or HSA. HSA is fundamentally identical to the "nested segmentation" procedure employed by Caterpillar. Two basic approaches exist through which this technique can be applied. One is customer-based; the other is product-based.

Customer-Based Approach to HSA

The customer-based approach to HSA is illustrated in Exhibit 9.4. With this technique, marketing managers employ their own judgment to decide how larger aggregate markets should be broken up into smaller sub-markets or market segments. The example in Exhibit 9.4 focuses on the household paint market. The process begins by segmenting the overall paint market (employing a geographic segmentation base) into urban and rural markets. These two markets are then further segmented based on user-type, such as professional painters and *Do-It-Your-Self* (DIYS). This later classification is shown only for the rural segment. In turn,

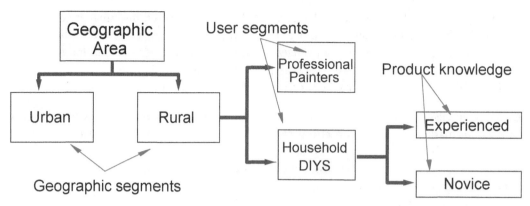

Exhibit 9.4 *Hypothetical Nested Segmentation of a Metropolitan Area Household Paint Market.*

the DIYS segment (if this is the segment the Firm chooses to target) could be segmented, again, based on the painter's degree of product knowledge, yielding experienced and novice segments.[15] Experienced users are likely knowledgeable. Novice users may need extensive help in selecting and using both paints and associated painting paraphernalia.

This example illustrates how easily this approach can be used to provide marketing managers with working segmentation schemes. The specific segmentation bases employed to create segments are those that managers feel will produce the most useful set of segments for further analysis and ultimate targeting. The approach focuses on identifying market segments from customers' perspective, which is generally the better tactic.

The Product-Based Approach to HSA

The product-based approach to HSA focuses on products rather than customers. Otherwise, the segmentation process is identical. The objective of this approach is to ultimately identify relevant **branded product-markets** in which the Firm competes. To illustrate, let's segment the beverage product-market. Begin with the overall beverage product-market shown at the top of the figure in Exhibit 9.5. The "beverage product-market" is subsequently broken down into more specific product types, beginning by differentiating between two product classes: "non-alcoholic" and "alcoholic" beverages. These two product classes comprise the first level of market segments.

Now consider only the alcoholic beverage segment. This segment can be sub-divided further into distinct product forms. This could include wine, beers, liquor, and specialty alcoholic beverages. Each product form may be treated as a distinct market segment within the "alcoholic beverage" product class.

In turn, each product form can be subdivided into more precisely defined product forms. Consider the beer product form (market segment). There are multiple types of beers (additional product forms): light beers, premium beers, specialty beers, craft beers, and so forth.

Finally, the next level entails branded product-markets. These are the specific brands for each product form. For example, the light beer segment consists of brands such as Miller Lite, Bud Light, Sam Adams Light, Coors Light, and so on.

When employing product-based HSA, market segments are typically equated with specific product forms. For example, we might talk about the "light beer segment" or the "premium beer segment." One assumption, of course, is that each product form segment contains a series of similar brands vying with each other for the available market share in that segment.

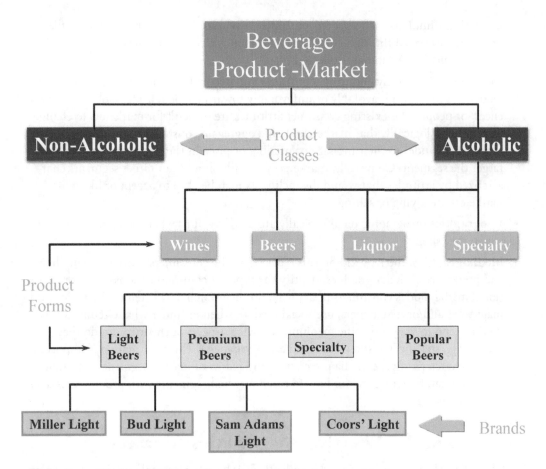

Exhibit 9.5 *Hypothetical Nested Segmentation of the Beverage Market.*

Marketing managers employ product-based HSA to define their "competitive set." If market segments are defined in terms of light beers, premium beers, specialty beers (and so on), the definitions suggest the specific brands should viewed as direct competitors. In the light beer segment, Miller Lite, Bud Light, Sam Adams Light, and Coors Light may be considered as direct competitors with one another.

→ Profiling Market Segments

Once market segments have been created or identified, segment customers must be exhaustively profiled. The major descriptors (variables) that are used to characterize consumer segments generally include their demographics, psychographics, needs and attitudes, geographic location, and media-graphics. Most of these descriptors have already been discussed as segmentation bases that are employed to initially create segments. Regardless, they should be used again to provide the richest possible profile for consumers in the segments.

- **Demographics** include the standard demographic traits discussed earlier in the chapter (age, income, education, occupation, etc.). Demographics are crucial for fully profiling customers in market segments at any level.

- **Psychographics** consist of preferred lifestyle traits and enduring personality traits. Lifestyle traits capture consumers' whole patterns of acting and interacting with other people and with various stimuli throughout the world. Personality captures unique psychological characteristics that lead to consistent and enduring responses to events or marketing stimuli as each arise in consumers' environments. Psychographic profiles are normally developed through consumer surveys in which data on activities, interests, and opinions (AIO data) are collected.

- **Attitudes** are relatively enduring, consistent and deeply-held consumer evaluations and tendencies to respond favorably or unfavorably toward particular ideas, objects, experiences, or people. Pre-existing consumer attitudes are difficult for marketers to change. This implies, logically, that marketers should aggregate consumers who share similarly favorable attitudes to their message or product or price in the same segment and then target the segment. Conversely, marketers generally should not target segments characterized by attitudes that would dis-incline its membership to accept or like what marketers are saying or selling.

- **Geographics** (geographic data) typically are used to tell us where customers live and where they shop.

- **Media-graphics**, the new kid on this block, describe consumers' media viewing habits and preferences. Media-graphics identify the types of communications and promotional media modes consumers prefer (e.g., do they watch TV, listen to the radio, read magazines and/or newspapers, use social media), when or under what circumstances do they tend to view a specific medium, and what aspects of the medium do they prefer (e.g., specific TV shows, magazines, newspapers). This information is important when characterizing the media preferences and habits of market segments such that marketers can better figure out how to reach targeted segments with product messages and incentives.

Requirements for Effectively Segmenting Markets

The ability of any Firm to segment markets effectively is based on several criteria. For segments to be attractive, useful, and viable as potential target markets, they should be:

Homogeneous Within, Heterogeneous Between

Consumers within segments should share similar wants and needs that are germane to the targeted product. Ideally, consumers also should be similar to one another on key demographic and psychographic characteristics that profile the segment. This is what is meant by the term "homogeneous within."

By contrast, these customers should be distinctly different from customers who populate other segments on these dimensions. This means that segments are "heterogeneous between." If these between segment differences are present, then one segment should respond differently from other segments to any given Firm's unique marketing mix efforts. If these sorts of critical differences do not discriminate between segments, why bother segmenting the market. A mass-marketing approach may be more appropriate.

Large, Measureable, and Profitable Enough

Marketers must be able to estimate the size of any market segments under consideration. The size, purchasing power, and customer profiles associated with the market segment must be large enough and measureable. Overall segment size is a function of the number of potential customers. Size alone, however, is insufficient to gauge the profit potential in a market segment. Marketers must also estimate both the market- and sales-potential within segments.

Market potential is a function of both the number of potential customers and their product purchase rates. Market potential provides a best-case estimate of the total sales available to all Firms competing in the segment. **Sales potential**, by contrast, is a best-case estimate of the Firm's possible share of the market potential. **Profit potential** estimates readily follow from the initial two estimates.

Accessible through Communications and Distribution Channels

Firms must be able to effectively and efficiently reach those segments it has chosen to target. This means that Firms must assure the existence of the appropriate distribution and communications channels required to reach customers in their target markets. If Firms cannot reach segments with their distribution and promotional efforts, they cannot market to them successfully. For example, no one has ever purchased anything new until they have been made aware that the "anything" exists.

Marketers must also identify the right media to communicate with customers in market segments. Media purchasing services, such as J. Walter Thompson (JWT), Mindshare, and GroupM, profile the users of TV, radio, print, and some electronic media on a range of demographic, geographic, psychographic, attitudinal, and behavioral dimensions.

Actionable

Firms must have adequate resources and expertise to ensure segments are properly served; ideally in a manner superior to their competitors. This might entail possessing the resources making it possible to gain access to the right supply chains (wholesalers and retailers), logistics systems (transportation, warehousing) and financial services. It also means possessing the necessary marketing expertise, such as a knowledgeable and experienced sales force, to effectively engage with business partners and consumers.

Access to distribution is essential. The key question: can the Firm effectively capture the most efficient supply chain(s) that will provide the best exposure for its products to targeted segments? The answer is not nearly as obvious as one might assume. In 1987, Elizabeth Arden, a division of Unilever, attempted to launch its Elizabeth Taylor line of fragrances. However, Arden quickly found that higher end retailers, the desired retail partners, were not willing to stock the brand. Only mid-tier retailers such as J.C. Penny and Sears seemed willing due to their desire to improve their fashion images.[16]

→ Market Targeting/Target Marketing

As noted earlier, your favorite books, TV shows, movies or music rarely provide deep insights into your psychological makeup or deepest needs. But your favorites do point the way toward the market segments to which you most belong. Strategic marketers understand that knowing the movie or book or website you favor reveals insights that can be used to predict your tastes, habits, and ultimately your wants, needs, and problems. Watch out. You are being targeted by marketers. For reasons that are good for them and often good for you.

But what is this thing called targeting? The **market targeting** decision entails decisions about which market segments, among those identified during the segmentation process, to pursue. Four targeting options exist. These are summarized in Exhibit 9.6.

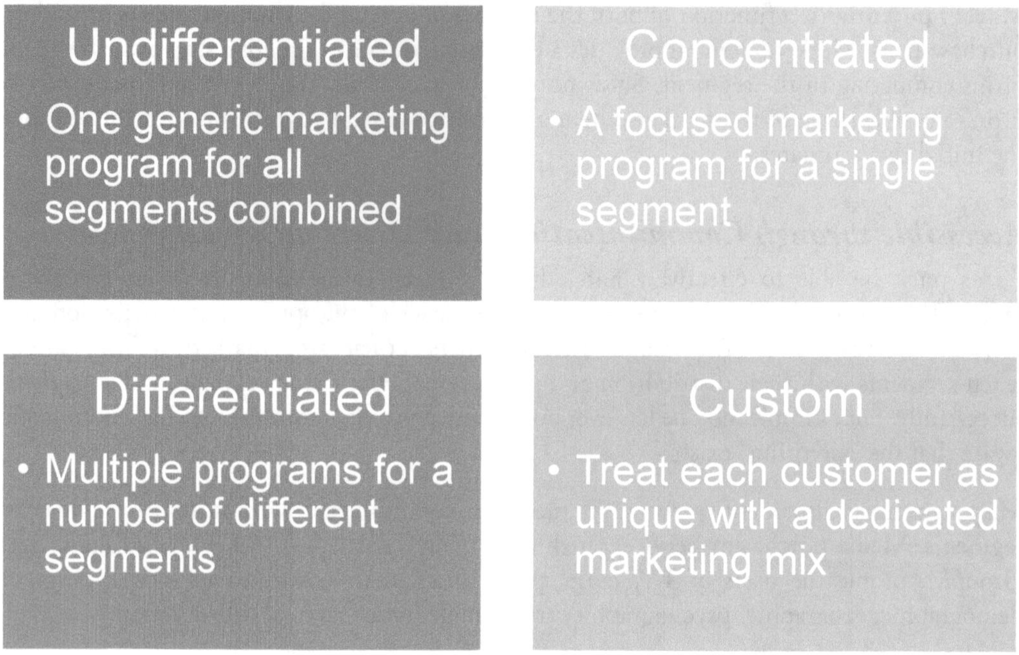

Undifferentiated	Concentrated
• One generic marketing program for all segments combined	• A focused marketing program for a single segment

Differentiated	Custom
• Multiple programs for a number of different segments	• Treat each customer as unique with a dedicated marketing mix

Exhibit 9.6 *Market Targeting: Selecting Market Segments—Four Choices.*

Undifferentiated Targeting

The undifferentiated targeting strategy assumes that no viable differences exist among market segments; namely, meaningful segments do not exist. There is one market segment (e.g., the whole market), generally one product or marketing provider, and one marketing mix approach that is most appropriate. Here, the Firm focuses attention on what is similar across consumers. The Firm has made the decision to aggregate consumers and to serve them with a single marketing program that appeals to a broader customer spectrum.

General merchandise retailers operating in rural communities frequently employ this targeting approach. Rural grocery stores might stock products geared to the average customer in its market area. Management assumes there are negligible differences in needs between customers. Consequently, an "average" range of products will appeal to the most people.

The undifferentiated targeting strategy is also well-suited to products in early stages of their product life cycles. Meaningful segments often do not exist in such newly created markets. Customers may be interested only in having their basic needs or newly identified problems satisfied. This was the case with Henry Ford's Model T. Ford customers, at that time, were interested in basic, reliable, and inexpensive transportation— and that was it. By using an undifferentiated strategy, Ford was able to exploit the tremendous scale economies associated with the mass production and marketing of a single model and keep prices low.

Differentiated Targeting

A differentiated targeting strategy assumes that multiple segments, characterized by meaningful customer differences, have been identified. Thus different marketing mix programs should be developed to reach each segment with the discrete values that the specific group of customers is most likely to desire. The assumption is that the Firm intends to pursue more than one of these segments also exists.

Large manufacturers of power tools produce different lines of tools. Each line is targeted toward buyers characterized by varying price, quality, and performance preferences. Black & Decker produces and promotes a number of product lines, including DeWalt, Porter-Cable, and Mac Tools. The Black & Decker and DeWalt lines target DIYS (Do It Your Self) consumers and professional builders, respectively. The DeWalt line is a premium brand. It is priced substantially higher than the Black & Decker line. Porter-Cable, a recent acquisition, is positioned similarly to Black & Decker. The Mac Tools brand targets professional automotive mechanics.

Concentrated Targeting

The concentrated targeting strategy unfolds when Firms target one or more products to a single segment through highly refined marketing communications, pricing, and distribution programs. This strategy is often used by smaller Firms who have limited resources, or by Firms that simply want to specialize on a limited portion of the market.

These Firms target niche segments. Marketers who pursue concentrated targeting pursue very large shares of narrowly defined, or niche, segments. Products, their associated messages, the pricing strategies, and even delivery or distribution programs are "fine-tuned" to satisfy the unique tastes, satisfy the challenging needs, or solve the vexing problems of highly specialized individuals or Firms.

Bugatti engages in niche targeting. As mentioned earlier, the Firm builds extreme high-end sports cars that few people can afford.

Customized Targeting

Customized targeting strategies involve tailoring (think of a tailored suit) marketing mix programs to satisfy the needs of individual consumers or companies. This targeting approach is most appropriate in B2B marketing, particularly when Firms market major equipment that must be custom designed. As these highly customized products are installed and used, customer employees often must be trained. Highly specialized after-the-sale-services are often also required. Successful relationship building and relationship management are each also critical, particularly over the longer-term. Fort-Worth Lockheed-Martin exemplifies the customized targeting strategy. The Firm focuses primarily on customizing its bleeding-edge, best-of-breed products for one customer—the US Armed Services. Second and third generation planes and arsenals are targeted to close American allies, such as Great Britain and Israel.

Consumer (B2C) products are less amenable to customized strategies. However, some consumer goods producers are taking steps to tailor aspects of their marketing to needs of individual consumers. For example, Ritz-Carlton Hotels maintains a database of its guests' preferences for such amenities as hypoallergenic pillows, radio and TV stations, Internet access, room service, or things as mundane as chocolate chip cookies. The information is used to tailor the service provided on the customer's next stay.[17] NIKEiD (http://www.nike.com) allows customers to customize clothing purchased from Nike. Customers can custom design shoes and accessories to endow them with their own "look and feel." The service is available online and in select retail stores.

Market Positioning

Market (or product or brand) positioning (hereafter simply called **brand positioning** or just **positioning**) is essential for effective marketing. A well-conceived positioning strategy can earn a substantial customer following, insulate the Firm from competition, and enhance the Firm's profit picture by permitting the Firm to raise overall prices. Once marketing managers identify the most viable target markets to pursue, the next logical step is to identify alternative positioning strategies. The objective is to select the strategy that provides the brand with a distinct personality or image (**brand image**) that can yield a differential competitive advantage in the market.

When marketers position products, brands, or organizations they are essentially creating a personality for the product, brand, or organization. This personality makes a statement to consumers about what the brand stands for with respect to important attributes, benefits, and competing brands. Proper positioning is critical for the long-term viability of any brand. Moreover, positions are not cast in concrete. Positions can change, or may need to be changed, over time as market conditions change, as demand for the brand changes, and as the relative positions (images) of competitive brands change.

In contrast to position, "positioning" is the process by which marketers attempt to establish or create position. Positioning generally is accomplished by developing marketing programs, i.e. designing marketing mixes that communicate the desired image. The elements of the marketing mix (product, price, promotion, and distribution) should work hand-in-hand to manage all aspects of customer demand for the brand. However, promotion tends to be the major tool employed for creating and managing position. This makes sense. Promotion is, after all, the primary mechanism through which marketers communicate with target customers. Indeed, many promotion strategies and techniques virtually mirror the different positioning strategies that can be used.

Positioning Methods

There are multiple dimensions on which brands can be positioned.

Competitive-Based Positioning

A common approach is to position relative to the brand's competitors. Competitive positioning entails using customers' existing perceptions of the Firm's competitors' brands as the basis from which to build and to eventually differentiate the brand's image. Developing a competitive position usually involves direct comparisons between competing brands. This positioning strategy is often referred to as product or brand "differentiation." Such comparisons are usually made via advertising. Comparative advertisements directly compare and contrast competing brands. Then, either directly or indirectly, they suggest or demonstrate why one brand is superior to the others.

Competitive positioning is illustrated by the advertising claims by the major burger chains made during the "Burger Wars." Each marketer claims its brand is better than the others on one or more dimensions; i.e., juicer, fresher, tastier, charbroiled—the list impresses. Wendy's, in its classic "Where's the Beef" advertising campaign, emphasized the size of their burgers relative to McDonald's and Burger King. Making claims of direct superiority is the most common competitive positioning strategy.

Firms can also competitively position their brands as being "different from but not necessarily better than" competitors' brands. This variant of competitive positioning entails emphasizing the fact the key brand features deliver different kinds of benefits. When Bayer Aspirin compared itself to Tylenol, a brand that is a hard-to-defeat beast in its marketing space, the advertisement simply said Bayer works better on a different type of pain than does Tylenol. Note the nuance.

Benefit-Based Positioning

Benefit positioning emphasizes the brand's ability to satisfy specific needs that customers may have. A unique brand personality may emerge as a function of an ability to satisfy these needs. (Brands can have personalities, too, as explained in Chapter 10.) When this positioning strategy is used, a brand's major benefits are highlighted in promotional materials. Benefit positioning is typically used for products that are purchased due to their form utility; that is, their functionality. Consumer non-durable goods such as toothpaste, soap, household cleaning supplies, canned goods, and personal care products are commonly positioned based on the benefits they deliver. Consumer durables such as refrigerators, dishwashers, and microwave ovens are also frequently positioned based on benefits. The symbolism or imagery that feeds consumers' self-concepts is less important for stimulating sales for these products.

Lifestyle-Based Positioning

When using lifestyle positioning tactics, Firms attempt to develop associations between the brand and some desirable lifestyle. In turn, those Firms seek to establish or exploit relationships that already exist between the desirable lifestyle and targeted consumer's ideal or actual self-concept. Humans continually strive toward idealized versions of themselves by engaging in behaviors that are consistent with their ideal self. Consumers diet to lose weight and gain love. They drive or wear the right brand so they will "fit-in."

When marketers position brands employing life style themes, they are developing brand images that reflect important dimensions of the consumers' life style or self-concept. Drawing on principles of classical conditioning, the brand is advertised in attractive lifestyle settings. Multiple ads employing similar themes are repetitively aired in mass media to generate "top-of-mind awareness" for the brand, and potentially, produce a conditioning effect. These strategies, if successful, psychologically endow brands with elements of attractive lifestyles. Over time the brand and the lifestyle image become synonymous to consumers.

Usage-Based Positioning

Brands can be positioned based on their **usage occasions**. Usage-based positioning requires that an image be created for the brand that strongly suggests when the brand should be used. Gatorade is normally promoted as a sports drink for replenishing lost electrolytes after a hard workout. However, Gatorade has aired ads that position the brand for use on other occasions. Some Gatorade ads promote its use during cold and flu seasons as an aid in replenishing lost fluids due to illness.

For similar reasons, coffee has been promoted and re-positioned as a "think drink." Ads produced by the coffee growers association in attempts to increase **primary demand**[18] for coffee ran a series of ads emphasizing that when you have something to talk over with someone, do it over a cup of coffee. Starbucks wins on this one.

Many people consume colas in the morning as a substitute for coffee. Recognizing this, Coke developed advertising as early as 1934 to further promote morning consumption. These ads were designed to position Coke as a coffee substitute and alternative morning "wake-up" call. After extensive testing, Coke offered its local bottlers a canned advertising program titled "Coke in the Morning."[19] More recently, Coke promoted Diet Coke as a way to "Kick Start Your Morning."

Part of an SSC&B advertising campaign in the early 80s was an ad for Heineken Beer that encouraged consumers to pick their own usage occasion. The copy in this ad was intended to be highly ambiguous, in that the viewer could read any usage occasion into the ad that he or she wished. The caption was, "Come to think of it, I'll have a Heineken." The picture was of a cold bottle of Heineken with water dripping down its length. The ad essentially said: "quench your thirst!" The specific usage occasion, however, was up to the consumer.

Price and Value-Based Positioning

Price positioning and value positioning are closely related. These two positioning strategies are distinctly different although, on the surface, both may appear to focus on providing customers with lower prices. **Price positioning** usually means establishing a low price image for the brand. Low price is the brand's key differentiating factor. Most advertising that promotes "lower prices" also implies that the advertised brand is of acceptable quality. The implication, therefore, is that customers can expect greater value.

In contrast, true **value positioning** can actually result in prices that are higher than the prices charged by competitors. A higher price is justified if benefits delivered to customers are substantially greater than those provided by competitors' brands. The key to positioning on value is to maximize the ratio of benefits received to the total cost of the brand (which includes its price). The brand's price is just one of the relevant "costs." From a practical perspective, this simply means that consumers tend to perceive more value in a brand when the benefits received from that brand, relative to the price paid, are greater than for competing brands. The emphasis on value generally means that the brand's quality continues to be an important component of the consumer's cognitive algebra.

→ Perceptual Mapping: A Tool for Assessing and Managing Positions

The strategic need to establish strong brand positions in order to compete more effectively has been well established. So how do Firms determine and measure their brand's positions? The process known as **perceptual mapping** offers a useful tool for ascertaining a brand's position relative to its competitors.

Let's create a **perceptual map** that displays 13 competing beer brands and, more germane in this setting, their relative market positions. Such maps can be created by collecting survey data from consumer samples. The survey would ask consumers to rate these brands on a series of, say, 13 attributes. The resulting data then can be analyzed with a statistical program that creates perceptual maps.

Exhibit 9.7 displays the perceptual map that emerged. The dots on the map represent the relative positions of each brand in this sample of consumers' "perceptual space." Dots located close to one another represent brands that consumers perceive as similar in some important ways. When dots are situated farther apart consumers perceived the respective brands as dissimilar in important ways.

The Heineken and Becks beer brands are located in the upper-left-quadrant of the map. Due to their close proximity, we can infer that these two brands are perceived as similar. At the same time, however, the map reveals that Heineken and Becks are perceived as materially different from the Miller Lite and Coors Light brands, which are each located in the lower-right-quadrant.

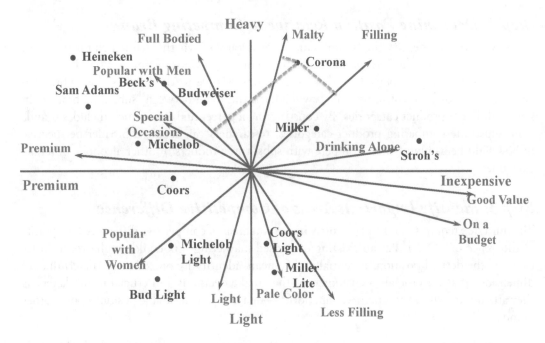

Exhibit 9.7 *Hypothetical Perceptual Map for Beer.*

The arrows displayed on the map represent the attributes used by consumers to rate each brand. Longer arrows indicate that its associated attribute is more important in the attempt to determine the proper location on the map for the brand. The location of each brand relative to each attribute arrow represents how closely that brand fits the attribute.

Take a look at the Corona brand, located in the upper-right quadrant. By drawing perpendicular lines between Corona's location and each attribute arrow, one can ascertain how Corona is perceived along each attribute. Perpendicular dotted lines have been drawn from Corona to the filling, malty, and popular with men attributes. Corona's positions along the lengths of each attribute vector indicate the degree to which Corona fits each attribute. Corona is clearly perceived as malty and filling by this customer sample. But the Corona brand is not as popular with men as are Beck's, Budweiser, Heineken, and Sam Adams.[20]

Developing Positioning Strategies: The Process

You should already understand what "position" is and why the concept is so important. The ability to develop, manage and strengthen the brand positioning process is critical to any Firm's success, survival, and longevity. The task of designing a successful brand positioning strategy, however, is always challenging. There are five basic steps.[21]

Step 1: Determine Brands in the Competitive Set

The first step is to identify and to define the entire set of relevant competitive brands. This collection will usually consist of the brands (branded competitors) operating in the defined market segment. When a Firm develops a positioning strategy for a light beer, the relevant competitive set would likely be other brands of light beer. But the set may include other regular beers, or expand more broadly to other alcoholic beverage categories, perhaps hard lemonades, wines, and ciders. The decision of how broadly to define the competitive set should hinge on the degree to which alternative alcoholic beverages are seen as substitutes for one another on different consumption occasions. Consumers may switch between beers, wines, ciders, or other beverages depending on the occasion.

Step 2: Determine Position Relative to Competing Brands

The next step is to identify the brand's current position vis-à-vis the defined competitive set. The task requires that the perceptual map outlined in the previous section be used. Perceptual mapping is normally employed to identify positions relative to the brand's closest branded competitors. However, consumers may switch back and forth between "substitute brands" in several different product categories. By constructing a perceptual map which includes brands from substitute competing product categories, researchers can secure a broader perspective of how light beers brands may compete with substitute products in other alcoholic beverage categories.

Step 3: Identify Important Areas of Competitive Difference

The third step requires that Firms identify important areas of competitive difference (i.e., points of difference or PODs) that an existing or revised marketing mix could emphasize in order to create the desired position. Essentially, this means identifying one or more "determinant" dimensions that are crucial to customers as they make decisions and crucial to marketers as they attempt to achieve competitive superiority—or a uniquely desirable position—over other brands.

The term "determinant" is actually a key marketing concept. For a given marketing mix, brand, product, or organizational dimension to be called determinant, the dimension must be perceived by customers as different from similar dimensions offered by competing marketing mixes, brands, products, or organizations. Moreover, the dimension on which this "difference" exists must be important to customers as they decide which product, from among an array of competitive options, to select.

The set of attributes employed in the perceptual mapping exercise from the last step represents a logical starting point for this task. Other sources of key determinant differences include:

- *Image differences* which imply the existence of distinct or unique brand personalities that may result from the use of brand marks, logos, or trade characters. Image differences also may result from the use of celebrity endorsers, brand extensions, co-branding, and brand licensing activities.

- *Benefit or attribute differences* of the sort that would confer functional superiority to the particular brands that featured them. Such brands would generally be perceived by customers as superior to competitive offerings in terms of their characteristics or functionality. This dimension would include any novel features or characteristics that are difficult for competitors to duplicate. And even if competitors did copy the feature or characteristic, the initiating brand should still occupy the "first-to-market" position in the minds of the market.

- *Services differences* of the sort that create a total service package, one that is uniquely superior to services provided by competitors. Strategically, this positioning process might entail developing a high quality training program, providing rapid and reliable delivery services, or providing timely and expert installation services. Each of these values could promote justified perceptions of competitive difference. Those differences, in term, could influence the perceived position of brands.

- *People differences* can be emphasized when a Firm's human resources constitute a distinct asset that can be leveraged to create a superior position. Credible, competent, and friendly sales personnel may prove crucial as a differentiator. Knowledgeable and empathetic customer service reps and clerks are obviously distinct assets. Such assets can be emphasized in the Firm's positioning strategy to enhance the Firm's perceived competitive position. When focusing on "people differences," Firms should focus primarily on "relationship marketing." Examples of Firms that position on their "people" are Walmart and New York Life.

Step 4: Develop the Marketing Mix to Convey the Desired Position

The Firm can create its desired market position by developing the appropriate combination of product, price, promotion, and distribution. There are no other options, no other paths exist, to this desirable end, as has been emphasized time and again in this book. The marketing mix is the primary tool at the marketing manager's disposal to establish and fine-tune the brand's personality and, in general, manage demand for the brand.

Step 5: Re-evaluate the Position over Time

Identifying the brand's desired position and creating the appropriate marketing mix to solidify that position is just the beginning. Brand position must be re-evaluated continually as relevant changes occur in critical marketing environments. Positions are monitored by employing the same perceptual mapping tools we've already discussed. Firms should regularly engage in perceptual mapping studies to identify changes that may be needed in their brands' perceived positions. General Motors, for example, holds an annual "image conference" in which the positions of is various brands are evaluated for possible changes. Perceptual mapping has traditionally been a key component of this review.

Regular re-evaluation allows a Firm to reposition brands as necessary. The ability to reposition may be critical for a brand's survival. Repositioning is the last topic explored in this chapter.

→ Repositioning

Repositioning occurs when a Firm strategically changes the brand's current image or personality. Changes to a brand's personality are required primarily when market conditions change, shifting the dynamics between competitors. The changes are necessary under three circumstances.

Current Brand Is Insufficiently Differentiated from Competitors

A brand may need to be re-positioned if its current image is too close to one or more major competitors. **Perceptual mapping** may suggest that the brand is simply too much like other brands targeted to the same market(s). These competitors may be brands produced by other Firms in the same product category, or brands existing in substitute product categories.

Closely competing brands may also consist of other brands in the Firm's own product line. For example, Procter & Gamble individually brands most of its products. P&G's detergent line is comprised of a number of individual brands including Tide, Cheer, Dash, Ivory Snow, Gain, Era, and Bold. Quite possibly, two or more of these brands are positioned too closely to one another. One brand's sales may be cannibalizing sales from another brand in the same product line.

Marketing "cannibalization" means stealing sales from other brands marketed by the same company. This can be a serious problem if the overall profitability of all brands taken together decreases as a result of the cannibalization. Subway and Starbucks have each earned reputations as Firms and brands that have sometimes cannibalized sales from existing store units by locating newer units too close to the original store.

Key Market Characteristics Change

Brands may require repositioning when key consumption-related market characteristics, such as demographic and psychographic compositions, change and the changes degrade demand. Examples include Pepsi's attempt to reposition to a wider demographic market when it forecast a decline in the number of teens and young adults that comprised its traditional target market. Mercedes extensively modified its positioning strategy for similar reasons. As market demographics shifted the then current personality of the Mercedes brand no longer successfully differentiated the brand.

Sales Are Insufficient to Justify Current Position

Repositioning may prove necessary when brands experience serious decline in sales and/or profits in their current markets. This essentially means that demand for the brand in this market is inadequate. Firms faced with this challenge often attempt to reposition the brand to new target markets in which sales and profit potential appear more promising. Two classic examples of repositioning as a result of declining market demand include Marlboro cigarettes and Miller High Life beer.

Marlboro actually began repositioning efforts in 1955 when it decided to change its "ivory tipped" woman's cigarette image. Initially, the Marlboro cast of men included a wide range of macho figures: sailors, farmers, and hunters were all depicted in the initial ads. When the Marlboro Man went national in 1955, sales reached $5 billion. This represented a 3,241% (yes, this number is correct) increase over 1954 when the brand's US market share was less than 1%. By the early 1970s, Marlboro was the number one cigarette brand in the world. Not until 1964 was the American cowboy employed as the primary positioning icon. At the same time the still familiar "Marlboro Country" theme was adopted. Thereafter, Marlboro sales continued to increase at a rate of about 10% per year. Notably, one of the original Marlboro men, Wayne McLaren, died of lung cancer at age 51, after going public against smoking.[22]

Miller High Life beer also illustrates the act of repositioning from an original segment to a more promising target market. Miller was originally targeted to women and promoted as the "champagne of bottled beer." Essentially, Miller was positioned as a substitute for table wine. This market did not meet the sales and profit expectations consistent with the company's objectives for the brand. As a result, in the mid-1970's Miller was repositioned to a higher beer-consumption market: the male, blue-collar market. The product itself was not modified. Modifications were required only in how the brand was promoted. Changes in advertising and supporting promotional materials were designed to shift Miller's brand personality to be more attractive to the male, blue-collar beer-drinker. Advertising themes subsequent to the repositioning decision have included "If you've got the time, we've got the beer," "Buy that man a Miller beer," "Miller Beer-Made in America," and "You work hard - stop and taste the high life." Each repositioning statement emphasized predominantly blue-collar themes.[23]

Endnotes

1. Russell Haley, "Benefit Segmentation: A Decision-oriented Research Tool," *Journal of Marketing*, 32 (July 1968): 30–35.

2. Richard S. Medlow, *New and Improved: The Story of Mass Marketing in America* (New York: Basic Books, 1990).

3. Kurt Badenhausen, "The World's Most Valuable Brands: Behind the Numbers", *Forbes* November 6, 2013, accessed January, 2015, http://www.forbes.com.

4. C.L. Tyagi and Arun Kumar, *Consumer Behaviour*, (Rajouri Garden, New Delhi: Atlantic Publishers and Distributors, 2004), 13.

5. Adopted from Charles Lamb, Joseph Hair, and Carl McDaniel, *Marketing 4*[th.] *Ed.* (Cincinnati, OH: South-Western College Publishing, 1998), 215.

6. Ellen Byron, "From Diapers to 'Depends': Marketers Discreetly Retool for Aging Boomers," *Wall Street Journal* (February 5, 2011), accessed January, 2015, http://www.wsj.com,.

7. Example adapted from a study discussed in Henry Assael, *Consumer Behavior and Marketing Action 2*[nd] *ed.* (Boston: Kent Publishing, 1984), 265.

8. Mark Huffman, "U.S. Beer Drinkers Shifting to 'Craft' Brands," *Consumer Affairs*, August 6, 2014, accessed January, 2015, http://www.consumeraffairs.com.

9. Corporate Design Foundation, "Harley-Davidson: Marketing an American Icon," *@issue Journal*, 2(1), accessed February 2015, http://cdf.org;
Sharon Schembri, "Reframing Brand Experience: The Experiential Meaning of Harley-Davidson", *Journal of Business Research*, 62 (2009): 1299–1310.

10. Robert M. McMath, "The Perils of Typecasting," *American Demographics*, (February 1997): 60.

11. George Brown, "Brand Loyalty—Fact or Fiction?," *Advertising Age* (June 19, 1952): 53–55.

12. Ross M. Cunningham, "Brand Loyalty—What, Where, How Much?", *Harvard Business Review*, 34 (January-February, 1956): 116–128.

13. George S. Day, "A Two-Dimensional Concept of Brand Loyalty," *Journal of Advertising Research*, 9 (September, 1969): 29–35.

14. "Caterpillar, Inc. 2013 Year in Review," accessed February 5, 2015, www.caterpillar.com.

15. Example is adopted from Roger Kerin and Robert Peterson, *Strategic Marketing Problems: Cases and Concepts 13*[th] *ed.*, (Boston, MA: Pearson Education, 2013), 105–112.

16. Robert F. Hartley, *Marketing Mistakes, 7*[th] *ed.*, (New York, John Wiley and Sons, 1998), 177–186.

17. James H. Gilmore and B. Joseph Pine II, "The Four Faces of Mass Customization," *Harvard Business Review*, January 1987, accessed February 2015, https://hbr.org.

18. "Primary demand" is demand for the total product category. In contrast, "selective demand" is the demand for single brands within that category.

[19] "A Morning Cola Instead of Coffee?" *New York Times*, January 20, 1988, accessed February 8, 2015, http://www.nytimes.com.

[20] Adopted from Richard Johnson, "Market Segmentation—A Strategic Management Tool," *Journal of Marketing Research* 8 (February 1971): 13–18.

[21] Example is adopted from David Aaker and Gary Shansby, "Positioning Your Product," *Business Horizons* 25 (3) (May-June 1982): 56-62.

[22] *Advertising Age*, "The Marlboro Man," March 29, 1999, accessed February, 2015, http://adage.com.

[23] Randall Rothenberg, "THE MEDIA BUSINESS: Advertising; Thompson Loses Miller High Life," *The New York Times*, November 17, 1988, accessed February, 2015, http://www.nytimes.com.

→ What Are Products?

Products are anything that can be offered to markets for the attention, acquisition, usage, or consumption of customers within those markets. This anything, of course, must be able to satisfy customer wants or needs. Physical goods, intangible services, actual places, real people, or ideas each can be products. Products are also anything that can potentially provide the basis for exchanges of values between buyers and sellers. Values are created only through a product's perceived or actual usefulness to customers.

Regardless of their core form or nature, products feature simple or complex bundles of tangible or intangible attributes. These attributes promise and deliver benefits, or values, that solve customer problems. When successfully marketed, products also profit marketers or marketing Firms, at least in the long-run.

Drill bits belong to a broad product category that delivers actual benefits and values related to the provision of holes. The hole might be small, but it is large enough to solve the problem for which a small hole was the solution; i.e., hanging up a portrait in your den. Or the hole might be large, say 29 inches wide and 2130 feet deep—the dimensions of the hole drilled to rescue 33 miners trapped in the San Jose mine in Chile during 2011. Same product (just a drill bit), same solution (simply a hole), wholly different sort of problem.

All products, regardless of their form, possess two levels or layers of characteristics. The first level is called the physical product. The second level is known as the enhanced product (Exhibit 10.1).[1]

The Physical Product

The physical product consists of the core benefits or values delivered by the product and its physical characteristics that allow the product to deliver these values. The importance of the physical product is self-evident; after all, it is what customers actually purchase. Customers buy products for the problem-solving benefits and values they deliver. Even within the same product category, the benefits and values can prove diverse. Cosmetics emerge from a product category that delivers benefits and values such as enhanced beauty, confidence, camouflage, sexiness, youthfulness or maturity (dependent on the consumers' age cohort), perhaps, an updated "look," or in the classic marketing description, "hope" for those using cosmetics' products.

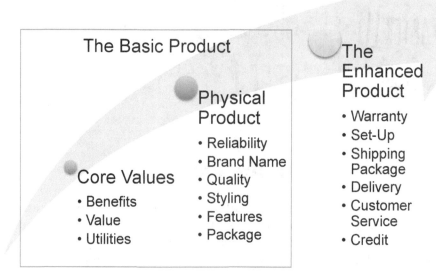

The Basic Product

The Enhanced Product
• Warranty
• Set-Up
• Shipping Package
• Delivery
• Customer Service
• Credit

Physical Product
• Reliability
• Brand Name
• Quality
• Styling
• Features
• Package

Core Values
• Benefits
• Value
• Utilities

Exhibit 10.1 *The Levels of a "Product."*

When they can afford or obtain it, customers chose the exact product that they sense is physically best-designed to satisfy their wants or needs. Well-designed physical products feature perfect unions of performance and purpose in ways that suggest meaning to customers. Apple knows this. Consequently, Apple always sweats design with an intensity few Firms have ever matched. Has this design intensity proven a key ingredient to Apple's success? Absolutely. Physical products usually should be designed in ways that simplify them to their fundamental natures as Apple has always done.

Customer needs can be complex. They exist at multiple levels. Consider an automobile purchase. At a fundamental level, customers purchase cars to satisfy basic transportation needs. However, higher level needs exist that automobiles may also satisfy. Consumers buy cars to address psychological and social communications needs, in addition to more fundamental transportation needs. Marketers should fully understand their customers' total need-sets and how their products might deliver benefits and values that fulfill those needs. The product's packaging, the style or look and feel of the product, its brand name and design, and functional characteristics such as its inherent quality, reliability, and durability are also part of the physical product.

Related Thoughts about Quality, Style, and Design

Quality can be defined as freedom from flaws. Quality's presence in products is also always directly proportional to those products' efficiency. "Proportional," in this context, means that the levels of quality and efficiency rise and fall together.

Quality once was, and some degree remains, a major positioning (differentiating) tool. General physical product quality, however, has never been higher than it currently is in the United States. (Of course, the overall quality situation remains less than ideal, particularly with respect to service provision.) But in many markets, the ability to develop physical products that feature high quality is no longer a sufficient differentiator. Not when all other competitors are doing the same thing. Instead, quality is more akin to an ante that must be laid on the table in order to sit and play or compete at a highly competitive (poker) game. High physical product quality is no longer just a nice-to-have. It has become a "must."

Style speaks more fundamentally to the physical product's appearance. Styles are also embedded in and derived from the website, packaging, or colors that accompany or complement physical products. The physical product's fit, feel (when you feel or handle it physically) and finish likewise speak and contribute to its style.

Design goes to the heart and functionality of products. Great design should strengthen the product's brand, contribute to its perceived or actual usefulness, and make the product more appealing. Style and design each can be managed by marketers to differentiate products and create desirable positions. Design can also be managed in ways that drive innovation. **Innovations**, as described in Chapter 11, are "new things" that are also "useful." The best designs move beyond simply solving existing or new problems through the development and delivery of new stuff. The best designs also make customers happy.

The Enhanced Product

The second level of product is the enhanced (or augmented) product. The enhanced product includes "extras" that build on, or supplement, the physical product. These extras are primarily services that include:

- Delivery
- Product set-up
- Warranties and guarantees
- Granting credit
- Providing post-sale servicing, such as repairs
- Customer service both before and after the sale
- Overall customer relations

The enhanced product delivers additional values to consumers. The enhanced product can be managed as a means to differentiate one brand from another. This often proves necessary because consumers are often unable to discern meaningful differences between physical products, even for major consumer durables such as microwaves, TVs, or refrigerators. In such situations marketers can make their brand stand apart favorably from the pack by designing an enhanced product that offers added value.

The Total Product

The two product levels function synergistically, in other words, as a whole, to create the "total product." The total product includes the product's benefits (fundamental and higher level benefits), the product's physical characteristics that embody or deliver these benefits, and service dimensions added to the product that deliver supplementary value. The customer's overall image of the product—its brand image—is, in part, a function of the total synergistic effect produced by these combined levels of the product. Marketers should keep the total product in mind as they create and manage the product's position in order to achieve greater profits. The best marketers surely do exactly this.

Movie theaters are products. The films theatres show and customers pay to experience are products, as well. But movie theaters, the product, are not really in the movie-showing business. They are more in the selling-candy-popcorn-soda business. That's where their real profits lie. Theaters, you see, must share 50% of your ticket price with the Firms that made and/or distribute the film. Yet theaters need films, just like Hollywood, Bollywood, or Europe's typically *film noir* needs theaters. So which is the physical product, the enhanced product, and the total product when the product in question is AMC Movie Theaters? The answer, we admit, is not clear.

→ Classifying Consumer Products

The traditional product classification scheme is based on the amount of effort consumers put into the purchase process (Exhibit 10.2). Three traditional categories of consumer goods exist: convenience goods, shopping goods, and specialty goods. **Convenience goods** are usually purchased with very little effort. **Specialty goods**, classified at the other extreme, require the most effort during the purchase process. **Shopping goods** generally reside in the middle of this amount-of-effort-expended continuum.[2]

Convenience Goods

Convenience goods, as noted, are purchased with little effort. Convenience goods include most products that we buy in grocery stores, convenience stores, hardware stores, drug stores, and the like. Ballpoint pens, candy bars, paper plates, soft drinks, or table salt are each convenience goods.

Characteristics of Convenience Goods

Convenience goods are usually:

- Relatively inexpensive; their purchase entails little financial risk.
- Purchased on regular or recurring bases for day-to-day lifestyle maintenance.

They are also often purchased impulsively or for variety-seeking purposes. Convenience goods are less expensive and less important than either of the other two product categories. These product traits create situations where simple in-store stimuli such as end-of-aisle displays, shelf coupons, or free samples are often enough to stimulate unplanned purchases.

Amount of effort expended in the purchase process

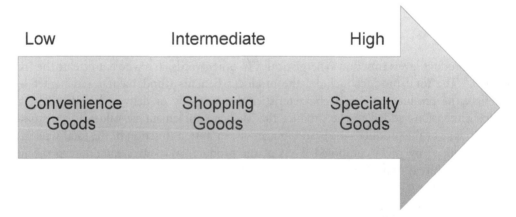

Exhibit 10.2 *The classification of consumer goods is based on how much effort consumers are willing to expend to acquire them.*

The classification label itself (i.e., convenience) suggests customers expend minimal effort when acquiring convenience goods. Convenience good purchases are usually labeled as routine purchasing decisions. Reconsider the Consumer Behavior chapter (Chapter 7) and its continuum of consumer decisions. Consumers often buy products to maximize time and place utility. They seek to purchase such products at the most convenient locations, generally without much thought. Consumers engage in no to little information search and rarely actively compare brands. Consumers will readily purchase substitute brands if their preferred brand is unavailable when purchasing convenience goods. The same description applies when one brand is perceived to have raised its price too high, even where consumers had a brand preference.

Convenience products can be classified more precisely into one of four additional categories. This second-order classification is based on the circumstances in which the convenience item was purchased. Staple goods are regularly purchased and consumed for basic lifestyle maintenance. Consumers typically restock staple goods when visiting supermarkets. Staple goods routinely end up on shopping lists. Consumers generally have multiple acceptable brands for a given staple good. When shopping for staple goods, consumers often switch between their accepted or preferred brands as a result of retail incentives such as coupons, specials, and attractive displays. Traditional staple goods include breakfast cereals, cooking supplies, milk, toothpaste and personal care products, and household supplies.

Emergency goods are purchased as the term implies—on an emergency basis. Consumers might run out and find they must restock the product quickly. Alternatively, a unique need might arise that requires immediate satisfaction. Ever buy an emergency umbrella on a rainy day at Six Flags? Or, make an emergency run to the drug store to buy medicine for a sick child on the weekend? Both are emergency products. Consumers are generally more concerned with time and place utility when making emergency purchases. These purchase conditions make consumers less price sensitive and willing to pay more to obtain the product when and where it is needed.

Variety-seeking goods and **impulse goods** are purchased without much prior planning. Consumers may switch between different brands of some convenience goods out of boredom, just to change things up. These brand-switching behaviors are known as variety-seeking. Consumers seeking variety may have preplanned the product purchase. Consumers "knew" they were going to purchase a specific product type and brand but changed their minds in-store, deciding to try something different. They sought variety. Consumer minds were probably changed through exposure to a marketing stimuli.

Impulse goods, by contrast, are unplanned. Decisions to buy the product type and brand are made on the spur of the moment as consumers are ostensibly shopping for other products. In-store promotional stimuli, such as displays, shelf coupons, and point-of-purchase promotions heavily influence consumers' purchases of variety-seeking and impulse goods.

Marketing Strategies for Convenience Goods

The marketing strategies employed for convenience goods are driven by their low-involvement nature. As noted, consumers more readily brand-switch when evaluating convenience goods. Marketers consequently should advertise their brands extensively throughout the appropriate mass media. Advertising costs are normally initiated and paid for by the Firms that manufacture convenience goods. National or regional advertising campaigns are employed to create demand for the brand at the consumer level. If successful, consumer demand will "pull" the product through the supply chain, from the point of manufacturing origin to the end-point of consumers' shopping carts. This advertising strategy, not surprisingly, is called a "pull" strategy.

Convenience goods should be distributed—made available—at an extensive level. Convenience goods marketers should sell through all qualified retail outlets that are willing to carry and promote their brands. The rationale is simple: because consumers will brand-switch in an instant, manufacturing brands must be well represented and ideally well placed on retail shelves. Consumers will rarely postpone purchases to search for their preferred brands.

Brands should be displayed in retail settings where customers can easily spot them. Convenience goods are often purchased based on a desire for variety or on an impulse basis. When consumers cannot easily see brands or find them difficult to reach (on shelves), the likelihood that those brands will be purchased impulsively or for variety diminishes. Indeed, convenience goods marketers often compete vigorously for preferred shelf space inside stores.

Shopping Goods

Sometimes, consumers make comparisons between brands and retail providers. Consumers are comparing alternative brands—called shopping goods—against one another or comparing the same shopping goods brand across multiple retail settings. When doing this, consumers engage in "shopping behavior." Shopping goods generally include clothing, jewelry, automobiles, computers, homes, major appliances, small appliances, recreational equipment, and gifts. Most consumer "durables"—lasting products that are expected to be used for a long time—are shopping goods.

Shopping malls, especially their department and specialty stores, are well-suited to market shopping goods. Mall environments make it easy and, equally important, enjoyable for consumers to engage in "shopping behavior." Consumers can readily make brand and price comparisons in malls. The Internet offers consumers similar opportunities to conduct comparison shopping easily and quickly.

Consumers usually actively seek information about alternative brands before making shopping good decisions. They then generally spend more time processing the information as they judiciously compare alternatives. Decision-making processes for shopping goods generally entail higher involvement. More effort is expended during shopping-good decision-making processes than for convenience or specialty goods. Decisions are rarely made impulsively.

The levels of monetary, functional, or social risk are much higher for shopping goods than for convenience goods. Consumers will more likely demonstrate, or express some feelings of brand loyalty for shopping products. Prices typically are higher for shopping goods. Shopping goods are often purchased either consciously or subconsciously to satisfy higher order social-, self-expression-, and self-concept-related consumer needs. Fashion items usually fit in the shopping goods category, that is, when truly expensive, high-end fashion items are not classified into another category; i.e., specialty goods.

Marketing Strategies for Shopping Goods

The marketing mix employed for shopping goods differs substantially from the one employed for convenience goods. The distribution for shopping goods is less intense than that required for convenience goods. Products are typically distributed through fewer numbers of more select, perhaps even elite, retailers. This distribution strategy is labeled "selective distribution."

Firms must successfully differentiate the product category (if they have launched new products) or brands (for existing products) when marketing shopping goods. Characteristics such as a product's basic functionality, reliability, and durability—along with quality—become substantially more important to consumers. When brands are successfully differentiated along any of these characteristics, price becomes less important to consumers. Consumers will often pay more for products that they perceive offer greater relative advantage or deliver an elite image. The extra value generated through these differentiating advantages justifies or offsets the higher prices in consumers' minds.

Specialty Goods

The final product category is the specialty good. Consumers typically possess very strong brand preferences for specialty goods. When such brand preferences exist, the consumer will accept no substitute. If you want a Ferrari, nothing else will do.

Specialty goods are usually more expensive. Typical examples include prestigious watches such as Rolex and Cartier; designer jewelry and clothes such as Armani and Dior; high-end sports cars, such as Bugatti and Lamborghini; and expensive perfumes such as Clive Christian (over $215,000 per bottle), Ralph Lauren's Notorious ($3,500 per bottle), Henri Alméras's Joy Perfume for Jean Patou ($800 per ounce), and Hermes Perfume 24 Faubourg ($1,500 per ounce). Indeed, Joy perfume has been consciously promoted as the "costliest perfume in the world," although clearly this is not true. Until recently Joy was sold only through a highly select number of retail partners, such as Lord and Taylor. This sort of selective distribution is the norm rather than exception with specialty goods.

Specialty goods are generally distributed through a limited numbers of selective supply chain partners. This restricted form of distribution is called "exclusive distribution." Manufacturers of specialty goods often develop close ties with specific retail partners; i.e., Joy and Lord and Taylor. In return for guaranteeing exclusive distribution rights to its product, Jean Patou demands that Lord and Taylor pay special attention to marketing its brand.

Specialty goods, however, are not always expensive consumer durable or luxury goods. Items that most consumers would view as convenience goods can acquire specialty status, depending on the consumer. Perrier mineral water, bottled in France, is promoted as a specialty product. Some consumers have developed strong brand preferences for Perrier. Thus they accord the brand specialty status, and often pay exorbitant prices as a result. Fuji, AquaDeco, Voss, Tasmanian Rain, and Finé are recent entries into the designer bottled water world, and have surpassed the specialty status of Perrier.

The takeaway: any product can earn a specialty status in the eyes of certain consumer segments. Products possessing some sort of designer status are the most likely candidates. To summarize, specialty goods exhibit the following characteristics:

- Specialty goods are associated with strong brand preferences and thus brand loyalty. Consumers become convinced that particular brands are superior to other alternatives and consequently will accept no substitutes. Consumers will spend considerable amounts of money, time, and effort to acquire preferred specialty brands.

- Specialty goods are generally purchased less frequently because they are usually more expensive. This is not always true, however. Recall Perrier bottled water. Perrier is certainly purchased much more frequently and is considerably less expensive than typical specialty goods, even other brands of designer bottled waters.

- The consumer's loyalty to retailers may prove as important as their loyalty to particular specialty good brands. Consumers may possess strong preferences for specific retailers due to their status, quality service reputations, in-store atmospherics, and other factors. When such retailer loyalties exist, consumers may also limit brand selections (preferences) to brands sold by those retailers. Specialty good marketers should develop close relationships with such retailers.

Marketing Strategies for Specialty Goods

Marketing programs for specialty goods should attempt to develop and emphasize strong brand preferences. The sorts of brand preferences that consumers associate with products that can suggest differentiating quality; invoke desirable levels of status; or convey desirable images to others about the specialty good "owner." This is why specialty goods are normally priced higher. Higher prices support their prestige image and exclusive-granting status. Look at me. I can afford to rock this bag and you can't!

The advertising themes for specialty goods, likewise generally focus on status and prestige. Attempts at comparative or competitive advertising will have little effect on changing consumers' attitudes toward their preferred brand. Pre-existing attitudes toward preferred brands are simply are too strong.

As noted, specialty goods are distributed on selective or even "exclusive" bases. A limited number of retail outlets, often only one or two, in a geographic area may be employed. Close, cooperative working relationships are developed with retailers in ways that are intended to mutually benefit producers and retailers. Yet because consumers normally know which brands they intend to purchase prior to entering stores, personal selling efforts rarely sway customers' attitudes or behaviors.

An Emerging Category: Positional Products

Certain physical goods or services (more about services below) are also increasingly being classified as positional products. Positional products are things or experiences that are valuable largely because other people cannot have or enjoy them. Expensive paintings on walls, sculptures in gardens, very expensive fine wines, extremely expensive stays in luxury accommodations and/or locations, exorbitantly priced bags on shoulders, or dresses on bodies fit into the positional goods category. Consumption, as readers have undoubtedly experienced, can prove competitive.

Customers, typically consumers, can elevate their social status, or social class positions, by displaying or using their goods in ways that "lesser" others can directly or indirectly observe. This all may be biologically predetermined. Which male peacock gets selected as a mating partner by female peacocks? One with the "good-enough-tail" or the one with the "best-tail"?

With most products, higher prices reduce demand. But positional goods, services, or experiences invert this economic law. When positional products are acquired, buyers are actually purchasing valued evidence that they have forked out a bundle and that you probably could not afford the same thing. When their prices are raised, the demand for positional purchases is rarely disturbed. Positional goods have inevitably achieved impressive amounts of brand equity (discussed fully in Chapter 12).

→ Classifying Organizational Products

The classification scheme for organizational goods is less intuitive than the classification for consumer goods. The organizational product classification scheme features seven major categories:

- Raw Materials
- Component Parts
- Fabricating or Component Materials
- Installations
- Accessory Equipment
- Operating Supplies
- Services

This classification scheme is based primarily on how the products are used, rather than customer purchasing behaviors. Because some organizational goods can be used in multiple ways, some products can be classified into more than one of the seven categories. Examples of these "dual category products" are highlighted below.

Raw Materials

Raw materials are "ingredients" used in the production of other products. Raw materials, by definition, must undergo extensive additional processing during their conversation into other products. The only initial processing received by raw materials is to preserve them during storage while awaiting shipping to production facilities. Additional processing may be required to make the product easier and/or less expensive to ship.

Raw materials include:

- *Mined Products:* Metal ores and ingots, coal, coke (coke is a fuel made from coal that possesses a high carbon content with few impurities), and other minerals extracted from the earth. Iron and other ores, for example, are generally shipped in largely unaltered states to smelters or other processing plants. Iron ingots produced in smelters result from separating iron from rock that contains iron. Iron bars are easier to ship than the ore itself.

- *Forestry Products:* Trees harvested from forests are converted by having their limbs trimmed as they are cut to uniform length to ease their shipping to mills (Exhibit 10.3).

- *Agricultural Products:* At their point of harvest cotton, corn, wheat, etc. are typically separated from the parent plant and minimally treated with insecticides. This process preserves the grain during storage or shipment.

Exhibit 10.3 *Raw materials include forestry products such as trees that may only have their limbs removed to make shipping easier.*

- *Crude Oil and Natural Gas:* Crude is a raw material until it is refined. The refined product is classified into other product categories. Raw natural gas (the raw material) is normally filtered for impurities before use. During this complex process natural gas is "cleaned" of impurities and various non-methane hydrocarbons to produce pipeline quality dry natural gas.
- *Ocean Products:* Tuna, when harvested from the world's oceans, may be frozen for shipment to a cannery or food processing plant.

These examples are raw materials because all fundamentally remain in their natural states, in other words, these materials retain the same basic form as when they were taken from their natural sources.

Component Parts

Component parts represent a "step up" from raw materials. These manufactured items have undergone extensive processing to become "parts." In turn, these parts are merged with other parts as they are assembled into more complex final products.

Component parts do not change in shape or form as they are combined to make finished products. They experience no further processing. Component parts can always be identified as unique components of final products into which they are incorporated.

Consider your car or notebook computer. Both products are made-up or constructed from arrays of component parts. Those parts were acquired from various sources and eventually delivered to a single manufacturing or assembly facility through myriad supply chains. These component parts are combined during manufacturing or assembly processes to actually make your car or computer.

Let's drill down further. Now consider just the mass data storage device that resides inside your computer. This hard drive is a component part. Your hard drive is assigned a part number by the manufacturer that distinguishes it from other parts. This part number will be keyed to all the unique specifications that characterize and effectively differentiate this particular drive. In turn, this hard drive consists of dozens of its own component parts. These parts have been assembled or combined to create the hard drive. This last point is important: multiple levels of component parts usually exist inside products.

Next, consider motor oil or antifreeze as each relates to your vehicle. Both can be treated as component parts under some circumstances, depending on their use. For example, when motor oil is placed in automobile engines when they are manufactured, it is a component part with an associated part number. In contrast, when motor oil is used as a lubricant for production machinery, it is an operating supply. The distinction, again, is based on how the product is used.

On the surface, some component parts don't appear to qualify as "parts." Dupont's Quallofil is an insulating material used in multiple applications. One natural application involves sleeping bags (think camping); after all, the material insulates. Thus you might view Quallofil as a fabricating material rather than a component part. Recall, however, the primary distinguishing characteristic of component parts. That is, component parts always retain their unique identity as they are integrated into other, larger products. Quallofil does not change form as it is stuffed into sleeping bags. Cut the bag open and the material is easily identifiable.

Fabricating Materials

Like component parts, fabricating materials are manufactured items that have undergone substantial processing before they are incorporated into more complex products. However, unlike component parts, fabricating materials will undergo additional extensive processing as they are made into new products. As a result of this additional processing, they lose their original shape and or become unidentifiable as a unique component of the final product. This is why Quallofil is a component part and not a true fabricating material.

Flour, by contrast, is a manufactured material that has undergone extensive processing to become flour. Flour, of course, originates from a raw material, usually wheat. Flour, in turn, is combined with other ingredients to produce baked food products such as bread.

Steel results from the extensive processing of iron during which it is alloyed with carbon and impurities are removed. In turn, steel experiences extensive additional processing as it is converted or reshaped into other products such as truck frames. Aluminum ingots are conceptually similar to the iron ingots that were used to exemplify raw materials. However, extensive processing is required to create aluminum. One does not simply melt aluminum from ore. This makes aluminum a fabricating material rather than a raw material.

Finally, chemical additives illustrate fabricated materials. Additives such as NutraSweet, a chemical sweetener, are combined with other ingredients to make food products. In the process, they lose their distinct identity. One can no longer tell NutraSweet from other ingredients used to make candy bars or soft drinks.

Installations

Installations typically consist of capital items, such as buildings, dams, and major production line equipment (Exhibit 10.4). Installations, as products, are typically expensive, capitalized

© supergenijalac/Shutterstock.com

Exhibit 10.4 *Installations include major items of equipment such as the assembly line depicted below to move car bodies through the assembly process.*

on balance sheets, and depreciated over time. Installations typically contribute substantially to the Firm's scale of operations. Installations permit Firms to do more of what they exist to do. For example, when General Motors buys robotized welding machines that allows it to build more cars, the Firm's scale has been increased. Similarly, when trucking companies buy more trucks they can transport more goods for their customers. The scale of those trucking companies increases. Each additional airplane purchased by American Airlines increases its scale of operations because it can carry more passengers and freight. Airplanes are installations for American Airlines.

Accessory Equipment

Accessory equipment is a step down from installations. Accessory equipment includes most office equipment, such as printers, computers, copy machines, and office mailing equipment. Accessory equipment is relatively inexpensive compared to typical installations. This is why accessory equipment is normally expensed when purchased rather than being depreciated over time. Most importantly, accessory equipment usually does not contribute directly to the production effort. Rather, such equipment simply supports day-to-day business operations.

Accessory equipment can contribute to the Firm's scale of operations, but not to the same degree as the installation. For example, portable hand tools and small power tools certainly contribute to scale to some degree. A forklift truck (Exhibit 10.5) is an example of accessory equipment that lies somewhat in the gray area between true accessory equipment and the installation. Forklift trucks are relatively expensive and, as a result, generally capitalized and depreciated over time. However, forklifts rarely contribute directly to scale. Instead they are used to support warehouse and production operations by moving finished goods, parts and materials, and goods in process.

© Jojie/Shutterstock.com

Exhibit 10.5 *A forklift truck is considered to be accessory equipment.*

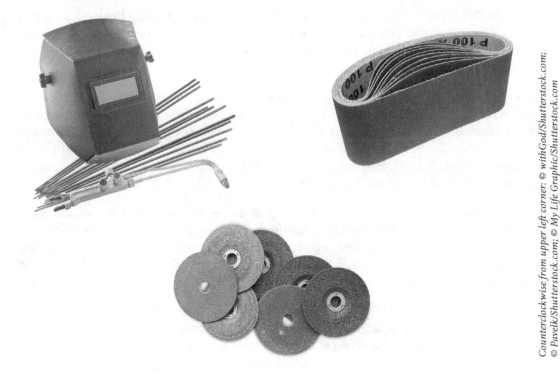

Exhibit 10.6 *Consumable supplies are usually considered to be operating supplies.*

Operating Supplies

Operating supplies are the "convenience goods of industrial markets" that are routinely used up in the daily operations of Firms. Operating supplies are short-lived items that facilitate routine operations. Consequently, they are repurchased frequently. Operating supplies include lubricating oils, light bulbs, many small office supply items, and janitorial supplies. These products are used up or consumed in daily operations and must be regularly restocked. Utilities are operating supplies. Heating fuels, water, and electricity are all consumed in the Firm's daily operations and are repurchased, essentially, automatically. Finally, various consumable production supplies, such items as sandpaper, welding rods, emery cloth, and solvents are considered operating supplies. (Exhibit 10.6)

Services

Services commonly purchased by business organizations include maintenance services, janitorial services, pest control services, accounting services, and consulting services. Companies often contract with service providers who specialize in these services areas rather than attempting to perform the service themselves.

→ The Product Mix and Product Lines

Most companies offer a range of products for sale. In fact, large consumer goods manufacturers typically sell wide varieties of product items across various product categories.

Consider the range of products sold by Procter & Gamble (P&G). P&G, as a large consumer goods manufacturing company, produces and markets a wide variety of products. Taken together, all individual product items produced and sold by P&G comprise its **product mix**.

In turn, P&G's product mix can be broken down into a series of **product lines**. For example, P&G boasts separate product lines for detergents, toothpastes, bar soaps, deodorants, disposable diapers, and coffees. The number of lines contained in the product mix is called the **product mix width**.

Each product line consists of multiple individual **product items**. Product items are the individual brands in each product line. **Product line depth** refers to the assortment of product items within any specific product line. Depth, naturally, can vary from one to any larger number. For example, P&G's detergent line consists of 14 individual brands; i.e., 14 individual product items. By contrast, P&G's product line of shaving implements (razors) features three brands: Gillette, Venus, and Braun.

Product line can be defined more specifically as groups of closely-related product items. "Closely-related" means that individual items in the line are similar to one another in function and/or characteristics. Product items may vary in terms of specific features, styles, and colors. But the product items all share sufficient commonalties in how they function to be classified in the same product line.

- LG features a line of DVD players in its product mix. These DVD players vary in terms of colors, styles, and specific features. However, they all function in virtually the same way and overlap in terms of physical characteristics.

- John Deere, a major manufacturer of industrial, agricultural, and lawn and garden equipment has a varied product mix. Deere's line of lawnmowers is extensive. The mowers all possess similar functional characteristics, but vary in terms of features, styles, and other characteristics.

Product lines within any Firm's product mix can be characterized as "consistent" or "inconsistent" with one another. Consistent lines are closely related to one another in terms of function, characteristics, or markets served. For example, P&G toothpastes, bar soaps, and deodorant lines are consistent with one another. Each is, after all, a personal care product. Lines that are inconsistent differ substantially from other lines in the Firm's mix along one or more key dimensions. The extent to which lines are consistent or inconsistent with other lines in their product mix is crucial when Firms are considering expanding their mixes. Generally, adding consistent rather than inconsistent product lines is less risky. For example, it would be least risky for Gerber to add another line of baby care products to its existing product mix, rather than a line of daycare centers.

→ What Is a Service?

Services, defined, entail the application of specialized competencies via the execution of actions, processes, and performance for purposes of benefitting other entities (usually customers). The ability to apply those specialized competencies often requires large amounts of skills, knowledge, and education. Plumbers, physicians, attorneys, CPAs, and professors each market services. None of these professionals could successfully provide their specialized services without substantial training and motivation.

Described more simply, services also entail actions performed by people or machines that deliver desired values to customers. These values can include a wide range of deliverables. Common deliverables include information (research services, education), pleasure (entertainment, travel), physical well-being (health, counseling), convenience (delivery services, dry cleaning), transportation (airlines, taxis), among nearly uncountable others.

The US economy is often characterized as a **service economy**. In 2010, 84% of all jobs in the United States were service-related and services accounted for over 80% of total GDP.[3]

The service component of the US economy obviously has grown rapidly. Consumer and business services are in demand because they provide access to experts who perform tasks that individuals or Firms cannot provide for themselves in a cost effective manner. Many service businesses are relatively inexpensive to establish and operate compared to most manufacturing, wholesaling, and retailing operations.

The Goods-Services Continuum

Capturing the essence of a service can prove difficult. The definition presented earlier implies that services are distinctly different from tangible products. This is not entirely true. Most intangible services feature a product component, just as many tangible products feature service component. In fact, one of the best ways to differentiate tangible products is to associate them with a desirable intangible service.

One decade after it had initially entered the US automobile marketplace, Hyundai still had trouble gaining traction. Apparently American consumers had difficulty accepting the notion that Korea could actually produce high-quality automobiles. Sure Germany, Japan, or even Sweden (Volvo) could manufacture great vehicles, and Korean firms obviously produced great electronics (hello, Samsung), but cars? Not so much. That is, until Hyundai became the first auto marketer to attach a 100,000 mile bumper-to-bumper or ten-year warranty to its brand. American consumers "suddenly" realized Hyundai must be a high-quality brand, after all. Its differentiation goal achieved, Hyundai was off to the races.

One can visualize products and services on a continuum (Exhibit 10.7). This continuum reflects a range between pure services on one end and pure goods on the other. Most goods and services reside somewhere toward the middle of this continuum. Few examples of pure services or pure goods exist. Even services such as dental care and health clubs boast "product" components. A dentist service encounter usually results in the acquisition of some physical products in addition to the service delivered. Free toothbrushes, tubes of toothpaste, dental floss and, of course, fillings, caps, retainers, and other less delightful products result from your visit. Many health clubs sell fitness accessories such as lifting gloves and straps, t-shirts, sweat towels, etc. Some even offer the equivalent of small cafés that provide protein drinks, smoothies, and other sport nutrition products.

Examples of pure goods also are rare. One might think that products such as wristwatches, shovels, and lawn chairs are pure goods. These products are purchased primarily for their form utility. The service dimensions that accompany these products tend to be less important.

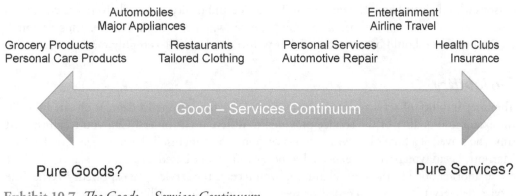

Exhibit 10.7 *The Goods—Services Continuum.*

However, a service dimension does exist. Such products feature an augmented service dimensions such as post-sale service, warranties, return policies or financing options.

Many goods and services simultaneously feature substantial physical and substantial components. Consider your favorite restaurant. You frequent this restaurant to receive both its service and excellent cuisine (we hope). The cuisine, clearly, is the product component. (So too is the physical restaurant.) The service component consists of the ambiance and quality attention provided by the restaurant and its wait staff.

Key Characteristics of Services

Four primary dimensions distinguish services from tangible products: intangibility, inseparability, variability, perishability.

Intangibility

Ever try to touch a service? Can you hear or smell services? Of course not. Services have no physical presence. They are actions, activities, experiences. When you buy a movie ticket, all you acquire is a promise you will view a movie. No guarantee exists that you will enjoy the experience. Workout at a health club, and you receive no takeaway, except perhaps feelings of accomplishment, exhaustion or both. Perhaps you hired a trainer to advise and motivate you during your workout. If the trainer delivered the promised service value, you may have left the gym with even greater feelings of accomplishment and even more exhausted, albeit with a bit less money.

Because services are intangible, consumers cannot judge service quality prior to actual delivery. Consumers often seek out cues in the service-delivery environment in order to predict the level of service they can expect. Would you hire fitness training services from someone who, upon visual inspection, was overweight, slovenly in appearance, and obnoxious? Probably not. Such signals suggest this trainer may deliver less than satisfying outcomes. Similarly, would you hire the services of a plumber who has received several seriously negative ratings on Angie's List or poor endorsements from the local Better Business Bureau? Again, we don't think so.

Inseparability

Services are produced and delivered by the service provider—usually at the location where the service is consumed. Services differ from tangible products in that they are produced and delivered at the same time. By contrast, products usually are produced in manufacturing facilities. They then flow through supply chains, which may include long periods of storage, before they are ready for delivery to customers. We discussed time utility in Chapter one.

Because services are simultaneously produced and delivered, they cannot be separated from the persons who deliver them. The quality of the service and utility (value) delivered to customers result from the efforts of the specific person or people who perform the service. Thus, as noted, service providers should be well-educated or well-trained as well as highly motivated.

Variability

The inseparability of services from service providers often results in degrees of variability in the extent and quality of the service provided to different customers. Can you recall the last time you stayed at a hotel? If it was part of a corporate or franchised chain such as Holiday Inn, Marriott, Hyatt, you probably expected some level of service based on your last stay somewhere else at another hotel in the same chain. Did you receive the service you expected? Maybe. The service delivery may have exceeded or met your expectations (delighting or satisfying you), or somehow fallen below what you had been lead to expect (leading to disappointment and dissatisfaction).

Every service employee is different. They "own" different life and professional backgrounds, motivations, personalities, moods, emotions, and attitudes toward their customers and jobs. Each and every difference can lead to different service experiences by customers even within in the same service delivery environment. This variability in service delivery is perhaps the most challenging problem facing service organizations. Service Firms must have in place quality, ongoing training and supervisory programs, and policies aimed at standardizing high levels of service delivery. When high-end professional service providers are having a "bad day", they must, according to J. W. Marriot marketer Ariadne Strutton: "Excuse themselves, walk through a closed door, return quickly, and begin having a 'great day'."

Perishability

Products can be stored until they can be sold. Not so with services. Services that go undelivered are lost. No revenue is earned. Ever miss a dental appointment? Get charged anyway? Many professionals charge for missed appointments. The block of time allocated to your appointment is lost and cannot be replaced, unless someone else was present, waiting to be "serviced."

The Services Marketing Mix

The marketing mix for services employs the same four tools that are used when marketing tangible products. These tools—the product, price, place, and promotion—are also used for the same purpose: to create differentiating value for intangible services, which here, are the products being marketed.

The Service Offering ("Product")

Selection of the service offering begins with the targeted customer segment. Service offerings should be designed to satisfy the identified needs of targeted customers and to differentiate the offering from those offered by competitors. Differentiation is key. Three primary pathways exist through which effective differentiation can be achieved:

- *Continuous Services Innovation:* Providers can differentiate service offerings via innovation. For example, Dallas-based Bonded Inspections specializes in non-destructive testing by using an array of innovative technologies in gamma ray, ultrasonic, magnetic particle, x-ray, and phased array penetrant systems wielded by a team of highly trained employees. Staying on top of current technologies and applying these methods to the needs of its diverse customer base differentiates the Firm, keeping it continuously ahead of competitors. Of course, innovations essentially will be replicated by competitors. Technological advantages can be sustained only when Firms continuously seek new technologies and identify new ways to improve basic service offerings.

- *Consistent Delivery:* Service providers can differentiate their brand values based on the quality of their service delivery by recruiting and training capable, expert service providers. Bonded Inspections continuously seeks experienced talent from a number of industries, including hiring top-notch technicians from competitors. Bonded also maintains relationships with a number of trade schools specializing in training on non-destructive testing technologies. Bonded differentiates its services by having programs that ensure its equipment and personnel consistently deliver a higher-quality service than its competitors. Technicians are incentivized to acquire additional certifications on existing and new technologies. An internal training program provides refresher training related to key testing technologies and the testing needs of clients.

- *Branding:* The variability and intangibility of services poses problems for branding the service. A well-branded product offers a promise of consistent quality. The same description applies to services. Failing to provide consistent quality from one service encounter to the next can degrade or destroy the service's brand image. However, options exist through which Firms can effectively brand services. First, service Firms should identify the distinct service image that they seek to promote and adopt a tangible object that epitomizes the image.[4] This image should be incorporated into the Firm's branding symbols and consistently employed in marketing communications. Prudential's "rock" symbolizes the strength and stability of its promise to customers. Allstate's cupped hands and slogan "you're in good hands with Allstate" suggest responsible and caring service. By employing such an image consistently across all marketing communications (i.e., advertising, specialty advertising, sales promotions, public relations and publicity releases, social media, and websites), providers can cement their brand icon with the quality of their service and reputation. Second, service Firms must identify the key elements of the service offering that are responsible for projecting and solidifying this image with customers. The Firm should institute measures to ensure that these specific elements are consistently provided at a superior level. Employee training and proper supervision are essential to minimize any variability in delivery. Firms should measure whether the outcomes they are seeking are actually being delivered to customers. Inside any Firm "what gets measured" is also "what will be delivered."

Pricing the Service (Price)

Price is variously labeled, in service domains, as rates (hotels, motels), fees (doctors, lawyers), charges (medical facilities), and fares (airlines, taxies, public transit). The pricing of services poses a major challenge for at least two reasons. First, the intangible and perishable nature of services means that if the service is not sold, the revenue opportunity is lost. Prices for products can be marked down to clear inventory. Services cannot. Second, services face capacity constraints. Unlike product manufacturing where additional production runs can match added supply with demand, services are produced as they are consumed. This means only so many service encounters can be provided in a given period of time. Just as revenue can be lost permanently if prices are too high, revenue is also sacrificed if the service is priced too low.

Each scenario points toward the need to price services in ways that manage revenue and capacity. During periods of slow demand, services marketers may employ "off-peak pricing" to encourage and elevate demand. Airlines, hotels, theaters, and restaurants reduce prices during slow periods (these periods are predictable) to shift demand away from peak consumption periods where the danger exists that all service requests may not be honored. Service requests that cannot be delivered result in lost revenue and, more seriously, lost customers.

Price influences consumers' preconceptions of service quality. Times will arise when few cues exist upon which customers can base their service quality expectations. Lacking other information consumers may consciously or subconsciously use price to gauge the quality of an anticipated service experience. As a general rule, attention to price is likely to be greater for higher-priced packaged goods, durable goods, and services than for low-priced consumer products, such as beverages. Higher prices suggest higher quality, particularly in the view of uninformed customers. Charging a price premium for the service offering may be justified if it is an important synergistic component of the Firm's brand differentiation strategy. Service providers attempting to differentiate on superior quality should price in a manner consistent with the image projected via their marketing communications.

Service Distribution (Place)

Most consumer services providers operate out of brick and mortar (B&M)—physical—storefronts or offices. In today's convenience-oriented societies, locating these facilities is just as important to service providers as it is for traditional retailers of consumer products. This is particularly true when direct customer/service provider interaction is required; for example, with hair salons, dentist and doctors' offices, banking services, dry cleaners, etc.

The advent of the Internet, particularly broadband wireless services that can be accessed via a wide variety of devices, has made it possible for service providers to connect more easily with their customers. Banks offer mobile "apps" and websites for their customers' convenience. You can order your favorite take-out from your smartphone. You can arrange for a variety of services directly from the provider's website, or use a third-party broker, such as Angie's List, to both research and purchase services. The world of services delivery has genuinely changed for the better.

Services Promotion (Promotion)

Well-planned and effective promotion programs (think integrated marketing communications) are absolutely essential for services to overcome their fundamental "intangibility," "variability," and "inseparability." Most services must rely heavily on promotion to communicate the promise of a quality service experience. The importance of communicating and managing quality of the service delivery is addressed in some detail in a subsequent section. The current discussion focuses more on the major forms of promotion that are typically emphasized by service Firms.

Personal selling is central to successfully marketing services. The inseparability of services, as you recall, means that the service is produced at the time it is sold. Face-to-face interaction between providers and customers is usually required for any service transaction to occur. Exceptions exist. Our Angie's List example earlier allows buyers to purchase services at a discount that will be delivered at a future agreed upon time. However, even in cases where the service is pre-sold or contracted, the service technicians that actually deliver the service still function as salespersons for their Firms. To the extent that technicians represent their respective Firms, they are ex post facto acting as salespeople. In addition, technicians may identify additional sales opportunities based on problems uncovered during service delivery. These problems may be addressed at that time, or future appointments may be recommended or arranged.

Advertising consumer services is essential for signaling the promise of a quality experience to prospective customers. Today, advertising for services encompasses a wide array of media well beyond traditional TV, radio, and print. The importance of Internet exposure via the provider's own website and third-party sites, including social media, continues to grow. Historically, certain professional services (lawyers, doctors) were not permitted to advertise in any form or media due to ethical concerns. The Supreme Court has since ruled such prohibitions as unlawful under anti-trust laws.

Managing the Service Experience

Delivering Quality Service Experiences

Customers often have trouble anticipating the quality of service to expect from providers. Services are produced at the point they are consumed (we call this inseparability). Few tangible characteristics of services exist that consumers can examine prior to purchase. How do consumers evaluate service offerings prior to purchase? How can marketers communicate to consumers that a quality service will be delivered? Consumers talk to other people about their experiences. Would you recommend this service? Did the provider do a good job at a reasonable price?

Positive word of mouth is crucial. The Internet makes it easier for consumers to compare service providers. Sites like Yahoo Local, Yellow Book, and Local.com provide listings of local service businesses, ratings, and reviews. Some companies offer substantial discounts for purchasing their services from such websites. Marketers often exploit these sites to differentiate their service offerings by providing quality information with reasonable promises, offering discounts to prospective customers visiting these sites, and encouraging customers to share satisfying experiences via positive reviews.

Service providers must offer tangible evidence to support their promises of professionalism and expertise. Certifications, degrees, endorsements, and positive publicity in local media offer some evidence. Most service Firms have their own websites containing evidence backing claims of quality delivery. Websites are employed to provide prospective customers with "blueprints" of anticipated service experiences; here is what we do and how we do it. Similarly, social media such as Facebook, LinkedIn or Instagram are excellent venues to encourage consumers to share their positive service experiences, and for service providers to manage any negative information that may be disseminated.

Judging the quality of a service during and immediately after delivery can prove difficult. Many dimensions of quality are hidden. How do you know whether the electrician who repaired a shorted switchbox did a good job? All we know for sure is whether the lights came back on. There is no way to know how long the fix will last, whether it was instituted according to code, or whether it will cause a fire. How do we know that the bathroom toilet was properly repaired so that it won't overflow again shortly after the plumber leaves? There are no 100% guarantees. But service providers can quell feelings of doubt in much the same way they assure consumers of promised service quality before the service is purchased. In addition, quality service Firms provide clearly-written and communicated service warranties, with prompt and professional follow-up should something go wrong.

Service Encounters and Managing Service Failures

Service encounters are key to quality service delivery and creating satisfied customers. However, some service encounters inevitably result in failure. Either the service is improperly delivered and rejected at the time of its delivery ("The haircut is wack. My girlfriend will hate it!") or the customer discovers the failure after delivery—the toilet overflows the day after being repaired. Whenever such failure is discovered, service providers must take quick, professional actions to correct the problem and convince the customer that their complaint will be resolved and won't happen again. Service providers can salvage the situation by demonstrating that they care and value continued positive customer relationships.

Failures can be minimized and more effectively handled with "failure planning." Providers should seek to understand where in the service delivery process things are most likely to go wrong. Regularly reviewing service encounters, talking with technicians, and listening to customers can uncover the common sources of delivery failures. Understanding probable sources of failures can be the best defense against these failures occurring or going undetected until it's too late and an irate customer must be placated.

Empowerment is key to successful service failure planning. Service technicians and other employees should be empowered to take action immediately when failure occurs. The more quickly failures are addressed, the greater the likelihood that positive outcomes will result and re-newly satisfied customers retained. With "customer service recovery," an empowered employee can take the initiative to offer immediate accommodations to ease customer complaints. Ritz Carlton, for example, empowers employees to spend up to $2,000 to rectify complaints. The Ritz Carlton objective is to "delight the customer," not just fix the problem.

Starbucks does many things well, including lattes. When service encounters with customers go bad, as occasionally happens everywhere, Starbuck's baristas leap into action. This is because they have been trained to *Listen* to the complaint; *Acknowledge* the complaint; *Thank* the complainer, while giving him/her a new cupful; and then *Explain* what went wrong—and why. *Listen, Acknowledge, Thank, Explain*; take the first letters from each word, then add one more "T" to thank—which makes sense because service providers should thank the customer more than once for bringing the complaint to their attention—and what word appears? That's right, LATTE.

→ Managing Products' Life Cycles

Forty-five plus years after their run ended, the Beatles remain history's most influential and popular band. Beyond question, John Lennon, Paul McCartney, George Harrison and Ringo Starr consistently created discontinuous, never-heard-before, musical innovations. These disruptive new products arrived in the form of new songs and albums that were gobbled up by 1960s-era consumers.

The Beatles were able to develop unique music because, as new product developers, the band consistently operated on intersectional edges between diverse musical genres. When creating new music the Beatles mixed, matched, and blended ideas acquired from musical disciplines as diverse as skiffle, beat music, 1950s rock & roll, the blues, pop-like ballads, Indian music, psychedelic music and, of course, hard rock. The Beatles' integrated multiple perspectives into these new songs (leveraging multiple perspectives). The Fab Four refused to be limited by past or then-current musical norms and practices (unleashing themselves from associative barriers). The band consciously took measured risks despite the prospect of failure. These creative choices and attitudes proved crucial as the Beatles developed successively more evolutionary music that elevated the band to the legendary status that it still enjoys to this day.

The Beatles disbanded in 1970, just seven years after first achieving unparalleled stardom. Experts agree that the life cycle of the product and brand called the Beatles ended far too soon. Each Beatle enjoyed a successful career as a solo artist. In fact, Lennon, McCartney, Harrison, and Starr each released solo albums in 1970. But the new product developed by George Harrison, the so-called "Quiet Beatle," proved the best-seller. Harrison's album was presciently and nostalgically titled, All Things Must Pass. Heed the phrase and the implications associated with these four words.

Products Have Life Cycles

Firms can neither succeed initially nor sustain success over the long-run unless they adeptly develop new products. After launch, the same Firms must also effectively manage these products throughout their life cycles. Marketing managers must manage such products while giving full strategic consideration to the influence of changing customer tastes; technological, socio-cultural or economic trends; and dynamic competitive practices.

New or established products, brands, and product categories (for example, automobiles, gasoline-powered combustion engines, or rubber tires) all face limited life spans. Believe it or not, Coke Classic or McDonald's will one day exit this world. This means, at net, all products must pass through product life cycles (hereafter, PLC). Depicted in Exhibit 10.8, products

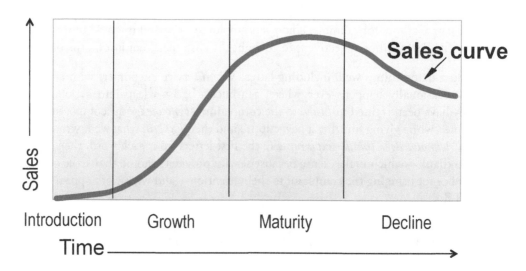

Exhibit 10.8 *The Product Life Cycle (PLC).*

progress through four life cycle stages: **introduction**, **growth**, **maturity**, and **decline**. Traditionally, the product life cycle was intended to depict how sales revenues typically change through time for a given **product category**, rather than for individual brands. However the PLC concepts and principles discussed here apply equally to entire product categories and individual brands in those categories.

No preset time-frame exists during which products must complete their life cycles. Only one thing is certain: all new products, eventually, *must pass*—reminiscent of the title of George Harrison's first solo album's title. In this regard, products, brands, or product categories are exactly like all other living things. Every dog, flea, tree, or person alive today one day will die.

After sometimes lengthy gestational periods (nine months for humans, up to 680 days for elephants, who knows how long for new products), living things, by definition, are always born—or introduced. During this introduction stage living things are labeled as "new." These new things, with good cause, are often carefully fed and nurtured. And when this happens, these living things are more likely to quickly enter a stage where they grow rapidly.

Growth is great, pretty much for everyone involved. But growth never lasts forever, not even if the once new things continue to receive careful attention and special types of resources. Consequently, after this growth stage ends, those once-new but now-older things (products, people, fleas, or trees) enter a third, mature stage in their life cycles.

The maturity stage for products, brands and product categories can last for very long times. In the end, however, living things always end up in the same place: the dirt, grave, or trash bin. We would point out, this is another compelling reason why Firms must successfully and perpetually execute NPD efforts.

→ Exceptions to Rules

All this so far makes sense, right? For as George Harrison wrote *All Things Must Pass*. Except, it turns out, perhaps Beatles' products themselves. In descending order from 10th to 1st place the top-ten best-selling music artists during 2000-2009, were:

- Jay Z, Creed, Linkin Park, Nelly, Kenny Chesney, Britany Spears, Toby Keith, Tim McGraw, and in essentially a dead-heat tie, the Beatles and Eminem.

Some camps report that the Beatles edged out Marshall Mathers during the 2009 Christmas season. That was when Apple first released Beatles music on its then still-new iTunes delivery service.

The PLC concept is still very much in play, however. Witness how some of the most successful new musical products/brands launched during the 2000s are now after-thoughts, while other artists' work essentially descended to laugh-line status, as in how could so many consumers have bought that stuff in the first place?

Consider three final Beatles takeaways or PLC values. First, the life cycles of products and brands should be actively managed. This has been true of the Beatles' now 45-52 year old product portfolio. Second, formerly new and successful products and brands can trend into, out of, and back into style or high demand. Third, technology always has its say and exercises its influence. Had Apple not intervened in the music marketplace with its new product, iTunes, The Beatles would not have been America's best-selling musical artist five decades after releasing their last new-to-the-world product.

The Introduction Stage

The Firm delivers a new product to market during the introduction stage. This initial PLC stage immediately follows the completion of the NPD process discussed in Chapter 11. Hopefully, the new product is sufficiently different from and materially superior to existing products competing in the same market space. If so, the new product faces little to no direct competition during the introductory stage.

The initial promotional goal should be build awareness of and demand for this new product class (i.e.; create **primary demand**), rather than the specific brand, through messages designed to educate and inform. This is critical given that no customer has ever purchased anything new until s/he first became aware of its existence and new values. A related promotional goal should be to stimulate trial. These promotional messages would be targeted primarily toward "innovator" and "early adopter" customer categories.

Distribution, at first, may remain limited or selective. "Selective distribution," in this context, implies that at launch only a few stores may carry the new product. Selective distribution might also imply that during this introductory stage, the new product is made available only in select geographic market segments. Distribution may remain selective until customers demonstrate broader acceptance of the product. Alternatively, the Firm might engage in "extensive" distribution—making the product available in all possible stores, targeted market segments, or distribution channels—right from the start. In either situation new distribution or supply chain relationships might need to be established. Securing new distribution relationships may prove challenging, however. Usually, when new products enter the market and seek space on retailers' shelves, other older products must exit that same shelf space. Or, alternatively, existing supply relationships may need to be strengthened to ensure the distribution support necessary to launch the new products successfully.

Prices may be markedly higher or lower as compared to competing or potentially substitute products. The decision to price high or low as the product enters the market normally pivots on the tactics the Firm employs as it manages the other three marketing mix dimensions. This decision similarly might be established to counter or match the closest competitor(s) current pricing strategies.

A penetration, or lower, pricing strategy might be pursued to build market share rapidly. Walmart's White Stag (targeting women) or George (targeting men) brands of apparel enter the market through penetration pricing strategies. The problem with penetration pricing, however, is that Firms not named Walmart invariably have more difficulty raising low prices than lowering higher prices. Walmart, however, rarely encounters unmanageable pressures to raise apparel prices due to how efficiently it manages supply chain relationships.

By contrast, firms such as Apple or Gillette prefer to unveil new products through **skimming-the-cream**, or **premium pricing**, strategies. One reason why each Firm does this is to recoup its product development costs quickly. Another, likely more dominant, reason is because they can. Apple, with its ever evolving line of iProducts, or Gillette with its Fusion product line, logically exploit the brand equity that each Firm has painstakingly earned across decades. Their brand equity permits such Firms to simultaneously maintain higher prices and market share. Each Firm typically "obsoletes" its own products before any competitor can update them, while developing new products that move the competitive bar higher as lower-priced, "me-too" products enter the same market space. The overarching strategy for both Apple and Gillette is to make price levels less important to loyal customers from the moment those new products enter their introduction stage.

Hybrid cars or solar-power-generating devices probably will remain in their introduction stages for some time. No one knows with certainty because futures are easier to create than predict. To be sure, however, neither product category's sales have taken off to the point where experts can comfortably classify them as growth-stage products.

The Growth Stage

During the growth stage competition arrives, perhaps slowly but inexorably, attracted by the promise of accelerating revenues and profits. Primary promotional goals include creating brand preference (i.e.; creating **selective demand**) and sustaining perceptions of differentiation. Sustainable success requires that Firms establish, within the collective mind of targeted segments, the notion that this still-new product remains different and better from all the others. Promotions are generally targeted at additional adopter category audiences (i.e., "early majority" and "late majority"). But targets also might include new segments.

Whatever pricing strategy was employed during blast-off likely will be maintained. At the least, the Firm should seek to maintain its initial pricing strategy as long as competitive efforts and overall environmental conditions permit.

Firms should strive to expand distribution channels and supply chain relationships as demand increases and more customers seek opportunities to purchase the product from different sources. Firms should attempt to lock in as many distribution relationships as possible during the growth stage. Securing these relationships will help Firms sustain sales and profits latter as sales inevitably level off and eventually decline during the latter stages of the PLC.

Years after their introduction, smart phones—at least globally—probably remain in their growth stage. Similar descriptions likely apply to 3D televisions, Blue Ray players, and Tablet PCs.

The Maturity Stage

The maturity stage features a general slowing or leveling-off of industry sales for the entire product category. Competitive pressures intensify to peak levels during this stage. Marginally competitive products are probably exiting the market, often not of their own volition. They simply cannot compete effectively any more. This trend creates opportunities for Firms that are able to differentiate their products effectively enough to remain profitable. By this time, everyone who might eventually purchase the once-innovative product is aware of it, and is either a repeat customer or someone who tried and decided to dump the product in favor of a superior alternative.

More than ever, the overarching strategic goal is to defend market share by differentiating the product from competitive offerings. Lower-level sorts of continuously-innovative NPD activities may transpire at this point. Firms may add or delete features from the original product to support differentiating efforts. These actions, in effect, give Firms something new to talk about in their promotional messaging.

Promotional efforts also might pointedly remind current customers why they once loved the product. Recall The Simple Minds song, "Don't You Forget about Me," the song that played over the closing credits in *The Breakfast Club*. That's the gist of reminder promotional messaging. By no means is all lost as products enter this stage. Innovative promotional campaigns can extend the mature life-spans of established brands for decades. Coca-Cola, London Fog, and Bayer Aspirin easily come to mind as products that have remained ensconced in their maturity stage for years if not decades.

Originally premium prices for now well-established brands will likely drop during this period. Firms would also seek to secure as much distribution as can be acquired, through as many retail outlets as possible, for the mature product. Extensive distribution is more the rule than exception.

Soft drinks, fossil-fuel powered automobiles, and laptop computers also have probably entered mature life cycle stages.

The Decline Stage

Many well-known products, brands, and product categories are experiencing decline. A list of sometimes unusual suspects includes:

- Yellow pages, classified ads, movie rental stores, landline phones, VCRs, CD players, ash trees (from which the best baseball bats are made), ham radios, answering machines, cameras that use film, milkmen, hand-written letters (imagine the love-lost here), honey bees, analog TV, and family farms.

Peruse this list carefully, however, you should note that classification in its decline stage does not mean the absolute end is near, or inevitable, for given products. Cameras that use film, and consequently film itself, are clearly in decline. Kodak knows this all too well. But true cameras and film will never go completely away, during a time horizon that anyone alive now will experience. Camera aficionados and artists will remain, and continue to demand "real" film.

Even when formerly favored product/brands begin to decline, Firms generally have the opportunity to exercise one of three strategic options. First, Firms can keep marketing the product. They might opt to reposition the old by rejuvenating and upgrading old value by adding new features or finding new uses. Arm & Hammer Baking Soda did this decades ago, around the time when legions of American women were leaving pure-homemaker roles and entering other sorts of bread-maker roles. Those women, naturally, began baking less. Less baking, less need for baking soda. In response to these highly threatening socio-cultural and economic environmental trends, Arm & Hammer widely promoted the fact that the old standby can be used in myriad numerous new ways. Turns out, having Arm & Hammer Baking Soda around can solve myriad other problems. Such problems include:

- Neutralizing odors, particularly in refrigerators; exfoliating skin; erasing crayon, pencil, ink and furniture scuffs; unclogging drains; removing tough stains from stainless steel; scrubbing pans; brushing teeth; deodorizing; cleaning-up minor oil and grease spills; and settling upset stomachs…to name a few.

Talk about products as problem-solvers. Old school marketers, clearly, can also be creative.

Second, Firms can harvest the mature product by reducing costs and continuing to market it, for example, to loyal or emerging niche segments. Buggy whips experienced rapid sales declines more than 100 years ago. The reasons was that a superior new product, the automobile, began replacing the long-dominant horse and buggy in a big way. Fewer buggies, fewer buggy whips. Automobile sales grew so fast because they presented a huge relative advantage over existing forms of transportation (e.g.; horses and buggies). Cars did not need to be fed, walked, or rubbed down every day. Rarely, if ever, did they crap all over the road. The sanitation problem that prevailed in New York City during the last 20 years or so before the first car traversed Broadway and Fifth Avenue was a sight to behold, smell, and avoid stepping in.

But back to buggy whips, and niche targeting. Consumer segments that purchase buggy whips because they have needs—or problems—that could be solved through buggy whips still exist. With the recent success of 50 *Shades of Gray*, the segment may expand from its erstwhile niche status. But probably not, we'll admit!

Third, Firms can divest and discontinue the product. Divestiture might entail liquidating leftover inventory, selling mature products outright, or licensing rights to other Firms who continue to market mature items.

→ Product Life Cycle Concept: Boon and Bane

"Boon" means benefit or advantage. "Bane" means nuisance or curse. (And it's okay for you to learn the meanings of new words, even when reading a marketing text.)

The PLC concept, like any successful idea, has since been converted into a popular product. Like any successful product, the PLC delivers certain discernable values. The PLC concept delivers two, once-new but still useful, values. First, the PLC concept is valuable as a teaching and learning device. (Note, there is no teaching without learning.) The concept provides a platform to teach students what marketing managers should do with their marketing mix and segmentation—targeting efforts at various stages during their products' life cycles. Second, the truest utility emerging from the PLC concept is this: if managers understand what stages of their life cycle their products are in, they will better understand how to market those products successfully.

Many things in business life are connected to good news/bad news stories. We just learned two good things about the PLC concept. The one problem with the concept is that marketing managers often struggle to accurately identify the exact stage in which their product belongs. In fact, the only way marketing managers can be certain about the stage a given product occupies is when they are looking backward, toward what has happened in the past. This creates another problem, of course, because managers develop strategies for purposes of moving forward.

Anyone living in Texas ought to find it relatively easy to drive to California. Wherever they are, Texas drivers just have to drive north or south until they encounter Interstate 10, 20, or 30. Then head west and keeping driving until you hit California. Getting to California from

Texas is that simple. Now imagine the problems that might arise on this trip if you, the driver, had to steer your car driving forward only by looking backward through the rearview mirror.

Great insight and power can gleaned from understanding the past. The further back into the past you are able to see, the further ahead you can see into the future—and all that. But how difficult would it prove to navigate moving forward when your head is exclusively struck in the past? The answer is quite difficult indeed.

Endnotes

[1] Based on a classification scheme proposed by Gary Armstrong and Philip Kotler, *Marketing: An Introduction, 11e* (Upper Saddle River, NJ: Pearson Education, 2013), 198.

[2] Louis P. Bucklin, "Retail Strategy and the Classification of Consumer Goods," *Journal of Marketing*, 27 (1) (January, 1963): 50–55.

[3] Cengiz Haksever and Barry Render, *Service Management: An Integrated Approach to Supply Chain Management and Operations* (Upper Saddle River, NJ: FT Press, 2013).

[4] Adopted from Allan C. Reedy, Bruce D. Buskirk, and Ajit Kaicker, "Tangibilizing the Intangibles: Some Strategies for Services Marketing," *Journal of Services Marketing*, 7(3) (1993): 13–17.

[5] Valarie A. Zeithaml, "Consumer Perceptions of Price, Quality, and Value: A Means-End Model and Synthesis of Evidence," *Journal of Marketing*, 52 (July 1988): 2–22.

[6] Cengiz Haksever, Barry Render, Roberta S. Russell, and Robert G. Murdick, *Service Management and Operations, 2nd Ed.*, (Englewood Cliffs, NJ: Prentice-Hall, 1999), 342–3.

[7] Bob Thompson, "The Key to Success with Employee Empowerment: Work Backwards from the Customer," *CustomerThink*, March 17, 2013, http://customerthink.com/key_to_ success_employee_empowerment_work_backwards_from_the_customer.

Chapter 11

DEVELOPING NEW PRODUCTS—AND YOUR CREATIVITY

Few people fully appreciate the nearly miraculous innovative processes involved in the evolution from whalebone corsets (circa 1850) to Spandex (today). Whalebone corsets and Spandex are notably different products. Yet each was developed to solve the same human "problem" or, stated differently, to satisfy the same human want.

The Western female desire to appear slimmer has not fundamentally deviated from at least the Victorian Era until today. Only the products developed to satisfy this desire have changed. Along the evolutionary path from whalebone corsets to Spandex the product solutions changed, most materially, in their effectiveness, discreteness, comfort, and ease of use. In this context, each change was and remains a determinant product feature. Each change delivered new differentiating values. Each change contributes to the fact that Spandex, the newly developed product, is incredibly superior to its whalebone predecessor.

The myriad processes through which new products (corsets) or new services (tax preparation services such Turbo Tax) are developed are collectively called New Product Development (NPD). NPD includes the development, marketing and positioning/repositioning of new ideas, places, or people (as professional, political, entertainment or celebrity brands).

→ NPD Is Important

World Changing

NPD exists as a mega business activity that profoundly influences your life, often for the better. The once-new products listed in Table 11.1 were recently ranked 50th to 1st in term of their importance and impact, since the development of the wheel, that is.[1] What, no "Angry Birds" or "Candy Land"? And Texans might rank air conditioning higher than number 44.

How many of these products resonate with you? Hint: the answer should be "all." Each product on this list has solved problems you have had, would have had, or never had, all because the products were developed and exist or because their creative new product offshoots were developed and exist. This "nifty-fifty" also created new civilizations; innovative business models; amazing technologies; scaled-up economies; and, as noted, slews of related new products. Each new product on this list changed the world.

The NPD activity is a similarly world-changing, paradigm-shifting affair. Paradigm is a word people occasionally use just to show off. Paradigms, however, are nothing more than "collections of ideas about how something should be done, made, or evaluated."

Table 11.1 • Most Important Innovations in History (Since the Wheel)

50	The Combine Harvester (1930s)	25	Alphabetization (circa 1000 BC)
49	Assembly Line (1913)	24	Telephone (1876)
48	Lever (circa 3000 BC)	23	Sextant (1757)
47	Nail (circa 2000 BC)	22	Green Revolution (1950s)
46	Anesthesia (1846)	21	Nuclear Fission (1939)
45	Television (1940s)	20	The "Pill" (1960)
44	Air-conditioning (1902)	19	Industrial Steelmaking (1850s)
43	Abacus (circa 3000 BC)	18	Automobile (late 1800s)
42	Paper Money (around AD 1200)	17	Compass (1200s)
41	Rocketry (1926)	16	Personal Computer (1970s)
40	Sailboat (4000 BC)	15	Airplane (1903)
39	Oil Refining (1859)	14	Gunpowder (10th century AD)
38	Scientific Plant Breeding (1920s)	13	Refrigeration (1850s)
37	Oil Drilling (1859)	12	Sanitation Systems (1850s)
36	Cement (around 1000 BC)	11	Nitrogen Fixation (leading to fertilizers; 1918)
35	Steam Turbine (1884)	10	Steam Engine (1712)
34	Gregorian Calendar (1582)	9	Internet (1960s)
33	Pasteurization (1863)	8	Vaccination (1796)
32	Cotton Gin (1793)	7	Internal Combustion Engine (late 1800s)
31	Archimedes' Screw (about 300 BC)	6	Paper (AD 200)
30	Moldboard Plow (1830s)	5	Optical Lenses (1200s)
29	Photography (1850s)	4	Semiconductor Electronics (1950s)
28	Radio (1906)	3	Penicillin (1928)
27	Mechanized Clock (1500s)	2	Electricity (late 1800s)
26	Telegraph (1837)	1	The Printing Press (1430s).

Survive and Thrive

NPD activity and output contributes materially to almost every Firm's ongoing survival. Almost all Firms must continuously develop new products or services. Thereafter, sizeable percentages of those new products, services, or ideas must succeed, or else those Firms will die. Firms that fail not execute NPD well will inevitably fade away.

How fast Firms die depends largely the industry in which they compete. For Firms to survive, much less thrive, they must grow, just like sharks succumb unless they continuously swim forward. Existing products, along with existing Firms, are rarely murdered. Instead, they slowly commit suicide, dying because they outlived their usefulness, having failed to change in ways that would have permitted them to offer what the world now sought.

Solves Problems, Known and Unknown

Successful new products or services offer the best solution to most Firms' most pressing problem. Most Firms' most pressing challenge derives from the needs they face to achieve genuinely sustainable differentiation in markets that have become increasingly commoditized and globalized. For points of differentiation to be sustainable, they must be grounded in sustainable competitive advantages (SCAs) that Firms create for themselves. Gillette Razors and Apple have long benefitted from the SCAs that their NPD acumen has conferred to them. These two global leaders have likewise greatly profited from the branding/pricing power that both Firms earned once they established reputations, respectively, for offering the latest, greatest blades or smart devices.

Marketing competitors will do the most damage (to each other!) when little to no differentiation exists between their product portfolios. In these commoditized markets, competition often devolves into price wars where, over time, each competitor secures similar sales but decreased profit margins. In fact, only consumers appear to win in such markets.

But do customers actually win in the absence of NPD? Is it possible that customers would actually benefit more from the new, superior, and differentiating values that effective NPD generates for them? Or, at least, might customers welcome the opportunity to select from amongst larger sets of viable solutions?

Minds have no way of knowing what their tongues desire until the satisfaction from a newly-revealed solution is made available for their tongue-to-taste. This principle is offered neither as mystery nor riddle. Instead, what is referenced here is a now-old product, sugar, that not long ago was viewed throughout most of the world as a startlingly delightful new product. The Western world (think Europe) did not enjoy much access to sugar until the 1500s. Even then distribution was limited. (India, notably, was enjoying sugar by AD 500.)

Imagine a world without the one-time new product called sugar. Consumers would experience less pleasure in that world. More germane, could you conceive how sensational sugar tastes if you had never experienced it? Trust us, you could not. The mind cannot imagine what the tongue does not know as a real thing. The right sort of NPD can prove powerful indeed.

Benefits Economies in Every Way

The outcomes generated by NPD generally but inevitably benefit societies, cultures, and economies. NPD, you see, increases productivity and economic growth. The most fundamental cause of growth in any economy is organizationally-produced, competitively-prompted innovation.

The 1990s are held up as the last great decade of sustained economic growth in the United States. Here's why: First, the Internet, invented in the 1970s (#9 on the Top-50 list), initially blossomed into a potentially profitable innovation during the 1990s. Second, original oil drilling services (#37 on the Top-50 list), called directional drilling, were perfected and made new—again during the decade. (This new product permitted new deposits of oil to be inexpensively discovered and extracted. Consequently, oil prices averaged around $12.00 a barrel during the decade. Notably, with the development of fracking, oil drilling was made new again/again during the 2000s.) Third, during 1980–1988 President Reagan's administration promoted the idea that the United States should develop a new product known as "Star Wars." Some experts, including us, argue that "Star Wars" financially forced the Soviet Union out of business, because the USSR could no longer spend enough to keep up in the Arms Race. America's 1990s economy boomed because of the resulting 1990s peace dividend. That Bill Clinton was President or the Republican Party dominated Congress had little to do with an essentially decade-long economic boom. The three radical innovations just noted--the Internet, directional drilling, and peace dividend—simultaneously increased economic efficiency, economic productivity and wages, and consequently consumer demand. Economic success was assured.

Promotes Your Success

NPD success is predicated on creative success. Turns out, that's good for you, too. As you learn more about NPD you will also learn more about becoming more creative, yourself. Which should prove hugely valuable, because from the moment you graduate you will be delivering whatever problem-solving value you are able to develop on a global stage. The performance of legal, accounting, medical, engineering, technology development and analysis, and information management functions is increasingly outsourced to India or China or other places, with more foreign country providers entering the scene every year. These international professionals are as smart and well-educated as you. Their technology works as well as yours; they are willing to work as hard as you. They are also delighted to work for 15 cents on your salary dollar!

This is one impact of globalization, up-close and personal. As you enter an information-driven marketplace of ideas will you possess the ideas and skill sets to compete successfully? You cannot "out-cheap" your global competitors. But you can "out-create," that is, outthink, them. Your learned ability to solve current and emergent problems more creatively may prove your ultimate survival skill.

⟶ What Is a New Product?

"The new is a glittering lure," as fictional marketer Don Draper said on the television show *Mad Men*. The allure of "new" always has and always will be desirable and a driver of sustainable marketing success. Most consumers love "new stuff." The New acts as a bait and hook that first catches eyes and then plastic cards. One question every Firm's managers must answer: Will we "do the new" ourselves, or will "the new be done to us?" We trust the answer is self-evident.

Three broad categories exist in which new products or services can be classified. The classifications begin with products that are genuinely new-to-the-world. They end with simple additions or deletions to existing products. From the miraculous to the mundane, the relevant range of new products include (Exhibit 11.1):

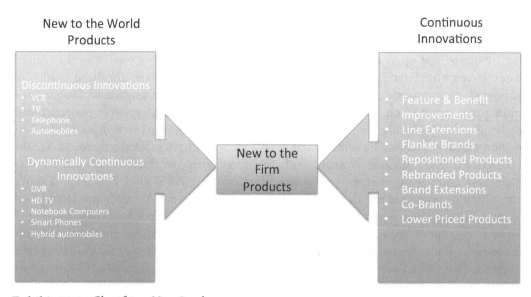

Exhibit 11.1 *Classifying New Products.*

New-to-the-World-Products

The first personal computer, first mp3 player or for that matter the first wheel were truly new-to-the-world products. These products are also called "discontinuous innovations" because they dramatically changed the solutions to existing consumption-related problems. Consumers had to learn new ways of solving old problems. Discontinuous innovations are usually based on new technologies. There is, for example, only one original telephone, the product developed in 1876 by Alexander Graham Bell. This truly discontinuous innovation dramatically changed the way in which the world's communications needs were met! Additional examples of such discontinuous innovations when the products were first introduced include VCRs, PCs, automobiles, aircraft, and electricity.

One implication: today's smart phones are merely highly evolved extensions of the unique, highly-innovative product that Mr. Bell developed. The core function and benefit of smart phones, after all, is still that they permit people to communicate orally, voice-to-voice, speaking with and listening to other people. These extensions of what was once the discontinuous innovation are called "dynamically continuous innovations." Such innovations are significant improvements on their parent innovation, but not nearly as disruptive in terms of the amount of re-learning involved to adopt the innovation for personal use. Additional examples of dynamically continuous innovations include notebook computers (based on the PC), DVRs (an outgrowth of VCR technology), commercial and military jet aircraft, and digital photography (derived from a synergy between film-based photography and computer technologies.)

New-to-the-Firm-Products

Instagram and WhatsApp once were, essentially, new-to-the-world products. But technically, each Firm became "New-to-the-Firm" products at the point that Facebook acquired them for inclusion in its rapidly expanding product portfolio. New-to-the-Firm products can also be derived from or based on continuous innovations (discussed next). Simple improvements, revisions, upgrades, etc. to existing products already produced by other Firms may offer opportunities for new-to-the-Firm products. Most private label products added to retailers' product portfolios are derived from existing brands already produced by other Firms.

Improvements, Revisions, Upgrades, Subtractions, Deletions to Existing Products

This specific NPD activity might involve adding health-enhancing vitamins or minerals to orange juice or removing unhealthy sugar or excessive caffeine from an existing cola product. Product additions or deletions could be initiated to create new or added value for existing or newly targeted customer segments. Also called "continuous innovation," this sort of less intense, but still useful creative endeavor is actually the most common type of NPD.

Professional baseball and football remain hugely popular products throughout the United States. Yet the marketers who manage how each product is delivered to targeted US markets are continuously changing their products. Product features that once dominated football are being eliminated in order to reduce the risk of permanent injury to players and preserve the game's brand image. Changes in how baseball is played are being instituted for purposes of speeding up the game and making it more TV-friendly. Each game seeks to preserve and/or upgrade its long-term value through NPD.

Other Types of NPD Efforts

Other useful marketing actions qualify as NPD-related endeavors. Most are also classified as continuous innovations. First, there are acts of repositioning. Repositioning is sometimes also called retargeting (remember Chapter 9), which occurs when existing products are repositioned for new uses, new applications, or new market segments. Bush's Baked Beans, for example, recently decided to reposition itself to parents as a "vegetable" that kids will eat and love. Parents, of course, often have trouble getting their children to eat vegetables, so if Bush's can help solve the problem all the better for the brand.

During the last 30, 10 or 5 or so years, respectively, think about how many times Madonna, Beyoncé, or Taylor Swift, along with their marketing handlers, have strategically changed and purposefully repositioned their personal brands? These artists, led by their marketers, engaged in repositioning efforts in attempts to make an "old, known-thing (them, their music and personae!) seem new, again." That is, before the old Beyoncé's brand, actually settles in permanently in the market's mind as actually being old. (We'll leave the Madonna brand out of the conversation because at the age of 57/58 her brand truly is chronologically older.) The reason why the imperative to make "known-things-appear-new-again" through NPD is so pressing follows from a lesson taught by Neil Young. The old rocker sang: "Once a story's told it can't help but get old." Acute repositioning needs inevitably arise as the fans of formerly new products "age-out." Of course, all the while the formerly new product is concurrently aging. Father Time always bats last and he always hits 1000.

Second, cost reductions can be classified as NPD. Here, Firms develop newer but less expensive versions of current products.

Third, certain personal endeavors, such as repositioning or rebranding one's personal values, represent NPD efforts. When one purposefully adds new skills or experiences, improves skills or abilities one already possessed, or refrains from behaviors or activities that had detracted or distracted others from one professional's or personal value, NPD has transpired. Products have already been broadly described as "anything" that can be offered to a market for attention, acquisition, use or consumption that might satisfy a need or want (and presumably profit the marketer.) "Anything" includes products, services, ideas, places, or persons.

⟶ Invention vs. Innovation

Invention

Invention refers to an aspect of uniqueness and/or something that is new. Uniqueness is reflected in the unique form, formulation, or function of the new thing. "Form" captures what is actually new about a new product. Formulation relates to the uniqueness of how a new product will be made, or formulated. "Function" relates to what the presumed new product does; that is, the unique new value or solution provided by the new product. Inventions are often patentable.

The mere act of invention never profits or benefits anyone, at least in the short-run, until and unless the marketing inventor can find or create awareness of "problems" that some substantially-sized targeted market segment cares about that the invention can also solve. Markets consequently may view inventions with a collective blah, as in "so what? who cares?" We are not discounting the imperative that marketers face to invent new, presumably unique solutions. That need is perpetual. Nor are we devaluing the premise that marketers can often succeed big by inventing solutions and then selling problems to previously unsuspecting customer groups who, with a bit of invention, suddenly discover they cannot live with the innovation that eventually emerged from the invention. We are just pointing toward certain risks that inventors face.

Still, inventions sometimes fall into the unfortunate category of solutions desperately seeking problems to solve. The then new RFID technology or Radio Frequency Identification Devices could have been characterized in this manner during the early 2000s. That is, until Walmart discovered a way to leverage the new technology as a means to solve certain tracking-related problems that arose inside their supply chains, and then forced suppliers to adopt RFID. Today the RFID market is worth approximately $9 billion.

Time and again, the invention of new solutions creates new markets. Think about the myriad treatments for depression, i.e., the drugs produced by the marketers known as "Big Pharma", and the myriad diagnoses for depression that emerged (by the marketing psychiatrists), and thus the presumed depression-related problems and needs and subsequent marketplace demand for anti-depressants grew, seemingly overnight, beginning during 1997, amongst American consumers. The point: inventions may address either practical (genuine) or merely salable (perceptual) customer problems.

Innovation

Innovation refers to an overall process whereby inventions are transformed into commercial products that can be sold profitably. For this to happen innovations must be capable of delivering practical or perceptual value that benefits some targeted segment. The members of that targeted market must be willing to give up something of value, usually money, in order to obtain or use the innovation. For a new something, often an invention, to be called an innovation, the element also must be useful. There are more inventions than innovations. Three basic types of innovations exist (Exhibit 11.2). These were introduced earlier within the context of our classification for new products. They are examined again here:

Discontinuous Innovations

This category of innovation is radical in nature. Discontinuous innovations are new products that require customers to learn new things, acquire new experiences, and adapt their current consumption behaviors before they can be properly used. A tall order, this.

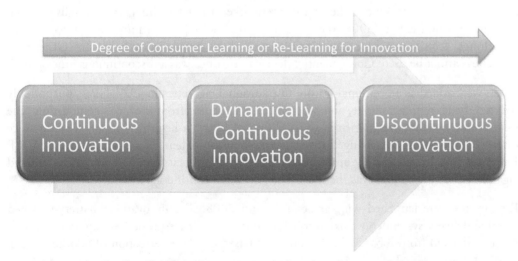

Exhibit 11.2 *The classification of innovations is based on how much consumer learning or relearning is involved.*

Genuinely discontinuous innovations are rather rare. All 50 new products used to introduce this chapter were discontinuous in nature; one might note, however, that the most recent of these products was the personal computer. The nearest precursor to the contemporary PC was introduced to the world during the 1970s.

Another classic example of discontinuous innovation, one that did not hit the nifty-fifty list, is the microwave oven. The microwave oven was available in the US marketplace for about 20 years before enough customers finally made enough personal accommodations to both their existing cooking and eating behaviors to permit sales to balloon.

Dynamically Continuous Innovations

This class of innovation generally arises when two or more concepts or product ideas are combined. But those ideas are combined in such a way that customers face gentle learning curves because they can still easily understand the new product and how it should be used. Now-classic examples of dynamically continuous innovations include the iPod, which moderately enhanced existing mp3 players and expanded Walkman-like technologies; hybrid cars such as Toyota's Prius; or flat-screen HD televisions, whose dynamically continuous value eclipsed the old technology's value at an amazing pace. Dynamically continuous innovations must deliver at least one significantly new benefit to the market.

Continuous Innovations

Continuous innovations include modest or ongoing upgrades of existing products, and include the lion's share of innovations. Continuous innovations do not fundamentally change customer behavior. Nor do they fundamentally change the dynamics of what marketers themselves are doing. Continuous innovations are based on the same idea, with minor tweaks or upgrades involved. Thus next year's Porsche 911, as compared to this year's model, is a continuous innovation.

Cigarette Break

Cigarettes can be used to illustrate the difference between discontinuous, continuously dynamic, and continuous innovations. These thin tubes of rolled paper contain finely-cut, carefully-cured tobacco leaves. The tubes are used to transmit a highly stimulating and addictive chemical into human bodies. This is both the value and benefit of cigarettes.

Sir Water Raleigh introduced the first cigarette-like product to his patron, English Queen Virginia, during the late 1500s. Then and now, the smoking act requires new users to learn new things, acquire new experiences, and adapt current consumption behaviors. Otherwise, cigarettes cannot be used. Consequently, the cigarette once was a discontinuous innovation.

Filters were added as an optional feature to traditional cigarettes in 1927. Filters purportedly reduced the level of tar, smoke, and other chemicals inhaled from tobacco's combustion. The oxymoronic benefit emerging from the addition of filters: a healthier smoke (a claim since disproven). Nothing else changed for smokers. Winston-Salem, North Carolina-based R.J. Reynolds, Inc., introduced the aptly named Winston brand as its first commercialized filtered cigarette. The only change was the filter. Winston was a continuous innovation.

E-cigarettes were launched with great fanfare in 2008. The innovation's battery-powered nicotine delivery system contains no tobacco. Instead, e-cigarettes deliver vapors laced with nicotine derived from tobacco. E-cigarettes are based on the intersection of two new ideas.

First, no actual tobacco (meaning no tar). Second, an e-delivery vapor-based chemical delivery system. The imputed benefit of e-cigarettes is that they help addicted smokers kick the regular cigarette habit. E-cigarettes are a dynamically continuous innovation.

Basis for Classifying Innovations

The classification of an innovation in one of these three categories depends upon two factors. First, how radically new and innovative the new product actually is. And second, the degree of learning and/or behavioral changes that must occur amongst targeted customers before they will be willing or able to adopt the innovation.

Inventions and Innovations Can Be Mothers

Invention and innovations are mothers of necessity. This means that the invention of something that is converted into something else new and useful (innovations) often creates presumed needs for the product. Who knew they needed a minivan before they saw one? Who needed mutual fund portfolios or cross-training shoes until each was available? Customers often don't know what they need in advance of their exposure to the new.

→ The Diffusion of Innovations

Diffusion, defined scientifically, entails the movement of atoms or particles—for simplicity's sake, objects—from areas of greater concentration to areas of lower concentration. Were a professor to open a large bottle of malodorous cologne at the front of your classroom, the aerated molecules would diffuse from the point of highest concentration; i.e. the top of the opened container, to the point of lowest concentration; i.e., the back of the room. This is how diffusion works in the physical world.

Diffusion, defined in marketing and NPD contexts, entails the rate of adoption—the rate at which the new product sells—of a new product throughout a particular market, population, nation, or global region. The adoption rate for any innovation is measured from the point at which the product is introduced to a new market, market segment, or social system to the point at which, theoretically, the last customer in the market, segment, or social system has learned about or adopted the new product for use. This process unfolds over time.

The adoption rate for innovations measures the velocity or speed at which new products, ideas, or technologies spread, or are adopted, throughout markets, market segments, or social systems. Naturally, not everyone in, say, a targeted segment adopts the innovation at the same time. Certain prospects within a given segment never adopt.

Customers and prospective customers have traditionally been classified into one of six categories based on the rate at which the new product is adopted (Exhibit 11.3). These adopter categories are:[2]

- *Innovators* (about 2.5%).

Innovators adopt innovations first. Customers in this category, on average, enjoy higher social status, are better informed and more knowledgeable about the innovation in question, possess the financial means to acquire the new item should they so desire, and are more willing to take more purchase or usage-related risks. Innovators possess myriad types of resources that permit them to recover from any losses that may arise due to the innovation's failure.

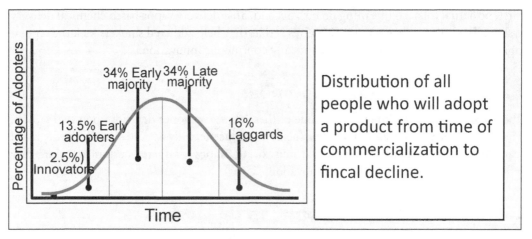

Exhibit 11.3 *The adopters of a new product are distributed along a normal distribution.*

- *Early Adopters* (about 13.5%).

Early Adopters are most likely to function as opinion leaders on behalf of the new products they purchased and/or use. (Note the purchaser and user may be different people). On average they enjoy high social status, are better educated, and possess greater financial resources in comparison to latter adopter categories. Early Adopters are, however, more judicious in their product choices than innovators. Early Adopters are extremely important to new product developers. Their propensity to evangelize favorably or unfavorably about their experiences with the innovation make them either a marketer's best friend or worst enemy. This category of adopters contains opinion leaders who readily pass on word-of-mouth about new products and can be instrumental in facilitating a new product's adoption and diffusion.

- *Early Majority* (about 34%).

While this group accepts the innovation earlier than some others, the Early Majority is likely to adopt the innovation much later than members of the initial two adopter categories. This segment enjoys above average social status. Members of the Early Majority likely know one or more Early Adopters. The Early Majority is much less likely to function as opinion leaders. Still, the Early Majority may influence some future adopters. Early Adopters, along with the next category, the Late Majority, comprise the mass market for the new product.

- *Late Majority* (about 34%).

We passed the hump and are sliding down the diffusion curve. The Late Majority is generally skeptical about various types of innovations. They are usually less well-off financially and lack social status. The Late Majority will exercise little, if any, opinion leadership. But given the comparative size of this cohort, Firms still attend carefully to the Late Majority as a significant proportion of the mass market for the new product.

- *Laggards* (about 16%).

Laggards "lag" meaning they adopt an innovation last. They value tradition more highly, are concurrently more satisfied and comfortable with how things are currently being done, and thus sense little reason exists to change. Laggards, in fact, may never adopt the innovation.

Compared to other adopter categories, laggards trend older, and lack financial resources and social status. But not always. This book's first author has been a laggard adopter or non-adopter of new technology his entire adult life. An e-book reader. Him? Not going to happen.

Not when the old book technology, once a great new innovation (see #1 on our List) itself, still delivers the differentiating benefits of never-breaking when dropped; having forever-battery lives; looking-great on shelves in the den or office library; and, in his perception, being easier to read.

→ Keys to New Product (Innovation) Success

New products will succeed or fail based on the degree to which they possess, demonstrate, or feature the following characteristics.

Relative Advantage over Existing Products

Unless they are brand-new-to-the-world products, innovations must supersede—at first replace and eventually exceed—the value of existing products in the minds of targeted segments. Tennis was introduced as a new product in England and France during the 1200s. By the 1500s the game had been widely adopted. The modern tennis racquet was introduced during the 1500s. The head (the striking area) of the original racquet maintained approximately the same size until 1976, even though the composition of racquets and their strings had evolved across the centuries.

In 1976 Prince Manufacturing, Inc. introduced the then-oversized Prince Classic tennis racquet. This racquet, along with other oversized branded racquets that quickly followed, featured a substantially larger sweet spot. The Prince Classic also provided players who were performing at all levels of proficiency, the immediate ability to hit balls faster and more accurately, as compared to the velocity and precision those players were previously able to generate with prior generations of racquets. The scale of the Classic's relative advantage over existing racquets was epic. The Prince Classic became the history's largest selling racquet, a record held to this day.

Comparatively Low Complexity

Complexity, in this context, is a reflection of the relative ease or difficulty associated with:

- Using the new product.
- Personally understanding the benefits and value delivered by the innovation once it's used.
- Communicating the value and benefits of the new product to others.

The Prince Classic was easy to use. The innovation was used; i.e., swung, exactly how prior racquets had been wielded. The only difference was a marked improvement in the Classic owner's ability to play tennis. Classic users, as well as competitors playing against Classic owners for the first time, clearly saw and experienced—one positively, the other player negatively—the new product's value. As far as communicating the value and benefits of the product to others, the Prince practically spoke for itself.

Compatibility

Compatible with what, obviously? Compatibility, in this context, with the existing ways in which tennis players were already using existing generations of tennis racquets; as well as with tennis players' existing attitudes, beliefs, likes or dislikes, and preferences. To the extent that tennis players, as noted, did not have to change any aspect of how they played the game, but instead simply played tennis better; and to the extent that tennis players valued winning (attitude-related), believed they were more likely to win when using the racquet (beliefs), and liked and preferred to win, which was demonstrably more likely once they had adopted the Classic, the new racquet was highly compatible.

Divisibility or Trialability

Divisibility, in this context, captures the ease with which new products can be tried out on a limited basis. Or take the Prince Classic tennis racquet out for a test drive. One author played tennis seriously during the 1970s. One day, after having been suffering a beat-down from a well-matched playing partner who had adopted the Prince, he asked if he could borrow his racquet and hit a few. Thereafter, game, set, match, as they say. A new Classic customer was born.

Other Factors Contributing to NPD Success

As you know, another highly effective but difficult to navigate pathway toward NPD success exists. The best way to create mega-successful innovations is to satisfy/solve hitherto unsatisfied needs/unresolved problems that customers did not realize they even had yet. Customers, that is, never knew they had a problem or need until after the opportunity for the solution suddenly arrived in their lives. Think anti-depressants or the iPod, as discussed during Chapter 1. Yet new product developers should check-off other boxes when seeking to elevate their prospects for success.

First, marketers should take all necessary and appropriate measures to ensure that only uniquely superior products are conceptualized, designed, produced, and actually delivered to pre-targeted markets. Otherwise, why bother developing anything that is new? The phrase "uniquely superior products" implies that Firms should only introduce new products to the market when they:

- Are truly higher in quality. Quality, defined earlier as "freedom from defects." Quality is important because it is directly proportional to efficiency; or …
- … Deliver legitimately superior features, attributes, benefits, solutions, and ultimately value to precisely targeted customer segments; or …
- … Are genuinely easier or less expensive to use.

In other words, Firms should develop new products that permit them to create either cost leadership-based, customer intimacy-based, or technological advantage-based differentiation. In fact, as discussed, the only three ways for any Firm to earn sustainable differentiation for its brand or product is through either cost leadership, greater customer intimacy, or technological advantage.

Second, marketers engaged in NPD should only deliver new products that are based on "well-defined-product/market-concepts." Product developers should only introduce new products to market when the innovations:

- Have been pre-targeted toward discernible, well-defined, and substantially sized and/or growing market segments.
- Deliver benefits that are different from those provided by other competitive products and that are also important to the customers in the targeted segment(s).

The benefits that will be delivered by the new product therefore can be described as determinant.

Third, new product developers should demonstrate a relentless commitment to achieve success despite the occasional inevitable failure and to engage in continuous, or ongoing, innovation. To successfully engage in NPD, Firms must understand competitors, customers, relevant marketing environmental conditions (trends, trends, and trends) and then develop new products that deliver exceptional value to new or existing customers.

Finally, as a prerequisite to innovative success, a formal and systematic NPD process should be established. This staged set of structured processes should permit new product concepts—ideas—to be discovered or created; then evaluated, retained or rejected; and, finally, once an idea is selected, "grown" into adulthood and eventually commercialized inside targeted segments.

→ How to Fail at NPD (Innovation)

Most NPD efforts fail. This prospect makes NPD successes all the sweeter and more profitable and underscores the challenging nature of the endeavor. New products, however, do not fail at the rates reported by many texts (reputedly up to 80-90%).

The failure rate for anything depends on how failure is defined. The fact is that many new products fail during the ideational stage (Stage 2); evaluation and screening of those new ideas (Stage 3); or prototype development and living plan stages (Stage 5). (Additional discussion about all six NPD stages follows.) In other words, most new products fail—are rejected—before actually entering the marketplace. Including such pre-market failures in the reporting drives up the overall NPD failure percentage. A more reasonable rate of failure, measured within one year of actual launch, is 40-50%.

Even so, more than half of new products fail within one year of launch, underscoring the need for this discussion. Prior results suggest that when the following factors are not accounted for or are addressed poorly, NPD failure rates rise substantially. Consequently Firms should pursue the following acts only if they are seeking to have their new products fail.

Overestimate Demand for the New Product

Pepsi Kona was a coffee cola that mixed the Kona Blend of coffee with the original Pepsi product. The highly carbonated drink tasted more like coffee than cola, and failed rather dramatically after it was introduced to market. The product's success prospects would have benefited from better marketing research. Pepsi Kona was test marketed only in one city: Philadelphia, PA. That was a mistake. Fact is, even if you have never been to Philadelphia you may know City of Brotherly Love's general citizenry, having famously thrown snowballs at Santa Claus during a Christmas parade, after merely booing him during prior parades, are not necessarily representative of the rest of the country.

Launch Products That Don't Deliver Sufficient Value

BlaK was another coffee-flavored soft drink that was introduced, and quickly pulled from the marketplace in 2006 by Pepsi's chief rival, Coca-Cola. The product failed to deliver sufficient value that differentiated it from existing products it was supposed to replace in customers' minds.[3]

Coca-Cola positioned the product as an energy drink that high school and college students could use to charge their study and exam-taking efforts. Red Bull never blinked as prospective BlaK customers brusquely rejected the low coffee-to-Cola ratio. The blended taste was less than appealing, while the excessive caffeine inured parents against serving the new product to younger children. Even the packaging was a dud. The thin, small (only eight-ounce), plastic-wrapped bottles further cheapened BlaK's image, degrading the overall perceived value of the new brand.

Launch Poorly Designed Products

Almost every technology-based product seems poorly designed when compared head-to-head with its Apple counterpart. Microsoft learned this lesson, the hard way, when it introduced Zune to counter Apple's smart devices. Apple products have always featured minimalist designs that simply work better. Microsoft's products, not so much. Zune was harshly criticized for technical problems that customers experienced as they used the product. Zune lacked an easily-accessible way to purchase and play music. Zune perished quickly.

Good new product design should solve customers' problems but also make them happy. This is challenging because they are so many customer personalities, needs, ideas, and options to evaluate. The best new product design is one that has been simplified to its most fundamental nature. The best new product designs also marry purpose with purpose in ways that communicate meaning. Easy to write; difficult to achieve.

Execute Marketing Mixes Poorly

Success, supposedly, has many mothers. Failure, of course, is an interminably sad orphan. While many scramble to grab credit for success, few will accept responsibility for failure.

The truth, actually, is when market mix strategies designed to launch new products fail, many mothers are probably responsible. Failure, at the marketing mix level, could result from deficiencies with the product itself (quality issues), promotion (the wrong messages, poor targeting), pricing (simply stated, too high or too low), and distribution (it cost too much to get the product to targeted market segments). Or some combination of two or three. Any one of these strategic shortfalls might lead to poorly positioned new products; insufficiently differentiated innovations; an inability to raise or lower prices or attract customers at current prices; a failure to successfully reach targeted markets at acceptable per unit costs; or some unholy alliance of one, two, or three of these innovation death-magnets.

Sometimes the most important element of the marketing mix, the product, simply sucks. Frito-Lay's fat-free, but olestra-laden WOW! Chips were extremely popular when first launched. Then suddenly the innovation died on Kroger's and Albertson's shelves. Products that cause persistent and uncontrollable anal leakage usually do.

Launch New Products Despite Disappointing Research

Products are sometimes ahead of their time. Apple's Newton MessagePad (get it, Isaac Newton, the physicist who discovered gravity when an Apple fell on his head) was the first tablet computer marketed to consumers. Actually it was called a "Personal Digital Assistant," or simply PDA, at the time. But the world simply was not ready for Newton in 1990, as marketing research had clearly indicated. While the same exact product concept became extraordinarily popular 15 years on, Apple failed to turn consumers on to the value of mobile computing at the time. Likely, the relative lack of Internet infrastructure at the time also doomed the Newton. This is actually a supply chain-based cause for the failure (Chapter 12).

Selling Dog Food Dogs Won't Eat

Most people enjoy or are at least okay with yogurt. Meanwhile everyone, presumably, assigns a high value to clean, shiny, healthy hair. Few people, however, were turned on by the prospect of rubbing Clairol's A Touch of Yogurt shampoo into their scalps. The new product was launched with large fanfare back in the 1970s. The product was launched in strategic (think, logical) response to a back-to-nature environmental trend that was driving shampoo product development at the time. Natural ingredients, including honey, various herbs, and fruits had recently been successfully integrated in other new shampoo products. But the jump into milk-based hair-care proved a bridge-too-far for parent company Procter & Gamble. P&G apparently had decided to leave no natural bridge unburned because, shockingly but true, the Firm had seen its Touch of Buttermilk shampoo crash and burn only three years earlier.

Most people repeatedly purchase the same approximately 150 or so products, which address 85-90% of their needs. Think how challenging things are for Firms as they struggle to get their new stuff on American consumers' radar. Even products that launch effectively often have trouble sustaining their success.

Targeting Segments Where Competitors Struck Back, Big-Time

You should have learned from Chapter 2 that when Firms choose a segment to target they also choose their dance partners, that is, their competitors. Firms should choose targets carefully.

The new product launch must have seemed like a good idea at the time. Samsung (who earned a 17.7% market share), Nokia (who earned a 5.8% share), Sony (1.6% share), I.G. (1.4%), Xiaomi (less than 1%), Huawei (less than 1%), and HTC (less than 1%) all must have thought that introducing new smart phones to the market during the 2014 Christmas season was a good idea. Apple, apparently, disagreed. Apple predictably entered "beast mode" and took the legs out under from each Firm's new product launch. The possible partial exception was Samsung. But even there, Samsung's new products were out-activated, i.e., outsold, by Apple phones by a nearly 3-1 ratio.

But competitors should compete, and NPD is unquestionably the best way to compete and grow market share, long-term. Consequently, we wish Apple's competitors the best, as well as Apple itself. Because in the end, consumers are the primary beneficiaries of their competitive struggles.

→ The NPD Process

Stage 1: Develop Tentative "Go-to-Market" Strategies

The initial goal during the NPD process (Exhibit 11.4) is to identify and to rank-order attractive market opportunities. During Stage 1, Firms should conduct SWOT and environmental analyses (as initially discussed during Chapters 2 and 3). One purpose of these analyses is to identify customer or prospect needs/problems that are not currently fully satisfied or resolved. Another purpose is to identify trending opportunities, threats, or competitive actions that would point the way toward product development opportunities.

Exhibit 11.4 *The New Product Development Process.*

Remember, "own the trend when it is your friend," just as Levi Strauss did when it introduced a new genre of men's pants, Dockers. The brand, of course, was a huge hit because Dockers was neither too dressy nor too casual but instead, just right. In fact, Dockers succeeded because they were positioned at the intersection of dressy and casual attire.

Once the most attractive and/or pressing opportunities are enumerated, they should be assigned a preliminary new product protocol. This protocol will generally guide future new product developmental efforts. The protocol summarizes the role the proposed new product could play in the Firm's existing product portfolio. The new product protocol also establishes tentative revenue, market share, and profitability goals for the new product. Finally, the protocol tentatively sets aside resources as should prove necessary to produce, promote, and distribute the new offering.

Stage 2: Develop Initial Concepts (Ideas)

New products are always born from new ideas or concepts. These new concepts, in turn, may have many different mothers, even though these ideas should also be associated with the insights and opportunities that were developed during the initial stage. Many more ideas should be cultivated at this stage than could ever be used. In fact, the large majority of ideas developed here will never be developed into prototypes, much less actually commercialized or brought to market. As many as 9 of 10 new-birthed ideas will be rejected during the next stage. Yet each concept should be created based on an initial assumption that each will help the Firm achieve the goals denoted during Stage 1.

This is the most important stage of any NPD process. Here, the presence or lack of "new product developer" creativity can make a literal life or death difference for the Firm. Various logical sources should be tapped routinely as places from which these ideas might originate.

Open-minded, forward-looking, growth-oriented firms should look toward competitor actions; employee and supply chain partner suggestions; related or unrelated research and development activities; customer suggestions and the general business press and blogosphere as viable sources of useful new concepts; as well as, of course, their own NPD teams or specialists.

Stage 3: Evaluate and Screen Initial Concepts

Stage 3 is where the concept tests mentioned earlier are executed. A logical, process-driven evaluation and screening effort should be undertaken. Concept tests essentially function as a "yes, this idea can go-forward to the next developmental stage/no, this idea must stop here" gateway. The purpose is to identify the one or two ideas, from an entire collection of concepts, that appear most likely to generate desirable new products. Desirable new products are those that can be successfully produced and subsequently priced, promoted and delivered in ways that will allow the Firm to achieve the goals outlined during Stage 1.

Ideas that fail to muster up during this stage are eliminated. Most ideas will be rejected for various reasons during this stage. Perhaps they are eliminated permanently. Yet some will likely be set aside for future reference. Managers may conclude that, while ideas are potentially viable, their time has not yet come. Apple likely reached this conclusion about the ideas that originally led to the Newton think-pad.

Questions to ask during the "go-forward/no-go-forward" concept testing stage might include: Will customers understand, care about and/or use the product that would be born from this product? How and why would customers use the new product? Do we have or could we reasonably acquire the resources including partnering supplier and distributor Firms that would prove necessary to produce and market this new product successfully?

Stage 4: Strategic Business Analysis

As if things were not already serious enough, the new product development game gets more serious still during this stage. The features, attributes, and benefits, along with the associated manufacturing and marketing costs associated with the proposed new product are now defined with great specificity. More detailed marketing strategies regarding how best to bring the new product to market, including designation of exactly which target markets to pursue, are developed during Stage 4.

During this stage, conclusive evidence should be developed about how well proposed new products fits strategically inside the Firm's current product portfolio. If they don't fit, they must go. Detailed financial projections associated with the product will also be concurrently prepared, or least nearly so. Again, product proposals that fail to measure up will be eliminated.

Stage 5: Move from Paper to Prototype

The first action-item during this stage is to develop a prototype. A prototype is a demonstrable and reproducible version of the actual product. Prototypes presumably one day soon will be produced either in mass or substantially greater numbers. Three-D printers are increasingly being used to develop prototypes.

A living or live marketing plan is also developed during this stage. Cost estimates become live budgets inside living marketing plans. Proposed manufacturing processes are transformed into functioning production facilitates (either owned by or partner to the NPD Firm). Marketing plans are fully "costed-out" as marketing mix activities aimed at creating new, or refocusing existing, positioning efforts are actively initiated. These marketing activities then are aggressively launched, employing genuine cross-functional teams, as (in the case of tangible products) designers, engineers and other organization members cope with the myriad of NPD issues and conflicts that must be addressed and navigated successfully.

Finally, the marketing commercialization test (test market), if required, is executed during this stage. These measurements and assessments of customer and prospective customer responses to the product and proposed marketing mix may or may not happen. The decision to test will generally depend based on the nature of the new product, characteristics of the relevant markets, and size of the Firm. When market tests are initiated, genuine products are exposed to actual or prospective customers under realistic market conditions. The purpose of test marketing is to determine whether customers will buy the new product and whether they will likely be unsatisfied, satisfied, or possibly delighted. Based on test results, new products might still be removed from further consideration, refined or sent out into the "brave new world" on an as-is basis.

You would be correct had you thought, gosh, lots of stuff is happening here. A three-headed set of semi-simultaneous actions unfolds during Stage 5.

Stage 6: "Taking It to the Street" (Commercialization)

"Takin' it to the Streets" was the title of a popular Doobie Brothers album. That's right, Doobie. As in joint, pot, weed, Mary Jane, reefer, hash, hemp or even marijuana's real name, cannabis. See how creative an entrepreneurial, new product-oriented language can become? But the original phrasing speaks directly to what must happen during this stage. The one-time baby product has grown up. The innovation has been nurtured and prepped long enough. Ready or not, now is the time to determine whether the new product can run on its own. Firms may roll out new products fast or slow; locally, regionally, or nationally; they may broadcast or narrowcast the fact a new sheriff has arrived. Whatever is done should be executed in accordance with the living marketing plan. But commercialize they must.

→ Managing the NPD Process

On average, successful new products create greater value for any organization than anything else that might reasonably happen—anything, that is, the Firm can also control. Firms can rightfully expect to gain most new market share and higher proportions of their overall sales revenues and profits from successful new products. Successful NPD offers most Firms their best opportunity to raise prices or sustain already premium prices.

The actual NPD process is difficult to manage successfully. This statement should not surprise. NPD is not an activity that people who are weak in spirit, will, or intellect can execute effectively. But if you can learn to manage and eventually master the NPD process your prospects are delightful indeed. You can expect to enjoy a challenging, emotionally-satisfying and financially-rewarding career.

The dual realities that the world has shrunk while globalization has expanded underscores why US managers must learn how to compete more effectively on a global stage. The surest road to this desirable destination runs right through NPD-land. US managers have no choice but to develop or sustain their ability to block foreign competitors who are routinely launching forays into their market space. Superior creativity, and concomitantly more successful new products are best ways to achieve this outcome, as well. The US auto industry would be much better off today had the former Big Four (i.e., General Motors, Ford, Chrysler, and American Motors) learned and applied these lessons several decades ago, going back to at least the

1970s. American consumers would absolutely purchase more new domestically manufactured automobiles if they believed those products delivered merely equivalent value to what many foreign automobiles provide. But too many domestic automobiles don't.

Orchestrating, Directing, Pushing Innovation

Today's world is full of extremely challenging problems. The low-hanging fruit, or easily solved problems, has all been picked. Most important challenges exceed the capabilities of any one individual to resolve. To solve the most pressing NPD problems, the combined expertise and views of people from diverse backgrounds who can bridge gaps between discrete points of view and skill-sets are required. NPD teams, rather than Han Solo lone-hero types, are usually required to generate and identify the best ideas that lead to the best new products. New product developers usually can either work together successfully as parts of functioning teams or fail by themselves.

But this diversity must be directed by someone. Successful new product developers (NPD leaders) must orchestrate the performance of teams. Diverse groups perform more effectively, but diverse groups are more difficult to manage and more challenging to work with because diverse views lead to more disagreement and conflict. Thus, while the results are better, people are less happy with the experience. Consider this as an acceptable loss. As Mary Follett Parker said in 1924, "contentious problems are best solved not by imposing a single point of view at the expense of all others, but by striving for a higher-order solution that integrates the diverse perspectives of all relevant constituents." This implies that if consensus is reached too quickly about how best to solve truly challenging NPD-related ideas, something is probably wrong.

New product innovation, like all innovation, consequently must be pushed. People who report to you or people to whom you report will rarely jump up and say, "I want to make exactly the sorts of changes that you recommend." Organizational roadblocks and "Debbie Downers" must be overcome; "Oh, thanks, but sorry, we don't do things that way around here." One way to gently move people toward the sorts of changes you are pushing is not just to list the shortfalls or opportunities you seek to correct or pursue (which are generally negative), but also to lay out the positive reasons why you want to make these changes.

Creating Art, Managing Science

As you have probably determined, successful NPD processes require more than a little "art." Perhaps surprisingly, however, effective NPD processes usually entail more management of "science" than the creation of "art."

Art supposedly creates more energy than was required to produce it. Artistic efforts, in any forum, are essentially grounded in intuition, emotions, hunches, or gut feelings. Risks must be taken.

Such qualities factor more heavily when NPD decision makers possess less experience or lack the proper tests and information on which to base their decisions. And the ability to be creative and think more creatively, accept manageable risks, and think outside one's comfort zones is hugely important to successful NPD. The normal person categorizes an object, and then forgets about it. The creative person, by contrast, is always open to new possibilities, looking beyond the normal categories to which objects have been assigned.

Science, by contrast, is empirically based or, alternately stated, empirically tested. The results derived from these tests support or invalidate (i.e., fail to support) certain relationships that are presumed to exist. Which of these three ideas should most reasonably be converted into a marketable product? How likely are consumers to "connect" with the solution that would result from this idea? Would our Firm have the resources to successfully deliver the proposed new product to our current target market?

Science is similarly based on established concepts; principles, laws and processes; and existing relationships between these concepts and those principles, laws and processes. Finally, as inferred, science is based on analysis of the results that emerge from those tests. "Empirical," in this context, means that NPD decision-makers collect information. Then that information is subjected to tests in order to factually, or empirically, answer questions about which new product idea should proceed to the next stage and which strategic or tactical actions should come next.

Art, artistic, and creative thinking is good, necessary, useful, and therefore appropriate at various stages during the NPD process. This statement applies especially to the second and third stages of the NPD process. But there is no denying that empirical testing and the adherence to accepted principles based on and derived from those tests should play the guiding role during the later stages of the NPD process. Bottom line: successful NPD demands greater mastery of science and tests than of art and creativity.

→ NPD Tests

NPD developers should never shy away from the value of or need for a good test. Three tests will likely prove integral to the success prospects of any NPD endeavor:

The Concept Test

NPD processes, indeed all innovative endeavors, always must begin with an idea. These ideas are often called product concepts. The concept test is conducted to determine whether intended new product users are likely to either want or need the proposed product that would result were the idea carried through to its logical conclusion. The logical conclusion, in any NPD context, entails the actual development and commercialization of the new product that was based on an initial concept.

The concept test determines, at a core level, whether "the dogs are likely to eat the dog food." Imagine a situation where you owned a dog, loved your dog, and sought to do everything reasonable and possible to ensure that your dog lived a healthy, happy, and long life. Easy to imagine, right? Now imagine a dog food marketer develops a new product, one that if consumed promises, essentially guarantees, a healthier, happier, and longer life for Butch. If reasonably priced, you'd probably grab that new dog food right off the shelves and serve it to Butch. Great product launch, right? Congratulations all around. But what if Butch himself refuses to eat this new, healthier fare? The new product will fail is what will happen. It literally doesn't matter what the owner wants if the dog won't eat the new dog food. Had a concept test been conducted, this problem would have been uncovered before the product was launched.

The Product Use Test

The product use test is conducted to reveal whether the prototypical product, once developed, will actually satisfy the customer want or need that it is supposed to satisfy. Meaning, at a granular level:

- Will targeted customers likely understand the new product and the values it delivers?
- Will adoption of the new product generally prove comparatively easy or disruptive to prospective customers?
- Will targeted customers understand how to use the proposed item?

The Marketing Commercialization Test (Test Market)

The marketing commercialization test determines whether the Firm already possesses or could acquire the resources to create an effective marketing mix plan. The test similarly assesses whether the Firm has available the resources, including the experience and supply chain partners, that would prove critical to the Firm's ability to efficiently deliver and promote the new product within its intended target segment(s). The mechanisms by which test markets are conducted were examined earlier in Chapter 6.

Two Basic NPD Strategies

Two basic strategies exist through which Firms can acquire new products, as well as entrée to newly targeted customer segments. The first method entails an acquisition, or "buy" strategy. The second approach is through the NPD process itself, which represents a "make" strategy.

When they employ the acquisition strategy, Firms may acquire an entire company, whole, or more simply purchase the rights to a patent or license (the right) to produce another organization's product. As of this writing, Google has acquired more than 170 companies. To date the largest is Motorola Mobility. This mobile device manufacturer was purchased for $12.5 billion. Microsoft acquired, on average, more than 10 new companies (and their products) a year between 2005 and 2008. If Microsoft, acknowledged seemingly forever as a "creative leader," is acquiring new Firms and products at this rate, imagine how many Firms and products less creative firms must be purchasing or acquiring.

The new product development approach entails developing original products, product improvements, product modifications, and new brands through the Firm's internal efforts. Those efforts can ensue through direct research and development, technological sources, internal marketing sources, direct NPD teams, or outsourcing practices. At other times the same Firms might save money and presumably lower risk and effort by copying competitor's products. Not for nothing did the phrase "imitation is the sincerest form of flattery" enter the Western cultural lexicon.

During NPD marketers strive to create new things (products or services) that promise practical or perceptual value to targeted customers. Hopefully, the values delivered through new products that are created are perceived by targeted customers as different from and better than the value(s) currently delivered by competing products. Achieve this outcome, and the new product may thrive. Fail to achieve this outcome, the new product will likely fail.

From the start, however, new product developers don't exactly understand what those new products will end up being. After all, every product always begins just as an idea. This new idea might be convertible into a new product offering that delivers value that appeals to somebody; ideally a large and identifiable targeted segment.

With ideas, as illustrated below, one thing can lead to another, often in unpredictable ways. That's where creativity comes in; that's why creativity is so important. New product developers don't exactly understand what the new item will cost to make. Those professionals, obviously, still should some possess a sense of a rough budget that outlines what this process is going to cost. These marketers may not know exactly how the new things will be distributed or promoted or priced. Again, however, new product developers should develop a reasonable sense regarding how these marketing mix elements will be managed.

Long trails of experience and verifiable results demonstrate that three factors contribute materially to the new product developer's ability to execute NPD processes effectively: planning, execution, and creativity. The same evidence reveals that all great new products originate from exactly the same source. That source, specifically, is a great idea that began inside some creative person's head.

The adjective "creative" generally involves the human imagination, as well as the ability to derive original ideas, especially when producing some form of art. Creative people essentially see and experience the same things, stimuli, as everyone sees and experiences. Yet in business and marketing contexts creative professionals are best able to go beyond "what everyone else sees" to visualize and develop something new that also has value. Creative people are more likely to develop great ideas. Creative people are similarly more likely to succeed during a future in which the marketplace of ideas becomes increasingly globalized and competitive. Finally, and reassuringly, despite your possible thoughts to the contrary, everyone can be taught how to become more creative.

You must be willing to do the hard work and take the appropriate risks that will prove necessary for you to become more creative. Which is okay. As most serious people learn moving forward through their lives, the only place where Success arrives before Work is in the dictionary. The pain of any extra work you do is temporary. But the cost of "you may suck" if you don't could last forever.

→ Creativity: Reflected in the Long-Tailed Consequences of Ideas

Creativity is crucially important because when the subject turns to NPD and the requirement that the process begin with great ideas—one thing, one idea, one product leads to another.

When Johannes Gutenberg had the idea that a printing press would be a good thing (the all-time #1 new product), legions of people began reading now more widely accessible books. Suddenly, many readers realized they had a problem: farsightedness. Awareness of this problem facilitated creation of a solution. We now call this innovation eyeglasses. Remember, our fifth most important new product of all time (optical lens).

But as craftsmen worked more precisely with glass and lenses, the telescope soon followed. Along with microscopes. These two new products facilitated huge advances in other disciplines. Think, for example, astronomy (and Galileo, and the pivotal astronomical- and religious-altering idea that the Sun did not revolve around the Earth) or microbiology (germs and infections). Wow, germs; there's a genuine consumer problem. Have no fear, once the problem was known, the third (penicillin), nineth (sanitation systems), and 34th (pasteurization) most important innovations in history soon followed as new product solutions. Penicillin, discovered to kill germs. Sanitation, developed to remove germs. Pasteurization, created to prevent germs. Marvelous marketing solutions, all. Each new product was birthed by a single idea, the idea for germs, or was it the idea for microscopes, or the idea for printing books?

Relatedly, these increasingly efficient European glassworkers improved technologies that made superior mirrors possible. More effective, more broadly available mirrors allowed more people to see themselves clearly for the first time. Whoops, another consumer problem for some creative person to solve. As people examined themselves more carefully, did they become more introspective or more self-critical? Perhaps both. If so, the initial consequence may have fostered philosophical debate and progress. The second probably dented self-esteem? If so, greater numbers of more effective camouflaging products (cosmetics) probably emerged. Or not. And you know, if we really wanted to extend this exercise, we could reference the facts that all-time new products numbers 31 and 9 (photography and the Internet, respectively), indeed have fostered philosophical debate and new processes, as well as decreased self-esteem. Otherwise known as the Facebook Effect. Which is creating more problems still …

Truth be sold, this seemingly farfetched chain of ideas, events, consequences and newly developed products as solutions to newly arising problems is actually "near-fetched." After all, "One Thing Leads to Another," as the The Fixx once sang.

→ Creativity Is …

Creativity is the ability to produce things—most importantly, ideas—that are novel (original) and also useful or adaptive. Compared to their less creative counterparts, creative managers excel at recognizing relationships, creating new associations and connections, seeing things others don't see, and seeing those things in original ways. Creative people usually work harder than others, likely because they love their work and earn so much more money while doing it.

Creative people are often polymaths. Polymaths possess broadly intersectional interests across multiple disciplines. Creative people are generally more venturesome and exploratory; they are more willing to take risks. The work done by creative people usually unfolds at the frontiers of what is known. But when people work on the creative edge, they are likely to get cut and to fail. (What do we think about this? We think: the heck with the "cutting edge," go for broke, go for blood, strive to create the "bleeding edge.")

True creatives, however, persist despite failure, usually because they believe in themselves and in the value of what they do. Creative people are often autodidacts. Autodidacts teach themselves instead of letting others feed them. Consider the uber-successful college drop-outs named Gates, Jobs, and Zuckerberg, three wise men who technologically framed the modern age. Creative people, quoting Bob Dylan, "don't follow leaders."

Growing Creativity

The act of invention, which ideally facilitates innovation (new and useful products), always involves an act of recombination. The reason is because ideas have sex. And what happens when two or more fertile ideas have unprotected sex? That's right, a new idea, a baby, often results. What can you do to create situations in which two or more fresh and useful ideas relevant to the problem that is driving the actual need for NPD can be developed and recombined? Five steps should be pursued. Each step is based on prior research.[4] The order in which these creativity-enhancing activities are executed is important. Consequently, you should:

- Create intersections,
- Develop multiple perspectives,
- Lower associative barriers,
- Avoiding creativity-defeating traps, and
- Respond properly to failure …

…in your professional and personal lives. The meaning as well as the "how-to" of each step is discussed below.

Step 1: Creating Intersections

Professionals become professional only after having consciously cultivated their expertise in a specific discipline during an extended period of time. This is a wonderful thing, of course. Their specialized expertise, combined with experience, permits professionals to adroitly solve problems arising in their fields of expertise. Professionals are in demand.

Unfortunately, their specialized expertise and experience often degrades the professional's creativity. This is because professionals rarely live, operate, or discover at intersections. Instead, professionals generally remain ensconced in disciplinary silos where everyone else thinks pretty much the same way about similar problems.

Accountants, engineers, operational analysts, logisticians, HR managers, and marketers, for example, all work in the same business world. They confront similar problems. But this diverse group of professionals rarely "see" or experience the same problems in the same way. Nor are they likely to develop and propose the same solutions to those problems, which is actually a good thing, particularly when these diverse groups of professionals elect to come together and share their divergent thoughts and ideas at a place called the intersection.

The intersection exists as a hypothetical or real place. Intersections exist in any location where ideas emanating from different business functions or disciplines (i.e., different points of view) have the opportunity to crisscross, recombine, "have sex" and consequently engender new ideas. But intersections can also arise and exist perpetually inside your own mind.

When this happens, you will become more like the creative masters who breed waffles with doughnuts (creating wonuts); Italian with Jewish cuisine (creating pizza bagels); Mexican chili with German frankfurters (creating chili dogs); or peanut butter with chocolate (creating Reese's Peanut Butter Cups). Nothing like three fast food geniuses to discover exciting new ideas that led to new products that led to more Americans having trouble fitting into their airplane seats.

Or, more seriously but no less creatively, more like the architectural and entomological (insect scientists) professionals who jointly created ideas facilitating designs that permitted large Sub-Saharan African office buildings to remain cool even when the electricity to power their A/C units failed. Which is a problem that arises frequently, by the way. The secret sauce for their creative success was no secret at all: the intersection. An intersection was established where builders could integrate core architectural principles with new ideas that entomologists learned from studying how African termites construct ventilation tunnels throughout their huge mounds that permitted cooling air to circulate. A remarkable spate of creativity emerged when discrete professional teams operated, cooperated, and solved huge problems at the intersection that was created between entomology and architecture.

People who consciously pursue the next four steps should become more creative because they will create more intersections in their minds.

Step 2: Developing Multiple Perspectives

Firms that seek creativity, hopefully all of them, can create more creativity by developing diverse—or intersectional—teams. Such teams might feature accountants, logisticians, and marketers. Those teams might then be asked to create batches of ideas that could lead to new products that will solve a pressing customer problem.

But we're trying to make you the hero, here. Let's concentrate on you and your mind. How should you create intersections there?

The first step involves consciously developing multiple perspectives—introducing diverse ways of thinking about the issues or problems—inside your own mind over time. Once you own multiple perspectives in your mind, intersectional thinking becomes more natural and easier for you to execute, not as a leap of faith, but as one grounded in intersecting facts.

Our prescription for creating multiple perspective in your own mind is simple. But then again, the best new ideas usually are, as discussed below. We recommend that you:

- Read the *New York Times* and the *Wall Street Journal* or do something akin to this. These two publications operate in the same world and address the same problems/issues every day. Each publication also inevitably develops resoundingly opposing views regarding the next best step to pursue solutions to or, say, their interpretation of the causes of the problem being discussed. You can expect to mine great value from the multiplicity of views that this activity will manufacture for you. Because as Mean Green Eagles Eagle himself, Don Henley wrote: "There is your side, there is my side, and then there is the cold hard truth." Note that we could have written listen to National Public Radio and a nationally networked conservative Christian station, or watch Fox News and MSNBC. The same exact same multiple-perspective enhancing outcomes would result.

- Eat lunch and talk, as often as reasonable, with people who look nothing like you. The fact that they look nothing like you increases the likelihood that the people hail from different cultures from you, view the world as, and knows things that are, different from you. You can learn a great deal from them—and naturally them from you as well.

- Experience other sources offering new perspectives, as well. If you're a real-time or pastime jock, read about the history of fashion. How were apparel problems solved in the past? Or, if you're a female fashion maven, read a treatise on the history of violence.

- Travel. Especially to places where there are lots of other people who are like you won't be. Off-the-beaten-path, unusual types of destinations, far away from maddeningly similar touristy crowds are preferable. Once you're exposed to difficult sets of cultural values, you can more easily extricate yourself from overly narrow self-imposed perspectives.

Never be like the uber-liberal or conservative politician who supports diversity in everything except thinking. Yet if you actually adopt the right open-minded perspective while creating these diverse views, all the good developed during Step 1 may come to naught. Unless ... which leads us to the next creative "must-do."

Step 3: Lowering Your Associative Barriers

"Buying-into" the value of and "acting-based-upon" what you learn from the intersection is easier said than done. The primary reason is because your potential creativity is likely inhibited by associative barriers. Associative barriers are essentially guaranteed to arise in professionals' lives because they already know so much about what they know. Professionals already understand how to solve obvious problems in their own disciplines.

These bonds of association are entirely beneficial; they're what make professionals pros. But because human minds operate best through association, human beings usually follow the simplest path, the path that is least disruptive and easiest to navigate. This tendency is self-defeating when the need arises to develop the sorts of creative ideas that are necessary to solve disruptive customer problems. Disruptive problems require true creativity, or intersectional thinking, and are difficult to navigate, because no established path exists.

The best way to diminish the creativity-negating impact of your associative barriers is to remain perpetually aware of their existence and how the presence of associative barriers injures your creativity. This task should prove easier for you now that you know associative barriers exist. Three others ways to lower your associative barriers follow:

- Learn differently: Employ learning strategies that permit you to learn as many different concepts as possible without getting overly bound-up narrow-minded ways of thinking about, or judging, those new ideas.

- Reverse assumptions: Your perpetual task as creative marketers is to derive as many new and useful ideas as possible about how to develop NPD solutions that will satisfy customers. Invert the purpose of this task. Instead, temporarily assume your job is to develop as many new ideas about how to create outcomes that would dissatisfy customers. Then create forward by doing the reverse of these "wicked" ideas.

- Wear different hats: You are what you are until you consciously choose to be someone else. Assume you are a marketing professional who has been assigned responsibility for creating nine innovative ideas that are intended to facilitate solutions for a particularly challenging problem. Now, adopt the mindset that an accountant, philosopher, or Lt. Colonel in the US Marine Corps would adopt were s/he charged with the same responsibility. Then create the requested ideas. Congratulations, you just switched perspectives; you also temporarily defeated your associative barriers.

Step 4: Avoiding Creativity-Defeating Traps

Too many professionals never succeed on large scales or stages, creatively or otherwise, for one of the worst reasons possible. Simply stated, they were afraid to try. The reason people are afraid to try is because the prospect of failure weighs so heavily upon them.[5] Human beings are wired to hate losing more than they love to win. Consequently they fear the prospect of failing by venturing too far forward creatively, which is an entirely voluntary misfortune. Don't be this person. In today's world you must rationally measure the prospects of acceptable risk against the prospects of success. For reasons already described, average levels of creativity will not ensure success in the world you are entering.

Stepping out and stepping up are challenging. People prefer the value of certainty. People are demonstrably willing to sacrifice the prospects of future creativity-engendered success to achieve more certainly now. What about you? As discussed, people assign more weight—more negative value, if you want—to the prospect of loss than to the prospect of gain. You? Truly creative people must take measured risks, particularly the risk of having their ideas eventually fail more often than not, in order to generate enough ideas for one to succeed.

The idea about innovation as a structured process has been taken to an extreme. Professionals who long for large success must be willing to take measured risks. Perhaps you can figure out a way to love winning more than you hate losing. Perhaps you can learn this to the degree that you become super-motivated to win. Fundamentally, this implies you won't become more creative by always remaining part of a strictly defined process. But you can become more creative by caring enough about the creative process and creativity to keep thinking about how to solve complicated problems better until you find the simplest possible way to solve them.

Step 5: Responding Properly to Failure (Fail Early, Fail Often)

Failure is no stranger to any business endeavor. Every Firm keeps doing what works until it no longer works or, in other words, fails. Winston Churchill wrote "Success often entails the willingness to go from failure to failure without loss of enthusiasm." The great man was not writing about NPD and creativity. But he could have been.

When the subject is becoming more creative, commit yourself to failing early and often, because few of the new ideas you develop will succeed to the point of actual transformation into new products. When striving to grow the quality of your creativity, remember: quantity of ideas is key to the eventual quality of any ideas eventually selected to progress through the NPD process. Thomas Edison, the inventor who eventually created the new and useful innovation known as the light bulb, failed more than 1000 times to invent a functioning bulb. Undaunted, he reportedly replied (paraphrasing) "I have not failed. Instead I have learned 1000+ ways to not make the light bulb."

To be creative one should divorce oneself from self-consciousness. One must take risks, including the risk of potential failure and embarrassment. But without question, one cannot fail one's way to success. Nor is there doubt, however, that those who succeed the most failed and often failed big-time at various points along their paths to success. But they surely learned something useful from most if not all of their failures.

Kemmons Wilson was the entrepreneurial founder of the once innovative *motel*. There had been *hotels* and *notels* (places you wouldn't tell anyone you'd slept in) for hundreds of years. But Wilson invented the innovation now called motels. "Mo" as in "motor" or attached to places of hospitality, places where travelers knew one could reliability and safely stay overnight during longer 1950s and 1960s automobile trips made possible by the innovation known as the US interstate highway system. Again, we see how one innovation leads to another. The motel chain (another innovation) he launched was called Holiday Inn. Decades after his initial success, Mr. Wilson was invited to present at a prominent university about business success and failure. A skeptical student stood up and asked (paraphrasing), "Mr. Wilson, how can you profess to teach us about failure. Look at how successful you are." To which Mr. Wilson replied (paraphrasing): "Young man, I have undoubtedly failed more than you have even tried." People usually learn more from aspiring or ambitious failures than from modest successes. What Wilson knew, and you should learn, is that one must develop new ideas and try new things or get passed by those who do. But you should fail in situations only where failure is not fatal.

→ Walking Further Down the Creative Path

If you are serious about becoming more creative, you should also engage more routinely in the following user-friendly behaviors.

"Capturing" for Yourself

Capturing require that you non-judgmentally preserve any new ideas whenever and wherever they happen to occur. Perhaps that is when you are exercising or talking to a friend. Goodness knows, in a "smart-phone world" many easy ways exist to capture new ideas. There are many other ways to capture new ideas.

Otto Loewi won a Nobel Prize for work based on an idea about cellular biology that he almost failed to capture. He had the idea in his sleep, woke up, and scribbled the idea on a pad. But the next morning he discovered that he could neither read his notes nor remember the idea. When the idea turned up in his dreams the following night, he used a better capturing technique: he put on his pants and went straight to his lab! Lucky man, in terms of the idea reappearing in his dreams; smart man, given that he took action right away.

Another story, perhaps anecdotal, applies. This one is about the professor who used to take power naps in his office. While thinking deep thoughts about profound problems, as professors do, he would hold keys in his hand with his hand hanging off the office couch as he was falling asleep. When he fell asleep the keys would fall from his hand, and wake him up. He would then immediately write down the last thought he could recall. He did so based on the now proven assumption sometimes our best creative thinking may occur in the intersection between consciousness and unconsciousness. We'll leave it up to you to determine whether the story is true. But the point to be taken is the value of capturing.

"Challenging" Yourself

To become more creative, you should lean-in-toward rather than away-from the challenge of taking on the task of solving the toughest, most important or most pressing problems. Marketers are, after all, problem-solvers. Almost by definition, then, the most creative marketers would be those who voluntarily seek out the most challenging problems to solve. Multiple behaviors, conflicting multiple thoughts, compete with one another in the midst of intellectually challenging situations. These forced interconnections—think intersections—create new behaviors and lead to new ideas. Tough times breed tough people, right? Why shouldn't tough problems breed more creative people, too?

Consciously seeking challenging assignments, the sort that involve important problems, may confer other professional values to you—lagniappe, if you will. Volunteer for the toughest tasks, and you will probably get noticed by your superiors. Even if you fail or fail to succeed completely, which is likely with the toughest problems, you position yourself more positively with your superiors. People just entering the professional workplace should do this whenever the first opportunity arises.

"Broadening" Yourself

The act of broadening oneself, with creative intent, entails the choice to mindfully expose oneself to more intersections. And consequently, to more intersectional thinking. As one's base of knowledge broadens and becomes more diverse, one should be able to create more interesting, and potentially more useful, inter-connections. The takeaway: elevate your creativity by learning interesting new stuff.

This genre of learning, of course, may require burdensome activities such as traveling more to new places or actually reading real books and articles as opposed to reading and sending all-texts, all-the-time. Once this sort of prescribed broadening happens, you may find it easier to engage in mind-wandering: the tendency to follow interesting, unexpected offshoots of the main task at hand. Your social intelligence should also expand, as should your capacity for learning implicitly and switching back and forth between tasks. Once one has broadened, one should retain or develop the ability to remain disciplined but open-minded enough to see other possibilities and opportunities without the urge to reject them out of hand.

"Surrounding" Yourself

We preemptively acknowledge that "surrounding yourself" is akin to "broadening yourself." Nonetheless, you should surround yourself with people, new ideas, and things that force you to step up your game; that is to say, to change or upgrade the quality of your thinking on a continuous, going-forward basis. This will require that you consciously manage your physical and social environments. The more interesting and diverse are the things and the people around you, the more interesting your consequent ideas should become.

Although we realize on one has complete control over this, choose your closest friends and professional associates the best you can. Why? Because, nine times out of ten, if you will show us your friends we can show you your future. Choose carefully.

We referenced tennis and tennis racquets earlier. You probably now know more about distant and recent tennis racquet history than anyone you know. There is one more thing you probably already knew about tennis: your game never improves when you play against people who are worse than you. Translating that tennis lesson to the creativity game: your creativity is unlikely to improve if you play with people who know less than you or you know the same things as you.

"Einstein-ing" Yourself

Albert Einstein knew creativity. He said: "You cannot solve problems by using the same sort of thinking that created them" [in the first place]. So, with a tip of the hat, the Apple, and 1984, "Think Different" from how you used to think.

Earlier in this book, we wrote: Often it is not what you don't know, but rather what you think you know for certain that gets you into trouble. Consequently, our final counsel related to how best to grow your creativity is to loosen your grip on [your] certainties to expand the range of possibilities. Watch what you think.

→ How to Identify the Best Creative Ideas

The first rule of story-telling is "make me care." The rules by which teams can determine whether an idea is sufficiently creative are, when considered collectively, surprisingly similar. Five "creative criteria" through which great new NPD ideas, or for that matter, great stories, follow:[6]

Simplicity

Ask: Is the idea simple enough to lead to a new product that customers will understand?

Simple new product ideas improve existing products or lead to the development of new products by revealing new solutions to old or new problems. Simple ideas should be easy for marketers to explain. They should be easy for customers to understand. Eyeglasses that permit people to read or watch TV while lying flat on their back; in-wall ironing boards that double as mirrors, or dustbins that allow sweepers to scrape all the dirt off the broom are each based on simple ideas.

Overly complex ideas are the NPD coward's way out. Being complicated is actually easy. True experts, by contrast, can explain complicated ideas in a simple fashion. Experts have the ability to coalesce complicated concepts into a few simple themes. In a marketplace of ideas, simplicity's virtue usually makes it the most desirable choice.

Unfortunately, achieving simplicity in an ideational context is not simple. Simple ideas should honor three principles. First, the ability to empathize by perceiving customers' needs and expectations as they relate to the idea. Second, the idea and any product emanating from the new concept should be distilled down to its essence—the most fundamental substance— and core value. Third, the core value of the idea should be sharpened to the point where the resulting product becomes easier for customers to understand or use.

In Retrospect

Ask: Does the idea appear obvious now that it has been created?

Why did it take so long for marketers to discover the idea that led them to design desks one could use while standing up (for health's sake)? Expert designers suggest, essentially as doctrine, if designs do not appear obvious in retrospect, get worried. Then consider starting over. Were he alive, Chief Apple Designer Steve Jobs would surely agree.

Seemingly Out of the Blue

Ask: Is the idea unexpected?

One could pretty much guarantee ideas will be more unexpected to the extent that they arrive from unexpected sources. PepsiCo, who owns Frito-Lay, asked Frito-Lay's new product development team to cut the salt in some new products while retaining the salty taste that salty snack consumers crave. The NPD team discovered the idea that led to new products that solved this marketing problem from osteoporosis (think human bones) researchers. Those medical researchers had created nanoparticles by smashing calcium into tiny pieces and re-growing them into eatable particles that tasted sodium-like, or salty.

This type of unexpected sourcing is actually quite common. Proctor & Gamble developers recently created an idea for reducing wrinkles in clothes taken right of the dryer by sourcing a polymer idea invented by a European computer chip expert.

Credibility

Ask: Is the idea credible?

The best explanation of the notion that ideas should be credible or believable is this: if the creator or creative team still believes in the problem-solving and commercial potential of the idea 72 hours after it was developed, then the new idea is probably credible. The reason why exemplification of credibility is a bit more difficult is due to the fact that every successful product has had, at one time, a credible idea at its root and point of origin.

But hang in there if you believe in the idea's value even as the critics criticize. Criticism frequently leads to more new ideas because it forces people to fully engage with the work (and ideas) of others. Criticism is also natural and should be expected. The German philosopher Arthur Schopenhauer wrote that all new (most substantial) ideas pass through three stages. First, the idea is ridiculed. Then it encounters outrage. Finally, the truth of the idea is acknowledged to have been obvious all along.

Walking in Their Shoes

Ask: Will current or prospective consumers "feel" an empathic connection with the idea and products emanating from it?

An empathic connection with consumers is crucially important because its presence will lessen the gap between the firm that is developing new products and those who buy or use them. The most effective ideas are those that permit customers to connect most closely with the resulting product or more closely with each other as a result of the product. Ask Apple, if you have a need for evidence.

To enhance the prospects that such empathic connections can be made, solicit and secure the right sort of feedback from intended or actual customers. Then actually listen. The act of listening, by the way, delivers all manner of non-coincidental relational benefits to listeners. The simple act of really, truly, actually, totally listening, as in listening without formulating your next response in your mind, listening with open mind and heart, listening without prejudice or bias, is one of the surest ways possible to demonstrate regard, respect, and even love for the speaker. Once speakers realize this is happening, and they will, all manner of affirming value will flow back toward the "listener." That value may arrive quickly, perhaps it arrives over time, but you may rest assured that it will arrive.

Endnotes

[1] James Fallows, "The Fifty Greatest Inventions since the Wheel," *The Atlantic*, November 2013, 56-68.

[2] Everitt Rogers, *Diffusion of Innovations, 5th Edition* (New York: Simon and Schuster, 2002).

[3] Steve Tanner, "Discontinued: Coca-Cola BlaK," *BevReview*, August 31, 2007, accessed April 13, 2015, http://www.bevreview.com/2007/08/31/discontinued-coca-cola-blak.

[4] Frans Johansson, *The Medici Effect* (Cambridge: Harvard Business School Publishing, 2006).

[5] Daniel Kahneman and Amos Tversky, "Prospect Theory: An Analysis of Decision under Risk," *Econometrica* 47 (2): 263.

[6] Chip Health and Dan Heath, *Made to Stick: Why Some Ideas Survive and Others Die* (New York: Random House, 2007).

CHAPTER 12 — BRANDS AND BRAND MANAGEMENT

→ What's in a Name?

The first rule of storytelling is "make me care." Successful brands exist as part of narratives—stories—that confer differentiating meaning to distinct systems of benefits that are purportedly delivered by the branded product. Successful brands "make customers care" about the product. This represents a huge win for any marketer.

Brands help customers. As part of the Firm's product strategy, branding helps customers identify specific products produced and sold by particular Firms. The branding act, successfully executed, permits consumers to associate positive and negative expectations with specific products. Without branding, consumers could not easily compare products, one against the others. Customer decision-making processes would then become more time-consuming and difficult for many products. A brand on a product (or its label, packaging, storefront, etc.) tells consumers what to expect from the product. A brand evokes meanings and associations that assist consumers as they evaluate a product's value. Established or trusted brands offer "insurance policies" that lowers risks otherwise might be associated with purchase.

Brands benefit marketers. Well-managed brands permit Firms to develop customer loyalty and raise or perpetuate higher prices. Successful brands make it easier for marketers to introduce new products. This is especially true when potential customers already trust or like the Firm due to prior positive experiences with its existing brands. Well-managed brands provide formidable barriers against successful imitation. They make it difficult for competitors to copy or dissipate the stronger brand's competitive advantage.

→ The Meaning of Brand

The definition of "brand" has evolved and is always evolving. The term brand was originally used to designate the owner of horses and cattle. Think about any branding scene you have seen in cowboy movies or television shows and you've got it. The purpose for which branding was initiated then—to identify a cow as belonging to one rancher and not another—is a primary reason why branding is used today. Is that sweater made (marketed) by Merona or DKNY?

The term **brand** was traditionally defined as a names, word, design, symbol, or other characteristic such as color or shape that identified one marketer's product, service, person, place, or idea as distinctly different from those being offered by other marketers. The meaning of "brand" is, in this sense, now what we refer to as **brand identifiers**.

Brands are now viewed as **psychological constructs** that exist in consumers' minds. The **brand** is assumed to capture all the meanings, images, sensations, experiences, and other content that customers associate with products or services offered by specific Firms. Or the meanings, images, sensations, experiences, and other content that consumers associate with a person, place, or idea.

Consider Coke as a classic example. What synapses fire up in your mind when you think of the brand "Coke?" Some may simply think "sugary soft-drink" and nothing more. But others may associate Coke with warm feelings grounded in pleasant past consumption experiences and/or occasions involving friends, family, or fun. The failure of New Coke, introduced to replace existing Coke, can be traced to a failure of marketing research to uncover the added associations that defined the brand "Coke" for many consumers. Coca-Cola, Inc., quickly brought back old Coke under the new name Coke Classic once this horrific mistake was recognized.[1]

Exhibit 12.1 expands our earlier view of product levels, extending the original terminology to capture this modern view of brand. The "core brand values" are the benefits, utilities, and values delivered by the brand as a member of its respective product category. The "physical brand" and "**extended brand**" are the branded equivalents of the physical and extended product, respectively. No surprise here. The primary difference occurs with the addition of a fourth branding layer—the "extended brand." This brand captures the various meanings, associations, usage experiences, emotions, and other associations consumers consciously or subconsciously attach to brands.

Exhibit 12.2 provides an alternative way of viewing the brand concept. A hypothetical **brand schema** for Apple's iPhone 6 is shown. This depiction represents the complex network of associations or "nodal concepts" that may pop into mind for iPhone 6 owners. Each oval or block in the schema represents an association. In turn, these associations are interlinked in complex networks in which triggering one concept can activate others. Nodes closest to the central node of "iPhone" are most likely to be activated first. These nodes are more closely and most strongly linked to the "brand."[2]

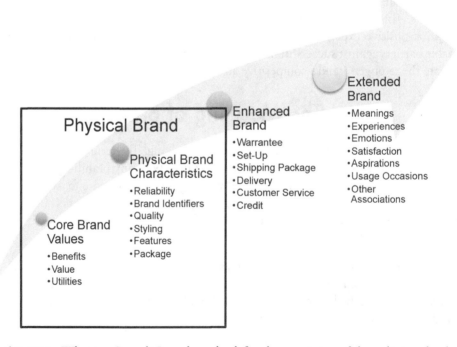

Exhibit 12.1 *What is a Brand? Brand can be defined as consisting of three distinct levels.*

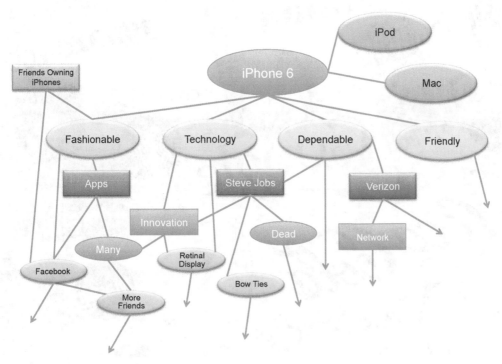

Exhibit 12.2 *A Hypothetical Brand Schema for the iPhone 6.*

The marketing manager's task is to create the meanings and solidify the associations in this schema that are most consistent with the Firm's desired position for its brand. Creating and managing associations for elements of the physical and enhanced brands are easiest. Management can most easily shape the meaning (nodes) and associations (linkages) of these inner-most levels of brand. The mechanism by which these are created and managed is, of course, the marketing mix. In contrast, structuring nodal linkages reflecting the extended brand are more problematic. Marketers can employ various forms of promotion, mainly advertising, to associate the brand with consumption occasions and positive emotions. But, ultimately, the associations at the level of the extended brand are defined by consumers themselves.

→ Brand Identifiers

As noted, brands have been historically defined in terms of **brand identifiers**. Brand identifiers uniquely identify the product or products (services) made by given Firms from those made by their competitors. Brand identifiers are anything that make it possible to distinguish the specific products or services owned by a particular Firm. Brand identifiers include brand names, logotypes (or logo), brand marks, trademarks, service marks, trade characters, and slogans.

A **brand name** is that part of a brand that is spoken or verbalized. Think of the brand name as "what you hear." For example, when you speak the name "Coke," you are verbalizing a brand name. Or, when you say "Levi's," you are using a brand name.

Logotype is the distinctive way the lettering is employed to spell the brand name. The colloquial for logotype is the term "logo." The distinctive ways in which Coca-Cola, Google, Twitter, Facebook, and Yahoo! are written uniquely identify the products or services offered by each Firm (Exhibit 12.3).

Exhibit 12.3 *Brand marks comprise the entire graphic brand identifier. The logo is a component of this graphic.*

A **brand mark** is the total visual component of a brand. Brand marks include the logotype, if distinctive lettering is employed to spell the brand name (also Exhibit 12.3). Brand marks (and logos) must occasionally be upgraded as consumers' tastes change. The Apple brand mark, for example, has experienced multiple changes since the brand's inception in the 1980s. The first brand mark for Apple boasted Isaac Newton seated under an apple tree. More recent variants of the Apple brand mark are contained in Exhibit 12.4.

Trademark. A trademark is any aspect of brand (i.e. brand name, brand mark, logo, slogan, etc.) that has been registered with the US Patent Office. Trademarks are legally protected. This means the trademark owner has legal recourse if another Firm attempts to copy any registered components of the brand. Slogans and jingles also can be trademarked. BIC's familiar slogans "writes first time, every time®," and "flick your BIC®" are trademarked. Registered trademarked brands or brand identifiers are usually acknowledged with the symbol "®." The symbol "TM" is also commonly employed to represent brands for which trademark protection has been applied for but not yet granted.

Trademark status even provides protection against other Firms using similar, but not identical, names. For example, Coors successfully sued a soft-drink manufacturer for trademark infringement when it employed the name *Corrs* on its drinks. The logotype *Corrs*, as well as the brand name, were very similar to those owned by Coors.[3] Similarly, Federal Express legally pursued a grocery store with a coffee cart named "Federal Espresso" due to name similarities.[4]

Firms can be very protective of their brands! And rightly so; strong brands possess substantial value and are enduring assets that can be reported on balance sheets. This value, referred to as **brand equity,** can be used to generate substantial additional revenue from brand licensing arrangements and a variety of family branding strategies. More about brand equity below.

Exhibit 12.4 *The Apple brand mark has evolved substantially over the years in response to changes in consumer preferences and styles.*

Exhibit 12.5 *The Pillsbury Doughboy is one of the most recognized trade characters of all time.*

A **Service Mark** is a trademark applied to services. *World Gym*, *Jiffy Lube*, and *Terminix* are registered service marks. Service marks can be legally protected in precisely the same fashion as trademarks. Slogans and jingles associated with service marks also can be trademarked. United Airlines' slogan, "Fly the friendly skies …" is trademarked.

Trade Characters are special cases of brand marks. Trade characters can be anything from cartoon characters (Geico Insurance and the Gecko) to real people (Progressive Insurance and Flo). Just as with any brand mark, the trade character uniquely identifies the brand it represents. The Pillsbury Doughboy is an all-time memorable trade character (Exhibit 12.5). The Doughboy appears in virtually all Pillsbury ads. Like the Pillsbury Doughboy, Speedy Alka-Seltzer ranks near the top of the memorable trade characters list. Speedy Alka-Seltzer was originally known as Sparky, but the name was changed by a sales manager, Perry L. Shupert, to reflect that year's promotional theme, "Speedy Relief." The Speedy Alka-Seltzer character was created in 1951. The original working model was six inches tall and appeared in more than 200 commercials over a 10-year period from 1954–1964.[5]

The Michelin Man Trade character (Exhibit 12.6), like most enduring trade characters, has been periodically updated to reflect changing consumer tastes and fashions. Changes are made gradually, so that no single change is especially noticeable. Trade characters may disappear only to be resurrected down the road. The Jolly Green Giant trade character was recently called back to active duty after a long hiatus. The Green Giant's personality has also been updated; the Firm's stated goal was to elevate the "giant from protector of the land" to a more accessible "cheerleader for every child in the quest for vegetables."[6]

Because they facilitate **iconic rote lear**ning—think back to Chapter 7 (Consumer Behavior)—for low involvement products, trade characters have been extensively employed to represent brands. The preceding examples sample some more successful trade characters seen in the mass media across decades. Most Firms that have developed successful trade characters show them off in their on-line "museums." Regardless, the aforementioned trade characters have long since taken their place in American culture.

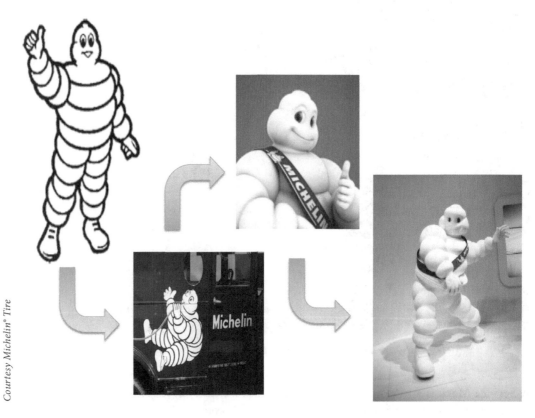

Courtesy Michelin® Tire

Exhibit 12.6 *The Michelin man has been around since 1898 and has gone through a number make-overs.*

→ The Generic Use of Brand Names

Generic brand names are names used to describe entire product categories. Typically, generic brands originated as trademarked brands owned by specific companies. However, over time, consumers began to equate the brand name with the product category as a whole. The generic brand names Nylon, Kerosene, Escalator, Cellophane, Thermos, and Aspirin (originally a Bayer trademark) were once the names of specific trademarked brands. Because the Firms that owned these names promoted them so well, consumers referred to all brands in their respective product categories by the Firm's trademarked name. The Firms that owned the generic brand names marketed so effectively that they purchased "ownership" of the word in the collective mind of targeted markets.

Brands that are probably becoming "generic" include Vaseline and Kleenex, among others. How often have you needed a tissue and said "I need a Kleenex?" Or, you need petroleum jelly and have said "I need some Vaseline?" Most people equate these brands with their entire product categories. The Firms owning these brands are concerned the courts may designate them "generic." If this happens, any marketer can then use the same name on their own products.

Firms employ various strategies to prevent their brands from becoming "generic" in use. The first, most obvious step is to trademark the brand. This action would provide some measure of legal protection but would not guarantee the safety of the brand. For extra protection, many Firms combine their brand name with the name of the product category in all marketing communications. For example, Kleenex is identified as "Kleenex brand facial tissue," Vaseline as "Vaseline brand petroleum jelly," or Rollerblade as "Rollerblade brand in-line skates." This strategy constantly reinforces the truth as well as the perception that each unique product is a specific brand within its respective product category; the brand is not synonymous with the entire category.[7]

A corresponding strategy is to develop and deliver advertising that specifically reminds consumers of the brand's trademark status. Xerox and Rollerblade have advertised that their brands are trademarked and should not be confused with the product category as a whole. Xerox's ad—"You can't Xerox a Xerox on a Xerox"—was intended to make just this point. The ad goes on to clarify the headline, emphasizing that they "don't mind at all if you make a copy on a Xerox copier," explaining that Xerox is just one brand of copier.

Google now uses a similar strategy. Google has issued strong warnings to media organizations directing that its trademark is not to be used as a verb. You can no longer say "Google it," or the equivalent. Rather, Google prefers that its trademark always be used as a noun; e.g. "Do an Internet search using Google."[8] Popsicle, a Unilever brand, emphasizes on its website that Popsicle is "POPSICLE® is a registered trademark …. and is NOT a name for just any frozen pop on a stick."

Finally, Firms might leverage their legal right to sue Firms infringing on their trademarks or engaging in activities that encourage consumers to use their brand names generically. For example, for years restaurants would serve Pepsi, RC Cola, and other cola brands to customers who asked for a "Coke." The brand name Coke was deemed by consumers as being synonymous with colas in general. In fear of losing its trademark protection, Coke filed suit against numerous restaurant chains to force servers to specifically state the brands that are available when customers ask for a "Coke," but Coke is not available. For example, a server might be required to say "We don't have Coke. Will Pepsi be OK?" The resulting debate developed quite a cult following.

These sorts of proactively-defensive, brand-protecting strategies make sense, by the way. Kleenex, Vaseline, Rollerblade, Google, and Popsicle, for example, should not be punished simply for doing marketing well. Or for, as a consequence, securing huge amounts of brand equity, market share, marketing power and pricing power for themselves and their brands.

Types of Brands

Brands can be owned by manufacturers, middlemen (i.e., in this context, intermediaries or retailers). Most brands have traditionally been owned by the product's manufacturer. Such brands are called **national brands** (older terminology), **manufacturer's brands**, or **producer's brands**. The brands Pillsbury and Green Giant (owned by General Mills) are producers' brands. Pillsbury and General Mills market their products under their own brands (Exhibit 12.7). Similarly, Black & Decker (power tools and small appliances) (Exhibit 12.8), and General Electric (larger appliances) are brands that are owned and supported by the manufacturers of these products. Notably, every General Electric product features the same GE brand. This makes sense, for reasons explained below.

Distributors' brands are owned and promoted by middlemen. Usually, this means a large grocery retailer such as HEB (Exhibit 12.9), Jewel, Kroger's, or Albertson's. Or, the brand is owned by big-box general merchandise discounters such as Target, Walmart, or K-Mart. Distributor's brands are also called **private labels**, **middlemen's brands**, and **store brands**. Middlemen have their brands produced to specifications by other manufacturers. Manufacturers then place the middleman's brand label on the product. Distributors' brands are becoming increasingly popular because they provide distinct advantages to middlemen and offer greater value to consumers. More than 20% of consumer packaged goods sold in 2013 were private label brands.[9] Private labels accounted for $112 billion out of $643 billion in total retail sales in 2013. Aldi, Save-a-Lot, Wegman's, HEB, and Kroger round out the top five in private label sales in the supermarket sector.[10]

Can: © Thinglass/Shutterstock.com;
Cake: © LunaseeStudios/Shutterstock.com

Exhibit 12.7 *Green Giant and Pillsbury are both producer's brands. Both Firms market their products under their own brands.*

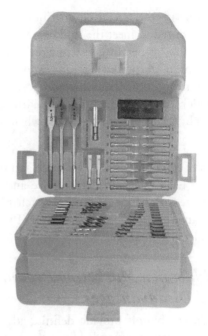

© Jeffrey B. Banke/Shutterstock.com

Exhibit 12.8 *Black & Decker produces lines of power tools and small appliances under its own brand.*

© Warren Price Photography/Shutterstock.com

Exhibit 12.9 *HEB is a major supermarket chain in the South with its own private label brands.*

The growth in the popularity of private labels is illustrated by private label colas. Private label soft drinks capture more than 15% of the total soft drink market. Sam's Choice, a Walmart private label manufactured by Cott Beverages, is promoted as comparable in quality to national brands, such as Coke and Pepsi, but at a substantial savings. Walmart suggests Sam's Choice branded products provide greater value to customers. An independent taste test sponsored by the *Wall Street Journal* confirms that private label colas taste about the same as national brands. Most consumers fail to notice any differences.[11]

Generic products can be distributor's brands. Like standard distributor's brands, generics are produced to meet the middleman's specifications. But their label is very plain, as in "not distinctive," generally consisting only of white labels with simple black lettering that provides the name of the product category and any other information required by law. Generic products today are most prevalent in pharmaceuticals. Generic drugs provide excellent alternatives with superior value to many branded pharmaceuticals. Indeed, most health insurance plans prefer that physicians prescribe generics whenever possible.

Generic products are increasingly being displaced by private labels as distributors add more lines of store brands at lower price and quality points. Target, for example, has three private labels. Each reflects different price and quality levels. Target's premier label, positioned to compete with national brands, is Archer Farms. Market Pantry and Up & Up are its mid- and low-range private labels, respectively. The Up & Up brand is essentially positioned equivalently to older generic products.

Middlemen Marketing Producer's Brands: Advantages and Disadvantages

Producer's brands provide definite advantages to the middlemen that sell them. Because these products are branded by their producers, most responsibility for promoting the brand is assumed by the manufacturer. Generally, manufacturers will spend heavily on advertising in mass media to stimulate consumer demand for their brands, referred to as "pull" promotion.

Producers also will provide promotional support to their distributors. For example, sales personnel may provide merchandising assistance to retailers in the form of free-standing displays and other **point-of-sale** materials, along with their assistance in setting up the displays. **Promotional allowances** also may be offered to partially offset the costs of advertising the producer's brand in local media.

The producer's brand is essentially pre-sold to consumers because of this "pull strategy." Moreover, the extensive promotional support provided by producers translates into stronger brand preferences and higher turnover rates for producers' brands on retail shelves. Although middlemen's margins (profits per unit) are generally lower for producer's brands, their higher turnover rates generally compensate for lower unit margins. The net is higher overall profits. The lower margins earned by middlemen selling producer's brands result from the higher costs incurred by producers for the packaging, promotion, and distribution required to support the marketing of their own brands.

Producers often seek to control, to the extent possible, how their brands are marketed at the retail level. These producers seek to control the images for their brands. Producers may insist on prime retail shelf and display space, demand that retailers participate in their sales promotions, and mandate that distributors promote their brands in local media. Large consumer goods producers, such as P&G, possess considerable power over middlemen due to strong consumer demand for its brands. This often makes it possible for such producers to pressure retailers into doing things their way, or risk having the manufacturer's products removed from the store. If the product is actually withdrawn, the retailer obviously loses sales for that brand. More importantly, the retailer may risk losing some customers who prefer P&G brands. Would you take this chance if you were the retailer?

Middlemen Marketing Their Own Brands: Advantages and Disadvantages

Middlemen are increasingly opting to stock their own brands. The consumption of private label products is growing across virtually all retail sectors. The reasons for their popularity are readily apparent. For starters, private labels generally provide more value to consumers. Private label brands are comparable in quality to national brands, but can be purchased at lower prices. This translates into greater value. As a result, today's value-conscious consumers are turning to private labels in greater numbers. Although national brands still enjoy higher turnover rates than do private labels, private labels are rapidly closing the gap.

Middlemen generally earn higher unit margins on their own brands, even though these brands are sold at lower prices than comparable national brands. There are two reasons why:

- First, private labels are produced to middleman specifications. Depending on the quality-level specified, the cost of ingredients and packaging materials may be lower for private labels.

- Second, and more importantly, private labels are not promoted as extensively as national brands. This creates costs savings that can be passed on to consumers in the form of lower prices.

Middlemen enjoy substantial freedom in terms of how their own brands are produced and marketed. Decisions about specifications and which producers actually make their brands are solely the middleman's responsibility. But middlemen must ensure that quality standards in their own brands are met. To receive the lowest possible prices from producers of their private labels, middlemen also must purchase in large quantities. If the resulting inventory fails to sell, losses may be substantial. An important point is that middlemen must bear substantial risks when stocking and selling their own brands.

Middlemen have sole responsibility for how private label brands are merchandised, priced, and promoted. Middlemen control all aspects of the marketing mixes for these brands. Of course the costs of advertising and other promotional activities are borne solely by these middlemen. This is only natural; higher levels of marketing control are inevitably associated with higher costs. The upside: no producer looks over the middleman's shoulder and exerts pressure to market the products in specific ways.

Middlemen may gain such a degree of "market control" from selling their own brands that greater loyalty to the store-brand results as consumer preferences emerge for their private labels. If consumers, for example, prefer the values delivered through Kroger brands, they must visit Kroger's to acquire the products.

Who Produces Middlemen Brands?

Middlemen contract or source the production of their private label products to outside producers. Many such producers exist solely to make middlemen's brands. Private label manufacturers generally fall into four categories:[12]

- Producers of national brands who execute contracts for private labels even though the store brands may compete side-by-side with their own national brands on the retail shelf. National brand producers understand they will lose some in-house brand sales in the process. But they also know that if they don't producce the private label products, another Firm will. Many national brands producers have excess capacity that can be absorbed through private label production. Manufacturer's incentives to keep production lines operating and personnel employed are essentially ubiquitous.

- Smaller manufacturers who generally specialize in precise product lines. These producers focus almost exclusively on producing private labels. The smaller Firms may be owned by larger producers who also make national brands.

- Major retailers and wholesalers who maintain their own production facilities dedicated to producing private label products for their own Firms. Tara Foods in Georgia is a private label manufacturer of peanut butter and other food extracts. Tara is owned and operated by Kroger. But Tara also produces private labels for retail grocery chains such as Albertson's, Safeway, and Jewel.

- Producers of regional brands may produce private label products for specific markets. These producers are similar to larger national brand producers in that they also exploit their expertise and excess capacity to increase production by contracting to produce private labels.

→ Brand Equity

Popular brands enjoy extra value and power because of the meanings that customers assign to them. The images or personalities of brands provide value beyond that attached to the more concrete or routine benefits offered by these brands. This added value is called **brand equity**.

Brand equity can defined as the extent to which customers are willing to pay more for this particular branded product as opposed to another branded product from the same product category. The power developed for and now associated with a specific brand provides the basis for brand equity. Brand equity's power is developed throughout skillful management of the marketing mix, and can emerge quickly (as occurred with Google or Facebook) or may take considerable time, even decades (as happened with Coca-Cola, in Japan, or Hyundai, in the United States).

When products or services earn brand equity, the propensity of customers to think first about the specific brand when encountering problems for which a known product category can provide a solution is high. When Firms earn brand equity for one or more products those products generally enjoy top-of-the-mind-awareness. Brand equity "captures" consumers' entire sets of perceptions and feelings about a product and its performance. These collective perceptions and feelings are typically favorable.

Some brands are worth far more than others. For example, as of this writing, the most valuable brand in the world is Google, which is valued at around $159 billion, closely followed by Apple at $148 billion.[13] Until 2009, the annually published lists of most valuable brands were generally dominated by traditional producers including Coca-Cola, IBM, Microsoft, GE, and McDonalds.

Marketers exploit the market power and pricing power of brand equity to boost profits in several ways. Brand equity:

- Can be used by the Firm to help launch new products. The Firm can employ one or more of family branding strategies such as **line extending**, **brand extending**, and **co-branding**, all to be discussed in subsequent sections of this chapter.

- Can be leveraged by licensing use of the Firm's brand to other Firms. A strong brand can be licensed to boost revenues, as Coke and Harley-Davidson have recently done.

- Permits Firms to charge higher prices or avoid having to lower their prices.

- Helps Firms attain and sustain greater market share, stimulate earlier trial, and invoke more favorable word of mouth.

- Develop more efficient communication programs (because customers are more responsive to advertising and promotional efforts initiated in support of well-differentiated brands).
- Helps Firms command greater customer loyalty and distribution power; meaning, at net, other Firms want to work with them in the supply chain.

→ Strategies for Branding Product Lines

Two fundamental branding strategies exist through which Firms can expand existing product lines. The first is called **family branding**. The second is known as **multiple branding**.

Family Branding

Family branding occurs when all or part of a Firm's product mix carries the same brand. The most common family branding strategies are corporate family branding and product line family branding. **Corporate family brands** exist when most items in the Firm's product mix are given the same family brand. In most applications, the family brand name is the company's **trade name**. Kraft, Heinz, Hunt, and Honda use the company's trade name as the brand name for most of their products. Additional descriptive wording is added to the trade name to inform customers of the specific type of product. For example, Kraft identifies the type of food product on the label immediately below the Kraft trade name (Exhibit 12.10). Similarly, the Pillsbury brand mark along with a descriptive name for the type of product is displayed on its packages (Exhibit 12.11).

An alternative to corporate family branding is assigning each product item its own brand, while also associating the brand directly with the corporate trade name by prominently displaying each brand on the package. General Mills and Kellogg's each use this approach. General Mills employs individual brands for its cereal products and links each brand to the company trade name on the package. The General Mills "G" adorns every package. Kellogg's similarly links its trade name with each individual brand, such as with its Rice Krispies and Special K cereals (Exhibit 12.12). The net effect is the same. The common images associated with General Mills' and Kellogg's trade names "rubs-off" on each of their products.

Cheese: © Steve Cukrov/Shutterstock.com;
Sauce: © Barry Blackburn/Shutterstock.com;
Mayo: © Barry Blackburn/Shutterstock.com

Exhibit 12.10 *The Kraft trade name appears on most products as part of its corporate family branding strategy.*

Exhibit 12.11 *The Pillsbury trade name appears on most of its products as part of its corporate family branding strategy.*

Exhibit 12.12 *The Kellogg's trade name appears on most products as part of its corporate family branding strategy.*

Product line family branding, as the name implies, occurs when the Firm uses different family brands for different product lines within its overall product mix. Sears uses this branding strategy. Sears' entire line of major appliances is given the Kenmore brand, the Firm's tools are sold under the Craftsman family brand, while Sears' exterior paints are identified by Weatherbeater family brand.

Advantages of Family Branding

Family branding offers distinct advantages when new products are launched. First, a known family brand creates immediate awareness for new products displaying the brand. Based on their knowledge or experience with the brand, consumers know what to expect from these new products. This awareness increases the likelihood of trial and adoption for continued use. Second, when the family branding strategy is employed, the new product entrant will not require the same level of promotional effort and expenditure as would new products introduced under new, unique, and consequently unknown brands. The new product has already been "promoted" to some degree because of prior promotions of other products under the family brand.

Family branding also provides greater shelf exposure for the family brand in total. Because multiple products all carry the same brand, consumers are exposed to the brand that much more as they scan retail shelves while shopping. This situation should engender greater top-of-mind awareness, easier "brand recall," and a higher propensity for **brand switching** within the family brand, rather than to competing brands.

Disadvantages of Family Branding

There are, of course, some disadvantages to family branding. First, the Firm may introduce a poor product under the family brand. Depending on how "bad" the new product is, negative feedback about other products bearing the family brand may spill over. We expect good images associated with the family brand to stimulate sales of new products. Correspondingly, bad images of new products may hurt sales for existing products. The Friskies family brand of pet foods is an extensive line produced by Carnation. Carnation once considered introducing a contraceptive dog food. Two brand names were considered: "Lady Friskies" and "Extra Care." Both were rejected and the new product was never commercialized. Carnation was afraid that sales of existing Friskies products would be hurt if the new dog food was not well received by consumers.[14]

The most serious limitation associated with family branding is probably that the new product may not fit the current family brand's image. Consumers may not think that it is logical or reasonable for the family brand to appear on the new product. This issue is called "perceptual fit." New family branded products possessing higher degrees of perceptual fit with the family brand are more likely to succeed. For example, what happens when you think of Goodyear? Should Goodyear use its family brand on a personal computer? Would that make sense? Likely not. The name Goodyear connotes blimps and/or rubber-products, particularly automobile tires, and automotive care. Goodyear's core areas of technological expertise are completely incompatible with those required to make personal computers. If dropped, would the computer bounce?

Consider Ben-Gay Aspirin? What is your image of Ben-Gay? Does this transfer favorably into what you would expect in an aspirin with the same name? Ben-Gay, produced by Pfizer, is a well-known brand associated with externally applied medications formulated to relieve muscle and arthritis-related pains. The product takes the form of a thick cream, arrives in squeeze-type packages, and boasts a definite and prominent smell. When applied, there is a distinct "heating" sensation as the medication takes effect.

Pfizer thought consumers would welcome Ben-Gay aspirin. Pfizer reasoned that Ben-Gay's pain-reliever image would smooth the path toward a successful new product launch. Consumers did not agree. Additional images associated with Ben-Gay (smell, how applied, heating action, etc.) probably caused them to question how well the aspirin would taste, smell, and work.[15] The new product failed.

Multiple Branding

Multiple branding is essentially the opposite of family branding. When employing this strategy, each product item in the Firm's mix receives its own, unique brand name. In contrast to family branding, there is little common imagery across products produced by the same Firm. Each brand consequently lives or dies on its own.

Individual branding is a sound strategy for Firms featuring large, diverse product mixes, particularly when individual product items vary in quality and functionality. Here, a family brand strategy would likely actually backfire. Because products possess different images due to their differing levels of quality and types of functionality, family branding may result in muddled or confused images of the company's values and expertise and what one might expect from a given product. P&G employs the multiple branding strategy over its extensive and varied product mix. The product mix includes a wide range of lines. Each line contains multiple product items. P&G's laundry detergent line, for example, contains ten brands: Tide, Bold, Bounce, Cheer, Downy, Dreft, Era, Gain, Ivory Snow, and Oxydol.

Advantages of Multiple Branding

Many Firms believe the *advantages* of multiple branding outweigh its disadvantages. The strategy eliminates the potential that confused images of the company and its products might arise amongst targeted segment. Multiple branding strategies simultaneously lower the probability that deficient or bad products will harm sales of other items in the product mix.

Multiple branding allows the Firm to exploit the presence of market segments. P&G targets different detergent brands to slightly different market segments. This targeting strategy permits P&G to pursue the entire detergent market. This outcome would prove more difficult if family branding were employed.

Firms like P&G also realize their products are essentially low involvement in nature. This condition creates situations where customers have a tendency to "variety-seek" between alternative brands. Most people, after all, enjoy trying something new and different once in a while. P&G provides consumers with multiple variety seeking alternatives in each of its product lines. The company prefers customers to variety-seek amongst its own brands, rather than switch to competitors' brands.

Disadvantages of Multiple Branding

The *disadvantages* of multiple branding are essentially the same as the advantages of family branding. New products are more difficult and more expensive to introduce under multiple branding strategies. The reason is that each brand possesses its own name and consequently must be promoted separately. The costs associated with creating awareness, interest, trial, and repeat purchase for each new product are higher than when family branding is employed. Scale economies of marketing are nearly nonexistent.

Finally, the introduction of a new brand likely will **cannibalize** some sales from the Firm's other similar brands. When P&G introduces a new laundry detergent, some sales will be cannibalized from other detergents. Cannibalization, however, is not necessarily bad. Major problems arise only when overall profits across all brands in the product line decrease as a result.

→ Strategies for Branding New Products

New product branding strategies fall into two categories: Those strategies employed to lengthen existing product lines and those designed to expand the width of the product mix.

Product Line Extensions

Product line extensions, also called **line extensions**, are new products introduced into a product line in which the producer already has product representation. Product line extensions are always *family branded*. Line extensions, therefore, are a special case of family branding. Each new cola introduced by Coke and Pepsi (both family brands) are simple variations (new taste sensations) of existing products. Coke and Pepsi routinely use line extensions to expand their brand portfolios (Exhibit 12.13). The high degree of similarity in characteristics and function, along with use of the same brand, make these brands product line extensions. When General Mills (an example of corporate family branding used earlier) and Kellogg's add new breakfast cereals into their existing lines, they are adding line extensions.

Product Line Flanker Branding

Flanker brands are a special case of multiple branding in which new products are added to an existing product line using different brand names. This is the strategy discussed above for P&G when new products (brands of laundry detergent) are added to its existing line of detergents. The advantages of flanker branding are exactly the same as discussed for multiple branding.

Exhibit 12.13 *Both Coke and Pepsi employ family branding to introduce new products in their respective lines.*

Product Category Extensions

New product introductions that are launched into different product categories (i.e. those in which the Firm does not currently have representation) are called **product category extensions** (or **category extensions**). The distinction between product line and product category extensions can be illustrated through Black & Decker's product mix. Whenever Black & Decker introduces new power tools into its existing power tool product line (e.g. a circular saw, or an electric screwdriver), it introduces line extensions. By contrast, when Black & Decker introduced its first small appliance (i.e.. the Black & Decker Coffee Maker), it engaged in product category extension using a family brand. However, subsequent introductions of new products into this new small appliance line would be considered *line extensions*. The distinction between the line and category extensions is illustrated in Exhibit 12.14.

Product category extensions may or may not be family branded. Black & Decker, as shown, employed family branding for category extensions. Procter & Gamble uses individual brands during most of its category extensions. Each new product introduced by P&G into new product categories as its **product mix width** grew and diversified was a product category extension. No family brands were employed.

Brand Extensions

A **brand extension** occurs when a new product is launched into a different product category (category extension) using the *family brand*. Brand extensions, therefore, are simply a product category extension that has employed the family brand.

BIC (Exhibit 12.15) exemplifies brand extension in action. A French company, BIC, introduced its first major product into US markets in 1959. This was the classic BIC pen. The memorable slogan "writes first time, every time" accompanied a massive promotion program. The pen was positioned based on reliability, low cost, and disposability. These benefits were driven home through some creative advertising. In an initial ad, the pen was placed into the barrel of a rifle and fired through a one-inch thick pine board. The pen-point went through the board and protruded on the opposite side. The barrel of the pen shattered, but the pen still wrote. This sent a strong image to viewers telling them what BIC stood for—very reliable, yet inexpensive and disposable.

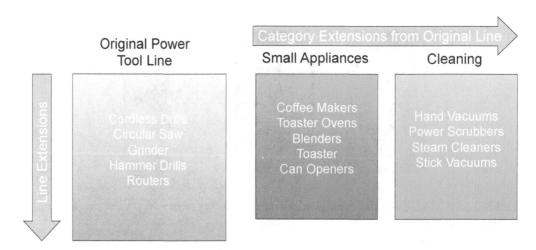

Exhibit 12.14 *Black & Decker Line and Category Extensions.*

Exhibit 12.15 *BiC was among the first Firm's to employ brand extension as a major growth strategy.*

Based on the success of the pen and image that was created, BIC launched a series of additional products under the family brand that it felt were consistent with this image. The BIC disposable lighters and disposable razors were the most successful.

GladWare is a brand extension based on the "Glad" family brand. The parent brand: GladBags. Glad's decision to brand extend into food storage containers appears logical. The Firm's reputation with bags provides an image base on which the new product could be introduced. Arm & Hammer employs brand extension as a mainstay of its overall growth strategy. Based on the reputation of its original baking soda brand, Arm & Hammer has extended into multiple lines of personal care and household products. Tupperware extended into toys (Tupper Toys). Then there is Apple. Apple has successfully brand-extended from its original computer lines into iPods, iPads, and iPhones.

Brand extension is the single-most used strategy for introducing new products.[16] The benefits to the Firm for employing a brand extension strategy should be obvious at this point: the same set of benefits accruing from family branding are in play. The Firm leverages an existing brand reputation (image) to reduce the risks and costs of new product introduction. Consumers' perceptions of the degree to which the new product "fits with" the parent brand's existing image are the best predictor of success when new brand extensions are launched.

Some brand extensions are quite successful; others are not. Prospects for success generally pivot based on the degree to which the brand extension possesses "perceptual fit" with the parent brand. The biggest risk in brand extending, therefore, is that no "family branding-effect" will result. In other words, there may be low perceptual fit and consequent image transference. Selling the new product under the existing family brand simply does not make sense to consumers. Previously discussed examples that illustrate the consequences of poor fit include Ben-Gay Aspirin and Gerber Singles. There are other examples of failed brand extensions:

- Dr. Pepper (soft drink) extending to a "Dr. Pepper Marinade" for beef.
- Zippo (cigarette lighters) extending to "Zippo The Woman" perfume.
- Arizona (the beverage) introducing "Arizona Nachos 'n' Cheese Dip."
- Smith & Wesson (firearms) launching Smith & Wesson Apparel.
- Samsonite (luggage) introducing "The Samsonite Outerwear Collection" line of clothing.[17]

Brand extensions are more likely to work when perceptual fit is high. The following examples illustrate conditions in which perceptual fit was high:

- The brand extension offers the same product in a different form, such as Starburst Jellybeans and Jell-O Pudding Pops.
- The new brand extension complements the original or parent product. The fact that Crest 3D White Toothpaste introduced 3D White pre-brush mouthwash and 3D White whitening strips makes sense.
- Brand extensions targeted to virtually the same target market (customer franchise) are more likely to be perceived as beneficial because customers already are familiar with the brand. Tupper Toys are targeted to the same consumers (moms) who buy Tupperware. Do you think moms who use Tupperware would perceive a high degree of perceptual fit with Tupper Toys?
- When brand extensions capitalize on distinctive ingredients (Arm & Hammer's baking soda) or tastes (Snickers Ice Cream bars) customers are more likely to "get the fit."
- Brand extensions that build on defined expertise associated with the parent brand will more likely succeed. Canon's reputation for superior optics (cameras) helped it launch copy machines. Similarly, Endust's reputation for fighting dust helped its electronic duster succeed.
- Ivory soap has the image of purity (even though it floats only due to air in the mixture). This distinctive attribute or benefit has been used to successfully launch a range of additional Ivory products, including shampoo.
- Brand extension is a major strategy employed by manufacturers of designer labels. Designer images; i.e., Polo, Guess, Calvin Klein, Dior, Prada, etc. are routinely used to launch other products under their respective family brands.

→ Brand Licensing

On the surface **brand licensing** (also called **trademark licensing**) is a branding strategy that appears nearly identical to brand extension. However, the two strategies are distinctly different. With brand licensing, the brand's owner simply rents the name to another manufacturer in exchange for a licensing fee. Coke licenses its brand name to various manufacturers of other products such as clothing and watches. Harley-Davidson extensively licenses the values and appeals of the Harley brand. Harley appears on a range of products including clothes, novelty items, and motorcycle accessories. There are also lines of Harley-Davidson beer, men's and women's colognes, and cigarettes.

The success of brand licensing arrangements, similar to brand extensions, hinges on the degree to which the licensed brand perceptually fits the new product. If it makes sense to consumers that the new product should be branded with the licensed brand, the arrangement is more likely to succeed.

→ Co-Branding

A co-brand is a type of brand extension. Co-branding occurs when two Firms jointly place their brands on a new product. Both brands are prominently displayed on the package to promote the alliance to consumers. The underlying logic of co-branding is that each brand contributes unique and uniquely appealing "meaning" to the new product. Together, the co-branded item can generate an image and a level of expectations from the product that neither brand can deliver alone.

Co-branding originated in the credit card sector. Seems almost all major companies now offer a Visa or Mastercard. Co-branding more recently entered the consumer food marketplace as a low-risk way to expand Firms' product mixes. Many food-related co-brands are tied to brand licensing agreements. Frito-Lay licensed the use of Warner Brothers' Loony Tunes characters to promote the Dorito's brand. Jack Daniels licensed its bourbon brand name to TGI Fridays for a variety of menu items. Kellogg's licensed the Disney brand for use on its Mickey's Magix breakfast cereal when launched in 2002. Kellogg's has engaged in multiple co-branding arrangements to help launch new products. Kellogg's Healthy Choice cereal resulted from a licensing agreement. Kellogg's understood it lacked a strong position to leverage when it first attempted to enter the "healthy" cereal category. In response, Kellogg's licensed the Healthy Choice brand to help it leverage the new product into this market sector. The cereal was produced by Kellogg's.[18] Additional examples of co-branding include:

- Breitling and Bentley collaborated to produce a Breitling for Bentley watch priced in excess of $5,000 each.
- Aston-Martin collaborated with Nokia to produce the Nokia 8800 priced at $1,640.
- Pottery Barn colors, a paint line co-branded with Benjamin Moore.
- Betty Crocker Hershey's Ultimate Fudge cake.
- Lipsmackers, a co-branded lip balm between Dr. Pepper and Bonne Bell.
- Dairy Queen co-branded its Blizzard with the Girl Scout Tagalongs peanut butter cookies and, most recently, with the movie Jurassic World.
- Fiat co-branded with Barbie to create the Barbie 500 to celebrate Barbie's 50th birthday.
- Michael Jordon and Nike collaborated to introduce Air Jordans.
- Tiger Woods co-branded with Gatorade to introduce Tiger Gatorade.

The concept of perceptual fit is also important in predicting the success of co-branded products.[19] However, the relationship becomes more complex. Consider, for example, the Tiger Gatorade co-brand. For the co-brand to be successful, consumers must perceive a fit between Tiger Woods (the partner brand) and a sports drink and, equally important, to perceive a fit between Tiger Woods (the partner brand) and Gatorade (the host brand.) To the extent that consumers perceive there to be a high degree of perceptual fit on both dimensions, the co-brand (Tiger Gatorade) has a higher likelihood of succeeding. Of course, once Tiger Woods' out-of-bounds non-golfing activities were exposed in the media, most of his endorsement and co-branding relationships were dissolved.

→ Over-Branding

Over-branding is a form of co-branding that generally is used to gradually change a brand's name over time. The goal is to avoid customer confusion and potential lost sales as the name change occurs. For example, when the Chix line of baby products was purchased by Dundee Mills in 1977, over-branding was employed to gradually change the Chix brand to Dundee during a five-year-period. Gradual changes were made to the brand mark. The first change involved superimposing the text "by Dundee" on the existing Chix brand mark. The new text was small and placed below the Chix brand mark. The Dundee name was subordinated in the combined Chix brand mark. Chix still held the superordinate—the top—position. As time passed, however, the positions on the combined brand mark were reversed. Dundee assumed the superordinate position on the brand mark. The Chix logo was eventually removed entirely. These gradual changes were justified based on Dundee's desire to avoid confusion or loss of existing Chix customers with the brand name change.

A second example of over-branding is provided by Nestlé's acquisition of the Alpo dog food brand. Nestlé entered the pet care business with the purchase of Carnation in 1985. Carnation developed the Friskies brand in the United States in the 1930s, and subsequently expanded to select markets in Europe and Asia. When Nestlé acquired Alpo, over-branding was employed to integrate Alpo into the Friskies product mix. Nestlé had no desire to eliminate the Alpo brand. Instead, the objective was to communicate that Alpo was now a member of the Friskies family. To accomplish this objective, the Friskies brand mark was added to the top of Alpo brand mark (over-branded). More recently, with the acquisition of Ralston-Purina by Nestlé, the Friskies over-brand has been replaced with the Purina trade name, essentially turning it into a corporate family brand.

→ Developing Effective Brand Names

Brand names can help make or break products. No single trait exists that makes a brand name "good." Rather, there are a number of characteristics, any one or combination of which, can result in a good brand name, given the right circumstances. These characteristics include:

- The brand name should be easy to pronounce and remember such as Dell, Coke, and Bounty.
- The brand name should be short, distinctive, and unique, such as Exxon, Compaq, IBM, Texaco, and Alka-Seltzer.
- A good brand name might suggest positive images, feelings, or associations as do Joy Perfume, Outback Steak House, and Therma Silk.
- A good brand name should communicate key product benefits and functions such as. Quick Metal, Frigidaire, Endust, Zip Drive.
- Good brand names should avoid verbal traps. The names Exxon and Acura have no pre-existing cultural meanings and can be used globally with little danger of being associated with negative or taboo associations.

A Technique for Developing Brand Names

Building a good brand name often focuses on creating the name around the key benefits delivered by the product. One approach is to identify descriptive words and part words (called "morphemes") that characterize the product's key benefits. These words and/or part words then can be combined to uniquely identify the brand. This approach has been used to successfully brand Duracell, Compaq (computers), Acura, Panasonic, Volkswagen, and Quick Metal (industrial adhesive).

The Quick Metal example illustrates how the process works. First, the major benefits of the product to its industrial customers were listed: the adhesive's strength, reliability, and ease of use. Based on these key benefits, descriptive words were identified that communicated or implied these benefits: durable, strong, metal, dependable, lasting, tested, simple, quick, and fast. Next, part words (morphemes) consistent with these adjectives were brainstormed: Dura, Stren, Meta, Depen, Las, Tes, Simp, Quik, and Fas. The brand name finally chosen was "Quick Metal."[20] This change in brand name was, in part, credited with boosting the product's sales from $320,000 to over $2,220,000.[21]

Endnotes

[1] Robert F. Hartley, *Marketing Mistakes 6th ed.*, (Hoboken, NJ.: John Wiley & Sons, 1995), 129–145.

[2] Semantic networks are the basis of much research into the meaning of brand. See for example, Michael Collins and Elizabeth Loftus, "A Spreading-Activation Theory of Semantic Processing," *Psychological Review* 82(6) (1975): 407–42.

Deborah Roedder-John, Barbara Loken, and Christopher Joiner, "The Negative Impact of Extensions: Can Flagship Products Be Diluted," *Journal of Marketing*, 62 (January 1998): 19–32.

[3] Bill Barnhart and Sally Saville Hodge, "Corr's Makes A Splash In Chocolate-drink War," Chicago Tribune, June 24, 1985, http://articles.chicagotribune.com/1985-06-24/business/8502100566_1_soft-drinks-beverage-digest-saturn-plant.

[4] United States Court of Appeals, Second Circuit, "FEDERAL EXPRESS CORPORATION v. FEDERAL ESPRESSO INC" (January 5, 2000), accessed February 26, 2015, http://caselaw.findlaw.com/us-2nd-circuit/1153856.html#sthash.6zs1ETMt.dpuf.

[5] http://www.alkaseltzer.ie/en/about-speedy/.

[6] Mike Hughlett, "Jolly Green Giant Goes Back to Work," *Star Tribune* (September 18, 2012), accessed February 27, 2015, http://www.startribune.com/business/170275366.html?refer=y.

[7] Kathy Rheintgen, "Branding 101: Proper Use of a Trademark—It's All In the Grammar," Healthcare Law Insights (May 24, 2003), accessed 27 February 2015, http://www.healthcarelawinsights.com/2013/05/24/branding-101-proper-use-of-a-trademark-its-all-in-the-grammar.

[8] Kravitz & Verna PLLC, "You Can't Google It. You Also Can't Xerox a Xerox, Still Generic Trademarks," November 4, 2013, accessed March 8, 2015, http://www.kravitzverna.com/trademark-law/you-cant-google-it-you-also-cant-xerox-a-xerox-still-generic-trademarks.

[9] *Private Label Manufacturer's Association*, accessed February 27, 2015, http://plma.com/storeBrands/marketprofile14a.html.

[10] Todd Hale, "How 10 Retailers are Pushing Private Label's Potential," Nielsen Newswire, March 11, 2014, accessed March 7, 2015, http://www.nielsen.com/us/en/insights/news/2014/how-10-retailers-are-pushing-private-labels-potential.html.

[11] E. Cherney, "After Flat Sales, Cott Challenges Pepsi, Coca-Cola," *Wall Street Journal*, (January 8, 2003): 81, 88.

[12] Private Label Manufacturer's Association, accessed March 8, 2015, http://plma.com.

[13] Millard Brown, "BrandZ Top 100 Global Brands," accessed March 8, 2015, http://www.millwardbrown.com/mb-global/brand-strategy/brand-equity/brandz.

[14] Irvin Molotsky, "Dog Food is Proposed, With a Secret Ingredient: Birth Control," *The New York Times*, (February 10, 1985), accessed March 7, 2015, http://www.nytimes.com/1985/02/10/us/dog-food-is-proposed-with-a-secret-ingredient-bith-control.html.

[15] Robert McMath, "Look Before You Leap," *Entrepreneur*, (April 1998), accessed March 7, 2015, http://www.entrepreneur.com/article/15414.

[16] Franziska Volckner and Henrik Sattler, "Drivers of Brand Extension Success," *Journal of Marketing*, 70 (April, 2006): 18–34.

[17] Robert Klara, "The Best (and Worst) Brand Extensions," *AdWeek*, (February 4, 2013), accessed March 1, 2015, http://www.adweek.com/news/advertising-branding/best-and-worst-brand-extensions-146966.

[18] George Lazarus, "Healthy Choice Gasps For Breath In Cereal Battle," *Chicago Tribune*, (January 08, 1998), accessed March 7, 2015, http://articles.chicagotribune.com/1998-01-08/business/9801080271_1_healthy-choice-conagra-kellogg-cereals.

[19] Kenneth Thompson and David Strutton, "Revisiting Perceptual Fit in Co-branding Applications," *Journal of Product & Brand Management*, 21/1 (2012): 15–25, available www.emeraldinsight.com/1061-0421.htm.

[20] Example adopted from Roger J. Best, *Market-Based Management* (Upper Saddle River, NJ: Prentice-Hall, 1997), 171–172.

[21] B. Abrams, "Consumer-Product Techniques Help Loctite Sell to Industry," *The Wall Street Journal*, April 2, 1981, 29.

CHAPTER 13

MANAGING SUPPLY CHAIN AND LOGISTICS RELATIONSHIPS

The purpose of supply chains is to create opportunities for Firms to achieve results collectively that those Firms could never achieve individually. Please keep this initial purpose in mind as you work through this chapter.

But for now, more simply, imagine a blazing campfire, full of fiercely burning logs. Now imagine pulling the logs from the fire one by one, until only one is left. How well will that single log burn and for how long? The answers are simple: "not well" and "not for long." That's because logs burn better together than they do apart. People or Firms often also perform better when working together rather than alone, particularly they work in a collaborative, cooperative, and cohesive fashion. In business and market settings, no individual or organization can operate for long in complete isolation from other individuals or organizations and the values that they produce.

The poet John Donne expressed similar views when he wrote: "No man is an island entire of itself; every man is … a part of the main." Donne's statement is true and applies to every marketing organization. No Firm can exist or operate as if it were an island. Every Firm instead exists, operates, and benefits materially from its participation as part of the mainland. Every Firm participates with others first as part of highly networked regional, national, or global economies and; second, as part of myriad relationships shared with other Firms.

No Firm exists today that can do everything by itself that must be done for it to succeed. Instead, even to simply survive, every US Firm depends on the successful execution of other partnering organizations. In modern business parlance, those partnering organizations exist, collaborate, and benefit mutually as part of what is now commonly called a supply chain. (For the historians among you, the **supply chain** used to be called the **marketing channel**.) Indeed, successful Firms routinely participate in dozens if not possibly hundreds of actively-engaged supply chain relationships, and receive or create value from each relationship.

You may have established a company in Eden, North Carolina, one you operated in your barn while you kept your regular professional job. J. Hoover Knives is such a one-man Firm that manufactures and markets world-class hunting knives at affordable prices. But owner Joe Hoover depends on steel manufacturers to produce the steel and other suppliers to supply the additional materials used to make his knives. He counts on various transportation Firms to bring or ship raw materials, component parts, or finished products to and from his production site. And, naturally, Mr. Hoover utilizes websites across the Internet to promote his products as well as process payments. Mr. Hoover likewise depends on the Firms that produced his foundry equipment and the tools he uses to sharpen and finish his knives. As you can see, successful entrepreneur though he is, Mr. Hoover is no one-man-band. He and his Firm, instead, participate in myriad supply chains.

Supply chains emerge from the mandate that B2B and B2C customer needs must be served in the best manner possible. Moreover, customers and their needs never stop changing. Therefore, supply chains operate in states of continuous change and must constantly adapt to those changes.

→ Write It Down: One Simple Product, One Stunningly Convoluted Supply Chain

We're not trying to discourage you, but facts are facts. Supply chains can be shockingly complex to manage or understand, even when seemingly simple products are being created and conveyed within and through their admittedly nebulous boundaries. There are various reasons why this description is true. Not the least of these is because complex, unpredictable, and at times less than completely rational human activities are always involved in supply chain management. But more factors than that contribute to the complexity of supply chains.

For now, however, let's ignore the human element (it comes up later) and remain entirely process-driven. Consider, for example, the supply chain processes by which J.J.'s Pizza, located in Denton, TX, is able to acquire, inventory, use, and ultimately benefit from the value delivered by one simple, old school technology. While no longer as predominant as it was a few years back, the technology certainly still exists and is used inside most Firms. The item in question: a *pencil*.

The pencil is a simple product based on a simple technology, right? Well, actually, not as simple as one might imagine. No single Firm in the world, in fact, is sufficiently-skilled, financially-able, or knowledgeable-enough to efficiently, effectively, and economically produce an ordinary pencil. And yes, we are discussing the old yellow pencil; the one that features wood, lacquer, print labeling, graphite lead, a little metal, an eraser, and nothing else. Instead of attempting to make one themselves, Firms are far better off purchasing pencils from a supply chain provider.

The number and complexity of supply chain partners (i.e., Firms) that must engage and cooperate with each other in a sophisticated business network in order for J.J.s wait-staff to use a pencil to write down "pepperoni + mushrooms" on an "extra-large" "thin crust" pie is absolutely, without reservation, guaranteed to amaze. Consider the following summary of what happens in various supply chain relationships that must be involved when this uncomplicated writing device is produced. The summary is based on the playful 1958 autobiography: *I, Pencil: My Family Tree as told to Leonard E. Reed*, actually written by Milton Friedman.[1] The story reveals how something as ostensibly simple as a pencil is actually the result of an extremely complex set of supply chain processes.

The supply chain processes involved in the production of pencils permit the logical division of labor between Firms and thus between people who possess specific types of resources, expertise, knowledge, and skills. The pencil supply chain processes in this case, and most cases, involve international trade. Pencil production processes require the successful development of specialized expertise based on each supply chain partner's ability to develop and exploit a core competency. Notably, more supply chain processes involved in pencil manufacturing were left out than featured in the discussion that follows. Our goal is to teach rather than torture you.

Managing Supply Chain Relationships to Make Pencils

The family tree of the common pencil actually begins, unsurprisingly, with a tree that is harvested. Usually, a cedar tree, perhaps one growing in Oregon, is taken for pencils. Cut down with what, however? As you could logically guess, various saws and engines and fuel for the engines and rope and other gear are involved, as are, indirectly, even food and coffee consumed by lumberjacks.

But focusing only on one element, from where do these saws arrive? Think about all the mining of ore, production of steel and its transformation into chain saws or axes that must transpire for such cutting instruments to be produced. Or consider the fuel, infrastructural and vehicular (drillers, refiners, trains, trucks, highways, waterways) sectors that must be engaged to bring the saws from point of production (where they are made) to their point of consumption (where they are used).

Once cut the cedar logs are shipped to a mill, let's say one in Northern California. Shipped how? Surely some form of rail, water, or highway transportation is involved. Or perhaps all three transportation modes are engaged at one or another times during the shipping process. The mill cuts the cedar logs into cedar slats and consequently refines them by kiln drying, polishing, and eventually tinting them. The process takes time; lots of skills and experience must be involved to do the right things right. How many people, machines, dollars, skills, and processes are involved in this stage? Who made, shipped, and installed the kiln? Where does the polish come from? What is used to apply it? What does tinting a pencil even mean? Too many people, processes, machines, and sets of unique expertise are engaged to reasonably list here.

A modern pencil's lead, which is not lead at all, boasts a similarly complicated heritage. Circa 1958, the graphite was mined in Ceylon, an island located off the Southeast coast of India that is now called Sri Lanka. Times change, though these processes and their complexity actually have not. The technology was too simple to bother upgrading it, we suppose. The graphite's miners, their tools, training, and expertise co-exist as part of pencil supply chains. In the day, graphite was combined with Mississippi clay in a process that also involved aluminum hydroxide. Do you see how both the plot and complexity of this homely writing instrument's story continues to literally thicken? For good measure, as the graphite supply chain extends toward the ultimate consumer, camellia wax from Mexico, paraffin wax, and hydrogenated natural fats that originated in US stockyards enter the so-called lead mix and its supply chain.

The cedar wood receives at least six coats of lacquer at some point in the pencil production process. Do you know all the ingredients that must be successfully acquired, measured, and blended to make lacquer? We don't either. But we do know that makers and marketers of castor beans (from the legume) and castor oil (from fish) are both involved. The skills and technologies involved in making a pencil grow less comprehensible and still more remote.

Pencils have labels. The labeling process involves applying heat to carbon black along with resin. We know baseball players rub resin onto balls and bats. But we are less certain about where resin or, for that matter, carbon black come from—except possibly from trees and coal. New processes, new people, new firms; new things and more processes that any single Firm that tried to make a pencil would have to learn do well. Or, more logically, as was the case when J.J.'s decided to make Denton's best pizza, and let someone else worry about making the pencils. Focusing on what J.J.'s and its Chicago-born owner do best, and all that. Aha! So that's why supply chains exist.

Pencils require a metal band. The band has a name, *ferrule*. It used to be made of brass, and perhaps some bands still are. Regardless, miners of zinc and copper were involved then, because these minerals are component elements of brass. Miners of nickel are also involved. But not just regular nickel; it turns out only black nickel is good enough. But the center of the ferrule requires no black nickel, which is another complicated supply chain story that would take more pages to explain than we have available.

Pencils wear a hat, known as a *plug*. Plugs once were made of rubber sourced from Southeast Asia; *factice*, manufactured from rape-seed oil; pumice, mined and processed in Italy; and cadmium sulfite, from the United States, which gives the plug its color. Ah, the supply chain complexity elevates further. Be thankful we are not discussing the pencil sharpener's life story.

The modest pencil, as produced through the networked collaboration and cooperation of a few dozen supply chains, is not so humble after all. Thousands of people and dozens of Firms can legitimately claim to have had a hand in its genetics and birth. *The whole economic world, in fact, exists as little more than a series of supply chains.* Do you understand more about why we have continuously emphasized the role and importance of creating and managing relationships successfully throughout this book?

→ Yes Butt ... What If Supply Chains Did Not Exist?

The book of Exodus reports manna miraculously appeared each morning to nourish the Israelites as they wandered, desert bound, for 40 years after leaving captivity in Egypt. This food source was noteworthy in another way. It could not be stored, another word for inventoried, for future use. Manna had to be consumed on the day of its arrival. No one knew how manna arrived in just the right form at the right time and place each morning from heaven; it was simply accepted as God's gift. Just like the food you store in your pantry or the toilet paper in your bathroom.

Ever wonder how all that arrives, seemingly seamlessly, at the final destination? Not at the final destination in your home, by the way, but at the grocery stores from which you purchase food and toilet paper. Or, for that matter, how many rolls of toilet paper does the Metroplex population (the area between and including Dallas, Fort Worth, and Denton, TX) use each day?

The answer to either question is hardly miraculous. But each is fascinating, complicated, important, and instructive, in its own right. The answer to the first question, of course, is the supply chain and logistics. The costs savings, to consumers and Firms; product assortments, made available for B2B and B2C customers alike; and economic stimulus, in the form of more jobs, enhanced tax revenues, greater capital, and economic investment generated by the supply chain infrastructure generated in and around the Metroplex are remarkable. But again perhaps predictably, this supply chain infrastructure's astoundingly beneficial effects are too often taken for granted, even by those benefitting most, as was true of the Israelites and manna.

The fact is that the integrated air, rail, and highway supply chain system operating within the triangulated region bounded by Dallas, Fort Worth, and Denton remains underappreciated by many. This is a shame. Because no supply chain network operating on either the left (West) or right (East) coasts can rival the positive local, national, and international impact of the supply chain mecca that resides and operates in North Texas.

Supply chains are typically neither glamorous nor sexy, except, surely, among Firms and people who reap huge financial gains from their supply chain participation. But then again, as a Michelin advertisement once suggested, your cars' tires are not glamorous or sexy either, even though your family's health depends upon them every day. Every North Texas resident benefits daily from the presence of their local supply chain systems and the value they create. Without the supply chain networks that operate in North Texas, the Metroplex would not function as the job-producing and corporation-attracting machine it has become during the last three decades.

What Is Logistics and How Does Logistics Relate to Supply Chains?

Before proceeding further, we should clarify the relationships between a number of processes and terms that are all intertwined in our discussion of supply chains. Exhibit 13.1 is useful for visualizing these relationships. Consider the five-level supply chain in the exhibit, beginning with providers of parts, materials, producers of forest products, mines, and agriculture on the left and ending with ultimate users on the right side. The top of the diagram illustrates the physical movement of products from one supply chain member to the next. The entire sequence is referred to as **logistics**. Logistics may be defined precisely as "inventory in motion or at rest throughout the supply chain." Logistics occurs within the supply chain. Logistics is about "me." Meaning, simply, logistical processes are about my Firm or your Firm, but only my or your Firm. Logistics is about my Firm's inbound (coming into the Firm) and outbound (going out of the Firm) and through-bound (passing through the Firm) flows of raw materials, component parts, finished products, financial resources, and ultimately information. Logistical managerial processes happen inside the Firm. The major logistics functions that must be performed include warehousing (inventory management), order processing, and transportation. Related to logistics, you will also encounter the terms: "**materials management**" and "**physical distribution**." Materials management is the movement of parts, materials, and other resources into the manufacturing process (i.e. into a manufacturing Firm). Similarly, the movement of finished goods from manufacturers to ultimate users (consumers) is called **physical distribution**.

The bottom of the exhibit provides alternate terminology for the organizations and people through which products move. The **channel of distribution** consists of the set of organizations and people through which finished goods move from producers to consumers. The channel of distribution typically consists of producers (manufacturers), wholesaling intermediaries, retailers, and consumers. The **supply chain** captures and expands on the channel of distribution. It is the totality of the organizations and people involved in moving goods from source providers to ultimate users. Supply chains consist of networks of Firms that systematically partner in an organized fashion with each other at each level of logistical systems. Supply chain managerial processes happen between Firms. These systematic supply chain partnering processes unfold with a three-headed purpose in mind:

- To maximize logistics values.
- To minimize logistics costs.
- To deliver expected levels of value and satisfaction to customers at every level in the supply chain. (By "level," we mean "Firm.")

Supply chain management is about "us." "Us" means everyone—the entire network of Firms involved in the supply chain working together, hopefully in collaborative, cooperative, and cohesive fashions, for the mutual benefit of every Firm engaged in the supply chain.

Supply chains may be compared to rivers. They will flow whether they are managed or not. But unlike some wild, remote rivers, the flows within supply chains should always be managed. Logistical and supply chain processes are each driven by two factors: the derivation and sharing of information, and the development and application of the proper metrics. The supply chain that possesses and exploits the best or most accurate information, likely because it has implemented and employed the best metrics, usually will win marketing competitions.

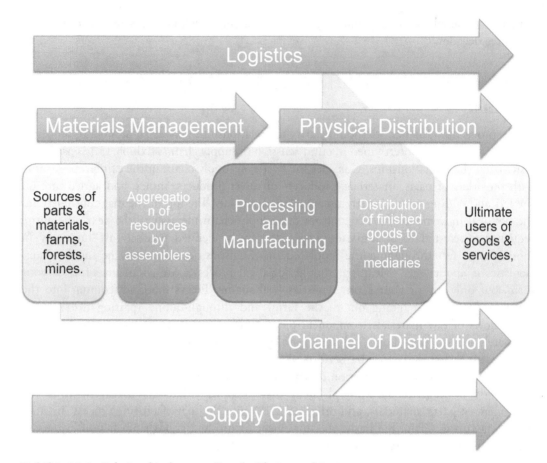

Exhibit 13.1 *Relationship between Supply Chains and Logistics.*

Defined academically, the **supply chain management** process involves planning, implementing, and controlling the flow and storage of products, services, and related information from point of origin to point of consumption, with the end goal of satisfying customer needs at the lowest possible costs.

Hopefully, those flows pass reciprocally (i.e., back and forth) from one Firm to another Firm. By partnering inside the supply chain, these reciprocal flows between Firms occur in a seamless fashion.

Supply chains are where most strategic marketing decisions occur. Decisions are made about which and how many products to make or develop, as well as to which markets or customers they should be targeted, as are decisions about how to price, distribute, and promote products' unique values. The supply chain is also where all resulting marketing activities are actually executed. These are each big deals.

You might be a cynical college student or a grizzled 50-something business owner. Regardless, you receive the same core values from the various supply chains that enhance your life, every day. The supply chain enables you to obtain the right product or service at the right time in the right place at a price that you, by definition, consider right. But, there is more than that to our story about the value of supply chains.

Manufacturers lust after the opportunity to create narrow product assortments in huge quantities. The ability to go "narrow and deep" lowers manufacturers' operational and production costs. This is because they then can exploit economies of scale. Economies of scale are cost advantages that Firms obtain due to their size, output, or scale of operation. The cost per unit of products produced generally decreases as fixed costs are spread over more units of output. More will be said about scale economies when we examine aspects of pricing in a later chapter.

China-based Foxcomm produces thousands of iPods, iPhones, and iPads for Apple every day. However, individual consumers want broad assortments of i-products in small quantities. This means that consumers only seek one iPod, one iPhone, or one iPad—or perhaps their Samsung counterparts—at a time. Supply chains transform the mass assortments made by manufacturers into the "onesies" generally sought by buyers. This is the **allocating** or **breaking-bulk** activity. This activity is a core value provided by supply chains. More will be said about this activity and other key supply chain activities later in the chapter.

Supply chain managers enjoy describing how their role is crucial to satisfying B2B and B2C customers alike. They further emphasize that supply chain management is crucial from cradle-to-grave or from "dust-to-dust," as they put it. This dust-to-dust phrasing, which may appear forced, overly cute or even Biblical in its origins, is actually absolutely apt. You have eaten, worn, or typed on nothing today that did not originate in the dirt. Dirt is also exactly the place to which each thing you've eaten, worn, or typed on will eventually return.

Sophisticated businesspeople inevitably recognize a great thing when they see it. They recognize a core marketing function, that when managed effectively, contributes directly to their bottom (profit) lines. Likely, this is because smart-money marketers understand this unpretentious supply chain formula, called the **profit leveraging of costs**:

> *If the net profit margin on each sales dollar earned is 5%, a supply chain operational savings of $5,000 yields the same return to the Firm's bottom line as would a sales increase of $100,000.*

Because the consequences for net profits will be the same, marketing strategists and managers should ask: Is it easier for our Firm to create supply chain, logistics, and distribution efficiencies that permit us to save $5,000 in supply chain costs. Or, is it easier for our Firm to increase top line revenues by $100,000, because the net profit outcome will be the same?

These are top-line versus cost-line income statement questions, of course. All strategists should ask them. We also believe all strategists should answer each question with a yes. That is, managers should seek to lower costs by developing greater supply chain efficiencies and seek to raise revenues by developing marketing effectiveness, which really means developing and delivering greater value to precisely targeted customers. Not coincidentally, Firms can enhance their capacity for increasing top line marketing revenues by improving their supply chain and logistical efficiencies—which, in turn, wraps around again to our prior discussion of better information and superior metrics.

An Under-Considered Supply Chain Benefit

Oh yes, the toilet paper question. How many rolls are consumed daily in the DFW Metroplex? According to Charmin statistics, American use an average of 57 sheets a day or 20,805 sheets per year. The average roll contains 500 sheets. For one American, an average roll should last about 8.77 days. The average consumer thus would use 41.6 rolls annually (365 days/8.77 days); a true dirt-to-dirt example, by the way.

No exact count of the Metroplex population exists. Estimates, however, generally settle around 6.8 million inhabitants. Thus, some 282,880,000 (6,800,000 times 8.7) rolls are used annually by the Metroplex population—or 775,014 rolls per day. Most toilet paper rolls arrive after originating from states as far away as Wisconsin, the nation's leading paper producer and home of Charmin. As noted, the fact that these rolls do arrive, as was true of the manna, is very much taken for granted. But what if one day they did not? Imagine that particular day within the supply chain.

Why What Madonna Sang in 1984 Matters More Today

Most of you will work in a knowledge economy. Eventually, if you are not doing so already, you will manage information as well as people all day long. But Madonna, the original "Material Girl," was right: "We're all living in a material world." The discussion just developed has answered one question and illustrated one point:

- The answered question: How does all that material (stuff) get into our homes, garages, and closets?
- The illustrated point, derived from the New Testament: "The branch must be connected to the vine in order for it to bear fruit."

Think about this statement, and its marketing implications, please. Who is the vine, and who is the branch, in any supply chain setting?

→ Supply Chains Used to Be Called "Marketing Channels"

What images come to mind when you hear the word "Channels"? Television would be the first thought for many, which is logical. After all, channels are the means through which television network marketers deliver various programing products (i.e., shows, movies, news content, sport events) to targeted consumers. How many different marketing channels, for example, does the Entertainment and Sports Programing Network employ to deliver content to viewers, listeners, or readers? Note, please, these are three relatively distinct market segments. ESPN has at its strategic command more than a few platforms, or channels, through which its live and recorded sports related content can flow and be monetized. ESPN features, for example, five or more ESPN television channels (ESPN1, ESPN2, ESPNU, ESPN-CLASSIC and ESPN-NEWS); ESPN, the Magazine; ESPN.com, the Website; ESPN-RADIO; and myriad ESPN-WATCH applications. Each channel option permits ESPN to deliver different products to different target audiences, just as would any other marketing channel.

For others, the word "channels" undoubtedly conjured images of waterways. The Danube River courses through and connects ten European countries (alphabetically, Austria, Bulgaria, Croatia, the Czech Republic, Germany, Hungary, Moldavia, Romania, Serbia, and Ukraine). Across millennia the Danube's flow served as a mechanism for marketing exchange for business, governmental, and military entities operating within these nations.

Regardless of which image of a "channel" popped into your mind (television or waterways), each implies the presence of a passageway. The term passageway speaks to real or imagined conduits or pipelines that allow certain activities and processes to occur. Such imagery is appropriate.

Marketing channels, as defined earlier in the chapter, amount to a group of independent Firms involved in the process of making a product or service (e.g., hunting knives, pencils, toilet paper, or ESPN content) available for use or consumption by organizations or consumers. These independent Firms could include manufacturers, wholesalers, agents, transportation and warehousing firms, retailers, and ultimately customers themselves. The classic or traditional marketing channel begins with a manufacturer, which makes and distributes product(s) through various wholesalers, warehouses, agents, and/or transportation firms downstream to, ultimately, a retailer or retailers. From there, these retailers market these products to end-user consumers. This process is illustrated in Exhibit 13.2 with a more concrete example. Consider a popular consumer good, Coors beer. The channel of distribution for Coors begins with the brewery in Golden, Colorado. Coors distributes its beer to most areas of the United States using a network of distributors (wholesalers) and retailers. Several distributors serve the Dallas-Ft. Worth area in Texas. In turn, these wholesaler are responsible for distributing Coors beer to local retail stores, such as 7-11s, Safeway Stores, Kroger's, and Winn Dixie stores, plus a large assortment of restaurants, bars, and private clubs. The channel of distribution for Coors is the typical distribution channel encountered for many consumer goods. It is the most traditional distribution channel for consumer products. We examine variations on this channel structure later on in the course.

Technically, channels of distribution provide the route by which ownership is transferred between buyers and sellers. It includes only those organizations or persons that take title (buy the product) and then transfer that title (sell the product) to another organization or person. The physical product may actually move through a different set of hands than does ownership. An example will clarify the distinction. Consider the channel of distribution for bulky commodities, such as coal and building materials. **Drop shippers** are wholesaling middleman that buy and sell bulky commodities, such as coal and building materials. These products are very expensive to handle and ship, relative to their unit value. As a result, when coal, say, is purchased by a drop shipper for resale to his or her customers, arrangements are made to ship the product directly from its point of origin to the customer's location. The drop shipper will never physically handle the coal. In order to minimize shipping and handling costs, the drop shipper buys the coal (takes title from the producer), but will have it shipped directly to the customer (e.g. a public utility). In this case, since the drop shipper takes title to the product,

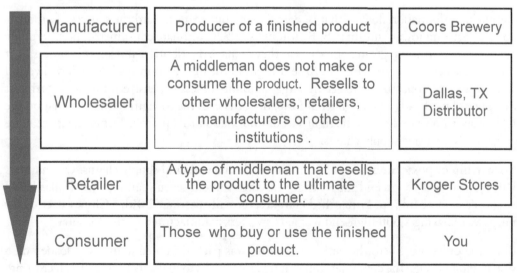

Exhibit 13.2 *A Traditional Channel of Distribution.*

the channel of distribution includes the producer of the coal, the drop shipper, and the final customer (the public utility). The product and its title have traveled different routes.

Generally, the physical product and its title move together through the channel. The case of the drop shipper is more an exception, rather than the rule. But, the point should be clear: the channel of distribution technically refers to the movement of title for the product, rather than movement of the product itself.

The term marketing channel was first used to describe the existence of a trade channel that bridges producers and users. In effect, channels exist to close gaps that otherwise would separate producers from consumers. Marketing channels can be logically compared to paths through which goods move or flow from marketers to buyers. This is why the traditional term "middleman" emerged as a way to explain product flows. Middlemen are now more commonly described as **intermediaries**.

Channel or supply chain intermediaries are individuals or organizations who mediate the exchange and creation of value in relationships involving two or more partners. Intermediaries, like channels or supply chains themselves, generate form, place, time, and ownership values (utilities) by bringing together sellers and buyers. Intermediary Firms or persons help channels or supply chains CRAM: **C**reate more value by increasing efficiency, facilitate more **R**outine execution of established processes, simplify **A**ssortments, and **M**inimize uncertainty within the channel or supply chain.

Getting in the Flow(s)

Flows, as they move reciprocally (that is, back and forth) inside traditional marketing channels or supply chains, are not limited to the flows of finished products. Physical flows of raw materials and component parts, as well as financial or payment flows, also exist. Yet, the flow of *information* may actually prove the most important channel or supply chain flow of all.

Properly managed information can knit supply chain partnerships together. A lack of information, or poorly managed information, can keep erstwhile supply chain partners at arms-length from one another. Either outcome can increase the likelihood that conflict will arise inside supply chain relationships.

Reciprocal information flows—that is, data moving upstream toward the sources of products and downstream toward ultimate B2B customers or B2C ultimate consumers—permit supply chain partners to attain greater efficiency as they manage distribution and logistics processes at the points where their Firms interact. The true gift of the information age in which we live and work is not the opportunity to secure larger amounts of less expensive information. Almost every one of us already has too much information. Instead, the true gift of the information age is the opportunity to develop the right sort of information that permits Firms to engage more collaboratively inside supply chains.

Ownership or **possession** flows also unfold inside channels and supply chains. One author's wife is an apparel design and supply chain executive. About seven years ago, her Dallas-based employer, a now bankrupt Firm called Harold's, formally partnered with a Chinese factory for purposes of having 4,500 high-end women's sweaters manufactured in that country.

Once the order was filled, the entire sweater lot was packed in a container and loaded on a ship in Hong Kong. The container ship required two weeks to make its Pacific Ocean crossing, eventually reaching its destination, Long Beach, CA. With its seal unbroken (meaning the container was unopened), the container was loaded onto a Burlington Northern Santa Fe train. A few days later the train arrived in Oklahoma City. At that time, the container was lifted from the train onto a tractor-trailer and driven a few miles south to Harold's warehouse in Norman, OK. The container's seal was then broken and it was opened.

Normally, "ownership" of the sweaters would have changed hands from the Chinese manufacturer to the US retailer at that point, meaning Harold's would have taken ownership at the point of delivery in Norman. This never happened. The sweaters, all of them, possessed a very undesirable new feature: a horrible smell (rats were in the container at the time of departure, all died, and decayed along the trip.). But Harold's was not out any money, although it did have to scramble to find enough sweaters for the Christmas Season.

The Firm never took ownership of the sweaters; it never paid for them. By all rights Harold's could have shipped the container and its entire contents back to China, cost-free. This did not happen. Instead, supply chain agents representing the Chinese manufacturer's interests had the sweaters cleaned. They then were sold through another supply chain to two alternative retailers. Who knows, if you bought a high-end but heavily discounted ladies' sweater at Marshalls or T.J. Maxx that Christmas season, you might have been part of this supply chain yourself.

Transitioning from Channels to Supply Chains

The transition from the traditional descriptor "marketing channel" to the contemporary "supply chain" is surprisingly simple to explain. All one must do is to take the traditional channel defined earlier (let's assume the manufacturer is General Motors) and add in GM's suppliers, You then have a contemporary supply chain. The GM supply chain begins with the source firms that provide GM with finished goods, raw materials, or component parts, or various types of information or expertise. The supply chain then continues with the manufacturer itself (GM), followed by the Firms involved in the transportation and warehousing of GM cars and trucks and, finally, the dealerships (retailers) that directly market GM's products to end-user consumers. GM likely participates in hundreds of supply chains. Figure 13.3 depicts a typical supply chain based on our example with GM.

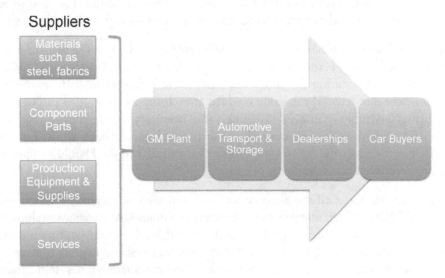

Exhibit 13.3 *GM's Supply Chain.*

GM participates in a wide range of supply chains featuring myriad suppliers for the best possible reason: developing relationships with other supply chain partners permits GM to focus on doing what it does best. Presumably, what GM does best entails designing cars and trucks, assembling the finished and component parts, managing the tools and technology that are necessary to manufacturer cars and trucks, and managing the marketing and branding of their vehicles. GM does not make GPS or stereo or windshield wiper devices; it certainly does not manufacture steel or plastic. But, GM obviously requires each of these and thousands of more parts to manufacture and market automobiles.

GM does not make tires, either. But the Firm surely needs tires; no substitute technology has yet emerged to replace tires. No problem, however. Goodyear is more than delighted to manufacturer tires for GM. This is a classic supply chain-facilitated win-win relationship. As noted, their partnership in this shared supply chain also allows Goodyear and GM to focus on doing what each does best.

From here the degree of supply chain complexity quickly multiplies. Normal tires for US vehicles, or for that matter Japanese or German automobiles, feature the following parts: plies, steel belts, cap piles, bead and chaffer, liners, sidewalls, sipes, and other critical items. We don't know what all the critical additional parts are and we don't even understand what sipes are, but we do know Goodyear doesn't produce all these parts itself. Goodyear has to source these tire materials and component parts from their suppliers.

The Firms that provide parts to Goodyear, as a partner to GM, also belong to one of the many supply chains in which GM participates. Notably, tires are but one of the approximately 30,000 parts—right down to the smallest screw—that are used to build modern automobiles. Now you see why, apart from the human element, supply chain relationships are so complex. The network of supply chains in which Firms participate gets very complicated, very fast. But as also shown, the availability of such supply chains, as well as the values that they provide, permit Firms to focus on their strengths.

Supply chains literally stretch halfway around the world and back again, sometimes to nearly where they began, in order to deliver the value you want. West Texas boasts one of the largest concentrations of cotton growers in the world, a fact that surprises many. HanesBrands, Inc. (better known as Hanes) is one of the world's largest consumers of cotton. Thus the fact that Hanes has built all those cotton T-shirt factories in and around Amarillo, TX, so as to be near the source of the cotton makes perfect sense. Except, as you know, this is not absolutely true.

The majority of T-shirt factories in the world are located up and down the east coast of Asia. Consequently, before any Hanes T-shirt can be purchased at an Amarillo, TX, Walmart, cotton grown within shouting distance of the city must travel about halfway around the world to somewhere in Asia. There, value is added at each supply chain level through various manufacturing, assembly, polishing, labeling, and inventory-management processes that unfold in and around Asian factories. Then the finished goods, here, white T-shirts, are shipped back again across the ocean via a supply chain similar to the Harold's shipping saga that was just recounted. Sans dead rats, of course.

Think, for a second, about all the farmers; fertilizer and seed marketers; irrigation systems; cotton pickers, balers, refiners and processors; bankers and financiers; warehouses; ships, trains, and trucks; factories, assemblers, polishers, and die and label makers; and manufacturers, wholesalers and retailers; and for that matter information systems experts that went into getting that inexpensive undershirt on your back. These corporate entities, and others that were not identified, are parts of the "cotton in the fields" (think dirt) to "T-shirts on your back" (on their way, eventually, back to the dirt) supply chains.

By the way, to underscore how complicated another seemingly simple product actually is, each cotton T-shirt contains about six miles of yarn. Moreover, you may find it interesting to learn that Michael Jordan, as the brand's primary spokesperson for more than two decades, is also part of Hanes' supply chain; he is part of the *information flow* from the manufacturer to the consumer within the supply chain.

Just think about how complicated this discussion might become had we considered the myriad supply chains in which Apple participates. We're assuming, of course, that iPads demand a few more component parts and more technical manufacturing processes than do Hanes' T-shirts. Because Apple, as is well-known, does not make or assemble a single part of any product it conceptualizes, designs, and brands. Again, myriad Firms generally located around the East Asian Pacific Rim are responsible for manufacturing Apple's products. These supply chain relationships, as was true of GM, permit Apple to focus on leveraging its three primary strengths: creativity, design, and brand management.

→ Supply Chains Are Critical Because ...

Any Firm's supply chain-related decisions directly affect every other marketing mix decision that it makes. The supply chains to which Firms belong influence the products that management elects to create, modify, or continue to market; how management prices those products; and how management elects to distribute, display, discuss, and promote them. Consequently managers should never make fundamental supply chain decisions in isolation from other marketing mix considerations.

Imagine, for example, your Firm designs women's apparel and has created a new blouse. Your Firm, fortunately, has the option of retailing the product through Walmart, Target, or Neiman-Marcus. That these three Firms might currently agree to market the same item is a bit of a stretch, we'll admit, but hypothetically this could happen. Do you believe that the decision to market your new product through Walmart, as opposed to Neiman's, would impact how the blouse was priced? Might the same choice affect the quality, type and feel (called "hand") of the fabric used to make the garment or even the materials from which the buttons it features are made? Perhaps even the brand name for the blouse? What the Firm would choose to say, communication-wise, about the product? We believe the answer to each question is "yes," too.

The Longer Run

Supply chain partnerships or relationships usually involve longer-term commitments to other Firms. At the least, they should. Consequently, management must define and establish relationships carefully, mindful of the need to understand and address present problems and accommodate future possibilities.

Supply chain partnerships are more like fully-committed marital relationships than dating relationships. Consider the consequences associated with the differences between the latter two relationships types. How difficult—emotionally, practically, and financially—is it to get married? The truth is that two heterosexual people who are not first cousins and who are of legal age rarely have much difficulty getting married. But how much more challenging— emotionally, practically, and financially—would it generally prove for the same two people, once married, to unhitch?

Supply chain relationships can similarly be entered into rather easily. And, supply chain relationships can also prove extremely painful to exit. Firms and managers consequently should choose supply chain partners carefully. To illustrate, how important to Japan's Nissan Motors is the dealer relationship it has in Jackson, TN? (Jackson is located about 80 miles east of Memphis yet is surprisingly isolated from other sizable cities. But Jackson features a

Nissan dealership and plays a prominent role in a Johnny Cash song.) The answer is "extremely important." The real question, however, is: How difficult and costly would it prove for Nissan to establish and fully implement another dealer relationship in Jackson? The answers are "very" and "a lot." The fact that supply chain relationship can be easily entered but usually only painfully exited underscores why strategists should rarely limit their supply chain partner options to only a few.

Polygamous Supply Chain Marriages? Why Yes, in Fact

The prior discussion underscores why strategically-minded retailers should enter relationships with multiple supply chain sourcing partners (manufacturers). The same discussion also underscores why manufacturers should engage with multiple partners at the retail supply level. Anyone else thinking about the adage never put all your eggs in one basket?

Dallas-headquartered Haggar Manufacturing, once the world's largest marketer of men's pants, brings its products to market through multiple retailers. The list includes Walmart, JC Penney, Dillard's, Kohl's, Macy's and so forth. Meanwhile, Plano-headquartered JC Penney buys men's pants from several supply chain sources. Penney's suppliers include Haggar, Levi Straus, Liz Claiborne, Dickie's, Ralph Lauren, and so forth. Even the Nissan dealership in Jackson, TN, also retails brands made by Volvo, Kia, and Hyundai. Think about how many supply chain relationships that Microsoft, Toyota, or your university must manage. That is, in the case of universities, just to ensure that enough eggs, milk, and toilet paper are available in its restaurants and dormitories to ensure that freshmen don't starve or catch diseases if it gets too cold outside.

Consider how many different supply chain partners supply tangible goods to Walmart in just the "lawn and garden" or "automotive parts" sections of its stores. Let's see, in just the first section we'll start with Firms that manufacture and market lawn mowers, rakes, leaf blowers, seeds, water hoses, seeds, plants, trees, fertilizers, flower pots, gardening gloves, wheelbarrows, living walls, saws, clippers, plastic sheets, liners, etc., etc., etc. No one assumes that just one manufacturer is producing all that different stuff, do they?

Walmart: Almost Always a Special Case

Supply chain relationships offer the last best chance for most Firms to achieve sustainable competitive advantage. This statement is never more apropos than when one thinks about Walmart. The supply chain beast that is Walmart has been a "killer" in its big box, discount retailer category for more than 50 years precisely for one reason: the efficiency with which its supply chain managers manage myriad supply chain sourcing relationships.

Walmart's competitors have rarely been able to match the competitive advantages (i.e., broad product assortments at generally lower prices) that the Firm has generated through its adroit and often ruthless supply chain management practices. In Walmart's mercilessly rational supply chains, functioning as the "Channel Captain" (a supply chain partner that, by virtue of some power it possesses, exercises disproportionate influence) dictates that:

- Suppliers will lower their prices in exchange for their receipt of the value known as higher sales volume available by selling through Walmart.
- Suppliers will track the status and location of each product throughout the entire supply chain.
- Drivers will never let trucks idle for more than 30 seconds.
- Unions will stay out, thus lowering employee-driven costs inside supply chains.

To its credit and gain, Walmart passes on these cost savings to consumers in the form of **everyday low prices** (the **EDLP** strategy). The low-cost value that Walmart offers customers is legitimate. The presence of this value has permitted Walmart to defeat competitors based on "cost leadership" advantages. Over time, as a consequence, Walmart has also cultivated *Customer Intimacy*-based advantages for its brand in selected consumer market segments.

Some consumer market segments, of course, continue to hate Walmart with a passion. But what was that comment we offered earlier about marketers should never try to change someone's mind? If a marketer doesn't like the tenor of the conversation, or the direction it is taking, either change or move on and target someone who does appreciate the values you offer. This is exactly what Walmart has done across the decades.

→ Supply Chains Functions—Values That Supply Chains Create

The need to specialize, or focus on doing and improving what Firms do best, was introduced in Chapter 1. The need to achieve such specialization invariably exists inside supply chains, too. In fact, the supply chain is the place where the best opportunity for most Firms to specialize actually materializes. Such specialization generally plays out in the form of one Firm's ability to perform a given supply chain function more effectively than a partner can perform the function for itself. In fact, the need to achieve and exploit specialization is why supply chains exist and why Firms participate in supply chain relationships.

Supply chain partners should concentrate on doing what they do best. Inside supply chains, manufacturers should manufacture, transportation firms transport, warehouses store and manage inventory, and retailers should retail. Not complicated, but a logical and important idea. Inside supply chains, the Firm that can perform a given function most effectively should perform the function. This focus, this opportunity to specialize, permits Firms to focus on leveraging and refining their core competencies. Core competencies, in fact, usually provide the foundation on which the differentiating values of Firms can be established, promoted, and delivered to targeted customer segments.

Typical Supply Chain Functions

Many supply chain functions exist, as shown below. These functions must be performed by some Firm. A focal supply chain question thus becomes who will perform them best?

One saying many readers have likely heard goes like this: "Gee, if we could just cut out the middleman, we could save money." But the functions performed by "middlemen" (i.e., supply chain intermediaries) can never be eliminated. Supply chain functions must be performed by someone, meaning some Firm. Otherwise, disappointingly few pencils, toilet paper rolls, or knives would arrive in intended customers' hands. You can eliminate the middleman, but not the functions that must be performed. Thus, back to our focal question in the first paragraph introducing this section: "Who will best perform the function?" The most essential supply chain functions are examined in the next few sections.

Matching

Matching is tantamount to bringing buyers and seller together and matching supply with demand. In the process, the exchange process is made more efficient. The sheer existence of middlemen in a supply chain effectively reduces the number of total transactions required to create the assortments of goods desired by consumers. For example, assume the scenario in which five consumers are interested in acquiring the goods produced by five manufacturers. In this scenario there must be a total of 5 × 5 = 25 total transactions to distribute the products offered by each of the five producers to each of the five consumers (Exhibit 13.4). In contrast, if a single large retailer (e.g. Best Buy) is placed in the channel between the producers and consumers, the number of required transactions can be more than halved (Exhibit 13.5)! Each producer and consumer needs only to engage in a single transaction with Best Buy, meaning that only 5 + 5 = 10 transactions now are required. Best Buy purchases the products from each manufacturer, combining these products into the quantities and assortments desired by each retail customer.

Negotiating

Matching also requires negotiating. As part of the buying and selling process, supply chain members negotiate several issues. But negotiations relate most often to final prices and product placement within retail settings. This latter function literally entails negotiating over shelf space. Producers typically desire prime shelf space (i.e. eye-level and at one or the other ends of an aisle), but there is only so much prime shelf space to allocate. The negotiating function is generally performed on behalf of manufacturers by various agents (manufacturers' representative or jobbers), or by the manufacturers' salespersons directly.

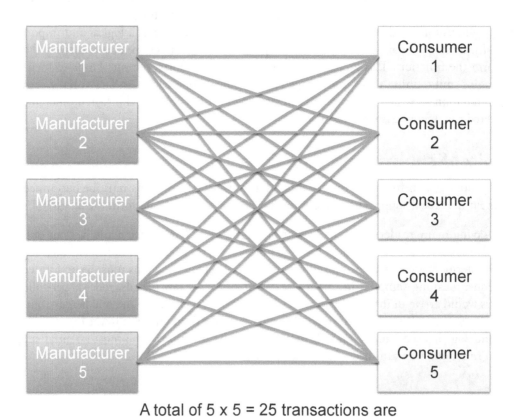

A total of 5 x 5 = 25 transactions are required!

Exhibit 13.4 *The number of transactions required for producers to reach consumers in the absence of intermediaries.*

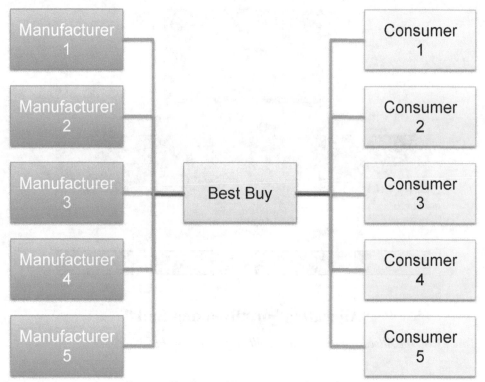

A total of 5 + 5 = 10 transactions are required!

Exhibit 13.5 *Total Transactions are reduced substantially when an intermediary is introduced into the supply chain.*

Allocating

Allocating, also called "breaking-bulk," means creating the "right sized" product assortment. Customers, meaning you, typically want to buy one or two tubes of toothpaste at a time, not a dozen (a dozen is called a "gross," by the way). Colgate concurrently seeks to make as many tubes of toothpaste as possible. The supply chain allocating function breaks up the large quantities produced by Colgate into smaller quantities at the retail level from which you will choose. The allocating function is typically performed when wholesaling middlemen buy from very large manufacturers and resell to smaller retailers. For example, Procter & Gamble will sell in large quantities to Core-Mark, a large grocery wholesaler that supplies a large number of independent and chain grocers. Core-Mark then resells in smaller quantities to its retail grocery customers (Exhibit 13.6). Similarly, allocating is performed when a large retailer such as Walmart buys directly from large producers for redistribution to its own retail stores.

Accumulating

Accumulating, also known as "making bulk," involves buying units of the same product from multiple sources of supply to create larger quantities that will be sold to customers preferring to buy in larger amounts (Exhibit 13.7). Middlemen who perform accumulating functions are typically referred to as "assemblers." Assemblers are commonly found in the agricultural and fishery industries. Large food products producers (Hunt, Campbell, StarKist) do not want to buy direct from many small farmers or fishermen. They prefer to buy in large quantities from wholesalers that have already pooled these smaller quantities. Buying in large quantities helps minimize ordering, shipping, and handling costs.

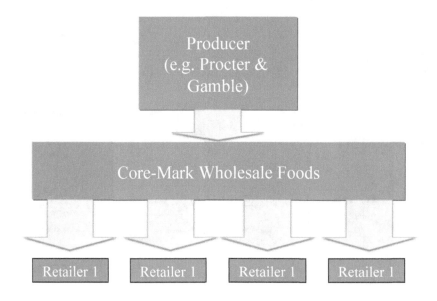

"Allocating" or "Breaking Bulk"

Exhibit 13.6 *The Allocating or Breaking Bulk Supply Chain Function.*

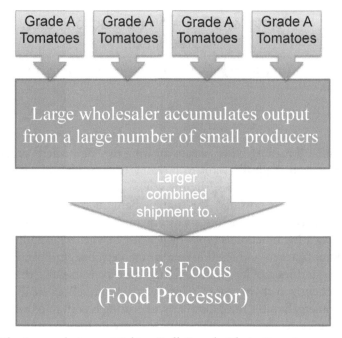

Exhibit 13.7 *The Accumulating or Making Bulk Supply Chain Function.*

Sorting

Sorting is a function typically performed by assemblers once "bulk" has been accumulated. When products are sorted, they are separated into categories based on differences in "grade," or some other aspect of "quality." Sorting is commonly done for agricultural products and raw materials. Eggs may be sorted and packaged into different sizes (medium, large, jumbo) and grades (A or AA) for sale in your local Kroger supermarket. Lumber products, such as 2x4 studs, may be graded according to number and severity of knots or splits. Grading systems for products such as these are essentially quality rating schemes.

Sorting also occurs in other product categories. An investment firm, for example, may sort investments based on "risk" and "return." Investment opportunities of similar risk may be grouped together into a single "mutual fund" that will be offered to clients. Typically, riskier investment portfolios offer the potential for larger returns. Investors who are more risk averse will gravitate to lower risk (but lower return) portfolios.

Assorting

Assorting means combining a variety of different products together to offer variety to customers. Retailers and wholesaling middlemen typically create assortments for their customers. Consider your local Kroger or Winn-Dixie. Each typically stocks in excess of 40,000 products on its shelves from which customers can choose. The assortments offered by Kroger and Winn-Dixie are driven by customer expectations and demands. Indeed, one of the primary keys to wholesaling and retailing success is matching the assortment of products to the wants and needs of customers.[2]

Storage and Inventory Management

The storage function is performed when products must be held for significant time periods before they are sold. In some cases, storage involves holding products until consumers are ready to buy them, as in the case of ski equipment and other seasonal products. Such products may be produced year-round, but may be held in storage until the onset of the appropriate selling season. The storage function is creating **time utility** for customers.

These days, most products are stored just long enough to perform any required accumulating, sorting, and allocating functions that needed to make them available to the next channel member. These functions generally are performed in specialized warehouses called **distribution centers**. These are large, typically single story facilities designed specifically for performing the accumulating, sorting, and allocating functions as efficiently as possible. For example, Core-Mark maintains a number of distribution centers at key points in the United States. These centers receive products from a large number of manufacturers in truckloads. Deliveries are received, sorted, accumulated, and reallocated to retailers in an efficient and timely manner.

Transportation

Transportation (shipping) involves the physical movement of finished goods, raw materials, and component parts. Such products are typically shipped in the United States by trucks, trains, barges or ships, airfreight, or pipelines. Each shipping medium is called a **transportation mode**. The term used when multiple transportation modes—trains, planes, automobiles, trucks, pipelines, barges, etc.—are employed to ship any item is **intermodal transportation**.

Communications

Communication occurs up and down throughout supply chains, including various forms of promotion targeted at intermediaries and ultimate customers. The most fundamental reason for communication up and down the supply chain is to create *exchanges*; actual buying and selling results in the transfer of ownership of products from one channel member to another.

Supply chain members employ a wide range of promotional activities to disseminate information about the availability and features of products to other members of the chain. For example, Nike may advertise its products to consumers on TV and point out that they are available at your local JC Penney's. Similarly, Nike may run advertisements in trade journals or participate in trade shows to announce its upcoming new lines in order to create interest with its wholesale and retail partners. Nike may also use its own sales people to provide merchandising assistance to its supply chain partners.

Similarly, retailers commonly advertise sales and special events in local newspapers and on cable TV to support its producer partners. These ads often are partially funded by manufacturers of the products advertised, as part of a cooperative promotional agreement.

The communications function also facilitates the *collection of information* about markets and the activities of other supply chain members. For example, manufacturers may rely on middlemen to collect information about consumers and competitors in order to improve their marketing activities. This may take the form of dedicated marketing research projects, or may be something as simple as passing along customer complaints, suggestions, and requests.

Financing and Risk Taking

By accepting ownership—buying the product—a supply chain member is **risk taking**, accepting some degree of risk. If products don't sell, spoil while in storage, or are otherwise damaged during shipment or storage before they are sold, losses are incurred. In some cases, losses can prove substantial.

A number of business entities provide **financing** to members of the supply chain, making it possible for them to engage in the myriad of supply chain functions previously discussed. Most supply chain members offer financing for their customers in the form of credit. This credit function amounts to allowing customers a period of time in which to pay their bills. Typically, 30, 60, or 90 days are quoted as payment due dates after the customer has been invoiced, or after the merchandise has been delivered. Longer payment terms essentially allow the buyer to generate some sales (and revenue) before the bill becomes due!

These functions are all essential. As noted earlier, the only relevant question is who will perform the function best, not whether the function will be performed. Some Firm will have to perform each of these supply chain functions. No function can be eliminated. However, supply chain members could choose to perform more of these functions themselves, if they can perform them better and at lower costs. This is exactly what Walmart hopes when it chooses to eliminate wholesaling intermediaries from its supply chains and establishes distribution warehouses with its own fleet of trucks. Only a few years post-launch, Walmart's trucking arm was already the world's largest.

Supply chain members exist, and succeed, because they add value. As you know, marketing success will accrue to the Firm that delivers the most value. Supply chain members add value by bridging *time*, the right time; *place*, the right place; and *possession* gaps that separate the producers of products and services from those that would use them.

How Supply Chains Bridge Gaps and Add Value

Consider this summary of how the supply chain for Larry the Lobster (not his real name) operates, adding value at each level. As of this book's printing, Larry or one of his friends or family members could be pulled from a trap off the Nova Scotia coast and be sold live immediately after the lobster boat docks for about $4.00 a pound. He will be eaten about eight days later in New York or Toronto, Canada or even Shanghai at an average price of about $52.50 a pound. Two-pounder Larry will have survived healthy, and as happy as lobsters can be, up to 16 minutes before he was eaten. At T minus 16 minutes Larry was dropped in boiling water, cooked for 14 minutes and served, two minutes later, steaming, on someone's plate.

This distribution miracle is possible because of the magic of the North American lobster supply chain and the supply chain functions performed by various Firms and individuals as Larry was trapped, extricated from the trap, placed in salt water on the boat; sold, then drugged by his new owner to an essentially comatose state; sold again, received a colonic (yes, a colonic is what you think it is; done for taste-enhancing purposes) from his third owner; sold, and then bound-up, claw-wise (hungry lobsters eat other lobsters in the tank); inventoried and shipped by yet another owner to some point on the North American continent or perhaps halfway around the world; whereupon, Larry finally visits another tank in a nice restaurant. All told, about 30 people and exactly five organizations owned, touched, and added value to Larry in route to your stomach. This, of course, is why the cost of a two-pound, $8.00 lobster multiplies as he ends his time on an expensive restaurant plate at the end of a highly specialized supply chain.

→ Primary Supply Chain Designs

Two basic supply chain designs exist: conventional supply chains and vertical marketing systems.

Conventional Supply Chains (CMS)

The first supply chain configuration is the conventional marketing system (CMS). Exhibit 13.2 described earlier in the chapter depicts the typical conventional marketing system. In a CMS, each level in the supply chain operates under independent ownership. In other words, the producers and their suppliers, as well as all downstream marketing intermediaries (wholesaling middlemen and retailers) are separate business entities. Each possesses its own goals, objectives, and priorities that can lead to conflict within the supply chain. Each of these independent supply chain members tends to make decisions in its own best interests. The interests of other members and concerns about the overall efficiency of the supply chain become secondary. In some cases, very large Firms possess the ability to impose their will on other members of their supply chains. As noted, these Firms are called **Channel Captains**. Traditionally, Channel Captains in supply chains have been large producers, such as Proctor & Gamble in consumer non-durable products, and General Electric in appliances. Their sheer size and the tremendous demand for their products have allowed these companies to make demands of, and extract concessions from, their suppliers, and also dictate how their products are handled by most middlemen. Today, however, Channel Captains are also just as likely to be large wholesalers, such as McKesson and Core-Mark; or large retailers, such as Walmart, Best Buy, and JC Penney.

JC Penney, wherein everything sold by the Firm is produced by another supply chain partner and often shipped or inventoried by another Firm, exemplifies a conventional marketing system. While Penney exercises substantial influence over what happens in its supply chains, the Firms with which Penney works operate as independent corporate entities. As such, Penney's partners can honor or reject its requests, terms, or prices based on their own free will. Consequently, conflict is much more likely to arise in conventional marketing systems.

Other huge Firms that operate in conventional marketing systems include McKesson, the world's largest pharmaceutical wholesaler. While mammoth in size and thus influential, McKesson neither manufactures nor retails drugs to end-use consumers (Firms such as CVS, Walgreen's or Walmart do this). "Big Pharma" Firms such as Pfizer or Eli Lilley focus on making and marketing pharmaceuticals. Pfizer and Lilly concentrate especially heavily on new product development (NPD), because that's where the best opportunity to make huge profits resides. Substantive pharmaceutical innovations can be patent-protected for up to twenty years. This patent-protection permits Firms to achieve monopoly-like profits. Not having to perform distribution-related supply chain functions (i.e., inventory management, shipping, warehousing, order processing) for themselves permits Big Pharma Firms to focus on NPD. Of course, neither McKesson nor Big Pharma Firms operate at the retail level of the supply chain. Firms such as Walgreen's, Walmart, CVS and thousands of other "Mom and Pop" pharmacies sell pharmaceuticals at the retail level.

Vertical Marketing Systems (VMS)

Vertically integrated supply chains, also known as vertical marketing systems (VMS), are of two types:

- **Corporate Vertical Marketing Systems** in which one member of the supply chain has vertically integrated, either forward or backward (or both), to own and control much of the supply chain.
- **Contractual Vertical Marketing Systems** in which there exist contractual agreements between supply chain members dictating how relationships between members should be conducted.

In either form of VMS, Channel Captains can exist, just as we saw in the Conventional Marketing System.

Corporate Vertical Marketing System

Kimberly Clark, as discussed previously, manufactures toilet paper. But the Firm also owns or controls access to the trees and mills involved in harvesting the raw materials and manufacturing the toilet paper, as well as various other Firms performing various functions that operate in its supply chain. Exxon-Mobil is also highly vertically integrated. Exxon owns the land or land rights below the water in which oil drilling is done, drilling Firms, oil refineries, and fuel stations. The Exxon supply chain is vertically integrated from "dirt to dirt." Insofar as Walmart owns and manages the world's largest trucking fleet and dozens of huge distribution centers, it operates a partially vertically integrated Firm. However, Walmart is still considered to operate within the confines of a Conventional Marketing System.

The term "vertical integration" captures the degree to which one Firm owns upstream supplier or source Firms and downstream shippers, warehouses, marketing agents and/or retailers. Exhibit 13.8 illustrates the conceptual differences between a CMS and a vertically integrated supply system, or Corporate Vertical Marketing System. (We prefer the term Corporate Vertical Supply Chain, but employ the traditional term in this book).

Contractual Vertical Marketing Systems

In contractual vertical marketing systems, supply chain functions are coordinated and controlled by legal contracts between supply chain members. There are three basic types of contractual VMS: (1) Voluntary Chains; (2) Retailer Cooperatives; and, (3) Franchises.

Wholesaler Sponsored Voluntary Chain

The voluntary chain is a contractual arrangement between a large wholesaler and a series of smaller, independent retailers. In this arrangement, retailers agree by contract to buy from only one wholesaler who, in turn, agrees to provide each retailer with all its products and required services. Voluntary chains are common in the grocery and hardware industries. In the hardware industry, a well-known voluntary chain is Sentry Hardware. Similarly,

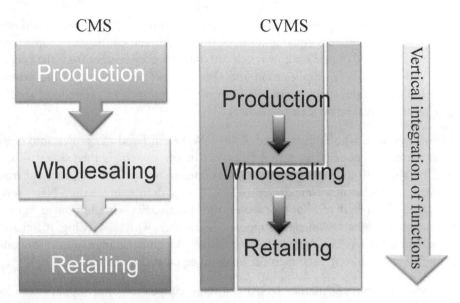

CMS   **CVMS**

Production

Wholesaling

Retailing

Production

Wholesaling

Retailing

Vertical integration of functions

Exhibit 13.8 *Common ownership of multiple channel levels distinguishes the Corporate Vertical Marketing System (CVMS) from the Conventional Marketing System (CMS).*

SUPERVALU sponsors a voluntary chain in the grocery industry. SUPERVALU, in fact, is the nation's largest grocery wholesaler. The giant supplies nearly 1,900 independently owned and operated stores with a competitive mix of branded and unbranded merchandise, as well as a wide range of services. These stores all operate under the SUPERVALU name.

SUPERVALU offers its member retailers a wide variety of services that allow them to compete effectively with large corporate grocery chains. These services include (among others):

- Market assessment, new store sales forecasting, competitive assessments
- Site selection
- Store design and layout, equipment, and fixtures
- Professional product and market research
- Financing, licensing, legal services, and insurance
- Management and training
- Merchandising assistance and cooperative promotion programs
- Computer hardware and software for retail applications

Retailer Cooperatives

Retailer cooperatives are a second form of contractual VMS. While the voluntary chain is organized by a wholesaler, the retailer co-op is set-up by retailers. However, the basic functions and advantages of both forms of contractual VMS are fundamentally the same.

Retailer co-ops are very common in both the hardware and grocery industries. In retail hardware, this form of VMS still accounts for a significant proportion of total industry sales—about 35%. True Value Hardware and Ace Hardware are representative examples of retailer-owned hardware cooperatives.

Associated Wholesale Grocers, Wakefern, Associated Foods Stores, IGA, and Certified Grocers probably are the best examples of retailer co-ops in the grocery industry. According to Hoovers, Associated Wholesale Grocers (AWG), is the nation's second-largest retailer-owned cooperative (Wakefern is the largest). AWG is jointly owned by over 350 retailers. There are roughly 850 supermarkets operating under the AWG banner in 10 Midwestern and Southern states. Members each own an equal amount of stock, with end-of-the-year profits passed on in the form of dividends based on how much merchandise they bought from the cooperative. Like SUPERVALU, AWG supplies food and nonfood merchandise, including private-label products. It also provides services ranging from market research and store merchandising to loan programs and real estate lease assistance.

Started by seven men who each invested $1,000, Wakefern Food has grown into one of the largest supermarket cooperatives and wholesalers in the eastern United States. The co-op is owned by about 40 independent grocers who operate nearly 200 ShopRite supermarkets in Connecticut, Delaware, New Jersey (where it is a dominant chain), New York, and Pennsylvania. About half of ShopRite stores offer pharmacies. In addition to name-brand and private-label products, Wakefern supports its members with advertising, merchandising, insurance, and other services. Although the holdings of members range in size from one store to 32 (Big V Supermarkets), each member holds an equal voting share.

The Independent Grocer's Alliance (IGA) is a retail cooperative that supplies branded and private-label grocery and nonfood merchandise to more than 3,000 supermarkets. IGA was originally operated as a voluntary chain by Fleming Foods. However, subsequent to Fleming's bankruptcy in 2003, IGA was restructured into a retail cooperative.

Certified Grocers of California distributes food and general merchandise to about 2,750 independent grocers in Arizona, California, Hawaii, Mexico, and the South Pacific. The food wholesaler and cooperative supplies dry groceries, frozen and prepared foods, meats, and deli items, as well as its own bakery and dairy goods. In addition to name-brand items, its offerings include the private labels Springfield, Gingham, Golden Creme, La Corona, and Special Value. The co-op also supplies member support services, including store remodeling, financing, and insurance. Certified serves about 680 retailers, many of whom own shares in the company.

Franchises

Franchises involve contractual agreements between a parent company (franchisor) and independent business operators (franchisees). In the contract, the franchisor grants the franchisee the right to operate under its trademark. The franchisor typically provides a wide range of management services to its members. The franchisee, in return, pays royalties or fees to the franchisor.

Franchise systems continue to grow in importance in our economy. As of 2013, franchise sales in the US generated roughly $839 billion in sales of goods and services and employed nearly nine million workers in 781,000 franchise establishments. Franchise sales for 2014 are expected to account for 4.5% of GDP. Food and Hospitality account for 65% of all franchises, followed by 29% in the services sector, and 6% in real estate and automotive.[3]

The **business format franchise** is the most common form of franchise operation. Indeed, this is the type of franchise most consumers normally envision when the term "franchise" is mentioned. In the franchise contract, the franchisee receives the right to sell goods or services, and has access to a wide range of services provided by the franchisor. Included in this category are virtually all of the fast food, consumer services, hotel/motel, and retail store franchises that dominate most local economies. Virtually every community has a McDonald's, KFC, Wendy's, Midas Muffler, La Quinta Motel, H&R Block, Subway, and/or a 7-11. With this form of franchise, the franchisee is purchasing a method of operation or a way to do business. The franchisee is buying a package that has been well-tested and proven to work! If the franchisee runs the business as intended by the franchisor, he or she is virtually guaranteed to succeed!

Franchising has distinct advantages over operating as an independent business. The biggest advantage to the franchisee is the tremendous *reduction in risk* associated with running one's own business due to the tested and proven format of the franchise operation. The franchisee is provided with management assistance, training, store designs, quality control and accounting systems, and group advertising and promotions. Equally important are the scale economies in purchasing and promotion provided by the franchisor. The franchisor possesses the overall size and, therefore, buying power to allow each franchisee to *compete on a cost and price basis* with larger corporate chains. In addition, by pooling the resources of a number of franchisees, the franchisor can run very sophisticated promotions that include advertising and sales promotions that individual franchisees could not afford on their own.

Franchisors also benefit from the relationship, because the franchisee must contribute some capital to establish the franchise; the *franchisor needs less capital for expansion* and can *expand more rapidly*. The *risk of doing business is essentially shared* with the franchisees.

Not all franchises are equally profitable. Unfortunately, some franchises are so poorly organized and managed that they essentially amount to scams. Moreover, some are much more expensive to establish than others. The least expensive franchises are usually in service industries. For example, a Rooter-Man franchise costs between $50,000 and $105,000 including all fees and start-up costs.[4] In contrast, the cost of setting up a McDonalds franchise will easily exceed $1,000,000.

A significant advantage to franchising is the ability to share promotional costs. Each franchisee typically contributes a small percentage of its profits to a common promotional pool. These funds are employed to create promotional programs that benefit all franchisees operating in a given geographic area. For example, McDonald's requires each franchisee to contribute 4% of gross sales annually to the corporate advertising and promotion budget.

→ Three Major Supply Chain Design-Related Decisions

Managers must make three discrete decisions as they ascertain which supply chain design to use and which partner, including possibly themselves, will perform a given supply chain function. These three decisions are examined below.

Types of Intermediaries to Use

The general menu of choices includes manufacturers; intermediary firms, including shippers and transportation specialists; wholesalers; warehouses; agents; retailers; and various marketing firms that specialize in delivering either branding, advertising, or promotional management functions. Decisions about which specific intermediaries are needed are largely a function of:

- The type of product and the market to which it is sold.
- The expectations of the customers who buy the product.
- The resource base of the company.
- How competitors are distributing their products.
- Relative costs and profits associated with employing different intermediaries.
- The range of services offered by the intermediaries available.

Determining the specific intermediaries to use based on these criteria entails an understanding of the fundamental differences between the types of intermediaries that serve different channels. This is why we delay our discussion of how specific intermediaries are chosen until we examine the types of wholesaling and retailing intermediaries in the next chapter.

How Many Supply Chain Intermediaries to Use

Supply chains in which there are few levels of intermediaries are called shorter, or more direct, supply chains. The shortest supply chain in which producers sell direct to end-users is called a **direct channel**. Direct channels are most common in B2B supply chains. Supply chains in which more levels of intermediaries separate manufacturers from end-use customers are described as indirect. **Indirect channels** are more common in B2C supply chains.

A related consideration is how many intermediaries are needed at each level in the supply chain. Three general levels of **distribution intensity** are commonly recognized, although these three levels actually exist on a continuum with one another (Exhibit 13.9). **Intensive distribution** attempts to achieve maximum retail exposure for a product. Every suitable retail outlet is targeted. This type of distribution is best suited to consumer *convenience goods* and some *shopping goods*. To a lesser extent, in the B2B arena, intensive distribution may be appropriate for some industrial supplies. Intensive distribution is appropriate whenever the product is such that customers will not go out of their way to find a specific brand and/or will easily accept substitute brands. If a specific producer's brand is not represented, consumers will switch to an available alternative. Soft drink and candy distribution are typical examples. Pepsi and Coke employ very intensive distribution through supermarkets, convenience stores, restaurants, and vending machines. Every appropriate retail facility is targeted for distribution. Similarly, Mars, the makers of brands such as M&Ms, TWIX, Milky Way, and Snickers employ intensive distribution via the same types of outlets.

Selective distribution limits the sale of products to a smaller range of retail outlets. This form of distribution is most appropriate for *shopping* and some *specialty products* that are tailored to meet the needs of well-defined market segments. For much the same reasons, selective distribution is employed for most *industrial equipment*. Producers can limit distribution to those middlemen that best reach the targeted segments. Polo and Tommy Hilfiger in fashion clothing and accessories are distributed through select retailers possessing images that are consistent with the desired positions of these brands. Both firms work hard to establish solid relationships with their retail partners to ensure that their products are properly represented to consumers. In return for limiting their distribution to these select retailers and, therefore,

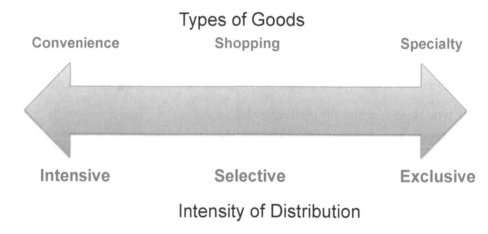

Exhibit 13.9 *The Continuum of Distribution Intensity.*

limiting the amount of retail competition, Ralph Lauren and Tommy Hilfiger expect these retailers to provide more support for their brands by acquiescing to their demands on how their products should be marketed.

Exclusive distribution is the most restricted form of distribution. This form of distribution is best suited to *specialty goods* and some *shopping goods*, as well as industrial equipment and installations. Specialty products such as Rolls Royce, Joy Perfume, and Rolex watches are sold through only a select number of highly screened resellers. Anytime the product requires extensive support by the retailer, producers are wise to consider establishing exclusive distribution arrangements. In return for assuring the reseller that it will face no competition in local markets for the producer's brand, the reseller generally agrees to carry an extensive inventory, provide considerable promotional and merchandising support, offer repair services, and agree to honor other special arrangements.

In the industrial arena, John Deere and Caterpillar distribute their products through tightly-controlled and heavily-supported networks of industrial distributors. Products sold by these Firms typically are high priced and require extensive servicing. Exclusive distribution agreements are often specified contractually. The contract outlines exactly the expectations of both parties with respect to inventory requirements, amounts and types of promotional support, any required personnel training, honoring of product warranties, provision for repair and maintenance services, pricing, credit arrangements, and payment terms.

Number and Types of Supply Chain Functions to Be Performed

The third decision involves determining which supply chain functions must be performed and which intermediaries are best suited to perform these functions; that is to say, distinguishing between those supply chain functions whose performance a given Firm would willingly outsource to a competent supply chain provider and those that the same Firm would prefer to control and consequently execute itself. We conceptually expand on this decision area in the next section, but will examine the implications for choosing specific partnering Firms (primarily intermediaries) in the next chapter.

→ One World-Changing Question (Seriously, It Is)

As referenced above, the question in question is who, as in which Firm, will perform what supply chain function? The question of which Firm will perform what function, in turn, relates to supply chain "design choices" made by managers. The advantages or disadvantages associated with one "design choice" as opposed to another generally pivot based on two criteria.

The first design choice criterion relates to customer needs, specifically, the satisfaction of customer needs. The second criterion relates to a "cost versus control" issue.

Which Supply Chain Design Is Best?

The question of which supply chain design is best for a given market context should begin, logically, with an analysis of customer needs. Indeed, customer needs should provide the basis for most strategic marketing decisions. That is, the satisfaction of customer needs should function as a determinant decision-making factor. Consequently, the best supply chain design choice is always the one that does the best job of satisfying customer needs at an *optimal cost*. Notably, optimal cost need not mean lowest cost.

The delivery of higher levels of supply chain customer service necessary to satisfy customer needs is simply going to cost more. There is no way around this fact. Yet the satisfaction of customer needs must be balanced against the Firm's strategic goals and cost constraints. For example, the needs of Walmart customers, on average, differ radically from the needs of Neiman-Marcus customers. So, on average, the nature of the costs associated with Walmart's or Neiman's supply chains differ, too—a great deal, in fact.

The second factor that should be considered when managers seek to determine which supply chain design is best for their firm is embedded in the following question:

> *Will my Firm be better off if it can lower costs by outsourcing the performance of a supply chain function to some other Firm or Firms inside our supply chain?*

If the answer is yes, then the Firm makes a "buy" decision. In other words, the Firm buys the performance of the marketing function from a supply chain partner. This decision presumably would allow each partner to focus on what it does best; i.e., to specialize.

Alternatively, managers should ask: Will my Firm be better off if it generally maintains greater control over how a given supply chain function is performed? If the answer is yes, then the Firm should opt for a "make" decision. Here, the decision-making Firm should perform the marketing function(s) itself.

Two Supply Chain Design Principles

Some basic supply chain principles will apply universally as managers ponder these questions. First, if a Firm performs a supply channel function itself, it pays more because performance of the function probably will cost more. But the Firm maintains control over how the function is performed.

Second, if the Firm engages another firm in its supply chain to perform a supply chain function, the decision-making Firm generally will pay less for the function to be performed. But the originating Firm will give up some control over how the function is performed, right?

How much do you or your Firm value control? Which outcome is worth more to your Firm? Is it achieving lower supply chain costs by outsourcing performance of the function? Or, is it maintaining control over how the function is performed, even knowing your Firm will pay more to have the function executed?

Most Firms opt for alternative one. Fewer select the second alternative. Presumably these latter Firms operate in marketplace and competitive contexts in which consistently high levels of product quality (i.e., freedom from defects) and/or customer service or possibly on-time performance are absolute "must-haves," as opposed to "nice-to-haves."

→ In the End, Supply Chain Relationships Are Prone to Conflict …

Although greater collaboration and cooperation between supply chain partners is the goal, conflict inside supply chain relationships is almost inevitable. Conflict arises for exactly the same reasons why clashes occur in most long-term human relationships. People always bring their personal goals to any relationship. Humans are inexorably wired to be concerned first about me and mine—my family, my Firm. When my goal comes into conflict with your goal, and neither is willing to bend, conflict will inevitably arise.

Worth nothing at this point, however, is that attempts to unilaterally (one-sidedly) apply power usually fail in today's supply chains. Walmart itself has seen many former source Firms walk away from the opportunity to sell through the world's largest retailer because they were no longer willing to bow to Walmart's expectations. Simplicity, a marketing of lawn equipment, recently terminated its relationship with the Arkansas giant because its management saw no profitable future in continuing the relationship. In an era where more competitive, information-driven, globally-accessible supply options are widely available, coercive power is now used less frequently than once was the case. (Note, we are not implying that Walmart coerces its source Firms.)

Things Got Really Ugly

Estee Lauder Co., the $10 plus billion-per-year marketer of female hopes and dreams, and one also would suppose male fantasies, now sells most of its flagship products directly online. This choice, made around 2000, created huge conflict with the various high-end retailers (Nordstrom's, Saks Fifth Avenue, Bloomingdales) who had made Lauder's Clinique line their top seller in the prestige skin-care and cosmetics market. At the same time Estee Lauder, in order to grow its Internet presence, also radically grew its chain of freestanding stores and catalogues. But Estee Lauder, at the time, was understandably and justifiably doing what it strategized was best for itself and its brands. Estee Lauder was simply being about "me and mine"—just like any Firm would be. Clearly, however, what Estee Lauder did encompassed more than making just cosmetic changes to its existing supply chain relationships. Launder's strategic moves created huge new sources of conflict between its manufacturers and channel intermediaries; its wholesalers, distributors, resellers, and retailers.

More than ever, the question of who "owns" direct access to final consumers inside this cosmetics supply chain remains perpetually up for grabs in an Internet-enabled world. When more cooperative supply chain relationships are in play, both partners "own" the customer and can work together more efficiently to develop mutually beneficial marketing strategies. Both partners ideally would more willingly share information as a necessary precursor to securing mutual access to customers. Thereafter, collaborative supply chain partners can more easily assume joint responsibility for managing the entire customer experience more effectively.

Conflict: Not Necessarily Bad

Let's continue this discussion bolstered by one common thought: conflict is not necessarily a bad thing. Once supply chain managers accept this fact, they will be prepared to develop climates within the supply chain that facilitate greater cooperation and creativity. Collaborative creativity facilitates innovation. Remember innovation—in this context, ideas leading to new and useful supply chain solutions. Innovation, in turn, represents productive change even, and perhaps especially, in the face of crises. Finally, remember that crises, as could easily be fomented by conflict, also represent opportune moments to institute necessary changes, and thus are terrible things to waste. As we said, conflict is far from a universally negative thing, particularly inside supply chains.

Moreover, when listening—that's right, just listening—is used as a means of steering conflict away from positional disagreement (the "me and mine" thing again) and, instead, toward an exchange of ideas and thoughts, supply chain managers will be better able to maintain energetic, fully-engaged participation in productive, enduring relationships. As supply chain managers acquire more mutually collaborative mindsets (because they are listening to each other), they should more readily seek resolutions that satisfy their "side" while still accommodating the other partner's "side." Conflict then slowly or suddenly transforms into opportunities to learn more, innovate better, and eventually grow superior solutions. Easier said than done, of course, but at least it has been said.

Key Ingredients for Resolving Conflict

Like newlyweds who never lived together before they got married, supply chain managers are frequently shocked by how quickly once cozy relationships turn south. Problems could arise not only around issues such as who performs what supply chain function, but also in more nebulous areas such as personal relationships between individuals operating in different corporate, regional, or international cultures. Perhaps the biggest stumbling block to successful partnerships is a lack of trust, which generally contributes to an absence of liking, which inevitably leads to two supply chain parties not wanting to play well together.

Without trust, things can get personal quick. As conflict arises, people generally gravitate toward one of two positions: digging in their heels, convinced they are right, or attempting to understand what is motivating their "foe's" misbehavior. How do you think that the absence or presence of trust would affect the position you would most likely occupy?

Think back to your last argument. What if you had trusted the other party so much that you took the position of trying to understand his or her position? Most likely, at that point, there would have been no conflict at all. Or, at the least, the dispute causing the conflict could have been resolved more quickly.

You may think, "Why should I be the calm and rational one who has to make it work? Why can't I be the unreasonable one every now and then?" We would suggest instead you would simply be the one who figured out first how best to manage the conflict. We assure you, under such circumstances, you would usually be better off.

As supply chain conflict arises all parties would benefit if they could agree, assuming the following statements are true, that:

- We are better off working together than separately.
- At the least, despite the nature of any specific conflict, we still respect each other.
- In the long run, which is where we're going together, sometimes the other side prevails (i.e., takes away more value), at others time my side will win, but eventually such things, like life itself, average out.

The heart, soul, and ultimate purpose of any supply chain—or interpersonal—relationship lies in understanding that we're better together than apart. This is no pie-in-the-sky philosophy. The increasing density and complexity of human knowledge, never ending deluges of global competitors, and the escalating difficulty of gaining sustainable competitive advantages in markets full of customer options means supply chain managers must learn to work together more collaboratively. Otherwise, they will fail alone; having fallen prey to the superiority generated within competing supply chains that have figured out how to work together better.

Additional insights about how best to address supply chain conflict as it arises follow:

- Understand conflict resolution styles. Evaluate your and your supply chain partners preferred methods of conflict resolution. Understanding each other will invariably provide a head-start to those seeking to resolve conflict.

- Give positive responses and honest feedback to supply chain partners as often as possible to avoid a negative atmosphere.

- Evaluate the value of the supply chain relationship. Ask whether winning this fight will move you closer to an optimal relationship or further away from the ideal.

- Check your ego at the door. Understand, always, the distinction between egomania and self-esteem. Which one do you think better serves your purpose? Use your ego. Never let it use you, because if your ego is left unbridled, it will. Supply chain managers should consciously avoid the "I" when attempting to resolve conflict. Your partners don't want to wade through your ego to get to the information they need.

- Decisions produce behaviors. Behaviors generate consequences. Be mindful of the consequences that your behaviors or non-behaviors engender as you attempt to resolve any supply chain conflict. And remember, consequences can be positive or negative, even though most people tend to reflexively consider consequences as negative.

- Pick battles carefully. Never take on everything that bothers you; otherwise there will be constant conflict and turmoil. Learn to distinguish between annoying behaviors or habits and actual problems that impede the effectiveness of the partnership.

- Don't feel guilty. As noted, healthy supply chain relationships are not conflict-free zones. Healthy relationships are those that have learned how best to deal more effectively, albeit never perfectly, with conflict.

- Understand and accept the cultural norms of the "other." Geographic, ethnic, and corporate cultural differences are in play in many supply chains. For example, what is polite in NYC or Beijing is not necessarily polite in Dallas, TX, or Charlotte, N.C. Such differences should be accounted for.

- Don't overthink what could go wrong in any conflict-resolution conversation. Look more broadly at the conversation as an opportunity to address a key issue that needs to be addressed. No one can plan an entire conversation; do your best and go with the flow. Little will be gained by wasting time or psychic energy wondering or worrying about what the other partner will accept. Instead, enter negotiations mindful of what is acceptable to you and your Firm. Use that as a starting point and work from there.

- Never rush through the awkwardness. Easy conflict resolution is not necessary for good conflict resolution. Conflict resolved too quickly is likely not resolved at all. Spend more time outlining the situation causing the problem rather than assigning blame. Then, both parties will enjoy a better, nonjudgmental grasp of the problem causing the conflict. There is no cliché in suggesting supply chain partners who understand the causes of any problem are well down the road to resolving it. No point in pointing out the other side's flaws given that your side probably has a few logs in its eye, as well.

- When it's over, it's over. Once the problem causing the conflict is resolved, get over it. Holding grudges about what happened only ensures further problems.

- Stay cool, or fake the cool until you make the cool. Over time, the person and thus the Firm that wants it least (with the least emotion) or appears to want it least typically holds the power advantage.

Formal Procedural Steps for Negotiating Conflict Resolution

The most broadly accepted procedural steps for resolving supply chain conflicts are to:[6]

- *Identify and Define the Problem.* Remember, problems well-defined are problems half-solved. As problems are defined supply chain partners should seek to distinguish the problem's symptoms from the core factors that are actually causing problems. The focus should be on these core casual factors.

- *Generate Possible Solutions.* Be sure to distinguish between facts and assumptions when framing the solution set. Focus on facts as much as possible. Make any assumptions clear.

- *Evaluate Possible Solutions.* When and where possible, use logic and mature judgment rather than personal biases. Do you want to get even or do you want the supply chain partnership to move forward toward a more positive place?

- *Select Solution(s).* Remember, there may be no single best solution; a combination of alternatives may be the preferred solution.

- *Evaluate the Results.* If things are not working out, it may be necessary to revisit the problem-solving process.

Closing Thoughts

While they do not exist in a "class by themselves," supply chain relationships do operate in a "class with a short roll." Being a member of a supply chain means interacting with other Firms. The world of supply chain relationships is unusual if not unique. This is because there is the potential for win-win relationships between supply chain partners. Markets reward supply chains in which its partners are mutually "winning." Markets would shift away from those supply chains in which there were "winners" at the expense of "losers," favoring an alternative supply chain in which partners were mutually winning. In fact, if the supply chain exchange relationship did not feel right to each buyer/seller who engages with others in the partnership, neither party would participate for long. Think about it.

By definition, every supply chain exchange relationship features a buyer and a seller. And, usually and unfortunately, either the buyer or the seller is actually right (the winner of more value!) and the other partner is wrong (loser of more value!). Why? Because either the value gotten from the seller is less than the value the buyer gave up to obtain the object of transaction, or the value given up by the seller was greater than the value the buyer gave up to obtain the object of the exchange.

The truth, then, is that one supply chain partner inevitably wins or loses, even if just by a little. Perhaps surprisingly, here at the end, we recommend that supply chain participants should try to avoid winning or losing too big. Yes, we believe supply chain partners should never "win too big," even when they can. This means, essentially, never take the last dollar off the table even when your current size or power would allow you to do it. Why? Because the individual or Firm from whom you take the "last dollar" may well spend the rest of his/her/its life wanting and waiting to get back at you—and one day that opportunity may arise.

Mighty oaks always begin life as little acorns, after all. Think about the long-term. After all, that is where we are all going to live, work, play—and succeed or fail.

Endnotes

1 Leonard E. Read, "I, Pencil: My Family Tree as told to Leonard E. Read" (Irvington-on-Hudson, NY: The Foundation for Economic Education, Inc., 1999), Library of Economics and Liberty, accessed 18 February 2015, http://www.econlib.org/library/Essays/rdPncl1.html.

2 "The Downside of Too Many Product Choices on Store Shelves," *Consumer Reports Magazine* March 2014, accessed February 19, 2015, http://www.consumerreports.org/cro/magazine/2014/03/too-many-product-choices-in-supermarkets/index.htm.

3 Franchise Businesses Projected to Again Grow Faster Than the Rest of the Economy in 2015," *International Franchise Association*, accessed 20 February 2015, http://www.franchise.org/franchise-businesses-projected-to-again-grow-faster-than-the-rest-of-the-economy-in-2015.

4 Rooter-Man Franchise, *Entrepreneur*, accessed February 16, 2015, http://www.entrepreneur.com.

5 Douglas McIntyre, "How Much Does it Cost to Own a McDonald's Franchise?", 24/7 WallSt, July 25, 2013, accessed February 13, 2015, http://247wallst.com/retail/2013/07/25/how-much-does-it-cost-to-own-a-mcdonalds-franchise.

6 Lou Pelton, David Strutton, and James Lumpkin, *Marketing Channels: A Relationship Management Approach* (New York: McGraw-Hill, 2002).

Chapter 14

KEY INTERMEDIARIES: WHOLESALERS, RETAILING AND FACILITATING AGENTS

This chapter examines wholesalers, retailers and facilitating agents, and the marketing and distribution functions each performs in supply chains. Wholesalers, retailers, and facilitating agents are each middlemen and are also known as **intermediaries** (Exhibit 14.1). Intermediaries exist to bridge the supply chain gaps that separate entities that produce (manufacturers) from those who ultimately consume (consumers). End-use customers, as in you or us.

Now do you see why the role that intermediaries play is so important?

Retailers (retailing intermediaries) exist and operate as the last link in supply chains. Retailers exist primarily to make retail sales to ultimate consumers; retailers earn most of their income from retail sales. **Retailing** includes all activities involved in selling goods and services to ultimate consumers for their own personal use.

Firms that primarily engage in wholesale transactions are called **wholesalers** (wholesaling intermediaries). **Wholesaling** activities include all functions involved in the distribution or marketing of goods and services from one business to other businesses. Wholesaling organizations either resell products, use products to make other goods, or use products to operate their businesses or organizations.

Wholesalers never produce or consume the products that they distribute or sell. Wholesaling intermediaries instead link manufacturers to retailers. Many wholesaling intermediaries buy products from manufacturers and/or other wholesalers and resell them to other business, usually retailers. Some wholesaling middlemen function as independent sales forces for the manufacturers they represent. These sales forces earn commissions when they sell those manufacturers' products.

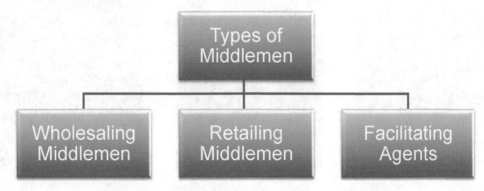

Exhibit 14.1 *Types of Middlemen (Intermediaries).*

Facilitating agents are the third type of supply chain intermediary. Facilitating agents are not directly involved in the transfer of title for products moved through the distribution channel. They do, however, provide a range of specialized support services that allow supply chains to function more efficiently. Banks, for example, are facilitating agents who provide the financial services that often prove necessary for other supply chain members (wholesalers and retailers) to establish and operate their businesses. Transportation firms, such as trucking companies and railroads, assist manufacturers and retailers by transporting products from point of production to point of consumption. Warehouses operated by third party operators provide access to various long-term and short-term specialized storage and inventory management facilities. These transportation firms and warehouses likewise function as facilitating agents.

→ Types of Wholesaling Intermediaries

Wholesaling middlemen fall into three broad categories: merchant wholesalers, agents, and manufacturers' sales offices and branches (Exhibit 14.2). Members of the first two categories (merchant wholesalers and agents) are each independent businesses. Merchant wholesalers and agents are not employees of, nor are they owned by, manufacturers.

Merchant wholesalers actually buy products from producers and then resell those products to other organizations. In other words, merchant wholesalers "take title" to the products they sell; they own them. Merchant wholesalers usually deliver a wide range of important services—supply chain functions—to both manufacturers and retailers.

Agents, by contrast, rarely if ever take title to the products they sell. Agents generally work on a commission basis. This means agents receive a percentage of the sales revenue they generate for manufacturers whose products they sell. Agents generally provide fewer services than merchant wholesalers for the manufacturers they represent.

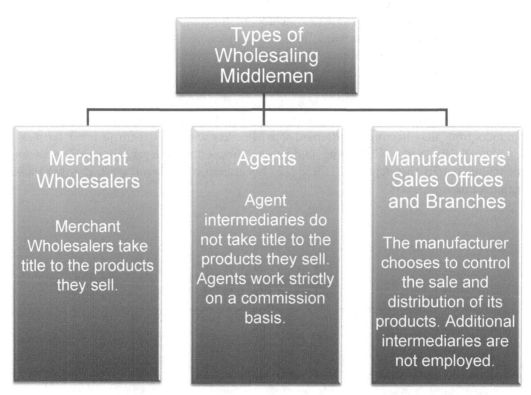

Exhibit 14.2 *Types of Wholesaling Middlemen (Intermediaries).*

Manufacturers' sales offices and **branches** are owned and operated by producers who engage, in part, in their own wholesaling activities.

Types of Merchant Wholesalers

Merchant wholesalers buy products from manufacturers and then resell them to other intermediaries, generally retailers. Merchant wholesalers are extremely important to the US economy. They handle or "touch" nearly 60% of all wholesale transactions. The remaining 40% is accounted for by agents, manufacturers' sales forces, and Internet distributors. Merchant wholesalers can be further classified into two basic types: full service and limited service. The appropriate classification depends on the range of services they provide to retailing and manufacturing supply chain partners (Exhibit 14.3).

Full Service Merchant Wholesalers

Full service merchant wholesalers can be further classified into three types: general merchandise merchant wholesalers, cooperatives, and specialty wholesalers. More than 75% of merchant wholesalers are full service merchants. The range of services that merchant wholesalers provide to manufacturers includes:

- Purchasing and owning inventory. Wholesalers bear substantial risk by actually purchasing products from manufacturers and granting credit to their buyers.
- Providing warehousing and, possibly, transportation functions for producers.
- Performing bulk-breaking and selling functions as necessary to "push" sales downstream to the next supply chain level. The fact that selling functions can be performed by wholesalers reduces the need for manufacturers to employ their own additional salespeople.
- Providing information about changing market and environmental conditions to manufacturers.

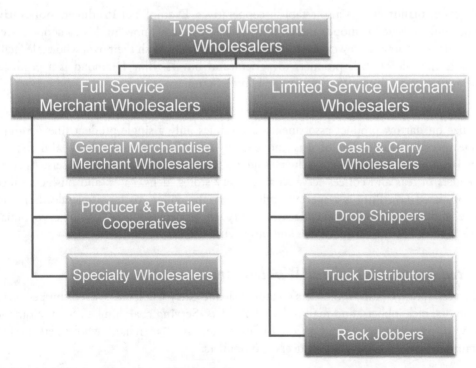

Exhibit 14.3 *Types of Merchant Wholesalers.*

Services that full service merchant wholesalers provide to retailers include the:

- Performance of part of the buying function. In the process, the wholesaler breaks bulk (allocates), accumulates bulk, and creates assortments to fit the retailer's requirements.
- Transference of title to retailers, often extending credit in the process.
- Providing storage and transportation services.
- Providing information about market conditions and competitor activities.

General merchandise merchant wholesalers carry a wide range of products, but usually stock each product line in only limited depth. These full service merchant wholesalers are the "department retail stores" of wholesaling. SUPERVALUE and McKesson are each general merchandise merchant retailers. These wholesaling behemoths carry huge assortments of manufactured products and provide impressive ranges of services to the retailers they support. SUPERVALUE serves the grocery industry. McKesson wholesales drugs and associated sundries. These large general merchandise wholesalers routinely stock entire stores from their shelves.

Full-service merchant wholesalers are called **industrial distributors** when they operate in organizational-goods markets. Grainger is a full-service industrial distributor of maintenance, repair, and operating (MRO) supplies, as well as small equipment used in a large cross-section of industries. Founded in 1927, Grainger is North America's leading wholesaler of MRO products for organizational use. With revenues exceeding $9 billion in 2013, the company employs over 22,000 people working in 400+ facilities in the United States, Asia, Europe, and Latin America.[1]

The *retail cooperative* is similar to a voluntary chain except that retailers, not wholesalers, have established the cooperative. Retailer-owned cooperatives, like Ace Hardware and True Value hardware, are particularly important in the hardware industry. In this sector, they account for a large proportion of industry sales. Associated Wholesale Grocers and Certified Grocers are grocery cooperatives.

Producers or manufacturers also establish cooperatives. Examples of **Producer cooperatives** include Sunkist, Blue Diamond, and Land-O-Lakes. You may know Sunkist, a cooperative in which numerous orange growers have banded together to establish their own wholesale facility to handle the sale of their products to agricultural buyers. Blue Diamond is a producer's cooperative serving almond growers in the United States.

Specialty wholesalers, also called limited line wholesalers, are full service intermediaries that specialize on narrow product assortments, sometimes only a single product line. Examples include specialty wholesalers of teas and coffees, specialty wholesalers of health foods or oriental foods, or automotive products sold exclusively to mass-merchandisers. Specialty wholesalers of teas and coffees serve small grocery stores, delis, cafés, and business offices. Houston-based Java Pura is a specialty wholesaler. The coffee roaster wholesales fair trade, organic, and limited production coffees. Specialty wholesalers like Java Pura are exceptionally knowledgeable about their industries and target customers.

Limited Service Merchant Wholesalers

Limited service merchant wholesalers include cash and carry wholesalers, drop shippers, truck distributors, rack jobbers, and mail order wholesalers. Serving coal, lumber, food, cosmetics, jewelry, or sporting goods industries, for example, these merchant wholesalers perform substantially fewer services for producers and retailers.

Cash and carry wholesalers offer minimal services to their customers, who are usually small retailers or service firms. Cash and carry wholesalers, however, will also sell to end-use (ultimate) consumers. Customers generally must physically visit the wholesaler's facilities, select merchandise, and often must pay cash. Examples include Sam's Club, Price Club, or Office Club. These wholesalers are popular with small businesses because of their low prices and self-service formats. As noted, most cash and carry wholesalers, such as Sam's Club, also sell directly to consumers.

Drop shippers are limited service merchant wholesalers. Drop shippers take title (they own the products), but never physically handle these products. Drop shippers are most common in "commodity" industries. For example, coal, coke, and various building materials are often purchased by drop shippers. But thereafter the products are typically shipped from their point of production directly to the buyer, usually an industrial user. Such products are quite bulky and their unit value is low relative to the costs associated with physically handling them. The drop shipper's objective is to minimize how much the product must be handled.

Truck distributors handle perishable or semi-perishable products that are delivered directly to small retail stores such as gas stations, convenience stores, small restaurants, hotels, business cafeterias, or delis. The products are usually national brands of dairy products, candies, breads and other bakery products, tobacco products, and snack foods. Small retailers often prefer to buy from truck distributors because they can buy in small enough amounts to limit spoilage on their shelves. Truck distributors provide frequent deliveries in small quantities, lowering the risk of financial loss for retailers. CD Hartnett is a truck distributor that serves Texas and contiguous states. Deliveries are made to convenience stores and small food service facilities providing over 6,000 **SKU's** (i.e., shop keeping units) with an in-stock fill rate of 99%.

Truck distributors are adding services to make themselves more valuable to customers and differentiate their services from other wholesaling competitors. For example, services offered by CD Hartnett to convenience stores include:

- Customized invoices, reports, and order guides with custom retails and profit margins.
- Proprietary logo products along with specialty advertising products.
- New and promotional items and specials.
- In-store planning and merchandise assistance, general merchandise programs.
- Rebate books and programs.
- Full deli support.
- Scanable shelf tags.
- EDI interfaces with all leading store computer systems.[2]

Rack jobbers are particularly common in the grocery industry. The shelves filled with toys, housewares, small hardware items, magazines, sunglasses, and greeting cards often are maintained and stocked by rack jobbers. Rack jobbers fill an important niche as they help small grocers engage in **scrambled merchandising** strategies. Rack jobbers provide a low risk way for smaller retailers to extend their product mixes. Rack jobbers set up displays and stock the shelves of these displays for retailers. Retailers merely provide floor space and consumers, which is a lot, but they never "own" products stocked by rack jobbers. Stated differently, rack jobbers retain ownership until consumers actually purchase products. Retailers are billed only after products have been sold. Because they sell their products on consignment, rack jobbers assume most of the risk of loss due to theft, damage, and product obsolescence.

Products can be wholesaled via mail order catalogs or through the Internet. An array of wholesale catalogs exists from which buyers can order products. Most catalogs are also digitally available. For example, Jillian Distributors of Austin, Texas is a wholesale distributor of products from more than one hundred different product categories. These categories include motorcycle gear, home and garden products, and home security equipment that is usually sold in bulk. Their customers are retailers of leather products and biker accessories.

Wholesale catalogs are often geared to specialty goods that are hard to obtain from traditional wholesalers. For example, Blue Ridge Knives is a catalog and Internet wholesaler of specialty knives that serves retail customers. Blue Ridge does not sell directly to consumers. With over 60,000 square feet of warehouse and office space, Blue Ridge stocks a wide selection of knives. Their physical catalog is available upon request to qualified dealers via the Internet.

Most general merchandise and limited service wholesalers now sell to traditional retail customers through the Internet as well as traditional supply chain venues. The lines between wholesale and retail sales via the Internet are blurring. This is because industrial distributors, such as Grainger, have expanded sales to include ultimate consumers. However, the consumer market still accounts for a small proportion of their overall sales.

Future of Merchant Wholesalers

Larger retailers and manufacturers are increasingly attempting to eliminate the wholesaler link from their supply chains. In particular, large retailers like Walmart often prefer to buy directly from producers. Manufacturers increasingly are pressured by retailers like Walmart to bypass traditional wholesalers. This trend threatens many wholesalers' future prospects.

Full service wholesalers have reacted to this threat in a number of ways. Many have upgraded their operations and added services to make themselves more important supply chain member— to both producers and retailers. Some are forming partnerships with other supply chain members, primarily by organizing into corporate or contractual vertical marketing systems. Numbers of mergers and acquisitions are also rising. Smaller, less efficient wholesalers are being swallowed up by larger operations in an attempt to achieve added operating efficiencies.

→ Agent Wholesaling Middlemen

The key distinction between merchant wholesalers and agents is that agents never own the products they sell. However, like merchant wholesalers, agent wholesaling middlemen are in business for themselves. They are not employees of the manufacturers for whom they sell. Agents primarily act as independent salespeople for the manufacturers they represent and are typically compensated on a commission basis. Depending on the specific industry, commissions can be as much as 20% of the wholesale price to retailer customers. Agents, in general, are expected to be experts for the products they sell. Small manufacturers that cannot afford their own sales forces rely heavily on the expertise of agents to sell their products for them. This permits manufacturers to concentrate on other issues meaning, presumably, they can focus on what they do best—making quality products.

Agents provide fewer services than merchant wholesalers. Sometimes agents may arrange for credit and delivery of products they sell. They also may provide physical facilities in which business can be conducted. For example, manufacturer's agents in the gift industry could maintain showroom space and offices in local merchandise marts. Retailers are invited to visit these showrooms to view the products made by the manufacturers the agent represents. Agents also tend to conduct a substantial amount of business on the road, visiting retailers' stores to show products and take orders.

Types of Agents

The most common types of agents are manufacturer's representatives, selling agents, brokers, commission merchants, and auction companies (Exhibit 14.4).

Manufacturers' Representatives

Manufacturers' representatives, also called **manufacturers' agents**, have grown in importance over the years, now accounting for over 30% of all sales by agent wholesaling intermediaries. These agents are independently-operated businesses. They are not employees of the manufacturers they represent. "Reps" essentially work as independent sales forces for the manufacturers they represent. Reps generally operate in limited geographic areas; most cover at most only a single state. Manufacturers who seek representation across wider geographic areas would usually need to hire additional manufacturers' agents to provide adequate coverage. In this case, the manufacturer will be represented by several reps, each covering a different geographic area or territory.

Exhibit 14.4 *Types of Agent Middlemen.*

Manufacturers' agents generally "rep" for more than one manufacturer. However, the manufacturers represented don't compete against each other. In the retail gift industry, for example, manufacturers' agents may represent several small gift producers, but each producer makes different types of gifts. The differing product lines, naturally, provide reps with a portfolio of products that complement one another. Then, when agents call on retailers, their various complementary products are made available for sale. Each retail sales call, therefore, will likely yield agency sales.

Reps are paid on a commission basis. In some industries, commissions are minimal. For example, reps involved with selling electronic components may make a commission of only 2 to 3% of sales. In contrast, commissions of 15% to 20% are more typical in the gift industry. Although a 20% commission may seem excessive, smaller manufacturers of gifts are more than willing to pay this rate because they have little experience in marketing. Nor do they have the resources to hire their own sales forces. Manufacturers' agents consequently solve their problems and satisfy this particular business need.

Manufacturers' agents also assist larger producers by helping them introduce new products or enter new markets. For example, a manufacturer's in-house sales force may not be experienced with a new product. An experienced agent may be engaged to generate initial sales for the item while the manufacturer's own sales force comes up to speed. Similarly, temporary contractual arrangements with reps are often used to help manufacturers penetrate new geographic markets or market segments. A manufacturer's rep presumably knows the new market better than the manufacturer's own salespeople. The end result is quicker, more efficient initial penetration of the new market product.

Selling Agents

Selling agents are similar to manufacturers' reps except that they sell a manufacturer's entire product mix in all markets served. Found mainly in the textile, apparel, food, lumber, metal products, and coal industries, selling agents function as independent marketing departments for the manufacturers they represent. Selling agents are granted exclusive rights to sell the manufacturer's products everywhere. There are no geographic limitations. Selling agents also enjoy the authority to decide how the product will be promoted, priced, and distributed. Selling agents are excellent alternatives for smaller, less well-financed Firms that lack the assets or expertise to market their own products. It sounds strange, we admit, but this sort of situation arises frequently.

Brokers

Brokers typically sell real estate, securities such as stocks and bonds, agricultural products, crude oil, or even scrap metal. Brokers are agent wholesaling intermediaries. Their primary function is to connect buyers and sellers. Brokers generally work on a commission basis for the seller in an attempt to locate viable buyers for the seller's products. Some brokers may represent buyers rather than sellers, but not both at the same time.

Brokers may assist in helping buyers and sellers with contractual negotiations, but they have no authority to set prices or finalize a sale. Buyers and sellers must reach agreement on final prices and other terms of the sale.

David J. Joseph brokers scrap metal globally. The Firm's brokers cultivate quality intelligence about scrap metal markets, including the identity of potential suppliers and scrap metal buyers. The Firm promotes itself as "the most experienced scrap metal brokerage team in the industry"… they "monitor markets in real-time and work out in the field (literally) to build the world's most reliable supply chain."[3]

Brokers are valuable assets for providing their principals (the sellers with whom they contract) with market information relevant to prices, market conditions, and the competition. Aside from finding buyers for their principals, providing expert, timely market information is a major function.

Brokers tend to be used only when needed. When a seller has product that must be moved, brokers are contacted for assistance in locating buyers. Once sales are finalized, the temporary arrangement between the broker and seller generally is terminated. But, of course, the relationship can be reignited when the need again arises.

Brokers, like other wholesaling middlemen, are attempting to solidify their positions inside supply chains by making their services more important to customers. By adding services and enhancing their knowledge of markets and market conditions, they hope to turn traditionally temporary relationships with sellers into more permanent relationships.

Commission Merchants

Commission merchants are agent wholesaling middlemen who work primarily in agricultural markets that sell grain, produce, or livestock. Unlike traditional brokers, commission merchants receive additional authority to set prices, establish terms of the sale, actually make the sale, and manage delivery of the product to buyers.

As the name implies, commission merchants work on a commission basis. They often take possession of agricultural products in small local markets, arrange for their transportation to larger regional markets, and then sell them. For example, a commission merchant may work with several local farmers in Eastern Colorado to sell their annual sugar beet crop in a larger regional market located in the Denver area. The commission merchant ensures that the farmer's crop is safely transported, temporarily stored, and is sold at the best possible price in that market.

Auction Companies

Auction houses bring buyers and sellers together in situations where multiple buyers are pitted against one another to extract the highest possible price for a product, given existing market conditions. Auction houses offer forums in which bidding can occur. Buyers can view products up for bid and respond to bids placed by competing bidders. Auction houses normally are paid a percentage commission based on the final bid price of the product.

Auctions are common in a variety of product categories including:

- Agricultural products such as tobacco, furs, livestock, and fruit.
- High value art, unique collectibles, and to liquidate estates.
- Used cars and industrial equipment.

Sotheby's auction house, probably the world's most publicized auction house, specializes in the sale of antiques, unique collectibles, art works, and estate liquidations for celebrities. For example, Sotheby's auctioned space suits used on Apollo 13 and has liquidated estates for celebrities such as Jacqueline Bouvier Kennedy Onassis.

Sotheby's has a unique history, dating back to 1744. A London bookseller, Samuel Baker, wanted to find a more effective way to connect buyers with sellers of private libraries. Baker's auction was born and business flourished. During the next 100 years some of the great libraries of the times, including those of Charles-Maurice de Talleyrand and Napoleon Bonaparte, were brokered through Baker's auction house. When Baker died in 1778 the auction house was taken over by his nephew, John Sotheby.[4]

Internet Auction Houses

The Internet auction house is a relatively recent supply chain innovation. Internet auction companies are springing up almost daily, providing a mechanism for consumers to auction a wide variety of products. Some major, traditional auction houses like Sotheby's now feature websites through which select products are auctioned.

Today, the premier Internet auction house is eBay. eBay bills itself as the world's largest personal online trading community. On the eBay site, visitors can buy and sell items in more than a thousand categories, including collectibles, antiques, sports memorabilia, computers, toys, beanies, dolls, figures, coins, stamps, books, magazines, music, pottery, glass, photography, electronics, jewelry, gemstones, and much more. eBay believes that much of its success is a function of the large number of items available. According to eBay, "If you want it, somebody's probably selling it on eBay."

Manufacturers' Sales Branches and Offices

Some manufacturers prefer to distribute products through their own facilities rather than using other intermediaries. The decision is often based on how much control the manufacturer desires over how its products are distributed and represented with customers. In the B2B arena, for example, a manufacturer of industrial installations or other major equipment may prefer direct distribution to its customers because the product may require custom design, installation, training, and servicing. At times, products may be highly perishable. Direct supply chains offering specialized handling may be required to avoid spoilage. Similarly, there may only be a few customers or those customers might be concentrated in limited geographic areas, such as in Houston or Silicon Valley. This dearth of customers or geographic concentration makes it more efficient for the manufacturer to serve customers with its own sales force.

Sales offices and **sales branches** are similar in that both are owned and operated by the manufacturer. However, sales branches maintain an inventory of the manufacturer's products while sales offices do not. The sales branch effectively functions as a full-service merchant wholesaler. Presumably, the sales office engages only in selling activities, providing services similar to those of agents.

→ Major Trends Affecting Wholesaling

The Emergence of Internet Wholesaling and Retailing

The single most important trend affecting both retailing and wholesaling is the emergence of the Internet and e-commerce. With the advent of e-commerce, manufacturers have an efficient mechanism for communicating with and selling directly to consumers. A digitized world threatens traditional wholesaling and retailing as we know it today. E-commerce channels will never entirely replace traditional channels. But the digital threat has already significantly eroded traditional wholesaler or brick and mortar retailer revenues in select industries.

One should expect an ongoing proliferation of e-catalogs that market vast numbers of specialty products. Well-known specialty catalogs all now feature web-based versions of their catalogs. Examples include Lillian Vernon, Lands End, and the Sharper Image. This trend has expanded to include traditional wholesalers. Grainger, for example, has dramatically grown its online business to the point that it is one of the largest Internet wholesalers of maintenance, repair, and operations (MRO) services. The company's ecommerce activities include the launch of iPhone and iPad apps that piggyback on its powerful new web platform to "offer a consistent purchase experience for customers across multiple purchase channels…"[5]

Convenience goods, such as groceries and personal care items, are likewise rapidly becoming more available via Internet sites as wholesalers and retailers each discover new ways to use the web to target specific audiences. Traditional grocery retailers are selling via the Internet. Walmart processes orders online for delivery and allows customers to pick up at the closest store. Amazon Grocery and Gourmet Foods offers free delivery on qualified orders. Artizone is an online grocer serving a variety of farmer's markets. Online grocery sales are making a big dent in traditional brick and mortar sales. By 2019, that will account for 12% of all retail grocery spending.[6]

Large Retailers Will Bypass Other Supply Chain Members

As some retailers continue to grow larger, there will be added pressure to bypass wholesaling middlemen and buy directly from manufacturers. Firms such as Walmart enjoy the resources to more efficiently perform the make-bulk, break-bulk, and assorting functions that ordinarily would be entrusted to wholesaling intermediaries.

Intermediaries Seek Differentiation

Traditional wholesaling intermediaries are existentially threatened by large retailers' consolidating efforts. They are solidifying and improving the supply chain positions they serve by adding "value" via providing more and better services, cutting costs, and improving profitability for themselves and channel partners. Some seek out or cultivate unique niches which can be served where threats to their existence can be minimized. They will strive to build better relationships with their retail customers.

→ Retailing and Retail Middlemen

Retailing Is?

Retailing includes all activities involved in making sales of goods and services to ultimate consumers for personal, household (non-business) use. Retail sales, therefore, entail the sale of products or services to ultimate consumers. The retail sales of products or services, by definition, are not made to business or other organizational buyers.

Retailers are firms that primarily exist for purposes of making retail sales to ultimate consumers. Although any business at any level of the distribution channel, from producer to retailer, can make retail sales, only retailers are in business *primarily* for this purpose.

Most retailing still occurs in traditional storefront retail establishments. Referred to as "in-store" retailing, these storefront operations include the traditional regional shopping malls and a variety of smaller, local shopping centers. Increasingly, however, retailing activities occur in less traditional non-store settings including telemarketing, televised shopping channels, catalog retailing, direct mail, and digital marketing. Indeed, one of the most exciting changes is the advent of "e-tailing," the sales of retail goods and services to ultimate consumers via the Internet.

Interesting Retailing Facts

US retail sales have grown dramatically since the early 1970s. Total retail sales exceeded $5 trillion in 2013. This is more than a 150% increase since 1992. These sales are generated by more than 1,500,000 retail stores that employ about 15% of the workforce.[7]

Retailing is not as profitable as many people envision. Retailers' investments and operating costs are quite high due to the ongoing need to interface directly with ultimate consumers. Substantial investments are made in buildings, equipment, décor, fixtures, inventory, security, etc. to create and cultivate an alluring, attractive, soothing, or seductive store atmosphere and to provide merchandise assortments that appeal to targeted consumers. Gross margins for retailers generally average close to 30%, while wholesalers' gross margins average less than 20% . But the operating expenses for retailers remain much higher than expenses of their wholesaling counterparts. The net difference translates directly into lower profits.

Most retailers are "independent"; the retailer operates as a single-unit entity. Actual form of ownership may be a sole proprietorship, partnership, or corporation, but the entity operates from a single storefront. Independent retailers are usually smaller operations, generally with total annual sales of under $1,000,000. Each retailer may account for a rather insignificant level of sales. But collectively independent retailers account for more than 50% of retail sales.

Independent retailers do not always operate out of their own storefronts. **Leased department retailers** rent floor space from host facilities. For example, Starbucks operates coffee shops inside Kroger's and Albertson's supermarkets and Barnes & Noble bookstores. McDonalds similarly operates restaurants inside some Walmart stores. Other common examples include branch banks, pharmaceutical departments, and restaurants in super markets.

Chain stores are groups of two or more stores that are owned and operated by one entity. Chain stores typically share a common name, merchandise selection, and method of operation. Chain stores that boast 11 or more retail units or locations are technically called as **corporate chain stores**. Chain stores with fewer than 11 units may still be structured as corporations, but are not technically referred to as corporate chains. Some independent retailers have entered contractual vertical marketing systems (VMSs) that closely resemble chain store operations. However, individual stores in the VMS are still independently owned and operated.

Corporate chains, because they are well-financed and centrally operated, typically enjoy distinct advantages over independent stores. Their sheer size and financial strength provides most corporate chains with significant scale economies in purchasing and operations that confer advantages over smaller competitors. Large chains have the resources to hire expert managers who "specialize" in their respective areas. Smaller retailers usually cannot afford this luxury; managers must be "jacks-of-all-trades."

The primary disadvantage of corporate chains is that little flexibility exists with respect to operational decision-making at individual store levels. Most merchandising, promotion, purchasing, and personnel decisions are centrally made at the corporate level. It is thus harder for individual stores to respond quickly to changing local conditions. This latter point is the single area where the smaller, independent operator tends to excel. Independent store operators can make decisions that allow the store to adapt merchandise selection and operations to fit local conditions without approval from anyone. Operators can adapt store services to fit the local needs of its customers and tailor the physical facilities and store image to fit local tastes and values. Stores can reflect the personalities of their owner/operators.

Independent retailers, particularly smaller independents, face definite challenges. The failure rate for these stores certainly is much higher than for chain stores. A critical question becomes one of how have these smaller independent retailers survived? Two factors can be cited that contribute to their continued viability:

- Smaller independent retailers, because of their operational flexibility, can tailor their merchandise, customer service, and store personalities to closely match their customers' wants and needs. This is particularly the case when high levels of customer service and unique merchandise assortments are important customer needs. The independent retailer enjoys a better opportunity to address such needs successfully.

- Smaller retailers have also entered into **Vertical Marketing Systems** with other retailers and/or wholesalers. **Voluntary Chains** and **Retailer Cooperatives** provide smaller independent retailers with the buying power and management expertise needed to compete successfully with the larger corporate chains.

→ Classifying Retailers: In-store Retailing

Retailers can be classified several ways. The best classification scheme, we believe, is based on the retailer's "method of operation." Fundamentally, retailers can be classified based on whether their operations occur in storefront locations. In-store retailers operate out of traditional fixed storefront locations. Customers must visit these locations to make purchases. This category of retailer includes limited line and general merchandise stores, such as department stores, convenience stores, supermarkets, and discount stores (Exhibit 14.5). Non-store retailers, by contrast, operate from locations that customers never visit. Non-store retailers include telemarketers, catalog retailers, e-tailers, and firms engaged in other forms of direct marketing (Exhibit 14.6).

In-store retailers can also be categorized based on their merchandise mix. A retailer's merchandise mix is the total combination of products the retailer makes available to customers. The retailer's **merchandise mix** is analogous to a manufacturer's product mix. **Merchandise breadth** is the variety of different product lines that comprise the merchandise mix. Retailers

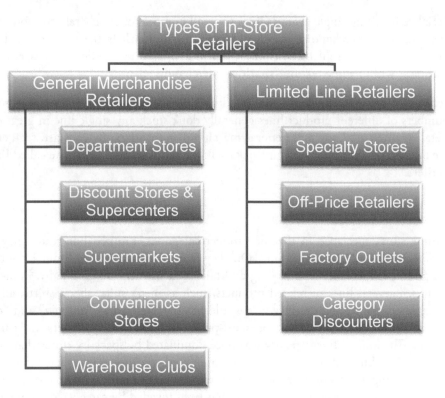

Exhibit 14.5 *Types of In-Store Retailing Middlemen.*

Exhibit 14.6 *Types of Non-Store Retailing.*

that specialize in selling single product lines or small numbers of closely related product lines feature a "**narrow**" merchandise breadth. **Merchandise depth** is the selection of brands, styles, colors, sizes, etc. available within a given line offered by retailers. Retailers offering limited choices within a line feature "**shallow**" merchandise depth.

Trade-offs exists between the depth and breadth of the merchandise mix. Retailers stocking large numbers of different product lines generally don't stock any single line in great depth. These retailers often are known as **general merchandise retailers**. By contrast, retailers that limit the number of lines they sell, but stock each line in substantial depth are called **limited line retailers**.

Limited Line Retailers

Limited line stores specialize in specific product categories. Limited line stores may sell a single product line, such as men's suits. Or, they may concentrate on a limited assortment within a given product line, such as "big and tall" sizes of men's suits. Finally, limited line stores may sell several lines of related products, such as men's suits, shoes, shirts, and ties. In each example, the related product mix would be characterized as "**narrow**" and "**deep**." Limited line stores include **specialty stores, off-price retailers, factory outlets**, and **category discounters**. The limited line category was once dominated by specialty stores that avoided price discounting. Limited line stores instead attempted to differentiate their offerings and values by providing an extensive assortment of quality merchandise and excellent customer service. More recently, however, this category has been invaded by category discounters, off-price retailers, and factory outlets that have interjected substantial price competition into the limited line arena.

Specialty Stores

Specialty stores can focus on selling a single line of products. LensCrafters does this with eyewear. Specialty stores can also focus on a subset of a product line (e.g. Sunglass Hut). Each line, however, is stocked in substantial depth to offer customers a wide range of choices. Specialty stores tend to sell consumer durable products and operate out of major regional and community shopping malls. Well-known specialty stores include The Gap, Gap Kids, Victoria's Secret, Bath & Body Works, or Barnes & Noble Booksellers. Most service retailers, such as banks and restaurants (particularly theme restaurants like Hardrock Café, Red Lobster, and On The Border) also fall into this category.

Specialty stores try to avoid price competition, maintaining manufacturers' **suggested retail prices** to the greatest extent possible. These retailers differentiate themselves from other retailers by precisely targeting customer segments with specialized product lines and by providing superior customer service and friendly, knowledgeable and even highly attractive sales staff.

Off-Price Retailers

Off-price retailers include stores such as Ross Dress For Less, Dress Barn, T.J. Maxx, DSW Designer Shoe Warehouse, and Marshall's. These stores typically sell brand-name merchandise that is priced very low. The prices charged by off-price retailers are often far below those offered by other discount stores for comparable merchandise. Bargain basement prices are possible because these retailers often purchase inventory at below-wholesale prices. How? By buying seconds, production overruns, discontinued, outdated or out-of-season merchandise. Increasingly, producers that used to sell exclusively to big-name retailers, such as Saks Fifth Avenue, Neiman-Marcus, and Lord and Taylor, are willing to sell excess inventory through the increasing ranks of off-price retailers. The strategy makes perfect sense in a nation where much of the citizenry has been worried about their personal economy for so long. Because of this low-price emphasis, off-price retailers provide only minimal customer services; a tactic that also controls costs. Manufacturers relatedly provide little support for these retailers in terms of promotional allowances, extended payment terms, or the opportunity to return unsold merchandise.

Factory Outlets

Factory outlets usually limit sales to products produced by a single manufacturer. True factory outlets, in fact, are owned and operated by the manufacturer. In this regard they exemplify **corporate vertical marketing systems**. Many major producers of consumer goods, even certain well-known brands, have established outlet stores. Examples include Tommy Hilfiger, Van Heusen, Corning, Levis, Calvin Klein, and Esprit. Customers are attracted to factory outlets because of the promise of quality branded merchandise at lower prices. Sometimes this promise has been kept; at other times, not.

Manufacturers have historically used their outlets to clear unsold merchandise and seconds. Most outlets today stock either the same merchandise that is sold through standard retailers or lower quality items produced specifically for the outlet. Given the dramatic increase in numbers of outlet malls (current sales exceed $24 billion annually[9]), more brand name outlets are apparently following the Van Heusen model and stocking marginally lower-quality, but clearly less expensive merchandise produced specifically for sale only in the outlet. The purpose, obviously, is to capture greater numbers of price conscious consumers, who numbers remain legion.

Category Discounters or "Category-Killers"

Category discounters are mass merchandise discounters that specialize in selling products in limited categories. Best Buy (consumer appliances and electronics), Staples (office supplies, furniture, computers, and software), Home Depot (home building supplies and equipment), and Bed Bath & Beyond (home decorating products) are each "category killers." Category killers offer deep discounts and probably the best selection of brands for the products they merchandise. As the name implies, the category killer's retailing strategy is to attract customers through relatively lower-priced offerings and broader selections, thereby "killing" the competition.

During the last decade, former category discounters have faced intense competition from Internet sales. A number of bankruptcies and mergers have resulted as killers were killed or forced to retrench. Circuit City and CompUSA each closed their doors. Office Depot and Office Max were acquired by Staples. Most remaining category discounters have sought insulation from the competitive forays of large discount stores (Walmart, Target, Kmart) or Internet retailers (e.g. Amazon) by offering price-matching guarantees, adding services difficult for Internet providers to match (e.g. Best Buy's Geek Squad), or improving their customer relationship management. Have no fears. Such competition is good for you, the consumer.

General Merchandise Stores

General merchandise retailers stock wider assortments of product lines than limited line stores. Traditionally, this category was dominated by department stores, discount stores, supermarkets, and convenience stores. However, more recent retail innovations in this category include supercenters and warehouse clubs.

Department Stores

JC Penney, Nordstrom's, Sears, Dillard's, and Macy's are department stores. Most department stores are owned and operated by corporate chains. In contrast to the narrow product mix of the limited line store, department stores offer a broad mix of product lines under one roof. Department stores organize related product lines by "department." A typical department store carries clothing, jewelry, cosmetics, electronics, furniture, appliances, gifts, and housewares lines.

Department stores usually offer a full range of services including credit plans, delivery, generous return privileges, hair salons, travel services, automobile insurance, and (occasionally) restaurants. Sales personnel are expected to be helpful, courteous, and knowledgeable. Even so, the quality of service has deteriorated in some stores. Each department in inside the store operates as an autonomous unit that is responsible for its own buying, merchandising, revenue, and profits.

The need to maintain high levels of service, stock inventories of a wide range of products, and maintain attractive shopping facilities contribute to higher costs and higher priced operations. Not surprisingly, department stores are facing serious competition from discount stores and limited line stores (particularly category killers) that offer the same or similar merchandise at lower prices. Some department stores, such as Nordstrom, have responded by modifying their merchandising and atmospherics to target upscale shoppers who are less price-elastic (discussed in Chapter 15). These stores focus on higher margin products such as clothing, jewelry, and cosmetics. Individual departments may operate as upscale specialty stores in which fixtures and merchandise are arranged to provide more attractive "atmospherics."

Discount Stores and Supercenters

The major national discount stores in existence today are Walmart, Kmart, and Target. Smaller scale discounters that operate more on regional bases include Big Lots, Dollar Tree, Dollar General, and Family Dollar. Both Dollar Tree and Dollar General are vying to acquire Family Dollar to stave off competition from other discounters, primarily Walmart. Dollar Tree appears to be in the best position to win the bid for Family Dollar. The acquisition will give Dollar Tree 13,000 stores in the United States and Canada[10] and make Dollar Tree one of the fastest-growing discount chains. Most merchandise is priced under $10.00 and is sold in a no-frills, low overhead, self-service environment.

Discount stores are general merchandise retailers. They feature a wide assortment of product lines, each provided in shallow, but reasonable, depth. Similar to department stores, discount stores organize their product lines by departments. But unlike department stores, discounters offer few services. The retail setting itself is also far more austere. These two related factors help keep costs and prices lower to attract price-sensitive consumers. Margins are low. Discount stores consequently rely on high volume to maintain profitability.

Discount retailing has been around since the early 1950s. The initial discounters operated regionally, often on a cash basis in Spartan-like facilities located in the warehouse districts of major cities. Prices were up to 30% less than in conventional department stores. Because of increased competition from other discounters and conventional department stores, discount stores have "traded up" over time, adding services, relocating to better sites, and improving merchandise selections. As a result some discount stores of the past, such as Target, are currently reclassifying their brands as conventional department stores.

Supercenters, pioneered in Europe, are combination supermarkets and discount stores. In addition to the expanded product mix resulting from combining the supermarket and discount store formats, additional services have been added including snack bars or fast food restaurants, dry cleaning, banking, check cashing, automobile servicing, and optical centers. Walmart Supercenter, Super Target, and Super Kmart dominant this category in the United States. However, select Kroger stores are now adopting this operating concept. Walmart's Supercenters range between 100,000 and 215,000 square feet in size. This is substantially larger than the typical supermarket's 20,000 square feet. Each supercenter is organized into approximately 40 departments including apparel, jewelry, lawn and garden, health and beauty aids, electronics, and a pharmacy. In addition, grocery areas generally include a bakery, a delicatessen, frozen foods, meat, dairy, and fresh produce departments. Supercenters also generally include vision centers, a Tire & Lube Express, and One-Hour Photo Processing. Some supercenters feature McDonald's restaurants. In 1991 in Medina, Ohio, Kmart opened the first of its 106 Super Kmart Centers. Each is a combined supermarket and discount store offering groceries, fresh foods, and general merchandise on a 24/7/365 basis.

Supercenters may be slowly dying, phased out incrementally as consumer demand shifts in favor of the greater convenience of e-commerce and preferences for smaller, local retail facilities over big-box retailers. Americans are now driving less and are returning to smaller, urban communities, eschewing large sprawling suburbs.[11]

Supermarkets

Today's supermarkets are large, self-service retail operations that carry complete lines of food products and carefully selected lines of complementary non-food items. Like most retailers, supermarkets are organized by department with centralized checkout facilities. Albertsons, Kroger's, Safeway, and A&P are nationally located corporate chains. Other supermarkets operate regionally. Winn-Dixie, for example, operates roughly 1,000 stores in the Southeast. H-E-B similarly operates 340 retail stores in Texas and parts of Mexico. Yet H-E-B is the 15th largest privately held US Firm. Sales in 2013 exceeded $20 billion.[11]

Price competition between supermarket chains tends to be intense. Profits after taxes average less than 1% of sales. Tight margins have produced some significant retailing innovations that have helped supermarkets control costs, improve efficiency, and improve margins. Examples include:

- Using technology to provide better customer service. Examples include barcode scanners that automate the checkout process and aid in managing inventory and purchasing; digital signs that update prices and locations of products and offer promotions; and fingerprint scanners or smartphone apps to scan bar codes and speed checkout. Self-propelled "smart" shopping carts that follow customers and lead them to items are currently being tested.[13]

- Vendor assistance arrangements in which vendors such as Frito-Lay manage the store's inventory and assist in restocking shelves.

- Expanding into more non-food, higher margin lines and services including video rentals, photo developing, financial institutions, pharmacies, and delicatessens.

- Adding multiple lines of private label merchandise (dealer's brands) that carry higher margins and provide customers with added value.

- Using promotional mechanisms to build store loyalty. Most supermarket chains offer rewards cards through which customers receive additional discounts, can enter cardmember sweepstakes, can earn special savings awards, and can earn bonus miles on airlines. These are called sales promotions, by the way.

Convenience Stores

Convenience stores, such as 7-Eleven, Quick-Trip, and Circle K are essentially mini-supermarkets. But mini-supermarkets with twist, given that they carry carefully selected lines of high-turnover consumer food and non-food products, along with various grades of fuel. Convenience stores have emerged as a major threat to supermarkets, as "rushed" consumers place more emphasis on time and place utility as they purchase. Consumers certainly pay higher prices for products purchased at convenience stores. But those that shop there apparently do so willingly.

This form of retail operation is growing at a rapid rate, with new innovations in convenience continually emerging. For example, most major oil companies now operate convenience stores and many have co-located with major fast food chains. Chevron has co-located some stores with McDonalds. Similarly, in addition to running its own "On the Run " convenience food stores, Mobil Oil has partnered with Blimpie and entered into a Taco Bell/KFC co-branding venture.

Warehouse Clubs

Warehouse clubs are large-scale, member-only, mass merchandisers that combine cash and carry wholesaling with discount retailing. The form of retailing is dominated by Costco (2013 annual sales exceeding $110 billion) and Sam's Club (annual sales of nearly $60 billion).[14]

Warehouse clubs typically stock between 3,500 and 5,000 products. The numbers may initially impress, but they are actually substantially less than the 40,000 items typical of most discount stores. Stores, again, are organized by department. These departments normally include food, beverages, books, clothing, appliances, housewares, automotive parts and accessories, tools and hardware, sporting goods, computers, consumer electronics, and furniture. Most warehouse products are known brands that enjoy preexisting customer preferences.

Warehouse clubs engage in wholesale- and retail-level selling. They attract smaller businesses who can purchase at wholesale prices. Consumers usually pay about 5% more for products than do business customers. Business and consumer customers each must be club members and generally pay a small annual membership fee.[15] In the past, consumer members had to be affiliated with government agencies, credit unions, schools, hospitals, banks, or other similar organizations in order to "qualify" for membership. Not so much, anymore. Membership requirements have been substantially eased in recent years as more clubs have emerged competing for the same finite customer segments. BJ's, a prominent discount club that currently operates exclusively in the northeastern United States, recently opened its memberships to everyone. BJ's charges $50 per year for a standard membership and $100 per year for a premium membership. The same pricing structure is used for businesses.

Membership fees account for only a small fraction of the wholesale club's total revenue. BJ's, for example, obtains only 1.8% of its $10.6 billion in revenues from membership fees. The right to pay for membership status actually functions as a subtle marketing trick. The fact that customers have already "paid" actually lures them repeatedly to the store. After all, who doesn't want to "get more for their money" [membership fee]. Memberships themselves also permit wholesale clubs to maintain customer information databases that can be used to:

- Target promotion activities, primarily direct mailings.
- Profile their customer base to better select merchandise and locate new stores.

Maintaining low prices forces warehouse clubs to restrict the number of services offered and closely control their operating costs, including marketing expenses. Promotion is primarily accomplished through direct mail and Internet advertising to members, public relations efforts, in-store marketing programs, and limited vendor-funded television and radio advertising during holiday seasons, including, say, Halloween. Some clubs use sales personnel to solicit potential business members and contact selected community groups to increase the number of consumer members. Free "trial memberships" and "one-day pass" promotions may be used to attract consumers. The purpose of these promotions is to eventually convert those consumers to paid membership status.

→ Classifying Retailers: Non-store Retailing

Non-store retailing occurs when products are not sold from fixed retail facilities i.e. retail brick and mortar (B&M) stores. Although the majority of retail sales are still made from B&M facilities, the revenue generated from non-store retailing is increasing rapidly. Currently, roughly 10% of consumer sales are generated by one or another type of non-store retailing. Four types of non-store retailing exist: direct selling, telemarketing, direct marketing, and vending (Exhibit 14.6).

Direct Selling

Direct selling occurs when there is face-to-face interaction between sales representatives and buyers either at home or in the work-place. Direct selling, also called door-to-door selling, is among the oldest retailing forms. Traditionally, salespeople made "cold-calls" on prospective buyers by canvassing neighborhoods. Today, most firms that employ direct selling are somewhat more sophisticated with their prospecting methods. Amway, Mary Kay, Kirby and Electrolux each attempt to identify potential buyers through other methods and then set appointments for salespeople. Prospecting methods include the use of contests, product or gift giveaways, or the use of coupons to solicit interest and leverage sales appointments. Referrals from friends and relatives are still commonly employed to identify prospects.

Household products (cooking utensils, vacuum cleaners, carpet shampooers, home cleaning products) and personal care products (cosmetics, health supplements) are often sold door-to-door. In general, direct selling probably is best employed for products that require extensive demonstration in an environment where the product is most likely to be used, i.e. the home. Kirby salespeople, for example, demonstrate their vacuum cleaners' benefits by cleaning select rooms in the prospect's home. Presentation, as a result, can be customized to fit the situation, offering a prime opportunity for salespeople to develop rapport and establish credibility with prospects.

Direct selling presents definite challenges to marketers. Sales commissions must be kept high to provide the necessary motivation for sales people to engage in the selling process. Sales commissions can be as high as 40 to 50% of the product's selling price, making direct selling the most expensive retailing form. This often inflates prices to consumers. Since door-to-door sales people are usually paid on a commission-only basis, there is tremendous pressure to "close" each sale. Too frequently, salespeople employ "high pressure" selling tactics to generate the close. Many practices are unethical; some are actually illegal. Most states now have "cooling off" laws that allow consumers to back-out of a sales agreement within a few days of the purchase, as discussed in Chapter 4.

High levels of energy and a unique personality are required to be an effective door-to-door sales person, This, combined with the negative image associated by consumers with most door-to-door selling and the increased difficulty in finding people at home, make it difficult to recruit and retain salespeople. Turnover rates are extremely high.

Party plan selling has evolved to lessen some of the more egregious aspects of door-to-door selling. With party plan selling, salespeople recruit prospects to host "parties" at their homes or in their places of work. The retailer's products will be displayed at the party; the salesperson is available to demonstrate. The "host" normally receives free products for his or her efforts. The party atmosphere helps overcome consumer skepticism and enhances the salesperson's credibility and likeability, all of which may translate into increased sales. The Magic Chef, Tupperware, Mary Kay, and Stanley Home Products frequently employ the party planning sales method.

Telephone Retailing (Telemarketing)

Traditionally, telephone selling or telemarketing involved using telephones to make initial contact with prospects and subsequently close sales. Prospects are identified in several ways. The traditional, but least efficient, approach was to make cold-calls based on names taken directly from phone books. **Cold-calling** has been automated with the advent of computer-assisted random digit dialing. Computers are programmed to randomly dial numbers within a defined block of numbers. When the computer senses that the phone has been answered, the call is either turned over to a sales representative or a recorded message is played. Random-digit dialing effectively defeats consumers' use of unlisted numbers. Probably the most efficient telemarketing methods employ lists generated from databases of the Firm's existing or past customers, or lists obtained from other sources. Such data-based marketing allows telemarketers to identify prospective customers based on similarities in product preferences, demographic profiles, and geographic locations.

Some marketers now assume a broad-brushed approach toward telemarketing, defining it to include all "marketing-related" activities conducted through phones. Redefined in this manner, telemarketing now encompasses using telephones to prospect for new customers, improve customer service, speed payment on past-due accounts, and gather marketing-related data.

Telemarketing faces tough challenges. Consumers understandably often view telemarketing activities as intrusive, as do your authors. And, as with door-to-door selling, telemarketers are sometimes unethical and unscrupulous, using high-pressure sales tactics on unsuspecting and/or vulnerable consumers. As a result, telemarketing practices have received substantial attention from legislative agencies. Laws exist at the federal and state levels restricting telemarketing activities. Individual states and the FTC have initiated "no-call" lists forbidding telemarketers to call consumers on these lists. Substantial fines, or worse, are levied for retailers who violate these new laws.

Direct Marketing

Direct marketers use the telephone and other traditional media to contact customers who can then purchase products via mail, telephone, or the Internet. The forms of direct marketing include direct mail, direct-response advertising, catalog sales, television sales, and e-tailing.

Direct Mail

Products are still frequently sold through direct mail solicitations. Many firms maintain mailing lists of current customers and/or purchase mailing lists of potential customers from secondary sources. Firms send letters, brochures, and samples to prospective customers who can then order via mail, telephone, or over the Internet. Many consumers prefer direct mail due its convenience and relative safety compared to visiting physical retail stores.

A continuing trend in direct mail by many credit card firms is the use of bill-inserts. Most major credit cards (VISA, American Express, Mastercard) and many oil companies or retailers that offer branded credit cards routinely include promotions or flyers for additional products.

Direct mail is probably the best way to communicate efficiently with well-defined target markets. Firms with limited promotion budgets that maintain databases of their customers may lean heavily on direct mail to communicate with them. BJ's Warehouse Club uses information from its membership database to target direct mail and email to existing customers for purposes of informing them about special sales, new products, and other events.

Direct-Response Advertising

Direct-response advertising occurs when marketers convey messages through magazines, newspapers, TV, radio, and other media to solicit sales from or build relationships with targeted customer groups. Consumers are encouraged to place orders through telephone, mail responses, or the Internet. Time Life regularly airs TV commercials promoting books, tapes, and CDs. Consumers are shown 1-800 numbers and encouraged to use credit cards to make purchases.

Some popular specialty catalogs initially employed ads in magazines and newspapers to sell their products. Only later did these retailers transition into catalog sales. Lillian Vernon, for example, began operations with a direct response advertisement featuring its purses in *Seventeen* magazine. The revenue generated from sales of this first product were reinvested to finance subsequent advertisements for other products. Lillian Vernon did not develop catalog operations until years later.

On-Line Retailing

On-line retailing is currently the fastest growing form of non-store retailing. Given the phenomenal growth in digitized communication across the world and the ever-increasing number of consumers who use smart devices, growth in this retailing medium should continue. Sales revenues in 2013 via the Internet reached nearly $350 billion. Nearly all traditional retailers feature websites that promote their brands and products.

The Internet provides a natural platform for augmenting sales from general merchandise and specialty catalogs. Again, nearly all traditional general line catalogs such as Spiegel, Sears, JC Penney, as well as the better-known specialty catalogs (Sharper Image, Lillian Vernon, Lands End, L.L. Bean, and others) now have online versions that are responsible for sales far in excess of those generated by their traditional catalogs. The printed catalog is quickly becoming obsolete and soon may become a memory.

Consumers' security concerns are still partially limiting e-tailing's expansion. With goods cause, consumers still fear that "hackers" will steal their credit card numbers or other personal information. There certainly has been several high profile hacker attacks during recent years. Home Depot, Target, T. J. Maxx, JC Penney, Jet Blue, and 7-Eleven, among others, have each been victimized by electronic thefts of massive amounts of their customers' credit card data. Most experts, however, still agree such concerns are generally overblown. A more pressing risk, actually, is that credit card information will be pilfered by unscrupulous clerks working in traditional retail settings. E-tailers, such as Amazon.com, invariably employ highly secure encryption technologies that reduce the likelihood of fraud. Most credit card vendors insure consumers against online fraud.

Television Sales

Television home shopping consists of dedicated TV shows or entire networks that are designed to introduce, promote, and sell consumer products. Consumers are encouraged to place orders via the phone or the Internet and pay with their credit cards. While myriad television shopping programs and networks now exist, the Florida based Home Shopping Network (HSN) pioneered this retailing form. However, QVC now dominates the television shopping market with earnings of $7.4 billion in 2009. HSN "lagged" with sales of just $2 billion. ShopNBC and Jewelry Television (JTV) are fast followers featuring revenues of $525 million and $300 million, respectively.[16] Television shopping programs usually specialize in selling limited numbers of product lines. The most commonly sold products, by far, are jewelry, clothing, electronics, and housewares.

The television home shopping format appeals to select consumers because they perceive prices are lower and that the sales personnel, on average, are friendlier and better informed than traditional retail personnel. The still evolving format surely does offer certain distinct benefits to marketers and consumers. On the marketing side, products can be easily demonstrated and plenty of time exists to explain the product's benefits. From consumers' perspective, they enjoy and consequently value the opportunity to shop from the convenience of their own homes. Greater convenience is a value that many consumers find nearly irresistible.

Vending

Vending machines account for an extremely small portion of retail sales, less than 1%. However, even that total still impresses. Vending sales in 2013 reached over $650 billion, however, vending sales have been declining by 1.5% per year since 1999.[17] In addition to vending machines that dispense products, video game machines, and bank ATMs fall into this category. Vending was historically employed to sell small, inexpensive, standardized products such as candy, snacks, soft drinks, newspapers, and cigarettes. Consumers generally value convenience when seeking these products and willingly pay a bit more when using vending machines.

Improved vending technology has recently made it possible to vend larger arrays of products, including sandwiches, canned foods, consumer electronics, and personal care items. More firms are now engaging in specialty vending targeted at defined audiences. Hotel vending machines, for example, dispense personal care items like toothbrushes, deodorants, razors, or laundry detergent. WeGoBabies markets a machine that dispenses baby supplies such as diapers and formula for desperate parents "stranded" in airports, zoos, museums or the like. Even consumer electronics, office supplies, and live bait are available from some vending machines. Best Buy offers vending machines that satisfy smaller, less expensive electronics needs. These can be found in major airports.

Vending is a comparatively expensive retailing format. Investment in equipment and costs of repairs are high. Losses from vandalism and theft can be daunting. To minimize such losses, vending machines should be placed in secure, high-traffic areas.

Newer vending technologies are being introduced to reinvigorate the industry. High-tech, millennial-friendly machines are creating new and more engaging vending experiences. Kraft Foods, for example, has partnered with Intel to create Diji-Taste, a vending platform that combines entertaining, engaging, and presumably tasty vending. Aside from vending products for immediate consumption, Diji-Taste machines feature programs that encourage buyers to sample new products and immediately share their experiences via social media. Diji-Taste will be located in high-traffic areas such as airports, train stations, healthcare facilities, and college campuses. Additional innovations include:

- The ability to pay using digital wallets, such as Apple Pay, Google-Wallet, and Softcard.
- Fast food, such as pizza, made to order. Let's Pizza has a vending machine that produces Pizza made to order in just 2.5 minutes.
- Single servings of drinks dispensed in re-usable containers.
- Twitter-activated vending machines such as Tweet for Tea's Twitter-activated vending machine that dispenses iced tea.

→ Strategic Retailing Decisions

Retailers are marketing managers. Like all marketing managers, they must make critical decisions about the marketing programs they manage. The steps in the marketing management process apply to establishing and managing retail facilities in the same way they apply to the management of products and services. Retail managers search for marketing opportunities and select the specific target markets they wish to serve. Retailers then must define the market positions they wish to achieve and structure key aspects of their marketing mix to create these positions. Critical decisions must be made in areas that affect the sustainability as well as the profitability of the retail operation. This section explores several more important retail management decisions including location selection, store image and retail atmospherics, determining the correct merchandise assortment, and customer service (Exhibit 14.7).

Selecting the Correct Retail Location

Location is absolutely a key determinant of retailing success. Put simply, whenever possible, retail stores should be located where members of the target market are likely to shop. Only rarely will consumers go out of their way to find products or to visit specific stores. As a minimum, locating close to complementary stores and in areas with adequate security, easy access, and ample parking are essential.

Exhibit 14.7 *Key Dimensions of Retail Strategy.*

One frequently arising location consideration: whether to locate in some type of shopping center or in a free-standing structure not associated with other stores. Shopping centers are planned groupings of retail establishments in which space is leased to specific retailers. Shopping centers themselves are usually owned and operated by a Firm that specializes in managing such facilities. There are several types of shopping centers: neighborhood shopping centers, community shopping centers, regional shopping centers, factory outlet malls, and power centers.

Neighborhood Shopping Centers

Neighborhood centers consist of a grouping of smaller convenience and specialty stores, including gas stations, fast-food restaurants, barbershops, hair stylists, delis, convenience or smaller grocery stores, and dry cleaning shops. There used to be something called "video rental stores" located in these neighborhood centers, but technology and innovation always have their way. Because lease rates tend to be low, many of the specialty stores, particularly restaurants, in these centers are independently owned (mom and pop) businesses. There is usually little organized planning aimed at creating a specifically desirable mix of stores in these centers. Smaller discount stores, such as Family Dollar or Dollar General, also may locate in neighborhood centers. Neighborhood centers generally target consumers living nearby, usually no more than one or two miles from the center's location. The draw or the attraction for consumers primarily is a combination of convenience and lower prices.

Community Centers

Community centers are larger, better organized, and better managed than neighborhood centers. Community centers' stores usually consist of specialty stores and convenience stores (the same as neighborhood centers), but also are anchored by one or more department stores. Community centers are centrally planned and managed by professionals. Special events and "side-walk" sales are often used to attract shoppers. Membership stores are generally selected to basically complement one another in terms of merchandise assortments. The objective is to create, across all stores in the center, a wide mix of products and services with substantial selections within lines.

Regional Centers

Regional centers are better known as the major shopping malls with which we are all familiar. These malls are anchored by several major department stores and are interspersed throughout with a variety of specialty stores. Most of these well-branded specialty stores belong to corporate chains or ownership groups. Regional centers consequently boast a much broader product assortment than neighborhood and community centers.

The Galleria in Dallas is anchored by a Westin Hotel, features an ice-skating rink, offers a five-screen cinema, and is populated by more than 200 select retail department stores, specialty stores, and restaurants for its patrons to visit. America's largest regional center is the aptly named Mall of America, located outside of Minneapolis. The mall contains over 800 stores, including 100 restaurants and nightclubs. The mall also hosts a theme park, hotels, miniature golf courses, and water slides. It makes wonderful sense that such a huge in-house shopping playground-paradise would be offered in a region where the average winter temperature in 16 degree Fahrenheit.

Well-planned and effectively-managed malls draw consumers from miles around. Many claim average customer bases exceeding 150,000 persons. Leasing rates in regional centers are high to offset the added costs of advertising, holding special events, employing extensive sales promotions, and maintaining positive public relations. Malls relatedly must employ large staffs to address marketing and management activities, facility cleaning and maintenance, and mall security needs.

Factory Outlet Malls

Factory outlet malls host a range of stores ranging from true factory outlets to small independently owned specialty stores. Smaller off-price retailers, such as Dress Barn and Payless Shoes, often are located in factory outlet malls. Traditional factory outlet stores are owned and operated by manufacturers. Examples include Van Heusen, Levi Strauss, Guess, Gap, Tommy Hilfiger, Liz Claiborne, Corning, Mikasa, Polo, and London Fog. Manufacturers use their factory outlets to sell leftover and irregular merchandise. Some manufacturers produce slightly lower quality products specifically for sale in their outlets. To avoid conflict with traditional retailers located in regional shopping malls, manufacturers who operate their own outlet stores often prefer to locate in outlet malls in outlying areas.

Factory outlet malls appeal to consumers seeking name brands at low prices. Outlet malls also can draw consumers from a wide geographic area. Like community and regional shopping centers, outlet malls employ a wide range of promotions and special events to stimulate traffic. Most factory outlet malls are unenclosed facilities ranging in size from 250,000 to 500,000 square feet. The Gainesville, Texas, Factory Stores features just over 400,000 square feet of shopping space.

Some larger outlet malls are difficult to distinguish from regional shopping centers. For example, Grapevine Mills, which is located Grapevine, Texas (outside of Dallas) is a fully enclosed 1.5 million square foot mall. The huge facility houses more than 200 well-known manufacturer and retail outlets, off-price retailers and unique specialty stores. In addition to a food court, the mall houses a variety of theme restaurants including Rainforest Cafe, Dick Clark's American Bandstand Grill, and the Eerie World Cafe. Entertainment destinations inside the mall include the Polar Ice Skating Arena, GameWorks, Lego Land, and AMC Grapevine Mills 30 Theatres.

Power Centers

Power centers are large un-enclosed shopping centers. Power centers are normally anchored by large category killers and off-price retailers rather than traditional department stores. Lowe's, Home Depot, Staples, Target, Walmart, Barnes & Noble, Bally's or LA Fitness Health Clubs, PETSMART, Old Navy, Best Buy, Bed, Bath & Beyond, and Toys-R-Us are typical rank and file store members in power centers.

Regional malls and power centers have evolved in complementary ways. Most power centers are located close to regional shopping malls to exploit the opportunity to share customer bases. Mall and power centers offer different, but again complementary, shopping experiences. Regional malls tend to focus more on fashion-oriented specialty and department store tenants. Power centers, by contrast, generally emphasize hard and soft goods not available in regional malls. The synergy between regional malls and power centers creates a retail destination that appeals to a much larger customer base than either retail format could draw by itself.

Store Image and Atmospherics

Store image is the sum total of everything its patrons think and feel about a store. A store's image is its personality. Creating the right store image is an important component of stores' positioning strategies. In stores such as Nordstrom, Niemen-Marcus or The Apple Store, tangible products are but part of the total consumption experience and thus their brand images. The total product experience delivered through such stores includes affiliated services, packaging, advertising, pleasantries, imagery, and so on.

Atmospherics—the subtle and overt internal and external physical characteristics of stores—are among the most important determinants of any store's image. Atmospherics encompass virtually everything that influences the store's internal and external appearance. When properly executed, atmospherics artfully capture and manage four tangible forms relevant to retailing environments: architecture; exterior structure; interior design and the design of window displays; plus music and at times even scents or how salespeople dress.

External atmospherics include building architecture and storefront, parking, landscaping, surrounding buildings, and the general drive-by appearance that contribute to the consumer's initial image of the store. External atmospherics can exercise a strong impact on retail patronage. The external appearance of theme restaurants, such as those offered by On the Border, Outback Steakhouse, Texas Roadhouse, or Medieval Times, triggers substantial initial traffic and contributes to customers' expectations and moods as they enter. Internal atmospherics include the decor, merchandise arrangement and crowding, general layout, background music, color schemes, scents, acoustics and noise levels, lighting, and cleanliness of stores. Well-designed and effectively-executed internal atmospherics can "manage" consumers' moods as they shop and can increase traffic, influence the amount of time consumers spend in the store, and can increase the incidence of impulse buying.

Retailers attempt to "touch" all five senses when developing the store's atmospherics. Retailers bombard our senses of sight, touch, hearing, smell and, in some retail settings, taste through positive cues. The Rain Forest Cafe, for example, blasts human senses with music, scents, and unique decors and sounds to create novel and exciting atmospheres for customers. Hopefully, taste, too, because such restaurants cannot focus on atmospherics to the exclusion of basics such as food and service. Just ask Bruce Willis or Arnold Schwarzenegger, former major investors in the now-defunct Planet Hollywood. Industry observers note that many theme restaurants face declining patronage and sales due to their failure to serve good food. These are restaurants, after all, and good food ultimately keeps customers coming back after their initial visits.

When designing and managing store image and atmospherics, efforts should be guided by one overarching retailing goal: to design in-store sensory space and experiences that increase the likelihood that customers experience certain predesignated emotions. Those emotions, in turn, should motivate customers to linger longer, return, more quickly, and ultimately buy more. In the most desirable scenario, those collective emotions occur routinely to solidify patronage behavior across time.

Merchandise Assortment

Maintaining the correct merchandise assortment from which customers can select is, without a doubt, among the most critical functions performed by retailers. Managers must choose and subsequently merchandise and market products that their customers will want. This means retailers should develop and then maintain a thorough understanding of their customers "wants, needs, and purchase-related characteristics." This understanding can be gained through marketing research and careful use of secondary data sources. For example, product manufacturers, wholesalers, and trade associations are sources of valuable information about consumers who buy their products. That many retailers make less than optimal decisions about what merchandise to stock is evidenced by their frequent use of markdowns and other price concessions required to move stale merchandise.

Selecting the optimal assortment of merchandise is complicated by the finite shelf space available in retail stores. Retailers must allocate this precious space to specific **SKUs** (i.e., **Stock Keeping Units,** or individual products items or brands sold by retailers) in ways that maximize profits per square foot of available space. Given the limited space and increasing number of new products retailers are pressured to stock, larger retailers are able to pressure vendors for certain concessions in return for stocking the vendors' brands. For example, they may be able to demand price breaks, added promotional support, or merchandising assistance. They may also demand that **slotting fees** (allowances) be paid as a hedge against the risks associated with stocking a vendor's new products.

Sophisticated retailers don't simply manage individual brands on their shelves. Rather, **category management** is employed with which **category managers** manage the profitability of a group of products, such as a product line or product category. Product categories, such as dental care products, fresh produce, seafood, hair care products, etc. are treated as profit centers. Profits across the entire category are evaluated. By working closely with vendors, category managers can improve product category performance by coordinating buying, merchandising, promotion, and pricing activities. Underperforming brands in the category certainly are candidates for removal, but so is the entire category if it does not perform well.

Customer Service

Courteous, helpful retail salespeople and others who touch customers are essential for survival in today's competitive retail environment. Convenient store hours, sufficient parking facilities, delivery, credit, return privileges, and expedient handling of customer complaints are other aspects of customer service that similarly contribute materially to satisfaction and repeat patronage. Superior performance on such service dimensions is often the only way that retailers can differentiate themselves from competitors. Retailers who seek to avoid direct price competition may offer better or more services to make it more difficult for consumers to make product-by-product comparisons strictly on a price basis. These retailers may bundle a variety of services with their products, offering different product/services combinations at different prices.

Endnotes

[1] Eric Slack, "Grainger," *Wholesale & Distribution International* (2014), accessed April 1, 2015, http://www.wdimagazine.com/index.php/sections/technology-automation/215-grainger.

[2] Taken from the CD Hartnett home page http://esite.cd-hartnett.com/public/home/welcome.jsp, accessed April 1, 2015.

[3] Taken from DJJ web site http://www.djj.com/brokerage, accessed April 4, 2015.

[4] Information extracted from http://www.sothebys.com/en/inside/about-us.html, accessed April 3, 2015.

[5] Eric Slack, 2014.

[6] Katherine P. Harvey, "Online grocery sales to reach $100B by 2019," UT San Diego, (November 3, 2014), accessed April 4, 2015, http://www.utsandiego.com/news/2014/nov/03/online-grocery-sales-near-100-billion-2019.

[7] *U.S. Census Bureau,* "Monthly and Annual Retail Trade 1992 – 2013," accessed April 4, 2015 http://www.census.gov/retail.

[8] Ibid.

[9] "2012 State of the Outlet Industry: Outlets Find the Happy Place," *Value Retail News*, (September, 2012): 12, accessed April 5, 2015, http://www.valueretailnews.com/pdfs/20 12stateoftheoutletindustry.pdf.

[10] Devika Krishna Kumar and Ramkumar Iyer, "Dollar Tree to Buy Family Dollar to Stave off Competition," Reuters, (Jul 28, 2014), accessed April 6, 2015, http://www. reuters.com/article/2014/07/28/us-family-dollar-st-offer-idUSKBN0FX0SX20140728.

[11] Ashley Lutz, "The Fate Of America's Dying Supercenters," *Business Insider*, (August 6, 2014), accessed April 6, 2015, http://www.businessinsider.com/the-fate -of-americas-dying-supercenters-2014-8#ixzz3WStdLJ9N.

[12] *Forbes*, "America's Largest Private Companies 2014," accessed April 6, 2015, http:// www.forbes.com/companies/he-butt-grocery.

[13] Andrea Chang and Tiffany Hsu, "Grocery Stores Adding Tech Features to Stay Competitive," *Los Angeles Times*, (September 08, 2013), accessed April 6, 2015, http://articles. latimes.com/2013/sep/08/business/la-fi-grocery-tech-20130908.

[14] Taken from BJs Wholesale Club Annual Report 2013, accessed April 6, 2015, http:// www.annualreports.com/Company/1646.

[15] Ibid.

[16] Lara Ewen, "TV Shopping Networks: Where are they Now?" *Rapaport Magazine*, (October, 2010), accessed April 6, 2015, http://www.diamonds.net/Magazine/Article. aspx?ArticleID=32790&RDRIssueID=54.

[17] *US Census Bureau*, "Monthly and Annual Retail Trade 1992 – 2013," accessed April 4, 2015, http://www.census.gov/retail.

CHAPTER 15 PRICING AND PRICE MANAGEMENT

→ Price Is ...

Price is the amount of money or other form of remuneration that is charged for products or services. More broadly defined, price is the sum of all the values that customers exchange, or give up, in order to receive the benefits, or values, associating with having or using a product or service.

Price is known by many logical and less logical names. Price is variously called rent, tuition, interest, fee, toll, wage, commission, dues, salary, bribe, blackmail, and more. Price is a measure of the utility that exists or is perceived to exist in a product. Utility was defined previously as a product's ability to satisfy wants and needs. The better a product satisfies customers' wants and needs, the more utility the product is perceived to possess. Price can be expressed in non-monetary terms. The price paid for a product, for example, may be another product (or service) that you offer in exchange. Exchanges of goods for goods, services for other goods, or services for services are quite common, even in modern industrialized economies such as ours.

Value is a commonly used (and abused) term. Marketers typically attempt to persuade buyers that values delivered through their brands exceed the values offered by competitive brands. Value is your perception of "what you get (obtain) in exchange for what you pay—or give up." In other words, the ratio between the utility you receive from a product and the price you give up in exchange for that product is its value.

Prices Should Change as a Product's Life Cycles Change

The relative importance of price as a tool that can generate competitive advantage generally shifts across a product's life cycle. During the introduction and growth stages of a product's life cycle, price usually is set high. The goal is to "skim" the market. There are several related reasons why Firms would charge higher prices at this point. First, customers are often less price sensitive during these initial two stages (think of innovators and early adopters). Second, Firms need to recover their new product development investment costs. Finally, production and marketing costs are typically higher at this point.

As a product's life cycle progresses, customers become more price sensitive and competitors enter the market. These pressures naturally force prices down as the product moves through its succeeding product life cycle stages (as you recall, maturity and decline).

Marketing Mix Elements Should Be Coordinated

Price is only one tool in the marketing mix. Price should never be established or managed in isolation from the other tools in the mix. Marketers should therefore evaluate how price affects and interacts with other marketing mix elements. Price and pricing management must be consistent with not only the qualities of the physical product, but also how the product is promoted and where it is sold. In other words, the elements of the mix must work together. This is obviously the case with brands that are positioned in ways to convey prestige or high quality images.[1] Price can function as a strong communication cue that helps create or sustain the appropriate positioning image.

Effective pricing decisions should begin with an understanding of how customer perceptions of the product's value impact their perception of whether the established pricing level is acceptable or unacceptable in customers' minds. "Acceptable pricing levels" are synonymous with "acceptable amounts of value" that customers would freely "give-up" through exchange in order to "get" a product that promises them even greater value. If we, as consumers, don't believe we're getting more value back from a product then we're paying out in terms of the price we pay to acquire the product, we will not pay the price. Customers almost always consciously or unconsciously evaluate the price associated with acquiring and/or using a product versus the benefits or values that they will receive if they choose to own and/or use the product. Any price paid by customers is their "cost." Any benefits received by customers are their "value."

You should remember, marketing success is predicated on the willingness of sellers and buyers to engage willingly in exchanges. You should also remember, buyers and sellers each also must believe they are winning. While this outcome is plainly impossible, all parties to the exchange must sense they are getting a better deal—taking away more value—than the other parties. Otherwise, sellers and buyers will not buy-from and sell-to each other. An exchange, of course, entails a "getting" of something that has value and a "giving up" of something else having value.

→ The Importance of Price

Price continues to be a major competitive tool in pretty much every Firm's marketing mix, but likely not always in the ways you would suspect. Pricing should be used as a strategic tool that concurrently creates and captures value for the Firm. Few customers wake up wanting to pay higher prices for anything. Yet the job of every marketer is to wake up each day seeking to convince customers that their product is worth paying more for, or, at the least, worth purchasing at the established price.

When deciding to purchase or not purchase anything, most customers first seek value. That is, customers generally search for and willingly pay more for what they perceive will prove valuable (to them). By voting with their wallets, customers signal what they are willing to pay. The responsibility of marketers is to frame and to deliver an attractive value proposition (through execution of the marketing mix), and make the brand's value appear worth the price—at almost any level. Marketers should do everything possible to make price matter less to customers as they determine which brand to purchase, or whether to purchase anything at all.

Price is the only marketing mix element that generates revenue for Firms. Each other marketing mix element represents a cost to the Firm. Price is also highly flexible, but easier to drop than to raise. When possible, Firms should avoid cutting prices too far or too fast to secure quick sales. Price cuts are literally the easiest differential advantage for competitors to match.

What happens when competitors match each other's price cuts? Two things. First, customers win. And second, each Firm loses insofar as their respective sales and market shares probably will not materially change while the profit margins of each Firm probably declines.

Price, for better or worse, is the number one tool that marketers currently use as they seek to differentiate their products. Yet the increasing price sensitivity of many customers, combined with their demands for greater "value," suggest marketers should monitor price and demand relationships very closely. Firms should be ready to adjust their marketing programs quickly if the need arises. However, price does not necessarily need to be set low to entice consumers and build demand. Consumers have become more heterogeneous in their preferences for products and brands, allowing consumer products companies to employ micro-segmentation strategies to finely tune their marketing programs aimed at increasingly smaller consumer segments. Paralleling this trend toward micro-segmentation, companies are also pursuing mass customization opportunities in which individual consumers often willingly pay premium prices for products customized specifically to their tastes.[2]

In some situations involving prestigious and extremely well-differentiated brands, the demand curve actually slopes upward. That means, when price goes up, demand goes up, too. In such cases, consumers are assuming that as price goes up, quality (and myriad other ancillary benefits such as, I can afford this "XX brand" bag, and you can't, so my status increases and I feel better about myself) goes up, as well. (Think **positional goods**.) In fact, with certain positional products such as high-end Chanel bags, the few rich people who actually can afford them are actually happy to pay a much higher price; a price that essentially serves as an exclusivity tax, and keeps less wealthy people from possessing the bag.

Price Competition vs. Non-Price Competition

When Firms use price as a differentiating tool, they engage in **price competition**. Firms that do battle on the basis of price competition attempt to achieve increased sales by reducing their prices. There is relatively less emphasis on the strategic use of other elements of the marketing mix to manage demand. Price competition is common in B2C or B2B settings where buyers essentially view products as commodities. Airfares and gasoline prices, for example, are subject to price-based competition because buyers view alternative brands as virtually identical. Firms competing in these industries often are forced into price wars with one another.

Firms that compete based on price often face serious challenges. First, price changes are very easily matched by competitors. As a result, price wars often occur in industries where customers are price sensitive and high fixed operating costs exist. In such situations, there is strong incentive to cut prices in order to maintain production volume at capacity, as with airline fares and gasoline prices. Second, government agencies, such as the FTC, closely scrutinize the pricing activities of Firms in industries prone to intense price competition. The FTC prosecutes Firms for "price fixing" activities in which competitors collude with one another to maintain prices at fixed levels to avoid price wars.

Non-price competition occurs when Firms compete on something other than price, or elect to de-emphasize price as a primary competitive tool. This certainly can help limit the probability of price wars, or at least a specific Firm's susceptibility to the effects of price wars. Essentially, Firms are engaging in non-price competition when they attempt to "differentiate" their brands by promoting the brand's superiority, higher quality, or unique image. Such Firms are attempting to create brand personalities that provide added "value" for the brand. They are attempting to build "brand equity."

The competitive implications for engaging in non-price competition are straightforward. Prices can be increased if Firms successfully differentiate their brands from those marketed by competitors. Customers are willing to pay more to receive the brand's perceived superior value. Of course, the risk always exists that, no matter how much Firms' try to differentiate their brands, consumers still won't bite. They may continue to view brands throughout the entire product category as virtual substitutes for one another. Non-price-based marketing strategies rarely work unless perceptions of real differences between brands can be created in the minds of targeted customer segments.

The Relationship between Price and Value

Price is now more important as a competitive and positioning tool because customers are increasingly seeking "value." Price invariably contributes substantially to buyers' value perceptions. Value, as noted earlier in this chapter, may be defined as the ratio between the benefits consumers perceive that they receive from owning and/or using the product and the "price" paid to acquire the product. In this context, price entails more than the direct monetary cost of products. Price can include additional costs associated with acquiring the product, such as travel time, cost of fuel, automobile wear and tear, or emotional frustration. Consumers consciously and subconsciously evaluate these tradeoffs as they assess the implied value implied with any charged "price."

According to Jack Welch, former Chairman of General Electric (GE), we are in the "value decade."[3] Note, however, "higher value" does not necessarily mean "lowest price." Higher value means that the price is "right" for the types and amounts of benefits received. From this perspective, value pricing does not hold the same connotation as does the aggressive use of lower prices or price cuts by Firms engaged in price competition. Value-based pricing is an attempt to increase the perceived ratio between benefits received and costs incurred. Value-based pricing does not automatically imply lower or the lowest price. There are several ways in which Firms respond to customers' demands for greater value:

- Many Firms accept that they will earn lower profits because they are offering customers more value for the same price. Typical responses to immediate competitive threats may entail providing higher product quantities for the same price, adding services, or bundling products. These are each short-term responses designed to negate threatening changes in consumer demand and competitors' marketing programs. These sorts of changes rarely provide sustainable competitive advantages. The reason why is that competitors can easily counter them by making additional adjustments to price and other elements of their marketing mixes. The fast food industry is replete with examples of this form of value-based pricing. Burger King's Value Menu and McDonalds' Extra Value Meals bundle several menu items together at lower prices than are charged for the same items when they are purchased separately.

- Firms often re-engineer existing products to improve quality and production efficiencies in order to tamp down manufacturing/marketing costs—and, of course, prices. Obamacare supporters, for example, believe that reforms to the US healthcare system mandated by the Affordable Health Care Act (AHCA) are forcing health insurers to re-engineer their products to provide greater value to consumers. The digital technology behind the AHCA is supposedly increasing transparency about prices and coverages associated with policies. Some suggest the changes spawned by the AHCA have driven the "most significant re-engineering of the American health system, by far the world's costliest, since employers began providing coverage for their workers in the 1930s."[4]

- Finally, Firms introduce new products that are more closely aligned with customers' wants and needs. Superfluous attributes and features are eliminated to control costs and hold the line on prices. Products are built from scratch for purposes of delivering predetermined amounts of customer value. This approach is clearly the most desirable marketer response, but also the hardest to execute successfully. The development of value-engineered new products is most likely to earn sustainable competitive advantage for Firms.

→ Major Pricing Decision Areas

Various factors should be evaluated before establishing the prices for products and services. Indeed, price setting entails more than determining products' base or list prices. Price-setting processes should involve the development of a pricing schedule wherein list price, price discounts, and allowances, and geographic pricing adjustments are identified. This pricing schedule becomes part of an overall pricing plan that features this price schedule and contingencies for managing price given changes in market conditions. The activities included in the pricing process are summarized below and in Exhibit 15.1. The detailed nature of each activity is subsequently discussed in its own section.

- *Analyzing the Pricing Environment.* Legal environment, competitive environment, economy, etc.
- *Identifying Relevant Costs.* Costs set the lower boundary, called the floor, for prices. Firms generally cannot price below costs per unit for long and remain profitable. The fixed and variable costs associated production (manufacturing) and marketing (think supply chain management) must be considered.

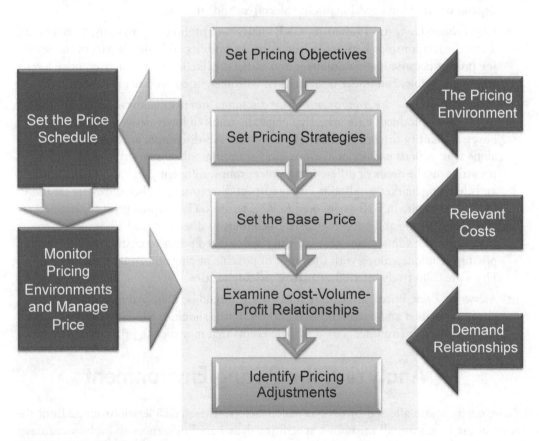

Exhibit 15.1 *The Pricing Process.*

- *Examining Price-Demand Relationships.* Demand considerations are critical due to the relationship between prices and the quantity of product that will be "demanded" by customers at those prices. In general, price is inversely related to demand; meaning, as price goes up, demand goes down. Managers should be able to predict the impact of a specific price or price change on resulting customer demand and profitability. This means being able to predict the shape of the demand curve faced by the Firm.

- *Set Pricing Objectives.* Pricing objectives should identify the role that price will play as a part of the overall marketing mix. This is the starting point in the price setting process. All subsequent steps are intended to achieve these objectives. Pricing objectives normally are framed in four areas: (1) to achieve specific levels of profit or profit-oriented objectives; (2) to achieve specific levels of sales or sales-oriented objectives; (3) to address or cope with competitors' actions or competition-oriented objectives; and (4) to achieve specific societal goals or social-oriented objectives.

- *Set Pricing Strategies.* Pricing strategies are the general approaches to pricing that will help achieve the Firm's pricing objectives. Different strategies are required to achieve specific types of objectives. Pricing strategies usually fall into one or four major categories: (1) Demand generation strategies in which prices are established to achieve sales and/or profit-oriented objectives; (2) Premium pricing strategies that usually focus on achieving profit-oriented outcomes; (3) Competitive pricing strategies in which prices are set to achieve competition-oriented pricing objectives; and (4) Product line pricing strategies that help the Firm achieve sales and/or profit outcomes that are established across entire product lines.

- *Set the Base Price.* Several pricing techniques are available to determine the "base/list" price to charge for products. Like pricing strategies, a range of different pricing techniques are available. The specific techniques employed by the Firm to set base price depend on the Firm's specific pricing objectives and strategies.

- *Cost-Volume-Profit (CVP) Analysis.* CVP analysis, or profitability analysis, attempts to assess the relationships between prices, costs, and profits. This step is part of the pricing process because it allows managers to gauge the likelihood that a given price level will be profitable, and under what market, customer, or environmental conditions.

- *Identify Required Price Adjustments.* Price discounts and price allowances are adjustments to the product's base price that generally result in lower delivered prices to buyers. Quantity-discounts, seasonal-discounts, cash-discounts, or trade-discounts along with various promotional-allowances are commonly employed in most industries to meet the needs of different customer groups, different purchasing situations, and changing market conditions. These sorts of discounts and allowances are far more likely to transpire in B2B as opposed to B2C settings. Geographic price adjustments allow for shipping and handling costs. In contrast to discounts and allowances, geographic pricing adjustments generally increase realized prices to customers. The specific pricing techniques, along with the range of possible pricing adjustments, adopted by Firms are collectively referred to as their **pricing tactics**.

- *Managing Price.* Prices, after being initially set, should be managed in response to changing market and competitive conditions. Firms should track daily changes in critical marketing environments to anticipate events that may dictate pricing adjustments.

→ Analyzing the Pricing Environment

Pricing decisions are affected by several major factors. These considerations range from the nature of the Firm's overall mission to specific analysis-based inferences about how customer demand may be affected by alternative prices that may be set.

Government Regulation and Pricing Legislation

No other area in marketing (and probably business in general) has received as much regulatory attention from governmental entities as have pricing activities. Two major pricing activities have received the most legislative focus across the decades: (1) horizontal and vertical price fixing activities; and, (2) price discrimination.

Horizontal Price Fixing

Horizontal price fixing entails pricing agreements between two or more Firms operating at the same supply chain level. Two or more manufacturers or intermediaries, for example, may maintain prices at some mutually-agreed-upon level. Firms engage in horizontal price fixing arrangements to negate the deleterious profit ramifications of severe price competition (e.g., price wars). Horizontal price fixing cases routinely arise. For example, Mrs. Baird's Bread was found guilty of price fixing in small towns in East Texas. Prosecutors claimed that from 1977 to 1993 management at Mrs. Baird's colluded with other producers in Texas and adjacent states to "fix" and maintain the per loaf price of bread at more than $.76. Bread is essentially a commodity. As a result, most consumers view alternative brands of bread as much the same. Under such conditions, price becomes a major choice criterion and a major component of the producer's marketing strategy.[5] More recently, Apple was convicted of colluding with five other publishers to fix the prices for e-books. The ruling was based on Section 1 of the Sherman Anti-trust Act.[6]

Acts of horizontal price fixing may not directly affect industry pricing activities. Two manufacturers may agree, for example, to uniformly restrict production output in order to drive prices up. In general, when supplies are restricted, prices increase as buyers compete for scarce supplies. The law of supply and demand is one law that almost always works.

All horizontal price fixing activities are strictly illegal under the Sherman Anti-trust and FTC Acts. The Sherman Antitrust Act prohibits Firms from engaging in activities that effectively restrain trade or tend to create a monopoly. The FTC Act prohibits "unfair practices" in general—horizontal price fixing is absolutely an unfair business practice.

Vertical Price Fixing

Vertical price fixing exists when producers or wholesaling supply chain intermediaries dictate the retail price of products. Unlike horizontal price fixing, vertical price fixing was legal until 1975. Before that time, the Miller-Tydings Act and McGuire Act rendered such "fair trade" practices (as they were then called) legal. The underlying rationale, which certainly appears logical, was that small retailers (who could not substantially lower prices due to their higher cost structures) could be severely hurt by the price-cutting activities of large-scale retailers (corporate-owned chains) who possessed cost advantages due to scale economies. The fair trade practice was also assumed to help producers protect the images of brands positioned on quality and/or prestige.

Fair Trade was repealed with the Consumer Goods Pricing Act of 1975. The argument for the legislative reversal was two-fold. First, Fair Trade laws actually provided little competitive advantage to smaller retailers. Second, consumers would benefit from any increased price competition that would result from their repeal.

Price Discrimination

Price discrimination is highly restricted by legislative action. Whenever producers or other intermediaries charge different prices to different customers for the same product sold in the same quantity, price discrimination has occurred. Interestingly, this discrimination may or may not be legal. The Robinson-Patman Act, passed in 1936, is the major piece of legislation governing price discrimination. Robinson-Patman dictates the circumstances under which price discrimination is or is not legal. Based on Robinson-Patman, price discrimination is illegal only under circumstances in which competition between buyers is harmed because of sellers' pricing activities. The Robinson-Patman Act does not pertain to prices charged to ultimate consumers. Because consumers are not in "competition" with one another for "customers," Robinson-Patman does not apply. The law only applies to the pricing activities of producers and middlemen when setting prices to other producers or middlemen (including pricing to retailers).

To illustrate how price discrimination can injure competitive interactions between buyers, consider the following. Assume a manufacturer has two major customers: Wholesaler 1 and Wholesaler 2. These wholesalers operate in roughly the same geographic area. They compete for the same customers. Assume that the manufacturer offers lower prices to Wholesaler 1 than to 2 because Wholesaler 1 is owned by a relative. If the lower price to 1 provides the Firm with a cost advantage that can be used against Wholesaler 2 (charging lower prices, for example), and that advantage harms Wholesaler 2's ability to compete in that market, then the producer has engaged in price discrimination. The producer's activities are illegal.

The Robinson-Patman Act covers more than just discrimination based on list prices. The law extends to various forms of discounts (cash, quantity, seasonal, etc.) and allowances for promotion. If any of these are provided to any buyer, they must be provided on a proportionate basis to all competing buyers. Again, this only applies when these buyers compete with each other and any potential price discrimination harms any Firm's ability to compete.

Competitive Conditions

The nature and intensity of competitive interactions in an industry often dictate the degree of discretion Firms have when setting prices. Recall from Chapter 4 our discussion of the forms of competition commonly encountered in industries. Price competition and the consequent impact of competitors on pricing activities tend to be strongest in those industries characterized by oligopolistic competition, monopolistic competition, and perfect competition.

Oligopolistic competition occurs in industries where there exist a handful of large competitors, each with substantial market share. Taken together, these large Firms dominate sales and market share for the industry. Depending on the industry, there may also be a pool of smaller competitors, each of which holds inconsequential market shares. The dominant competitors typically are the **price leaders**. These Firms set and broadcast prices to other industry members. Smaller Firms are expected to stay in line. These latter Firms are **price followers**.

Monopolistic competition exists in industries characterized by a large number of competitors all vying with each other for market share. No single competitor dominates. Each attempts to compete by changing its products and services to offer a value bundle that helps differentiate it from competitors' offerings. Firms try to emphasize branding and positioning as their major marketing tools in the hopes that price competition can be avoided. However, price still plays a major role in signaling value to consumers. Individual Firms cannot deviate too far from prices charged by competitors without degrading value perceptions of their brands. Attempts at differentiating are appropriate, but do have their limits.

Perfect competition exists in industries characterized by many small companies each producing and selling essentially the same product or service. True situations of perfect competition rarely exist. Agricultural and other natural products markets such as forestry, fish, gas and oil, and ores tend to come closest. For example, agricultural markets are characterized by many small producers of products that amount to commodities for which one source of supply is generally undifferentiated from any other (i.e. the output of one producer is no different than that of any other producer of the same product). Significant differences between products from alternative suppliers normally are negligible and price competition can be severe to the point that price wars may occur.

Regardless of the specific form of competition faced, it is imperative that Firms fully understand the pricing activities of their primary competitors. This goes beyond simply tracking their prices. Firms must "read between the lines" and try to decompose the underlying rationale associated with competitors' pricing activities. Have their pricing objectives and strategies changed? Why? What will be any likely additional changes to their prices and price setting activities? Will there be associated changes in other elements of their marketing programs to complement price changes?

State of the Economy

The general state of the economy will significantly affect Firms' pricing activities. Key economic factors affecting pricing activities either directly or indirectly include inflation, recession, and employment. Not all Firms and product categories are equally affected by economic change. Firms must understand which specific changes affect them and how. Monitoring key economic trends should be an ongoing component of the Firm's intelligence collection processes, just as it is important to stay on top of market, customer, and competitive conditions.

Recession, consumer confidence, and employment affect consumers' ability and willingness to spend. The relationships between these economic conditions and spending are complex, but in general as recessionary conditions hit the economy, consumer confidence and employment both decline translating into less spending. Firms often respond by reducing prices in an attempt to boost demand and spending. Price reductions in some cases tend to be supported by decreasing costs, also driven by these recessionary pressures. However, this is not always the case. Price reductions may be required to stimulate demand, but costs may not follow suite. In such cases, profits will be reduced or even become negative until economic conditions improve.

Inflationary conditions can also affect consumers' buying power. Wages often lag behind the cost and price increases resulting from inflationary pressures. However, Firms may not be able to reduce prices under inflationary conditions since virtually all components of Firms' supply chains are also subject to these same inflationary pressures, driving up costs of parts and materials, utilities, labor, and other inputs to production. Given that costs must be covered in the long-term if Firms wish to remain profitable, what options do Firms have when costs increase? Several alternatives are available. These are examined in a later section as part of our examination of the various costs affecting pricing.

→ Identifying (and Understanding) Relevant Costs Driving Price

As noted, the relevant costs of making and marketing products determine floors below which prices for those products cannot be set.

Fixed Costs

Fixed costs are costs that do not change as production increased or decreases. No matter how many units are produced and sold, these costs (in total) remain about the same.

Typical examples of costs that are "fixed" in nature include:

- Rent: no matter how many units are made within the production facility, rent remains the same from month to month.
- Salaries: managers receive the same salary no matter how much product is made in a given time period.
- Taxes: many taxes, such as real estate taxes, do not change with production volume.
- Plant and equipment: costs related to plant and equipment include depreciation, rent, maintenance contracts, etc. These are generally constant. Equipment maintenance, however, could change with output, if additional production results in the need for more maintenance.
- Advertising: costs to advertise in various media generally are treated as fixed. Total advertising costs usually vary by marketing program rather than by production and sales volume.

The graph in Exhibit 15.2 plots total fixed costs as a function of production output. The line parallel to the **units produced** axis emphasizes that these costs remain constant with increases (or decreases) in production per time period.

Variable Costs

Variable costs typically remain constant on a per unit basis. However, total variable costs will rise or fall directly with increases or decreases in production and sales levels. Increases in production volume per period result in higher levels of total variable costs.

Typical examples of variable costs include:

- Labor: laborers are paid an hourly rate. The more hours worked (i.e., more production), the higher the total costs for labor.
- Parts and materials: the costs of parts and materials used to build products remain constant on a per unit basis, but their totals obviously grow as output increases.
- Utilities: the costs of heat, electricity, water, etc. are largely variable because their total volumes (and total costs) are generally tied directly to overall production volume.
- Commissions: sales commissions are variable because they are not paid unless the salesperson sells the product. Total sales commissions increase as sales (and production) increase. This is one cost that Firms are delighted to see increase, by the way.

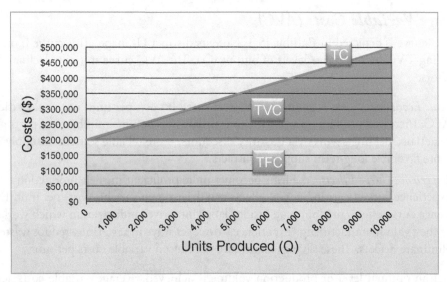

Exhibit 15.2 *Total Fixed, Total Variable, and Total Costs as a Function of Production Volume (Q).*

Exhibit 15.2 also plots total variable costs as a function of production output. Note the constantly increasing nature of the total variable cost curve. Given the behavior of fixed and variable costs as a function of production volume, **total costs** are obtained by adding fixed and variable costs together. From a graphic perspective, the total cost curve is obtained by plotting total variable costs on top of total fixed costs. The significance of the total cost curve will become apparent when **breakeven analysis** is discussed below.

Average Costs

The fixed and variable costs examined above have **average cost** equivalents. These average costs are obtained by dividing the relevant total fixed or total variable cost by the number of units produced.

Average Fixed Costs (AFC)

Average fixed costs are obtained by dividing total fixed costs by the appropriate level of output. Exhibit 15.3 demonstrates the behavior of the average fixed cost (AFC) curve with increased levels of output. Note, as output increases, the AFC curve declines as TFC are spread over a larger number of units. This cost decline is typically attributed to economies of scale. Scale economies are realized when the Firm's investment in larger, more efficient production facilities yields greater volume capabilities relative to the fixed costs associated with these facilities. By achieving the level of production volume for which the facility was designed, the Firm can achieve a substantial reduction in AFC. Note the nonlinearity of the curve, with most of the decreases in AFC being attained at lower production volume levels. The flattening of the curve as it moves to the right suggests that, after achieving some level of "optimal" production volume, coaxing further significant efficiencies may be difficult.

Average Variable Costs (AVC)

The AVC curve is depicted in Exhibit 15.3. Note its distinct U-Shape. This curve is obtained by dividing TVC by respective levels of output (Q). The AVC curve initially declines due to two factors:

- *Scale Economies.* Scale economies can affect variable costs per unit, just as they did for AFC. Increased production volume can translate into volume purchases of parts and materials, yielding savings via quantity discounts, more reliable sources of supply, and more favorable long-term supplier contracts.

- *Experience Curve Effects.* As Firms becomes more proficient in their production efforts, experience curve (learning curve) effects can drive down variable costs per unit. Experience curve effects predominate inside "labor-intensive" industries in which workers, as they gain manufacturing "experience," discover ways to save time, reduce waste, and eliminate defects. These savings contribute to reduced variable costs per unit.

But after an optimal level of production volume is achieved, average variable costs actually may increase. Increases in variable production costs emerge from factors such as the need to pay labor overtime, over-utilized facilities that require increased maintenance costs, increased material waste, and rising defect rates. These increased costs are called "diseconomies of scale."

Average Total Costs (ATC). The ATC curve is obtained by summing the AVC and AFC curves (Exhibit 15.3). The ATC curve usually mirrors the AFC curve because of the sheer magnitude of fixed costs relative to variable costs at low levels of production volume. The ATC curve increases at higher levels of production volume primarily due to the increase in AVC.

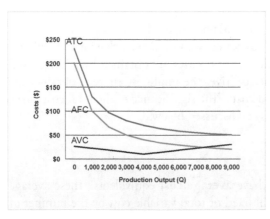

Exhibit 15.3 *Average Costs.*

The Price Floor Revisited

The nature of fixed, variable, and average costs underscores why costs define the "price floor." The Firm cannot price below its average total costs and remain profitable for long, particularly if price is set lower than average variable costs (AVC). Marketers may price below ATC, but not AVC. This practice is referred to as **marginal pricing** and is employed to keep production lines operating during periods of slow sales. The idea is that price can be reduced to the point that average (unit) variable costs are just covered. Any additional margin (profits per unit) that is generated will help cover fixed costs.

Costs are also a major component of several pricing techniques. **Cost-based** pricing tools specifically account for the importance of covering fixed and variable costs when establishing the base price for a product.

How Firms Cope with Increases in Costs

Given that costs must be exceeded over the long-term in order for Firms to stay in business, what options do Firms have when costs increase? Several options are available:

- Raising prices is the easiest response. But the option is not always possible or desirable.

- Reducing product sizes is a tactic often used by producers of consumer goods. The strategy is to maintain price, but reduce the size of the package and hope consumers don't notice. Candy manufacturers did this during the 1970s when sugar prices increased dramatically. Similarly, a beer producer in the Pacific Northwest toyed with an 11oz can. Toilet paper producers have recently been accused of "de-sheeting" rolls by fluffing individual sheets with air but decreasing the total number of sheets without reducing the apparent size of the role.[7] Weber's Law, as discussed during Chapter 7, has been employed by manufacturers to predict how much a stimulus (such as price or package size) can be changed before the change is noticeable.

- Reducing product quality is usually the least desirable response to higher costs. This was done by Schlitz when facing with rising costs for ingredients involved in brewing beer. Unfortunately, consumers noticed a distinct change in taste. Schlitz has never recovered lost market share as a result. Similarly, Hershey Foods has been accused of substituting lower quality ingredients for the cocoa butter credited with giving its chocolates their "creamy" taste.[8]

→ Analyzing Demand Relationships

Virtually all pricing decisions are impacted by customer demand for given products. As noted, demand is generally inversely related to price. This means that as price increases demand usually, but not always, declines. Firms must be able to predict the resulting impact on demand for the prices charged for its products; that is, to forecast the nature of demand curves for their products.

Types of Demand Curves

Demand curves are usually similar to the downward-sloping curve in Exhibit 15.4. Higher prices, simply stated, typically lead to smaller quantities of units demanded. As price increases from $5 to $20 per unit, the quantity demanded drops from 60 units to 5 units. The downward sloping demand curve reflects this inverse relationship and illustrates the **law of demand**.

However, demand curves can also slope upwards. Such curves (Exhibit 15.5) illustrate inverse demand relationships. Inverse demand relationships, wherein higher prices actually stimulate higher demand, often arise for products in which higher prices connote higher quality or prestige. The lower part of the curve up to price P1 represents prices for which inverse demand exists. Note that at price P1, the curve tips over; a normal demand curve (consistent with the law of demand) takes over for further increases in price. The bend in the curve at P1 illustrates: (1) prices can be set too high, even for prestige goods or (2) at some point customers will not pay more for additional quality.

Prices along Demand Curves Are Not Always Profitable

Some prices on a given demand curve will prove unprofitable for Firms. The task of managers is to identify a price on the demand curve that is acceptable to customers and at which the Firm can earn a profit. On typical downward sloping demand curves (Exhibit 15.6), prices at either extreme will usually result in losses. There are two reasons for this:

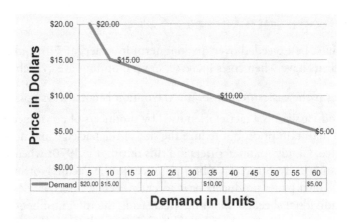

Exhibit 15.4 *The Law of Demand.*

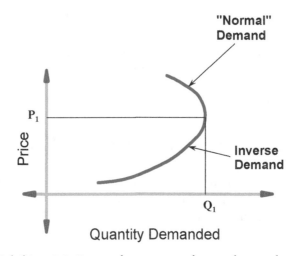

Exhibit 15.5 *Demand curves can show a direct relationship between price and demand. Such curves are characterized as "inverse demand curves."*

- When prices are high (left side of the curve), the profit-contribution-per-unit will be high. Price, you see, greatly exceeds each unit's variable costs. However, total demand may dip too low to generate enough revenue to cover total fixed costs.[9]

- Similarly, when prices are very low, sales volume may be high. But the profit-contribution per unit may be low or negative. The total contribution to profits consequently may be too small to cover fixed costs, even given larger numbers of units sold. When prices are set lower than average variable costs, the situation is worsened.

Price Elasticity of Demand

The "elasticity" of the relationship between price and quantity demanded is important. Price elasticity of demand expresses the degree to which changes in price affect changes in quantities demanded/sold and the associated revenues produced. When total revenue increases as a result of lowering price, demand is **price elastic**. When total revenue declines due to price cuts, demand is **price inelastic**.

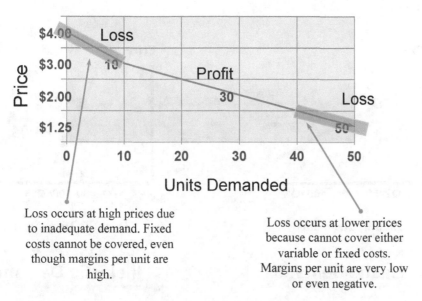

Loss occurs at high prices due to inadequate demand. Fixed costs cannot be covered, even though margins per unit are high.

Loss occurs at lower prices because cannot cover either variable or fixed costs. Margins per unit are very low or even negative.

Exhibit 15.6 *Not all prices on demand curves are profitable.*

Elastic Price-Demand Relationships

Exhibit 15.7 illustrates a situation where demand is price elastic. In "elastic demand" situations customers are very sensitive or responsive to price changes. As shown in Exhibit 15.7 a price increase from $6.00 to $8.00 has a substantial effect on demand. The result is a decrease in Total Revenue (TR) from $600 to $400.

The reason why TR increases as price decreases is that the percentage change in demand is greater than the associated percentage change in price. To determine why this happened, examine the formula for computing the coefficient of price elasticity:

$$(1) \qquad e = \frac{\dfrac{Q_2 - Q_1}{\frac{1}{2}(Q_2 + Q_1)}}{\dfrac{P_2 - P_1}{\frac{1}{2}(P_2 + P_1)}}$$

In this formula, the numerator reflects the percent change in demand. The denominator measures the percent change in price. The result, e, or elasticity, is the percentage change in demand associated with each percentage change in price. The denominators in the expressions for percent change in price and percent change in quantity are the midpoints between P1 and P2 and Q1 and Q2, respectively. This permits the formula to yield the same *e* value, regardless of whether price is raised or lowered (i.e., P1 and P2 are reversed).

Using the price/quantity data from Exhibit 15.7 illustrates how the formula for *e* works:

$$(2) \qquad e = \frac{\dfrac{Q_2 - Q_1}{\frac{1}{2}(Q_2 + Q_1)}}{\dfrac{P_2 - P_1}{\frac{1}{2}(P_2 + P_1)}} = \frac{\dfrac{400 - 600}{\frac{1}{2}(400 + 600)}}{\dfrac{8 - 6}{\frac{1}{2}(8 + 6)}} = \frac{\dfrac{-200}{500}}{\dfrac{2}{7}} = \frac{-.4}{.286} = -1.4$$

When price is increased from P1 to P2 in this example ($6.00 to $8.00), demand decreases from 600 units at Q1 to 400 units at Q2. The percentage change in demand is 40% (numerator), while the percentage change in price is 28.6% (denominator). The result is a value for elasticity,

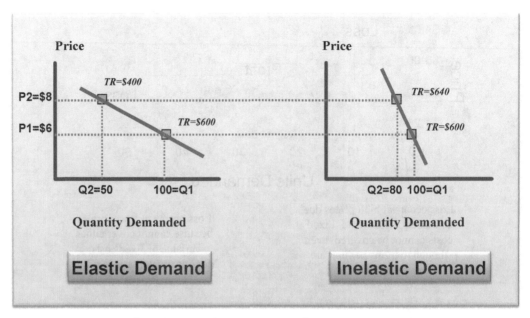

Exhibit 15.7 *Demand can be price-elastic or price-inelastic.*

$e = -1.4$. This value for e tells us that demand decreases by 1.4% for each 1% increase in price. This example clearly illustrates elastic demand because the absolute percentage change in quantity demanded exceeds the absolute percentage change in price (i.e. 1.4% > 1.0%).

The following conditions will generally lead to situations where demand is price elastic:

- *Brands are Similar:* When the brands are similar or if consumers merely perceive that few differences exist between alternative brands in a given product category, price becomes a key criterion that customers will employ when making choices. Consumers usually gravitate to the least expensive alternative. The marketer's job, as always, is to create differentiation; i.e. differentiate their brands—for their sake, hopefully along determinant differences (meaning along determinant attributes).

- *No Time Pressure:* The more time consumers have to engage in comparison shopping, the greater their tendency is to look for the best price.

- Involvement Is Low: Low involvement products or purchasing situations imply that customers experience little perceived risk when they purchase and use the product. The product is relatively unimportant to the consumer. Consequently price is more likely to be emphasized in the choice process.

- *Little Brand Loyalty Exists:* When significant brand preferences do not exist, consumers tend to brand-switch as they seek variety. Switching behavior is easily induced by perceived price differences between brands.

Inelastic Price-Demand Relationships

When demand is price inelastic, customers are less sensitive to price changes. Note that given the same increase in price ($2.00), demand only decreases from 100 to 80 units. The associated change in total revenue, however, is from $600 to $640. Revenue actually increased by $40. There is a direct positive relationship between changes in price and changes in total revenue. Price increases are associated with increases in total revenue. Similarly, when price decreases, total revenue also decreases. We just described an ideal scenario for marketing managers wishing to raise prices. Computing the coefficient of elasticity results in $e = -.777$:

$$(3) \qquad e = \frac{\frac{Q_2 - Q_1}{\frac{1}{2}(Q_2 + Q_1)}}{\frac{P_2 - P_1}{\frac{1}{2}(P_2 + P_1)}} = \frac{\frac{80 - 100}{\frac{1}{2}(80 + 100)}}{\frac{8 - 6}{\frac{1}{2}(8 + 6)}} = \frac{\frac{-20}{90}}{\frac{2}{7}} = \frac{-.222}{.286} = -.777$$

Note that the percent change in price is still 28.6% i.e. the same change as seen in the elastic demand condition in equation (2). The percentage change in demand, however, now is –22.2%. As a result, $e = -.777$, meaning that demand decreases by only .777% for a 1% change (increase) in price.

Factors that contribute to situations where demand is price inelastic, as might be expected, are essentially the opposite of those discussed for elastic demand.

- *Brands Are Highly Differentiated:* when brands are perceived as very different from one another with respect to their characteristics, benefits, and inherent quality, consumers experience more difficulty when attempting to compare them on a price-to-price basis. Customers are subsequently less price sensitive.

- *Strong Brand Loyalty Exists:* consumers who are already loyal to one brand are less likely to switch based solely on price differences. Indeed, consumers may willingly pay significantly more for their preferred brands. This is often true of products that are positioned based on prestige. Demand curves for brands that are perceived as prestigious are far less price elastic, unless demand is inversely elastic.

- *Emergency Purchase:* in emergency situations where time utility assumes paramount importance, consumers will typically accept higher prices. Think about an umbrella available for sale on a rainy day at Six Flags. Or, the higher prices you pay at convenience stores for emergency purchases of staple goods.

Estimating Demand Curves

Firms should understand the nature of the demand curves that they face. Firms employ a number of tools that assist them as they attempt to predict demand at different prices. These tools include:

Historical sales data at different prices can be compiled to gauge the effect of price changes on demand for existing products. This technique draws on historical price-quantity data maintained in the Firm's MkIS to plot a demand curve. A fairly extensive sales history is needed to produce statistically reliable estimates. Moreover, managers must eliminate or account for competing but independent causal factors that may affect demand. This is an unreasonable assumption for Firms that engage in extensive promotion and selling activities.

Surveys are frequently used to project demand at alternative prices for new products, or in situations in which material changes in marketing and operating environments invalidate the use of historical data. Surveys will typically examine a series of prices within a relevant price range and then tabulate the number of potential buyers who indicate they "would buy" at each price. These surveys are generally called "buyer-response surveys." They produce "demand curves" showing the percentage of prospective buyers who replied that they would purchase at a given price.

Test markets are the best way to project demand curves because actual behavioral data are collected linking product purchases to prices charged. Test markets for crafting demand estimates can be done in several ways:

- Multiple test cities can be selected in which different prices are set. A different price would be used in each city.
- Prices can be varied across retail stores in the same city. This approach can be combined with the multiple city approach to provide additional information on how price and demand may vary based on local market conditions.
- Prices can be varied over time in one or more cities in the same retail stores.

Employing syndicated data services that record consumers' purchases of products via scanned UPC codes can enhance all three forms of test market. This "observational data" provides the added benefit that it allows researchers to monitor competitors' prices and the prices of complementary/substitute products for comparison purposes.

→ Setting Pricing Objectives

The primary goal of the pricing process (Exhibit 15.1) is to produce a pricing plan that contains a price schedule (i.e. actual price lists, adjustments for discounts and allowances, adjustments for shipping and handling) along with contingency plans for managing price given changes in market conditions. The first step in this planning process is to identify specific pricing objectives. These objectives, once established, guide the remaining steps in the process. These objectives also dictate the role that price is expected to play in the Firm's marketing mix. Accordingly, all pricing objectives and activities must be consistent with the objectives established for the other three elements of the marketing mix. The four "Ps" must be managed such that they can work together to create and capture value from customers and, of course, help the Firm achieve its overall strategic goals.

The Range of Pricing Objectives

Typically, pricing objectives fall into four categories:

- *Profit-focused objectives* in which price is set to help the Firm achieve some specific level of profit.
- *Sales-focused objectives* in which price is set to achieve some desired level of sales revenue.
- *Competition-focused objectives* in which price is set to avoid competitors' reactions, or to elicit some specific response from competing Firms in the industry.
- *Socially-focused objectives* in which price is set to achieve a desirable societal state or to avoid a negative state.
- *Psychological objectives* in which price is purposely employed to signal quality and/or prestige.

Profit-Focused Pricing Objectives

Profit-oriented pricing objectives help the Firm achieve a desired level of profitability. Generally, profit-oriented objectives take two forms: (1) pricing to achieve a desired target return and (2) pricing for profit maximization.

Target Return Pricing Objectives

Target return pricing objectives set a specific level of return on investment (ROI) or return on sales (ROS) as the pricing goal. The objective is usually specified as a percentage return. For example, a manufacturer of farm and construction equipment, such as Kubota, may specify a 15% or 20% return on investment (ROI). ROI is measured as the ratio between the Firm's net profit and its investment in the plant and equipment required to generate that profit. For example, assume a manufacturer has $276,000 invested in the manufacturing process for a new product. If the net profit (before taxes) from sales of the new product is $29,000, the ratio between the $29,000 profit figure and the initial $276,000 investment is the Firm's ROI:

$$(4) \qquad ROI = \frac{\$29,000}{\$276,000} = .105 = 10.5\%$$

Large manufacturers, particularly industry leaders, normally employ ROI pricing objectives. This is due to their relatively large investments and their ability to exercise at least partial control over the prices paid for products in their respective industries. In addition, Firms can easily determine whether target-return pricing objectives have been met.

By contrast a wholesale grocery supplier, such as Fleming Wholesalers, may specify a 10% return on annual sales (ROS) as its pricing goal. ROS pricing objectives are popular with intermediaries (wholesalers and retailers) because they emphasize profitability as a function of sales, rather than investment in facilities.

Profit Maximization Pricing Objectives

Profit maximization, where price is set to maximize profits, is probably the most common pricing objective. Usually, this pricing objective is applied to single products, but it can also apply for entire product lines. For example, Gillette may price razors fairly low to stimulate demand, but price replacement razor blades relatively high. Prices for both the razors and replacement blades may be specifically set to maximize profits across both complementary products taken together.

Profit maximization pricing objectives are typically employed for new products, prestige products, and products for which high quality standards are important. In these situations, price usually is set relatively high to appeal to the first purchasers of products i.e., innovators and early adopters. However, high prices do not necessarily maximize profits. When demand for goods and services is price-elastic, lower prices will stimulate added demand. Total revenue and profits will increase. But when demand is price inelastic, lower prices may yield lower revenues and profits. When demand is price inelastic, profit maximization is better achieved by judiciously raising prices, up to a point.

Sales Volume-Focused Pricing Objectives

Sales volume focused-pricing objectives target achieving a specific level of sales volume. Volume can be expressed as unit sales, in dollars, or as a share of the market (**market share**). Profitability is not specifically the main concern. However, the implicit assumption is that increased sales volume, in whatever form, results in improved profitability over time.

Sales Volume Pricing Objectives

Sales volume objectives usually are framed or stated as a desired percentage increase in sales volume over a specific time horizon, such as a quarter or a year. Firms employing sales volume pricing objectives generally seek rapid sales growth because of the implicit assumption (an assumption that is not always correct) that increased profits go hand-in-hand with increased sales volume.

Sales volume objectives usually translate into aggressive pricing activities in which list prices are set low to stimulate demand. Sales volume objectives also are usually accompanied by aggressive price promotion activities. These promotion activities might include systematic discounting, couponing activities, rebates, among others. "Deep discounting" by off-price retailers, such as Ross or TJ Maxx, and warehouse clubs (Sam's or Costco) reflects the popularity of sales volume pricing objectives. The extremely low prices offered by these retailers emerge from their ability to buy seconds, overstocked, and left-over seasonal merchandise at low costs.

Emphasizing sales volume objectives can generate problems for Firms if they do not control their costs. If they myopically pursue sales growth, Firms may overspend on promotion, supply chain support, and other marketing activities. Profits fall as a result.

Market Share Pricing Objectives

Sometimes it makes sense to frame sales volume pricing objectives relative to industry sales volume. In this instance, Firms are setting market share pricing objectives. **Market share** is the ratio between the company's sales volume and overall industry sales volume. Price is established to achieve a desired level of market share, or to maintain existing market share. The underlying rationale is that Firms possessing superior market shares in an industry generally enjoy increased power over distributors and suppliers, greater "self-presence" and market awareness, and lower unit costs for their products. Large, powerful manufacturers, for example, might demand that smaller retailers provide premium shelf space, more support for special promotions, and accept larger inventories.

Market share gains often can be "bought" with aggressive pricing. The potential drawback, as noted, is that competitors can easily match these price reductions. Price wars can ensue. The end result, usually, is a temporary shift in market share. That is, unless a distinct competitive advantage such as dramatically lowered costs that competitors cannot match accompanies the increases in market share.

The use of market share objectives have proven particularly attractive in high-tech industries that sell products such as computers, calculators, digital cameras or DVD players, and other electronic equipment. In these industries, increases in market share often translate into unit cost reductions (declines in average fixed and average variable costs) due to scale economies and experience curve effects. In turn, these cost savings lead to further possible price reductions and additional gains in market share.

Competition-Oriented Pricing Objectives

Certain pricing objectives focus specifically on how pricing activities may affect competitive interactions within the industry. Indeed, Firms that are satisfied with existing sales volumes and profits may adopt pricing objectives that maintain the "status quo." Competition-oriented objectives range from stabilizing prices in the industry, meeting competitors' prices, altogether avoiding price competition if possible, or pricing to discourage competitive entry.

Price stabilization amounts to a "don't rock the boat" pricing objective. Price stabilization is a common pricing objective in mature industries where products tend to be highly standardized (e.g. building materials, oil refining, chemical production, and steel and other metals production). One or two Firms tend to function as price leaders in such industries. These price leaders set prices that are reasonable for most Firms in the industry, expecting other Firms to follow their lead and approximately match that price. Smaller Firms act as "price followers" as they pursue a **meet the competition** pricing objective. Price followers are unlikely to price significantly below the price leader because any price cut will easily be matched by other Firms. A price war may eventuate; a struggle which smaller Firms, with their smaller cash reserves, are likely to lose.

When *avoiding price competition* Firms may seek to escape the negative ramifications of price competition. Rather than competing on a price basis, Firms may price at market rates and differentiate their brands' values by emphasizing other elements of the marketing mix.

Firms may price to *discourage competitive* entry by adopting pricing objectives intended to discourage competitors from entering the market. This is usually a pricing objective associated with new product introductions. Firms that anticipate significant reductions in unit costs due to scale economies and/or experience effects may purposely price below competitive levels to quickly acquire market share. Some Firms actually may price below initial unit costs, knowingly accepting a loss for a period of time. However, if the low price is successful at stimulating significant demand, scale economies and experience effects may be achieved before competitors can respond with their own product introductions. If potential competitors perceive a significant cost disadvantage resulting from their late entry, they may stay out of the market entirely. The low price established by the pioneering Firm has effectively discouraged competitive entry.

Socially-Focused Pricing Objectives

Socially-oriented pricing objectives focus on social concerns that are facing the Firm or are important to the Firm. Nonprofit organizations such as zoos, museums, or charities view the delivery of public service and creation of public values as major components, if not the primary components, of their missions. For such organizations, pricing levels are established that ensure the patronage of cross sections of socio-economic groups with varying levels of discretionary incomes. Prices may be set below costs to make their services affordable to as many people as possible. These artificially low prices are often only possible because these organization are subsidized by public or private funds that might arrive in the form of tax breaks, federal or corporate grants, or corporate or private donations.

Traditional for-profit businesses are increasingly evaluating moral and ethical issues when setting prices. As they should. After all, as you have learned, Firms that are viewed as socially responsible and/or ethical in their business dealings generally enjoy greater brand equity and positioning advantages. For example, in the pharmaceutical industry, prices for life-saving drugs often are set substantially lower than warranted based strictly on marketing and economic considerations. In the pharmaceutical domain, the nature of the product and the "life and death" problems and solutions involved often lead to situation in which demand is highly price inelastic. In other words, the sorts of situations that support extremely high prices. But management may forego the added profits associated with higher prices, choosing instead to set prices low to ensure the drug's wide-spread availability and enhance their Firm's reputation for "fair play."

In some cases, pricing to achieve social objectives may lead to higher rather than lower prices. Firms may keep prices for certain products high for purposes of discouraging consumption. Interestingly, the product's manufacturer may not be solely responsible for its high price. For example, average prices for packs of cigarettes now exceed $6.00. More than 30% of this price can be attributed to the cigarette taxes imposed by the federal government. These onerous tax rates ostensibly were imposed to offset the skyrocketing health care costs that are associated with smoking-related illnesses. However, because higher taxes inevitably stimulate price increases, taxes can also be used to discourage demand for a given product. At some point, taxes imposed on cigarettes may drive cigarette prices high enough to substantially limit the product's consumption. There are limits to what the market will pay even for addictive products, such as cigarettes, that practically market themselves; that is, once users get hooked.

Higher prices also can emerge from the adoption of social-objectives that guide how other components of the marketing mix are structured. **Green movement** products are often priced higher due to their natural ingredients and their manufacturers' professed environmental concerns. Many consumers are philosophically "all-in" for the values delivered by green products. After all, who doesn't care enough about the environment to want a better future world for their born or yet-to-be-born grandchildren? But, when push comes to shove, so-called green consumers often don't spend the extra "green" that almost always is necessary to buy them. Most consumers, being only human, are unwilling to sacrifice their own short-term welfare (by paying more than they have to, given that less expensive non-green alternatives are available) in exchange for creating long-term benefits for others they do not know.

Firms that adopt socially-oriented marketing and pricing objectives should be applauded. Unfortunately, Firms that do so often place themselves at a competitive disadvantage. Making products and engaging in marketing activities that contribute positively to society's well-being often place Firms at cost (and price) disadvantages relative to competitors.

Psychological Objectives

Firms adopt psychological pricing objectives when they are concerned with employing price in conjunction with other elements of their marketing mixes to support claims of high quality or status. Prices for designer labels of perfumes, jewelry, clothing, and some automobiles are often positioned far above the associated products' actual costs. Perfumes, for example, that are priced at $400 or more per ounce cost only about 5% of that amount to produce.[10]

→ Setting Pricing Strategies

The pricing strategies available to marketing managers fall into five areas:

- Market entry pricing strategies focus on setting prices that facilitate entry into new or emerging markets. The market entry strategy includes, ironically, both penetration pricing and market skimming pricing.

- Value pricing and discounting strategies. The typical focus here is to deliver lower prices for purposes of satisfying price sensitive consumers.

- Product mix pricing strategies focus on managing the pricing function in situations where Firms are concerned about the impact of pricing on profits across the entire product mix. A price change for one product may impose dramatic effects on the sales of related products.

- Psychological pricing strategies are clearly intended to achieve psychological objectives. A number of specific strategies are available, some of which also are cited in one or more of the other four categories of pricing strategies.

- Competitive pricing strategies directed toward either avoiding direct competitive actions or encouraging direct competitive responses.

Market Entry Pricing Strategies

Market entry pricing strategies can focus on two divergent goals. The strategy, for example, can focus on setting higher prices to secure higher margins from price inelastic adopter segments (i.e., generally, Apple-type or Prada-type customers). Or, market entry pricing strategies can focus on establishing relatively lower prices to stimulate demand and secure higher market share among price-sensitive segments (i.e., generally, Walmart- or Ross Dress for Less-type customers).

Market Skimming Pricing

Market skimming pricing or "price skimming" involves setting initial prices high and then progressively lowering prices over time as products progress through their life cycles. During the introduction and growth stages of products' life cycles buyers often are price inelastic. The relevant, and consequently targeted, adopter categories are innovators and early adopters. These adopter categories generally possess substantially more discretionary buying power. Each category is also often substantially more willing to take the sort of measured risks that motivate them to try out new things.

Notably, there are few direct competitors in the market during the introduction or growth stages. However, the threat of competitive entry is high when competitors sense that large profit potential exists in the industry or sector.

Finally, when R&D and/or production/marketing costs are unusually high, strong incentives will exist to price higher during these initial stages. Higher prices would prove necessary in order to generate the margins necessary to recoup costs quickly.

Market skimming pricing is more likely to succeed when the effects of competitors' responses can be minimized for a significant period of time. Essentially, that is, when competitors are denied access to markets long enough for price-skimming Firms to reap their anticipated high profits. You might logically be thinking: how can one Firm ethically and legally deny potential competitors ready access to markets? Competitors would typically experience reduced access to markets under conditions where:[11]

- Key technologies are patent protected. Patent holders enjoy protection for 17 to 20 years. Competitors must find ways to produce their versions of the product that they not infringe on existing patents. Thus we see, as we have seen previously, the value of as well as the need for greater creativity.

- Access to key raw materials is limited. Firms can cultivate exclusive rights to key raw materials either by owning them outright or entering long-term partnerships with suppliers at favorable prices. The result may be distinct competitive advantages that effectively deny potential competitors access to markets. Again we see, as previously seen, the value and importance of supply chain relationships.

- Economies of scale with associated large capital investments are high. In many industries Firms must enjoy access to substantial financial resources in order to invest in the plant and equipment needed to provide the necessary scale to compete effectively in that industry. Imagine the resources required for Firms to begin producing microprocessors and effectively compete, head-to-head, with Intel, and its *Intel-Inside* brand equity advantage.

- Access to necessary supply chain relationships are limited. Entry may be discouraged if competitors cannot obtain access to adequate distribution for their products. For example, in highly competitive retail grocery sectors, food producers may not be able to convince retailers to allocate shelf space to new, unproven products. After all, every shelf we've ever seen in US grocery stores is already full-up. This condition leads to the ever-pressing need for **slotting fees** and incentivizing sales promotions such as **spiffs** and **push money**.

- Strong brand differentiation and preferences exist. Potential competitors may find it difficult to gain market access if existing Firms have created strong brand preferences or loyalties for their products. This condition, however, is unlikely to arise for lower involvement products, such as convenience goods. This specific "entry barrier" will more likely arise for Firms that market shopping and specialty goods.

Market Penetration Pricing

The objective of market penetration pricing strategies is to employ low prices to stimulate rapid demand for associated products. Price is set low to induce price-sensitive buyers to purchase the product. Firms basically "buy" market share with their low prices. Penetration pricing is a demand generation strategy that assumes that the market is fundamentally price elastic. Recall that when demand is price elastic, lower prices generate increased demand and gains in total revenue. Sales-focused pricing objectives are usually paired up with demand generation strategies. Sales volume pricing objectives seek to achieve specific unit sales, dollar sales, or market share outcomes. Sales volume-oriented objectives are more appropriate when Firms are interested primarily in pricing at levels that will produce substantial sales growth. Increases in unit sales volume, in turn, promote increased profits.

Penetration pricing is more appropriate when:

- The market is highly price elastic, meaning that customers are sensitive to price changes and will be attracted by lower prices.
- Average Total Costs (total costs per unit sold) can be reduced via scale economies and/or experience curve effects as sales volume increases. The decrease in unit costs contributes to greater overall profitability at the low price, and actually may foster further price decreases as manufacturing and marketing costs simultaneously continue to decrease in lockstep.

Value Pricing and Discounting Strategies

Value Pricing

The purpose of value pricing is to stimulate increased demand by enhancing a product's perceived value. Generally, added value is created by lowering the product's price and heavily emphasizing the implied "added value" in the Firm's promotion program.

Value pricing is frequently employed by Firms that market consumer convenience goods, including fast food. Wendy's, Burger King, and McDonalds all employ combo pricing in which several fast foods are bundled together into "value meals" at prices lower than if each item had been purchased separately.

When using this strategy Firms may opt to maintain the same pricing levels while adding benefits or enhancing their products' quality. This "new and improved" strategy is employed across many consumer convenience good categories.

Odd Pricing

Odd pricing means price is established at a point other than even dollar values. Examples include prices such as $.49, $4.95, and $199.99. Some retailers assert that these psychologically-lower prices increase sales beyond what would be obtained even if price were changed by a few pennies (up or down) to create an "even price."

Several explanations have been offered for why odd prices may work. Most explanations are based on anecdotal rather than empirical evidence. Most credible explanations focus on the belief that "odd prices" produce customer perceptions of a "discount." In our opinion, if odd pricing does work, its effectiveness is a function of how customers "read" in our culture. Think about it. You read left to right. We're all a bit lazy when scanning price tags during most shopping trips. We consequently tend to truncate digits located on the right. For example, a price of $19,999 for a car may be interpreted as $19,000 rather than $20,000![12] Of course, this catches us off-guard just for a moment. We quickly realize what the "real price" is.

Second Market Discounting

Second market discounting first assumes that primary markets exist for products for which standard, higher price are employed. The second assumption is that one or more secondary markets also exist for which demand for those products might be more price elastic. The customers who comprise these secondary markets should be targeted through lower prices.

Second market discounting would generally be employed only when excessive production capacity exists for products that cannot be sold effectively to primary market customers. The strategy permits Firms to sell excess output in secondary markets at lower prices. Second market discounting is not an appropriate strategy if customers in the primary and secondary markets routinely "communicate" with one another. If the primary market learns that discounts are offered to other customer markets, someone will get upset. This problem frequently arises with products such as health club memberships. Some clubs discount heavily to secondary markets (such as students in a college town), while other membership fees for non-students (the primary market) remain high. Once the differential pricing policy becomes "public" knowledge, clubs have sometimes lost substantial proportions of their higher revenue customers.

Systematic Discounting

A popular retailing strategy, systematic discounting also supports sales volume-oriented pricing objectives. Systematic discounting is conceptually similar to second market discounting. The intent of each approach is to target additional customer groups (secondary markets) that are substantially more price elastic.

With systematic discounting, retailers employ sales promotion (more on this topic in the next two chapters) and other forms of discounting at predictable time intervals. These discounts include coupons, special pricing programs, and rebates, among other incentives. Potential customers can predict when discounts will occur and may purposely wait for "the sale" to happen. Customers attracted by systematic discounting are generally folks who like that specific retailer's merchandise, but are hesitant to buy it at normal prices. These price-sensitive customers then wait for a sale; they generally will not buy substitute products from alternative retailers during the waiting time. Systematic discounting assumes a core "primary" market of relatively price inelastic customers exists. This segment will continue to buy at the regular price; they sense no need to postpone purchase until the "sale" arrives.

Periodic but predictable sales that occur at major department stores, such as Dillard's or Foleys (Red Apple Sale), exemplify this strategy. Sales tend to occur at specific times of the year. The foreseeable nature of such sales encourages customers to delay purchasing certain products as they anticipate material savings on more preferred items.

Unsystematic Discounting

As logic would dictate, unsystematic discounting is basically the opposite of systematic discounting. A potential drawback to systematic discounting, as noted, was that primary market customer may postpone purchases; they learn to wait for "sales." When retailers randomly discount, the predictability associated with the timing of the sale disappears. There is less danger that customers in the primary market will postpone purchases and wait for the sale. Nothing is perfect, however. One downside is that sales to more price elastic secondary markets may suffer. These people may buy substitute products or brands from other retailers, rather than wait for the next sale at their preferred store. However, this may not necessarily be true of all price-sensitive buyers. Some may purposely visit retailers hoping to "hit" sales. While there, customers may purchase other items at regular prices.

Multiple Product Pricing Strategies

Multiple product pricing strategies, also called **product line pricing** strategies, focus on pricing products across a number of product items, usually within a single product line. The price on each product in the line is established mindful of that price's impact on the sales and profitability of other items in the product line. The usual pricing objective is to maximize profits across the entire set of products.

Captive pricing occurs when basic or base products are sold at low prices (possibly even given away). The catch, however, is that customers must buy additional complementary products at regular prices to realize the base products' benefits. Marketers may eat a loss on base products, but secure substantial profits on complementary captive products. This strategy works when no alternative sources of supply exist for captive products, or alternative products are inferior in quality and/or higher priced. Examples of captive pricing include:

- Razors and razor blades: razors are sold at relatively low prices bundled with limited supplies of blades. Firms depend on replacement blades sales to earn reasonable profits.
- Cameras and film: the Kodak disk camera was priced quite low. But its unique film was expensive to develop. Kodak was the sole source of supply for the film. All exposed film could only be developed by Kodak. A great strategy, when a Firm enjoys the power to execute it.
- Cell phones and airtime: many cell phones are either given away or provided at reduced prices in package deals. Of course, customers are contractually locked into a provider for a specified period of time.
- Color printers and ink cartridges: manufacturers of bubble-jet printers (e.g. HP, Cannon, Brother, and Epson) price their printers low in order to encourage sales in what are, now, highly competitive markets. Firms' reduced margins are off-set by the extra profits attained by charging relatively high prices for ink cartridges (or the captive product). Some third-party ink cartridges and refill services are available from web-based companies, such as inkcartridges.com.

Bundled pricing is typically employed for products for which multiple options or accessories are available, or for which extra services may exist. Rather than price each product or service separately, some are "packaged together" and priced as one item, usually at a discount. Industrial examples abound. Equipment producers and/or resellers bundle basic products with accessories and service contracts. Customers are charged total prices that are lower than the totals that would be charged were all items purchased separately. Examples in consumer markets include:

- Discounted options packages available on most new cars.
- Bundled computer hardware and software as standard packages sold through major "discount" retailers such as Staples, Cons, and Best Buy.

Psychological Pricing Strategies

Psychological pricing strategies use price as a cue to other real or imagined characteristics or benefits that customers assume products will deliver or confer.

Quality Pricing

The existence of a price-quality relationship is well-established. *Ceteris paribus* (all things being equal), most people assume higher prices reflect higher quality in products. Because this pre-assumption exists, some Firms manipulate the "psychology" involved and set prices higher to bolster their quality image. Unacknowledged economic and pricing principles are often involved when this strategy is used. First, often, if marketers want to attract attention and ultimately a crowd, they should charge ridiculously high prices. Second, many people, in the end, highly value and truly desire things or experiences they cannot afford. But the best marketers understand, one day those same consumers might be able to afford that Mercedes or Rolex, or take that trip to New Zealand.

Consumers are more likely to infer quality from price under the following circumstances:

- When it is difficult to judge products on their own characteristics. Sometimes, as you realize, identifying quality based solely on a product's physical characteristics is too challenging. So consumers tread an easier path, one promising less resistance, by using price as a surrogate quality metric.

- When consumers lack experience with the product category, they may not know what to look for and are much more likely to employ simple cues (like price) to make their decisions. In fact, their inexperience often accounts for why consumers may not be able to judge a product's quality based on its physical characteristics alone.

- The use of price as an indicator of quality is particularly likely when buyers perceive that substantial differences in quality do exist between brands. This expectation, combined with any difficulty associated with evaluating the product based on its physical characteristics, suggests consumers may use price as a heuristic—or shortcut—from which they can judge quality.

Prestige Pricing

Prestige pricing is a psychological pricing strategy that is closely related to quality pricing. Prestige pricing is commonly used by perfume, fur, jewelry, fashion clothing, and watch marketers. Joy Perfume, by Jean Patou, exemplifies the strategy. The Joy brand aspires to connote status, prestige, and extremely high quality. Joy is priced at over $100 per ounce. This price contributes substantially to the perception of prestige (and quality) that its marketer seeks. A strategic failure to establish pricing levels that are consistent with the desired image might significantly harm sales. Demand for prestigious brands such as Joy is price inelastic. Indeed, inverted demand curves may exist for such brands. As price increases, demand increases due to the brand's enhanced image.

Reference Pricing

There are two forms of reference pricing. Retailers typically employ each. The first is the strategy whereby moderately priced products are displayed next to higher priced versions of the same product in the retail setting. Because of their close proximity to one another, the moderately priced version may appear significantly more attractive. This is essentially a psychological pricing strategy. The reference product can be a similar item in the same producer's line, or it may be a competitor's product.

There is, for example, a New York City restaurant called Norma's that actually does charge $1,000 for a caviar and lobster omelet. Few consumers buy this dish. But the fact that this product costs $1,000 makes the other menu items, which surely are extremely expensive themselves, appear less pricy. This form of reference price-based anchoring works because, when making decisions, our minds assign disproportionate weight to the first information they receive. When consumers encounter exorbitant prices first, everything else that follows seems like a much better deal.

A second reference pricing approach is illustrated by the pricing practices of retailers that predominantly display "reference prices" for brands on their shelves. These reference prices are the prices charged for the same or similar brands by competing retailers. Used in this manner, the reference price induces perceptions of value—a comparative bargain. If reference prices are exaggerated, the practice is illegal. Firms must be able to establish that their reference price is truly being charged by competing marketers in their geographic region.

Reference pricing is employed by some Internet retailers. Overstock.com regularly displays its prices alongside manufacturers' suggested retail prices for the same brands. The digital world has made it easier for consumers to engage in price comparisons for brands. But the same world has concurrently made it easy for "e-tailers" to present false information when presenting price comparisons. Overstock.com faced a recent court ruling charging it with providing deceptive reference price information. The Court ordered the company to pay $6.4 million in restitution and penalties. Overstock.com's defense focused on claims that older pricing laws are outdated in today's highly competitive and rapidly changing e-commerce environment.[13]

Loss Leader Pricing

Primarily a retail pricing strategy, leader pricing is used mainly to generate store traffic. The retailer promotes certain key items for sale at "value" prices. Customers are lured into the store to take advantage of these loss leaders but end up buying other items at regular prices. Because of these extra, usually unplanned purchases, the retailer makes a profit on the total basket of items purchased. Leader pricing has traditionally been used for well-known, national brands for which consumers immediately recognize "value" prices. Increasingly, however, private brands and even commodities (steaks, ground beef, etc.) are promoted as loss leaders. The major key to success is that consumers must believe they are receiving appropriate value.

Bait and Switch Pricing

Bait and switch pricing is an unethical (and sometimes illegal) pricing strategy that some retailers still employ. With bait pricing, retailers promote low, highly attractive prices for products that are actually available in limited supply or which are not present at all inside the store. The idea is to attract—"bait" or "lure"—customers into retail settings and then switch the customer to higher priced, higher margin products. If the promoted product is not stocked (i.e. the "stripped down" version must be specially ordered), the practice is referred to as "bait and switch." This practice is illegal.

Everyday Low Pricing

Another value pricing strategy, everyday low pricing (EDLP) means prices are offered at consistently low levels with few or no additional price reductions. This strategy is common with large discounters such as Walmart, Sam's Club, Family Dollar Store, and Costco. Retailers employing EDLP believe that by maintaining consistently low prices overall, across a broad assortment of products, profitability is higher than when constant discounting resulting in fluctuating prices is employed. In addition, promotion and advertising costs are substantially reduced since there is no need to promote sales prices with an EDLP structure.[14] EDLP strategies are not possible, however, unless the Firms' supply chain business model support them. Supply chains, as you recall, are the last, best place for most Firms to carve out costs savings.

High-Low Pricing

High-Low pricing is a form of systematic discounting that entails alternating price between high (regular) and low (sale) levels. Aggressive promotional tactics are employed in conjunction with the sales (low) prices to solidify consumers' perceptions that prices are indeed "low." The strategy is usually employed by larger department stores and supermarkets. As was true of systematic discounting, retailers use the regular price to appeal to less price sensitive customers while relying on sales prices to attract more price sensitive buyers.[15] Studies indicate that high-low pricing is substantially more profitable than EDLP for retailers.[16]

Competitive Pricing Strategies

Competitive pricing strategies are used either to avoid direct competitive actions or to force such actions to occur.

Penetration Pricing

Penetration pricing, as noted above, is essentially a demand generation strategy in which prices are set low for purposes of stimulating demand. Penetration pricing also can be employed with new products to discourage competitors from entering into a market early in the product life cycle. If Firms anticipate the opportunity will arise to attain lower unit costs because of scale economies and/or experience curve effects as demand increases, price can be set low when products are first introduced. Prices can even be set below initial unit costs. The assumption is that lower prices will dramatically stimulate demand, allowing Firms to accumulate market share quickly and to move down the cost curve rapidly. At the same time, low initial prices signal competitors that little opportunity for profits exists in the market. Market entry by competitors thus should be temporarily discouraged. By the time competitors opt to enter (if at all), the originating Firm has progressed far down the cost curve and possesses distinct costing (and pricing) advantages that competitors will struggle to match.

Texas Instruments has employed this pricing practice (Exhibit 15.8).[17] Before introducing its now-classic hand-held calculators, TI projected likely unit costs based on anticipated cost reductions. Initial prices for its calculators then were set based on these unit cost predictions. For example, if unit costs at the cumulative production volume Q_1 were predicted to be P1, the initial price of the product (at Q_0) could be set a P_0, a point well below the product's initial unit costs. TI anticipated losses would be incurred until cumulative production and sales reached

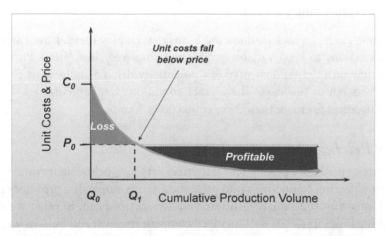

Exhibit 15.8 *TI's use of penetration pricing for tapping the calculator market depended on the ability to predict cost reductions accruing from scale economies and experience effects.*

Q_1. The initial low price allowed them to "buy" substantial market share quickly. The signal sent to competitors: you can't make a profit, so don't even try to enter and compete with us. You'll lose!

Meet-the-Competition Pricing

Meet-the-competition pricing is a "don't rock the boat"; "follow-the-leader" strategy. Here, Firms typically follow the lead set by major competitors. Prices are set at about the same level as signaled by industry leaders. Actual prices could be slightly higher or lower, but not different enough to upset the major players and initiate a price war. The assumption is that Firms shift their competitive emphasis to other areas of the marketing mix, in other words, Firms compete on the basis of superior features, benefits, quality, promotion, or distribution as they differentiate and position their offerings. This strategy can prove doubly advantageous. First, it may bend the demand curve facing the Firm. Second, if this happens, the Firm might elect to price higher than competitors while avoiding negative responses.

The meet-the-competition strategy is common in oligopolistic industries dominated by one or two large producers. The steel, coal, and building materials industries also employ these strategies because they manufacture difficult to differentiate products (thus the difference between this strategy and the last one.) Essentially, these industries produce commodities. Dominant players within such industries become the "price leaders" who enjoy substantial power to dictate prices. Other Firms follow the lead established by the dominant Firm or Firms.

Undercutting the Competition

This strategy is employed by Firms wishing to aggressively use price as the major competitive tool in their marketing mixes. Firms that pursue this strategy seek to become the lowest priced competitor in their sector. Those Firms must possess the sorts of intrinsic cost advantages that will permit them to remain the low price market alternative. When challenged by others companies, and a price war ensues, Firms must have sufficient on-hand cash reserves to weather periods of declining or negative profits.

Some Firms are positioned such that this strategy does not illicit strong competitive reactions. An example is the "deep discounting" practiced by off-price retailers such as Marshall's or T.J. Maxx. Prices trend extremely low. But the merchandise usually consists of "left-overs" or "dated" fashions appealing to price sensitive or value-seeking customers. Collectively, these customers constitute a different sort of segment who are more than happy to purchase and wear or use less than cutting-edge gear.

More threatening examples include domestic Firms that employ inexpensive labor in overseas supply chain locations to keep variable production costs very low. These Firms price their products very low on international markets, potentially driving indigenous producers with higher labor costs out of business. These exact conditions have endangered domestic (US) clothing manufactures for more than three consecutive decades.

Predatory Pricing

Firms that practice predatory pricing set their prices very low, below their costs in some cases, with the intent of forcing competitors into price wars. Firms employing predatory pricing tend to be larger Firms with substantial cash reserves. The sort of Firm, in other words, that can weather resulting losses until less well-financed competitors crash and burn or withdraw from the market. Once competitors are eliminated, prices can be raised to normal or even higher levels. The surviving Firm now has a monopoly on the market. John D. Rockefeller (Standard Oil) and J.P. Morgan (General Electric and Carnegie Steel) each made their first tens of millions—back when $10,000,000 was real money—by using this exact strategy during the late 1800s. The practice, obviously, has been around for a while.

Predatory pricing has long since been ruled strictly illegal. However, some Firms still use this strategy. Consequently, cases of predatory pricing periodically surface. Procter & Gamble (P&G) was accused of dumping Pampers brand diapers on the Israeli market at prices more than 40% below prices of local producers. P&G increased its market share from 6% to 16% as a result. This dramatic share-shift threatened the viability of local producers.[18] Walmart is periodically accused of predatory pricing activities, facing at least three separate predatory pricing charges. Government agencies in Wisconsin, Oklahoma, and of all places, Germany accused the mega retailer of pricing products below costs intending to force local competitors out of the market.[19]

→ Setting the Base Price

We turn now to an examination of specific methods for setting base or list prices for products.

Categories of Pricing Methods

The pricing methods available for establishing list prices can be categorized as cost-based, demand-based, or competitor-based in nature. **Cost-based** pricing techniques focus on setting prices that are high enough to cover, or exceed, costs. Several methods are available to do this. Supply chain intermediaries generally use different sorts of cost-based pricing methods than manufacturers; even manufacturers operating in the same supply chain. Cost-based pricing methods often fail to consider the impact of resulting prices on demand. In contrast, **demand-based** or customer-based pricing methods focus on setting prices with likely-customer-reactions in mind. Price is often set to achieve some desired level of customer demand. Finally, **competition-based** pricing methods result in prices that are set primarily with competitors' prices in mind.

Cost-Based Pricing Methods

Cost-Plus Pricing

Cost-plus pricing, also known as average cost pricing, is primarily used by manufacturers. The simple pricing method entails tabulating all relevant costs involved in making and marketing a single unit of the product and then adding a predetermined percentage amount to capture profits. The resulting sum is the selling price. What could be easier? Relevant costs considered during this tabulation process are the basic fixed and variable costs, as examined above.

The mechanism by which cost-plus pricing works is straightforward. One begins by computing the total fixed and total variable costs associated with a specified level of production. The desired level of profits is then added to these costs. The resulting total is divided by the number of units produced (and hopefully sold), to obtain the price per unit that must be charged. The relevant formula:

(5) $$\text{Price} = \frac{\text{Total Costs} + \text{Desired Profit}}{\text{Units Produced}}$$

Assume that a manufacturer can produce and sell 10,000 units of a product. Assume, further that total fixed costs (TFC) associated with producing the product are $500,000 and that total variable costs (TVC) are $200,000 (i.e. $20 per unit). If the manufacturer also seeks a profit of $50,000, the appropriate price is directly obtained from the above formula:

$$(6) \quad \text{Price} = \frac{\text{TFC} + \text{TVC} + \text{Desired Profit}}{\text{Units Produced}} = \frac{\$500,000 + \$200,000 + \$50,000}{10,000} = \$75$$

The price should be $75 each.

Cost-plus pricing processes basically use what is known about the shape of the average total cost (ATC) curve. Recall that average total costs declines with the number of units produced and sold (Q). Thus, the ATC curve is obtained by dividing TFC+TVC by each possible value of Q. For the current pricing example, when Q is 10,000 units, ATC is $70 per unit (i.e. $700,000/10,000 units = $70). Because we seek a $50,000 profit across these 10,000 units, this translates into $50,000/10,000 units = $5 per unit in desired profit. Price, therefore, is $70 + $5 = $75 per unit. Exactly the same result as obtained using the above formula.

The various advantages associated with cost-plus pricing account for its widespread use:

- Relevant fixed and variable costs are easy to compute and should be readily available from existing accounting data.
- Ready access to relevant cost data makes it easy to compute list prices.
- Cost-plus pricing approaches are especially attractive because they ensure that all costs of production and sales are covered. Firms will be profitable if they can sell all units produced at the price set.

Yet cost-plus pricing suffers from certain limitations. The most serious is that prices are not tied to customer demand. If Firms can't sell their inventory at the established price, they fail to achieve desired profit levels and/or to cover relevant costs. Prices are often set too low when the cost-plus method is used—meaning that available customer value is not captured. The market may be willing to pay more than the price computed based on cost-plus criteria. Finally, when this strategy is used, the incentive to improve efficiency in order to control production and selling costs is dampened, particularly if the product is selling successfully at the price set using cost-plus methods. Yet most Firms, most of the time, should strive to lower their costs of doing business.

Markup Pricing

Manufacturers often successfully use cost-plus pricing due to the limited number of products they typically produce. This circumstance makes it relatively easy to calculate relevant fixed and variable costs. The typical supply chain intermediary, however, is not as lucky. Supermarkets, for example, must stock thousands of individual products. Each product must also be priced. Thus, it is virtually impossible for retailers to employ cost-plus pricing in the same way as a manufacturer.

Such intermediaries, instead, employ a different form of cost-based pricing called markup pricing. When this strategy is used, some preset amount is added to the cost of the product to obtain the selling price to the next level in the supply chain. Markups usually are expressed as a percentage of either the cost of the product or the projected selling price of the product. Wholesalers, for example, may employ a 10% markup based on their costs from the producer as they price the product forward through the supply chain to retailers. Retailers, in turn, may use a 25% markup based on their costs from wholesalers when they establish retail prices for consumers.

Two versions of markup pricing exist:

- Markup based on cost.
- Markup based on selling price.

Markup Based on Cost

Prices set by using markup based on cost is easily visualized. Indeed, the procedure is compatible with most consumers' conceptualization of a markup. When employing markup based on cost, the dollar amount of the markup is computed by multiplying the desired markup percentage by the associated cost of the product. Price is then obtained by adding the dollar amount of this markup to the original cost of the product. Assume a retailer's cost to acquire a product is $5. If the retailer requires a 30% markup based-on-cost to cover overhead and provide adequate profit, the appropriate price is:

(6) $$\$5.00 + (.3 \; x \; \$5.00) = \$5.00 + \$1.50 = \$6.50$$

The required 30% markup was multiplied by the $5.00 cost. The result is $1.50. This dollar amount was added to the $5.00 cost to yield price. The resulting $6.50 price covers the $5.00 cost of the product and provides an extra $1.50 to cover additional overhead and provide a little profit to boot!

The general formula for computing price using markup based on cost is:

(7) $$\text{Price} = \text{Product Cost} + (\%\text{Markup x Product Cost})$$

By multiplying the desired percentage markup (expressed as a decimal value) by cost, we determine how much (in dollars) must be added to cost to obtain the appropriate selling price.

Markup Based on Selling Price

The formula for computing price when the markup is based on selling price, rather than on cost, is more complicated:

(8) $$\text{Price} = \frac{\text{Product Cost}}{1 - \dfrac{\text{Desired Markup}}{100}}$$

The formula suggests that the required selling price is developed by dividing the cost of the product (the amount paid by the retailer or wholesaler for the product) by one minus the required markup percentage. The resulting total yields the amount required to cover the product's cost to the middleman, plus permits something extra to cover additional overhead costs and provide a reasonable level of profit. A simple example illustrates the formula's application and highlights the differences with markups based on cost. Assume the wholesaler's cost for a product is $100 and that a 50% markup (based on selling price) is required to cover additional costs and allow for profit. The price, therefore, should be:

(9) $$\text{Price} = \frac{\$100}{1 - \dfrac{50}{100}} = \frac{\$100}{1 - .5} = \frac{\$100}{.5} = \$200$$

Applying the formula in Equation (9) yields a price of $200. The equivalent cost and markup data assuming price is computed using a markup based on cost yields a much lower price of $150. We leave it to you to verify the results from Equations (7) and (8). The price is obviously substantially higher when markups based on selling price are used. This makes sense. The percent markup remains the same (50%). But the percentage is now multiplied by a larger number (price rather than cost) to identify the dollar amount that must be added to cost. For a given percentage markup and product cost, the actual dollar markup will always be larger for markup based on selling price than for markup based on cost.

Computing price via markup based on selling price is the most common markup pricing method employed by intermediaries (particularly retailers). This is primarily because the strategy is consistent with how Firms express mark-downs, expenses, and profits. All are expressed as a function of selling price. Consider the last "on-sale" purchase that you made at your favorite department store. You may have purchased an on-sale item that was advertised as marked down "50%." This mark-down meant that the product was being sold at a 50% reduction from the original selling price. Thus, if the selling price was originally $100, you would now pay only $50. Expenses and profits are expressed similarly.

Thus far, our markup pricing examples have only evaluated pricing from one level to the next level in the supply chain. For example, a wholesaler pricing to a retailer or a retailer setting final selling prices to consumers. However, markup pricing can be used through entire supply chains. Manufacturers may use the approach to identify a "suggested retail" price to consumers. The process is a simple extension of markup pricing (using either form of markup). The manufacturer first determines the costs associated with making the product and establishes its desired level of profit. Next, the manufacturer identifies the markups sought by all supply chain members up to and including the retailer. Based on this information, the manufacturer can compute the required selling price to each supply chain member using the appropriate markup pricing formula (i.e. based on cost or based on selling price). The following example illustrates how forward chain markup pricing would work for a manufacturer who wants to establish a "suggested retail" price that would be pre-printed on the product. Assume the following:

- The manufacturer's relevant costs for making the product are all variable and are $25.60 per unit.
- The manufacturer desires a 20% markup based on selling price to cover its overhead and allow for a reasonable profit.
- Wholesalers require a 10% markup based on selling price.
- Retailers need 30%, also based on selling price.

The required markups are sequentially applied to get the price to each level in the supply chain as follows:

- Since the manufacturer's variable costs are $25.60 per unit and it desires a 20% markup to cover overhead and capture profit, the appropriate price to the wholesaler must be: $25.60/[1−.2]=$32.00.
- Since the wholesaler seeks a 10% markup to cover overhead and capture profit, the price to the retailer must be: $32.00/[1−.1]=$35.56.
- Since the retailer also needs a 30% markup, the price to consumer must be: $35.56/[1−.7]=$50.79.

Target Return Pricing

The objective of target return pricing is to obtain a specific return on investment (ROI) or return on sales (ROS). We illustrate this pricing process using ROI—or the ratio of net profit to the capital investment required—to generate that profit.

To apply this pricing technique, Firms must understand their costs as well as the product's "standard volume" of production. Standard volume is typically set at 90% of plant or production capacity. The target return pricing method assumes that the Firm will eventually sell its entire standard volume at the price set. The formula for computing a target price is:

(10)
$$\text{Price} = \frac{\text{Total Investment x Target \% ROI}}{\text{Standard Volume of Production}} + ATC$$

We begin by computing Average Total Costs (ATC) for the product at the stated standard level of production. The additional amount needed to yield the desired ROI is then added to the ATC. "Total Investment" x "% Target ROI" yields the dollar amount of the total return on investment that is desired. When this amount is divided by standard volume, the result is the per unit amount that must be added to ATC to get "price."

The following example demonstrates how the formula works. Assume a manufacturer wishes to set its product's price high enough to generate a 20% return on its investment of $2,000,000 in a new plant. Standard volume is estimated at 700 units (90% of plant capacity). Average Total Costs are estimated at $2,850. Price is derived through the following formula:

(11)
$$\text{Price} = \frac{.2 \text{ x } \$2,000,000}{700 \text{ units}} + \$2,850 = \frac{\$400,000}{700} + \$2,850$$
$$= \$571 + \$2,850 = \$3,421$$

The dollar amount of the desired ROI is $400,000 (found by multiplying the specified 20% ROI by the $2,000,000 investment). Dividing this $400,000 by the 700 unit standard volume yields a required per unit return of $571. When this per unit return is added to ATC (computed from the fixed and variable costs for producing the product), the resulting price is $2,850 + $571 = $3,421.

Target returns pricing has limitations:

- Firms that have small capital investments probably will not want to use the procedure. The increment in ATC to obtain selling price will not be large enough to generate a reasonable level of profit.

- The method assumes that the entire standard volume can be sold and that standard volume can be achieved. This is the most serious problem associated with all cost-based pricing methods.

Demand-Based Pricing Methods

Demand-based pricing methods specifically account for the impact of price on the quantity of the product that will be demanded. In general, these techniques are theoretically superior to the cost-based methods previously employed. However, some are very difficult to use.

Value pricing for consumer products can be conducted through a number of approaches. Most approaches involve consumer surveys or marketing experiments. These tools were examined when we reviewed methods for estimating demand curves.

Establishing value-based prices often proves easier for industrial products, as opposed to consumer products. Organizational buyers are generally more objective and careful; i.e., more highly involved, when they make purchase decisions. **Economic Value Analysis (EVA)** pricing is the value-pricing tool that is usually employed by marketers of industrial goods. The objective of EVA pricing is to generate a price that provides total life cycle costs to customers that are lower than those provided by a reference product (generally, a competitor's product). Exhibit 15.9 summarizes the underlying logic of EVA pricing. The total life cycle (TLC) costs incurred by buyers of a competing (reference) product (left side of Exhibit15.9) are compared with the total life cycle costs incurred by buyers for using the seller's product (right side of Exhibit 15.9). Three types of total life cycle costs come into play for both competitors' product and the seller's product:[20]

- *Start-up costs* are required to make products operational. Start-up costs include items such as custom design of the product, training costs for the buyer's employees, installation costs, and re-tooling costs.
- *Post-purchase costs* are required to keep products operational over their expected life, including maintenance costs, utilities, direct labor, repairs, and upgrades.
- The *delivered price* of the product.

As Exhibit 15.9 demonstrates, the seller estimates these costs, as they relate to buyers, for both the competitor's product and for its own product. Remember, these estimated costs are the costs that the buyer incurs when using either the marketer's product or the reference product. Marketing Firms, presumably, seek to demonstrate that buyers will incur lower total life cycle costs when they use their product rather than the competitor's reference product. It remains possible to charge higher prices than the prices charged by competitors and still successfully close the sale based on total life cycle costs-savings. That is, price can be set higher if associated TLCs come in at the same or lower amount than the TLC provided by the reference product. This situation is illustrated in Exhibit 15.9, where, as you see, the seller's start-up and post-purchase costs to the buyer are lower than those associated with using the competitor's product. This circumstance makes it possible to price higher than the competitor but still deliver lower TLC—or overall—costs to the buyer.

Competition Based Pricing Methods

Various techniques exist through which prices can be established based on "competitive" conditions. The simplest approach is to examine the prices currently charged by competitors and price at the "going rate." Going-rate pricing is frequently used by B2C marketers. However, for B2B or industrial products, several somewhat more sophisticated approaches

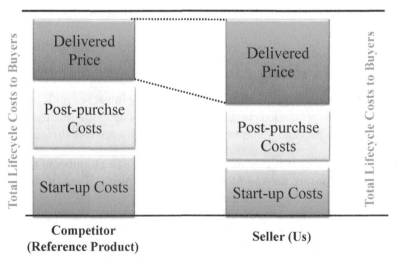

Exhibit 15.9 *Value pricing industrial products using Economic Value Analysis (EVA).*

are available. For starters, the EVA procedure presented above fits here. Given that the EVA pricing methods employ a reference product (usually a competing product), they exemplify competitive pricing methods.

Competitive bidding is probably the most widely-used competitive pricing approach in industrial markets. Competitive bidding represents a highly specialized activity. The activity itself is often driven by state-of-the-art mathematical pricing models. Demand is generally already understood; the Firm, you see, is bidding on a known quantity. The focus of competitive bidding, therefore, turns toward examining the Firm's own costs and estimating the likelihood the bid can be "won" at a price sufficient to cover these costs and generate a reasonable profit. Because other competitors also bid on the project, higher prices lessen the odds of winning the bid.

→ Conducting Cost-Volume-Profit Analysis

Cost-volume-profit analysis (CVP Analysis) consists of a series of tools and techniques designed to assess the profit impact of charging different prices for products. This section examines one such tool—breakeven analysis. Breakeven analysis is one of the most frequently used business tools. It can be applied to a wide range of business problems and decisions, in addition to price-related evaluations.

What Is Breakeven Analysis?

Breakeven analysis entails an attempt to identify the level of sales, measured either in units or dollars, at which "breakeven" occurs. Specifically, breakeven analysis determines unit or dollar sales amounts where total revenues equal total costs, or, alternatively stated, where profits equal zero.

Breakeven analysis provides an indirect way to examine the impact of price on profitability. A more direct approach is to build a pro forma income statement (profit and loss statement) that attempts to project an accurate numerical estimate for expected profits. *Pro forma* projections, however, rely on obtaining solid estimates of the number of units that would be purchased at different target prices. A reliable assessment of the demand curve thus is necessary to produce realistic *pro forma* income statements. Yet this assumption would generally prove unreasonable; the "production task" requires too much time and expense, and is prone to error due to the influence of uncontrollable forces.

This is where the need for breakeven analysis reenters the picture. Breakeven analysis does not require that precise estimates of demand at the price under evaluation be available. This makes breakeven analysis an ideal technique for "backing into" profitability estimates when precise estimates of demand are not available and cannot be reasonably developed. But when they know the "breakeven point," managers can more readily estimate the likelihood that actual sales will surpass the computed breakeven point. Developing breakeven points is easier than precisely pinpointing actual unit or total sales anticipated at specific pricing levels.

Assume, for example, the computed breakeven point for a product is 100 units. Decision makers then can estimate the likelihood, or probability, that at least 100 units will be sold. If decision makers believe actual sales will likely exceed "breakeven," the analysis indicates the price being considered is viable. By contrast, when management believes sales levels likely will not reach the calculated breakeven point, alternative prices should be evaluated.

Allow us to re-emphasize. Breakeven analysis is extremely useful. The tool specifically benefits Firms who are uncertain about how much demand will result from charging a specific price. By employing breakeven analysis, marketers can acquire general insights about how many units must be sold in order to cover all relevant costs involved in making and marketing the associated product. Knowing their relevant "breakeven point," managers can project the likelihood that sales will exceed (or not exceed) breakeven.

Breakeven analysis, therefore, is best described as a technique that allows Firms to logically examine the potential profit impact of charging a particular price. The technique is also extensively used to evaluate the profit impact of changing various marketing mix and/or production programs that affect the costs associated with making and marketing products. Marketers may use breakeven models to identify the level of sales in units needed to offset increases in advertising or sales promotion expenditures or to assess the profit impact that would result when personnel are added to the sales force.

The Breakeven Point: Its Relationship to Revenues and Costs

Exhibit 15.10 graphically illustrates how a typical breakeven analysis is conducted. The "X" axis represents the number of units produced or sold. The "Y" axis represents both costs and total revenues. The cost dimensions on this graph should look familiar. When conducting breakeven analyses, the relevant costs are fixed and variable costs. You should be familiar with each by now. Both total fixed costs (TFC) and total variable costs (TVC) at increasing levels of output are summed to generate the total cost (TC) curve. However, this is the first time you see the total revenue curve (TR). The TR curve begins at the origin, where the X- and Y-axes intersect, and steadily increases to the right as output increases.

The breakeven point is the sales level where TR=TC (total revenue equals total costs). Any sales in excess of those required to achieve breakeven generate profits. This is illustrated in Exhibit 15.10 by the fact that to the right of the breakeven point TR>TC (total revenue exceeds total costs). In contrast, to the left of the breakeven point, TR<TC —total revenues are lower than total costs. This latter situation results in a loss to the Firm. There are no profits.

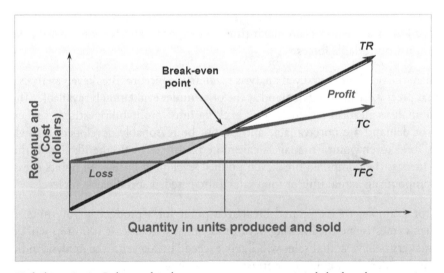

Exhibit 15.10 *Relationship between costs, revenues, and the break-even point.*

Conducting Breakeven Analyses

Building a breakeven analysis is not difficult. For those familiar with Excel, the process may already be evident. One starts by building a spreadsheet that contains the relevant revenue and cost data. Then, from these data, the relevant curves are plotted on the breakeven graph.

Assume we want to conduct a breakeven analysis in which the price under consideration is $100 per unit and average variable costs (AVC) have already been estimated at AVC = $50. Similarly, total fixed costs (TFC) are $200,000. The resulting spreadsheet in Exhibit 15.11 contains six columns. The first column contains the values for the "X" axis. This is nothing more than the range of production or sales in units. The range of output ("Q") varies from 0 to 10,000 units. The second column, total revenue (TR), is obtained by multiplying price per unit (P) by each value of Q in the first column. The first entry in the total revenue column will, of course, be "0." After all, no units have been produced and sold. Remaining entries in the total revenue column range from $100,000 to $1,000,000.

The third column contains fixed cost information. Assuming that total fixed costs involved with producing and selling the product are $200,000, all entries in the TFC column will be the same—$200,000. This reflects the fact that fixed costs in total do not change with level of output. It does not matter whether output is zero units or 1,000 units. Fixed costs remain $200,000.

The fourth column tabulates total variable costs. Entries are obtained by multiplying values of Q by AVC = $50. Therefore, total variable costs will be zero when output (Q) is zero. TVC increases to $500,000 at 10,000 units.

Entries in the total costs (TC) column are, obviously, obtained by adding total fixed costs (TFC) and total variable costs (TVC). You should pick a few entries in the table and verify for yourself that the values in the total cost column correctly reflect the sum of total fixed and total variable costs at their respective levels of output.

The breakeven point can actually be identified directly from the data in the table in Exhibit 15.11. Note that, at 4,000 units of output, the values in the total revenue (TR) column and the total cost (TC) column are exactly the same—$400,000. Four thousand units, therefore, is the breakeven point. At this level of sales, total revenue equals total costs, and profits are equal to zero. We have conveniently added a sixth column containing profit (TR-TC) to the spreadsheet, confirming that profits do indeed equal zero at the 4,000 unit point. Exhibit 15.12 contains the resulting breakeven graph. Sales in excess of 4,000 units will yield a profit, while sales below 4,000 units result in a loss.

Mathematics of Breakeven Analysis

The graphic approach to breakeven analysis provides a solid conceptual understanding of the breakeven point and its relationship to both revenues and costs. However, the breakeven point can be found much more easily via direct computation. The formula for breakeven in units sold (Q) is:

(12)
$$BE(Q) = \frac{TFC}{Price - AVC}$$

Q	TR	TFC	TVC	TC	Profit
0	$0	$200,000	$0	$200,000	-$200,000
1,000	$100,000	$200,000	$50,000	$250,000	-$150,000
2,000	$200,000	$200,000	$100,000	$300,000	-$100,000
3,000	$300,000	$200,000	$150,000	$350,000	-$50,000
4,000	$400,000	$200,000	$200,000	$400,000	$0
5,000	$500,000	$200,000	$250,000	$450,000	$50,000
6,000	$600,000	$200,000	$300,000	$500,000	$100,000
7,000	$700,000	$200,000	$350,000	$550,000	$150,000
8,000	$800,000	$200,000	$400,000	$600,000	$200,000
9,000	$900,000	$200,000	$450,000	$650,000	$250,000
10,000	$1,000,000	$200,000	$500,000	$700,000	$300,000

Exhibit 15.11 *Break-even data in an Excel spreadsheet.*

The breakeven point in units (BE (Q)) is found by dividing total fixed costs (TFC) by the difference between price per unit and average variable cost per unit (P – AVC). The latter difference (P – AVC) is called the **unit contribution** (UC) or simply **contribution**. This is the per unit amount that is available to cover total fixed costs.

An example illustrates the computational procedure and helps clarify the meaning of the unit contribution. Using the data from our prior breakeven analysis (Exhibit 15.12), the breakeven point in units is found by:

$$(13) \qquad BE(Q) = \frac{TFC}{P - AVC} = \frac{\$200,000}{\$100 - \$50} = 4,000 \text{ units}$$

Total fixed costs are, again, $200,000. These costs are divided by the difference between price, which is $100 per unit and average variable costs per unit ($50). This difference is $50 per unit. Fifty dollars is the contribution per unit that is now available to help cover the $200,000 in fixed costs. Each unit sold contributes $50 to cover fixed costs. This means that we must sell $200,000/$50 = 4,000 units to fully recover the $200,000 in fixed costs. This 4,000 units is the breakeven point.

Sometimes it is useful to compute the breakeven point in dollars rather than units. Of course, a simple way obtain the dollar breakeven point is by first computing breakeven in units, as we have already done. The result then is multiplied by the selling price. In our previous example, the dollar breakeven is obtained by multiplying 4,000 units by the $100 price tag. The result is $400,000. Not surprisingly, both the 4,000 units and $400,000 breakeven values correspond to the breakeven points on the X- and Y- axes, respectively, from our earlier graphic analysis (Exhibit 15.12).

Breakeven in dollars can also be computed directly by dividing total fixed costs (TFC) by the percentage contribution margin (also called the contribution margin). The percentage contribution margin is obtained by dividing unit contribution (P- AVC) by price (P). Percentage contribution margin is, therefore, a ratio between the dollar unit contribution and the original selling price. The computation is:

$$(14) \qquad BE(\$) = \frac{TFC}{\dfrac{P - AVC}{P}} = \frac{\$200,000}{\dfrac{\$100 - \$50}{\$100}} = \$400,000$$

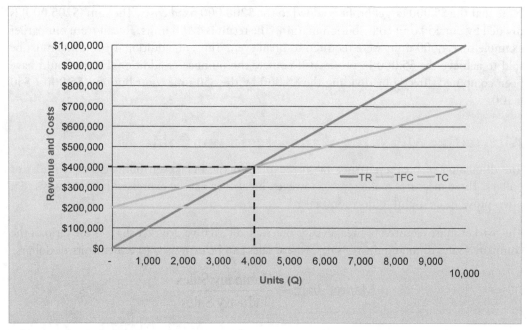

Exhibit 15.12 *Break-even analysis based on Excel data.*

Basic breakeven analysis, as presented above, is immensely useful. Even if we stopped here with our presentation of breakeven, you will carry away an application that will be one of the most important tools you will use in your business career. However, breakeven analysis has many additional applications, or "extensions." For example, the breakeven model, with a simple modification, can be employed to solve for the level of unit (or dollar) sales required to achieve some desired level of target profit. The modifications needed in the breakeven formula are:

$$(15) \qquad \text{Target Q} = \frac{\text{TFC} + \text{Target Profit}}{\text{P-AVC}}$$

Note that the additional desired profit is treated as an additional fixed cost in the revised formula. The numerator in the formula is now TFC + Target Profit. In addition, since the formula is solving for the level of sales required to achieve a target level of profits, it no longer makes sense to call the result "breakeven" or use the variable name BE(Q). We have substituted the variable "Target Q" for "BE (Q)."

Conceptually, treating the target profit as an added fixed cost makes sense. Achieving the desired profit requires selling more units beyond those required to breakeven. The exact number of extra units that must be sold is a function of the unit contribution (i.e. P-AVC), just as in the standard breakeven model.

Our last example can be extended to illustrate how this works. TFC remains at $200,000, but now let's add the stipulation that we want to earn $5,000 in incremental profit beyond breakeven. Unit price is still $100 and AVC is $50. This means that the unit contribution is still $50. The formula becomes:

$$(16) \qquad \text{Target Q} = \frac{\$200,000 + \$5,000}{\$100 - \$50} = 4,100$$

Note that the $5,000 target profit is added to the $200,000 fixed costs. The sum ($205,000) is divided by our $50 unit contribution margin. The result is 4,100 units. Recall from our earlier example that 4,000 units were required to breakeven. Thus, an additional 100 units must be sold to achieve the $5,000 in profits. Of course, the number of additional units could have been computed directly by dividing the $5,000 by the $50 unit contribution - $5,000 / $50 = 100.

Alternative Measures of the Breakeven Point

The discussion of breakeven thus far has expressed the breakeven point either in units or dollars. These measures make sense. However, breakeven can be expressed in other ways that often prove more useful to decision makers.

The market share required to breakeven is one such alternative. Market share is the ratio of the company's sales to total industry sales, where sales can be expressed in either units or dollars:

(17) $$\text{MarketShare} = \frac{\text{Company Sales}}{\text{Industry Sales}}$$

Market share, as discussed earlier, is the Firm's "share" of industry sales. Using market share is sometimes more useful than using "units" or "dollars" when conducting breakeven analyses. Management may struggle to judge the likelihood that specific breakeven points expressed in units or dollars can be achieved. No mental baseline may exist against which the resulting value can be compared. But, when the breakeven point is transformed into market share, the required market share may be immediately revealed as reasonable and obtainable, or conversely, as impossible to achieve. This would be particularly true for new products or when the Firm is entering new markets in which it has little prior experience. As an example, assume the estimated breakeven point for a newly proposed product is 500,000 units. This may seem like an impossible amount to achieve by just examining the magnitude of the result. Now assume that this breakeven estimate is transformed into the market share required, and that the resulting breakeven market share is only 1%. The outlook changes dramatically; the 500,000 unit goal now appears more attainable given the overall size of the market is obviously very large.

Breakeven also can be expressed in terms of room-nights-sold or occupancy rates in the case of hotels and motels. Room-nights-sold is equivalent to computing breakeven in units. The result is an estimate of how many rooms must be rented, on average, during a specified period in order to breakeven. An alternative measure is "occupancy rate." This is the proportion of rooms in the respective hotel or motel that must be rented, on average, to achieve breakeven. Like market share, it is sometimes easier for management to visualize the proportion of rooms that must be rented to breakeven instead of the absolute numbers of rooms rented or room-nights that must be sold.

Breakeven When Multiple Product Items Are Considered

Most Firms sell a mix of products, not single product items. Thus, it is often necessary to project the levels of sales for a number of products sold at different prices needed to breakeven.

This problem can be addressed, again, by extending the breakeven model. All that must be done is substitute a weighted average unit contribution or weighted average contribution margin percentage into the denominator in the formula. This is done by computing a weighted average price and a weighted average AVC across all products in the mix. These weighted averages then are used in the standard breakeven model.

As an example, assume that a Firm sells three products. Their associated prices and costs are shown in Exhibit 15.13. Each product is sold in the ratios indicated. These ratios reflect the proportion of total company sales accounted for by the specific product. Product 1 accounts for 30% of sales, product 2 for 40%, and product 3 for 30% of total sales. From these data, weighted average prices and AVC are computed as shown in Exhibit 15.13. The weighted average price across all three products is $1.50; the weighted average AVC is $.65. Therefore, the weighted average unit contribution is: $1.50 - $.65 = $.85. Similarly, the weighted average contribution margin is $.85/$1.50=.5667. Substituting these values into the breakeven formula for computing breakeven in dollars yields:

$$\text{(18)} \quad BE(\$) = \frac{\$75,000}{\dfrac{\$1.50 - \$.65}{\$1.50}} = \frac{\$75,000}{.5667} = \$132,345$$

Breakeven in dollars (BE ($)) is $132,345. BE ($) for each product item can be found by multiplying this result by each of the product's sales ratios. For example, BE ($) for product 1 is $132,345 x .3 = $39,703.50. Similarly the BE ($) for products 2 and 3 are $52,938 and $39,703.50, respectively.

The unit breakeven points for the total product mix and for each product are also easily computed. Divide the fixed cost estimate ($75,000) by the weighted average unit contribution margin ($1.50 - $.65) = $.85. The result yields the total number of units across all three products that must be sold – 88,235 units. Breakeven values in units for each product are found by multiplying the 88,235 by each product's sales ratio. The BE (Q) for product 1 is 26,470 units; product 2 is 35,294 units; and product 3 is 26,471 units.

→ Identifying Pricing Adjustments

Once base price is set using one or more of the tools just discussed, the price schedule must be adjusted with a consideration of a range of discounts, allowances, and geographic pricing modifications. These adjustments are simultaneously strategic and tactical in nature. They permit managers to adjust the ultimate delivered price to meet the needs of different customer groups and adapt to changing market conditions.

Product	Ratio	Price	Weighted Price	AVC	Weighted AVC	Unit Contribution	Weighted Average Contribution
	(1)	(2)	(1)x(2)	(3)	(1)x(3)	(2) - (3)	[(2)-(3)]x(1)
1	30%	$1.30	$0.39	$0.50	$0.15	$0.80	$0.24
2	40%	$1.50	$0.60	$0.65	$0.26	$0.85	$0.34
3	30%	$1.70	$0.51	$0.80	$0.24	$0.90	$0.27
Sum	100%		$1.50	-	$0.65	=	$0.85

Exhibit 15.13 *Weighted prices and costs are used to compute a weighted average unit contribution.*

Discounts

Discounts are reductions to base price. Manufacturers provide a range of price discounts to their distributors to compensate them for performing their marketing functions, or to influence their marketing activities. The most commonly employed discounts are trade, quantity, cash, and seasonal discounts.

Trade Discounts

Trade or functional discounts are reductions in list price (price to the ultimate user) provided to intermediaries in exchange for their performance of their prescribed supply chain functions. Trade discounts are the markups quoted to wholesaling and retailing intermediaries. A manufacturer, for example, may quote retailers a 25% trade discount from the suggested retail selling price to cover the retailer's costs and provide a reasonable level of profits to the retailer. If the suggested retail selling price is $100, then the amount of the discount will be $25. The retailer price, then, is $75. Similarly, the manufacturer may quote the wholesaler that sells to this retailer a chain discount of an additional 10% after allowing for the retailer's discount of 25%. The wholesaler's functional discount is 10% of the $75 price to the retailer, or $7.50. The wholesaler can expect to pay $100 - $25 - $7.50 = $67.50 for the product.

Quantity Discounts

Quantity discounts are employed to incentivize customers to buy larger amounts. The more items purchased, the lower the price per item, for example. The primary purpose of a quantity discount is to generate additional sales revenue. However, quantity discounts also can help reduce the seller's storage, shipping, and general selling costs. There are two types of quantity discounts:

Noncumulative Quantity Discounts

The amount of a noncumulative quantity discount is a function of the size of a single order or sale. For example, Snapper (a producer of power lawnmowers) may quote Home Depot noncumulative quantity discounts of 3% on orders of 500 to 1,000 units, 5% on orders between 1,001 and 2,000 units, and 7% on orders over 2,000 units. Such discounts are used to generate larger orders.

Noncumulative quantity discounts are usually quoted as price cuts. However, they sometimes can be offered as free products. Credit card companies, for example, may offer frequent flier miles to buyers of other products. The miles are distributed in direct proportion to how much of the product is purchased or, how much money is charged to the credit card in a single transaction.

Noncumulative quantity discounts usage is regulated by provisions of the Robinson-Patman Act. To avoid charges of price discrimination, producers must offer the same discounts to all buyers, as long as equal quantities are purchased.

Cumulative Quantity Discounts

Rather than basing the quantity discount amount on how many products are purchased in a single order, cumulative quantity discounts are based on how much is purchased during an agreed-upon time frame. Clearly, many individual orders may be involved. The time period covered by the discount could vary from 30 days to one or more years. Such discounts encourage repeat purchases from customers across time and support the development of longer-term customer relationships. The discount simultaneously helps marketers reduce costs that otherwise would be associated with competing for each individual sale.

A plumbing supply and equipment wholesaler, for example, may offer smaller contractors a cumulative quantity discount based on how much they purchase across one year. Smaller contractors are less likely to have the financial resources to buy everything they need at once (to qualify for a noncumulative quantity discount). The cumulative discount may "lock-in" the smaller contractor to the wholesaler. Closer working relationships may evolve, meaning the contractor is less likely to "shop around."

Cumulative quantity discounts are attractive to organizational buyers who would rather avoid carrying inventory. For example, small convenience stores, preferring to maintain fresh products on their shelves for their customers, employ truck distributors to restock their shelves on a regular basis. The truck distributor delivers small individual orders and may offer a cumulative quantity discount to encourage the store to place future orders from the same distributor.

Seasonal Discounts

Many products are purchased by customers on a seasonal basis. This makes sense. Skiing equipment generally is in greatest demand in the winter. Air-conditioning systems will more likely sell during summer months. Yet Firms that manufacturer these products yearn to keep their production facilities operating year-round. If possible, they would also like to avoid costly storage expenses for producing and shift inventory costs further down the supply chain toward the buyer.

The practice of "forward dating" is a special case of seasonal discounting in which the producer offers a seasonal discount but does not require the buyer to receive and pay for the merchandise until a later point in time. The producer gets the order and can plan production, but does not get paid and still must inventory the merchandise. The buyer (wholesaler or retailer) is the real winner. The buyer receives a substantial discount and generally does not have to pay for the merchandise until after some initial sales have been made. Moreover, the buyer avoids all the costs and risks associated with storing the merchandise until it can be sold.

Service Firms offer their versions of seasonal discounts. Airlines and tourist resorts usually offer lower rates during the off-season to encourage bookings. Health clubs offer lower rates during summer months when many potential members shift their recreational and exercise activities to other areas. Some phone services still offer lower prices for airtime on weekends and evenings.

Cash Discounts

Cash discounts are offered to customers to incentivize them to pay bills quicker. Cash discounts, if correctly used, can dramatically improve marketers' cash flows. A sample quote for a cash discount: "2/10, net 30." The "2/10" means the seller is offering a 2% discount from invoice if the buyer pays the bill within 10 days of the invoice date. Otherwise, the entire invoiced amount (with no discount) is due in 30 days (i.e. the "net 30").

Allowances

Allowances are similar to discounts in that they are reductions from list price. Allowances are offered primarily to middlemen to offset their marketing costs. Several types of allowance exist: promotion allowances, stocking allowances, trade-in allowances, and push money.

Promotion Allowances

Promotion allowances are reductions to list price that compensate intermediaries, primarily retailers, for promoting the manufacturer's products in local media. Most promotion allowances are quoted as percentage reductions from list price. However, some allowances may be offered in the form of free goods. Procter & Gamble may offer a large grocery chain a 1% promotional allowance or, alternatively, may provide the retailer with a certain number of free cases of the product on promotion. Of course, the implicit assumption is that the promotion allowance (in whatever form it exists) will be "spent" on local promotion activities (which are usually specified by the manufacturer).

Stocking (Slotting) Allowances

Slotting allowances are incentives provided, generally to supermarkets, to allocate shelf-space to the manufacturer's products. Usually, slotting allowances are used for new products and are provided in the form of dollar incentives or free merchandise. Because new product introductions are always risky and retail shelf-space is always limited (and also full), retailers often demand slotting allowances to offset their costs of stocking new merchandise. These costs include such things as adding the item to the computer database, reconfiguring shelves, re-allocating storage space, and modifying promotional materials.

Trade-in Allowances

Trade-in allowances are price reductions granted for trading-in older, used items when purchasing new products of the same type. Trade-ins are typically encountered when consumer shopping goods, such as automobiles and major appliances, are sold. They also are used for boosting sales of industrial equipment. Trade-ins offer customers price reductions without actually lowering the list price of the product. In addition, the trade-in can be an added source of revenue (and profits) when there is substantial demand for used products of that type.

Push Money Allowances (PMs)

Manufacturers and wholesalers sometimes provide monetary allowances, or "spiffs," to retailers. The retailer is expected to pass on the PM to its retail sales personnel as an added incentive to aggressively sell the manufacturer's products. PMs are most commonly used in industries that rely heavily on personal selling such as the furniture, consumer electronics, and cosmetics industries. PMs are normally used to boost the sales of new products and/or slower moving items in these lines.

Geographic Pricing Adjustments

Geographic price adjustments are anomalous in that they generally add to the realized product price, rather than reduce it. These price adjustments amount to adding shipping and handling costs for the product onto its list price. These costs are sometimes absorbed by marketers to assist in closing the sale. But usually, there is an upward price adjustment that increases the ultimate delivered price to buyers. Questions about who will pay shipping and handling costs, and the size of these costs directly affect supply chain buyer-seller relationships. The amounts of money involved may be huge. Shipping and handling charges are quoted to buyers in several ways.

Free-on-Board (F.O.B) Pricing

Prices are quoted as F.O.B. to a specified location. For example, prices quoted as **F.O.B. plant** or **F.O.B. mill** means that the seller pays the costs associated with placing the product onboard the specified shipping medium (e.g., truck, train, etc.). The buyer, however, assumes all shipping and handling costs from that point forward. The customer also assumes title to—"ownership of"—the product at this point. When prices are quoted F.O.B., mill buyers pay the lion's share of shipping and handling costs and assume most risk.

Prices, however, can also be quoted as **F.O.B destination** or **F.O.B. delivered**. In either case, marketers assume most of the shipping and handling costs and risk. Title does not pass from marketer to customer until the product is received and approved.

The form of F.O.B. pricing that is used exercises a dramatic impact on buyers' realized prices. If prices are quoted F.O.B. mill, buyers located geographically further from the marketer's location pay higher realized prices because transportation costs increase. At some point, it becomes less expensive to purchase from local suppliers, even at higher list prices, in order to receive lower transportation costs. When this happens, sellers may be forced to quote prices as F.O.B delivered in order to compete with local suppliers in distant markets.

F.O.B. delivered pricing is sometimes called **freight absorption pricing**. In reality, F.O.B delivered pricing is an extreme form of freight absorption pricing in which marketers assume all transportation costs. In less extreme situations, sellers may pay a portion of the freight costs for buyers residing or operating far way. The amount "absorbed" is usually enough to make the seller's delivered price competitive with the delivered prices of local suppliers. Freight absorption pricing is attractive to sellers who have excess production capacity and face high fixed costs. The incremental revenue generated from selling in new geographic areas helps the Firm cover these fixed costs. As long as the revenue generated from selling to customers in distant markets exceeds the Firm's variable production and selling costs (including any freight costs that have been absorbed), freight absorption pricing is appropriate..

Delivered Pricing

Prices quoted as "delivered" mean that shipping and handling costs have been "built into" the list price. Two basic types of delivered pricing are usually employed: uniform delivered and zone delivered. **Uniform delivered pricing**, also called "postage stamp pricing," is typically used when transportation costs account for a relatively small proportion of the product's list price. There is little material difference in the freight paid by customers located in widely divergent geographic areas. Firms determine the average shipping and handling costs to all customers in all geographic areas served. This average shipping and handling cost is then built into the price. Delivery charges are not quoted separately. With uniform delivered pricing customers closer to the point of origin (producer's location) clearly are paying more than their fair share of delivery costs. These customers are essentially subsidizing delivery to more distant buyers. This subsidization is called **phantom freight**.

Zone delivered pricing partially alleviates, but never eliminates, the problem of phantom freight accruing from uniform delivered pricing. Zone delivered pricing divides the market area into multiple "zones," with a different delivered price set in each zone. Customers in more distant zones receive higher delivered prices than do customers located in zones closer to the producer's location.

Zone delivered pricing must be employed with caution to avoid allegations of price discrimination. For example, assume a producer sells to two customers. Customer A is in a zone closer to the producer, and customer B is in a second zone more distant from the producer. Assume also that customers A and B are actually physically close enough to one another such that they are in direct competition with one another. The lower delivered price given to customer A (in the closer zone) may provide it with a competitive advantage over customer B (more distant zone). If the advantage is significant, customer B's viability in the market could be harmed. In this case, the seller could be held liable and charged with price discrimination under the Robinson-Patman Act.

→ Managing Price and Pricing Activities

As noted, the ultimate objective of the pricing process is to generate a price schedule that contains list prices and associated pricing adjustments for relevant customer groups. However, this price schedule is not static. It must be continually revisited as elements of the pricing environment change. Changes in market and competitive conditions, the economy, legislation, societal expectations, and global conditions may dictate revisiting the pricing process and revising the schedule. Firms must track such changes in critical marketing environments to anticipate events that may dictate pricing adjustments.

→ Pricing Points to Ponder: Strange but True

True story. About 100 years ago, along the Florida gulf coast, stone crabs, if they registered at all, did so as junk catch; pests that snagged nets and had to be laboriously cut loose. Then an oceanic Steve Jobs-type had a clever idea. Don't toss them; sell the stone crabs—not at the bottom of the price market but toward the top—as a delicacy appreciated by the sophisticated. In this way, a nasty nuisance was transformed into a luxurious delicacy. What started with fishermen bitching ended with Disney-like lines at Joe's Crab Shack.

Two final pricing principles are revealed. First, sometimes if you want to attract a crowd, charge a ridiculous price. And second, in the end, lots of people value what they cannot afford.

Endnotes

[1] Frank Alpert, Beth Wilson, and Michael T. Elliott, "Price Signaling: Does It Ever Work?" *Journal of Product & Brand Management*, Vol. 2, No. 1 (1993): 29-41.

[2] CIO Journal, "2015 Consumer Products Industry Outlook," *The Wall Street Journal* (January 8, 2015), accessed March 8, 2015, http://deloitte.wsj.com/cio/2015/01/08/2015-consumer-products-industry-outlook.

[3] Noel M. Tichy and Stratford Sherman, "Jack Welch's Lessons for Success," *Fortune* (January 25, 1993), accessed March 8, 2015, http://archive.fortune.com/magazines/fortune/fortune_archive/1993/01/25/77396/index.htm.

[4] *The Economist*, "Shock treatment: A Wasteful and Inefficient Industry is in the Throes of Great Disruption," accessed March 8, 2015, http://www.economist.com/news/business/21645741-wasteful-and-inefficient-industry-throes-great-disruption-shock-treatment.

[5] *The New York Times*, "A Guilty Verdict For Mrs. Baird's" (February 15, 1996), accessed March 26, 2015, http://www.nytimes.com/1996/02/15/business/a-guilty-verdict-for-mrs-baird-s.html.

6   Andrew Albanese, "Apple Loses: Judge Finds Price-Fixing in E-Book Case," *Publisher's Weekly* (July 10, 2013), accessed March 26, 2015, http://www.publishersweekly.com/paper-copy/by-topic/digital/content-and-e-books/article/58166-apple-loses-judge-finds-price-fixing-in-e-book-case.html.

7   Serena Ng, "Toilet-Tissue 'Desheeting' Shrinks Rolls, Plumps Margins," *The Wall Street Journal* (July 24, 2013), accessed May 3, 2015, online.wsj.com/article/SB10001424127887323971204578626223494483866.html#printMode?KEYWORDS=%22Kimberly-Clark%22.

8   Laura T. Coffey, "Chocoholics Sour on New Hershey's Formula," *NBC News Today* (September 19, 2008), accessed March 24, 2015, http://www.today.com/id/26788143/ns/today-today_food/t/chocoholics-sour-new-hersheys-formula/#.VRG1JJPF_Ds.

9   Contribution per unit is defined as the selling price per unit minus the variable costs for that unit. Contribution per unit is the amount that each unit can contribute, in dollars, to covering fixed costs.

10 David L. Kurtz, *Contemporary Marketing 17e*, (Boston: Cengage Learning), 602.

11 Michael Porter, *Competitive Strategy: Techniques for Analyzing Industries and Competitors* (New York: The Free Press, 1980).

12 Mark Stiving and Russell Winer, "An Empirical Analysis of Price Endings with Scanner Data," *Journal of Consumer Research*, Vol. 24, No.1 (June 1997): 57–67.

13 Susana Kim, "Overstock.com Defends Itself After Court's Deceptive Pricing Ruling," ABC News (January 10, 2014), accessed March 28, 2015, http://abcnews.go.com/Business/overstock-plans-appeal-courts-deceptive-pricing-ruling/story?id=21479695.

14 Stuart Hirshfield, "The Squeeze," *Apparel Industry Magazine* (August 1998): 60–64.

15 Peter J. McGolderick, Erica J. Betts, and Kathy A. Keeling, "High-Low Pricing: Audit Evidence and Consumer Preferences," *The Journal of Product and Brand Management*, Vol. 9, No. 5 (2000): 316-331.

16 Stephen L. Hock, Xavier Dreze, and Mary E. Purk, "EDLP, Hi-Lo, and Margin Arithmetic," *Journal of Marketing*, Vol. 58, No. 4 (October 1994): 16-27.

17 Pankaj Ghemawat, "Building Strategy on the Experience Curve," *Harvard Business Review* (March 1985), accessed April 1, 2015, https://hbr.org/1985/03/building-strategy-on-the-experience-curve/ar/1.

18 Raju Narisetti, "Israel Accuses P&G Of Dumping Diapers," *The Wall Street Journal* (June 6, 1996), accessed March 28, 2015, http://www.wsj.com/articles/SB834013719298393500.

19 Stacy Mitchell, "Wal-Mart Charged With Predatory Pricing," *Institute for Local Self Reliance* (November 1, 2000), accessed March 28, 2015, http://ilsr.org/walmart-charged-predatory-pricing.

20 See Kenneth N. Thompson, Barbara J. Coe, "Gaining Sustainable Competitive Advantage Through Strategic Pricing: Selecting a Perceived Value Price, *Pricing Strategy & Practice*, Vol. 5, No. 2 (1997): 70–79.

    John L. Forbis and Nitin T. Mehta, "Value-Based Strategies for Industrial Products," *Business Horizons* Vol. 24, No. 3 (May-June, 1981): 32–42.

CHAPTER 16

AN INTRODUCTION TO MARKETING COMMUNICATIONS— THE LAST "P"

Take an object or idea or a service, place or person; an "entity" about which most people know little to nothing. And those who know anything usually could care less. Now imagine your job is to elevate this "entity" to a position where it becomes the temporary center of these people's world. Only highly creative or absolutely inspirational scientific, historical, or fictional writers could produce this result, right? But this ambitious result is exactly the communication outcome that marketers are routinely expected to generate.

Marketing is an action word, which means "market-ing" is a gerund. (Any word ending in "ing" that is used as a noun and also conveys the meaning of the verb, as in "to market," is a gerund.) Market-ing, then, is something in which individuals or Firms engage - or do. Marketers can never do marketing well unless they also do communicate-ing well.

Knowing this, we finally turn toward a discussion of marketing communication or promotion. Promotion is likely the topic most readers thought would be addressed first in this book. But we have purposefully waited until now, near the end of the book, for a dedicated discussion of marketing communications.

The reason why is simple: if you, as a marketer, have nothing to say, does it matter whether you have endless venues, or what we would call communication channels, through which to say it? And with the onset and proliferation of digital marketing, marketers pretty much do enjoy endless venues or channels, through which to deliver promotional communiqués. So congratulations. If you've read and understood this book to this point, you now understand enough about how marketers can and should create differentiating values and favorable positions aimed at establishing equity for their brands. Consequently, you are now ready to understand how marketers can and should package and deliver their value propositions via the messages embedded inside their marketing communications. Which is great, because to succeed in any professional role, you must communicate effectively. There was less value, however, in demonstrating all the power of promotional persuasiveness until you had learned the basics of marketing well enough to know how to effectively exercise this communication power.

→ The Role Promotion Plays as Part of the Marketing Mix

Promotion is a key component of every Firm's marketing mix; it is one of the "4 P's." Promotion exists and operates as the communication weapon, or tool, in marketers' value-creation arsenals. Primary traditional communication media include personal selling, newspapers, magazines, outdoor advertising, and television. Digital media include emails, Twitter, or other social networking sites. All of these marketing communications media are subsumed under the five basic categories of promotion: advertising, personal selling, sales promotion, publicity, and public relations. Together, these five forms of promotion are referred to as the promotion mix.

Advertising

Advertising is any form of communication that is conveyed via a "non-personal medium," meaning a medium that does not employ personal face-to-face contact, and is paid for by some sponsor. Usually, the sponsor is the producer of the product or service, but it can also be a retailer or other supply chain intermediary that is responsible for some aspect of the product's sales. Typically, advertising is delivered via "mass media" (non-personal media) such as television, radio, newspapers, outdoor, and magazines. However, any visible surface that can attract and hold the customer's attention can be a useful advertising medium. We see ads placed on the backs of restroom stall doors (stall malls, or "the writing on the stall", get it?); handles of grocery carts and floors of grocery stores; walls in sports stadiums, and even asphalt on automotive racetracks. Other useful forms of advertising include direct mail, specialty advertising, and Internet advertising via a growing pool of digital media, including social media.

Traditionally, the advertising message is generally one-way, meaning that the message's recipient cannot ask questions or otherwise exchange information with the advertiser. Thus, advertising via traditional mass media is considered to be impersonal in nature. However, the growing use of Internet advertising, particularly via various social media, is negating this traditional one-way flow perspective. Advertisers are aggressively interacting with consumers via social media by monitoring online conversations and often engaging and even directing those conversations.

Traditional mass media, in particular, reach large numbers of people quickly at a low cost per exposure. However, the cost of developing and airing advertisements in some media can be prohibitive for many Firms. For example, the costs of airing a 30-second TV ad during the 2015 Super Bowl exceeded $4.5 Million.[1] This figure does not take into account the costs associated with developing the advertisement. These costs might easily exceed $1,000,000. The advent of local cable TV has helped reduce the costs of TV advertising, making this medium accessible to smaller Firms.

Personal Selling

Personal selling is an oral, one-on-one, often face-to-face communication between prospective buyers and sellers. The primary purpose of such one-on-one communication is to "close" sales. Indeed, personal selling is considered to be the only promotional medium capable of "closing" a sale and directly generating revenue for the Firm. However, the communication process inherent in personal selling is also very useful for ascertaining the customer's wants and needs, imparting customized information to customers about products or services, and for developing customer relationships, even if the contact does not immediately result in a "sale."

Sales Promotion

Sales promotion supports and augments advertising and personal selling efforts. It consists of activities that provide short-term incentives aimed at inducing desired responses from customers, the Firm's salespersons, and supply chain intermediaries. Sales promotion is a paid form of communication that is temporarily used to stimulate purchases, as well as enhance salesperson and dealer effectiveness. Sales promotion includes, but is not limited to, the use of coupons, games, contests, free samples, rebates, frequent-flyer programs, in-store displays, in-store product demonstrations, free gifts, and travel vacations for salespeople.

As noted, sales promotion activities are intended to support traditional advertising and personal selling efforts. For many consumer goods, advertising is used to generate awareness and interest in the product. The use of sales promotion at the point of sale, such as coupons and aisle displays, may trigger the actual sale. In general, sales promotion is great for stimulating new product trial and encouraging brand switching for consumer convenience goods. Since most convenience goods are low involvement in nature, consumers can be influenced to engage in unplanned or impulse purchasing via the use of free samples, coupons, product demonstrations, and aisle displays.

Publicity and Public Relations

Publicity is any message about a product, organization, person, or event that is communicated via non-personal media and is not paid for by a sponsor. Usually, employees working for the communications medium determines the content of the message. For example, a TV station may run a story about a product or a company that is deemed to be "newsworthy." The company or product that is the subject of the news story does not pay for or directly sponsor the message.

Publicity can be both positive and negative. In either case, the message is often perceived as very believable because it is communicated by an "independent" and usually credible third-party. Firms often receive positive publicity in the media when introducing new and innovative products, or when engaging in activities that bolster popular social causes. Negative publicity can be extremely damaging to the Firm. For example, the negative publicity experienced by Toyota a few years ago due to sticky gas pedals had a major, albeit short-term, effect on its corporate image and the sale of its products.[2] Or consider what has recently happened to Blue Bell ice cream sales in Texas.

Public relations is an attempt by Firms to manage the publicity it receives. Public relations efforts generally either seek to enhance the image of the Firm and its products, or to communicate important company information to key publics. The usual targets (publics) for public relations efforts include the Firm's existing and potential customers, government agencies, advocacy groups, and the general public. Public relations departments in Firms primarily focus their efforts on external communications media by aggressively going after positive publicity. Typical goals are to garner positive news releases, arrange interviews between the media and the Firm's spokespersons, lobby governmental agencies, support charitable events, and engage in corporate (institutional) advertising. However, public relations efforts also can have an internal focus that includes company newsletters and magazines, annual reports for stakeholders, and myriad programs and activities geared to building positive employee relationship. Internally directed marketing activities are called, not surprisingly, "internal marketing."

→ Determining the Composition of the Promotion Mix

The promotion mix elements should complement one another. This means, in brief, the promotional elements should work together to deliver and reinforce the key message or messages being conveyed sent to the target audience. Times and places will arise while it is more appropriate to use personal selling rather than advertising, or sales promotions rather than direct marketing. The relative emphasis that should be allocated to each promotional element primarily depends on five related factors: (1) characteristics of the product or service being promoted, (2) characteristics of the segment or segments being market, (3) characteristics of the marketing organization itself, (4) competitors' promotion activities, and (5) the Firm's promotion objectives.

Characteristics of the Product

Specific characteristics of the product that determine the composition of the promotion mix include: the type of product and its unit value, the product's service requirements, the complexity of the information that must be communicated, and the product's stage in its life cycle.

Type of Product and Its Unit Value

The product's unit value impacts the type of promotion employed. One or more forms of advertising should be emphasized when less expensive consumer products, such as consumer convenience goods, are marketed. Marketers must appeal to mass markets to generate sufficient sales. Advertising is employed primarily through a "pull strategy" for the dual purposes of creating brand awareness and differentiating the brand from competitive offerings. Packaged goods, such as those purchased in retail supermarkets and discount stores, exemplify convenience goods.

Sales promotions can prove useful when consumer packaged goods are being marketed due to their low-involvement nature. Low-involvement products are purchased frequently, low priced, and low risk. When evaluating consumer packaged goods, customers are price sensitive. They engage in extensive impulse buying. Coupons, premiums, gifts, and/or price deals can easily stimulate impulse buying behaviors. Finally, personal selling is used primarily to influence intermediaries (wholesaler and retailers) to stock the product and to support the efforts of these middlemen.

For expensive products, such as durable shopping goods and most industrial products, personal selling is usually more important. Customers who purchase these higher value products generally demand more information and often welcome the "expert" advice that only face-to-face salesperson exchanges can provide. Sometimes, salespeople are essential for demonstrating how consumer durables are used. Think about the Kirby vacuum salesperson who provides extensive in-home demonstrations.

Most shopping and specialty products are "durable products," meaning that they are longer-lived. Durable goods are used over sustained periods of time. But eventually, they are replaced. Household appliances, automobiles, clothing items, or recreational equipment exemplify durable products. Advertising can prove important. Durable goods' features and benefits, after all, must be communicated, attended to, and ultimately understood by targeted customers and prospects. Consumers are more likely to experience post-purchase cognitive dissonance when purchasing major durable products. Advertising and personal selling can each prove useful in reassuring consumers, post-purchase, that they have certainly made a great decision.

Personal selling inevitably plays a primary role in the promotion mix for most industrial goods, particularly installations and major equipment, where product customization and demonstration are often essential. The interpersonal two-way, give-and-take interactions that ensue between customers and sales representatives are essential in order to establish credibility, foster trust and overcome dissonance; to inform, create awareness among and persuade customers and prospects; and finally, to truly understand the most-pressing pain-point problems of those customers. Personal selling efforts are necessary to establish the mutually beneficial and long-term relationships that contribute so much to successful supply chain partnerships.

Service Requirements

Some consumer and many industrial products require significant pre- and post-sale servicing. Consumer products that must be customized (e.g. computers, tailored suits, custom homes) rely heavily on salespeople to communicate the product's benefits and bundle the proper package to satisfy customers' specific needs. Industrial salespeople are well-suited to satisfying the servicing requirements of industrial equipment items that require substantial customization, training, and post-sale servicing.

Amount and Complexity of Information Communicated

Advertising is generally more appropriate when communications messages are simple or when the products' benefits are easily observed. When messages are complex or when products benefits must be extensively demonstrated (e.g. computers, vacuum cleaners, DVD players), personal selling is more appropriate.

Stage in the Product Life Cycle

The composition of the promotion mix varies depending on the products' life cycle stage. During introduction, the Firm's main promotion objectives are to generate primary demand for the product category by informing consumers of the product's existence. The overarching communication purposes are to introduce and highlight the product's benefits and stimulate trial.

- Advertising is used extensively during this stage to create awareness and stimulate product trial.
- Sales promotions, such as coupons and free samples, are employed to induce trial.
- Personal selling is employed to reach intermediaries and persuade them to stock and promote the product.

During the growth stage of the product life cycle, as competitors enter the market, promotion objectives shift to building selective demand (demand for your Firm's brand) by differentiating the brand from competitive brands. Promotion is used to build and sustain brand preference. Brand preference, once established, elevates the prospect of repeat purchases.

- Advertising should communicate brand superiority by promoting the brand's differentiating characteristics relative to competing brands. Comparative advertising in which competing brands are directly referenced in advertising messages is often employed beginning in this product life cycle stage. Because a larger number of consumers purchase the product during growth, advertising usually is more economical than other forms of promotion. The cost-per-exposure—i.e., eyeballs or ears reached—is lower for most forms of advertising than for other promotion tools.
- Less emphasis is placed on sales promotions during the growth stages. Sales promotions' incentivizing values are typically not necessary at this point because of the product's increasing acceptance and the growing market.
- Personal selling is still essential for reaching supply chain intermediaries. Existing supply chain partners should be nurtured and supported, and new relationships developed to foster continued growth.

The maturity stage of the PLC is the most expensive from a promotion standpoint. There is intense competition between brands during the maturity stage. Consequently, promotion expenditures reach their pinnacle. The promotional focus remains on fostering selective demand for the brand. But the communication effort is intensified.

- Now, advertising generally predominates within the promotion mix. New advertising campaigns may be required to announce product improvements, reach additional target segments, and demonstrate new ways that consumers could use the product. Advertising's main objectives continue to focus on differentiating the brand. The purpose, fundamentally, is to "buy market share" from competitors.
- Sales promotions again become important to support any revised advertising themes. But the primary reason to use sales promotions at this point is to tempt consumers into "brand switching." Coupons, point-of-sale devices, premiums, and price incentives are needed to entice consumers away from competing brands.

During the decline stage, promotional efforts are generally lowered in an effort to "harvest" remaining profits from the now-old brand. Intense promotion efforts may be targeted to still profitable market segments or niches. For the most part, however, promotions are pruned to cut costs and increase profit margins.

Characteristics of the Target Market

The type of customer toward whom product/brands are directed and the way in which these customers make purchase decisions affect the relative emphasis that should be placed on various elements of the promotion mix.

Type of Customer

The composition of the promotion mix varies depending on the basic type of customer targeted:

- Ultimate—or final—consumers are typically reached via advertising and sales promotions. A "pull" promotion strategy tends to predominate in order to create demand by consumers for products (Exhibit 16.1).
- Personal selling, sales promotions, and, to a lesser extent, trade advertising are employed to reach intermediaries: retailers and wholesalers. The primary objective is to convince intermediaries to stock products or to emphasize their sales. Greater reliance is placed on discounts and direct payments to middlemen (such payments are called "push money") that support intermediaries' promotional efforts. These incentives are intended to "push" demand for the product through the supply chain's various levels.

Type of Buying Decision

When consumers engage in high-involvement, extensive decision making, promotional mixes must be structured to provide consumers with ample information related to the product's characteristics, brand performance, availability, and price. Hence, print advertising and personal selling are generally emphasized. Types of products that normally would be involved here include major appliances or automobiles.

By contrast, consumers engaged in low involvement decisions—perhaps they are variety-seeking or mired in inertia—are much less receptive to information. Little active information search and alternative evaluation occurs with low involvement decisions. Consequently, high imagery media, such as TV and billboards, could be used to stimulate brand awareness. Sales

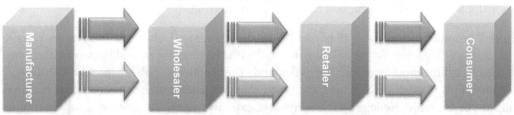

Push Strategy: Promotion directed at middlemen "pushes" product from one level in the channel to the next.

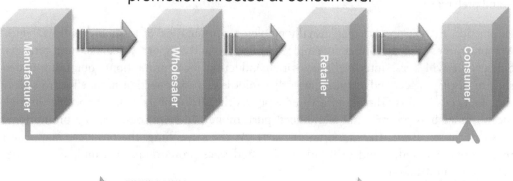

Pull Strategy: Product is "pulled" into the channel due to promotion directed at consumers.

Exhibit 16.1 *Push and Pull Strategies.*

promotions (coupons, gifts, and premiums) and in-store conditions (displays, added shelf-space, free sample, etc.) are likewise effective for stimulating product trial and brand switching when high involvement decision conditions prevail.

Influencing Factors within the Firm

The two major organizational-related factors should influence the structure of the promotion mix that is used. The first factor is the supporting marketing mix strategies. The second is the available promotional budget.

Supporting Marketing Mix Strategies

The emphasis placed on alternative promotion tools depends on the level of synergy sought with other elements of the Firm's marketing mix. (Synergy exists when the interaction of two or more elements produces a combined effect greater than the sum of their separate effects.) Consistency between all elements must be present to support the Firm's overall marketing objectives and strategies. Here, the Firm's reliance on supply chain intermediaries to support the selling effort and the Firm's branding strategy are particularly relevant.

Manufacturers often rely heavily on intermediaries to support their efforts. Considerable resources are directed at middlemen to provide sales incentives and generally support their sales efforts. Using these "push promotion strategies" producers heavily "promote" to wholesale and retail intermediaries. In turn, retailers actively promote the product to ultimate consumers. Push strategies rely heavily on the aggressive selling efforts of the manufacturer's sales force to work with wholesalers and/or retailers. In addition, producers employ a wide range of promotions directed at intermediaries to motivate their selling efforts. Examples include dealer contests for middlemen's sales personnel, trade shows, slotting fees for retailers, promotional allowances, and added sales commissions in the form of "push money." Again, see Exhibit 16.1 for the distinction between "push" and "pull."

A "pull promotion strategy" builds sales by promoting aggressively to the final buyer, usually the ultimate consumer. By stimulating demand with the final buyer, middlemen are forced to stock and sell the product to satisfy this demand. The product is "pulled" into the distribution channel. Pull strategies rely heavily on advertising and sales promotion directed at the final buyer. For example, Kellogg's Cereal employs extensive television and print advertising to create demand for its cereals with consumers. Coupons, gifts, and premiums are employed at the point of purchase to stimulate trial and brand switching behaviors, as well as to create brand preference.

In practice, marketing managers usually employ a combination of push and pull strategies. Manufacturer's sales personnel are employed to sell to and support wholesalers and retailers. Salespeople will assist intermediaries with conducting local promotions, obtaining added shelf or display space, and encouraging other middlemen to apportion more effort to selling the producer's brands. The manufacturer supports the efforts of its own salespeople through incentives such as promotional allowances, push money, in-store coupons, and promotional aids (brochures, flyers, free-standing displays). At the same time, the producer may invest in extensive TV, radio, and print advertising and sales promotions to stimulate consumer awareness and demand.

Branding Strategy

Firms that use different forms of family branding strategies, such as brand extension or co-branding, do so in part to obtain scale economies in promotion. The meaning attached to the brand name held in common by the Firm's various products stimulates "meaning transfer" from existing brands to any new products that may be introduced. The net result is that less promotion should be required because of the common imagery associated with the family brand.

By contrast, Firms that employ individual or multiple branding strategies cannot rely on the shared image delivered by the family brand. Instead, each brand must stand alone. New brands, therefore, require heavy promotion expenditures to gain market awareness and acceptance.

Promotion Budget

The selection of elements of the promotion mix is highly dependent upon the funds that are available for promotion activities. Indeed, this may be the most critical limiting factor for many Firms when deciding how to promote their products. Generally, Firms with limited resources are locked into employing less expensive promotional techniques such as Internet sites and social media, printed media such as flyers and brochures, specialty advertising, direct mail, and phone book listings. These Firms do not have the money needed to invest in more efficient mass media, such as TV, radio, and print.

Four ways in which promotional budgets are determined are discussed below.

Competitors' Actions

Much of any Firm's promotional efforts may be geared to responding to and countering the promotional activities of competitors. The objective is usually to add, retain, or regain market share. Ongoing "cola wars" between, primarily, Pepsi and Coke have been fierce. In this industry, a 1% change in market share entails untold millions of dollars in sales. Coke and

Pepsi have each invested heavily in creative mass communications in TV, radio, print media, and outdoor ads. This investment has been supported with creative use of coupons, games, contests, publicity schemes, and public relations. The objective is simple: protect market shares.

Major automotive manufacturers likewise constantly respond to one another's promotion activities. Advertising, rebates, special credit terms, and the like are commonplace, particularly during the end of the fiscal year. As one model year ends and another begins, manufacturers and dealers each seek to trim inventories in anticipation of next year's sales and profits.

The Hierarchy of Communications Objectives

The task of blending or mixing the elements of the promotion mix into a unified and integrated whole to achieve the Firm's communication objectives is hugely important. Well-managed promotional activities normally are geared to achieving desirable communication objectives. These communication objectives are often framed and referred to as a "hierarchy of communications objectives." These objectives constitute a hierarchy because objectives at lower levels must be met before Firm's can hope to achieve objectives at the next higher levels. The communications hierarchy of objectives, in order of precedence, include (Exhibit 16.2):

Generating Customer Awareness

By definition, without awareness of a product and its comparative value, no one will be buy it. Marketers first must create brand awareness as a foundational first step toward achieving any other communication goal. No alternative path to successful communication exists. Customers must be aware of a product's existence. Before consumers can form impressions of products, let alone develop brand preferences, they must be aware that the product exists in the market. In fact, many new product failures can be traced to a basic lack of brand name recognition; consumers simply were not aware that the brand existed![3] Middlemen generally refuse to stock new products that lack brand recognition; preferring brands from well-known

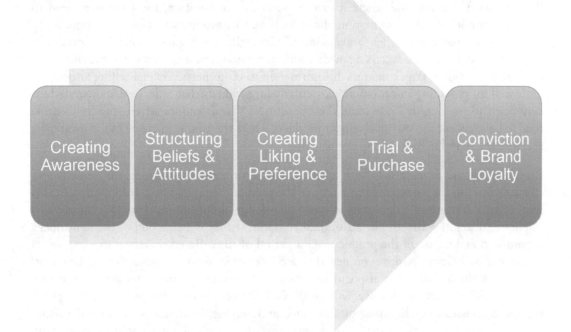

Exhibit 16.2 *The Hierarchy of Communications Objectives.*

manufacturers that are supported with large promotion budgets. Even then, retailers may insist on slotting fees before allocating precious shelf space to new brands. The mass media are excellent for creating awareness. In particular, TV, outdoor, and to a lesser extent, radio with their large exposure rates do an excellent job of building awareness.

The objective of creating awareness is easier when distinct consumer wants and needs exist that are, essentially, waiting to be satisfied. Marketers are quite capable of creating customer wants, or least bringing those wants to the point of awareness within consumers, by skillfully managing their promotional communications. Marketers, as you recall, are not able to create basic human needs, no matter how adroitly their communication efforts are managed. Nor do marketers need to do this. States of felt deprivation arise easily enough all on their own inside consumer hearts and minds. The desire to fit in, love and be loved, feel safe, eat, drink, sleep or have sex, naturally-arising human needs, one and all, would still motivate and drive human choices and behaviors even if there were no marketers or marketing messages. Instead, through their strategic promotional messaging marketers can influence the products/brands that we want to help us feel "like we belong" when we experience the need "to fit in."

Teenage American boys "need" to eat because they get hungry. But when this hunger need kicks in they want a burger and fries or pizza. This specific want arises in large part because fast food marketers and their marketing messaging have influenced them throughout their lives. Marketing communications can create consumer wants. Marketing communication do not have to create, nor can they create, human needs.

Structuring Brand Beliefs, Attitudes, and Differentiating the Brand

Awareness is usually not enough, in and of itself, to generate a purchase. Additional customer knowledge must be imparted about product/brand characteristics, benefits, availability, prices, new values, etc. Customers often must acquire and digest additional knowledge about new or existing products before deciding to purchase. Marketers should deliver the sort of knowledge that leads message recipients to perceive that the promoted product is "different from" and "better than" competing product options. This is the essence and goal of differentiation. As a minimum, consumers must be educated about such things as the product's characteristics, the benefits it delivers, and where it can be obtained. In addition, the Firm may need to communicate important information about itself and its products to suppliers, community groups, middlemen, and other "stakeholders." Generally, for higher involvement products, the Internet and printed advertising media, such as newspapers, magazines, and brochures are the best at providing large amounts of information to customers. Personal selling also works quite well for providing information, particularly for products that must be demonstrated for consumers to thoroughly understand their benefits. TV and outdoor advertising (billboards) tend to be excellent for low involvement products where the goal is to create brand awareness and link the brand name to a few key benefits.

Brand images are developed from more than just information concerning the benefits and characteristics of the associated product; i.e., the product being branded. Information in this sense shapes consumers' cognitions or basic knowledge about brands. However, image also implies a substantial affective or attitudinal component that is a function of the consumer's exposure to and/or use of the product over a period of time. Based on repeat use (exposure) consumers will form positive or negative attitudes that tend to guide future behavior. However, attitude formation also can be influenced by some promotional activities at this stage. Specifically, for low involvement products, it is possible to shape positive attitudes via the use of classical conditioning by linking brands to highly attractive emotional themes with TV and some print media. To a lesser extent, conditioning techniques employing the mass media can also assist in shaping consumer's attitudes toward higher involvement products such as automobiles. For example, imagery-laden ads for the 2016 Jaguar F-Type are specifically designed to elicit a positive affective response from viewers that, in part, may help in structuring consumers' attitudes toward the car.

Developing a solid, positive brand image is probably the single most important communications objective Firms strive to achieve. Strong brand images translate into added value for the brand; strong positive brand images yield positive "brand equity." Strong brand images essentially tie consumers and channel members to the brand. Images are created, in part, by providing information via the media just examined.

Differentiating the brand from competing brands is an important promotion objective, particularly during the late growth and maturity stages of the product life cycle. As the number of competing brands increases, Firms often turn to promotion to emphasize the important differences between their brands and those of their competitors. If the brand can be effectively differentiated, the brand's market share can be stabilized and the brand's sales will be less susceptible to price competition. The key to effectively differentiating the brand is to emphasize differences with competitors on the product's determinant attributes. Determinant attributes are those that are important to consumers when they compare and choose between brands. Actual meaningful or perceived differences must also exist between those attributes and the same attributes associated with competing brands. A specific product attribute can be important, but if competing brands all perform equally on that attribute, consumers cannot use it to choose between brands. Ultimately, choice is driven by comparing brands on their points of difference, not their similarities.

Creating Liking, Preference, and Desire

Continuing to solidify customers' beliefs and attitudes toward brands should walk these customers closer to trial and purchase. This "solidification" leads to customer desire, liking, and/or preference, for products and/or brands. At this stage, marketers are establishing the consumer's "want." Interestingly, consumers may want a particular product but elect to not purchase the "something" until a specific problem arises that the product/brand can address or resolve. For example, a student may want high-speed Internet access at home, but may not take the plunge now because adequate access is already available on campus and the student does most of his/her work while on campus. A sufficient need does not exist. Similarly, customers may fervently desire (the need and want exist) something now but find they must wait to acquire the product/brand until they can afford it. The liking, preference, and desire for a Mercedes E-class sedan, for example, may already be embedded deeply within your mind and buying soul due to your lifelong exposure to Mercedes' sophisticated marketing communiqués. Still, you're likely a few years away from possessing the financial wherewithal to reasonably afford the E-class option. But once you have acquired the financial stroke, Mercedes wins, because the German brand earned prime positioning real estate in your mind years ago.

Stimulating Trial and Purchase

Inducing trial is most easily accomplished for low involvement products via the use of coupons, free samples, displays, and other point-of-sale techniques. Inducing trial for higher involvement products such as automobiles and major appliances is more difficult because of the relatively high costs and inherent risk associated with the purchase and use of such products. Automobiles can be test driven, but more extensive trial generally requires that products be purchased. To some extent, the risk of trial can be offset by offering consumers generous return policies and warranties. Of course, the better job that is done in structuring consumers' beliefs and attitudes, as well as differentiating the brand per the previous step in our hierarchy of objectives, the easier it becomes to stimulate trial and subsequent purchase.

Establishing Brand Conviction

Successfully inducing trial and purchase is essential for ultimate conviction to a brand. Positive rewards based on purchase and use of a brand positively reinforce the brand purchase decision, walking the consumer one step closer to conviction and brand loyalty. Successful reminders (more about the topic follows), calls-to-action (i.e., get your fanny into Best Buy before close of business this Saturday because there is a "huge, never-to-be-repeated" sale on Samsung smart phones), leads to the creation of brand equity and, ultimately, brand loyalty.

Other Communications Objectives

In addition to the traditional hierarchy of communications objectives, which is probably best suited to new product adoption and diffusion, there are a number of additional communications objectives that are more applicable to products already in the Firm's portfolio.

Managing Demand

Promotion is employed to manage demand for products during all stages of the product life cycle, but of specific interest are the increasing use of "de-marketing" and advertisers' ongoing attempts to keep a product alive by increasing the amount and frequency with which a product is used. Particularly during the late growth and maturity stages of the product life cycle, Firms strive to increase the frequency and quantity of product purchases. Specific strategies targeting these objectives were examined in earlier chapters. Clearly, promotion plays a major role in achieving these objectives. Specifically, advertising in the mass media is ideal for demonstrating new uses for products. The generous use of sales promotions such as coupons, samples, games, and the like can stimulate added consumption.

De-marketing

When supplies are limited, products may need to be de-marketed. Promotion is used to encourage consumers to purchase less, or at a later date. Similarly, Firms engage in de-marketing to reduce the demand for products that are subject to abuse. With no small irony, ads geared to de-marketing alcohol and tobacco products are *actually* sponsored by Firms that produce these products. But fortunately, and sensibly, they are also sponsored by the American Cancer Society, the American Heart Association, and various public interest entities.

Managing Corporate Image

Managing the company's image is an increasingly important communications objective, particularly for Firms that are continually under fire by special interest groups and governmental agencies. Firms make extensive use of the mass media, particularly TV and print, and social media to explain their actions to interested publics and to improve their corporate images.

Influencing Intermediaries to Stock the Product

When producers rely heavily on middlemen to support the Firm's selling efforts, considerable resources are directed at these intermediaries to provide sales incentives and generally support their sales efforts. Firms rely heavily on the aggressive selling efforts of the producer's sales force to work with wholesalers and/or retailers and employ a wide range of sales promotions directed at middlemen to influence them to stock the product and further motivate their selling efforts.

→ Communication Media and the Message Matter Greatly

Marshall McLuhan famously suggested that when the subject is successful communication, the "medium is the message." More recently, we've increasingly realized that the most critical medium in most professional settings is the actual person delivering the message. Your voice, poise, presence, and appearance are part of your communications capital and ultimately your value. The more you invest in improving each, the greater the return you will earn. In particular, appearance—your own "look" and/or that of the objects being marketed—does matter. Perhaps this strikes you as threatening; perhaps as opportunity, but this circumstance should strike you as fact. Because it is.

Appearance is tremendously important in communications settings because the fact that it matters is biologically predetermined. To classify, categorize, or stereotype anything and everyone that is communicated as either desirable or undesirable—good as in "benign, beneficial, or opportunity" or bad as in "malignant, harmful, or threat"—is an innately human activity. Not true? Consider that as humans we even classify chairs and sofas.

The next thing we hope you learn is that marketing messages matter greatly. For example, the core Democrat marketing party's message: "Give us power so we can do great things for you." The core Republican marketing party's message: "Give us power so we can give you the power and ability do great things for yourself." Two great political parties' respective messages, summarized in 11 and 17 words, respectively. Your choice. A nation's future hangs in the balance. You better believe marketing messages matter.

But what do marketers have to do to create and deliver messages that are capable of moving markets? Read on and find out.

Determining the Message's Content, Source, and Format

The message's content or appeal is often nothing more than the key selling points or ideas that must be emphasized in the communication. These can be the major benefits the product delivers, the characteristics of the product that distinguish it from those of competitors, links to key behavioral motivators (such as dimensions of lifestyle or self-concept), or other reasons why the target audience should listen to what the advertiser has to say. Two basic types of appeals are commonly employed:

- *Rational appeals* focus on communicating information about concrete benefits, functions, or characteristics that are associated with the product.
- *Emotional appeals* attempt to elicit affective or emotional responses from target audiences. Humor, fear, and sex appeals are the most common emotional appeals.

The message source can be as important as its content. The source of the message is the apparent originator of the message. The source can be a person, a company, or an inanimate figure, such as a cartoon character. The perceived credibility of the source (source credibility) can be important for assuring acceptance of the message. The extent to which a source is seen as credible is directly related to its perceived expertise and trustworthiness.[4] Expertise is special knowledge the source is known to possess as recognized by others. Trustworthiness is a function of the source's perceived objectivity, honesty, and integrity. These characteristics are drivers of how believable the source is perceived to be. The expert source who is perceived to have no reason to mislead can exert a powerful influence on shaping the consumers' perceptions and opinions. Friends and family, and other non-commercial sources of information usually are perceived to be more trustworthy than are commercial sources. However, friends or family may not be perceived to be all that expert with respect to some products or issues. In contrast, salespeople often are perceived as very knowledgeable, but score low on trustworthiness because they are attributed with the "selling" motive.

Celebrities are often used to endorse products because they can lend a degree of perceived credibility to a message that can enhance its persuasive effect. Celebrities who endorse products related to their areas of specialization are easily viewed as experts. Think of Michael Jordan endorsing Nike athletic shoes or Tiger Woods endorsing Nike Gear or Gatorade. Celebrities also tend to score high on trustworthiness because of their status and charisma with certain audiences. Celebrity endorsers can influence audiences in other ways as well. Their celebrity status can attract and sustain the consumer's attention, making it easier for marketers to get the message across. Celebrities also can be powerful "aspirational referents" to consumers, meaning that consumers may identify with or desire to emulate the celebrity. Buying the endorsed product makes it possible for the consumer to communicate his or her identification with the celebrity.

The use of celebrity endorsers is not without clear dangers. Mike Tyson, Madonna, and Michael Jackson were dropped by Pepsi Cola because of their tainted images and the potential negative effects on the Pepsi brand and its sales. More recently, Tiger Woods and Lance Armstrong were dropped by the majority of their sponsors for less than ethical behaviors. The fear that a celebrity endorser will become a liability for a brand has led some Firms to use dead celebrities who obviously won't do anything to generate negative publicity. Coors once ran as series of ad employing the then-deceased John Wayne as an endorser by editing segments from his movies into the ads. For similar reasons, some Firms are using animated characters as endorsers, such as Looney Tunes characters used by Frito-Lay and Chevrolet.[5] As for the Gecko or Tony the Tiger, neither has ever gotten embroiled in any sex- or drug-related scandals. At least not yet.

Message format considerations focus on how best to structure the message to achieve the greatest impact. Designing the message to attract and hold attention, enhance the likelihood of positive attitude formation or change, as well as reduce the likelihood of miscomprehension are key concerns with selecting the right message format. Usual considerations include use of one-sided vs. two-sided arguments, use of comparative advertising, or the order in which key message points are presented.

One-Sided Versus Two-Sided Messages

A one-sided message only points out the product's good points. Bad points are ignored. Most advertisements use one-sided messaging because advertisers are afraid of pointing out their products' deficiencies. However, pointing out deficiencies and then refuting them can actually reinforce perceptions of a products benefits and lead to improved sales. For example, Avis used the refutation approach in its early ads. The ads begin by pointing out that Avis was not the largest car rental company and then essentially discounted the "deficiency" by stating "...we try harder." In general, one-sided ads work better when consumers are less educated, already agree with the advertiser's position, or already prefer the advertiser's brand.

By contrast, with two-sided ads, both sides of the positive-negative "argument" are presented. Consumer tendencies to counter-argue against positive points consequently may be diffused. This is because the advertisement has already pointed out the weaknesses. In fact, it may have even refuted them.[6]

Comparative Advertising

When using comparative advertising, a Firm's competitors are named. Banned until 1976, the use of comparative advertising has since proliferated. Most comparative ads are one-sided. In other words, the message only emphasizes the merits of the advertised brand and the weaknesses of competing brands. Comparative ads often influence consumers' attitudes. People who are already using competing brand named in comparative ads are more likely to notice and pay attention to the ads. Next thing you know, they consider switching brands. Comparative advertisements provide consumers with more information and rational bases on which to choose one or another brand. Indeed, this was the exact rationale cited by the FTC when it reversed its stance on the use of comparative advertising.[7]

Order of Presentation

This issue focuses on whether the strongest points in the communication should be presented first or last. Attention and interest are enhanced when the strongest message points are presented first. Primary ordering surely makes more sense when audiences are unlikely to attend to the whole message. Hit recipients with key points right away.

→ Four Basic Communication Principles

The first, most basic communication principle is well-known. Indeed, it is almost self-evident. For communication to actually occur, the "intended marketing message" must be received and understood by the "intended customer target" in the manner in which the originating or initiating marketing sender intended. This principle applies to marketing and all other communication processes.

Messages are essentially bilateral, or two-way, in the traditional communication process model (Exhibit 16.3). The sender, here, the marketer, develops and initiates a message. This message then is conveyed through some communications medium, which is also known as a communication channel. In turn, essentially on the other end of this dyadic communication exchange process (dyadic means two persons or two parties), the receiver, or customer, responds to his or her receipt of the message. As described, the marketing sender of this message must package this central idea in such a way that it can be understood by the receiver in the intended manner. This is called encoding a message. Without encoding, successful communication has not occurred. At the exact time they receive messages, receivers decode them. Decoding is the process by which receivers interpret, make sense of, and assign meaning to the message.

Many is the time, as you might expect, when either the encoding or decoding process goes awry. Then there is, as the prison warden said to the inmate character played by Paul Newman in the movie *Cool Hand Luke*, "a failure to communicate." The warden then proceeded to hit Luke in the head with a shovel because of the communication breakdown. But we will have none of that here.

There is one other major impediment to successful communication: noise. Noise is any physical/psychological barrier, distraction, or interference that impedes the recipient from successfully decoding the message. In today's heavily congested traditional and Internet-mediated media marketplace "noise levels" are higher than at any point in history. This condition only intensifies the communication challenge that all marketers confront today.

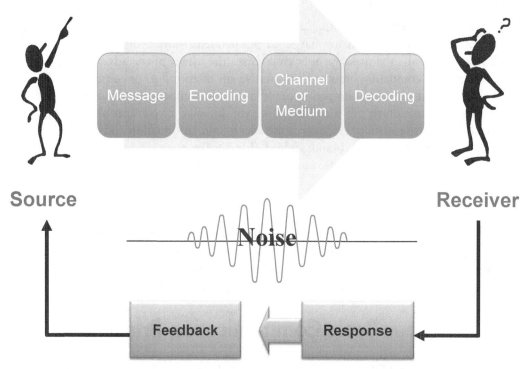

Exhibit 16.3 *The Communications Process.*

The second communication principle is when communicating with customers, marketers should emphasize the product **f**eatures, **a**ttributes, and ultimately **b**enefits (FAB) that are viewed as most important (valuable) to customers. If marketers fail to communicate key product values to customers, customers are unlikely to appreciate or even be aware the value exists. Most US customers live in low-involvement, low-information consumption worlds; just like most US voters.

Consequently, any failure to persistently focus communication efforts on establishing the presence and value of key differences in the minds of targeted customers represents an unpardonable error. The best marketing communications almost inevitably focus doggedly on emphasizing a unique selling (value) proposition. As discussed in Chapter 6, marketing research is often needed to determine which product values (solutions) are most important to customers. Moreover, different target segments usually value different sorts of benefits or solutions more highly. Firms generally should target different marketing messages to different market segments, as part of the unique marketing mixes and concomitant value propositions developed for each customer segment they target.

Whenever possible, marketers should emphasize features, attributes, and/or benefits that meaningfully differ from those offered by competitors' products. This is the third communication principle. Marketing success, as you know, is predicated on standing-out rather than fitting-in; making old-things-appear-new; and making new-things-known. In other words, success is grounded in effective differentiation.

Once the second and third communication principles are fulfilled, marketers will focus on communicating the "determinant" product/brand differences in their messaging, a desirable outcome, indeed. The word determinant means "decisive." Examined earlier in the chapter, determinant communication messages must emphasize differences between the brand being promoted and competitive brands. Moreover, the differences emphasized in the message must be important to customers as they deliberate which brand to select. During most of their promotions during the last five or six years Southwest Airlines has emphasized the tagline "Bags Fly Free." Most if not all flyers enjoy saving money when they travel, right? Consequently, most travelers perceive that "Free Bags" is important. By promoting this difference relative to legacy airline competitors such as American Airlines, Delta Airlines, or United Airlines, Southwest logically and effectively grounded its ongoing communication efforts in genuine, effective, and determinant brand differences.

A fourth communication principle is that marketers will communicate better once they consciously choose to live in the real rather than some ideal version of the world. Living out this reality makes it easier for marketers to accept that part of their job, the communication part, is to *manipulate* others. Now clearly, this manipulation should only be executed to the extent that it benefits prospects/customers over the long- or short-run, which is consistent with the case we have built throughout this book.

The primary role of marketers is to develop and thereafter to deliver the best possible need-satisfying product/brand value to targeted customers. This task is executed in order to solve customer problems. The primary role of marketing communicators, meanwhile, is to develop the best possible messages and thereafter to deliver those messages through the best possible communication channels to precisely targeted marketing segments. This task is executed for purposes of informing, reminding, and/or persuading prospects or customers that the particular marketing value delivered by the Firm's product represents the market's most logical choice. The Firm's product is the best choice because it best solves customer problems.

Marketers should also accept the need to manipulate because they should understand the extent to which most customers need to feel unique at the same time they need to feel that they fit in. "How can marketers "thread that particular needle" without too much manipulation?" In marketing often the most productive way to promote the value of a product is not to describe how much you will benefit from consuming the product, but rather to emphasize how much you will suffer if you don't consume the product. This is manipulation, to be certain, but this is also an ethically sound persuasive tactic that is driven by the purpose of satisfying or solving customer needs or problems.

Marketers still should be judicious whenever they execute manipulative communication efforts because, in the end, customers will decide which marketing communication mostly makes sense and which mostly makes noise. Which brings us to the issue of sincerity. The secret to success in a surprising number of quarters, Hollywood, leadership, and marketing, for starters, is an ability to demonstrate the appearance of sincerity in one's communications.

Is it true then that once you can fake sincerity you have got it made, communication-wise? We'll leave it up to readers to ascertain whether we just delivered a sincere lesson in the preceding sentence. In other words, were we manipulating (yuck) or teaching you another useful concept (yea) by writing that sentence. Your call.

These four baseline communication principles are useful and nearly universal in their application. But they alone are far from enough to ensure marketing promotional success. Marketers seeking breakout communicative success should also honor three additional keys to successful communication. These follow.

→ Other Keys to Marketing Communication Success

First Key: Begin with Ends in Mind

Marketing communications presumably should always deliver one or more of the following communication outcomes: remind, inform, or persuade (influence). Alternatively, marketer communicators might incentivize (motivate) targeted customers.

Reminder communications should remind targeted recipients why they once loved the marketing object of communication. Reminder communications tell customers, in effect: "Don't You Forget about Me." This simple message should be delivered with the same compelling and memorable spirit that The Simple Minds did as they sang this song as the classic 1985 movie *The Breakfast Club* was ending. Reminder messages should generally prove more useful during the maturity or decline stages of products' life cycles; that is, after the product/brand is already well-known. Most people, including customers, need to be reminded more often than they need to be instructed or persuaded. People generally know the right thing to do. Sometimes they just require prompting to do it.

Informative messages create awareness of something new, special, different, or better that is happening now or available. No one has ever bought any new product or participated in any special marketing experience until s/he was informed or made aware of the "new" or "special" thing. The pivotal New Testament book of Romans (Chapter 10, Verses 14–16), written by the Apostle Paul, discusses a thing or two about the need to create awareness; to strategically inform others about something new and special.

Key verses read: "How then will they call on him in whom they have not believed. And how are they to believe in him [at the time of writing, a new, innovative idea and product] of who they have never heard? And how are they to hear [about the new idea and product] without someone [a marketer] preaching [communicating, or in this case spreading the good news]. As it is written, "How beautiful are the feet of those who spread the good news!" The Bible, it seems, gives a historical shout-out to marketers who inform the world about anything that is good, or, in *Marketing from Scratch*'s language, anything that is valuable. Informative messages generally would be more appropriate during the introduction or growth stages of a product's life cycle.

Persuasive communications persuade. To persuade in communications contexts, marketers should demonstrate, through carefully designed messages, how and why making the choice that they are advocating will help customers achieve their goals. This approach to persuasion epitomizes the marketer as "need-satisfier" and "problem-solver." Who wouldn't be persuaded by such a marketer and message? Persuasion, at its core, can prove that simple.

Persuasion is the centerpiece of business activity. You want to succeed in business, right? Then learn how to persuade others. Customers, for example, must be persuaded to buy products. Employees must be persuaded to agree with or contribute to strategic plans. Investors must be persuaded to invest. Supply chain partners must be persuaded to partner and participate collaboratively in mutually beneficial relationship. Not coincidentally, customers, employees, investors, or supply chain partners each will be persuaded by exactly the same thing: the perception that they are taking away at a little more value from the exchange relationship than they are putting into the exchange relationship.

Just as everyone wants to be more powerful, everyone wants to be more persuasive. The ability of marketers to develop perceived or actual values in their products provides the basis for most marketing persuasion. These values, naturally, are subsequently disseminated (delivered) to others through communication efforts. After actually persuading others, marketers may not know whether it was their message or how they said it that generated the outcome. Consequently, marketers should concentrate great attention when developing and delivering each value.

When making decisions in either B2C or B2B settings, potential or actual customers almost always respond to incentives if those potential or actual customers are logical or rational. But not everyone, as you know, is "logical" in the same way. Hence, the need for segmentation and targeted marketing, which grants marketers the opportunity to position, develop, and deliver uniquely designed marketing mix values to each targeted customer segment (see Chapter 9). Communicating these values is a key element of the unique marketing programs developed by marketing Firms. Marketing promotions should provide incentives, create new incentives, and/or emphasize incentives that, in the views of message recipients, prove value-enhancing.

An incentive is something that inspires decision-makers into action. When doing something or buying something becomes more or less costly (less or more incentivizing) in terms of, say, money, risk, time-expended, stress, inconvenience, or prestige than doing or buying something else, which "something" do you believe rational people are going to do? Taylor Swift and her marketing team understand the power of a communicative incentive. When releasing her 1989 album, Ms. Swift offered three extra songs on the album to fans who purchased the whole thing as opposed to downloading songs individually. Any guesses regarding who sold the most albums during 2014?

Incentives generally differ from motivations. Incentives, which are often delivered through sales promotions (more about these in Chapter 17), are essentially legal "bribes" aimed at enticing customers to do something, now. Buyers' motivations for purchasing are more likely to be affected by advertisements or publicity, include "gifting" customers with opportunities to achieve valued benefits. These benefits are diverse, encompassing the product's functional utilitarian benefits, status, prestige, ability to earn higher returns, acquiring recognition, demonstrating affection or regard for others or even for yourself (because, after all, you deserve that premium-priced beverage, bag, or vacation experience. Go ahead, you've earned it and you're worth it!).

Incentives are powerfully good or powerfully bad communication tools. Loose use of incentives can trigger unintended and undesirable consequences. Think about the marketing incentives (i.e., huge price subsidies) that the Affordable Health Care Act is providing to some folks who earn just enough (actually, not quite enough) money to qualify them for health care subsidies. Consequently, Obamacare customers who receive such financial incentives may be incentivized to not work harder or longer to make more money because if they do, their health care incentives, or subsidies, would disappear. Not saying they would, but the possibility is worth consideration.

Second Key: Frame Messages and Choices Carefully

When communicating, marketers should frame the choices they present to actual or prospective customers as decisions that potentially lead to losses, rather than gains, if the decider chooses poorly. Gains or losses relating to money, efficiency or time; or social standing, companionship or love, for example. We learned during Chapter 11 how much more attention and power people ascribe to the prospect of failure (a loss) than they do the prospect of success (or winning). The prospect of loss, frankly, is far more motivating than the prospect of gain.

Fail to engage with Fidelity Investments and its Green Line counsel and risk losing money and a more secure future. Fail to wear Old Spice and blow your chances with the ladies. Eat a cereal other than Wheaties and no championships for you.

The ease with which information is recalled and thus the probability that it will influence behaviors is influenced by the impact said information makes as it enters minds. Human minds respond most instinctually to and consequently are most influenced by three factors: fear, extreme tension (stress), and/or novelty (or "the new"). You're well aware by now of the glittering allure of the new.

Human brains are hard-wired to allocate more attention to things that appear threatening. These instinctual responses account for the disproportionate impact that fear and stress exercise in our lives. In the distant past, strangers, starvation, or sabre-toothed tigers (correctly named the sabre-toothed cat or *Smilodon fatalis*) actually were real-time threats to the survival of our ancestors. Those instincts were passed genetically from generational survivor to generational survivor right up to contemporary times. Negative information, communicated through marketing or other media (e.g. interpersonal or socially networked sources) is consequently stickier and more viral-like than is positive information. Bad, depressing, or scary marketing information, once communicated, is difficult to dislodge and spreads more quickly than good or positive information.

Human behaviors, when viewed collectively throughout market segments or entire markets, are rather predictable. Positive emotions, for example, make people more vulnerable than negative emotions. This is largely because positive emotions are more future-oriented, while negative emotions often resolutely adhere us to the present. Gratitude and joy, over time, yield better health and deeper human connections. But in the short-term, each positive emotion exposes people to greater risk of rejection and loss. Why? Because while negative emotions tend to insulate, positive emotions expose us to elements of rejection and heartbreak. Fear or sadness, by contrast, generate immediate defensive responses, largely because they protect people from emotional attack. Fear and sadness also motivate people to acquire shielding resources in response to times of stress or great need of the sort that would invoke fear. Fear spreads quicker than a virus. The fact that "if it bleeds it leads" on television, newspaper and website front-pages is grounded in this knowledge.

Smart marketers understand these things and often exploit them. For example, what proportion of negative to positive message do politicians employ in their marketing communications? Watch television during election season, and you will quickly see how big a role fear plays in contemporary political communications. Political advertisements will likely feature ominous background music; quick cuts highlighting shadowy and shady figures; and/or sonorous-voiced narrators offering alarming assertions about our "side's" vulnerability to myriad threatening possibilities, if the wrong choice is made. More often than not the core political message boils down to one "big idea": be scared, in fact, very afraid.

Or consider, how vigilantly teenagers and 20-somethings work to maintain or enhance their online reputations? Do teens engage in these activities driven more by their fear-of-falling-behind others' putative enjoyment of better stuff/experiences? Or is it simply FOMA, or the fear of missing out?

Fear, for most of us, is often little more than False Expectations Appearing Real. But fear unsurprisingly remains the most powerful human emotion. Stress is a huge motivator, as well. Few people have ever awakened at 2:35 AM, unable to return to sleep, because they were experiencing happiness or peace of mind. Smart marketing communicators exploit their awareness of this, too. Hopefully, however, not on you, because by now, you should also understand that while well-grounded fears do protect us from real dangers, our tendency to over-fear the prospect of failure often prevents us from pursuing genuine opportunities (Chapter 11).

These descriptions of customer and marketer behaviors are generally unflattering. They remain accurate, however. Marketers should always leverage their insights about human nature when communicating with customers, so long as they act in concert with appropriate ethical standards. Marketers should do the right thing because it is the right thing, not because the doing gives them something else to brag about. Consciously choosing to do right for and by others invariably offers marketers the opportunity to better themselves, as pointed out in Chapter 4.

Third Key: Honor the "Cs" of Good Communication

When messaging, marketers usually should explain their product/brand and the core differentiating values it delivers as Clearly, Concisely, and Compellingly as possible.

Clearly, so that the message might be better understood. Marketing messages, almost all messages, should be structured such they can be understood, not deciphered.

Concisely, because "brevity is the soul of wit." Whenever possible, marketing messages should feature both soul and wit. Wittiness, or humor, is frequently used and quite useful in marketing messaging. Humor provides message recipients with needed exercise and keeps customers' brains engaged. Engaged customer brains are always a positive for effective marketing communication, where the primary task is to structure and deliver messages and essentially beg for the customer's attention.

Compellingly, because, doggone it, effective marketing messages are either attention-worthy, memorable, persuasive or some combination of the preceding three traits. Creating compelling messages never proves easy. But then again, simply creating anything that is new and useful never is. Compelling messages differentiate, meaning that these messages deliver compelling value propositions that differ from and are better than the propositions delivered in competitors' messaging. Then and only then can marketers begin the task of building memory structures inside consumers' minds about the foundational value proposition.

The average human attention span—the amount of time one can allocate to a task without becoming distracted—was traditionally about 30 seconds. In an age where Internet and satellite television channel browsing has become rule rather than exception, attention spans have dramatically shortened. Internet users, for example, spend less than one minute on the average website.[8] A popular Calgary, Canada radio station only plays songs that have been edited to half their original length.[9] The station boasts "twice the songs." Perhaps, however, it should also report half-the-music. Technology driven multi-tasking has made many people feel far more time-pressed. Consequently, now, more important than ever before, marketers need to make their point quickly in whatever messages they construct.

Four other keys have been shown to contribute directly to contemporary communication success. Let's call these the "4-C's." The first key entails instant Comprehension. What does it say about Americans that they eat so much fast food so fast? We actually have no idea (presumably, Americans are hungry and hurried). But one clear consequence of this fast-food-analogy is that marketers should deliver instantly understandable messages.

In *Thinking, Fast and Slow*, Nobel Prize Economist Daniel Kahneman describes two different but equally effective frameworks through which people make decisions. The first is called "thinking fast." The second, "thinking slow."[10] "Thinking fast" occurs when people make decisions without really being aware of how they are making decisions. The fact is, absent substantial mental effort (or what we have called "involvement"), people don't "think" about the decision. "Thinking slow" arises when customers are highly attentive to, and thinking hard about, the decision we are making; similar to solving calculus equations, which most people are loathe to do.

Most consumer purchase decisions involve "thinking fast." Consumer brains generally default to purchase decision-making processes that are largely automatic and subconscious. When "thinking-fast" happens, consumer decisions are based on the quantity and depth of memory structures that have already been created through prior exposure to comprehensive communications about the brand. People have evolved to make simple, fast decisions when they evaluate new or known information. When communicating, marketers had better make their point, comprehensibly, and get to the point, quickly.

The second "C," or communication key, is Connection. To influence or be memorable, messages must resonate favorably with and trigger positive responses from targeted recipients. The term "resonate" is routinely used in contemporary language, as in, "that particular political message appeared to resonate with voters" or "the new brand's image resonated with targeted users."

But what does the word resonate mean in this context? Resonate implies messages should be designed specifically to affect or appeal in personal or emotional ways to targeted customer segments. Messages, in brief, should strike "resonate chords" with consumers to whom the messages are exposed.

Credibility of the message, which often includes the messenger is the third key to communication success. The importance of credibility was introduced earlier in this chapter. The value proposition is simple. For messages to be effective, recipients must believe what marketers are saying. Otherwise, they will rarely purchase what marketers are selling. Successful marketing, and thus successful communication, depends in no small measure on the presence of trust. Credible messages and messengers are trustworthy; i.e., such as mega-credible endorser Bill Cosby, until recently America's Dad. Trust is reciprocity flavored by emotion. Trust is knowing that you will get-back more or less the same amount of value that you give-out, over time. Trustworthy exchange partners can be counted on to tell the truth and honor their promises or commitments. Marketers and Firms that consistently message and behave in credible or trustworthy ways earn all manner of regard and respect from message recipients. Credible messages, like trusted brands, are powerfully but properly coercive. Good reputations deliver direct value to marketers. The more trust that marketers earn, the more business they will capture.

The CONTAGIOUSNESS of messages—our fourth key to communication success—gives messages legs (diffuses or spreads them around). In the process, contagiousness can enhance the trustworthiness or credibility of messages. When messages are contagious, people exposed to them often "talk-up" the messages and pass them along to others through various interpersonal, traditional, and digital means. This process tends to lend even greater credibility to the message.

These people are frequently called endorsers or evangelists. Evangelists, or evangelicals, are not bad words, although contemporary American culture sometimes appears inclined to designate them as such. The terms are simply ancient Greek words that mean bringer, or spreader, of good news. The good news could be about anything, including marketing messages, products/brands, or experiences. When marketers meet or exceed customer expectations, honor all promises they make, or engage quickly in service recoveries of the sort explained in Chapter 10 when things go wrong (as inevitably will happen), customer endorsements will likely be positive. Consequently, the news, for marketers, will likely be very good.

There's more, however. Customers can opt to trust what other customers tell them, or to trust what marketers tell them. Customers might also choose to trust neither. But other customers, probably either their friends, family members or co-workers, have no vested interest when spreading good (positive endorsements) or bad messages (negative endorsements) about given Firms, products, or brands. Other customers instead are simply reporting what they really believe about what they've seen or experienced. This does not apply to marketers themselves, who always have financial interests vested in what they say. So who are customers going to believe or trust?

The value of any favorable word-of-mouth endorsement that emerges from friends, family members, or co-workers of potential or actual customers is difficult to measure. Consumers who spread the good word as a product or brand evangelists are not trying to sell something for profit. Friends, family, etc. endorse because they actually like; they recommend because they actually believe; they advocate knowing their advocacy will never benefit them financially. Consumers who are the recipients of advocacy messages realize this to be true. As a result, this realization is the primary source of the extraordinarily persuasive power embedded in word-of-mouth. Word-of-mouth (WOM) endorsements are often best friends or worst enemies to organizations as they market and message.

Consumer initiated and positive WOM, you see, redeems marketers from their original sin of saying what they say for—like Cuba Gooding's character in the movie *Jerry McGuire*—the money. And many marketers, as many consumers suspect, indeed will say anything to gain the green. Not so the WOM-initiating friends or family members of these consumers. Friends and family members say what they say about brands or companies because they really believe it.

→ More about Word-of-Mouth and e-Word-of-Mouth

Word-of-mouth entails informal person-to-person communication between a non-marketing communicator and a customer about the ownership or characteristics of a brand, product, service, organization, or marketer.[11] Product, service, or branding information obtained from family members, friends, associates, and neighbors is more influential than information received through marketer-controlled communications, for reasons just explained. The power of WOM communications derives from the fact that somebody whom the message recipient knows and likes becomes the credible, believable, and trustworthy face of the brand. When the associated message is positive, WOM is marketers' most powerful type of promotion.

Almost everything in life, however, exists as a good news/bad news story. Moreover, marketing exists as a significant part of everyone's life. And the bad is more prevalent and powerful (influential) than the good in WOM communication settings. This tendency is especially apparent in e-retail online settings, which are rife with e-WOM and where most visitors check online reviews before buying anything. These de facto social networking sites integrate the "social" (peer to peer) with the "search" (key words) through the "D" ("Digital" communication transmission). When using social media, customers expect negative posts or tweets. Consequently, they often discount the otherwise negative effects in favor of judging how effectively the purportedly offending Firm handled the issue; i.e., the quality of the offending Firm's "recovery" response. Hope always exists that effective marketers might convert "injured" customers into brand loyalists, and subsequently into evangelists who advocate what is good about the Firm.

Bad news or potentially threatening events are more memorable than good news or soothing circumstances. Messages that create "better-watch-out" effects in the minds of recipients will grab more consumer mind-space; those messages will climb higher on the metaphorical ladders discussed during Chapter 1. The negative, as you know, is also simply more interesting to most of us. As mid-20th century American poet, story-teller, and satirist Dorothy Parker famously said: "If you don't have anything good to say about someone, come sit right by me." Ms. Parker was hardly unique in revealing this ironically humorous observation about human behavior. Gossip entails two or more people telling things about a third that the "third-party" would prefer not be known. Too often for Firms' liking, these third-parties are marketers for their brands, products, or messages. Negative WOM, which is hard to resist and perhaps more difficult still not to spread, is akin to marketing gossip. And, truth-be-told, who does not like gossip?

This potential threat of negative WOM for marketers and their brand-related communications has heightened exponentially during the last 15 or so years, an era during which the Internet came of age. The Internet makes scale-free, low-cost connectivity possible between a) marketers and customers, b) customers and marketers, and c) customers and customers. Wherever scale-free, low-cost connectivity exists, huge numbers of networked users also exist. Within these networks, good and bad messages about messages and brands flow reciprocally in quick, open, and largely unfettered fashions. E-WOM exists simultaneously as communication opportunity and communication threat to marketers.

E-WOM communication, like traditional WOM, entails any positive or negative accounts offered by potential, current, or former customers about products, brands, or marketing organizations. The impactful difference, however, is that these beneficial or harmful endorsements are potentially made available to hordes of humans (think herds of Zombie-like creatures from *The Walking Dead*) through Internet-mediated communication channels. These communication channels include various marketing media, including instant messaging, Twittering, Websites, blogs, social networking sites, Instagram(s), emails, and text messaging.

Text messaging, for example, is a contemporary, largely customer-driven channel through which e-WOM is widely disseminated. The average American teenager sends about 2000 texts per month. For teens and increasingly for people in their 20s and 30s, texting is their default communication mode. More than 97% of texts are read, and 90% are read in the first three minutes of receipt. This percentage is about four times higher than the rate at which emails are read.[12] Baby Boomer parents of Millennials and Generation X children are slowly or suddenly realizing their texts were read, even if there was no response. This same parental cohort has mostly given up hope that phone calls would be listened to in a similar fashion.

This is the contemporary world in which most marketers now communicate. Marketers must remain vigilant at all times for signs of trouble, because bad news spreads basically at the speed of light in an e-world. Yet this watchfulness itself will not assure that the promised levels of product/service quality and problem-solving value that were communicated to customers will actually be delivered. That's because, try as they may, things inevitably go wrong in the lives of products/brands and marketers/marketing organizations. But because they are vigilant, individual marketers and Firms will be better able to engage in quick-response service recovery efforts or other restorative practices when things, including communication efforts, fail to work as planned. Simply being observant and responsive permits Firms to avoid a good deal of negative WOM and e-WOM that otherwise would certainly arrive.

→ Integrated Marketing Communication

The ultimate secret formula for achieving sustainable marketing communication success is not a secret. First, accept environmental change as normal and permanent. Second, adapt constantly in response to these ever-changing environmental circumstances. The entire world, not just the marketing world, has changed dramatically during the last 10–20 years. Change is not necessarily good nor is it necessarily bad. Change just is. Change is also inevitable, and always necessary for progress to occur—including communicative progress.

Environmental and technological change, of course, can generate growth and facilitate appropriate improvements, particularly among the Firms that are first to spot and respond to the changes. Integrated marketing communications (IMC) is one the most important changes and improvements that marketers themselves have developed during recent decades. IMC was introduced in response to environmental and technological changes and the marketing communication challenges that those environmental and technological changes wrought.

Today's integrated marketing communications (IMC) effort involves every department in the Firm becoming involved in developing and communicating messages to customers, channel members, other stakeholders, and publics to create a unified image of the organization and its products.[13] Probably the real strength of the IMC concept lies in the two-way communications that are emphasized between the Firm and all relevant audiences. By exchanging information with these audiences, rather than just directing information toward them, stronger relationships are nurtured. This two-way exchange implies that the Firm must thoroughly understand the information needs of its audiences. Marketing research is absolutely essential to fully characterize relevant target audiences in terms of information needs, media viewing habits, and likely responses to communications activities.

Worth emphasizing again, IMC is a communication process that was developed to ensure that all elements of a Firm's marketing communications are fully integrated with one another, are directly relevant to customers to whom they are directed, and yield a unified message that is consistent across media and time. The IMC process may be compared to a song composed by four rock band instrumentalists. The guitar might function like advertising; the piano might prove akin to sales promotion; the bass like public relations and publicity; and the drums similar to personal selling. The goal shared among the four composers: create a process that permits each instrument to blend-together in ways that generate a memorable, attention-worthy, and exciting and/or emotionally-evocative song. Substitute the word "message" for the word "song" and you should have a better sense of what should unfold during the IMC process.

Still, in either the music-development or promotion message-development setting, this integrative task is challenging. Each musical instrument, after all, delivers differing musical values every bit to the extent that advertising, sales promotions, public relations and publicity, and personal selling likewise deliver differing communication values. For example, there are times and places when musicians should emphasize guitar licks, rather than piano chords; just like there are times and places when marketers should emphasize public relations rather than some other promotional messaging activity.

Rising Trends; Germane Changes

The media marketplace has recently changed at a speed and to a degree that exceeded almost everyone's expectations. Hundreds of television stations/networks and thousands of social networking and other online media sites are suddenly competing for finite consumer mind-space and time resources. Not that many years ago there were only three television networks. If a well-resourced marketer wanted to reach 50% of American consumers it could advertise three times on Bonanza during the 1960s or five times on Seinfeld, as recently as the late 1990s. Expensive, yes; effective, absolutely.

Today, dozens if not at times hundreds of stations are available on everyone's television sets. Still, viewers struggle to settle on which channel to watch every bit to the extent that marketers cannot identify the best one to use as a message delivery vehicle. This makes sense. The number of options customers are given impact what they choose, if they choose anything at all, and how satisfied they are with their choices. The basic point is that it is usually better to give consumers fewer rather than more choices. Is there any wonder why marketers have so much trouble reaching consumers and consumers, in turn, often have so much trouble making good choices? The effects of DVRs on marketing communication efforts should also be considered. The DVR innovation is radically changing the traditional advertising media model because it permits consumers to time-shift (watch programs or sporting events when they want to watch them) and essentially skip advertisements by speeding through them.

Then again, not long ago, there were exactly zero social networking or Internet-mediated sources of information through which marketer-to-customer, customer-to-marketer, or customer-to-customer communication exchanges could occur. Talk about a changing marketing and communications environment! Social media and mobile devices have also become remarkably more important to consumers and to marketers. Seemingly endless reservoirs of vanity and self-interest drive much of consumers' use of social media. Again, these conditions are neither good nor bad. But the same digital trends that make marketers' communications efforts potentially more rewarding for both marketers and consumers simultaneously make said communication efforts more difficult to execute successfully.

An abundance of media options has led to a deficit of customer attention. The communication efficacy of many marketer messages has declined so far that sometimes the only ones who really still believe in the effectiveness of advertising or the accuracy of marketing claims are advertisers and marketers. No, actually, things have not quite gotten that bad, but things are bad enough.

Modern media usually either deliver affirmation or fear. As they enter the contemporary media world, fewer consumers desire to hear the truth as opposed to hearing that they're "right." Relatedly, do more consumers visit their favorite media site to be informed or to be affirmed?

The media—for whom good news is an oxymoron—loves a crisis and appears to actively foment crises whenever possible. News media (CNN, Fox, the *New York Times*, even the *Wall Street Journal*) today often operate as if they were in the news-production rather than the news-reporting business. News cycles come and go out of date, essentially becoming unsellable, unusable, and unbelievable, with tremendous velocity.

All of which means another onslaught of new information is soon to appear? Is anyone surprised that fewer people are paying attention anymore?

This attention-deficit trend is very much alive online. Fifty-six percent of digital ads are never "in view."[14] "In view," in this context, is defined on being on-screen for more than one second. Marketers are paying the online media to deliver illusory messages, because these messages are generally never seen.

Domestic consumer market segments are now more splintered and fragmented than at any point in history. This change has similarly created various opportunities and threats to marketing organizations. The sort of creative destruction originally discussed by Austrian economist Joseph Schumpeter is currently raging throughout the developed world. (The creative destruction concept suggests, correctly in our view, that in order for new things to be created and accepted in the business world, older things must be rejected and destroyed. These things include products, brands, business models, technologies, organizations, etc.)[15]

Once again we can report that this market segment disintegration is neither good nor bad. Instead this environmental trend represents and imposes an ongoing challenge that contemporary marketers must overcome in order to communicate effectively. Marketers, in fact, are increasingly addressing this demographic and media-diversity inspired fragmentation with great effectiveness. They now target precisely-tailored messages to precisely-identified customer segments with greater precision than ever. Go online, purchase one book from a particular genre, say, a vampire mystery, and instantly receive seven or more "you might also like" recommendations. That's modern marketing messaging; that's contemporary marketing communication; that's precisely targeted marketing communication.

These still-trending environmental changes have contributed to a more diverse marketplace and a communication environment in which it has become difficult to earn and sustain the sort of message credibility and believability and customer attention that is necessary for marketing communications to succeed. These conditions are likewise contributing to communication environments in which many customers are ignorant of and apathetic about anything outside their Facebook (or other social networking sites) worlds. Consequently, these customers don't know and surely don't care about what marketers say. Too many Americans voluntarily live in low-information worlds.

Why Integrated Marketing Communication Is Important

Customers generally don't make distinctions between the message sources used by Firms. Why should they? Customers have no obligation to pay attention or think extensively about marketing messages. Consequently, the differing media and communication messages employed by any Firm should be structured such that they collectively provide a single, crisp, and unifying message. Consider the meaning of the word, integrated. Integrated means to strategically put together various, often independent, parts or elements and combine them into a more effective whole. Then tag the well-known suffix "marketing communication" onto the word. That's integrated marketing communication.

The messages delivered through integrated marketing communications should be Clear, Consistent, and Compelling. IMC messages should also be focused on a single determinant idea or point-of-difference (POD) that the singular marketing message conveys as it is delivered through various communication media to which targeted consumers may be exposed. The various communication media through which marketing organizations might deliver their messages include traditional media such as television, radio, newspapers and magazines, or even billboards.

Say or think what you will about billboards as communication venues, but they are a media that never interrupts your favorite television or radio programing. Well-placed and effectively-designed billboards are also quite likely to grab your attention at least several times a week, which is more than can be said from most other traditional media. Billboards work exceedingly well as you are stuck in traffic, "parked along your favorite" highway cum parking-lot.

Non-traditional communication channels through which marketers deliver messages include increasingly important digital sources such as websites, blogs, social networking sites, or emails. Experts have long believed that humans communicate and connect with one another much better when they interact face to face. But as the use of digital media has proliferated, does this traditional communication premise still apply, especially among younger cohorts? The answer is unclear. One thing is more certain: as screen time rises, direct human-to-human interaction decreases proportionately. Marketers and teachers alike understand this trend all too well. For years, each group has watched younger people perform mindless vanishing-attention acts.

The use of IMC allows marketers to "target and touch" the same segments from different angles. IMC likewise enables marketers to target different segments with the same message at the same time. Marketing communicators similarly don't generally care about the particular source from which customers receive messages. Instead, their primary concern is whether customers receive messages in the first place.

The use of IMC ensures a higher probability that marketers will enjoy media continuity. As noted, the same message is supposed to be conveyed across all media used by the marketing communicator when IMC principles are followed. The memorability or the recall of advertising and other forms of promotional messaging deteriorates across time. But by staying on air or the web and thus by staying top-of-the-mind, IMC's media hardens and sharpens the memory structures associated with brands.

IMC Delivers ...

The use of IMC makes it possible for marketing communicators to achieve communication objectives through the coordinated use of different promotional approaches that supposedly complement one another. Those communication objectives, you hopefully remember, include the generation of greater customer awareness; the development of additional customer knowledge; the cultivation of more liking and preference for the product/brand among customers; the execution of successful customer reminders and/or calls-to-action; the expansion of brand equity and brand loyalty amongst targeted customer segments; and, ultimately, the developing of greater marketer and/or branding persuasiveness. The successful use of IMC permits marketing communicators to deliver clear, consistent, and compelling messages as these classic promotional mix elements are integrated to create synergistic effects through a comprehensive communications plan.

The use of IMC fundamentally requires that consistent brand-related messaging be delivered across traditional and digital marketing communication channels. Rather than simply using differing media to "tell and sell" an overarching branding narrative (which is, on the surface, not a bad thing), the IMC approach provides greater assurance that the respective strengths of each communication channel will be leveraged by the Firm to create more favorable communication outcomes than any channel would have achieved individually.

The extensive application of basic IMC principles by marketing organizations as diverse as President Barak Obama's two successful presidential campaigns, the viral-like outcomes engendered by *The Walking Dead* production organization, or the Target store brand's repositioning has triggered various shifts in how Firms market to consumers and other customers. These shifts include trends that are moving:

- From preferred use of traditional marketing communications to greater engagement with digital/interactive communications.
- From greater use of mass media (ABC, NBC or CBS, or *Time* magazine) to more specialized media (Twitter, Instagram, and Spotify).
- From low-accountability in the terms of the effectiveness of communication expenditures (i.e., what advertisements are and are not working effectively) to high-accountability in terms of communication-spend effectiveness.
- From limited, one-way buyer-seller connectivity to more pervasive, two-way (reciprocal) connectivity.

→ Determining the IMC Budget

Communications budgets are established in various ways. The most commonly employed methods for setting budgets include the percentage of sales method, competitive-parity method, affordable method, and the objective and task method.

Percentage of Sales Method

With the percentage of sales method, the budget is set at some fixed percentage of the previous year's sales or next year's forecasted sales. For example, if sales of $1,500,000 are anticipated for next year and the promotion budget is limited to 5% of sales, the total promotion budget will be $75,000. The percentage of sales method is probably the most commonly employed method of budgeting because of its simplicity. The drawback to this technique is that expected sales drive the size of the promotion budget; in other words, anticipated sales revenue determines or causes promotion expenditures. In theory, the relationship should be the other way around; promotion should "cause" sales to occur. This type of thinking can lead to a reduction in the promotion budget when sales are down. But of course this is exactly the time when promotion may need to be increased in order to reverse the sales decline.

Competitive Parity Method

When budgets are established with this method, the size of the budget is driven by how much one's competitors are spending. Generally, this information can be obtained from competitors' annual reports, from trade association data, and from costing the different types of promotions in which competitors are engaged. This latter technique is referred to as "decomposing" competitors' promotion and can be used to gauge the size of the promotion budget as well as provide insight into competitors' objectives, strategies, and tactics. Determining how much one's competitors are spending on promotion is always wise. But Firms should never assume that their budget should be set at the same level. Competitors may be over- or under-spending based on their own promotion objectives. Your objectives may be very different, suggesting that a different budget may be needed.

All You Can Afford Method

With this method, the communications budget is essentially equal to any money left over after all other expenditures have been met. With this method, budgets tend to be higher when times are good and virtually non-existent when sales are down. This budgeting method, therefore, suffers from the same limitation as does the percentage of sales method: the level of revenue generated determines the size of the promotion budget.

Objective and Task Method

Using this method, budgets are set by first identifying exactly what communications objectives are being pursued and then setting the budget to achieve them. The objective and task method of budgeting is, realistically, the best approach to employ, although not normally the easiest. It is the only approach that specifically allocates promotion dollars to achieve specific objectives. In other words, the communications expenditures cause sales, not the other way around. When the objective and task method is used, the overall communications budget is built up from specific budgets allocated to each promotional activity that is needed to achieve objectives.

Because the basic purpose of promotion inherently involves persuasion, the Firm's promotion activities are subject to scrutiny from a variety of sources. Indeed, promotion has been highly criticized on several grounds. Various laws exist that constraint promotional activities. The purpose of these laws is to ensure that Firms never intentionally/unintentionally mislead consumers and other audiences with their communications. Laws exist at federal and state levels. Other private organizations have also established regulations that provide promotion guidelines. The following reviews certain major criticisms of promotion and key federal laws/regulations that have emerged as a result of these criticisms.

→ Legal Constraints on Promotion

Firms' communications programs have long faced criticism from various publics. These publics include consumers themselves, advocacy and watch-dog groups, government agencies, and the general public. Certain criticisms are summarized below.

Promotion Misinforms Consumers

Firms have been accused of misrepresenting the truth, or flat-out lying about a product's benefits and characteristics with their communications. Some promotional claims absolutely exaggerate a product's benefits. For example, most of you can probably cite examples of ads for different brands of the same product type that all claim they are the "best," provide the most value, or make some other claim that attempts to emphasize superiority over the competition. Clearly, such claims are exaggerated; they all can't be the best. These rather mild claims of superiority are generally called "puffery." Communication that goes beyond simple puffery, however, is troubling. These latter communications making more extreme claims may be declared as deceptive or even fraudulent. Such claims may be illegal and the responsible Firms are subject to investigation and possible prosecution. More discussion about puffery is provided in the next chapter.

Promotion Is Unjustifiably Expensive

Corporate communication efforts can prove extremely expensive. As noted, the average 30-second 2015 Super Bowl ad cost in excess of $4.5 million, up from $1.6 million in 2000. When costs of production are included, the total price tag is prohibitive for all but the largest Firms. Opponents of promotion argue that exorbitant costs substantially inflate the costs of products to consumers, while hindering the ability of smaller Firms to compete. However, if promotion is successful at stimulating added demand for the Firm's products, the added promotion costs may be offset by dramatic declines in production and other marketing costs due to increased scale economies. These lower costs can be passed on to consumers as lower prices. This argument, however, does not rectify any negative impact on smaller competing Firms. Indeed, the one-sided competitive advantage is exacerbated by the lower prices now offered by larger, better financed Firm's.

Promotion Can Classically Condition Some Consumer Groups

Critics of beer, wine, and cigarette advertising have claimed for decades that advertisements for these products classically condition consumers into buying products that are ultimately harmful to both the consumer and the broader society. While there may be some truth to these claims with respect to the ability of promotion to influence some segments of the population for some types of products, the effects of promotion to effectively "brainwash" consumers are exaggerated. The net effect of most promotion is too weak of a stimulus to make people do things against their wills. Advertisers simply do not have that kind of control over consumers.

Federal Laws and the Federal Trade Commission

Three major federal laws; the Federal Trade Commission Act, The Robinson-Patman Act, and the Lanham Trademark Act, have been established to regulate promotion activities of Firms engaged in interstate commerce.

The Federal Trade Commission Act

The Federal Trade Commission Act of 1914 prohibits unfair competitive practices. False, misleading, and deceptive advertising are included within the scope of the Act. Prior to 1938, per the FTC Act, the courts had to prove that false or deceptive advertising harmed competitive interactions before action could be taken. This limitation was rectified with passage of the Wheeler-Lea amendment to the FTC Act in 1938. This latter piece of legislation expanded the meaning of "harm to competitors" to include any injury to public interests resulting from promotional practices. The FTC was granted the authority to make advertisers modify their communications if they were deemed unfair. The FTC can require that Firms fully disclose (full disclosure) in its promotions all data necessary for a consumer to make safe and informed decisions. In addition, the FTC can force Firms to substantiate (substantiation) its claims with evidence of all claims that are made in its communications.

The FTC has a series of solutions available to it should it rule that a Firm has been engaged in false or misleading messaging. The primary solutions include:

- *Consent Decrees* are the simplest form of "remedy." Offending Firms agree to stop their deceptive claims. This is the least drastic remedy.

- *Cease-and-Desist Orders* are employed when advertisers refuse to engage in the consent decree. The FTC can use Cease-and-Desist orders to force Firms to remove offend-ing communications from circulation. Unfortunately, Firms can appeal Cease-and-Desist orders and continue to air the offending communication while the case is under appeal.

- *Corrective Advertising* is the next most extreme remedy available to the FTC. The offending Firm is forced to retract the false or misleading claims of which it is accused. The Firm must pay for any promotion required to correct its false claims. And the Firm must use the content and a media schedule specified by the FTC. The FTC's forced use of corrective advertising has been fundamentally ineffective in its attempts to reshape consumer's false impressions about product claims. In fact, corrective advertising was not ordered by the FTC for more than 25 years until 1999. At that time, Novartis Consumer Health was required to run $8 million in corrective advertising for Doan's Pills. Novartis, while promoting Doan's, falsely claimed that the pills were more effec-tive at alleviating back pain than those of competing Firms.[16] Probably the most widely publicized case of corrective advertising required Warner-Lambert Co.'s Listerine to spend over $10 million to correct 40 years of previous messages claiming that regular use of the product could essentially cure the common cold. The FTC required Lister-ine to run corrective ads in 1977 and 1978 for 18 months stating that "Listerine will not help prevent colds or sore throats or lessen their severity." However, the net impact of these ads was negligible. Most consumers of the era still attributed Listerine with the ability to fight the common cold.[17]

- *Fines (restitution)* are the most severe remedy available to the FTC. Such penalties can be mandated along with the other remedies cited above. The FTC may stipulate that fines are paid to the government and/or to those consumers who may have been harmed by claims made in the Firm's ads. For example, in 1991 Pfizer was forced by the FDA to pay 10 states a total of $70,000 to settle charges relating to misleading advertising for its Plax mouthwash for treating and preventing gum disease.[18] Hardly a substantive amount even in 1991.

The Robinson-Patman Act

The Robinson-Patman Act, better known for regulating pricing activities, also limits Firms' use of promotional allowances as they attempt to incentivize middlemen. Sellers must offer promotional allowances to intermediaries on a proportionally equal basis, meaning that the magnitude of any allowances offered must be in proportion to the magnitude of sales made to that intermediary. Otherwise, the seller may be subject to charges of price discrimination. Promotional allowances can include a diversity of payments or services ranging from actual dollar payments to the assistance of sales persons in setting up displays or giving away free samples. In general, the courts have ruled that "proportionally equal" means proportionally equal to the dollar amounts of the product purchased from the seller.

The Lanham Trademark Act

The Lanham Trademark Act of 1946 grants Firms the opportunity to acquire trademark protection for their brands and brand identifiers. Lanham offers Firms exclusive rights to the use of words, names, symbols, and combinations of letters or numbers, or other distinctive devices (slogans and distinctive packaging) that uniquely identify their brands.

A 1988 revision to the Lanham Act (Trademark Law Revision Act) made it illegal to make false claims about the Firm's own brand when making comparisons with competing brands. Based on the Trademark Law Revision Act, advertisers are able to file civil suits based on false claims made about their brands in comparative ads. In 1996, Campbell Soup Company successfully defended ads for its Prego brand spaghetti sauce against a suit brought by its largest competitor, Ragu. Campbell ran a series of demonstration ads designed to show that Prego was thicker than Ragu. The Court upheld the legitimacy of the claim.[19] In another case, U-Haul International was awarded over $42 million in damages by the US Court of Appeals for the Ninth Circuit Court for violations of the Lanham Act by a competitor, Jartran. Jartran aired a series of comparative ads that made deceptive comparisons with U-Haul of rental rates and truck sizes.[20]

Other Federal Regulatory Agencies

In addition to the Federal Trade Commission, the Federal Communications Commission, the Food and Drug Administration, and the Bureau of Alcohol, Tobacco, and Firearms are involved in regulating some aspects of Firms' promotion activities.

The Federal Communications Commission (FCC)

The FCC, established in 1934, cannot directly regulate a Firms' promotional activities, but it does have jurisdiction over some media industries (radio, television, and telephone) that may carry the Firm's communications. In this capacity, the FCC can indirectly control some message content aired via these media, such as obscenity and indecency in ads. The FCC can refuse to grant licenses and renewals of licenses to Firms in these industries that air programming (including ads) that are counter to the public interest.

The Food and Drug Administration (FDA)

Created in 1906 by the Pure Food and Drug Act, the FDA has jurisdiction over aspects of food and prescription drug labelling and branding. This law sets the standards for the content of labels placed on products. The FDA dictates that labels on products must identify the contents of the package (i.e., its ingredients, the size and locations of labels on the product's packaging), and the names and addresses of the producer, packer, or distributor.[21] Since product labelling usually parallels the content of the product's advertising, the FDA essentially has some control over the content of the advertising as well as the labelling of products. Thus label claims must be:

- Truthful and not misleading.
- Supported by legitimate, reliable, and research data that is publicly available.
- Based on accepted medical and nutrition principles.

In 1993 food labelling requirements were strengthened to standardize across products how the nutritional content of food products must be identified. Exact definitions and guidelines were spelled out for how terms such as "low fat," "low cholesterol," and "high fibre" are used on packages.

The FDA also controls prescription drug products. This control permits the agency to dictate the labelling and content of advertising messages aimed at both consumers and the medical industry for these products. Since many pharmaceutical Firms promote directly to consumers in an attempt to "pull" their products into distribution channels, the FDA can require that the same detailed information be provided to consumers that may otherwise have only been provided to physicians.

Bureau of Alcohol, Tobacco, and Firearms (BATF)

The BATF regulates the advertising of alcohol, tobacco, and firearms indirectly due to its ability to superintend the production and distribution of these products. The BATF grants and renews permits to manufacturers of these products. As a result, BATF dictates content that must appear on the labelling for these products. This includes mandating that facilities (i.e. retailers) selling these products prominently display warning labels identifying the hazards associated with using these products.

The Internet: Mediator of Marketing Communication

Modern communication technologies exercise roughly as much influence on human behaviors as the messages that they carry. Think about what was just written. This is a big deal. The primary reason why this is true is because modern communication tools (phones, email, social networking sites) essentially function as extensions of our bodies.

Phones first provided ordinary ears distant and eventually global reach. Television next extended ears and eyes in ways no one could have anticipated when the first black and white screens appeared. More recently, the reach and grasp of the Internet has proven inescapable. Extraction from the crowd is now impossible, unless users decide to toss their Internet-enabled devices. The Internet has made the information world more dominant. As screens have shrunk, the role played in our lives by the information those screens convey has grown. Is the Internet sucking us into a dwarf world or hurling us untethered into a giant universe? The answer is debatable.

This much is known, however: every time new-generation communication technologies are adopted, the consequences alter how consumers receive, process, and perceive (make sense of) information, including marketing communications. Consumers adopting these new technologies inhabit new realities that have been fundamentally altered by their acceptance of these new communication tools.

Each new-generation technology creates new markets for marketers to pursue and new communication channels through which to deliver messages. Each new-generation communication technology creates new environments in which customers think, decide, and consume. Technology creates new markets and environmental trends. The emergence of new markets and environments often destroys old markets and environmental trends. The entire marketing communication and promotional process has been effected for better or worse (depending on the Firm) by the proliferation of Internet-mediated media and channels. Marketing communicators have had no choice but to acknowledge and adapt to these technologies themselves. As they have.

Digital Marketing and Social Networking

Digital marketing, formerly better known as e-marketing or Internet-marketing, has been around for a while. So has the "social network." Long enough that digital marketing and social networking are no longer viewed as new or mysterious. Long enough to prompt some critics to suggest that digital marketing hasn't made marketing better. Long enough to induce still other critics to argue that social networking sites have made human interactions worse. Most readers, we suspect, would disagree with the preceding statement. Perhaps your view depends on whether you prefer texts and tweets or hugs and handshakes. As for your authors, we're agnostic.

But one important communication consequence is clear: new social media have given consumers another way to keep score. And consumers have leapt into this scorekeeping game in a big way. You have got 50 Twitter followers. Congratulations. But what about your friend with 500? Make you feel bad? Or Lady Gaga with 37 million? Make you feel worse, still? In an era driven by tweets, reality shows, and Facebook, everyone sees everything and almost everyone suffers by comparison to someone. This can prove problematic. Most consumers' Facebook friends, for example, post only a Sports Center highlight reel of their lives, leaving others feeling comparatively worse about their own lives. Still, when opportunities to make social comparisons (or established hierarchies such as social class) arise, people instinctively sort themselves out into higher and lower positions.

Communicating marketers should care about this consumer sorting process because they have the power to make consumers feel better or worse about themselves by presenting them with images of others who are higher or lower in status than them. Not pretty, not nice, but absolutely true. But little need exists for digital marketers to do this because social networking sites such as Facebook regularly permit consumers to do this to themselves. If most of the people in your Internet world appear better or worse off then you, no imagination is necessary. One irony: high-status folks usually don't feel better than the lower caste because they too are always being exposed to someone better off than them. Social network-ing actually often unfolds more like social comparison-ing, even among competing grandmothers.

A couple of related thoughts about consumers' online decisions and their subsequent happiness are worth considering. The more that consumers' decisions are motivated by an effort to impress other people, the lower the happiness boost for consumers. In the generally wealthy, on a global scale, US marketplace consumers enjoy ample opportunity to engage in exhibitionist or positional spending. So they do. Those same consumers enjoy ample opportunity to experience disappointment when expected happiness never arrives or proves fleeting. Again, they do, and as a result often buy again and again. Good outcomes for the economy, and for marketers, but for consumers and their emotional health? Often, not so much. Social networking creates situations where what consumers value and truly want often no longer matter as much as they did in an analog world. A useful test: would you still make the same purchase if no one was there to impress?

Over time, the value of any social network is defined not only by who is on it, but who is excluded. Which brings us to Facebook, the world's largest meritocratic democracy, an epoch-shifting cultural phenomenon, and social networking platform though which marketers can deliver messages and consumers can make comparisons.

Facebook's World, for Now

People are rarely highly motivated by what marketers say. Consumers are more likely to be motivated by what other people associated with particular Firms and brands do or say. Times arise, however, when marketers should distribute messages suggesting that you (individual consumers) are the thing making a given brand cool. And they do. Marketers also understand they need to insert that message in the right spot, once they have found the right spot, in order to reach the right customers. Marketers increasingly know that Facebook and similar social networking sites, represent the right spots on which to place their messages.

Facebook radically differs from traditional media. The algorithm that drives Facebook is configured to "measure" consumers' level of engagement with others who are like them. Facebook tracks what individual consumers, and other people who resemble those users, "like," comment on, and share. This makes Facebook a segmentation dream machine for marketing Firms. Facebook is also configured to show users more things related to what they have already indicated interests them. This capability also functions like catnip for marketing Firms because the social networking site also functions as a self-perpetuating target marketing and positioning tool. These are the two primary reasons why marketers persistently promote on Facebook.

But there is a third reason. Just as there is a "get and give" in any exchange, it takes "two to tango." Marketers would not go to Facebook unless customers were on Facebook. Facebook is able to successfully attract and retain users because it also operates as a self-perpetuating optimization machine for consumers. Imagine that when you turned on the television it ranked every episode of every show in terms of your past preferences, just for you. Or, when you went to a bar, only the people you liked, had been hanging out with, and were willing to let in were there.

We sense, however, that fewer consumers truly love Facebook anymore. At least not to the extent they did just a few years ago. (No surprise there. Facebook is no longer new, which means, by definition, Facebook is growing older inside the most important place: its current and future "fans'" minds. And, as you realize, younger people are not naturally inclined to love "old" stuff.) Users, however, still like and use Facebook for what it can do for them. There's no question about this. But people probably don't want to perform their lives publicly in the same way today they did five years ago.

Digital technology should bring, enhance, and improve human and marketing interactions. Has Facebook? Clearly, it has. Otherwise, the once new product would not have succeeded on such a global scale. Facebook succeeds because it trades value-for-value, based on an exchange process that the site expects/asks users to make. Post all your pictures, give us all your information, tag all your friends, and so on, forever. In return, you get an optimized social life. Any output is only as good as its input. How long will the current quality of customer information be sustained?

Firms that market digitally have grown reliant on Facebook's powerful message distribution abilities. Many marketers now act like kittens nuzzling up against their mama cat, mewing and jostling among siblings for nourishment. The nourishment these Firms seek, of course, is attentive eyeballs and ears from the proper demographic and psychographic segments.

This transformational movement toward Facebook and other social networking sites has weakened traditional marketing media. Print magazines and newspapers, cable and analog television programing and networks, and traditional radio stations each grounded their success in their ability to reach large, known, demographically and psychographically well-defined consumer segments. But more and more and more still of their more attractive (to marketers), less than 40-year-old consumers have absolutely abandoned traditional media. Fortuitously, one must assume, many of these customers ended up in the same place. Yes, you know where; you are probably there, too. Marketing communicators increasingly know how to currently reach them: visit Facebook, select options from pull-down menus—18 to 24 year old males from TX who closely follow college football—and targeted advertisements magically materialize in the feeds of these precisely defined demographic and psychographic segments.

Facebook will continue to serve as an alluring potential savior to marketing communicators until one day it is no longer effective. Newer technologies always win in the end as product life cycles and creative destruction have their say. After all, we live in a world that Myspace, Napster, and Donkey Kong once ruled. Father Time, as will you eventually learn, always bats last and hits 1.000.

→ Marketing Messaging: Subtle, Subversive, Sophisticated

Marketing messaging has steadily evolved across the years to the point where brand-related messaging, as communicated through brand logos and symbols, has generally grown quite sophisticated.[22] Even seemingly simple branding signs or icons are not so simple in terms of the intended messages being delivered. Then again, this should not surprise you. You learned earlier in this book that there is nothing simple about achieving simplicity.

Coke, the drink, as in what is now known as Coke Classic, originated as a syrup version of a French wine coca product. The iconic brand name of this drink, the product, emerged through an intersection of two key ingredients: extracts of "coca" (cocaine, yes really) and "kola" (caffeine extracted from the kola nut).

McDonald's customers supposedly have long unconsciously recognized the golden arches as being symbolic of a pair of nourishing breasts. McDonald's wanted to change its logo, even back in the 1960s. But fortunately Mickey D never got around to it. Of course, the now struggling brand would never consider ditching the iconic image. McDonald's, however, has notably decreased the Golden Arches' size (Exhibit 16.4).

Look carefully at the FedEx brand symbol. Can you find the hidden message? There is an arrow situated between the letters E and X. The arrow reflects the shipper's commitment to forward thinking, forward movement, and forward-looking hopes for the future.

The arrow in the Amazon logo, a symbol that curves like a smiley face, is intended to underscore one of Amazon's primary goals, as stated in its mission, which is to keep customers satisfied. The arrow stretches from A to Z in the word Amazon, underscoring the wide variety

Exhibit 16.4 *McDonald's arches have been substantially toned done in recent years, but the iconic symbol is not likely to go away entirely.*

of products that are available through Amazon. The actual use of the brand word "Amazon" was surely no accident. The Amazon River is far and away the world largest and most powerful. Founder Jeff Bezos' ambitious idea and goal was to birth a baby that one day would grow up to be the worlds' largest retailer—online or otherwise. Bezos is currently not far off his goal. The Amazon brand mark and some of those discussed below are illustrated in Exhibit 16.5.

The white lines passing through the IBM logo give the appearance of the equal sign in the lower right hand corner. Big Blue apparently wanted to reflect equality. The globe in AT&T's brand is three dimensional. 3-D captures the growing depth and range of products that AT&T remains committed to providing its customers. The Adidas logo represents a mountain. The mountain underscores the obstacles people must overcome along their pathway toward success. Great semiology for a company that develops, at its core, training shoes.

The Google logo features four primary colors in a row before they are broken by a secondary color. Google was signifying its playfulness within making the logo big or overwhelming. The logo also signalled the brand did not play by the rules.

With its roots in aviation, the BMW brand was designed with its roots in mind. The blue and white represent a propeller in motion, with the sky peeking through. The star in the rival Mercedes-Benz logo represents the company's dominance in style and quality over land, air and sea. The "volk" in Volkswagen means people (in German); the "wagen" car. Hence, the Volks-wagen was and remains the "car of" or "car for" the people.

BMW's competitor, Toyota, has long used a logo that features three ellipses. These ellipses symbolize three hearts. The heart of the customer, of the product, and of progress—with unbounded future opportunities for continuous improvement. Very Japanese, these messages.

Exhibit 16.5 *Iconic brand marks that speak metaphorically.*

*Clockwise from upper left: © Radu Bercan/Shutterstock.com; © nattul/Shutterstock.com; © Rob Wilson/Shutterstock.com;
© 360b/Shutterstock.com; © 360b/Shutterstock.com; © Helga Esteb/Shutterstock.com; © FooTToo/Shutterstock.com; ©
desk006/Shutterstock.com; © OlegDoroshin/Shutterstock.com*

From the start the NBC peacock logo was extremely colourful. This rainbow of color was supposed to drive viewers toward the then new product, color televisions, NBC, the Corporation, had a stake at the time in the development of color television.

The bitten-into Apple symbol signifies the bite from the forbidden tree of knowledge. The bite itself is supposedly representative of a computer byte. Apple, the corporation, originally purchased the rights to the now famous Apple logo from the Beatles. The Fab Four used the exact same logo when it became the first band to launch its own record label, which was called, yes, Apple. Only two artists were signed by the Apple record label. The first was James Taylor, who carved out a rather impressive career during the ensuing decades. The second artist was the until-recently largely forgotten English rock band, Badfinger. Badfinger, however, authored the song "Baby Blue" in 1972. This was the song Vince Gilligan choose to play during the last seconds and over the final credits of the iconic show, *Breaking Bad*. The opening lyrics ("Guess I got what I deserve …") of "Baby Blue," along with the song title itself, perfectly captured the core value of the spectacularly pure ("pure" being its determinant characteristic) new product that lead character Walter White developed in the show that many say is the greatest drama of all time.

Marketing messages, you see, are everywhere. Just like marketing itself. But the best marketing messages, as you long since should have ascertained on your own, would rarely, if ever, arrive accidentally.

Endnotes

1. Nathalie Tadena, "Super Bowl Ad Prices Have Gone Up 75% Over a Decade," *The Wall Street Journal* (January 12, 2015), accessed April 19, 2015, http://blogs.wsj.com/cmo/2015/01/12/super-bowl-ad-prices-have-gone-up-75-over-a-decade.

2. Brain Ross, Joseph Rhee, Angela Hill, Megan Churchman, and Aaron Katersky, "Toyota to Pay $1.2B for Hiding Deadly 'Unintended Acceleration'," *ABC News* (March 19, 2014), accessed April 25, 2015, http://abcnews.go.com/Blotter/toyota-pay-12b-hiding-deadly-unintended-acceleration/story?id=22972214.

3. Joseph Pereira, "Name of the Game: Brand Awareness," *The Wall Street Journal* (February 14, 1991): B1, B4.

4. P.M. Homer and L. R. Kahle, "Source Expertise, Time of Source Identification, and Involvement in Persuasion," *Journal of Advertising* (Vol. 1 1990): 30–39.

5. See excellent discussions on this topic provided by Brian D. Till and Terence A. Shimp, "Endorsers in Advertising; The Case of Negative Celebrity Information, *Journal of Advertising*, Vol. 27(1), (Spring, 1998): 67-83.

   Margaret F. Callcott, "A Content Analysis of Animation and Animated Spokes-Characters in Television Commercials," *Journal of Advertising*, Vol. 23 (4), (1994): 1–12.

   Kevin Goldman, "Dead Celebrities are Resurrected as Pitchmen," *Wall Street Journal* (January 7, 1994): B1, B2.

   Cyndee Miller, "Some Celebs Just Now Reaching Their Potential—And They're Dead," *Marketing News* (March 29, 1993): 2, 22.

6. Mark I. Alpert and Linda L. Golden, "The Impact of Education on the Relative Effectiveness of One-Sided Communications," in Bruce J. Walker et al., *Proceedings of the American Marketing Association Educators' Conference*, Series No. 48 (1982): 30–33.

   Carl Hovland, Arthur A. Lumsdaine, and Fred D. Sheffield, *Experiences on Mass Communications* (New York: John Wiley, 1949), 182–200.

   W. E. Faison, "Effectiveness of One-Sided and Two-Sided Mass Communications in Advertising," *Public Opinion Quarterly* 25 (1961): 468–469.

7. William L. Wilke and Paul W. Farris, "Comparative Advertising: Problems and Potential," *Journal of Marketing*, 39 (October 1975): 7–15.

8. "Turning into Digital Goldfish," *BBC News Sci/Tech* (February 22, 2012), accessed June 12, 2015, http://news.bbc.co.uk/2/hi/science/nature/1834682.stm.

9. "Your Favorite Songs, Abridged," *NPR All Things Considered* (August 7, 2014).

10. Daniel Kahneman, *Thinking Fast and Slow* (New York: Farrar, Straus and Giroux, 2011).

11. David Strutton, David Taylor, and Kenneth Thompson, "Investigating Generational Differences in e-WOM Behaviors: For Advertising Purposes, Does X =Y?," *International Journal of Advertising*, Vol. 30 No. 4 (2012): 559–586.

12 "Conversational Advertising – Mobile Squared," *Totango* (June, 2010), accessed April 26, 2015, http://www.docstoc.com/docs/119372644/Conversational-Advertising ---Mobile-Squared#.

13 Adapted from Tom Duncan, "The Concept and Process of Integrated Marketing Communications," *Integrated Marketing Communications Research Journal* (Spring 1995): 3–10.

14 David Murphy, "56% of Google's Online Ads are Never 'Seen'," *PC Magazine* (December 7, 2014), accessed April 26, 2015, http://www.pcmag.com/article2/0,2817,2473243,00. asp.

15 Joseph Schumpeter, *Capitalism, Socialism and Democracy* (New York: Harper and Brothers, 1942).

16 "Doan's Pills Must Run Corrective Advertising: FTC Ads Claiming Doan's Is Superior In Treating Back Pain Were Unsubstantiated," *Federal Trade Commission* (May 27, 1999), accessed April 24, 2015, https://www.ftc.gov/news-events/press-releases/1999/05/ doans-pills-must-run-corrective-advertising-ftc-ads-claiming.

17 "Corrective Advertising," *Advertising Age* (September 15, 2003), accessed April 24, 2015, http://adage.com/article/adage-encyclopedia/corrective-advertising/98418.

18 Philip Mattera, "Pfizer: Corporate Rap Sheet," *Corporate Research Project* (August 27, 2014), accessed April 24, 2015, http://www.corp-research.org/pfizer.

19 Judann Pollack "Prego Prevails in Battle Over Comparative Ad Ragu Has Sued Over Spot That Claimed Rival Spaghetti Sauce Was Thicker," *Advertising Age* (September 16, 1996), accessed April 24, 2015, http://adage.com/article/news/prego-prevails-battle-comparative-ad-ragu-sued-spot-claimed-rival-spaghetti-sauce-thicker/77150.

20 "Jartran is Confident, But it Faces Hurdles," *The New York Times* (March 14, 1983), accessed April 24, 2015, http://adage.com/article/news/prego-prevails-battle-comparative -ad-ragu-sued-spot-claimed-rival-spaghetti-sauce-thicker/77150.

    Jeffrey A. Babener, "Chasing the Competition," *MLM Legal* (February 1994), accessed April 24, 2015, http://www.mlmlegal.com/chasing.html.

    "U-haul International, Inc., an Oregon Corp., Plaintiff-appellee, v. Jartran, Inc., a Florida Corporation, and James A. Ryder, defendants-appellants, 793 F.2d 1034 (9th Cir. 1986)," *Justia US Law*, accessed April 24, 2015, http://law.justia.com/cases/federal/ appellate-courts/F2/793/1034/119304.

21 "Guidance for Industry: A Food Labeling Guide (3. General Food Labeling Requirements)" *U.S. Food and Drug Administration* (January 2013), accessed April 24, 2015, http://www.fda.gov/Food/GuidanceRegulation/GuidanceDocumentsRegulatory Information/LabelingNutrition/ucm064866.htm#3.

22 Naldz Graphics, "Branding and Logos—The Stories Behind the Evolution of Some of the Worlds' Biggest Brands," Form Advertising, accessed April 25, 2015, http://www. formadvertising.co.uk/branding-and-logos-the-stories-behind-the-evolution-of-some -of-the-worlds-biggest-brands.

CHAPTER 17

ADVERTISING, SALES PROMOTION, PUBLICITY, PUBLIC RELATIONS AND PERSONAL SELLING

"If the circus is coming to town and you paint a sign saying 'Circus coming to the fairground this Saturday', that's advertising. If you put the sign on the back of an elephant and walk it through town, that's [direct marketing]. If the elephant walks through the mayor's flower bed, that's publicity. And if you give the mayor free tickets [in exchange for his troubles] and get the mayor to laugh about the elephant, that's [a mixture of sales promotion and public relations]. If the town's citizens go the circus, and buy a ticket, that's sales."

P.T. Barnum, famous entrepreneur and principle partner in the Ringling Brothers and Barnum & Baily Circus, offered this humorous take on marketing promotions during the late 1800s. [The parenthetical additions are ours.] Left unsaid by anyone until now, however, is that if the circus intended for these things to happen, its marketing team should be congratulated. The circus would have done a fine job of managing key elements in its promotional mix. The circus was able to deliver an integrated message that permitted the brand to put its best face forward.

→ Elements of the Promotional Mix

The four "P's" of marketing provide a means by which any Firm's product, price, place (supply chain) and promotional factors can be mixed and managed in ways that deliver differentiating value to targeted B2C or B2C segments. Note the phrase "mixed and managed in ways." It infers more than one way exists to combine the elements of the marketing mix in order to deliver unique and uniquely desirable value to targeted customer segments. For example, the mixture of food ingredients and proportions that yield any truly tasty or healthy dish are rarely thrown together arbitrarily. Similarly, marketing mix elements—the ingredients that marketer's mix to create, deliver, pronounce, and capture customer value—should never be combined haphazardly. Not if the planning Firm wants to succeed, that is.

Speaking of useful recipes, consider the following formula. This formula would never guarantee but still should enhance the prospects that you eventually will succeed as a marketer. Our formula for marketing success:

Take 3 cups of innovative ideas, 1 cup of goodwill, 2 pinches of possibilities, 1.75 cups of leadership, 2 spoonfuls of teamwork, 2 cups of market vision, 3 cups of creativity, 3 tablespoons of willingness to tackle challenging problems, and 1 large pinch of hope. Mix vigorously and then leap forward—fast.

Now, back to our regularly scheduled promotional discussion.

→ The Means through Which Marketers Communicate

The promotional mix exists as part of every Firm's marketing mix. The components and scope of the promotion mix were introduced in the last chapter. In this chapter we explore the key components of the promotion mix in detail.

Promotions provide the means through which marketers communicate with key external audiences. For Firms that feature any size or scale, typical promotional mix elements include advertising, personal selling, public relations, direct marketing, and sales promotion. The primary purpose of the promotional mix is to communicate the message that the promoting Firm is able to deliver differentiating value to customers through its combined product, price and supply chain offerings. Promotional mixes should be managed in ways that simultaneously create branding value in the minds of targeted customers and capture financial value from those customers.

What specific messages should readers take away from the preceding paragraph? To answer, consider four marketing truths. First, the price of any product, fundamentally, is whatever customers are willing to pay. Second, customers never wake up wanting to pay higher prices, although many are manipulated into willingly paying more as a consequence of their exposure to marketing communications. Third, all customers do wake up seeking more value, especially more value for their money. This statement remains true even when customers willingly pay materially more money to shoulder, say, Prada bags, even when nearly as prestigious and equally functional bags are available at lower prices. This is because certain customers believe the Prada brand delivers materially more value to them and thus to their personal brand. Fourth, by voting with their feet (i.e., buying brand A as opposed to brand B, or choosing to buy nothing at all), buyers determine and demonstrate the amount they are willing to pay. These four marketing truths always exist, and will always exercise influence, with the occasional exception of certain non-discretionary market offerings. These offerings would typically include health care; energy-related products such as gasoline or electricity; and certain other life staples. Each non-discretionary product satisfies genuine needs rather than perceptual wants. Each product, in other words, is something you actually cannot live without; that is, at least not in a modern Western economies.

Marketers must acknowledge and account for the presence of these four marketing truths. This is why the first and overarching responsibility of marketers is to develop and deliver their best possible value proposition to targeted customer segments through the effective management of their entire marketing mix. Then, when marketers focus attention specifically on their communications efforts, they should frame and deliver their best possible value proposition by managing and manipulating the promotional element of their marketing mix. This promotional task requires that marketers initially develop and subsequently deliver messages that do more than merely communicate the brand's value. Delivered messages, however, should also elevate the market's perception of the promoted brand's value. When each communication outcome is achieved, the product will appear worth acquiring even at higher current prices.

This is exactly the type of value and message that the Louis Vuitton brand has successfully created and delivered since the Firm began marketing in 1854 on Rue Neuve des Capucines in Paris, France—a high-end address indeed. Its elevated product/brand image, equity, and value is reflected in the high-end prices that Louis Vuitton charges. And in the high-end prices that Vuitton's customers willingly pay.

→ Mixing Promotions

The elements that collectively comprise the promotional mix each feature comparative communication strengths (advantages) and weaknesses (disadvantages). What this means practically is that advertising is better at achieving certain communication outcomes than is sales promotion. Thus advertising should be emphasized when those specific outcomes are sought. Or, for example, that personal selling generally generates better communication outcomes than direct marketing in certain communication contexts. Personal selling should be used as the Firm's primary mode of communication in those contexts. The comparative strengths and weaknesses of all five promotion mix elements are described. Each promotional element is also defined and its use is discussed.

→ Advertising

We all know what advertising is. Indeed, we all live in a world in which we can ignore but cannot escape the hydra-like reach of advertising. Correspondingly, we all know or believe there is too much advertising in our lives (another story explained below). But in all likelihood we mostly don't know the actual definition of advertising. Until now.

Advertising is any form of one-way, paid (with sponsor identified) and non-personal marketing communication that is aimed at targeted consumers and delivered en masse through electronic, print, or Internet-based media with the purpose of informing, reminding, or persuading targeted consumers or Firms about the values or differences that are associated with a product/brand. The preceding statement may be the longest sentence in this book, yet every phrase is important. Consequently, their underlying implications are broken out below.

The "one-way" phrase is important because it underscores that traditional advertising does not feature an immediate feedback loop where customers can respond or react back to the advertising firm. Its "one-way" nature indicates that if customers don't understand or are turned-off by the key advertising message, marketers have no opportunity to quickly adjust the message, or to even apologize and explain.

The phrase "paid (sponsor identified)" is meaningful for two reasons. First, the words indicate that advertising space must be purchased by some marketing entity. (Only rarely, such as with public service announcements, would exceptions arise.) Second, the phrase underscores that the organizations, individuals, or movements that buy advertisements and consequently are responsible for their message content must be identified. This is a good thing for all of us. Can you imagine, for example, what might be said in political advertising if candidates and their marketing teams never had to "own" their advertising messages and its truths and consequences? Things are already challenging enough, ethically-speaking, in that particular advertising sector. They are so bad, in fact, that the famous adman David Ogilvy, who died in 1999, famously suggested "Political advertising ought to be stopped. It's the only really dishonest kind of advertising that's left."[1] Yet no contemporary expert could claim, in good conscience, that conditions on the political advertising front have improved since Ogilvy uttered these words.

The word "non-personal," as applied to advertising, is equally material. Advertising messages are distributed to intended audiences through mass media. Traditional mass media have included television, radio and printed materials such as newspapers, magazines, or billboards. More recently, mass media include various Internet-based sites and technologies. Mass media were traditionally non-personal in nature. They did not feature immediate feedback loops in the same manner that personal selling or certain new media do. A great deal of planning and forethought therefore should be dedicated to message development and media selection when Firms advertise through traditional mass media. Marketing research results should almost invariably play an important role when larger Firms are involved.

Advertising: Strengths and Weaknesses

Advertising features several advantages or strengths. Advertising is effective at reminding and informing recipients, so long as they actually receive and pay attention to messages, which is, of course, far from a *fait accompli*—a done deal. Yet exquisitely designed—or at times appropriately sexy, fear-inducing or humorous—advertising messages can grab recipient attention. Still, it is extremely difficult to actually differentiate one's message in a world where consumers are exposed to somewhere between 4,000 and 5,000 advertising messages a day. (Experts disagree on the exact count.) Because they pay for advertising media space, marketers can control what they want to say, and to some degree, who receives the message, a strength.

Another strength of advertisements is that they are also good at conveying emotions and stimulating emotional responses from customers exposed to them. We don't even like cats. But any time Sara McLachlan keys up "In the Arms of an Angel," and the Society for the Prevention of Cruelty to Animals shows a cute kitten (okay, they're all cute), our hearts are tugged. Sustained advertising campaigns can also successfully build branding and positioning strategies, over time. Does anyone not know that GIECO Insurance "Can save you 15 or more percent in 15 minutes" or that "Budweiser is the King of Beers" and has really cool horses?

Certain disadvantages or weaknesses are associated with the use of advertising. Advertising, as a promotional element, is not as persuasive as some other forms of marketing communication. More troublesome still, is anyone really paying attention? The answer is: not so much, anymore. As discussed in the previous chapter, when distributed online, 56% of ads are never even in view—"in view" defined as being on screen for more than a second. Advertisers are paying for illusory impressions of those ads, though they are not actually seen. The proliferation of DVRs, Netflix, or pay-for-play cable shows that do not even contain advertising are each well-known environmental trends. Each trend is also a known advertiser's enemy that beats down advertising effectiveness. And, it is fact that fewer and fewer people even read paper media such as newspapers, magazines anymore. Meanwhile, consumers' attention spans and trust in the media are apparently declining in lockstep. Not a pretty picture, at net, as these trends relate to the present and future of advertising.

An old advertising proverb attributed to Philadelphia retailing Guru John Wanamaker suggested: "I know 50% of my advertising doesn't work, I just don't know which half."[2] Wanamaker's half might have to be further halved again today to 25%, or so. And finally, back to the fact that advertising is non-personal and one-way. If members of targeted markets are not "getting" or "buying-into" the message, no short-term corrective mechanism exists. With other promotional elements, specifically, personal selling, the opportunity exists to adjust the message or presentational style, or simply ask for a do-over.

Advertising: Featuring MAD Breadth and Depth

The origins of advertising are truly ancient. Messaging that *Madmen* would proudly claim as advertising goes back at least as far as pre-Christ Roman times (around 50 BC). At that time, carefully-crafted, aesthetically-appealing artistic images of gladiators and their genuine fights-to-the-death contests were created and posted throughout Rome. The purpose of this imagery was promote upcoming gladiatorial bouts, according to archeologists and historians. The first known US advertising promoted R. Lorillard's snuff and tobacco products, produced in Reidsville, N.C. Lorillard's advertisements were placed in New York City newspapers in 1789. The first genuine brand name advertised on a larger scale throughout the United States was "Bull Durham," another North Carolina tobacco product. The central idea that drove this advertisement's value proposition underscored the notion of "How Easy It [was] to Roll Your Own"—when smokers used Bull Durham products, of course.

The breadth and depth of use of advertising in the contemporary United States is astounding. American firms annually spend more than 180 billion dollars on advertising.[3] This total, by way of perspective, exceeds the entire Gross National Product (GNP) of some 185 countries. Put another way, only 35 nations in the world boast a GNP larger than the amount US Firms, as a whole, annually spend on advertising. During 2011, 26 US Firms each spent more than one billion dollars. Notably, 2011 was not a great year for the US economy, meaning advertising expenditures were actually down, as well.

But really, why is so much spent on advertising? After all, experts widely acknowledge that advertising, with rare exceptions, does not work effectively in this modern era; an era, obviously, characterized by extraordinary consumer cynicism, customers who often have the attention spans of fruit flies on crack, incredible amounts of advertising clutter (marketing promotions overload) and noise (other media- and life-induced distractions), several thousand media outlets through which advertising messages potentially might be conveyed, and a rapidly growing consumer capacity and willingness to void advertisements from their lives. At net, these collective trends underscore the degree to which the prospect of reaching large amounts of prospective customers with advertising messages that are attended to and understood by intended audiences is growing smaller and smaller.

When the subject of "why-we-still-have-all-this-advertising" arises, at least one other confounding factor exists that should be considered. All we ask is that you think about Bud, Miller, Coors, well-branded domestic beers, one and all. Is there anyone reading this now who has not long since learned, by dint of their lifetime exposure to advertising, that:

- Budweiser is the "King of Beers"
- Miller "Tastes Great and is Less Filling"
- Coors is "brewed with pure Rocky Mountain spring water" (except when Coors is brewed in Eden, N.C. Eden has two beautiful rivers running through it, but no Rocky Mountain springs within about 1,650 miles).

Sounds like mission accomplished, then, at least for these three brands. We ask, again, why all the advertising?

The answer does not relate to some variety of marketing madness, but rather just plain ole *MAD*. This MAD should not be confused with MADD (Mothers against Drunk Driving), which is, by the way, a successful marketing organization that has effectively disseminated its "Don't Drink and Drive" message through a combination of emotional- and fear-based appeals.

The MAD to which we refer harkens back to the implied US-USSR (Soviet Union, or Russia today) nuclear pact that successfully kept the world from nuclear war-induced conflagration from about 1950 all the way to about 1990. Throughout this entire period, the United States enjoyed the capacity to destroy the USSR several times over, should it have chosen to push the button and unleash the nuclear missiles at their intended targets. (Sounds like marketing there, doesn't it.) The USSR, of course, possessed essentially the same—truthfully, a little less—capacity to destroy the United States.

But as you know, because you are all alive and well today, during the entirety of the 40-year-long Cold War neither adversary pushed the button. That's because each side understood the true meaning of the acronym, MAD or Mutually Assured Destruction. For a US president to have pushed the button first would have achieved nothing but the assurance that he would have killed most Russians about 15 minutes after the USSR would have unleashed its nuclear arsenal and killed most Americans. Utter destruction (as in a global extinction event), after all, was mutually assured. (Now you know why your parents and grandparents may be screwed up. They lived through these times fully aware that this sort of annihilation could actually occur.)

Holy cow, the amazing thing about what we just wrote is that it is all TRUE. Less amazing, but more germane in this context, is that the same exact set of lessons apply to modern advertisers. Coors, Miller, Bud and innumerable others competing in other sectors are "caught in a trap" (like the lyrics of the old Elvis song "Suspicious Minds"), from which Firms cannot extricate themselves. Coors, Miller, and Bud, metaphorically, found themselves in a circular firing squad, with loaded .44 Magnums pointed at each other's heads, or brands. And the first beer brand that lowers its weapon by halting or even cutting back its incessant advertising during national sporting events—(because men, the primary beer drinker aka preferred target segment, love their broadcasted spectator sports, which subsequently serve as the preferred advertising medium)—will slowly fade away. The remaining two brands, the ones that continued to advertise, would slowly or quickly blow them away. That's because the beer brand that exits the advertising stage first will lose share of mind along with share of market.

So it's not advertiser madness, but rather the prospect of MAD that keeps us, the common viewer, up to our eyeballs in advertising that we have already memorized by heart but ironically never cared about. The world of advertising, as you now realize, is MAD.

Types of Advertising

There exist a number of different types of advertising. Some were mentioned in our previous discussion. These different types of advertising tend to serve different objectives and target audiences. More will be said about both advertising objectives and target audiences in later sections of the chapter. For now, however, it is useful to briefly review the distinctions between the different types of advertising.

Product Advertising

Most advertising falls into this category. Logically enough, product advertising focuses on promoting Firms' branded products and services. Product advertising dominates virtually all media from radio and TV to Internet advertising and advertising on social media. Product advertising comes in many shapes and forms varying between the inexpensive locally produced fact-based ads for your local plumber to expensive humorous high-imagery ads produced by

Coors and Budweiser. Ultimately, all such ads have similar objectives that are directed at walking buyers through one or more steps in the hierarchy of promotion objectives introduced in the last chapter. Several forms of product advertising exist, based largely on the product's stage in its life cycle. These include pioneering advertising, selective demand advertising, and reminder advertising.

Pioneering Advertising

Pioneering advertising, also called informative advertising, is purposed toward creating awareness and trial for new products that are in the introductory stages of their product life cycles. This form of advertising is used to develop primary demand for the product category, rather than demand for individual brands. Advertising will be used primarily to inform consumers of product characteristics, benefits, price, and availability. For more complex products, ads may demonstrate their benefits or how the products are to be used.

Selective Demand or Persuasive Advertising

As products move through their life cycles, the nature and purpose of advertising changes. During growth and maturing stages, advertisers should focus extensively on differentiating their brands from competitors' brands. The focus becomes one of persuasion; persuading consumers to buy or continue to buy the advertiser's brand. A special case of selective demand advertising is comparative advertising in which advertisers directly compare, usually by name, their brands against those of competitors. Watch any ad for McDonald's or Burger King. Invariably each compares itself against the other, either indirectly or by name. The FTC issued a ruling in 1979 that encourages such comparisons in advertising, as long as they are truthful, arguing that consumers are armed with more data upon which to make informed choices.[4]

Reminder Advertising

As products move into late maturity and eventually into decline, reminder advertising is employed to keep the brand in consumers' minds. Letting them know that the brand is available and continues to be a viable choice. (Recall The Simple Minds song reference "Don't You Forget About Me" that was made earlier.) This is exactly the outcome—no forgetting— that reminder advertising is seeking to achieve for its associated brands.

Institutional Advertising

Institutional advertising promotes organizations rather than products. Specifically, institutional advertising is intended to promote the image of an organization by highlighting specific activities in which the organization is engaged, people who represent the organization, and/or ideas and points of view espoused by the organization. BP, for example, has engaged in extensive institutional advertising subsequent to the now infamous Gulf oil spill in 2010. These ads are intended to "clean up" its image (pun intended) by talking about the steps it has taken to clean up the Gulf and prevent future similar disasters.[5]

Advocacy Advertising

Advocacy advertising is a type of institutional advertising in which Firms attempt to message their positions on some important issue. The purpose is to sway the opinions of targeted audiences. Often the general public is the primary target audience. Typically advocacy advertising does not promote products or services. Corporations or other Firms can sponsor ads, but nonprofit organizations and private advocacy groups pay for most. Some example follow. In 2010, Focus on the Family ran a Super Bowl ad supporting the pro-life cause. The ad starred former professional football player Tim Tebow thanking his mother for giving him life.[6] Kellogg's "Share Your Breakfast" campaign used Facebook as the primary medium for its 2011 award-winning advocacy campaign. In its ads, Kellogg urged consumers to submit their breakfast photos. Kellogg, for each photo, donated money to a nonprofit organization that provided free breakfasts to schoolchildren. Diet Coke's "Red Dress Online Initiative" used traditional and online media to draw attention to women's heart disease as the number one killer of women.[7]

The Advertising Process: Six Key Advertising Decisions

Management in any Firm that advertises must engage six major advertising decisions or actions. These decisions/actions are collectively called the advertising process. Management, in the following order, must: identify the target audience, establish objectives, set a budget, develop an advertising strategy (which entails choosing an advertising medium and developing an advertising message), execute the resulting strategy, and, once executed, evaluate the effectiveness of the strategy. These steps are summarized in Exhibit 17.1. We examine the first four decision areas below. An examination of the final step, evaluating advertising effectiveness is reserved for later in the chapter.

Identify the Target Audience

In most cases, the target audience or audiences toward which advertising is directed will be the target market or markets to which the Firm's products are targeted, in other words. the Firm's target market or markets. However this is not always the case. Sometimes the target audience(s) for advertising may be quite different from the Firm's target market(s). For example, Exxon may target its products to consumers (in both B2B and B2C markets) of petroleum products, but may target government agencies and environmental activist with its institutional advertising.

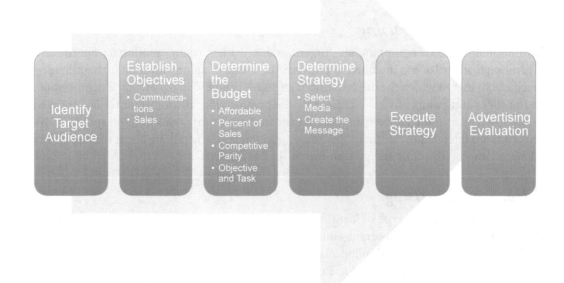

Exhibit 17.1 *The Advertising Process.*

Establishing Objectives

Most, if not all, advertisers face three primary questions while establishing objectives. The answers to these questions will guide the choices made about which objective(s) to pursue. The three questions are: Do managers primarily seek to inform (for purposes of creating awareness) those who are exposed to the message? Or, do managers primarily seek to persuade (for purposes of getting people in stores and/or making sales) message recipients? Or, finally, do managers seek to remind recipients about something as a result of those recipients' exposure to the advertising message?

These objectives, you should note, are highly similar to the communication objectives outlined in Chapter 16 under the guise of "the hierarchy of communications objectives." The beginning point in all advertising should be determining what the advertising is intended to accomplish. The advertising objectives that marketing managers choose to emphasize should be based on what is happening with respect to:

- Other elements of the Firm's marketing mix.
- The Firm's general positioning strategy.
- The nature of the Firm's intended targeted audience.
- The life cycle stage of the product featured in the advertisement.

Over time, of course, advertising can build desirable images or positions for brands or Firms. Advertising can similarly substantially strengthen existing images or positions for brands or Firms.

Setting the Advertising Budget

Advertising objectives must already exist before any effort is made to establish an advertising budget. Otherwise, the effort would prove pointless. Essentially, what happens during this stage is that managers determine or establish their best estimates of how much it will cost to reach their objectives. Just as discussed in the last chapter (Chapter 16) for budgeting the overall promotion program, Firms typically pursue one of four alternative advertising budgeting methods.

First, there is the affordable or all-you-can-afford method. We could never, in good conscious, recommend this method. At its core the affordable budgetary approach entails the Firm spending all the money on advertising that it believes it can afford. The problem with this method is that its use is not tied to any specific communications objectives.

The percentage-of-sales method is also frequently employed. Here, Firms set aside a pre-set percentage of their revenues earned during a particular period (generally, a quarter or a year) and spend that amount on advertising. Practically speaking: if the Firm allocated 3% of revenues toward advertising and generated revenues of $1,000,000 during the reporting period, it would spend $30,000 on advertising during the upcoming reporting period. If sales volume increased to $1,500,000.00, advertising expenditures would rise to $45,000. But what if revenues dropped? Advertising expenditures would naturally and correspondingly drop, which is probably not the wisest course of action for most Firms if their revenues are declining.

The percentage-of-sales method is better than the all-you-can-afford approach. After all, some measure of planning and forethought is involved. As emphasized in this last chapter, the appeal and utility of the percentage-of-sales method, however, is undermined by a fatal flaw. While practitioners probably are well aware that advertising efforts ultimately determine sales, the method, in application, is based on the opposite logic. By computing the advertising budget as a percent of projected sales, advertisers are implicitly, and incorrectly, assuming that sales causally drive advertising expenditures. This assumption is simply wrong. Advertising budgets should be set to achieve specific communications objectives. The correct causal relationship is that advertising causes sales. As practiced, however, the percentage-of-sales budgetary method is not causally tied to achieving any advertising objectives.

The competitive parity approach to advertising budgeting essentially entails emulating what competitors are doing. If competitors increase advertising expenditures, your Firm raises its expenditures, and so forth. There is, however, one compelling shortfall associated with the competitive parity method. The approach assumes that your Firm's competitors are experts when it comes to advertising expenditures. This is an assumption that few true experts would comfortably endorse.

In oligopolistic markets, where fewer but generally powerful competitors "bunch-up," actually playing follow-the-leader games when it comes to pricing, the competitive parity approach finds some logical footing. This happened in the domestic airlines industry a few years back. At that time, American Airlines decided to begin charging for passengers' third bags. Every major US airline except Southwestern then quickly lined up behind American, as you know all too well. If its competitors had not quickly followed suit, American would have quickly dropped their bags-also-need-a-ticket strategy. The objective and task method to establishing an advertising budget is, in our view, the most sensible path to follow. This "best" method entails establishing prioritized communication goals, and then determining what it will take, advertising spend-wise, to achieve each successively more important goal. This three-part budgeting method is based on an identification of the communication results or outcomes to be achieved, the advertising strategies and techniques required to achieve those results, and the costs associated with executing those specific advertising strategies.

Developing an Advertising Strategy

Developing a successful advertising strategy requires a two-part process. The first stage entails selecting the proper advertising channel or source or media. The second stage requires that the best possible message, that is, the most memorable, believable, distinctive, sticky, and/or contagious message, be developed for and delivered through the advertisement itself.

Select Advertising Media

Strategy Development Part 1: The first activity involves selecting the appropriate advertising media. Rising media costs and increasingly fragmented consumer markets make this choice more important today than ever before. There really are hundreds of television stations and myriad websites or digital vehicles through which consumers themselves rollout highlight reels of their lives. Media should be selected such that it (or they) match(es) up appropriately with the particular market segment(s) (or intended audience(s) for the advertising) that the Firm is seeking to reach and inform, remind, or persuade. What does this statement mean?

Let's assume, for example, that many people reading this book are aged 20–25; enrolled in college; female; and are interested in becoming or staying fit and healthy. Suppose we have just developed a great product that, if used, promises a healthier future for you. What is the best way for us to inform you about the existence of this product and persuade you about its benefits? More specifically, what advertising media should Firms that are marketing fitness and/or health products use to reach you with their advertising messages? For starters, a Firm might use Pinterest or a social networking site such as Facebook as a means to convey messages targeted at this group. There are likely certain television programs or networks that this particular target segment is more likely to watch. These programs or the networks that broadcast them presumably would also function as appropriate media through which health-related advertising messages might be effectively delivered to this segment.

Every Firm that advertises must decide where to "place" its messages. Various media alternatives exist apart from the few just mentioned. These would include television, as noted; radio, there are more than 14,000 radio stations in the United States; magazines, of which there are 19,000+; newspapers, which most of the people reading this book rarely encounter anymore, except possibly online; outdoor media; and of course a myriad range of digital sources such as smart phones, emails, Facebook, tweets, and various social networking sites.

Media selection is critical to advertising success. Fortunately, various sources of secondary information are already available to assist marketers in their media selection efforts. The media choice process appears simple, on its face: marketers must align their media choices, and advertising platforms with the media consumption preferences of those individuals comprising the targeted segments. Marketers advertising a new Beyoncé release had best not select *The History Channel* as an advertising medium. *The History Channel* viewership demographic is notably older and more masculine than are the typical Beyoncé fans. Yet marketers that are advertising slow-paced, river-based tours of historical old European capital cities likely would be pleased indeed with the results generated by a choice to advertise on *The History Channel*.

Creating the Advertising Message

Strategy Development Part 2: The second part of developing advertising strategy entails creating an effective advertising message. During this stage Firms first must decide on the exact nature of the primary message that it eventually will seek to communicate to targeted audiences. Messages typically should emphasize the most important customer benefit or value associated with the brand that is being advertised. This specific message-building approach involves the development of a "Big Idea"—that's what it is really called in the marketing world. Nike's "Just Do It," now that is a classic Big Idea. The Big Idea should be capable of bringing the message to life in a memorable way. Going forward, this compelling creative concept should likewise be able to function metaphorically as a sturdy hook on which additional messages could be hung going forward across the years. Burger King's simple but memorable "Have It Your Way" creative concept operated as a sustaining and self-perpetuating hook on which subsequent messages were hung for more than 20 years.

Then, one year, Burger King, the famous "Home of the Whopper," inexplicably decided its old message was stale. And frankly, Burger King never quite recovered its advertising mojo. Remember the creepy, scary, almost pedophile-like Burger King "King"? The "King" was not a good core message; not when one of your primary target audiences is children. Children, you know, are a special consumer-type who almost never visit restaurants without also dragging their parents along—two for one, if you will, for the marketer! Someone has to pay for and drive those kids.

By contrast, consider the beauty of Master Card's "Priceless" (which signals to customers, buy what you want, through Master Card's assistance, and damn the price because the value acquired for your life experiences and memories is worth any price!); Miller Lite's "Tastes Great, Less Filling" (experience more fun and fewer calories while drinking); or Intel's "Intel Inside" (a well-branded guarantee of performance). Each Big Idea functioned as a highly successful durable hook upon which decades of successful advertising campaigns were and continue to be launched. As has been true of Walmart's "EDLP," coupled with the smiley face (providing welcome assurance of savings, everyday!). And unlike BK, each Firm was strategically-wise enough to not fix what was not broken with the Big Idea that drove their promotional messaging.

When creating effective advertising messages Firms also must identify the type of message appeal to use. The reason why is because most advertising messages simultaneously include informative and persuasive content. These two elements often become so entangled in advertising messages that it becomes difficult to tell them apart. Basic informative advertising messaging content would typically include the brand name, a brief presentation of key features and benefits, and possibly price. Yet even highly persuasive messages generally still must contain informative elements in order to succeed. This bundle of informativeness and persuasiveness likewise must grab customer attention in a noisy and crowded advertising world. The same informative and persuasive content should coalesce in appeals that deliver basic rationales as to why customers should purchase this brand, as opposed to buying another brand or buying nothing at all.

There are a number of alternative message appeals from which advertisers can select. The range of alternative appeals is summarized in Table 17.1. However, one of three basic advertising appeals is generally selected to drive the message's theme. These optional appeals are fear-based, sex-based, or humorous in nature.

Table 17.1 • *Some Key Advertising Appeals*

Fear Appeals are employed to scare people into buying or not buying and using certain products. Michelin's ads emphasizing keeping one's family safe by selecting the correct tires and American Cancer Society ads aimed at de-marketing cigarettes and other tobacco products are among the better examples.

Sex Appeals are intended to either make one feel more attractive by using a product ("Ultrabrite gives your mouth sex appeal"), attach sexual imagery to the product (the Oui ad for perfume linking the brand to an attractive woman in a provocactive setting), or employ a "sexy" celebrity to endorse the product (Paris Hilton for Carl's Junior).

Humor Appeals are employed to gain attention and, hopefully, create a positive "affective" response to the ad that can rub off on the product. The idea is "like the ad, like the brand." Humor can be quite effective with both as long as the humor does not dominate the message to the point that viewers cannot recall the brand or its values.

Slice of Life appeals show the product being used by the "typical consumer" in a normal setting. Personal care and home maintenance products are often advertised using this form of appeal. A Tide commercial, for example, may show the average homemaker enjoying brighter, cleaner laundry as a result of using Tide's latest formula.

Lifestyle appeals show the product being used within the context of someone enjoying a specific lifestyle orientation or experience. Think of the typical Mountain Dew ad showing young adults enjoying the refreshing coolness of mountain lake while swimming and partying.

Demonstration ads show the product actually being used. The objective is to specifically highlight key benefits or features. Bounty paper towels employ demonstration ads in which the brand is demonstrated in a way that emphasized its absorbency and strength.

Testimonial ads attempt to use endorsers who appear likeable and believable to attest to the product's utility and value. The endorsers can be real people or paid celebrities. Weight loss products often use testimonials from real people who have successfully used the product to lose weight. Celebrities experiencing successful weight loss also have been employed. Jenny Craig for example has used both types of endorsers. Most recently they have used Marie Osmond as a celebrity spokesperson.

Personality Symbols are essentially trade characters (recall our discussion of trade characters from chapter 10) that have been created to represent the product. Examples include the Pillsbury Dough Boy, the GEICO Gecko, Betty Crocker, Progressive's Flo, Speedy Alka-Seltzer, and the Michelin Man.

Emotional appeals build a mood or image surrounding the product and its use. Usually there is no attempt to link the brand to any specific benefits or features. All that is desired is to create an emotional response to the ad that may "rub off" on the product. Common products advertising using emotional appeals include perfumes, jewelry, and designer clothing. Imagery is the essential element for success.

Fear-based appeals present harsh or gentle and overt or subtle arguments to customers that they can avoid some negative experience if they are "smart enough" to choose the alternative being advocated in the advertising message. The advertising narrative unfolds something like this: here's the problem (you're overweight!), and thank goodness, we're here with the dietary solution. Just listen, do as we suggest, and, yes, buy our product so that what you are afraid of does not happen.

The entire alcohol industry often plays gently into consumers' fears in its advertising. The culture of drink throughout America will continue to dominate for many reasons. But one underestimated reason is because alcohol advertisers subtly but successfully position the choice to drink as one that provides confidence for insecure people; clarity for folks who are uncertain; or solace for lonely and wounded people. By the way, alcohol consumption is also elevated by the fact that it helps users attain the soothing bliss of obliviousness, which is not generally a theme emphasized in advertising. So don't lay all the blame at marketers' feet.

Sex-based appeals suggest to customers or prospective customers that the object or offering being advertised will enhance their attractiveness. Sex-based appeals are used across a wide range of product categories, but beer advertising would surely come to mind first for many. Developing successful advertising messages for beer is easier than developing them for industrial bolts, and the task becomes easier still when some simple rules are followed. "Sex sells" is more than a marketing cliché. Sex really does gain attention, and without first establishing attention nothing would ever be sold. And what is the easiest way to have sex? Buy her a drink, or if you're a her, be "man-enough" to buy him a drink. Obviously, the drink that should be purchased is the one featured in the message. Of course we're exaggerating a little to make a point, but just a little!

This advertising appeal is pure stimulus-and-response, positive reinforcement-based brain association 101. Or, as some witty beer marketer one day might advocate: it's simply "Bottoms Up" in more ways than one. Lest anyone be offended here, we're genuinely writing the truth, hopefully in a humorous way. Which brings us to …

Humorous appeals suggest directly or indirectly to their intended audience that the product being promoted is more fun, exciting, or cooler than alternative products. Returning to beer, of course beer advertising has used humor so effectively for so long that the beer industry has begun poking fun at itself. Australia's Carlton Beer purposely mocked stupidly funny, big-budget beer promotions with its own stupidly funny, big-budget beer advertising. This ad (YouTube it) is one of the wittiest advertisements of all time. Humor works well because it softens hard brand images. Effective humor also increases likability for the brand, which is a key outcome because we don't make friends with things or people we don't like. The use of *Peanuts* characters, particularly, Snoopy, in its advertising has taken the harsh edge off its messaging, making Metropolitan Insurance Co. more likable. After all, with rare exceptions but with good cause, no one really likes their insurance company, but everyone loves Snoopy. But most importantly, humorous appeals are effective because they attract attention and create "buzz." To be certain, positive "buzz" or WOM is a wonderful thing to create, especially in a connected digital world. Funny, as you already knew, can prove viral. When events or ideas shown online capture an in-the-moment humorous buzz, they generally stick and quickly spread.

Turning toward the appeal inside the appeal, you should understand that fear-based, sex-based, or humor-based messages appeals can be presented inside of broader appeal structures. Fear-based appeals, for example, might be positioned inside advertisements grounded in "slice-of-life/slice-of-death" or "more or less-desirable lifestyle presentation" backdrops. Sex-based appeals might be ensconced inside of fantasy- or musically-based advertisement context. Personality symbols, brought to life in the form of cartoon characters (i.e., Pillsbury Doughboy, the Gecko, Tony the Tiger) or testimonial evidence provided by experts (Michael Jordan, an actor impersonating a financial advisor) might be employed to provide more suitable contexts for humorous appeals.

Effective Message Appeals Should …

Regardless of the appeal featured in the message, messages ideally should be:

- Memorable (easy to recall and remember)
- "Believable"
- Distinctive (from similar messages offered by competitive brands)
- Focused on some determinant feature, aspect, benefit, or problem-solving capability that is associated with the brand/product.

For any message to prove determinant in the minds of customers or prospects, the feature, function or benefit emphasized in the message must be different from and better than what competitors are saying or offering in their messages. What we're saying is that determinant messages first must establish a point of differentiation or point of difference (POD). And, second, members of the target audience must perceive that this POD is important for choosing between alternative products or brands as they engage in the decision making process.

The word "believable," as related to advertising messages, merits its distinguishing quotation marks. This is because advertising message "believability" should be taken with a large grain of salt; a grain of salt generically known as puffery, that is. Puffery, defined formally, is a promotional statement or claim that is based more on subjective rather than objective claims. Puffery, defined in an advertising context, include messages that knowingly offer exaggerated claims about brands, people, or products. These claims may be exaggerated to the point of making a claim that no reasonable person would take seriously. Mountain Dew's longstanding advertising campaign humorously emphasizes that customers who "Do the Dew" somehow receive essentially magical powers. "Dew Doers," as you've probably seen, acquire abilities enabling them to leap off waterfalls, land safely, and then skip across the top of the water below. This is obviously puff. Puffery has been around a long time, and that's no exaggeration.

Advertising messaging matters, greatly. Where would Nike be today without messages such as "Just Do It," "Gotta be the Shoes," "Chicks Dig the Long Ball," "You Don't Win Silver, You Lose Gold," "There is no Finish Line," "I am Not a Role Model," or "Winning Takes Care of Everything." Or is Nike's long-standing success all the result of the quality of their shoes, after all?

→ Measuring Advertising Effectiveness

Reach and frequency are two important success metrics for any advertiser. The metric known as reach captures the percentage of consumers within a targeted market who are exposed to a given message during a specified period of time. Reach measures "how many?"

The metric known as frequency captures the number of times consumers comprising the targeted market are exposed to a given message during the same specified period of time. Frequency measures "how often?"

The three-hit-rule also exists as an informal but seemingly universal principle. The rule suggests that in order for a "messaging" Firm or individual to influence a recipient's behavior (persuade) or teach the recipient something important (inform) the recipient must be exposed to the message at least three times. During the first hit, the sender explains what s/he is about to explain. During the second hit, the sender explains the message. During the third hit, the sender explains what s/he just explained.

→ Advertising's Greatest Hits—Oldies but Goodies

While the promotional element of the marketing mix is struggling in today's digital environment, advertising has had its day and undoubtedly will continue to have its say. Some of the greatest hits from the golden age of advertising are discussed below. Each is grounded in a singularly compelling and uniformly long-lasting Big Idea. Let's see how many of this advertising slogans you already know.

"A Diamond is Forever": DeBeers' iconic slogan has been used continuously since 1946. Honestly, the slogan will probably last forever, unlike, unfortunately, many marriages that these supposedly forever products purportedly permanently seal. Decades later, the advertising pitch received a huge promotional boost when Sean Connery starred in an iconic James Bond film that was called *Diamonds are Forever*.

"There're G-r-r-eat!": Tony the Tiger entered the world as celebrity spokesperson and product endorser back in the 1950s. His catchphrase has since taken its place as one of the most memorable, and longest running advertising slogans. Tony himself has evolved across the decades. He now stands upright, for example, has visited more than 40 countries, and has a wife and daughter.

"Nothing Sucks like an Electrolux": You really have to admire the edginess of this before-its-time message. Or not. We'll leave that up to you. The Swedish vacuum cleaner marketer introduced this slogan to the United States back in the 1960s. Trust us, at that time a lot less could be shown or said in advertising. Most Americans, including some marketing experts, naively assumed that something had been lost or gone wrong in translation. This was not true. Electrolux had sought to be edgy in their pun, and succeeded, even by today's standards. Electrolux was onto something, for sure. This humorous but also persuasive appeal, encapsulated in a slogan that very much captures the core benefit of the brand, is still used today.

"Nothing Outlasts the Energizer": This similarly ageless slogan was launched in the 1980s. Since then, the alternatively cool or annoying (your choice, but either way, you cannot take your eyes off the creature), drum-beating, shade-wearing and ever-lasting pink rabbit has since appeared on more television shows or YouTube videos than the Kardashians. (Maybe.)

"The Best Part of Waking Up is Folger's in Your Cup": The slogan rhymes speaks directly to the allegedly appealing flavor of the brand, and has been featured in every Folgers ad since the 1960. The jingle (lyrics) is accompanied by its own music and each have been rearranged and sung across the years by artists as renowned as Aretha Franklin and Randy Travis.

A nice list, this. But this "Fab Five" (the most recent version of this phrase came out in a series of cell phone advertisements starring Dwayne Wade and Sir Charles Barkley) list also could include Apple's "Think Different"; Wheaties "Breakfast of Champions"; Wendy's "Where's the Beef"; or M&M's (the original version) "Melts in your Mouth, Not in your Hand." Or we could have referenced Alka-Seltzer's "Plop, Plop, Fizz, Fizz: Oh What a Relief It Is"; Pepto-Bismol's "Nausea, Heartburn, Indigestion, Upset Stomach, Diarrhea" (can you believe the brand said, and kept repeating this?); or Viagra's slickly subtle "If you Experience an Erection Lasting More than Four Hours." These ten words, which are actually presented as a warning, provide a potent endorsement for this brand's actual power, as it were. (Yep, a four-hour erection will solve the problem, male recipients of the advertising must be thinking, while their partners must be thinking, yep, that would be a real problem.)

Even immortal advertisements such as "Gimme a Break, Gimme a Break (Break me off a piece of that Kit-Kat Bar); "Rice-A-Roni, the San Francisco Treat"; or American Express's "Don't Leave Home Without It," could have been on the list. As could "Hooray Beer": "Parkay, Butter"; "Hey Mikey … He Likes It!" (Life Cereal); or "My bologna has a first name… its O-S-C-A-R" (as in Mayer). Finally, who could forget, after exposure to their messaging, master advertising spokespeople such as Captain Crunch; the Keebler Elves; Snoopy; the Gecko; Flo; or Subway's own Jared; Mike (Tyson); Michael (Jackson); or Michael (Jordan); or the granddaddy of them all, Bill (Cosby), whose advertising star recently extinguished, probably forever.

→ Sales Promotions

Sales promotions, as defined, include a variety of short-term incentives that offer value to B2C or B2B targets. Sales promotion incentives, for example, can be aimed at encouraging purchases amongst targeted consumers and encouraging them to purchase the promoted item now, or at least in the short-run. These are called sales and market-share communication objectives.

Sales promotion incentives also might be used to improve and otherwise motivate the sales efforts of a partnering intermediary, or to secure preferred product placement or treatment from partnering intermediaries inside existing or potential supply chains. These are called retailer-related communication objectives.

South Korea-based Samsung sells electronic and digital products through various US retailer partners including, for example, Best Buy. Best Buy, of course, carries and sells various other well-known electronic and digital brands. Samsung, naturally, would prefer that Best Buy's well-trained, highly-motivated, generally-knowledgeable sales teams allocate greater attention and effort to selling its products rather than Apple brands. Samsung could employ sales promotions for purposes of incentivizing Best Buy to encourage its sales teams to emphasize Samsung brands in their sales efforts. Samsung might offer attractive price discounts to Best Buy (who first must actually purchase the products from Samsung before selling them to anyone) in exchange for Best Buy's agreement to push its sales force in directions sought by Samsung. These price discounts are a form of sales promotion.

Or, in a more likely sales promotion scenario, Samsung might provide promotional allowances (actual money) directly to Best Buy. This action would be taken in exchange for Best Buy's agreement to establish contests through which the salespeople who sell the most Samsung products earn cash bonuses, special trips, or some other incentivizing rewards. The type of sales promotion activity is driven by a sales force objective. It is usually called, as we have mentioned before, "push money" or a "spiff."

Finally, sales promotions are often employed to increase an existing product's visibility, as a sort of reminder or employed as a means to inform the market that a new product has arrived. The prospect exists, albeit in limited form, that the use of sales promotion incentives in B2C settings might facilitate longer-term relationships with customers. The underlying rationale is simple, but sound: get customers to try the product by using any ethical means necessary, and the new customers may end up loving the product, apart from any associated incentives, and decide to purchase the product again exclusively because of the special value that the product itself delivers. The promotion stimulates initial trial. But after a satisfying experience, the merits of the product take over to foster additional sales.

Sales promotions may be defined, or as least described, in another way: when Firms are promoting their brands' values, but not using either advertising, personal selling, direct marketing, or public relations to do it, then these Firms, by default, are using sales promotions to deliver their messages. Sales promotions could be viewed metaphorically as a "bucket" into which any promotional effort that cannot be definitively described as advertising, personal selling, or publicity and public relations can be placed.

Sales Promotions Tools

The most commonly used sales promotion tools are coupons, samples, refunds or rebates; the use of contests, sweepstakes and games; patronage or loyalty related rewards (think "frequent-flyer miles" or "credit card points"); and those supply chain incentives that we called spiffs. (More commentary about spiffs below.)

Various Firms, operating at various times and in different market sectors, will use one or more of these sales promotion tools as part of their integrated marketing communication programs.

Coupons are tickets or documents that can be exchanged for price discounts, usually in retail settings. They are typically distributed directly to customers by manufacturers of consumer packaged goods and are delivered to prospective users through a wide variety of media. These media include direct mail, coupon envelopes, magazines, and newspapers; various digital sources, including mobile devices such as cell phones; and directly through retailers themselves. Ironically, the use of coupons encourages a backhanded but absolutely ethical and legal form of price discrimination because only price-conscious consumers are likely to take the time and effort to use them.

Samples, as defined in a sales promotion context, might include a "freebie" portion of food or other products (cosmetics come to mind) in malls, grocery stores, or your own mailbox. Free samples of non-perishable items are often delivered through direct mail, in fact. The purpose of free sampling is to introduce and inform customers about new products, and to encourage customers, very directly, to take the sampled product for a "test drive" to try it out. Many Firms now offer free samples through their websites. Essentially, this is done in exchange for certain key customer information and the implied promise that customers will use the product. Who knows, after they try it, they, like Mikey, may like it. Thank you Quaker Oats, Life cereal, and Rob McEnany.

A rebate is a give-back to customers by way of a refund, price reduction, or a return on what has already been paid to purchase a product. The most common form is the mail-in rebate. Mail-in rebates entitle a refrigerator buyer to mail back a coupon, receipt, or barcode to receive a check that reimburses part of the purchase price, with the amount of the check indicated and agreed-upon prior to purchase. From the perspective of marketers, the beauty of rebates is that they encourage purchase, which makes sense. Incentives, after all, usually do work. But many consumers fail to redeem the rebates. Customer failure to execute their rebate prerogative likely has never bothered any marketer. And why should it? After all, any money saved by not having to pay out rebates goes directly to the Firm's bottom line. Rebates, in so many words, often function as the promise of a price-discount that marketers make and would keep but often never have to fulfill. Strange but true.

Sweepstakes, contests, and games are forms of sale promotion where one or more prizes are granted to the winner or winners. Typically, sweepstakes are drawings in which consumers (usually) submit an entry that entitles them to take part in and potentially win one or more prizes. Games and contests, in contrast, are competitions where the winner or winners are entitled to prizes. Games and contests can be directed at either consumers or at sales forces working at one or more levels of the supply chain. If directed at consumers, the objective is to motivate sales. If directed at the sales force, the objective is to motivate or incentivize extra effort, and improved performance.

Point-of-purchase (POP) materials are specialized types of sales promotions that include end-of-aisle displays, window signs, special display racks, shelf coupon dispensers, and displays near, on, or next to check-out counters. Their purpose is to draw consumers' attention to new products and products that are on a special offer. POP displays are also used to promote special events such as seasonal sales. POP displays are a powerful tool for stimulating unplanned purchases in retail stores. Eye-catching displays, particularly at the ends of aisles, attract attention, and generate substantial impulse buying. In smaller retail outlets, POP displays are often supplied by the manufacturers of products, and restocked and maintained by their salespeople.

Loyalty or patronage sales promotions are used to encourage and incentivize repeat, or loyal, purchasing behavior amongst key customers, and to offer premiums, special deals or price discounts as purchases grow. Today's most popular loyalty programs are generally offered by the airline and credit card industries. Customers accumulate "points" over time, as they are earned in exchange for loyal or persistent patronage. Those points eventually can be redeemed for books, cash, travel discounts, gift cards or, in the case of airlines, free or heavily discounted flights. Retailers such as Best Buy and Amazon offer "rewards" programs that give loyal customers points with each purchase. These points can be used as cash toward future purchases.

The word "spiff" traditionally has been defined as an immediate bonus that is offered in exchange for a sale. Spiffs were first awarded in 1947 as prizes to employees who sold high quantities of electrical products. Spiffs, you recall, were introduced earlier. More about them follows below.

Sales Promotions: Advantages and Disadvantages

The primary strength of sales promotions, and the chief reason why more money is spent annually on sales promotions than on advertising in the United States is because they work. The use of sales promotions is extremely effective at changing recipient behavior, especially in the short-run.

The Center for Responsive Politics estimates that $3.87 billion was spent on political advertising during the 2014 midterm campaign. Sounds like a lot, doesn't it? But a single private firm, Proctor & Gamble, spent about one-third more on advertising—$4.9 billion—during 2013. Let those advertising numbers, multiplied across tens of thousands of firms, sink in for a moment. Yet we just told you more money is spent on sales promotions than on advertising. The economic impact that can be attributed and indeed is allocated to the power of sales promotions specifically, and marketing communications generally, is something to behold. The United States is truly "ground zero" for the marketing world, and we're alternatively blessed or damned to live in it.

Still, thoughtfully-critical readers might be excused for thinking: this cannot be so. We are exposed to all this advertising; it's too much—it drives me crazy. And yet we've just been told that even more resources are allocated to sales promotion. Well, then, even though I do receive (and even use) the occasional coupon, why am I not more aware and the recipient of more sales promotions? The reason why most people are not more aware of the magnitude of sales promotion expenditures is because the majority of these expenditures occur upstream in supply chains, beyond the eyes and ears of most of us, who mostly are just ordinary consumers. These expenditures are allocated mostly in the form of spiffs or push money.

Another strength of sales promotions is that they can be used in several flexible ways. This latter strength likely derives from the fact that many different types of actionable sales promotions exist, as just explained.

The primary weakness of sales promotions is that their use builds customer loyalty to the deal. That is, loyalty generally accrues to the sales promotion incentive being offered, rather than to the brand being purchased, as a result of the sales promotion. With the exception of customer loyalty and reward programs, sales promotions are simply not effective at building or sustaining lasting relationships with customers. Customers who purchase products/brands or who visit store locations to purchase the promoted product do so because they have been "lured-in" by the sales promotion itself, not because of any value they sense is inherent in the brand, any experience they might have with the brand, or the relationship that said customers might otherwise develop with the brand or the retailer.

Certainly it remains possible that after customers use the promoted product or visit the retailing locale they end up loving one or both. But history and experience have shown that the sort of customer who is incentivized by sales promotions is more likely be loyal to the deal rather than the branded product or store. Consequently, as soon as another branded product or store offers an equivalently sexy or even sexier deal, off they will scurry, turned-on, incentivized, and/or motivated by the next "cute" sales promotional deal that sashays along.

A secondary, but still important downside associated with sales promotions is that such incentives are easily duplicated by competitors or abused by customers, or may lead to sales promotion wars. As with traditional price wars, this form of combat typically leaves the warring competitors with skinnier profit margins, but with market shares that net-out roughly the same.

There is also the fact that sales promotions alone would rarely provide the basis for successful promotional campaigns. "Special deals" cannot be extended forever. And when they end, revenues often crater. Advertising support is needed to convert customers who tried the promoted product into loyal users or repeat buyers, usually by reinforcing the notion in the minds of customers that they have a made a great choice.

Why Is So Much Money Spent on Sales Promotions?

For various reasons, the use of sales promotions has grown rapidly during the last 25 or so years. The reasons for this growth include the short-term pressures to earn material returns that are regularly imposed on marketing managers. Don't tell me what a good (sales) year you had last year. Tell me how many products you moved out of inventory last month. What have you done for me lately?

No one should be surprised then, that to their general detriment and in contrast to the longer-term orientation employed by many global competitors (particularly Asian Firms), US businesspeople generally place more emphasis on short-term results. No one, including us, can criticize US managers for pursuing this tact, because those domestic decision makers are generally rewarded based on what they have accomplished in the short-run. In a world where advertising-based promotions are increasingly ineffective, and where it is too expensive to send out salespeople to "close" sales with customers in every nook and cranny, what promotional element are you going to use if you do not use sales promotions? Rational businesspeople use what works, which is sales promotion, at least, as noted, in the short-run.

Relatedly, the world of global business really has flattened in a way that makes *The World is Flat* author Thomas Friedman proud. What are we talking about? Here, we reference the fact that the incredible expansion of global competition has made domestic (US) rivalries fiercer than ever. Did you realize that even 20 years ago the Big Three domestic automobile manufacturers still dominated domestic market share? Those times are far away in the rearview mirror at this point. In response to this trend, US managers are increasingly wielding their most effective promotional weapons to stand out favorably in an increasingly crowded room. Naturally, managers use what works. Just a few years back, the domestic auto industry got into trouble for using rebates so often that American customers quickly wised-up to the tactic, and were able to see it coming. At that point smart customers increasingly waited to purchase the new season's vehicles until General Motors, Ford, or Chrysler attached a rebate to the sales deal.

The attitudes of B2C and B2B customers have changed. Less loyalty exists toward all manner of institutions throughout the United States. These institutions include the government, religious organizations, schools, and business organizations, including their brands. Americans, with good cause, have generally turned into a more cynical, "prove-it-to-me," "show-me-the-money" (thank you *Jerry McGuire* and Cameron Crowe) bunch. Today, consumers and B2B customers alike are also more concerned about prices and their costs. This is especially true in the midst of the long-tailed aftermath of the 2007–2010 Great Recession from which most of country has still not recovered. These two trends intersected to create situations where customers who were less brand loyal became more likely to brand-switch, given the slightest incentive. And when customers, generally, are receptive to the price cuts and cost savings derived from incentives, the value of these spiff-like incentives increases in lockstep.

→ Public Relations and Publicity

Public relation (PR) efforts intended to build or sustain "good relations" or relationships with various publics, or groups, that people, organizations, or nations believe are important. Public relations entails Firm-initiated communications efforts that seek to manage the collective emotions, opinions, and beliefs held about the Firm or its brand by various publics who are important to the Firm's future success prospects. Key "publics" typically would include customers and prospective customers (in either B2C or B2B segments); stockholders and potential investors; intermediaries, suppliers and prospective supply chain partners; employees and management; or various groups such as environmentalists, financiers, and governmental or regulatory entities who have a stake or interest in the Firm's activities. Effective PR efforts help create desirable images for Firms and their brands, induce audiences into thinking that these images indeed are desirable, and create/strengthen relationships between their customers and those Firms. Perhaps most importantly, PR routinely helps Firms or human brands "pick up the pieces" as quickly as possible after something has hit the fan so hard that their carefully cultivated images have "come a cropper."[8]

Publicity management, as a subset of PR, entails non-personal, indirectly paid or unpaid communiqués that relate and contribute to the narrative that a Firm would prefer to have written, pronounced, or discussed about its brand, products, people, activities or strategies, etc. PR can and should be used to build or promote existing brand equity. PR can and should be used to announce great new breakthroughs or products. PR can and should be used to clean up the mess after screw-ups arise.

The League

The National Football League (NFL) has long been one of the world's best-managed, most-respected brands. No so much anymore. In quick order, the League suffered six plus one consecutive hits to its image during the 2014/15 season. First, there was spousal abuse, as exemplified by Ray Rice and other players. Second, there was child abuse, in the person of superstar Adrian Peterson. Third, negative publicity about a spate of traumatic head injuries and related suicides came to light involving numerous former and current players. Fourth, there were multiple rape convictions, exemplified most prominently through the imprisonment of former Super Bowl hero Darren Sharper. Fifth, this was all topped by the sensational murder conviction of a former New England Patriot star, Aaron Hernandez. Finally, there is Tom Brady's four game suspension resulting from "inflategate." On the plus-one front, Commissioner Roger Goodell was even accused of being caught in a cover-up, a knowing lie, by many media leaders. Despite unstintingly high television ratings (Americans love their violent games), these branding travails have not gone unnoticed. Long-term core NFL sponsors such as Coca-Cola, Anheuser-Busch, and Proctor & Gamble all rattled their sabers as they purportedly considered withdrawing their advertising in response to concerns about their brand images being damaged due to their close affiliations with the League.

Time to call in public relations and roll out the positive publicity, as is now being done. Time will tell how well those public relations-driven image-building efforts are working.

Public Relations and Publicity: Strengths and Weaknesses

The underlying strength of any positive messages delivered through either public relations-related sources is that such information is purportedly more credible. These messages are more credible because marketers do not have to commit the original sin, as discussed earlier (Chapter 16), of paying for or delivering the messages themselves. When public relations are used, someone else, is at least nominally speaking for the marketer and its brand.

Firms generally do not pay for PR press releases or new stories. Instead, PR staffers develop and circulate information and attempt to manage perceptions of events as well as news cycles. In many cases well-managed PR efforts create more media buzz more quickly and less expensively than advertising.

Yet even the strongest people, institutions, or promotional elements are usually imbued with certain inherent weaknesses. This is true of public relations and publicity messages, as well. To begin with, because PR is not paid for by marketers, the messaging element is not controlled by marketers. Convince key media to report on even the most positive new product launch is also difficult—unless, one can only assume, your brand name is Apple.

Oncologists, i.e., cancer physicians, have long coveted the so-called "Magic Bullet." For that matter so too have cancer survivors, most without consciously being aware of the possible rewards. "Magic Bullet," as used in this context, is a catch-all medical phrase used to describe the sort of cancer treatment that targets only cancer cells rather than indiscriminately targeting the body's other fastest-dividing cells, as does chemotherapy and radiation, or wrecking understandable violence on cancer survivors by cutting cancerous cells from their bodies. The only "Magic Bullet" developed by the pharmaceutical sector to date is a drug known by the brand name Gleevac. Gleevac successfully treats chronic mylegenous leukemia without delivering any punishing side effects upon the cancer survivor, which is fantastic news. But have you heard anything about this not just good but great news story from the media? It's doubtful that you have. As you know, given what you learned earlier, the same media are much more likely to report on what went wrong rather than what went right with most new product introductions.

Perpetual Needs

The world of business and marketing and indeed the world itself unfolds and intertwines in ways that perpetually create both the opportunity and need for public relations to step up and in, for purposes of cleaning up the mess.

Consider what the following entities all hold in common: British Petroleum (BP) and the Gulf Coast Oil spill; Hurricane Katrina, New Orleans and the George W. Bush Administration; fallen politicians or governmental workers such as Senator John Edwards, the aptly-named representative Anthony Weiner; or the Secret Service; Lance Armstrong and doping and lying about it; Tiger Woods and cheating and lying about it; the Affordable Health Care Act and its badly fumbled and misrepresented rollout; Obamacare architect and economist Jon Gruber and "the stupidity of the American voter"; and Chris Brown, R. Kelley, and France's Perrier brand.

Two things, actually. First, their personal, professional or corporate brands were all badly and at times permanently dinged by predictable or unexpected disasters that they visited upon themselves (through their behaviors) or that nature visited upon them. Second, each person, brand, corporation, or organization then went on to further damage their brands by badly mismanaging, or having "experts" in place who badly mismanaged, their rehabilitative public relations efforts.

What do Johnson & Johnson (a Fortune 500 member and multinational maker of medical devices, pharmaceuticals, and related products) and David Lettermen have in common? Two things, again. First, seemingly out of the blue, each brand was violently assaulted. The attack on the brand equity of Johnson & Johnson was utterly other-inflicted. In 1982, a horrible person (no specific person was ever completely linked to the crime) laced Extra Strength Tylenol with cyanide. The action led to the painful deaths of seven customers.

The attack on David Letterman's brand equity, was infinitely less profound and also utterly self-inflicted. Letterman, a married man, was "sleeping with" several female employees. He was therefore violating the rights of the male employees in his production company. Apparently, Mr. Letterman was never sexually attracted to and therefore never slept with male employees, thus denying them any opportunity to engage in potentially career-enhancing "pillow talk." And one of his former associates, a frienemy if there ever was one, was going to rat him out.

But yes. There was that second thing that Johnson & Johnson and David Letterman had in common: each branding entity masterly managed its public relations response to its respective threat, and quickly rebounded through tactics that elevated the branding power of Johnson & Johnson and Letterman to levels that neither had previously reached.

The long and short of each entity's response collapses to this singular point. Johnson & Johnson and Mr. Letterman each stood up, did not try to hide, deflect blame, equivocate, or spin in any way. Each entity publicly "owned" its problem, instantly, and resoundingly demonstrated that it was up to them to develop and deliver the best possible solution. As Johnson & Johnson and Letterman quickly did.

Johnson & Johnson promptly removed all Tylenol-related products from every shelf in the land and immediately instituted measures that led to tamper-proof and child-proof packaging for all its pharmaceutical products. The Firm apologized, assumed complete accountability, and delivered all possible restitution to injured parties that it could. Tylenol owned a huge US market share at the time of the cyanide incident. Its market share collapsed to zero, literally overnight. But through its actions Johnson & Johnson quickly reestablished the equity and power of the Tylenol brand (ever notice how much more expensive is Tylenol than its branded and generic competitors?) and regained the entire market share, plus some, that it lost during the episode. More than three decades later, the Johnson & Johnson's Tylenol public relations and new product development responses still reign as the unsurpassed model for how to effectively manage a true corporate crisis.

The Letterman affair obviously was far less meaningful. But he too masterfully managed his personal and professional branding crisis. How? By telling the truth. How else? By taking full responsibility and ascribing no blame or fault to anyone and anything else. How did he do it? By using the first ten minutes of his show that aired on October 1, 2009, or the day before the scandal was to break, to take full ownership and responsibility, sans any excuses, and to throw himself upon the mercy of the market. His preemptive public relations foray worked magnificently. Contrast that with the nearly contemporaneous Tiger Woods sex scandal, in which the golfer and his PR team failed to take any of the remedial actions that Letterman and his team had taken. Negative Letterman buzz died in days. The Wood's scandal went on to play out a seemingly interminable life all its own with one after another women, day after day, announcing their non-public relations with Tiger. The Tiger brand has never fully recovered. Of course the fact that, to date, he has never won another major hasn't helped, either. Marketers probably "love winners more" than they "hate those caught up in extramarital sex scandals"— especially when it comes to celebrity spokesperson serving as the human face for their brands.

Public Relations' Functions and Tools

The functions routinely performed by public relations professionals include management of media relations, publicity, and lobbying and investor relations. Public relations experts generally handle and manage the public relations promotional function through the use of:

- News (press) releases, generally initiated to counter the negative or accentuate the positive.
- Speeches, in terms of either writing or delivering them.
- News conference and grand openings, including fun events, such as General Motors displaying its new, youth-targeted vehicles on campus.
- Website management, blogs, and tweets.

→ Personal Selling

Personal selling, like other promotional mix elements, exists fundamentally to inform, remind, and persuade prospects or customers. Personal selling is also routinely used to establish or strengthen relationships with prospects or customers. But the core strength of personal selling is that it is far and away the most influential tool in most Firms' promotional mix. The primary purpose of personal selling is to shape the purchasing decisions made by carefully targeted individuals or groups. The primary objective is persuasion.

Personal selling, as defined, entails two-way person-to-person interactions in which message receivers (prospective or actual B2B or B2C customers) provide instantaneous feedback to senders' (salespeople's) hopefully influential messages. Feedback arrives in the form of actions, words, expressions, and body language initiated by customers or prospects. Personal selling, at its core, is a conversation between two or more people. Personal selling, naturally, is personal, generally involving face-to-face, phone-to-phone or more recently Skype-to-Skype type interactive communications between message senders and receivers. More than two individuals are often involved because teams of buyers and/or sellers are frequently used. Buying and selling teams are especially prevalent in supply chain exchange settings (B2B exchanges). Unlike advertising's non-personal nature, personal selling is, well, personal.

At least four exchange conditions exist in which the use of personal selling is usually appropriate. First, when the unit sales volume involved is sufficiently high. Second, when the prices of individual or bundled products being sold are sufficiently high to justify the higher costs associated with personal selling efforts. Third, when products being marketed are so complex that their precise use or benefits must be explained or demonstrated to customers. Finally, when the problem-solving capabilities of products must be customized in order to successfully match and resolve customers' special problems or needs, personal selling should generally be used. When all four of these pre-conditions are present the use personal selling is not only appropriate but likely also necessary.

Types of Personal Selling

Many of us think of inside selling in a retail setting when the term "personal selling" is tossed around. For example, consider salespeople on the showroom floors of Best Buy or JC Penny. This person is technically called an inside order taker. His or her job is to take orders, answer questions, make "suggestive sales," and generally assist customers at the point of sale. There are however, a number of other forms of personal selling:

- Order getters are salespeople tasked with generating new business. Their task is to find new customers and increase sales to existing customers. Usually associated with B2B, this form of selling is commonly called creative selling since it draws heavily on the ability of the salesperson to prospect and qualify prospective customers.

- Delivery salespeople, such as the Dr. Pepper route delivery person, are responsible for delivering and stocking products for which an order has already been placed. This type of salesperson, however, can make additional sales while servicing existing accounts.

- Outside order takers are traveling salespersons who visit customers in the field and generate orders in the process. This form of selling is most common in B2B supply chains. The Kubota salesperson calling on its regional distributors, as well as larger agricultural and construction businesses is an example.

- Missionary salespeople don't actually get involved in making sales. Their job is to provide B2B customers and prospective customers with information, assist in promotion activities with the Firm's supply chain partners, and generally work to build goodwill. If customers request additional products they are referred to the Firm's field sales personnel. This type of salesperson is common in the pharmaceutical industry. Missionary reps (called detail salespersons) service pharmacies, hospitals, and physicians. These salespersons normally are compensated via salaries.

- Sales engineers are technical experts in industries where products must be tailored to the needs of specific customers. Often trained in engineering or the sciences, these sales people offer their technical expertise to advise clients on product specifications and functions, and assist with systems design and installation. Sales engineers may not be directly involved with making sales, leaving this to other members of the sales staff.

- Team selling is employed by Firms in industries selling complex products and solutions to B2B customers. IBM, Xerox, EDS, Procter & Gamble, Drop Box, and Oracle are among the Firms heavily engaged in team selling. The selling task is simply too complex to be handled by a single person. The sales team consists of a mix of personnel with a variety of skills. Typical members include sales personnel, representatives from R&D, engineers and other technical specialists, operations experts, and financial advisors.[9]

The Personal Selling Process

The personal selling process features six steps (Exhibit 17.2). Each step or stage is examined briefly below.

Prospecting and Qualifying

Prospecting is the process of identifying prospective customers. This is probably the most critical step in the selling process. It makes no sense to waste time attempting to sell a product to someone who does not need, let alone want, or who cannot afford the product. Identifying prospects can be as easy as encouraging referrals by existing customers. In general, however, the task is more onerous. Firms typically will attempt to characterize likely customers in terms of easily identifiable geographic and demographic characteristics and then employ various directories and databases to locate people with these characteristics.

In the B2B arena, various federal agencies and trade associations maintain indexes of businesses that can easily be tapped for sources of leads. Increasingly, sales people are posting their professional profiles on social media such as LinkedIn to network with other professionals who may qualify as potential customers. LinkedIn's Sales Navigator, Sales Genie, and Hoovers offer dedicated prospecting services keyed to public and private databases. Services such as Accela Communications and Touchstone Communications will data mine website visitation data as well as tap existing databases to assist Firms in culling out likely prospects for further contact.

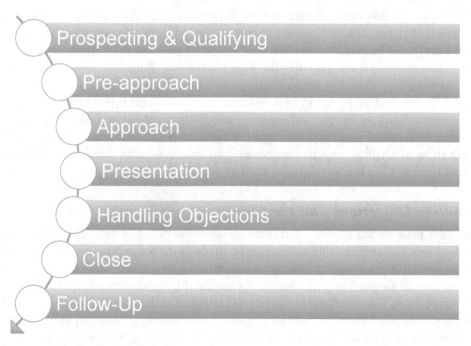

Exhibit 17.2 *The Personal Selling Process.*

B2C sales prospecting relies on tried and true procedures such as cold calling, inquiries by email, social media, or inquiries made to the sellers' websites. Sales promotions are employed to solicit interest in Firm's products. The objective is to generate interest that leads to requests for further information.

Once prospective customers have been identified they must further be "qualified." The key questions are: does the prospect need and want the product? And, does the prospect have the resources to buy the product? In many cases the product may be too expensive to buy outright and must be financed. If so, the next question becomes: can the prospective buyer obtain the required financing? In the case of B2B sales an additional qualifying dimension is the likelihood that the prospect will buy enough to justify investing in a long-term relationship.

The Pre-approach

The pre-approach is primarily a consideration with B2B selling. This is a homework step in which as much is learned about the prospect as possible. This task is much easier for public companies due to the extensive information disclosure requirements imposed on them. The resulting data are available via the SEC's Edgar database, Hoover's, The Wall Street Journal, Standard & Poor's 500 Directory, and Dun & Bradstreet's Million Dollar Directory. Of course, sellers can tap the websites for both public and private companies for a wealth of information.

The Approach

The approach is the initial contact with a qualified prospect. Armed with knowledge generated via the last two steps, the seller is prepared to contact the prospect and, potentially, make an initial presentation. In B2B selling it is rare to close a sale on the first visit. Rather, the first presentation is geared more to introductions and further information collection to learn more about the company and its needs. This is a time to build rapport with the buying organization; an essential first step in creating meaningful and lasting B2B relationships.

The Presentation

A formal presentation may not occur on the first visit to a prospect's office, as noted in our description of the approach. However, at some point a formal presentation will be made in which a case must be made for why the seller's product provides differentiation value beyond those values offered by competitors. The presentation may range between formal deliveries using presentation software to simpler one-on-one conversations. Purely canned presentations in the B2B context usually are to be avoided in favor of a hybrid presentation in which the seller listens as much, or more so, as he or she speaks.[10] However they're delivered, presentations should be professional-grade and highlight key value propositions. Ideally, salespeople should be perceived as credible, expert, dependable and truthful—just like Allen Chick, one of Edward Jones & Co.'s leading financial advisors.

Handling Objections and the Close

Every sales presentation will be interrupted by questions posed by prospective buyers. These questions may be framed as objections to points made by the seller. Such objections are offered as reasons why the prospect may be hesitant to commit. Astute sellers will view these objections as opportunities for providing additional information, further confirming the values provided by their products. This literally means that good salespeople should welcome objections. Every objection, if handled correctly, can be converted into additional selling points. Objections signal that the prospect has been paying attention and is weighing the merits of the seller's offer.

At some point, the seller must ask for the sale. This is the "close." Aside from prospecting for leads, this is probably the next most important step in the selling process. Without a close, no sale is made. All buyers expect the close. But amazingly, their fear of rejection often makes salespeople reluctant to initiate this final step! Yet it must be done and need not be difficult. Indeed, there are a number of alternative formats for closing sales that may ease the task for the reticent seller:[11]

- The assumptive close assumes the buyer has made a positive decision and only minor points need to be clarified to "finalize the details of the sale." For example, the salesperson may ask "Would you prefer delivery by UPS or FedEx?" Or, "Will you pay cash, or can we assist you with financing?"

- With the standing-room-only close the seller frames the sale as urgent to receive, for example, a special price or free gift before some deadline passes. For example, an LA Fitness salesperson may offer to "waive your enrollment fee if you sign-up today."

- Using the sharp angle close the buyer asks for a concession, such as free delivery or additional features. The salesperson's response could be: "If I can do this for you, will you place your order now?"

- The final objection close is used if the seller is confident that the customer understands and agrees with the differentiating values of the salesperson's product. The close is initiated by asking the buyer for an objection, one which should not occur if all has gone well to this point: "Is there any reason why we can't process your order and proceed with the shipment next week?"

Follow-Up

Follow-up includes post-sale activities that provide added value to buyers and provide feedback to sellers. Once the close is delivered and the sale is made there still are details of the sale that may remain including dates, times, and mode of delivery; payment and financing arrangements; arranging for installation of the product; and, training of the buyer's employees (as appropriate). It is essential the sellers absolutely track the status of the order as it moves to the buyer. In this way irregularities can be identified and rectified before they become problematic. This is the first real step to ensuring long-term customer relationships are developed and nurtured.

Advantages and Disadvantages of Personal Selling

Multiple advantages are associated with the use of personal selling. For starters, the initial sales messages can be a *priori* tailored to precisely address the needs of the audience. But because personal selling efforts involve two-way, interactive, and reciprocal conversations, anticipated sales messages can be modified on the run in response to recipients' more or less auspicious reactions to the initially planned messages. Salespeople also enjoy the opportunity to dictate to whom they present, at least over time. This second advantage reduces the amount of wasted effort. The third advantage of personal selling is that it offers marketing Firms their best opportunity to close sales. Salespeople can address customer objections or concerns in real time and directly acquire the customer's promise or commitment to purchase the product. The best salespeople are very good at achieving each communication outcome. These exact abilities, of course, are what makes them the best.

There are disadvantages, of course; nothing is perfect. First, personal selling is far more expensive to execute on a per-customer-reached basis than is any other promotional element. Training even the most talented individuals to become effective salespeople also costs a great deal. And unfortunately, one of two things is likely to happen once that training is complete:

salespeople fail to sell successfully, despite their expensive training or salespeople sell well and some other company hires them away now that they are well-trained and experienced. (Of course, a third possibility is that the salesperson succeeds, sticks around, and the salesperson and selling Firm each enjoy ample financial returns.) And ironically, one key strength associated with personal selling, its flexibility, can actually morph into a disadvantage. Different salespeople may alter key aspects of the selling message to the point where clear, consistent, and compelling presentation of the product's core values are not being delivered. When this happens, core Integrated Marketing Communication (IMC) principles of the sort introduced during Chapter 16 are being ignored.

→ Direct Marketing

Direct marketing, broadly defined, includes various types of direct communications initiated with and targeted toward B2C or B2B customers. These direct contacts are initiated to produce certain customer responses. These responses might include requests for additional information, visits to the soliciting retailer, or actual orders to purchase brands being promoted through direct marketing efforts. Direct marketing messages can be delivered through snail-mail (you will likely such solicitations in your actual mailbox today); catalogs; telephone calls; direct response advertising and infomercials, in magazines or on television or radio; or through digitally-mediated communication sources such as tweets, texts, or emails.

Advantages and Disadvantages

Direct marketing efforts often can be interactive, similar to personal selling efforts. This is a clear advantage of direct marketing. Messages also can be prepared quickly, specifically tailored, and adjusted to address the needs of targeted recipients. This capacity opens up the possibility of establishing closer relationships with customers. Direct marketing has been around for a long time but still remains one of the fastest growing promotional mix elements.

The promotional tactic, however, is still characterized by a number of shortfalls. For starters, direct marketing efforts are expensive, in terms of both money and time. Their preparation and delivery requires extensive use of a wide-reaching, perpetually-updated marketing research databases. Direct marketers are also increasingly confronting growing consumer concerns about invasions of their privacy. This is probably why direct marketers have recently experienced material declines in the numbers of favorable consumer responses to their promotional overtures.

→ Other Communication Elements

Other product and brand-related factors exist that can be leveraged to communicate desirable messages to customers. Product design is one such factor. Great design can drive innovation—as noted, products and ideas that are new and useful—and yet great product design is also a consequence of innovation. The perception or reality that innovation exists also can facilitate branding power. In turn, the presence of branding power strengthens marketing communications. Branding power, when bundled with effective communications, creates greater customer loyalty to the brand, which ultimately sustains higher profits.

Great product designs generally feature an intriguing blend of form and functionality (performance). Great product designs directly communicate; in effect, pronounce, the presence of quality or the absence of flaw. Want to give your promotional team as well as your customers something to talk about? Start with design. Did Apple just chime in with a resounding Amen?

The prices of product/brands (strategically pricing higher or lower than competitors) also communicate volumes about the brand. Rising prices, or already high prices, may signal the brand is in high demand (the style is hot, better get the brand now because it may be unattainable in the future) or cool (wow, if I could rock that brand I would be cool, too). Falling prices, or already low prices, basically may signal the opposite. Falling prices may "tell" customers something is wrong with the brand. Falling prices likewise might signal to customers that they should hold off acquiring the brand now because the price may be lower next month.

Carrie Bradshaw jokes aside, Manolo Blahnik shoes are an expensive, top-ten luxury brand in anybody's book. Blahniks are sold in high-end speciality shops and prestigious retailers such as Niemen-Marcus or Nordstrom's. What would be said about the quality, cache or position-earned status of Manolo's kicks if they suddenly showed up on Target's shelves? And we are not knocking Target Stores because over time, the Target brand has effectively developed and communicated an appealing lower price/higher quality/cooler design positioning cache all its own, despite the credit card theft issues that the Target brand has been trying to address, with mixed results. The 2015 Lilly Pulitzer roll-out comes to mind.

The distinctive shapes or styles of products similarly send messages about the quality, panache, and spirit of respective brands. The style and shape of the Jaguar automobile has been distinctively identifiable as "Jaguar" for several consecutive decades running. Meanwhile, as noted, the Mercedes-Benz star implicitly communicates the brand's dominance in style and quality over land, air, and sea. Even the nature of packaging or sounds of their engines can deliver pointedly positive messages about brands. Consider Hershey's chocolate; the packaging looks exactly like the product inside. Or, Harley-Davidson—the distinctively Harley sound of the Harley bike has actually been patented. "Zoom."

Finally, note that the retailers, as supply chain partners, through which manufacturers/marketers choose to distribute their brands, speak directly about those brands. The descriptive statement just written about Manolo Blahnik would similarly apply to the Rolex brand if its wares suddenly began appearing on Walmart's shelves.

→ Push Versus Pull Promotional Strategies, Revisited

The distinction between push and pull promotion was introduced in the last chapter. Below, we further develop the discussion. Supply chains begin with originating source Firms. From there, supply chains flow through to producers and intermediaries (including wholesalers and retailers) all the way, ultimately, to end-user consumers like us. These Firms exist and operate as buyers and sellers in a series of interconnected buyer-seller relationships. Raw materials, component parts, finished goods, services, and information flow from their points-of-origin and production to their points-of-consumption and eventually to their point of disposal or recycling. As you remember, supply chains operate from "dirt-to-dirt."

All Firms participate in supply chains. This means all Firms must make certain basic decisions about the types of promotions that they will use to inform, remind, or persuade prospective and actual customers about their products/brands and the values associated with those brands. These Firms must make promotional decisions related to how they might best develop and deliver informative or persuasive (or even reminder) information is ways that initiate new or strengthen existing relationships with other Firms or consumers.

Promotion within and through the supply chain, when taken as a whole, can be broken into two broad strategic categories. The two categories are, in no particular order, are known as pull and push promotions.

Pull Promotions

A pull promotional strategy describes informative, reminder or persuasive supply chain communications that are targeted directly at end-use consumers. The most basic communication goal of pull promotions is to stimulate the desire for a specific product/brand among final users or ultimate consumers. The demand that hopefully emanates from the communication effort is thereafter assumed to pull demand for the desired product from its originating source firm throughout the entire supply chain to end use consumers.

Folgers' coupons for a new coffee product that might fall out of the Sunday newspaper illustrate a pull promotional strategy. This classic sales promotion message, which often entails delivery of price-related incentives such as coupons, is conveyed directly from Folgers, the manufacturer, to consumers through the Dallas Morning News or Fort Worth Star Telegram, the communication or messaging medium. Then, coffee drinkers presumably would visit Tom Thumb or Kroger's and encourage the retailer(s) to carry the couponed merchandise to facilitate redemption, that is, if the grocery stores do not already do this. Or, if the couponed product is already present in the store, the consumer would be incentivized by the coupon's cost savings to purchase the specific coffee product. Notably, grocery retailers are also involved in and benefit from this promotional pull-based transaction.

Marketing manufacturers regularly use pull promotional strategies. Men of a certain age who remain sexually active sometimes experience performance problems. This same market

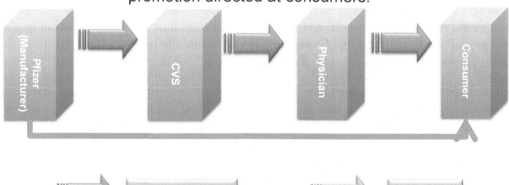

Exhibit 17.3 *Push and Pull Strategies.*

segment also often finds it difficult to discuss their problem with others. Realizing these things, pharmaceutical marketers consciously coined a more palatable name for this problem during the late 1990s—after they, as innovative marketers, had developed its solution. The kinder, gentler name, actually an acronym, was ED. Since that time, Pfizer, Eli Lilly and Bayer Healthcare have struggled to "own the word" that best epitomizes the solution for ED. Say hello to the now well-known Viagra (Pfizer), Cialis (Eli Lilly), or Levitra (Bayer Healthcare) brands. ED, by all accounts, is easier for male egos to accept or discuss as a problem than is impotence or erectile dysfunction. And a male consumer must discuss the problem, with his physician, no less. This set-up returns us to the question of how pull promotional strategies actually work.

Pull promotional strategies presume that, when they are properly motivated or incentivized, ultimate consumers can dramatically influence and stimulate the flow of products throughout entire supply chains; that is, when these end-users are properly informed or incentivized to do so. This is why Pfizer, the marketing/manufacturer who operates at the opposite end of the supply chain, delivers its advertised message about Viagra's marvelous solution directly to end-users. Anyone who has watched a televised college or professional football game during the last 16 to 18 years can readily attest to the preceding statement as fact.

By this point, the logic driving Pfizer's targeting (men have the problem), positioning (men in these ads are always powerful-looking and women always attractive) and media selection (men watch football on television) strategies should be evident to all. Pfizer hopes targeted consumers' exposure to pull advertisements will persuade them to visit their physician to discuss the problem and ask him/her to write prescriptions for Viagra by name. When this happens, demand for the brands is pulled throughout the entire supply chain. The promotional sequence— the bottom half of Exhibit 17.3 (a repeat of Exhibit 16.1) summarizes this process. It unfolds like this: Pharmaceutical manufacturer (Pfizer) advertises directly to the consumer (Joe Cool) who demands a prescription from his physician (Dr. House), who in turn writes a prescription that is filled by the retail pharmacist (CVS) who orders and stocks the product from Pfizer (the manufacturer, again).

Only rarely would physicians be contractually obligated to write prescriptions for Viagra. Physicians certainly have the option of prescribing Cialis, Levitra, or other marketing solutions to the ED problem. That is why physicians are often "incentivized" by Pfizer salespeople's offers of free drug samples or pizza for their staff; free trips to exotic locales, where they can learn more about new products at medical conventions; or attractive speaking fees in exchange for sharing their expertise and experience with others. These sales promotion incentives fall into the broad category of pull promotions, as well.

Pull strategies often are used during new product launches. They are executed in an attempt to entice consumers into creating early demand for the new product. Apple employs pull advertising and publicity-based promotional strategies each time it launches a new generation iPhone. Pull strategies are frequently employed to stimulate or sustain loyalty as mature products confront stronger price competition.

Pull strategies occasionally prove so effective that their use resurrects marketing dinosaurs, which are products or brands from another era that have long since lost their buzz. Here, we could be discussing the resurgence in the sales of Beatles music that transpired from 2000 to 2009 in correspondence the introduction of new music technologies as discussed during Chapter 11. Or we could be discussing a popular plaything for children throughout the 1950s and 1960s that eventually went off the boil. Yo-yos, you see, had lost their mojos by the time the 1990s arrived. So during 1995-6, Duncan, the world's large yo-yo marketer, decided to go straight to the kids. Hoping to lure youngsters away from then burgeoning video game-time,

Duncan offered kids real money, $25.00, if they could perform tricks. The communication goal was to trigger a resurgent interest in yo-yos amongst kids and force retailers to carry more yo-yos on prime shelf space.

Duncan's pull promotional approach worked, for a while, before technology's powerful lure depressed sales again. Since then, "Kids these days [increasingly] just want to live in their own f——king little worlds in their own bedrooms watching Netflix and becoming obese," according to prestigious British magazine *The Economist*.[12] Now may be an opportune time for Wham-O, the famous Hula Hoop marketer, to renew pull promotional efforts on behalf of the iconic brand. Somebody, or something, needs to get kids moving again.

Push Promotions

Push strategies target promotional mix efforts directly at the next downstream (i.e., toward the end-user) intermediary, as opposed to end-use consumers themselves (top half of Exhibit 17.3). This is the most important difference between push and pull promotional strategies. Supply chains exist as actual linked-together networks of buyer-seller relationships. When push promotions are used, one supply chain partner, functioning as seller, "pushes" its promotional efforts against the next link, now functioning as buyer, in the supply chain. Eventually the erstwhile buying Firm transforms into a seller who directs its promotional mix further downstream in the supply chain as the product ultimately flows eventually toward the final-user.

The following paragraphs illustrates how this process actually works, beginning with a Firm that mines and processes iron ore. That iron ore is quickly combined with other ores and transformed into steel by a steel mill. The resulting raw steel is subsequently converted into thousands of screws by a screw manufacturer. Those screws are then used in the manufacturing of diesel truck engines produced by Cummins. Hopefully sooner than later the engine is integrated, intact, into a Ram truck. Shortly thereafter Chrysler, operating as mothership to the Ram brand, "pushes" the finished truck onto the lot of an independent dealership that sells, among other brands, Ram trucks. Finally, a salesperson or sales team, working for the dealership, sells the truck to you.

Someone or some marketing team, operating inside each of these Firms, had to sell raw materials, component parts of finished products, to the next link in the supply chain. This is only natural and this is exactly how much of the B2B world operates. After all, nothing happens in business until someone sells something. This is how push promotions unfold inside supply chains. Each succeeding supply chain members' job is to push for ever-evolving, ever-more-valuable materials, components, and finished products throughout all six levels of the supply chain just reported. Naturally, various other intermediary levels including manufacturer's agents, warehouses, transportation or shipper firms, and wholesalers also operate inside this supply chain.

Personal selling and sales promotions typically play major roles during push promotional processes. Manufacturers' representatives might call on wholesalers to promote sales orders and offer sales assistance. Sales promotions, for example, might offer 15% off the normal lot price in exchange for Albertson's (the buyer's) promise that it will give Green Giant's (the seller's) new brand of corn preferred shelf space. The hypothetical action in which Green Giant just engaged is usually called a "slotting allowance." Note the use of "slot," as a synonym for the term "space" on grocery shelves. Space is always limited on grocery shelves. No one, then, should be surprised that grocery stores often must be "incentivized" to carry new products. And naturally, stocking new grocery products in slots on grocery shelves requires that older products be removed.

When effectively employed, push promotions can generate a sort of domino effect. Push sales promotions are typically launched by manufacturers and aimed at intermediaries, or resellers. The success of push promotions depends on how receptive intermediaries are to the promotional message and/or incentives. The use of push promotions allow supply chain members to exercise greater control over what is said and how things are said about their products.

Either, Both, But Never Neither

Marketing organizations usually do not rely exclusively on either the push or pull promotional strategies. Instead, they generally employ both push and pull elements together. Pfizer, Eli Lilly, and Bayer Health Care, the pharmaceutical firms mentioned earlier, collectively spend billions of dollars on their respective push and pull marketing communications. Both promotional forms are used because the Firms are seeking to develop long-term relationships with Firms operating at various levels of their supply chains, including, naturally, end-use consumers.

Don't and Do

Mr. Barnum, the fellow introduced this chapter began, is also famous for allegedly having said, "There's a sucker born every minute." A truism, unfortunately. But we know by now you have learned enough to never willingly take advantage of said suckers, because you've also learned to value long-term mutually beneficial relationships, along with an enhanced reputation for your Firm and its brand over any short-term exploitative value that might be secured. Whatever your Firm is showing or telling, or demonstrating or explaining, had best emanate from a position of truth. There is no substitute. Because in the Internet world, of all past or future worlds, the world has grown too small for anything but truth.

Once the material has been taught by a teacher as masterful as Dr. Fred Cassell, one realizes that the New Testament Book of Romans has more than a few good words to say about marketing, especially when marketing messengers themselves have something good to market. These words are (we have inserted the verbiage contained in the brackets):

"How then will they call on him in whom they have not believed? And how are they to believe in [a new product/an idea] of whom they have never heard? And how are they to hear [the product or idea] without someone preaching [disseminating the good news]? And how are they to preach [inform, remind, persuade and built relationships] unless they are sent? As it is written, "How beautiful are the feet of those who preach the good news!" (Romans 10:14-15).*[13]

A rather strong endorsement, you hopefully agree, for the importance and value of marketing promotion. Especially when and if something worthwhile, something delivering differentiating value to others, is being truthfully communicated by the marketer.

Endnotes

[1] John Nichols, Robert McChesney, *Dollarocracy: How the Money and Media Election Complex is Destroying America* (New York: Nation Books, 2013), 105.

[2] Ralph Keyes, *The Quote Verifier: Who Said What, Where, and When* (New York: St. Martin's Press, 2006), 2.

3 "Total US Ad Spending to See Largest Increase Since 2004," *eMarketer* (July 2, 2014), accessed April 27, 2015, http://www.emarketer.com/Article/Total-US-Ad-Spending-See-Largest-Increase-Since-2004/1010982#sthash.2KtneusE.dpuf.

4 John E. Villafranco, "The Law of Comparative Advertising in the United States," *IP Litigator*, Vol. 16, No. 1 (January/February 2010): 1–7.

5 Cain Burdeau, "BP Ad Campaign Following Gulf Oil Spill Deemed 'Propaganda' By Some," *Huffington Post* (January 8, 2012), accessed May 4, 2015, http://www.huffingtonpost.com/2012/01/08/bp-ad-campaign-gulf-oil-_n_1192600.html.

6 Michael Hiestand, "Super Bowl Ad with Tebow Creating Buzz," *USA Today* (January 27, 2010): 3C.

7 Neil Kokemuller, "Examples of Advocacy Ads," *AZCentral*, accessed May 4, 2015, http://yourbusiness.azcentral.com/examples-advocacy-ads-12699.html.

8 "Come a cropper" means 1. to fail completely, or 2. to experience a hurtful, damaging, or embarrassing fall. In the current context, the implication is that the Firm's carefully crafted brand image been extensively damaged.

9 Tawheed Kader, "Sales Teams Are Making a Big Comeback at Tech Firms," *Entrepreneur* (July 23, 2014), accessed May 5, 2015, http://www.entrepreneur.com/article/235855.

10 Greg W. Marshall, Daniel J. Goebel, and William C. Moncrief, "Hiring for Success at the Buyer-Seller Interface," *Journal of Business Research* 56 (April 2003): 247–255.

11 Thomas Metcalf, "Top 10 Sales Closing Techniques: Learn How to Seal the Deal," *Small Business*, accessed May 4, 2015, http://smallbusiness.chron.com/top-10-sales-closing-techniques-learn-seal-deal-70629.html.

12 "Oh! You Pretty Things," *The Economist* (July 12, 2014), accessed May 4, 2015, http://www.economist.com/news/briefing/21606795-todays-young-people-are-held-be-alienated-unhappy-violent-failures-they-are-proving.

13 *Holy Bible: New Revised Standard Edition* (Grand Rapids, MI: Zondervan Publishing House, 1989), 150.

Chapter 18 Negotiating and Marketing Successfully Inside Asian Supply Chains

→ **Beast Mode**

By producing tangible stuff and successfully marketing the stuff mostly to Westerners, China has remade itself and the global economy. China was responsible for less than 3% of global manufacturing output as recently as 1990. Just 25 years later China's share is nearly 25%.

Read the following and weep, if you're a high school educated American worker: Chinese Firms produce about 80% of the world's air conditioners; approximately 70% of its mobile phones, and around 60% of its shoes, which means American Firms are no longer making those things in large numbers. Or read it and rejoice, if you're the average American consumer. Whenever Chinese workers wake up and go to work American customers get a raise because of all the less expensive consumer goods now made available to them in American markets. The role played by China on the global economic stage is strangely paradoxical, as are many other things about China. (For non-English majors, a paradox exists whenever two opposing arguments hold an equal claim on the truth.)

The steep upward arc of China's economy has shaped supply chains that not only penetrate deep into the Chinese interior and northbound/southbound along its east coast, but also deep into other South-East Asian nations. A "Factory-Asia" now abides astride the world. This Factory produces about half of the tangible products manufactured in the world each year. China has gracefully mimicked the footsteps of former and current Asian Tigers nations Japan, Taiwan, and South Korea. Each nation's now long-standing economic success predates that of China. In the case of Japan and Taiwan, it precedes by decades. Experts assumed that China's economic muscle would diminish, at least by degrees, as the lead baton passed to other lower-manufacturing-cost areas of the world, as wages have progressively risen in China. This baton's passing, you see, would permit the now-lower-cost-manufacturing-regions of the world to produce their way to prosperity. But despite the fact that its work force demanded and now enjoys notably higher wages, China's grasp appears stronger than ever. Lost-cost products that do exit China travel only comparatively short distances to South-East Asian nations, whose cultures, not-coincidentally, are dominated by Chinese cultural values. These two conditions have only strengthened the dominance of "Factory-China" cum Factory-Asia. Apart from its mammoth scale (globally first in population and third in square miles), the primary reason why Chinese culture is so influential is that the Chinese write the way they have written for thousands of years. Chinese language symbols and signs are read and understood in all parts of Asia, even where no Chinese is spoken. This means the thoughts and principles of great

Chinese leaders and thinkers have been able to spread quickly and influence many people over about the last 6,000 years.

Okay, no more ancient sociocultural Asian history lessons. Time now to learn more about how American Firms should manage their Asian supply chain relationships more effectively.

→ Culture Matters

What strategies should domestic Firms pursue when negotiating and marketing inside international supply chains that begin or end inside the United States but also include Asian Firms as partners? The answer's simplicity may surprise. Professionals who manage American Firms that engaged in such supply chains should employ every marketing principle presented earlier throughout this book. That's it, that's all that is necessary. Subject to one stipulation, one caution, of course. Business principles, after all, become principles only after they have been proven to demonstrate what works well or poorly over time and across contexts. Principles likewise become rules-of-thumb because their application has been shown to prevent managers from going out-of-bounds. Good principles, in effect, operate like "child-bumpers" in bowling alleys. Finally, principles emerge as fundamental "must-dos" because they permit managers to discriminate more easily between good, bad, or so-so strategic, tactical, or personal choices.

By all means, then, US Firms operating in Asian supply chains should apply all lessons taught through the principles that were presented earlier in this book. But what about that "stipulation"? Domestic managers should not negotiate or market inside international supply chains until after they understand the culture dominating inside the Chinese Firm(s) with which their Firm is partnering or seeking to partner. Global marketers always must understand to the degree possible and reasonable the foreign cultures with which they are dealing. Cultural norms, beliefs, and behaviors always influence how individuals from those cultures make sense of situations and eventually make decisions, as you recall from Chapter 4.

Follow these two prescriptions: one, understand and execute relevant principles and, two, comprehend and react in accordance with relevant foreign cultural norms and beliefs. Follow these two prescriptions and any domestic Firm's prospects for international marketing success profoundly elevate. Fail to understand one, the other, or both prescriptions, and any Firm's prospects of international marketing success crater because domestic managers won't know what they don't know and consequently they would become more prone to fumbling or "getting-rolled" or exploited by their foreign partners.

To more fully appreciate and comprehend why understanding cultural differences is so important to global managers, let's temporarily stay home and consider college football, the death penalty, and some-not-so-subtle geography-based subcultural differences that prevail between "The South" and every other US geographic region. Major subcultural differences exist and operate inside America. These differences are reflected in the differing beliefs, norms, and behaviors that dominate within the region.

College football, for example, is really important in The South. Other regions, not as much. Consequently, Southeastern Conference football tends to dominate college football year after year.

The death penalty is also viewed differently in Southern culture. During about the last 30 years (since the death penalty was re-implemented in the US) about 1,144 people have been executed in the South (east to west from Georgia to Texas). Texas executions dominate in the South reaching 524 since 1976. About 85 people in the West and 174 in the Midwest have been executed. Only four people have been executed in the Northeast. The South is more an Old Testament eye-for-an-eye culture. This subcultural value reigns more resolutely throughout larger portions of The South's population. Understand now, as a result of simple cultural values, why domestic and foreign cultural differences matter so much?[1]

Asian Culture Also Matters; Especially Inside Global Supply Chains

Throughout this chapter when we write about "Asia" or "Asian" we are, naturally, referring primarily to the Chinese people and Chinese Firms. After all, soon enough China will emerge as the world's largest economy. China, in fact, has already been branded the "World's Factory." But in the following text we do not refer exclusively to China.

The insights developed below apply in near-equal measure to other Asian nations such as Singapore, Vietnam, Taiwan, Malaysia, Thailand, South Korea and the like. This is because the cultural business practices of most Asian nations with which American Firms primarily trade are dominated by ancient Chinese values and beliefs. These Chinese values and belief systems have migrated into and exercise dominant influences on other Asian nations' business practices. The league of Asian nations that has been influenced materially by ancient Chinese cultural values also includes Japan, to a level that induces chagrin inside that nation.

Read on to discover best practice and actionable lessons about how best to enculturate oneself into the eccentricities of Asian business cultures. The following discussion concentrates on Asia because the relationships American Firms engage in with Asian partners are already so important and are likely to become more important still in the future. But before focusing on the supply chain consequences of Asian cultural values, let's examine some factors behind certain key differences prevailing between three business cultural spheres that currently dominate the world.

Three Dominant World Business Cultures

Fossil fuel issues notwithstanding, three cultural networks (i.e. spheres) dominate the contemporary global economy.[2] Each sphere emerges from infrastructures grounded in culturally-specific worldviews and values. Each worldview has been shaped by specific points of pride and prejudice, unique histories of legendary victories and humiliating defeats, and culturally-specific shades of past evils, venality, and disorder. In other words, the modern business world fundamentally exists and operates in three discrete cultural spheres.

The world's oldest continuous cultural network, the Sino-sphere, is currently its most vibrant. The global influence of Chinese culture is reinforced though links with the some 70 million ethnic Chinese living outside China. Many descend from individuals who moved abroad during China's imperialist expansion from the 12th to 15th centuries. Their predecessors settled and imbued Chinese cultural values into regions that have since morphed into Asian tigers such as Vietnam, Malaysia, Myanmar, Singapore, and Indonesia. More recently, Chinese businesspeople, investors, and students have migrated by the millions to the United States, Taiwan, Hong Kong, Canada, and various African nations.

Another of the world's rising cultural networks, the Indo-sphere, emerged more through organic means than through centralized processes because of its democratic underpinnings. Ethnic Indians comprise less than 1% of the US population, but account for 13% of graduate students at America's elite universities. In Great Britain ethnic Indians earn at least 10% more than the average income. In the United States, Indian households boast the highest median income of any ethnic segment. The top five destinations for Indians' international investments each boast large émigré Indian populations: the United States, Great Britain, United Arab Emirates, Singapore, and Mauritius. Tata, an Indian conglomerate led by a British-educated executive, employs more manufacturing workers in Britain than any other Firm.[3]

Clearly suffering from years of iterating crises in confidence and more tangible factors, yesteryear's bullyboy, the Anglo-sphere, still packs a punch. The Anglo-sphere mightily influences global business and diplomacy, although no longer at dominant levels of the past. Trading and cultural links between Great Britain and its former colonies (the United States, Canada, India, Hong Kong, Singapore, Ghana, to note a few) indicate tight tribal connections. Trade flow rates between Britain and its former colonies are 13% higher than chance would prescribe, capital flows 24% higher, and, remarkably, flows of people and information are 93% higher. English remains the world's lingua franca—wielded reflexively and systematically to make communication possible between people who do not share a common language. This alone underscores the Anglo-sphere's global business impact.[4]

While the three spheres increasingly overlap as technology flattens business and social worlds, each sphere's unique cultural history injects radically differing biases into cross-cultural supply chain interactions. Resulting misperceptions and misunderstandings can prove dramatic when managers from any two of these three cultures interact.

Let's now focus our discussion on an examination of the pressing cultural biases within Sino- and Anglo-spheres and speculate on how Anglo-American managers can best respond to these biases. Why are we skipping an examination of the Indo-sphere? Simple. India once was a British colony. India unquestionably benefitted economically and has been changed permanently from the imposition and ultimate integration of certain British rules, language, customs, and values. It's doubtful that idiosyncratic Indo values could be teased out as wholly independent from the Anglo-sphere's business values. The second reason is that the Sino- and Anglo-cultural spheres are currently more globally determinant and more closely tied economically to each other than either is with the Indo-sphere.

Dealing with Asian Partners: Far from Easy

The legendary American diplomat Henry Kissinger wrote that "America needs to understand China, but it need not fear China." Well, yes and no, Dr. Kissinger. While most surely we agree America should understand more about China and other Asian nations, how many executives with skin in a global business game believe they have nothing to fear from their Asian partners? Not many, we suspect. Consider this opinion, from a voice less known and influential than Dr. Kissinger's. This veteran of dozens of relationships with Asian supply chain partners, recently said: "… don't know why I got up so early to go in to talk with them. All they're gonna do is try to mislead me about everything [i.e., meeting quality specifications, honoring cost agreements, hitting shipping deadlines], anyway."

Sincere words, uttered spontaneously during March 2013, by Bonne Strutton as she left home at 4:30 a.m. to lead an early morning conference call from her Fort Worth office. The call connected her Dickies' Manufacturing's supply chain sourcing team with executives from a prospective Asian manufacturing partner. Despite her misgivings, the manager grudgingly made the call and eventually negotiated an agreement.

The US manager enjoyed few other short-term, economically-viable partnering choices in an environment characterized by skyrocketing cotton prices, uncertain consumer demand, and little unused Asian manufacturing capacity. And the eventual Asian partner did offer attractive cost-to-quality production ratios for items featured within product lines that drove much of Dickies' revenue. Naturally, the Asian partner knew these factors, understood their implications, and conducted negotiations accordingly, offering ostensibly reasonable commitments to lock down the contract. But as predicted, the Asian manufacturer quickly failed by substantial margins to honor key promises. One might argue the Asian managers simply exploited their comparative advantage in this negotiation. As the US manager implied, costs were higher than negotiated; shipments arrived domestically three or more weeks late; and unacceptably high percentages of garments were flawed. Had the Asian Firm consciously deceived in triplicate?

This story is no anomaly. It is not fictional; this actually happened. Three negative outcomes were forecast in advance of the agreement, and unfolded as predicted. Each outcome is attached to metrics that are crucial to success within any domestic or global supply chain. While some problems resulted from asymmetrical power enjoyed by the Asian Firm, could the American executive have negotiated more effectively? We argue yes.[5]

For many domestic Firms partnering in Asian supply chains, patterns of negotiated "promises made, but not kept" too often proves to be the rule rather than the exception. Contracts, the written form of promises, are not legally binding for Asian Firms. Some have no intention of following through with negotiated deals from the beginning. What about "win-wins"; acknowledging and respecting the inherent value available for each party in long-term relationships; or mutually pursuing and profiting from collaborative competition? Do these values, highly esteemed amongst American managers, still apply in American-Asian supply chain relationships? In theory, each should. In creativity-driven relationships, such concepts may be relevant. In horseshoe-shaped supply chains (more about this topic later!), American-based Firms such as Apple ideate and create/design prototypes; Asian manufacturing partners produce and ship finished products globally; and then Apple again manages branding and retail-level promotional efforts in the United States.[6] But within less creativity-driven domestic sectors, i.e., ones in which most domestic Firms manage supply chain relationships with Asian partners, these concepts bear little semblance to workaday reality.

American supply chain managers recognize that many Asian partners now enjoy opportunities to leverage greater market power than they have traditionally possessed. Increasingly, Asian managers understand that foreigners need China and other Asian nations (with 2.5+ billion consumers) more than Asia needs foreign Firms. This leverage now enables many Asian partners to negotiate from positions of strength. But more significantly, domestic marketers must address the presence and impact of various Asian cultural differences during negotiations. Such differences may trigger routine violations of what most domestic marketers believe are acceptable negotiating practices. These two conditions—one new, another old (but rarely considered) news—are converging. Many American marketers may need to change the tactics they use to negotiate with prospective/actual Asian partners. As for you, you should learn these new marketing negotiating tactics in advance of the need to use them.

→ Negotiating Games American Marketers Should Play

"China is not communist in name only" despite what many believe.[7] China is a communist nation whose capitalist-like economic policies are developed and executed through centralized processes. This means when China wants to build a road, dam or factory it does so without concern that environmental, unionized or special interest groups will coalesce to block the effort. Most Asian nations operate with similar efficiency. Thirteen long years would not have been required to rebuild destroyed World Trade Towers in Asia. Asian nations' overarching business strategy is to leverage centrally-efficient manufacturing-branding power, to exploit their consumer market scale to build trade alliances with other nations (Chile, Ghana, etc.), and to dominate the 21st century global economy.[8] This centralized orientation filters down to how individual Firms are subsidized by Asian governments.

Whether the "Asian Tiger" nations achieve this macro-goal is not the subject of this chapter. Instead, this chapter develops seven tactics designed to enable domestic marketers to negotiate more effectively with Asian supply chain partners. Some negotiating approaches are strategic. Others are tactical. Each, however, is designed to negate cultural disadvantages that domestic marketers routinely confront when negotiating with Asian supply chain partners. Evaluate them from Western perspectives, and the tactics appear unorthodox. But each is grounded in one or more core Asian cultural values and largely mirrors how Asian supply chain partners negotiate with foreign partners (i.e., US marketers). The prospect of negotiating from positions of comparative disadvantage and dwindling power relative to Asian partners may appear intractable to many domestic marketers, perhaps with good cause. Yet domestic Firms should not constrain themselves by addressing otherwise solvable negotiating problems through "restrictive" Western mindsets destined to leave the problems insoluble. These approaches offer a primer on how to fight a dragon like a dragon.

→ Asian Managers Differ from Western, and Western Managers from Asian

Even today, three of six factors that traditionally favorably distinguished Western economies from most former developing economies remain resolutely foreign in Asia. These are: rule of law, inviolate property rights and free competition, relatively unfettered by government's visible hand. These conditions challenge American supply chain partners in the best of times. When these conditions are paired with the fact that Asian supply chain managers study American culture far more than Americans study the Asian culture, the challenges facing domestic marketers compound. In contrast to their American counterparts, Asian negotiators usually exploit all "lessons learned." Traditional American negotiating behaviors by now are ridiculously predictable in Asian eyes. In fact, many domestic negotiating approaches, when played out in Asian settings, are so predictable they are practically irresponsible.

Despite insistently gracious trappings and other appearances to the contrary, Asian marketers do not assume international partnerships should be negotiated in the same manner as Americans typically do. In large part this condition may follow from historically embedded cultural circumstances summarized by Kissinger.[9] Kissinger argues Americans still generally believe most problems are solvable, and base this belief on their understanding of US national history. Once a problem is solved, Kissinger suggests, previously formidable challenges usually recede from American consciousness. He notes these two factors are significant, and exist "in part because our [domestic] history has been short and very successful." By contrast, recorded Asian history extends back more than 5,000 years. At times, that history has proven both stunningly successful and disastrous. Consequently, "in their [Asian] mind no problem has a final solution; every problem is an admission ticket to another problem."[10] For Asian supply chain managers, history is a revered, heavily-referenced reality. These psychological-cultural/historical differences radically separate Asian from Americans managers. They deeply color the dominant value systems and strategic/tactical approaches each nation's negotiators normally bring to the table.

→ Another Cultural Problem: Americans are WEIRD

Consider any group of individuals primarily acculturated in the United States. That is, most of the people who make up your class. Now imagine these individuals must negotiate with Asian counterparts. How weird are these people? The answer, extremely WEIRD as in heavily Westernized (in world views); well-Educated; living in an Industrialized society where genuine scarcity, deprivation or clawing to survive are someone else's problems; Rich, by global metrics, and Democratic in their decisive values and decision criteria.

And when members of this group negotiate with non-Western people who possess at least vestigial and perhaps firsthand memories of a society where genuine scarcity, deprivation and clawing to survive were most everyone's problem; and who are strikingly undemocratic in their decisive values or decision criteria, the Westerners' WEIRD-natures may undermine their negotiating effectiveness. Meanwhile, Asian individuals culturally-programmed not to be WEIRD may be better equipped to exploit the increasingly challenged, but still present, WEIRD senses of Western well-being, fair play and cultural complacency.

In the past, an unattractive cultural arrogance, hopefully bred from correctable ignorance, frequently injured domestic marketers' negotiating effectiveness in Asia.[11] Even today, US supply chain managers frequently appear ill-equipped or unwilling to overcome their cultural shortcomings. This should not surprise. Most marketers' in-country exposure to Asian culture is limited to stilted five-star encounters at Hong Kong or Shanghai facilities or Potemkin-like visits to showcase factories and worker living quarters. Such cultural detachment leads to ignorance, which rarely facilitates bliss in American-Asian negotiations. Equal "negotiating playing fields" may only be attainable if marketers' interactions with Asian counterparts demonstrate greater insight into and respect for Asian culture. A good way for domestic supply chain managers to demonstrate said understanding and respect is to project Asian cultural tactics back at their potential or actual Asian partners.

An inversion of American versus Asian Firm power bases is ongoing. This inversion will continue. After all, who borrows from whom? Perhaps America's most powerful economic days are gone.[12] But the issue is already irrelevant. Even today only two basic methods exist through which domestic marketers can negotiate more effectively with Asian supply chain partners. A right way, which entails:

- Employing negotiating approaches drawn from and consonant with historically-based cultural experiences of Asian supply chain partners and exploiting opportunities to secure negotiating advantage as are found in those new cultural insights.

And a wrong way, which entails:

- Continuing doing what US supply chain managers have traditionally done; i.e., negotiating in states of comparative ignorance about relevant Asian culture, while ignoring threats to American negotiating success that seem to flow naturally from this comparative ignorance.

→ Culture: American Weakness, Asian Strength?

Americans often view the world as if every issue or problem arrived strictly in shades of black or white. In other words, they think dualistically. This sort of "either-or" managerial thinking is typically a double-edged tool. Like most tools, when wielded in the proper context, dualistic thinking is useful. Dualistic reasoning helps people organize knowledge or solve routine strategic problems quickly. However, dualistic thinking often impedes those negotiating with Asian partners. For starters, when they think in overly dualistic ways, domestic marketers' cultural comfort zones tend to narrow. Dualistic thinking contributes to an illusion that things must be one way or the other. Not surprisingly, the one right way tends to be "my way." Marketers negotiating primarily from dualistic mindsets often miss the full range of opportunities, options, or tactics available. When negotiating with Asian supply chain partners or prospects who now know how to say "no," and can back up their thumbs down, the effectiveness of dualistic negotiating approaches is degraded.

When negotiating, domestic marketers' dualistic tendencies may fundamentally oversimplify the complicated nature of supply chain relationships with Asian partners. Simplifications can clarify, but also artificially separate parties while eliminating potential options. Among many American managers, a sort of "Asia burn-out" has already taken hold. This makes it easier for marketers to define their Firm and any Asian counterpart as separate groups—truly "us and them." This perspective is antithetical to supply chain efficiency and to negotiating success. From this point forward, during any negotiation only small mental steps are required for marketers to proclaim "our" (American) actions as just/necessary, rational or defensive, while proclaiming "their" (Asian) actions as immoral/unnecessary, illogical or aggressive. Suddenly, but subtly and irrevocably, little strategic latitude exists for marketers to enter or exit negotiations effectively.

During negotiations, marketers operating primarily from black or white approaches would tend either to be overly cooperative and trusting as they engage with Asian partners, or excessively dedicated to erecting self-defense barricades. Open or receptive arms have their place in most human interactions. But being candid when negotiating with Asian supply chain partners often leads to victimization. Such victimization typically plays out in promises made but broken. Yet while clenched fists portend greater short-term security, they foreclose much opportunity to prosper mutually in a manner that still characterizes most American-Asian partnerships. Opportunities for conflict and deceit inevitably will arrive, emanating in all shades of intensity from either side, during American-Asian negotiations. By default, domestic marketers' negotiating strategies should be fluid. Dualistic thinking lessens the likelihood such finely tuned adjustments can be made. When focusing too intently on either passive or aggressive negotiating limits, the precise adjustments essential to secure successful negotiating outcomes will prove more difficult to make.

Culturally and historically, Asian negotiators think differently than Americans about the nature of supply chain relationships. The expression *Shang chang ru zhan* chang means "the marketplace is a battlefield."[13] (All future *Bing Fa* quotes come from this same source). As endemic to Asia's cultural lexicon as treat others the way you would like to be treated is to American culture, the adage underscores how important business victories are to the Asian. Asian negotiators are culturally conditioned to accept and be motivated by the notion that a Firm's success promotes their nation's welfare as surely as the outcome of battles, undermining the appeal of "win-win" propositions. Imbued with this understanding of what true business competition represents and requires, Asian negotiators invariably play hard ball.

In Cantonese, *Bing* means soldier. *Fa* translates as skill or law. The phrase *Bing Fa* functions as an inclusive cultural synoptic for all manner of "strategic thinking." As an organized body of thought, *Bing Fa* was first developed for military purposes by Lao Tzu, Chuang Tzu, Sun Tzu, and others, beginning about 2,700 years ago. Evolving actively for another 1,000 or so years, *Bing Fa* principles have been applied to most human interaction in Asia. Every Asian supply chain negotiator has intensively studied the *Bing Fa*.

A prominent *Bing Fa* law prescribes to managers: "Combine in yourself the dove and the dragon, not as monster but prodigy." Educated Asian managers extract two explicit lessons from this specific law. Each is applied widely and, when applied, places dualistic thinkers at distinct negotiating disadvantages. The first lesson speaks directly to the yin and yang. Knowledge and use of the yin and yang imbues Asian negotiators with a classic "rope-a-dope" antidote through which American propensities for thinking and acting dualistically are easily parried and eventually exploited. The original "rope-a-dope," of course, entailed boxer Mohammed Ali allowing the younger, stronger George Foreman to punch himself out before lashing out violently and victoriously himself during the famous "Rumble in the Jungle."

Were they to follow the yin and yang, *Bing Fa* (i.e., strategic thinking) during negotiation, domestic marketers would visualize that they stand on one side of a door while their counterpart stands on the other. Unfortunately, Americans rarely summon such images. Their Asian counterparts do, and understood that the door freely swings in two directions. Asians also understand that as negotiations begin only two movements are available to either party: push or pull. Pushes are yang movements; direct, active, and characteristically American. But yang can quickly exhaust energy, assets, and good will. Knowing this, false Asian acquiescence and/or seeming reticence, driven by culturally-imbued patience and respect for the longer view, follow in short order. Pulls are yin movements; receptive, yielding and "come closer into my [Asian] trap from which no easy extrication is available." Few Americans recognize the degree to which negotiating success or failure pivots on whether they manage or ignore the interplay of these forces from the opening bell.

The second dove and dragon lesson is best summarized by a Japanese author who wrote "An elevated spirit is weak and a low spirit is weak."[14] Asian supply chain negotiators are culturally wired to understand that balance is the key to defending ground successfully, taking the offensive or developing creative solutions to vexing problems during negotiations. Too much yang, negotiators become too aggressive, domineering and, ultimately, vulnerable to Asian "rope-a-dope." Too much yin, ¬negotiators fail to reach their goals, as they attempt futilely to capitalize on actual or feigned Asian weakness.

→ Un-WIERD Negotiating Tactics

On average, Asians do not like Americans. This statement is true and absolutely understandable, from the Asian perspective. Consequently, students still reading this book should deal with it. But Asia supply chain partners need American supply chain partners. Thus America is tolerated; American and Asian economic self-interests broadly intersect, so myriad supply chains connect as business is conducted. The Asian race believes it is racially superior to whatever agglomerative ethnic constituency it believes comprises the American race. Provocative? Yes. But true? Again, yes. But had the terms Asia or Asian been transposed with America or American in any of this paragraph's preceding sentences, would the resulting statements be less true?

Asian culture teaches that conflict and harmony reside at opposite ends of a continuum. The domestic American culture, by contrast, rarely leads marketers to view conflict and harmony in a similar fashion. But domestic supply chain managers are capable of grasping the argument that to achieve greater harmony with Asian partners, they must comprehend the culturally-instilled ways in which Asian partners view and treat conflict. Conflict is endemic to Asian culture and history. But American culture and history also manifest an uncanny penchant for conflict. Opposition to things American is normal to Asia; need an obvious parallel be stated? For decades, no matter what business American Firms conduct in Asia or Asian Firms conduct in America, powerful domestic entities have found their presence distasteful.[15]

The following discussion ensues from one premise: more favorable outcomes will be achieved by domestic supply chain managers who manage in accordance with guidelines prescribed in the *Bing Fa* for any conflicts that arise during negotiations with Asian partners. Supply chain managers who blithely or ignorantly do otherwise will unnecessarily expose themselves to double jeopardy. Not only will conflicts continue to arise, during, and after completion of negotiations, but the marketers' Firms will more likely be victimized by deceit on the part of their Asian partners. Seven un-WEIRD negotiating approaches follow. Each has its origins in *Bing Fa*.

Tactic 1: Negotiate by Embracing the Unusual as Normal

Negotiations with Asian partners may exhibit few patterns or follow many rules that are easily discerned by culturally-challenged—WEIRD—domestic marketers. Before entering negotiations, then, supply chain managers should learn as much as possible about Asian culture. In the doing, they broaden their Asian cultural comfort zones. Consequently, they will come to embrace the unusual as normal. As cultural comfort zones expand, marketers more readily tolerate greater adversity and ambiguity. Less obviously, but perhaps more significantly, supply chain managers should retain more composure when confronting (now less) unexpected or seemingly unfair turns of events. Greater composure, in turn, expands marketers' range of strategic options.

Even when vicarious, wider Asian cultural exposure yields experiences and insights that should facilitate greater latitude within which marketers can maneuver objectively and respond creatively. Creative latitude instills more of a sense of self-control and confidence. Creativity is largely grounded in one's ability to identify and exploit previously unexplored or unconsidered intersections, generally between known and previously-unknown factors.[16] You were introduced to "intersections" in Chapter 11. Exposure to all aspects of Asian culture therefore may prove valuable to supply chain negotiators, not simply for purposes of practical self-defense, but also as sources of creative responses and empathetic insight.

By expanding cultural comfort zones, negotiators unconsciously sop up new insights into how their counterparts strategically think. Such insights will always spur supply chain managers' abilities to engage effectively in the intellectual "thrusts and parries" that characterize negotiations. But such insights should prove especially propitious in negotiations with Asian partners who no longer appear quite so foreign. Still, domestic partners should not become "too Asian" in their behaviors. Being a culturally well-informed version of an effective negotiator is preferable to being a faux imitation of an Asian negotiator. Culturally well-informed and well-mannered individuals should be better received than puffed-up Americans whose presumed expertise in-things-Asian transmutes into arrogance. As they learn Asian culture, marketers will accept that Asian negotiators will be complicated, cunning, and deceptive—and prepare accordingly.

In this domain, domestic managers should take heart and draw solace from knowing that America's oldest historical enemy-turned-partner (Great Britain) and oldest historical partner-turned-whatever (France) have acted exactly the same way for 200+ years. Finally, supply chain managers should accept the strong likelihood that Asian negotiators will seek to make up some of the rules themselves. And all cultural and practical signals indicate such expectations should be honored.

Tactic 2: Negotiate Beginning with Hard Ends in Mind

Before negotiating conflicts arise, supply chain managers should precisely understand exactly what outcomes they seek, what ground they will fight and die for, if necessary, or retreat from based on strategic concession. Regardless of context, not having goals in the face of negotiating conflict can prove almost as daunting as not achieving them. Goals bring focus. Focus promotes order, strengthens purpose, and diminishes impulsivity. Abstract targets are notoriously difficult to hit; the vague cannot be benchmarked. But Asia hosts thousands of corporations that for 30+ years running have experienced extraordinarily (by Western standards) accelerated change. That's no overt "stop-sign." But this condition may signal "dangerous-curves-ahead" for domestic Firms. In such environments, goals that in one quarter appeared wise to negotiators may prove fools' errands in the next. This condition partially overturns the conventional wisdom just discussed about the imperative for precise goals. But another, more culturally exacting reason exists regarding why negotiating goals should be precise but fluid or tenuous.

It is this: Asian cultural values are also deeply impacted by a Confucian concept called *Beng Qing*—literally, human feelings. *Beng Qing* rigidly dictates the human component can never be eliminated from any negotiation. Western practices also clearly pay homage to the human element in negotiations, but not to this degree. The Asian ledgers in which accounts for the human (feelings) element are reconciled are scrupulously kept.

When American negotiators encounter confrontation, the prescribed cultural response is to label it a problem to be solved through strategic or informal "horse-trading." Not so for Asian managers, culturally-programmed as they are to embrace conflict as opportunities for creative expression. Notably, *Beng Qing* prescribes that details related to how human feelings will be squared should be left open to future interpretation. Thus domestic marketers leave little to chance by reaching agreements in accordance with *Beng Qing*. In fact, culturally-attuned marketers may incur future obligations from Asian negotiators that lead them to confer more generous terms informally than would result were more detailed, strictly goal-driven Western-style negotiations concluded successfully.

The trick is no trick: marketers need only create future obligations through inexpensive gestures or concessions, then wait to call chits in subtly when partners can repay only with something more valuable. Execution requires keen perception and a subtle touch. But if domestic marketers are not subtle and perceptive, they should not be the ones participating in American-Asian supply chain negotiations. Learn more about Beng Qing, and supply chain managers will understand negotiation conflict is not something to be avoided. Instead, conflict should be welcomed as an opportunity to secure future value. Their Asian counterpart managers surely will.

Tactic 3: Before and During Negotiating, Anticipate and Prepare for Conflict

This third tactic begins where the second ends. Domestic managers should always anticipate conflict will arise during negotiations with their Asian partners and prepare accordingly. Specifically, domestic managers should classify conditions that merit responses or non-responses. They should also deliberate whether they will react quickly or dispassionately, as conflict arises and the occasion calls. Reasons exist for marketers to let conflicts play out their normal Asian courses and exert leverage consistent with *Beng Qing*, as described. But facts are stubborn, and one fact is that fresh conflict is still pliable. Consequently, new conflict is typically more easily resolved than old. Domestic supply chain managers should also consider responding quickly. Asian negotiators are well-acquainted with each approach to managing conflict; after all, each comes from Sun Tzu, whose *Beng Fa* suggests: "He who excels at resolving difficulties does so before they arise. He who excels in conquering enemies does so before their threats materialize."

Not surprisingly in a culture that values balance and yin and yang, domestic marketers enjoy two culturally-acceptable approaches through which negotiating conflict can be addressed. Regardless of the approach used, marketers should not permit fear, ignorance, or cultural/spatial distance delay their responsiveness or receptiveness to conflict. Delay too long and conflicts may polarize into rigid stances. Extreme negotiating skill or power on the part of American marketers then may be required just to break even. Any supply chain negotiator's ability to anticipate and respond quickly or cautiously, as circumstances dictate, to conflict follows from an ability to make small adjustments before more pronounced disagreement arises. This requires that attention be paid to the smallest cultural details that engendered or may defuse the conflict.

Supply chain managers should enter all Asian negotiations knowing what their inviolate issues are, where borders must be drawn, and their reactions should such territories be violated. Each contingent response should be established based on insight about the powerful role pre-designated limits can play in strengthening or undermining negotiated supply chain partnerships with the Asian. Hard boundaries could be established in some areas (sanctions incurred upon late delivery), soft boundaries in others. Where soft boundaries prevail (production costs can rise due to various uncontrollable environmental factors), Asian supply chain partners can receive the benefit of the doubt.

Their negotiating success may depend in part on whether supply chain partners first distinguish essential from nonessential concerns and goals. Vital interests should be maintained as centers of attention, metaphorical nuclei around which protective boundaries are built in advance of conflict and attack. Limits should be communicated early and clearly. No doubts can be permitted to exist with Asian negotiators, particularly because the two cultures define space and territory differently. By fighting smaller fights at the beginning of negotiations, potentially larger fights can be avoided down the road.

Tactic 4: Never Resist Resistance; Always Retreat Gracefully

Americans typically push harder when resistance is encountered. To WEIRD minds pushing back makes sense; the pushback is only natural. But resisting resistance is culturally inappropriate, and often self-defeating during negotiations with Asian partners. Like it or not, resistance to American negotiators' proposals will perpetually emerge. Yet culturally-attuned well-adjusted marketers understand, as conflict arises during negotiations, their Asian partners can never be wrong (unless they breech a hard boundary). Once the "not resisting resistance" approach is accepted, supply chain managers can more readily accept and eventually more easily respond to whatever opposition comes their way. Asian negotiators will resist in all kinds of ways, some rational, some outlandish by WEIRD standards. Domestic marketers will secure nothing by judging such behaviors. Disapproval will carry no water. Instead, success pivots on the creativity, logic, and cultural appropriateness of the American response.

On that last characteristic, cultural appropriateness, *Bing Fa* delivers decisive insight. The cultural text counsels: "Travel where there is no enemy." Consider a conventional supply chain negotiation in which domestic political entities engage. When conflict arises, each party widens its stand (no new taxes) and hardens its positions (no Medicare cuts). Asian negotiators, by contrast, are culturally-habituated to understand if they retain flexibility during conflict, they can blend with and redirect attack. Marketers should learn to subtly adjust initial positions so that adjusted positions more closely parallel those of Asian partners. Post-adjustment, supply chain managers occupy new positions from which Asian resistance can be more easily deflected. A *Bing Fa* parable involving a boulder rolling down a hill effectively illustrates the how-to in this lesson. Anyone attempting to stop the large stone directly will be crushed. Yet people could run beside it, nudge it, and retain their safety while slightly altering the course of the stone. Effectively resisting resistance emanating from contemporary Asian partners may prove analogous to the runaway boulder parable; after all, in each people must step up against the powerful forces of nature. Conflict inevitably rolls downhill and gains momentum. But domestic supply chain managers still can retain balance while moving alongside and subtly maneuvering the stone's position. But remember, hard-ends and thus defined boundaries should exist. As ground is given, the integrity of those boundaries must be maintained during gracefully assertive retreats.

All Asian negotiators have inculcated another axiom from *Bing Fa* into their thinking: the notion that "Retreat is another form of advance. Good men should not fight losing battles." To achieve ultimate goals, supply chain managers may need to learn to accept temporary defeat graciously, and by escaping intact, preserve and build strength for future conflicts. Domestic managers would benefit from accepting what Asian negotiators already believe: no disgrace follows from changing soft-boundary objectives in Asia.

Supply chain managers should understand the unusual is usual when negotiating with Asian partners. Once this empathetic insight into Asian thinking exists, domestic negotiators can more easily parallel the flow of any attack and impose small adjustments to its movement. Asians know this, too, avidly studying the Western mind, because Chuang Tzu taught "understand one's adversary thoroughly; lead him to where he is without fault." Chuang's *Bing Fa* also advises "become your opponent" and suggests leaders should cultivate an empathetic understanding of opponents and their objectives and where their hard boundaries begin and end "before entering conflict." Americans following this *Bing Fa* will more easily reach solutions giving both parties almost all of what each wants and more of what either needs.

 Supply chain managers must create alternatives to every expectation and exit strategies for each negotiation. When initial efforts are rejected, American Firms should retreat as gracefully as possible to hard boundary positions. Extremely Asian in character, graceful retreats entail smooth transitions from original to alternative positions through an open-ended process. Planning for the prospect of failure/retreat is an act of foresight because, paradoxically to many WEIRD minds, failure can prove friend or foe in a culture of yin and yang. The process of planning for failure honors and accommodates the unpredictable nature of Asian negotiations. In Asia, continuous refinement of one's views epitomizes intelligence.

Tactic 5: When Negotiating Leverage Deceit

Americans typically still idealize traditions of openness and fair play. (Think about how touchy/feely, "do-the-right-thing" things got during the Chapter 4 discussion.) While Western culture is marked by numerous deceptions, skillful deceptions are rarely characterized as heroic (the "Trojan Horse" is one notable exception). Not so within Asian culture. A likely reason is because Sun Tzu wrote battles should be won "by offering enemies a bait to lure him, then feigning disorder and striking him." *Bing Fa* texts agree: deception lies near the heart of successful warfare; victory must be achieved through any means necessary. While Americans most likely occasionally engage in the practice, the term "deception" likely invokes negative connotations among many marketers. Yet when dealing with Asian partners marketers should callously set themselves straight on such naïve views. Their cultural naiveté has rendered many Americans vulnerable to exploitation in prior dealings with Asian negotiators.

The ability to mislead opponents has long been admired by Asian managers, who have mastered the tradition. While Asian negotiators clearly possess their own take on honor, the definition of what constitutes an ethical negotiation differs across Asian and Western culture. Supply chain partners should never negotiate with Asian partners until after they have become more than nominally conversant with Asian ways of guile, opportunism, and deception.

Some suggest the Asian art of deception entails two basic tactics.[17] First, there is concealment, which usually entails hiding truths about weaknesses or intentions. The "real" is concealed by demonstrating false strengths or feigned intent. Shows of false strength entail tactics of deterrence or bluffing. Negotiators may demonstrate false strength by embellishing the actual market positions or assets of their Firms. While concealment is still practiced, the tactic has serious flaws in a world where global information is available to anyone with an Internet connection.

Demonstrations of false weaknesses (disclosing the false), a second tactic of deception, is a common Asian negotiating practice. As students of Sun Tzu, who advised soldiers to "pretend inferiority and encourage the enemy's arrogance," Asian negotiators often create scenarios in which their organizations appear less than they really are. While WEIRD minds might view such deception as counterproductive (i.e., why feign weakness?), Asian negotiators don't. They recognize the tactic can prove useful in negotiating contexts where Western negotiators lack the motivation or see no value in crushing weaker partners or opponents. Marketers should negotiate with Asian partners aware that some form of deception likely will be used. If the American Firm's comparative strengths appear too enticing, marketers should be wary. When exploiting the Asian Firm's apparent weakness, marketers may be entering a trap.

Once its omnipresent nature and cultural origins are understood, marketers can more easily counter Asian deception. But supply chain managers also should understand that Asian negotiators did not simply study historical culture to execute deceptions effectively. They also study to detect deceivers more effectively themselves. Maintaining deceptions, generally requiring development of new chains of lies, is difficult, time-consuming and distracting. The sort of singular focus that appears key to success in many negotiations would then likely become more difficult to muster or sustain. In most negotiations, marketers should practice honesty as the default choice. Still, when dealing in a culture of deceit, suggesting marketers should not reserve a place for illusion themselves appears naïve. But deceit should be used sparingly, selectively and wisely, and only in extraordinary circumstances.

Tactic 6: Act Like Ladies or Gentlemen

Opponents in conflicted supply chain negotiations should be treated with genuine respect. Tactics even touching on any aspect that might denigrate one's counterpart should be rejected out of hand. The polite approach has little to do with common courtesy. Instead, giving face is a strategic imperative born of cultural and business pragmatism.

Confucius wrote in the *Analects*: "Gentlemen call attention to the good points in others; they do not call attention to their faults. Small men do the opposite." This is called "giving (opponents) face," and in Asia the act represents far more than a nice-to-do. Business-wise, as discussed, appearances deceive, especially in Asia. Partners may be far more capable than they initially appear. Individuals with whom supply chain managers are at loggerheads may acquire fresh knowledge, skills, assets, or allies that make them formidable adversaries or even more impressive partners in the future. The short- and long-term interests of domestic managers are best served by reflexively giving face to all Asian negotiators regardless of any havoc or deceit playing out during actual negotiation processes.

Throughout Asia, face is the reflection one sees in the eyes of one's peers. Face measures one's standing in a community. Lose it, and the Asian manager's self-identify diminishes. Stripping face from Asian negotiators is probably the worst tactical mistake domestic marketers can make. The possibility of future relationships is essentially eliminated. Because of the role face plays, marketers should avoid appearing aggressive in their negotiating efforts. Overt demands should never be employed to resolve conflict. Even seemingly innocuous questions such as "Do we have a deal?" go too far. Asian partners may have substantial difficulty responding to such "ultimatums," because acquiescence might diminish face.

Logic suggests anything which should not be taken away quite likely should be given. Such is the case with face. Domestic marketers should acknowledge their negotiating partner's position, value, and dignity; even the opponent's self-worth should be fed. An act sure to be interpreted as a sign of the marketer's cultural IQ, giving face is a genuine no-lose proposition. Negotiations can be pushed forward ahead toward closure by inquiring politely whether additional information is needed before a decision can be made. Selling partners are culturally expected to defer to buying partners. Acting otherwise is rude. Cultural ignorance is exposed.

Sometimes Americans act as if they believe respect for opponents indicates weakness. "Warriors," they believe, must remain supremely confident. Honoring opponents' value is a nonstarter because marketers might gain confidence for future contests. Asian negotiators arrive with no such pretensions. Educated Asians know from *Bing Fa*: "If I can fight and win, I fight. If I cannot fight, I escape." When negotiation conflict arises, Asian partners would be culturally more inclined to respect and accept their supply chain partner's potential for high performance or, perhaps, receipt of a lucky break.

Tactic 7: Never Die with Bullets in Your Chamber

Many domestic Firms participating in supply chains with Asian partners occupy precarious positions and always have, the recent historical evidence suggests. And for various reasons unfolding beyond most Firms' control, their negotiating positions likely will become weaker in the future. At net: WEIRD Western negotiators could follow every approach recommended above—learn and apply cultural lessons, avoid silly mistakes, perform honorably—and still have Asian rugs pulled out from under them through lies and deceit, indefensibly unusual events, performance or capability misrepresentations, or activities not broached above, such as technology theft, product knock-offs, or cyber-assault.[18]

Does *Bing Fa* have final words of wisdom for supply chain managers confronting such circumstances? It does, suggesting: "In death ground, fight!" Long ago, Asia learned surviving worst-case scenarios requires acknowledging and understanding the dangers, and American Firms should do both. Beyond that, no one-size-fits-all cross-cultural solution exists for such situations. After all, no two scenarios are alike. What is known, however, is that negotiating success may depend on timely and accurate analyses of the immediate direct threat. "In death ground, fight" implies marketers should consolidate all energies and assets into a single focused strike, aiming at jugulars or knees when no other way out exists. A strong will to win may prove the determinant factor. No measure of skill or cultural acuity can compensate for a lack of intensity in one's efforts to exercise the universal right to defend one's assets and rightful gains. In the end, intensity of conviction may win Asian partners' respect; culturally-speaking, they obviously understand "death ground" imperatives. And *Bing Fa* actually suggests "using non-coercive measures when confronting a determined enemy."

On death ground, then, supply chain managers should revert to the previously discounted American cultural state; that is, zero-doubt, dualistic reasoning. When confronting an absolute negotiating crises, zero-doubt negotiating positions should be underpinned by dead serious, in-opponents' faces logic. Dualistic (all in) negotiating thrusts imply utterly black-and-white commitments to principles or positions exist, and will be defended until all bullets are fired. *Ceteris paribus*, more unified domestic negotiators or teams will triumph. The death ground principle should hold at all levels, from pivotal verbal disagreements to worst-case conflicts.

Zero-doubt negotiating approaches should be used only when no other alternatives exist. A short-term solution, dualistic approaches taken too far (beyond possible resolution of precipitating crises) leads easily to overextension. No opportunity exists to revise a zero-doubt strategy. Used beyond the short-term, zero-doubt thwarts learning, flexibility and the prospect of creatively negotiated supply chain solutions.

→ Negotiate Smarter, Not Harder

The Asian supply chain negotiating threats and challenges discussed above are genuine, and more pressing than ever. *The Wall Street Journal* suggests that the American economy has never faced the sort of challenge now being thrown in its face by Asian competitors. Asia, according to the *Journal*: "Now plays the game of capitalization almost as well as we, and our response for now seems to be a mixture of fear and disbelief."[19] Now that Asian businesspeople are playing America's game so well, the time may be past due for American negotiators to turn back on them the same cultural rules that the Asians heretofore have executed so effectively against American interests. Ignorance of or apathy about crucial Asian cultural values should not continue to make one nation's interests vulnerable to other's tactics. Supply chain managers should fight dragons with dragons.

The question of how to negotiate more effectively with Asian partners remains a sensitive subject. America's stakes are high even as insights about best practices remain inconclusive. This chapter addresses this question, underscoring the degree to which being "culturally-aware" often may be more important than being "functionally-smart" when outsiders negotiate with Asian partners. Not only does it point out approaches that Asian negotiators routinely employ that have traditionally worked to their benefit, the chapter also reveals various cultural underpinnings driving their use. But the chapter's primary contribution follows from its development of new (to US marketers) negotiating approaches grounded in *Bing Fa* and Beng Qing standards. Too few supply chain managers are accounting for the negative impact certain Asian cultural values are exercising on negotiating outcomes. Now that these Asian culturally-based negotiating approaches are available, marketers should consider the suitability of using them for assertive or defensive purposes.

→ Global Supply Chain as Horseshoes— Things Going Better than You Think

To understand one last important thing about most global supply chains that link Asian and American Firms, you should also consider the horseshoe. The horseshoe provides a model to visualize the relationship among three aspects of marketing: ideation and product development; manufacturing; and positioning, branding, and supply chain management. These aspects will shape Asian-American economic relationships for years to come. The horseshoe also illustrates how a new Asian threat against future domestic interests is inexorably emerging.

A horseshoe, propped upright on its base, mirrors the contour of most global supply chains currently linking Asian Firms, typically operating near the point of physical production, to US Firms, typically operating near the point of those products' final destinations. Or so many individuals erroneously assume. Actually, supply chains always extend from the beginning point of any physical product's conception to an end point where the product is marketed, acquired, and ultimately consumed. To illustrate, if a product's point of ideation occurred in Fort Worth, Texas, when, say, a Dickies Manufacturing designer combined a new style and fabric for next season's work uniforms, and then that new product was produced by Asian manufacturers and assemblers and sold next year in the States as either a Dickies or private label brand, the supply chain in question began and ended in the United States, which is good for American interests.

Obviously, at least one and probably numerous Asian Firms performed key supply chain functions between those beginning and ending points. Just as obviously, Dickies, primarily due to the product concept and design, brand management and marketing/retailing functions it performed near the supply chain's beginning and end points, should, and generally does, command the lion's share of any profits generated.

Revisiting the horseshoe metaphor, assume new product ideation and positioning begins on, say, the left prong of an inverted horseshoe, moves down around the curve to the lower portions of the horseshoe during manufacturing and assembly processes and finishes high up on the other prong when branding, sales and distribution efforts are executed. So the horseshoe works, but applies fully only if each vertical prong is embedded in American soil. Repeated thousands of times weekly, the opportunity, as well as the practical necessity, to partner with Asian Firms in such supply chains represents both an economic opportunity and risk to many US Firms.

→ An Emergent Threat

So far, a broad cross-section of US interests generally have benefited when American and Asian Firms partner. Domestic interests have benefited because domestic Firms have typically excelled at supply chain originating idea generation and concept/prototype design as well as at the concluding high value-adding ends of the global supply chains that actually brand/position, distribute, and retail/sell those products. And what of the lower value-adding but still critically important supply chain activities situated along our metaphorical horseshoe's base? For some time now that is where Asian supply chain partners typically performed the required product manufacturing/assembly functions. That lower supply chain rung is where Asian Firms have been connected—going and coming, but rarely at supply chains' beginnings or ends, where the real creativity and money is—with American Firms and their end use customers.

Because of this, the global trade bottom line thus far remains a net win for American interests. Domestic Firms have won, as they have earned higher profits. American consumers have won, as they enjoy more choices and lower prices. And, despite persistent complaints about outsourcing, the domestic economy has also won.

The iPod and iPhone experiences exemplify how US interests have subtly won this supply chain tug-of-war, and how Asia, while never losing outright, finishes second place. Both the iPod and iPhone were conceived and created as a prototype by Apple, a famous American company. These products are and will continue to be assembled by many different Firms in Asia. Both are marketed at the American retail level through various American companies. And Apple shareholders, myriad US retailers, and millions of domestic consumers have thrilled to the result.

But how much longer are these comparatively easy wins likely to continue for less creative domestic corporations? Just like business failure is rarely fatal, business success is never final.

For good reason, Asian Firms are inexorably attempting to invert the horseshoe. One thing motivating all consumers, Firms, or nations to act, is their own self-interests. To date, Asian Firms generally have performed in relative satisfaction on the bottom rung of our metaphorical supply chain horseshoe. They have done so based on their government's understanding that doing so was necessary to ratchet Asia's economic station from where it was to where it is today.

Asia economies, of course, routinely produce more than millions of physical products. They also produce tens of thousands of engineers and scientists annually, many, in fact, manufactured in great American universities. Want to bet whether Asian business and governmental strategists are not similarly aware of their relatively disadvantaged global supply chain positions and are not working toward turf-grabbing (i.e., supply chain "function") efforts that better serve their interests? Especially in a global economy where most of the thousands of containers returning from Asia from American shores—after having arrived in the States brimming with consumer and electronic goods—hold scrap metals and other recycled materials. Or in a world where Chrysler recently partnered with Asian interests to deliver $10,000 "Cherry" cars—an idea originating in Asia—to the United States American interests should begin readying their responses.

→ Takeaway

If a US Firm found itself performing the same relatively less rewarding global supply chain functions as those performed by most Asian Firms, presumably it would attempt to secure performance control over additional higher value-adding supply chain functions. Not surprisingly, increasing numbers of Asian Firms are doing exactly that. Examples abound where Asian Firms are demanding that more ideation, design, research and engineering (i.e., more of the more creative activities) supply chain functions be performed in Asia by Asian Firms. In fact, their Asian partners recently made those exact demands to signature American Firms such as Intel, Microsoft, and Google. And, on several fronts, those same American Firms have relinquished performance of key supply chain functions to their Asian partners.[20]

Nothing about this trend is wrong. To the contrary, nothing less than national self-interest is being pursued, on a global scale, through the large and small actions of uncounted Asian Firms. The struggle for power, influence, and ultimate control over which Firms perform which critical supply chain functions has always existed. One difference here is that this particular supply chain tug-of-war involves global implications. A second difference is that this trend portends badly for the interests of many American Firms, and thus the entire domestic economy.

Large-scale movements in the performance-allocation of critical supply chain functions generate large-scale consequences. Incremental movements, in the same domain, generate incremental effects. But when the trend in question involves national economies as mammoth as these, is any consequence incremental? American Firms need not react with alarm or hostility, but they might reasonably respond to this trend like the threat it is. And, on a case by case basis, they might prepare to respond strategically in ways that ensure their current levels of control over future supply chains.

The time is right for American Firms facing such Asian threats to consider their responses. At the least, individual Firms should identify key supply chain functional areas—lines in the sand—which they would defend vigorously if turf-grabbing efforts ensued from Asian partners' camps. Those "lines" should prove easy to identify; examine the horseshoe. Then those Firms should determine how best to strengthen and preserve their relative supply chain positions.

The time is similarly beyond past for American marketers and marketing students to learn how to become, and thereafter remain, more creative because realistically, Americans and American Firms cannot hope to "out-cheap" or out-work" more highly motivated Asians and Asian Firms. But if you remember anything from Chapter 11, you already knew this is true, and why.

So what will you do with your recently acquired knowledge about marketing, creativity, and marketing more creatively? Hopefully, something. In closing, remember these thoughts. The two most basic mistakes most American, or for that matter Asian people make, are: (1) trying to control the uncontrollable, while (2) failing to control the controllable.

Can you control your level of creativity? Should you control it? The answers, for most of you, are yes and yes.

But you already knew that, didn't you?

Endnotes

1 *Death Penalty Information Center*, "Number of Executions by State and Region Since 1976," accessed May 8, 2015, http://www.deathpenaltyinfo.org/number-executions-state-and-region-1976.

2 A. Wooldridge, "The Power of Tribes," *The Economist* 402/8729, 2012): 68.

3 Ibid.

4 Ibid.

5 A. Hupert, "Conflict Resolution vs. Conflict Avoidance in Asian Business Part 1: Rock and a Soft Place" (October 7, 2009) accessed April 4, 2015 and April 7, 2015, http://www.Asiannegotiation.com/conflict-management-and-Asia/conflict-resolution-vs-conflict-avoidance-in-Asian-business-part-1.

6 D. Strutton, "Horseshoes, Global Supply Chains, and an Emerging Asian Threat: Creating Remedies One Idea at a Time," *Business Horizons*, 52(1) (2009): 31–43.

7 R. McGregor, "Five Myths About the Asian Communist Party," *Foreign Policy* 184, (January/February, 2011): 38-40.

8 S. Ordoi-Larbi, "Ghana: EcoBank, Bank of Asia to Boost Africa-Asia Trade Relations" (April 11, 2011), accessed April 7, 2015, http://inwent-iij-lab.org/Weblog/2011/04/11/ghana-ecobank-bank-of-Asia-to-boost-africa-Asia-trade-relations/.

9 B. Luscombe, "Ten Questions for Henry Kissinger," *Time Magazine* (June 6, 2011): 64.

10 Ibid.

11 D. Strutton and L. Pelton, "Scaling the Great Wall: The Yin and Yang of Resolving Business Conflicts in Asia," *Business Horizons* (40/5, 1997): 22–34.

12 F. Zakaria, "Are America's Best Days Behind Us?" *Time Magazine* (March 3, 2011): 28-35.

13 C.-N Chu, *The Asian Mind Game* (New York: Maxwell MacMillan International, 1991).

14 M. Musashi, *A Book of Five Rings: The Classic Guide to Strategy* (Boston: Shambhala Publications, Inc, 1982).

[15] William Safire, "Asia's 'Princelings' Play it Smart," *International Herald Tribune* (February, 1997): 18.

[16] F. Johannson, *The Medici Effect* (Boston: Harvard Business School Press, 2005).

[17] J. D. Hamilton and D. Strutton, "Two Practical Guidelines for Resolving Truth-Telling Problems," *Journal of Business Ethics* (13/11, 1994): 899–912.

[18] R. Clarke, "Asia's Cyber-Assault on America," *Wall Street Journal* (June 15, 2015): A15.

[19] A.W. Batson, "Soon Made in Asia: High-Tech Products; Intel Investment Shows How Nation's Economy is Climbing Value Chain," *The Wall Street Journal* (March 23, 2007): B4.

[20] James Fallows, "China Makes, the World Takes," *The Atlantic Monthly*. (July/August, 2007): 48–73.